# Vauxhall/Opel Astra
# Owners Workshop Manual

## John S. Mead

**Models covered**

*(4732 - 9AP1 - 304)*

Hatchback, Sport Hatch & Estate with petrol engines, including special/limited editions
1.4 litre (1364cc), 1.6 litre (1598cc) & 1.8 litre (1796cc)

*Does NOT cover 1.6 litre/2.0 litre turbo engines, 1.6 litre VVT engine or dual fuel models*
*Does NOT cover TwinTop models*
*For coverage of diesel models, see manual no. 4733*

© Haynes Publishing 2010

ABCDE
FGHIJ
KLMNO
PQRS

A book in the **Haynes Owners Workshop Manual Series**

ISBN **978 1 84425 732 4**

**British Library Cataloguing in Publication Data**
A catalogue record for this book is available from the British Library.

Printed in the USA

**Haynes Publishing**
Sparkford, Yeovil, Somerset BA22 7JJ, England

**Haynes North America, Inc**
861 Lawrence Drive, Newbury Park, California 91320, USA

**Haynes Publishing Nordiska AB**
Box 1504, 751 45 UPPSALA, Sverige

# Contents

## LIVING WITH YOUR VAUXHALL/OPEL ASTRA

## MAINTENANCE

# Contents

## REPAIRS AND OVERHAUL

### Engine and Associated Systems

### Transmission

### Brakes and suspension

### Body equipment

## REFERENCE

## Index

The Vauxhall/Opel Astra-H model was introduced in the UK in May 2004 as a replacement for the previous Astra, the 'G' model. It is available in 3- and 5-door Hatchback and Estate versions with 1.4, 1.6 and 1.8 litre petrol engines and various diesel engines (not covered in this manual). All engines are of the normally-aspirated four-cylinder, in-line type, featuring double overhead camshafts. 1.6 and 2.0 litre turbocharged engines are also available, but are not covered in this manual.

The manual gearbox is of the five-speed all synchromesh type, and a four-speed electronically-controlled automatic transmission is available as an option on 1.8 litre models. An 'Easytronic' manual/automatic transmission is also optionally available on 1.4 and 1.6 litre models.

All models have front-wheel-drive with fully-independent front suspension, and semi-independent rear suspension with a torsion beam and trailing arms.

A wide range of standard and optional equipment is available within the Astra range to suit most tastes, including electro/hydraulic power steering, air conditioning, remote central locking, electric windows, electric sunroof, anti-lock braking system, electronic alarm system and supplemental restraint systems.

For the home mechanic, the Astra is a relatively straightforward vehicle to maintain, and most of the items requiring frequent attention are easily accessible.

## Your Vauxhall/Opel Astra manual

The aim of this manual is to help you get the best value from your vehicle. It can do so in several ways. It can help you decide what work must be done (even should you choose to get it done by a garage), provide information on routine maintenance and servicing, and give a logical course of action and diagnosis when random faults occur. However, it is hoped that you will use the manual by tackling the work yourself. On simpler jobs, it may even be quicker than booking the car into a garage and going there twice, to leave and collect it. Perhaps most important, a lot of money can be saved by avoiding the costs a garage must charge to cover its labour and overheads.

The manual has drawings and descriptions to show the function of the various components, so that their layout can be understood. Then the tasks are described and photographed in a clear step-by-step sequence.

References to the 'left' or 'right' are in the sense of a person in the driver's seat, facing forward.

## Acknowledgements

Certain illustrations are the copyright of Vauxhall Motors Limited, and are used with their permission. Thanks are also due to Draper Tools Limited, who provided some of the workshop tools, and to all those people at Sparkford who helped in the production of this manual.

**We take great pride in the accuracy of information given in this manual, but vehicle manufacturers make alterations and design changes during the production run of a particular vehicle of which they do not inform us. No liability can be accepted by the authors or publishers for loss, damage or injury caused by any errors in, or omissions from, the information given.**

**Vauxhall Astra 1.8 SRi Hatchback.**

Working on your car can be dangerous. This page shows just some of the potential risks and hazards, with the aim of creating a safety-conscious attitude.

# General hazards

### Scalding

• Don't remove the radiator or expansion tank cap while the engine is hot.
• Engine oil, automatic transmission fluid or power steering fluid may also be dangerously hot if the engine has recently been running.

### Burning

• Beware of burns from the exhaust system and from any part of the engine. Brake discs and drums can also be extremely hot immediately after use.

### Crushing

• When working under or near a raised vehicle, always supplement the jack with axle stands, or use drive-on ramps. *Never venture under a car which is only supported by a jack.*

• Take care if loosening or tightening high-torque nuts when the vehicle is on stands. Initial loosening and final tightening should be done with the wheels on the ground.

### Fire

• Fuel is highly flammable; fuel vapour is explosive.
• Don't let fuel spill onto a hot engine.
• Do not smoke or allow naked lights (including pilot lights) anywhere near a vehicle being worked on. Also beware of creating sparks (electrically or by use of tools).
• Fuel vapour is heavier than air, so don't work on the fuel system with the vehicle over an inspection pit.
• Another cause of fire is an electrical overload or short-circuit. Take care when repairing or modifying the vehicle wiring.
• Keep a fire extinguisher handy, of a type suitable for use on fuel and electrical fires.

### Electric shock

• Ignition HT voltage can be dangerous, especially to people with heart problems or a pacemaker. Don't work on or near the ignition system with the engine running or the ignition switched on.

• Mains voltage is also dangerous. Make sure that any mains-operated equipment is correctly earthed. Mains power points should be protected by a residual current device (RCD) circuit breaker.

### Fume or gas intoxication

• Exhaust fumes are poisonous; they often contain carbon monoxide, which is rapidly fatal if inhaled. Never run the engine in a confined space such as a garage with the doors shut.

• Fuel vapour is also poisonous, as are the vapours from some cleaning solvents and paint thinners.

### Poisonous or irritant substances

• Avoid skin contact with battery acid and with any fuel, fluid or lubricant, especially antifreeze, brake hydraulic fluid and Diesel fuel. Don't syphon them by mouth. If such a substance is swallowed or gets into the eyes, seek medical advice.
• Prolonged contact with used engine oil can cause skin cancer. Wear gloves or use a barrier cream if necessary. Change out of oil-soaked clothes and do not keep oily rags in your pocket.
• Air conditioning refrigerant forms a poisonous gas if exposed to a naked flame (including a cigarette). It can also cause skin burns on contact.

### Asbestos

• Asbestos dust can cause cancer if inhaled or swallowed. Asbestos may be found in gaskets and in brake and clutch linings. When dealing with such components it is safest to assume that they contain asbestos.

# Special hazards

### Hydrofluoric acid

• This extremely corrosive acid is formed when certain types of synthetic rubber, found in some O-rings, oil seals, fuel hoses etc, are exposed to temperatures above 400°C. The rubber changes into a charred or sticky substance containing the acid. *Once formed, the acid remains dangerous for years. If it gets onto the skin, it may be necessary to amputate the limb concerned.*
• When dealing with a vehicle which has suffered a fire, or with components salvaged from such a vehicle, wear protective gloves and discard them after use.

### The battery

• Batteries contain sulphuric acid, which attacks clothing, eyes and skin. Take care when topping-up or carrying the battery.
• The hydrogen gas given off by the battery is highly explosive. Never cause a spark or allow a naked light nearby. Be careful when connecting and disconnecting battery chargers or jump leads.

### Air bags

• Air bags can cause injury if they go off accidentally. Take care when removing the steering wheel and/or facia. Special storage instructions may apply.

### Diesel injection equipment

• Diesel injection pumps supply fuel at very high pressure. Take care when working on the fuel injectors and fuel pipes.

⚠ *Warning: Never expose the hands, face or any other part of the body to injector spray; the fuel can penetrate the skin with potentially fatal results.*

# Remember...

### DO

• Do use eye protection when using power tools, and when working under the vehicle.

• Do wear gloves or use barrier cream to protect your hands when necessary.

• Do get someone to check periodically that all is well when working alone on the vehicle.

• Do keep loose clothing and long hair well out of the way of moving mechanical parts.

• Do remove rings, wristwatch etc, before working on the vehicle – especially the electrical system.

• Do ensure that any lifting or jacking equipment has a safe working load rating adequate for the job.

### DON'T

• Don't attempt to lift a heavy component which may be beyond your capability – get assistance.

• Don't rush to finish a job, or take unverified short cuts.

• Don't use ill-fitting tools which may slip and cause injury.

• Don't leave tools or parts lying around where someone can trip over them. Mop up oil and fuel spills at once.

• Don't allow children or pets to play in or near a vehicle being worked on.

The following pages are intended to help in dealing with common roadside emergencies and breakdowns. You will find more detailed fault finding information at the back of the manual, and repair information in the main chapters.

## If your car won't start and the starter motor doesn't turn

☐ If it's a model with automatic transmission, make sure the selector is in P or N.
☐ Open the bonnet and make sure that the battery terminals are clean and tight.
☐ Switch on the headlights and try to start the engine. If the headlights go very dim when you're trying to start, the battery is probably flat. Get out of trouble by jump starting (see next page) using a friend's car.

## If your car won't start even though the starter motor turns as normal

☐ Is there fuel in the tank?
☐ Is there moisture on electrical components under the bonnet? Switch off the ignition, then wipe off any obvious dampness with a dry cloth. Spray a water-repellent aerosol product (WD-40 or equivalent) on ignition and fuel system electrical connectors like those shown in the photos.

**1** Remove the engine cover and check that the wiring to the ignition module is connected firmly.

**2** Check that the airflow meter wiring is connected securely.

**3** Check the security and condition of the battery connections.

Check that electrical connections are secure (with the ignition switched off) and spray them with a water-dispersant spray like WD-40 if you suspect a problem due to damp

**4** Check all multiplugs and wiring connectors for security.

**5** Check that all fuses are still in good condition and none have blown.

# Jump starting

When jump-starting a car using a booster battery, observe the following precautions:

✔ Before connecting the booster battery, make sure that the ignition is switched off.

✔ Ensure that all electrical equipment (lights, heater, wipers, etc) is switched off.

✔ Take note of any special precautions printed on the battery case.

✔ Make sure that the booster battery is the same voltage as the discharged one in the vehicle.

✔ If the battery is being jump-started from the battery in another vehicle, the two vehicles MUST NOT TOUCH each other.

✔ Make sure that the transmission is in neutral (or PARK, in the case of automatic transmission).

 **HAYNES HiNT** *Jump starting will get you out of trouble, but you must correct whatever made the battery go flat in the first place. There are three possibilities:*

**1** *The battery has been drained by repeated attempts to start, or by leaving the lights on.*

**2** *The charging system is not working properly (alternator drivebelt slack or broken, alternator wiring fault or alternator itself faulty).*

**3** *The battery itself is at fault (electrolyte low, or battery worn out).*

**1** Connect one end of the red jump lead to the positive (+) terminal of the flat battery

**2** Connect the other end of the red lead to the positive (+) terminal of the booster battery.

**3** Connect one end of the black jump lead to the negative (-) terminal of the booster battery

**4** Connect the other end of the black jump lead to a bolt or bracket on the engine block, well away from the battery, on the vehicle to be started.

**5** Make sure that the jump leads will not come into contact with the fan, drive-belts or other moving parts of the engine.

**6** Start the engine using the booster battery and run it at idle speed. Switch on the lights, rear window demister and heater blower motor, then disconnect the jump leads in the reverse order of connection. Turn off the lights etc.

# Wheel changing

 **Warning: Do not change a wheel in a situation where you risk being hit by other traffic. On busy roads, try to stop in a lay-by or a gateway. Be wary of passing traffic while changing the wheel – it is easy to become distracted by the job in hand.**

## Preparation

- [ ] When a puncture occurs, stop as soon as it is safe to do so.
- [ ] Park on firm level ground, if possible, and well out of the way of other traffic.
- [ ] Use hazard warning lights if necessary.

- [ ] If you have one, use a warning triangle to alert other drivers of your presence.
- [ ] Apply the handbrake and engage first or reverse gear (or Park on models with automatic transmission).

- [ ] Chock the wheel diagonally opposite the one being removed – a couple of large stones will do for this.
- [ ] If the ground is soft, use a flat piece of wood to spread the load under the jack.

## Changing the wheel

**1** Lift the floor covering and unscrew the spare wheel clamp nut. Lift out the spare wheel.

**2** Remove the tools from the carrier stored beneath the spare wheel.

**3** On models with steel wheels, use the special tool to pull the wheel trim from the wheel. On models with alloy wheels, use the screwdriver provided inserted at the wheel bolt holes to prise off the trim.

**4** Slacken each wheel bolt by half a turn.

**5** Locate the jack head below the jacking point nearest the wheel to be changed; the jacking point is indicated by an arrow in the sill. Turn the handle until the base of the jack touches the ground ensuring that the jack is vertical. Raise the vehicle until the wheel is clear of the ground. If the tyre is flat make sure that the vehicle is raised sufficiently to allow the spare wheel to be fitted.

**6** Remove the bolts and lift the wheel from the vehicle. Place it beneath the sill as a precaution against the jack failing. Fit the spare wheel and tighten the bolts moderately with the wheel brace.

## Finally . . .

- [ ] Remove the wheel chocks.
- [ ] Stow the jack and tools in the correct locations in the car.
- [ ] Check the tyre pressure on the wheel just fitted. If it is low, or if you don't have a pressure gauge with you, drive slowly to the nearest garage and inflate the tyre to the correct pressure.
- [ ] Have the damaged tyre or wheel repaired as soon as possible, or another puncture will leave you stranded.

**7** Lower the vehicle to the ground, then finally tighten the wheel bolts in a diagonal sequence. Refit the wheel trim. Note that the wheel bolts should be tightened to the specified torque at the earliest opportunity.

# Identifying leaks

Puddles on the garage floor or drive, or obvious wetness under the bonnet or underneath the car, suggest a leak that needs investigating. It can sometimes be difficult to decide where the leak is coming from, especially if the engine bay is very dirty already. Leaking oil or fluid can also be blown rearwards by the passage of air under the car, giving a false impression of where the problem lies.

 **Warning: Most automotive oils and fluids are poisonous. Wash them off skin, and change out of contaminated clothing, without delay.**

 *The smell of a fluid leaking from the car may provide a clue to what's leaking. Some fluids are distinctively coloured. It may help to clean the car carefully and to park it over some clean paper overnight as an aid to locating the source of the leak.*
*Remember that some leaks may only occur while the engine is running.*

## Sump oil

Engine oil may leak from the drain plug...

## Oil from filter

...or from the base of the oil filter.

## Gearbox oil

Gearbox oil can leak from the seals at the inboard ends of the driveshafts.

## Antifreeze

Leaking antifreeze often leaves a crystalline deposit like this.

## Brake fluid

A leak occurring at a wheel is almost certainly brake fluid.

## Power steering fluid

Power steering fluid may leak from the pipe connectors on the steering rack.

# Towing

When all else fails, you may find yourself having to get a tow home – or of course you may be helping somebody else. Long-distance recovery should only be done by a garage or breakdown service. For shorter distances, DIY towing using another car is easy enough, but observe the following points:
☐ Use a proper tow-rope – they are not expensive. The vehicle being towed must display an ON TOW sign in its rear window.
☐ Always turn the ignition key to the 'On' position when the vehicle is being towed, so that the steering lock is released, and the direction indicator and brake lights work.

☐ Only attach the tow-rope to the towing eye provided with the tool kit in the luggage compartment. To fit the towing eye, remove the circular cover from the front or rear bumper, as required, then screw in the towing eye anti-clockwise as far as it will go using the handle of the wheel brace to turn the eye. **Note that the towing eye has a left-hand thread.**
☐ Before being towed, release the handbrake and select neutral on the transmission. On models with automatic transmission, special precautions apply. If in doubt, do not tow, or transmission damage may result.

☐ Note that greater-than-usual pedal pressure will be required to operate the brakes, since the vacuum servo unit is only operational with the engine running.
☐ The driver of the car being towed must keep the tow-rope taut at all times to avoid snatching.
☐ Make sure that both drivers know the route before setting off.
☐ Only drive at moderate speeds and keep the distance towed to a minimum. Drive smoothly and allow plenty of time for slowing down at junctions.

## Introduction

There are some very simple checks which need only take a few minutes to carry out, but which could save you a lot of inconvenience and expense.

These *Weekly checks* require no great skill or special tools, and the small amount of time they take to perform could prove to be very well spent, for example:

☐ Keeping an eye on tyre condition and pressures, will not only help to stop them wearing out prematurely, but could also save your life.

☐ Many breakdowns are caused by electrical problems. Battery-related faults are particularly common, and a quick check on a regular basis will often prevent the majority of these.

☐ If your car develops a brake fluid leak, the first time you might know about it is when your brakes don't work properly. Checking the level regularly will give advance warning of this kind of problem.

☐ If the oil or coolant levels run low, the cost of repairing any engine damage will be far greater than fixing the leak, for example.

## Underbonnet check points

◄ **1.4 litre**

**1** *Engine oil level dipstick*

**2** *Engine oil filler cap*

**3** *Coolant reservoir (expansion tank)*

**4** *Hydraulic fluid reservoir*

**5** *Washer fluid reservoir*

**6** *Battery*

◄ **1.6 litre**

**1** *Engine oil level dipstick*

**2** *Engine oil filler cap*

**3** *Coolant reservoir (expansion tank)*

**4** *Hydraulic fluid reservoir*

**5** *Washer fluid reservoir*

**6** *Battery*

◄ **1.8 litre Z18XE**

1 *Engine oil level dipstick*
2 *Engine oil filler cap*
3 *Coolant reservoir (expansion tank)*
4 *Hydraulic fluid reservoir*
5 *Washer fluid reservoir*
6 *Battery*

◄ **1.8 litre Z18XER**

1 *Engine oil level dipstick*
2 *Engine oil filler cap*
3 *Coolant reservoir (expansion tank)*
4 *Hydraulic fluid reservoir*
5 *Washer fluid reservoir*
6 *Battery*

# Engine oil level

## Before you start
✔ Make sure that the car is on level ground.
✔ Check the oil level before the car is driven, or at least 5 minutes after the engine has been switched off.

**HAYNES HiNT** *If the oil is checked immediately after driving the vehicle, some of the oil will remain in the upper engine components, resulting in an inaccurate reading on the dipstick.*

## The correct oil
Modern engines place great demands on their oil. It is very important that the correct oil for your car is used (see *Lubricants and fluids*).

## Car care
● If you have to add oil frequently, you should check whether you have any oil leaks. Place some clean paper under the car overnight, and check for stains in the morning. If there are no leaks, then the engine may be burning oil, or the oil may only be leaking when the engine is running.
● Always maintain the level between the upper and lower dipstick marks (see photo 3). If the level is too low, severe engine damage may occur. Oil seal failure may result if the engine is overfilled by adding too much oil.

**1** The dipstick is brightly coloured for easy identification (see *Underbonnet check points* for exact location). Withdraw the dipstick.

**2** Using a clean rag or paper towel remove all oil from the dipstick. Insert the clean dipstick into the tube as far as it will go, then withdraw it again.

**3** Note the level on the end of the dipstick, which should be between the upper (MAX) mark and lower (MIN) mark. Approximately 1.0 litre of oil will raise the level from the lower mark to the upper mark.

**4** Oil is added through the filler cap. Unscrew the cap and top-up the level. A funnel may help to reduce spillage. Add the oil slowly, checking the level on the dipstick frequently. Avoid overfilling (see *Car care*).

# Coolant level

 *Warning: Do not attempt to remove the expansion tank pressure cap when the engine is hot, as there is a very great risk of scalding. Do not leave open containers of coolant about, as it is poisonous.*

## Car care
● With a sealed-type cooling system, adding coolant should not be necessary on a regular basis. If frequent topping-up is required, it is likely there is a leak. Check the radiator, all hoses and joint faces for signs of staining or wetness, and rectify as necessary.

● It is important that antifreeze is used in the cooling system all year round, not just during the winter months. Don't top up with water alone, as the antifreeze will become diluted.

**1** The coolant level varies with the temperature of the engine. When the engine is cold, the coolant level should be slightly above the KALT/COLD mark on the side of the tank. When the engine is hot, the level will rise.

**2** If topping-up is necessary, **wait until the engine is cold**. Slowly unscrew the expansion tank cap, to release any pressure present in the cooling system, and remove it.

**3** Add a mixture of water and antifreeze to the expansion tank until the coolant is up to the KALT/COLD level mark. Refit the cap and tighten it securely.

# Tyre condition and pressure

It is very important that tyres are in good condition, and at the correct pressure - having a tyre failure at any speed is highly dangerous. Tyre wear is influenced by driving style - harsh braking and acceleration, or fast cornering, will all produce more rapid tyre wear. As a general rule, the front tyres wear out faster than the rears. Interchanging the tyres from front to rear ("rotating" the tyres) may result in more even wear. However, if this is completely effective, you may have the expense of replacing all four tyres at once! Remove any nails or stones embedded in the tread before they penetrate the tyre to cause deflation. If removal of a nail does reveal that the tyre has been punctured, refit the nail so that its point of penetration is marked. Then immediately change the wheel, and have the tyre repaired by a tyre dealer.

Regularly check the tyres for damage in the form of cuts or bulges, especially in the sidewalls. Periodically remove the wheels, and clean any dirt or mud from the inside and outside surfaces. Examine the wheel rims for signs of rusting, corrosion or other damage. Light alloy wheels are easily damaged by "kerbing" whilst parking; steel wheels may also become dented or buckled. A new wheel is very often the only way to overcome severe damage.

New tyres should be balanced when they are fitted, but it may become necessary to re-balance them as they wear, or if the balance weights fitted to the wheel rim should fall off. Unbalanced tyres will wear more quickly, as will the steering and suspension components. Wheel imbalance is normally signified by vibration, particularly at a certain speed (typically around 50 mph). If this vibration is felt only through the steering, then it is likely that just the front wheels need balancing. If, however, the vibration is felt through the whole car, the rear wheels could be out of balance. Wheel balancing should be carried out by a tyre dealer or garage.

**1** *Tread Depth - visual check*
The original tyres have tread wear safety bands (B), which will appear when the tread depth reaches approximately 1.6 mm. The band positions are indicated by a triangular mark on the tyre sidewall (A).

**2** *Tread Depth - manual check*
Alternatively, tread wear can be monitored with a simple, inexpensive device known as a tread depth indicator gauge.

**3** *Tyre Pressure Check*
Check the tyre pressures regularly with the tyres cold. Do not adjust the tyre pressures immediately after the vehicle has been used, or an inaccurate setting will result.

# Tyre tread wear patterns

### Shoulder Wear

**Underinflation (wear on both sides)**
Under-inflation will cause overheating of the tyre, because the tyre will flex too much, and the tread will not sit correctly on the road surface. This will cause a loss of grip and excessive wear, not to mention the danger of sudden tyre failure due to heat build-up.
*Check and adjust pressures*
**Incorrect wheel camber (wear on one side)**
*Repair or renew suspension parts*
**Hard cornering**
*Reduce speed!*

### Centre Wear

**Overinflation**
Over-inflation will cause rapid wear of the centre part of the tyre tread, coupled with reduced grip, harsher ride, and the danger of shock damage occurring in the tyre casing.
*Check and adjust pressures*

*If you sometimes have to inflate your car's tyres to the higher pressures specified for maximum load or sustained high speed, don't forget to reduce the pressures to normal afterwards.*

### Uneven Wear

Front tyres may wear unevenly as a result of wheel misalignment. Most tyre dealers and garages can check and adjust the wheel alignment (or "tracking") for a modest charge.
**Incorrect camber or castor**
*Repair or renew suspension parts*
**Malfunctioning suspension**
*Repair or renew suspension parts*
**Unbalanced wheel**
*Balance tyres*
**Incorrect toe setting**
*Adjust front wheel alignment*
**Note:** *The feathered edge of the tread which typifies toe wear is best checked by feel.*

# Brake and clutch fluid level

 *Warning: Brake fluid can harm your eyes and damage painted surfaces, so use extreme caution when handling and pouring it. Do not use fluid which has been standing open for some time, as it absorbs moisture from the air, which can cause a dangerous loss of braking effectiveness.*

## Before you start
✔ Make sure that the car is on level ground.
✔ Cleanliness is of great importance when dealing with the braking system, so take care to clean around the reservoir cap before topping-up. Use only clean brake fluid.

## Safety first!
● If the reservoir requires repeated topping-up, this is an indication of a fluid leak somewhere in the system, which should be investigated immediately.
● If a leak is suspected, the car should not be driven until the braking system has been checked. Never take any risks where brakes are concerned.

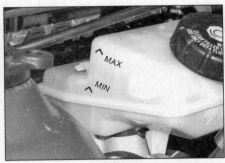

**1** The MAX and MIN marks are indicated on the side of the reservoir. The fluid level must be kept between the marks at all times.

**2** If topping-up is necessary, first wipe clean the area around the filler cap to prevent dirt entering the hydraulic system. Unscrew the reservoir cap.

**3** Carefully add fluid, taking care not to spill it onto the surrounding components. Use only the specified fluid; mixing different types can cause damage to the system. After topping-up to the correct level, securely refit the cap and wipe off any spilt fluid.

# Washer fluid level

● Screenwash additives not only keep the windscreen clean during bad weather, they also prevent the washer system freezing in cold weather – which is when you are likely to need it most. Don't top-up using plain water, as the screenwash will become diluted, and will freeze in cold weather.

 *Warning: On no account use engine coolant antifreeze in the screen washer system – this may damage the paintwork.*

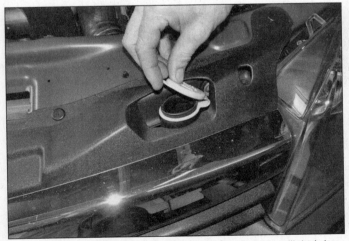

**1** The reservoir for the windscreen, rear window and headlight (where applicable) washer systems is located on the front left-hand side of the engine compartment. If topping-up is necessary, open the filler cap.

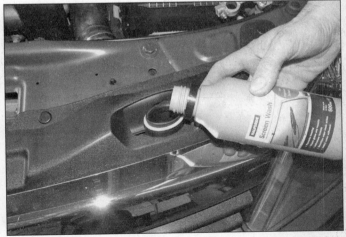

**2** When topping-up the reservoir a screenwash additive should be added in the quantities recommended on the bottle.

# Wiper blades

**1** Check the condition of the wiper blades; if they are cracked or show any signs of deterioration, or if the glass swept area is smeared, renew them. Wiper blades should be renewed annually.

**2** To remove a windscreen wiper blade, pull the arm fully away from the screen until it locks. Swivel the blade through 90°, then lift it off the pivot peg on the wiper arm. Don't forget to check the tailgate wiper blade as well which is removed in the same way.

# Battery

**Caution: Before carrying out any work on the vehicle battery, read the precautions given in 'Safety first!' at the start of this manual. If the battery is to be disconnected, refer to 'Disconnecting the battery' in the Reference Chapter, before proceeding.**

✔ Make sure that the battery tray is in good condition, and that the clamp is tight. Corrosion on the tray, retaining clamp and the battery itself can be removed with a solution of water and baking soda. Thoroughly rinse all cleaned areas with water. Any metal parts damaged by corrosion should be covered with a zinc-based primer, then painted.

✔ Periodically (approximately every three months), check the charge condition of the battery as described in Chapter 5A.

✔ If the battery is flat, and you need to jump start your vehicle, see *Roadside Repairs*.

**HAYNES HINT**

*Battery corrosion can be kept to a minimum by applying a layer of petroleum jelly to the clamps and terminals after they are reconnected.*

**1** The battery is located at the front, left-hand side of the engine compartment. Check the tightness of battery clamps to ensure good electrical connections. You should not be able to move them. Also check each cable for cracks and frayed conductors.

**2** If corrosion (white, fluffy deposits) is evident, remove the cables from the battery terminals, clean them with a small wire brush, then refit them. Automotive stores sell a tool for cleaning the battery post . . .

**3** . . . as well as the battery cable clamps

# Electrical systems

✔ Check all external lights and the horn. Refer to the appropriate Sections of Chapter 12 for details if any of the circuits are found to be inoperative.

✔ Visually check all accessible wiring connectors, harnesses and retaining clips for security, and for signs of chafing or damage.

**HAYNES HiNT** *If you need to check your brake lights and indicators unaided, back up to a wall or garage door and operate the lights. The reflected light should show if they are working properly.*

**1** If a single indicator light, stop-light or headlight has failed, it is likely that a bulb has blown and will need to be renewed. Refer to Chapter 12 for details. If both stop-lights have failed, it is possible that the switch has failed (see Chapter 9).

**2** If more than one indicator light or headlight has failed, it is likely that either a fuse has blown or that there is a fault in the circuit (see Chapter 12). The main fuses are located behind the trim panel on the left-hand side of the luggage compartment. Turn the catches and open the cover for access to the fuses.

**3** Additional fuses and relays are located in the fuse/relay box on the left-hand side of the engine compartment. Refer to the wiring diagrams at the end of Chapter 12 for details of the fuse locations and circuits protected.

**4** To renew a blown fuse, remove it, where applicable, using the plastic tool provided. Fit a new fuse of the same rating, available from car accessory shops. It is important that you find the reason that the fuse blew (see *Electrical fault finding* in Chapter 12).

## Lubricants and fluids

Engine . . . . . . . . . . . . . . . . . . . . . . . . . . . . . . . . . . . . . . . . .   Multigrade engine oil, viscosity SAE 0W/30, 0W/40, 5W/30 or 5W/40 to specification ACEA A3, ACEA A3/B3, ACEA A3/B3/B4 or higher

Manual transmission . . . . . . . . . . . . . . . . . . . . . . . . . . . .   Vauxhall/Opel gear oil (09 120 541)

Automatic transmission. . . . . . . . . . . . . . . . . . . . . . . . .   Vauxhall/Opel automatic transmission fluid (09 117 946)

Easytronic transmission . . . . . . . . . . . . . . . . . . . . . . . .   Vauxhall/Opel gear oil (09 120 541)

Power steering reservoir . . . . . . . . . . . . . . . . . . . . . . . .   Vauxhall/Opel steering fluid (90 544 116)

Cooling system. . . . . . . . . . . . . . . . . . . . . . . . . . . . . . . . .   Vauxhall/Opel silicate-free coolant (93 170 402)

Brake/clutch fluid reservoir . . . . . . . . . . . . . . . . . . . . .   Hydraulic fluid to DOT 4

## Tyre pressures (cold)

**Note:** *Pressures apply to original-equipment tyres, and may vary if any other make or type of tyre is fitted; check with the tyre manufacturer or supplier for correct pressures if necessary.*

| Normal load (up to 3 passengers) | Front | Rear |
|---|---|---|
| **1.4 litre models** | | |
| 185/65 R 15, 195/60 R 15, 215/45 R 17, 225/40 R 18 . . . . . . . . . . . . | 2.3 bar (33 psi) | 2.1 bar (30 psi) |
| 195/65 R 15, 205/55 R 16 . . . . . . . . . . . . . . . . . . . . . . . . . . . . . . . . . . | 2.0 bar (29 psi) | 2.0 bar (29 psi) |
| **1.6 litre models** | | |
| 185/65 R 15, 195/60 R 15, 215/45 R 17, 225/40 R 18 . . . . . . . . . . . . | 2.3 bar (33 psi) | 2.1 bar (30 psi) |
| 195/65 R 15, 205/55 R 16, 225/45 R 17 . . . . . . . . . . . . . . . . . . . . . . | 2.0 bar (29 psi) | 2.0 bar (29 psi) |
| **1.8 litre models** | | |
| 185/65 R 15, 195/60 R 15, 215/45 R 17, 225/45 R 17, 225/40 R 18 . . . | 2.3 bar (33 psi) | 2.1 bar (30 psi) |
| 195/65 R 15, 205/55 R 16 . . . . . . . . . . . . . . . . . . . . . . . . . . . . . . . . | 2.0 bar (29 psi) | 2.0 bar (29 psi) |
| **Fully laden** | | |
| **1.4 litre models** | | |
| 185/65 R 15, 195/60 R 15 . . . . . . . . . . . . . . . . . . . . . . . . . . . . . . . | 2.5 bar (36 psi) | 2.9 bar (42 psi) |
| 195/65 R 15, 205/55 R 16 . . . . . . . . . . . . . . . . . . . . . . . . . . . . . . . | 2.1 bar (30 psi) | 2.5 bar (36 psi) |
| 215/45 R 17, 225/40 R 18 . . . . . . . . . . . . . . . . . . . . . . . . . . . . . . . | 2.3 bar (33 psi) | 2.1 bar (30 psi) |
| **1.6 litre models** | | |
| 185/65 R 15, 195/60 R 15, 215/45 R 17, 225/40 R 18 . . . . . . . . . . . . | 2.5 bar (36 psi) | 2.9 bar (42 psi) |
| 195/65 R 15, 205/55 R 16, 225/45 R 17 . . . . . . . . . . . . . . . . . . . . . . | 2.1 bar (30 psi) | 2.5 bar (36 psi) |
| **1.8 litre models** | | |
| 185/65 R 15, 195/60 R 15, 215/45 R 17, 225/45 R 17, 225/40 R 18 . . . | 2.5 bar (36 psi) | 2.9 bar (42 psi) |
| 195/65 R 15, 205/55 R 16 . . . . . . . . . . . . . . . . . . . . . . . . . . . . . . . | 2.1 bar (30 psi) | 2.5 bar (36 psi) |
| **Space-saver temporary spare tyre** | | |
| All models. . . . . . . . . . . . . . . . . . . . . . . . . . . . . . . . . . . . . . . . . . | 4.2 bar (61 psi) | 4.2 bar (61 psi) |

# Chapter 1
# Routine maintenance and servicing

## Contents

## Degrees of difficulty

**Easy,** suitable for novice with little experience

**Fairly easy,** suitable for beginner with some experience

**Fairly difficult,** suitable for competent DIY mechanic

**Difficult,** suitable for experienced DIY mechanic

**Very difficult,** suitable for expert DIY or professional

**Lubricants and fluids** . . . . . . . . . . . . . . . . . . . . . . . . . . . . . . . .    Refer to *Weekly checks* on page 0•18

## Capacities

**Engine oil (including oil filter)**
1.4 litre engines . . . . . . . . . . . . . . . . . . . . . . . . . . . . . . . . . . . . . . .    3.5 litres
1.6 litre engines . . . . . . . . . . . . . . . . . . . . . . . . . . . . . . . . . . . . . . .    4.0 litres
1.8 litre engines . . . . . . . . . . . . . . . . . . . . . . . . . . . . . . . . . . . . . . .    4.5 litres
Difference between MIN and MAX dipstick marks . . . . . . . . . . . . . . .    1.0 litre

**Cooling system**
1.4 litre engines . . . . . . . . . . . . . . . . . . . . . . . . . . . . . . . . . . . . . . .    5.6 litres
1.6 litre engines . . . . . . . . . . . . . . . . . . . . . . . . . . . . . . . . . . . . . . .    5.9 litres
1.8 litre engines . . . . . . . . . . . . . . . . . . . . . . . . . . . . . . . . . . . . . . .    5.9 litres

**Transmission**
Manual transmission . . . . . . . . . . . . . . . . . . . . . . . . . . . . . . . . . . .    1.6 litres
Automatic transmission (at fluid change) . . . . . . . . . . . . . . . . . . . . .    4.0 litres (approximately)
Easytronic transmission . . . . . . . . . . . . . . . . . . . . . . . . . . . . . . . . .    1.6 litres

**Washer fluid reservoir**
Without headlight washers . . . . . . . . . . . . . . . . . . . . . . . . . . . . . . . .    2.4 litres
With headlight washers . . . . . . . . . . . . . . . . . . . . . . . . . . . . . . . . . .    4.0 litres

**Fuel tank** . . . . . . . . . . . . . . . . . . . . . . . . . . . . . . . . . . . . . . . . . . . .    52 litres

## Cooling system
Antifreeze mixture:
    50% antifreeze . . . . . . . . . . . . . . . . . . . . . . . . . . . . . . . . . . . . . . .    Protection down to -40°C

## Ignition system
Spark plugs:
    Type . . . . . . . . . . . . . . . . . . . . . . . . . . . . . . . . . . . . . . . . . . . . . . .    Bosch FQR 8 LEU2
    Electrode gap:
        1.4 litre engines . . . . . . . . . . . . . . . . . . . . . . . . . . . . . . . . . . . . . .    0.9 mm
        1.6 litre engines . . . . . . . . . . . . . . . . . . . . . . . . . . . . . . . . . . . . . .    1.35 mm
        1.8 litre engines:
            Z18XE . . . . . . . . . . . . . . . . . . . . . . . . . . . . . . . . . . . . . . . . . . . .    1.35 mm
            Z18XER . . . . . . . . . . . . . . . . . . . . . . . . . . . . . . . . . . . . . . . . . . .    0.9 mm

## Brakes
Friction material minimum thickness:
    Front brake pads . . . . . . . . . . . . . . . . . . . . . . . . . . . . . . . . . . . . . .    2.0 mm
    Rear brake pads . . . . . . . . . . . . . . . . . . . . . . . . . . . . . . . . . . . . . . .    2.0 mm
    Rear brake shoes . . . . . . . . . . . . . . . . . . . . . . . . . . . . . . . . . . . . . .    1.0 mm

## Torque wrench settings

| | Nm | lbf ft |
|---|---|---|
| Oil filter housing cap to filter housing (paper element filter): | | |
|    1.4 litre engines | 25 | 18 |
|    1.6 litre engines | 12 | 9 |
|    1.8 litre engines: | | |
|       Z18XE | 12 | 9 |
|       Z18XER | 25 | 18 |
| Oil filter housing retaining bolt (1.8 litre engines) | 45 | 33 |
| Roadwheel bolts | 110 | 81 |
| Spark plugs | 25 | 18 |
| Sump drain plug: | | |
|    1.4 litre engines | 10 | 7 |
|    1.6 and 1.8 litre engines | 15 | 11 |

The maintenance intervals in this manual are provided with the assumption that you, not the dealer, will be carrying out the work. These are the minimum maintenance intervals based on the standard service schedule recommended by the manufacturer for vehicles driven daily. If you wish to keep your vehicle in peak condition at all times, you may wish to perform some of these procedures more often. We encourage frequent maintenance, because it enhances the efficiency, performance and resale value of your vehicle.

If the vehicle is driven in dusty areas, used to tow a trailer, or driven frequently at slow speeds (idling in traffic) or on short journeys, more frequent maintenance intervals are recommended.

When the vehicle is new, it should be serviced by a dealer service department (or other workshop recognised by the vehicle manufacturer as providing the same standard of service) in order to preserve the warranty. The vehicle manufacturer may reject warranty claims if you are unable to prove that servicing has been carried out as and when specified, using only original equipment parts or parts certified to be of equivalent quality.

## Every 250 miles or weekly

☐ Refer to *Weekly checks*

## Every 10 000 miles or 6 months – whichever comes first

☐ Renew the engine oil and filter (Section 3)*

**\* Note:** *Vauxhall/Opel recommend that the engine oil and filter are changed every 20 000 miles or 12 months if the vehicle is being operated under the standard service schedule. However, oil and filter changes are good for the engine and we recommend that the oil and filter are renewed more frequently, especially if the vehicle is used on a lot of short journeys.*

## Every 20 000 miles or 12 months – whichever comes first

☐ Check all underbonnet and underbody components, pipes and hoses for leaks (Section 4)
☐ Check the power steering fluid level (Section 5)
☐ Check the Easytronic clutch hydraulic fluid level (Section 6)
☐ Check the condition of the brake pads, calipers and discs (Section 7)
☐ Check the condition of the rear brake shoes – models with rear drum brakes (Section 8)
☐ Check the condition of all brake fluid pipes and hoses (Section 9)
☐ Check the condition of the front suspension and steering components, particularly the rubber gaiters and seals (Section 10)
☐ Check the condition of the driveshaft joint gaiters, and the driveshaft joints (Section 11)
☐ Check the condition of the exhaust system components (Section 12)
☐ Check the condition of the rear suspension components (Section 13)
☐ Check the bodywork and underbody for damage and corrosion, and check the condition of the underbody corrosion protection (Section 14)
☐ Check the tightness of the roadwheel bolts (Section 15)
☐ Lubricate all door, bonnet and tailgate hinges and locks (Section 16)
☐ Check the operation of the horn, all lights, and the wipers and washers (Section 17)
☐ Carry out a road test (Section 18)
☐ Reset the service interval indicator (Section 19)

## Every 40 000 miles or 2 years – whichever comes first

☐ Renew the pollen filter (Section 20)
☐ Check the auxiliary drivebelt and tensioner (Section 21)
☐ Check the operation of the handbrake and adjust if necessary (Section 22)
☐ Check the headlight beam alignment (Section 23)

## Every 2 years, regardless of mileage

☐ Renew the battery for the remote control handset (Section 24)
☐ Renew the brake and clutch fluid (Section 25)
☐ Renew the coolant (Section 26)*
☐ Exhaust emission test (Section 27)

**\* Note:** *Vehicles using Vauxhall/Opel silicate-free coolant do not need the coolant renewed on a regular basis.*

## Every 40 000 miles or 4 years – whichever comes first

☐ Renew the air cleaner filter element (Section 28)
☐ Renew the spark plugs (Section 29)
☐ Renew the timing belt, tensioner and idler pulleys – 1.6 and 1.8 litre engines (Section 30)*
☐ Renew the automatic transmission fluid (Section 31)

**\* Note:** *The normal interval for timing belt renewal is 54 000 miles or 6 years for the 1.8 litre Z18XE engines, and 90 000 miles or 10 years for all other engines. However, it is strongly recommended that the interval used is 36 000 miles on vehicles which are subjected to intensive use, ie, mainly short journeys or a lot of stop-start driving. The actual belt renewal interval is therefore very much up to the individual owner, but bear in mind that severe engine damage will result if the belt breaks.*

## Every 100 000 miles or 10 years – whichever comes first

☐ Check, and if necessary adjust, the valve clearances – 1.6 litre and 1.8 litre Z18XER engines (Section 32)

## Underbonnet view of a 1.4 litre model

1 Engine oil level dipstick
2 Engine oil filler cap
3 Air cleaner assembly
4 Front suspension strut upper mounting
5 Washer fluid reservoir
6 Airflow meter
7 Brake (and clutch) fluid reservoir
8 Power steering fluid reservoir
9 Coolant expansion tank
10 Battery
11 Fuse/relay box

## Underbonnet view of a 1.6 litre model

1 Engine oil level dipstick
2 Engine oil filler cap
3 Air cleaner assembly
4 Front suspension strut upper mounting
5 Washer fluid reservoir
6 Airflow meter
7 Brake (and clutch) fluid reservoir
8 Power steering fluid reservoir
9 Coolant expansion tank
10 Battery
11 Fuse/relay box

## Underbonnet view of a 1.8 litre Z18XE model

1 Engine oil level dipstick
2 Engine oil filler cap
3 Air cleaner assembly
4 Front suspension strut upper mounting
5 Washer fluid reservoir
6 Airflow meter
7 Brake (and clutch) fluid reservoir
8 Power steering fluid reservoir
9 Coolant expansion tank
10 Battery
11 Fuse/relay box

## Underbonnet view of a 1.8 litre Z18XER model

1 Engine oil level dipstick
2 Engine oil filler cap
3 Air cleaner assembly
4 Front suspension strut upper mounting
5 Washer fluid reservoir
6 Airflow meter
7 Brake (and clutch) fluid reservoir
8 Power steering fluid reservoir
9 Coolant expansion tank
10 Battery
11 Fuse/relay box

## Front underbody view

1   Exhaust front pipe
2   Steering track rods
3   Front suspension lower arms
4   Front brake calipers
5   Engine mounting front torque link
6   Engine mounting rear torque link
7   Right-hand driveshaft
8   Manual transmission
9   Engine oil drain plug
10  Air conditioning compressor
11  Front subframe

## Rear underbody view

1   Exhaust tailpipe and silencer
2   Rear suspension torsion beam and trailing arms
3   Fuel tank
4   Handbrake cables
5   Spare wheel well
6   Rear coil springs
7   Rear shock absorber lower mountings

## 1 General information

**1** This Chapter is designed to help the home mechanic maintain his/her vehicle for safety, economy, long life and peak performance.

**2** The Chapter contains a master maintenance schedule, followed by Sections dealing specifically with each task in the schedule. Visual checks, adjustments, component renewal and other helpful items are included. Refer to the accompanying illustrations of the engine compartment and the underside of the vehicle for the locations of the various components.

**3** Servicing your vehicle in accordance with the mileage/time maintenance schedule and the following Sections will provide a planned maintenance programme, which should result in a long and reliable service life. This is a comprehensive plan, so maintaining some items but not others at the specified service intervals will not produce the same results.

**4** As you service your vehicle, you will discover that many of the procedures can – and should – be grouped together, because of the particular procedure being performed, or because of the proximity of two otherwise-unrelated components to one another. For example, if the vehicle is raised for any reason, the exhaust can be inspected at the same time as the suspension and steering components.

**5** The first step in this maintenance programme is to prepare yourself before the actual work begins. Read through all the Sections relevant to the work to be carried out, then make a list and gather all the parts and tools required. If a problem is encountered, seek advice from a parts specialist, or a dealer service department.

## 2 Regular maintenance

**1** If, from the time the vehicle is new, the routine maintenance schedule is followed closely, and frequent checks are made of fluid levels and high-wear items, as suggested throughout this manual, the engine will be kept in relatively good running condition, and the need for additional work will be minimised.

**2** It is possible that there will be times when the engine is running poorly due to the lack of regular maintenance. This is even more likely if a used vehicle, which has not received regular and frequent maintenance checks, is purchased. In such cases, additional work may need to be carried out, outside of the regular maintenance intervals.

**3** If engine wear is suspected, a compression test (refer to the appropriate part of Chapter 2) will provide valuable information regarding the overall performance of the main internal components. Such a test can be used as a basis to decide on the extent of the work to be carried out. If, for example, a compression test indicates serious internal engine wear, conventional maintenance as described in this Chapter will not greatly improve the performance of the engine, and may prove a waste of time and money, unless extensive overhaul work is carried out first.

**4** The following series of operations are those most often required to improve the performance of a generally poor-running engine:

### Primary operations

a) Clean, inspect and test the battery (refer to Weekly checks).
b) Check all the engine-related fluids (refer to Weekly checks).
c) Check the condition and tension of the auxiliary drivebelt (Section 21).
d) Renew the spark plugs (Section 29).
e) Check the condition of the air cleaner element, and renew if necessary (Section 28).
f) Check the condition of all hoses, and check for fluid leaks (Section 4).

**5** If the above operations do not prove fully effective, carry out the following secondary operations:

### Secondary operations

All items listed under *Primary operations*, plus the following:
a) Check the ignition system (Chapter 5B).
b) Check the charging system (Chapter 5A).
c) Check the fuel, exhaust and emission control systems (refer to the appropriate Parts of Chapter 4).

# Every 10 000 miles or 6 months

## 3 Engine oil and filter renewal

> **HAYNES HiNT**
> *Frequent oil and filter changes are the most important preventative maintenance procedures which can be undertaken by the DIY owner. As engine oil ages, it becomes diluted and contaminated, which leads to premature engine wear.*

**3.3 Removing the oil filler cap**

**1** Before starting this procedure, gather together all the necessary tools and materials. Also make sure that you have plenty of clean rags and newspapers handy to mop-up any spills. Ideally, the engine oil should be warm, as it will drain more easily, and more built-up sludge will be removed with it. Take care not to touch the exhaust or any other hot parts of the engine when working under the vehicle. To avoid any possibility of scalding, and to protect yourself from possible skin irritants and other harmful contaminants in used engine oils, it is advisable to wear gloves when carrying out this work.

**2** Access to the underside of the vehicle will be greatly improved if it can be raised on a lift, driven onto ramps, or jacked up and supported on axle stands (see *Jacking and vehicle support*). Whichever method is chosen, make sure that the vehicle remains level, or if it is at an angle, that the drain plug is at the lowest point.

**3** Remove the oil filler cap from the camshaft cover (twist it through a quarter-turn anti-clockwise and withdraw it) **(see illustration)**.

**4** Using a spanner, or preferably a suitable socket and bar, slacken the drain plug about half a turn. Position the draining container under the drain plug, then remove the plug completely **(see Haynes Hint)**.

**5** Allow some time for the oil to drain, noting that it may be necessary to reposition the container as the oil flow slows to a trickle.

**6** Position another container under the oil filter, located on the front left-hand side of the cylinder block. Two different types of filter may be encountered. On 1.4 and 1.6 litre engines, the oil filter is of the paper element type. On 1.8 litre engines the oil filter may be either a paper element type or a metal canister type. Proceed as described under the following sub-Sections, according to engine.

> **HAYNES HiNT**
>
> *As the drain plug threads release, move it sharply away so the stream of oil issuing from the sump runs into the container, not up your sleeve.*

3.7 Oil filter (arrowed) on 1.4 litre engines

3.12a Fit a new sealing O-ring to the oil filter housing cap . . .

3.12b . . . then clip the new oil filter element to the cap

3.13a Fit the cap and filter element assembly to the oil filter housing . . .

3.13b . . . screw the assembly into place and tighten the cap to the specified torque

3.15 Using an oil filter removal tool to slacken the canister-type filter – 1.8 litre engines

### 1.4 litre engines

7 Move the container into position under the oil filter housing **(see illustration)**.

8 Unscrew the oil filter housing cap and withdraw the cap together with the filter from the oil filter housing.

9 Withdraw the filter from the oil filter housing cap.

10 Use clean rags to remove all remaining oil, dirt and sludge from the oil filter housing.

11 Remove the sealing O-ring from the oil filter housing cap.

12 Fit a new sealing O-ring to the oil filter housing cap then clip the new oil filter element to the cap **(see illustrations)**.

13 Fit the cap and filter element assembly to the oil filter housing and screw the cap into position. Finally, tighten the cap to the specified torque **(see illustrations)**.

### 1.6 and 1.8 litre engines

14 Move the container into position under the oil filter.

15 Where a canister-type oil filter is fitted, use an oil filter removal tool to slacken the filter initially, then unscrew it by hand the rest of the way **(see illustration)**. Empty the oil from the old filter into the container. In order to ensure that all the old oil is removed, puncture the 'dome' of the filter in two places and allow the oil to drain from the filter completely.

16 Where a paper element-type oil filter is fitted, unscrew the filter cap and withdraw it, together with the element, then separate the element and remove the O-ring seal from the cap **(see illustrations)**.

17 Use a clean rag to remove all oil, dirt and sludge from the filter sealing area on

the block. Where a paper element-type oil filter is used, if required, the oil filter housing can be removed from the cylinder block by unscrewing the retaining bolt. The housing can then be thoroughly cleaned and refitted to the block with a new sealing ring **(see illustration)**. Tighten the retaining bolt to the specified torque.

18 On the canister-type filter, apply a light coating of clean engine oil to the sealing ring on the new filter, then screw the filter into position on the engine. Tighten the filter firmly by hand only – **do not** use any tools.

19 On the paper element-type filter, locate a new O-ring seal in the groove on the retaining cap, then locate the new element in the cap and insert them both in the filter housing. Screw on the cap and tighten to the specified torque.

3.16a Separate the paper-element type filter from the cap . . .

3.16b . . . then remove the O-ring seal – 1.8 litre engines

3.17 The oil filter housing can be removed from the cylinder block by unscrewing the retaining bolt – 1.8 litre engines

## All engines

**20** After all the oil has drained, wipe the drain plug and the sealing washer/O-ring with a clean rag. Examine the condition of the sealing washer/O-ring, and renew it if it shows signs of damage which may prevent an oil-tight seal. Clean the area around the drain plug opening, and refit the plug complete with the washer/O-ring. Tighten the plug to the specified torque, using a torque wrench.

**21** Remove the old oil and all tools from under the vehicle then lower the vehicle to the ground.

**22** Fill the engine through the filler hole in the camshaft cover, using the correct grade and type of oil (refer to *Weekly checks* for details of topping-up). Pour in half the specified quantity of oil first, then wait a few minutes for the oil to drain into the sump. Continue to add oil, a small quantity at a time, until the level is up to the lower mark on the dipstick. Adding approximately a further 1.0 litre will bring the level up to the upper mark on the dipstick.

**23** Start the engine and run it until it reaches normal operating temperature. While the engine is warming-up, check for leaks around the oil filter and the sump drain plug.

**24** Stop the engine, and wait at least five minutes for the oil to settle in the sump once more. With the new oil circulated and the filter now completely full, recheck the level on the dipstick, and add more oil as necessary.

**25** Dispose of the used engine oil and filter safely, with reference to *General repair procedures* in the Reference Chapter of this manual. Do not discard the old filter with domestic household waste. The facility for waste oil disposal provided by many local council refuse tips and/or recycling centres generally has a filter receptacle alongside.

# Every 20 000 miles or 12 months

### 4  Hose and fluid leak check

**1** Visually inspect the engine joint faces, gaskets and seals for any signs of water or oil leaks. Pay particular attention to the areas around the camshaft cover, cylinder head, oil filter and sump joint faces. Similarly, check the transmission and (where applicable) the air conditioning compressor for oil leakage. Bear in mind that, over a period of time, some very slight seepage from these areas is to be expected; what you are really looking for is any indication of a serious leak. Should a leak be found, renew the offending gasket or oil seal by referring to the appropriate Chapters in this manual.

**2** Also check the security and condition of all the engine-related pipes and hoses. Ensure that all cable ties or securing clips are in place, and in good condition. Clips which are broken or missing can lead to chafing of the hoses pipes or wiring, which could cause more serious problems in the future.

**3** Carefully check the radiator hoses and heater hoses along their entire length. Renew any hose which is cracked, swollen or deteriorated. Cracks will show up better if the hose is squeezed. Pay close attention to the hose clips that secure the hoses to the cooling system components. Hose clips can pinch and puncture hoses, resulting in cooling system leaks. If wire-type hose clips are used, it may be a good idea to update them with screw-type clips.

**4** Inspect all the cooling system components (hoses, joint faces, etc) for leaks. Where any problems of this nature are found on system components, renew the component or gasket with reference to Chapter 3 **(see Haynes Hint)**.

**5** Where applicable, inspect the automatic transmission fluid cooler hoses for leaks or deterioration.

**6** With the vehicle raised, inspect the fuel tank and filler neck for punctures, cracks and other damage. The connection between the filler neck and tank is especially critical. Sometimes, a rubber filler neck or connecting hose will leak due to loose retaining clamps or deteriorated rubber.

**7** Carefully check all rubber hoses and metal or plastic fuel lines leading away from the fuel tank. Check for loose connections, deteriorated hoses, crimped lines and other damage. Pay particular attention to the vent pipes and hoses, which often loop up around the filler neck and can become blocked or crimped. Follow the lines to the front of the vehicle, carefully inspecting them all the way. Renew damaged sections as necessary. Similarly, whilst the vehicle is raised, take the opportunity to inspect all underbody brake fluid pipes and hoses.

**8** From within the engine compartment, check the security of all fuel hose attachments and pipe unions, and inspect the fuel hoses and vacuum hoses for kinks, chafing and deterioration.

### 5  Power steering fluid level check

**1** The power steering fluid reservoir on RHD vehicles is located on the left-hand side of the engine compartment between the transmission and the bulkhead. On LHD vehicles, the reservoir is located between the engine and bulkhead on the right-hand side of the engine compartment. The fluid level should be checked with the engine cold.

**2** Wipe clean the reservoir and filler cap, then unscrew the filler cap from the top of the reservoir **(see illustration)**. The filler cap has a bayonet fitting and has a dipstick incorporated into it.

**3** Wipe all fluid from the dipstick with a clean rag. Refit the dipstick, then remove it again. Note the fluid level on the dipstick which should be up to the MAX mark **(see illustration)**.

**4** If topping-up is necessary, obtain a clean funnel and a long length of flexible pipe to fit the end of the funnel. Insert the pipe

*A leak in the cooling system will usually show up as white- or antifreeze-coloured deposits on the area adjoining the leak.*

**5.2 Power steering fluid reservoir filler cap (arrowed)**

**5.3 The fluid level should be up to the MAX mark (arrowed) on the dipstick**

down behind the engine and into the top of the reservoir **(see illustration)**. Using power steering fluid of the specified type (see *Lubricants and fluids*), top-up the reservoir by means of the funnel and tube until the level is up to the MAX mark on the dipstick. Do this slowly and carefully, checking the level with the dipstick frequently. Take care not to overfill the reservoir.

**5** When the level is correct, remove the funnel and tube and refit the reservoir filler cap.

### 6 Clutch hydraulic fluid level check – Easytronic models

**1** The clutch hydraulic fluid level markings are on the side of the fluid reservoir located on the front of the transmission. The use of a mirror will be helpful.

**2** Check that the level of the fluid is at or near the MAX marking on the side of the reservoir **(see illustration)**.

**3** If topping-up is required, unscrew the filler cap and pour in fresh fluid until the level is at the MAX marking. Retighten the cap on completion.

### 7 Brake pad and disc check

**1** Firmly apply the handbrake, then jack up the front and rear of the vehicle and support it securely on axle stands (see *Jacking and vehicle support*). Remove the roadwheels.

**2** For a quick check, the pad thickness can be carried out via the inspection hole on the caliper **(see Haynes Hint)**. Using a steel rule, measure the thickness of the pad friction linings. This must not be less than that indicated in the Specifications.

**3** The view through the caliper inspection hole gives a rough indication of the state of the brake pads. For a comprehensive check, the

**6.2 Clutch fluid reservoir (1) on Easytronic models**

**5.4 Use a clean funnel and a long length of flexible pipe to top-up the reservoir**

brake pads should be removed and cleaned. The operation of the caliper can then also be checked, and the condition of the brake disc itself can be fully examined on both sides. Chapter 9 contains a detailed description of how the brake disc should be checked for wear and/or damage.

**4** If any pad's friction material is worn to the specified thickness or less, *all four pads must be renewed as a set*. Refer to Chapter 9 for details.

**5** On completion, refit the roadwheels and lower the vehicle to the ground.

### 8 Rear brake shoe check – models with rear drum brakes

**1** Chock the front wheels, then jack up the rear of the vehicle, and support it securely on axle stands (see *Jacking and vehicle support*).

**2** For a quick check, the thickness of friction material remaining on one of the brake shoes can be observed through the hole in the brake backplate which is exposed by prising out the sealing grommet. If a rod of the same diameter as the specified minimum friction material thickness is placed against the shoe friction material, the amount of wear can be assessed. An electric torch or inspection light will probably be required. If the friction material on any shoe is worn down to the specified minimum thickness or less, all four shoes must be renewed as a set.

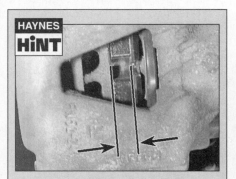

**HAYNES HiNT**

*For a quick check, the thickness of friction material remaining on the inner brake pad can be measured through the aperture in the caliper body.*

**3** For a comprehensive check, the brake drum should be removed and cleaned. This will allow the wheel cylinders to be checked, and the condition of the brake drum itself to be fully examined (see Chapter 9).

### 9 Brake fluid pipe and hose check

**1** The brake hydraulic system includes a number of metal pipes, which run from the master cylinder to the hydraulic modulator of the anti-lock braking system (ABS) and then to the front and rear brake assemblies. Flexible hoses are fitted between the pipes and the front and rear brake assemblies, to allow for steering and suspension movement.

**2** When checking the system, first look for signs of leakage at the pipe or hose unions, then examine the flexible hoses for signs of cracking, chafing or deterioration of the rubber. Bend the hoses sharply between the fingers (but do not actually bend them double, or the casing may be damaged) and check that this does not reveal previously-hidden cracks, cuts or splits. Check that the pipes and hoses are securely fastened in their clips.

**3** Carefully working along the length of the metal pipes, look for dents, kinks, damage of any sort, or corrosion. Light corrosion can be polished off, but if the depth of pitting is significant, the pipe must be renewed.

### 10 Front suspension and steering check

**1** Apply the handbrake, then raise the front of the vehicle and securely support it on axle stands (see *Jacking and vehicle support*).

**2** Inspect the balljoint dust covers and the steering gear gaiters for splits, chafing or deterioration.

**3** Any wear of these components will cause loss of lubricant, and may allow water to enter the components, resulting in rapid deterioration of the balljoints or steering gear.

**4** Grasp each roadwheel at the 12 o'clock and 6 o'clock positions, and try to rock it **(see illustration)**. Very slight free play may

**10.4 Check for wear in the hub hearings by grasping the wheel and trying to rock it**

be felt, but if the movement is appreciable, further investigation is necessary to determine the source. Continue rocking the wheel while an assistant depresses the footbrake. If the movement is now eliminated or significantly reduced, it is likely that the hub bearings are at fault. If the free play is still evident with the footbrake depressed, then there is wear in the suspension joints or mountings.

**5** Now grasp each wheel at the 9 o'clock and 3 o'clock positions, and try to rock it as before. Any movement felt now may again be caused by wear in the hub bearings or the steering track rod end balljoints. If the track rod end balljoint is worn, the visual movement will be obvious.

**6** Using a large screwdriver or flat bar, check for wear in the suspension mounting bushes by levering between the relevant suspension component and its attachment point. Some movement is to be expected, as the mountings are made of rubber, but excessive wear should be obvious. Also check the condition of any visible rubber bushes, looking for splits, cracks or contamination of the rubber.

**7** Check for any signs of fluid leakage around the suspension struts, or from the rubber gaiters around the piston rods. Should any fluid be noticed, the suspension strut is defective internally, and should be renewed. **Note:** *Suspension struts should always be renewed in pairs on the same axle.*

**8** With the vehicle standing on its wheels, have an assistant turn the steering wheel back-and-forth about an eighth of a turn each way. There should be very little, if any, lost movement between the steering wheel and roadwheels. If this is not the case, closely observe the joints and mountings previously described. In addition, check the steering column universal joints for wear, and also check the rack-and-pinion steering gear itself.

**9** The efficiency of each suspension strut may be checked by bouncing the vehicle at each front corner. Generally speaking, the body will return to its normal position and stop after being depressed. If it rises and returns on a rebound, the suspension strut is probably suspect. Also examine the suspension strut upper mountings for any signs of wear.

## 11 Driveshaft check

**1** Firmly apply the handbrake, then jack up the front of the car and support it securely on axle stands (see *Jacking and vehicle support*).

**2** Turn the steering onto full lock then slowly rotate the roadwheel. Inspect the condition of the outer constant velocity (CV) joint rubber gaiters while squeezing the gaiters to open out the folds **(see illustration)**. Check for signs of cracking, splits or deterioration of the rubber which may allow the grease to escape and lead to water and grit entry into the joint. Also check the security and condition of the retaining clips. Repeat these checks on the inner CV joints. If any damage or deterioration is found, the gaiters should be renewed as described in Chapter 8.

**3** At the same time, check the general condition of the CV joints themselves by first holding the driveshaft and attempting to rotate the wheel. Repeat this check by holding the inner joint and attempting to rotate the driveshaft. Any appreciable movement indicates wear in the joints, wear in the driveshaft splines or loose driveshaft retaining nut.

## 12 Exhaust system check

**1** With the engine cold (at least an hour after the vehicle has been driven), check the complete exhaust system from the engine to the end of the tailpipe. The exhaust system is most easily checked with the vehicle raised on a hoist, or suitably-supported on axle stands, so that the exhaust components are readily visible and accessible (see *Jacking and vehicle support*).

**2** Check the exhaust pipes and connections for evidence of leaks, severe corrosion and damage. Make sure that all brackets and mountings are in good condition, and that all relevant nuts and bolts are tight. Leakage at any of the joints or in other parts of the system will usually show up as a black sooty stain in the vicinity of the leak.

**3** Rattles and other noises can often be traced to the exhaust system, especially the brackets and mountings **(see illustration)**. Try to move the pipes and silencers. If the components are able to come into contact with the body or suspension parts, secure the system with new mountings. Otherwise separate the joints (if possible) and twist the pipes as necessary to provide additional clearance.

## 13 Rear suspension check

**1** Chock the front wheels, then jack up the rear of the vehicle and support securely on axle stands (see *Jacking and vehicle support*).

**2** Inspect the rear suspension components for any signs of obvious wear or damage. Pay particular attention to the rubber mounting bushes, and renew if necessary (see Chapter 10).

**3** Grasp each roadwheel at the 12 o'clock and 6 o'clock positions **(see illustration 10.4)**, and try to rock it. Any excess movement indicates wear in the wheel bearings. Wear may also be accompanied by a rumbling sound when the wheel is spun, or a noticeable roughness if the wheel is turned slowly. The wheel bearing can be renewed as described in Chapter 10.

**11.2 Check the condition of the driveshaft gaiters (1) and retaining clips (2)**

**12.3 Exhaust mountings**

**4** Check for any signs of fluid leakage around the shock absorber bodies. Should any fluid be noticed, the shock absorber is defective internally, and should be renewed. **Note:** *Shock absorbers should always be renewed in pairs on the same axle.*

**5** With the vehicle standing on its wheels, the efficiency of each shock absorber may be checked by bouncing the vehicle at each rear corner. Generally speaking, the body will return to its normal position and stop after being depressed. If it rises and returns on a rebound, the shock absorber is probably suspect.

## 14 Bodywork and underbody condition check

**Note:** *This work should be carried out by a Vauxhall/Opel dealer in order to validate the vehicle warranty. The work includes a thorough inspection of the vehicle paintwork and underbody for damage and corrosion.*

### Bodywork damage/ corrosion check

**1** Once the car has been washed, and all tar spots and other surface blemishes have been cleaned off, carefully check all paintwork, looking closely for chips or scratches. Pay particular attention to vulnerable areas such as the front panels (bonnet and spoiler), and around the wheel arches. Any damage to the paintwork must be rectified as soon as possible to comply with the terms of the manufacturer's anti-corrosion warranties; check with a Vauxhall/Opel dealer for details.

**2** If a chip or light scratch is found which is recent and still free from rust, it can be touched-up using the appropriate touch-up stick which can be obtained from Vauxhall/ Opel dealers. Any more serious damage, or rusted stone chips, can be repaired as described in Chapter 11, but if damage or corrosion is so severe that a panel must be renewed, seek professional advice as soon as possible.

**3** Always check that the door and ventilation opening drain holes and pipes are completely clear, so that water can drain out.

### Corrosion protection check

**4** The wax-based underbody protective coating should be inspected annually, preferably just prior to Winter, when the underbody should be washed down as thoroughly as possible without disturbing the protective coating. Any damage to the coating should be repaired using a suitable wax-based sealer. If any of the body panels are disturbed for repair or renewal, do not forget to re-apply the coating. Wax should be injected into door cavities, sills and box sections, to maintain the level of protection provided by the vehicle manufacturer – seek the advice of a Vauxhall/ Opel dealer.

## 15 Roadwheel bolt tightness check

**1** Where applicable, remove the wheel trims from the wheels.

**2** Using a torque wrench on each wheel bolt in turn, ensure that the bolts are tightened to the specified torque.

**3** Where applicable, refit the wheel trims on completion, making sure they are fitted correctly.

## 16 Hinge and lock lubrication

**1** Work around the vehicle and lubricate the hinges of the bonnet, doors and tailgate with a light machine oil.

**2** Lightly lubricate the bonnet release mechanism and exposed section of inner cable with a smear of grease.

**3** Check the security and operation of all hinges, latches and locks, adjusting them where required. Check the operation of the central locking system.

**4** Check the condition and operation of the bonnet and tailgate support struts, renewing them both if either is leaking or no longer able to support the bonnet/tailgate securely when raised.

## 17 Electrical systems check

**1** Check the operation of all the electrical equipment, ie, lights, direction indicators, horn, etc. Refer to the appropriate sections of Chapter 12 for details if any of the circuits are found to be inoperative.

**2** Note that the stop-light switch is described in Chapter 9.

**3** Check all accessible wiring connectors, harnesses and retaining clips for security, and for signs of chafing or damage. Rectify any faults found.

## 18 Road test

### Instruments and electrical equipment

**1** Check the operation of all instruments, warning lights and electrical equipment.

**2** Make sure that all instruments read correctly, and switch on all electrical equipment in turn, to check that it functions properly.

### Steering and suspension

**3** Check for any abnormalities in the steering, suspension, handling or road 'feel'.

**4** Drive the vehicle, and check that there are no unusual vibrations or noises.

**5** Check that the steering feels positive, with no excessive 'sloppiness', or roughness, and check for any suspension noises when cornering and driving over bumps.

### Drivetrain

**6** Check the performance of the engine, clutch, transmission and driveshafts.

**7** Listen for any unusual noises from the engine, clutch and transmission.

**8** Make sure that the engine runs smoothly when idling, and that there is no hesitation when accelerating.

**9** Check that, where applicable, the clutch action is smooth and progressive, that the drive is taken up smoothly, and that the pedal travel is not excessive. Also listen for any noises when the clutch pedal is depressed.

**10** Check that all gears can be engaged smoothly without noise, and that the gear lever action is smooth and not abnormally vague or 'notchy'.

**11** On automatic transmission models, make sure that all gearchanges occur smoothly, without snatching, and without an increase in engine speed between changes. Check that all of the gear positions can be selected with the vehicle at rest. If any problems are found, they should be referred to a Vauxhall/Opel dealer.

**12** Listen for a metallic clicking sound from the front of the vehicle, as the vehicle is driven slowly in a circle with the steering on full-lock. Carry out this check in both directions. If a clicking noise is heard, this indicates wear in a driveshaft joint (see Chapter 8).

### Braking system

**13** Make sure that the vehicle does not pull to one side when braking.

**14** Check that there is no vibration through the steering when braking.

**15** Check that the handbrake operates correctly, without excessive movement of the lever, and that it holds the vehicle stationary on a slope.

**16** Test the operation of the brake servo unit as follows. Depress the footbrake four or five times to exhaust the vacuum, then start the engine. As the engine starts, there should be a noticeable 'give' in the brake pedal as vacuum builds-up. Allow the engine to run for at least two minutes, and then switch it off. If the brake pedal is now depressed again, it should be possible to detect a hiss from the servo as the pedal is depressed. After about four or five applications, no further hissing should be heard, and the pedal should feel considerably harder.

## 19 Service interval indicator reset

**1** With the ignition switched off, the display on the instrument panel must show the trip odometer.

**2** With the ignition still switched off, depress and hold the trip odometer reset button located on the instrument panel.
**3** With both the brake pedal and the reset button depressed, switch on the ignition, wait until the service interval display changes (approximately 10 seconds).
**4** After approximately 10 seconds the display will show the service symbol and the maximum mileage before the next required service, followed by 'InSP'. When '- - -' appears in the display, release the reset button and switch off the ignition. When the button is released, the odometer reading will appear again.

# Every 40 000 miles or 2 years

## 20 Pollen filter renewal

**1** Remove the glovebox as described in Chapter 11.
**2** Undo the two screws and remove the facia lower panel below the glovebox **(see illustration)**.
**3** Release the expanding rivet and remove the passenger's side footwell air duct **(see illustration)**.
**4** Undo the three screws and remove the pollen filter access cover from the side of the heater/ventilation air distribution housing **(see illustration)**.
**5** Withdraw the pollen filter from the housing **(see illustration)**.
**6** Fit the new filter using a reversal of the removal procedure; make sure that the filter is fitted the correct way up, as indicated on the edge of the filter.

## 21 Auxiliary drivebelt condition check

### Checking

**1** Due to their function and material make-up, drivebelts are prone to failure after a long period of time and should therefore be inspected regularly.
**2** Apply the handbrake, then jack up the front of the vehicle and support it on axle stands (see *Jacking and vehicle support*). Remove the right-hand front roadwheel and the wheel arch liner cover for access to the right-hand side of the engine.
**3** With the engine stopped, inspect the full length of the drivebelt for cracks and separation of the belt plies. It will be necessary to turn the engine (using a spanner or socket and bar on the crankshaft pulley bolt) so that the belt can be inspected thoroughly. Twist the belt between the pulleys so that both sides can be viewed. Also check for fraying, and glazing which gives the belt a shiny appearance. Check the pulleys for nicks, cracks, distortion and corrosion. If the belt shows signs of wear or damage, it should be renewed as a precaution against breakage in service.

### Renewal

**Note:** *The manufacturers recommend that the tensioner roller is checked and if necessary renewed at the same time as the drivebelt.*
**4** If not already done, apply the handbrake, then jack up the front of the vehicle and support it on axle stands (see *Jacking and vehicle support*). Remove the right-hand front roadwheel and the wheel arch liner cover for access to the right-hand side of the engine.
**5** For additional working clearance, remove the air cleaner housing as described in Chapter 4A.
**6** If the drivebelt is to be re-used, mark it to indicate its normal running direction.
**7** On 1.4 litre engines, support the engine and remove the right-hand engine mounting with reference to Chapter 2A. **Note:** *On these engines, the engine mounting locates within the auxiliary drivebelt run.*
**8** Note the routing of the drivebelt, then, using a Torx key or spanner (as applicable) on the pulley centre bolt, or the raised projection on the tensioner arm, turn the tensioner clockwise (1.4 litre engines) or anti-clockwise (1.6 and 1.8 litre engines) against the spring tension. Hold the tensioner in this position by inserting a suitable locking pin/

**20.2 Undo the two screws and remove the facia lower panel below the glovebox**

**20.3 Release the expanding rivet and remove the passenger's side footwell air duct**

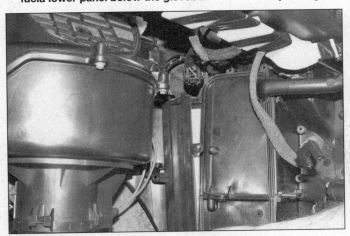

**20.4 Undo the three screws and remove the pollen filter access cover from the side of the air distribution housing**

**20.5 Withdraw the pollen filter from the housing**

**21.8a Auxiliary drivebelt tensioner on 1.4 litre engines**

*1  Tensioner body*                    *2  Locking pin/bolt*

**21.8b Auxiliary drivebelt tensioner on 1.8 litre Z18XE engines**

*1  Locking pin/bolt*
*2  Turn the tensioner as indicated to release the tension*

**21.8c Auxiliary drivebelt tensioner on 1.6 litre and 1.8 litre Z18XER engines**

*1  Raised projection on tensioner arm*
*2  Locking pin/bolt hole*

bolt through the special hole provided **(see illustrations)**.

9  Slip the auxiliary drivebelt off of the pulleys.

10  Locate the auxiliary drivebelt onto the

pulleys in the correct routing. If the drivebelt is being re-used, make sure it is fitted the correct way around.

11  Turn back the tensioner and remove the

locking bolt, then release it, making sure that the drivebelt ribs locate correctly on each of the pulley grooves.

12  On 1.4 litre engines, refit the right-hand engine mounting with reference to Chapter 2A.

13  Refit the air cleaner housing, then refit the wheel arch liner and roadwheel, and lower the vehicle to the ground.

## 22  Handbrake operation and adjustment check

1  With the vehicle on a slight slope, apply the handbrake lever by up to 3 clicks of the ratchet, and check that it holds the vehicle stationary, then release the lever and check that there is no resistance to movement of the vehicle.

2  If necessary, adjust the handbrake as follows.

3  Chock the front wheels then jack up the rear of the car and securely support it on axle stands (see *Jacking and vehicle support*).

4  From inside the vehicle, unclip and remove the access panel in the centre console, beneath the handbrake lever **(see illustration)**.

5  The handbrake cable adjuster nut is situated is situated by the handbrake lever inside the vehicle, unclip the cover from around the handbrake lever **(see illustration)**.

6  Move the handbrake lever to the fully released position, then turn the cable adjuster nut anti-clockwise to remove all tension from the cables **(see illustration)**.

7  Depress the footbrake five times, then fully apply and release the handbrake lever five times.

8  With the handbrake lever set on the second notch of the ratchet mechanism, rotate the adjuster nut clockwise until a reasonable amount of force is required to turn each wheel. **Note**: *The force required should be equal for each wheel.*

9  Now pull the handbrake lever up to the third notch of the ratchet mechanism and check that both rear wheels are locked. Once this is so, fully release the handbrake lever and check that the wheels rotate freely. Check the adjustment by applying the handbrake fully whilst counting the clicks emitted from

**22.4  Unclip and remove the centre console access panel**

**22.5  Unclip the cover from around the handbrake lever . . .**

**22.6  . . . for access to the handbrake cable adjuster nut (arrowed)**

the handbrake ratchet and, if necessary, re-adjust.

**10** On completion of adjustment, refit the handbrake lever cover and centre console access panel, then lower the vehicle to the ground.

### 23 Headlight beam alignment check

Accurate adjustment of the headlight beam is only possible using optical beam-setting equipment, and this work should therefore be carried out by a Vauxhall/Opel dealer or service station with the necessary facilities. Refer to Chapter 12 for further information.

# Every 2 years, regardless of mileage

### 24 Remote control battery renewal

**1** Using a screwdriver, prise the battery cover from the ignition key fob **(see illustration)**.
**2** Note how the circular battery is fitted, then remove it from the contacts **(see illustration)**.
**3** Fit the new battery (type CR 20 32) and refit the cover making sure that it clips fully onto the base.
**4** After changing the battery, lock and unlock the driver's door with the key in the lock to synchronise the remote control unit.

### 25 Hydraulic fluid renewal

**Note:** *It is not possible for the home mechanic to bleed the clutch hydraulic system on Easytronic models. Refer to Chapter 7C for additional information.*

⚠ **Warning: Hydraulic fluid can harm your eyes and damage painted surfaces, so use extreme caution when handling and pouring it. Do not use fluid that has been standing open for some time, as it absorbs moisture from the air. Excess moisture can cause a dangerous loss of braking effectiveness.**

**1** The procedure is similar to that for the bleeding of the hydraulic system as described in Chapters 9 (brake) and 6 (clutch).
**2** Working as described in Chapter 9, open the first bleed screw in the sequence, and pump the brake pedal gently until nearly all the old fluid has been emptied from the master cylinder reservoir. Top-up to the MAX level with new fluid, and continue pumping until only the new fluid remains in the reservoir, and new fluid can be seen emerging from the bleed screw. Tighten the screw, and top the reservoir level up to the MAX level line.

> **HAYNES HiNT**
> *Old hydraulic fluid is invariably much darker in colour than the new, making it easy to distinguish the two.*

**3** Work through all the remaining bleed screws in the sequence until new fluid can be seen at all of them. Be careful to keep the master cylinder reservoir topped-up to above the MIN level at all times, or air may enter the system and greatly increase the length of the task.
**4** Bleed the fluid from the clutch hydraulic system as described in Chapter 6.
**5** When the operation is complete, check that all bleed screws are securely tightened, and that their dust caps are refitted. Wash off all traces of spilt fluid, and recheck the master cylinder reservoir fluid level.
**6** Check the operation of the brakes and clutch before taking the car on the road.

### 26 Coolant renewal

**Note:** *Vauxhall/Opel do not specify renewal intervals for the antifreeze mixture, as the mixture used to fill the system when the vehicle is new is designed to last the lifetime of the vehicle. However, it is strongly recommended that the coolant is renewed at the intervals specified in the Maintenance schedule, as a precaution against possible engine corrosion problems. This is particularly advisable if the coolant has been renewed using an antifreeze other than that specified by Vauxhall/Opel. With many antifreeze types, the corrosion inhibitors become progressively less effective with age. It is up to the individual owner whether or not to follow this advice.*

⚠ **Warning: Wait until the engine is cold before starting this procedure. Do not allow antifreeze to come in contact with your skin, or the painted surfaces of the vehicle. Rinse off spills immediately with plenty of water. Never leave antifreeze lying around in an open container, or in a puddle in the driveway or on the garage floor. Children and pets are attracted by its sweet smell, but antifreeze can be fatal if ingested.**

*Cooling system draining*

**1** To drain the cooling system, first cover the

**24.1 Prise the battery cover from the ignition key fob**

**24.2 Carefully remove the battery from the contacts**

expansion tank cap with a wad of rag, and slowly turn the cap anti-clockwise to relieve the pressure in the cooling system (a hissing sound will normally be heard). Wait until any pressure remaining in the system is released, then continue to turn the cap until it can be removed.

2 Position a suitable container beneath the right-hand side of the radiator.

3 The coolant drain plug is located at the bottom of the radiator right-hand end tank. Unscrew the drain plug and allow the coolant to drain.

4 When the flow of coolant stops, refit and tighten the drain plugs.

5 As no cylinder block drain plug is fitted, it is not possible to drain all of the coolant. Due consideration must be made for this when refilling the system, in order to maintain the correct concentration of antifreeze.

6 If the coolant has been drained for a reason other than renewal, then provided it is clean and less than two years old, it can be re-used.

### Cooling system flushing

7 If coolant renewal has been neglected, or if the antifreeze mixture has become diluted, then in time, the cooling system may gradually lose efficiency, as the coolant passages become restricted due to rust, scale deposits, and other sediment. The cooling system efficiency can be restored by flushing the system clean.

8 The radiator should be flushed independently of the engine, to avoid unnecessary contamination.

### Radiator flushing

9 Disconnect the top and bottom hoses and any other relevant hoses from the radiator, with reference to Chapter 3.

10 Insert a garden hose into the radiator top inlet. Direct a flow of clean water through the radiator, and continue flushing until clean water emerges from the radiator bottom outlet.

11 If after a reasonable period, the water still does not run clear, the radiator can be flushed with a good proprietary cleaning agent. It is important that the manufacturer's instructions are followed carefully. If the contamination is particularly bad, remove the radiator, insert the hose in the radiator bottom outlet, and reverse-flush the radiator.

### Engine flushing

12 To flush the engine, the thermostat must be removed, because it will be shut, and would otherwise prevent the flow of water around the engine. The thermostat can be removed as described in Chapter 3. Take care not to introduce dirt or debris into the system if this approach is used.

13 With the bottom hose disconnected from the radiator, insert a garden hose into the thermostat opening. Direct a clean flow of water through the engine, and continue flushing until clean water emerges from the radiator bottom hose.

14 On completion of flushing, refit the thermostat with reference to Chapter 3, and reconnect the hoses.

### Cooling system filling

15 Before attempting to fill the cooling system, make sure that all hoses and clips are in good condition, and that the clips are tight. Note that an antifreeze mixture must be used all year round, to prevent corrosion of the engine components.

16 Remove the expansion tank filler cap.

17 Fill the system by slowly pouring the coolant into the expansion tank until it is up to the filler neck.

18 Top-up the expansion tank until the coolant level is up to the KALT/COLD mark on the side of the tank.

19 Refit and tighten the expansion tank filler cap.

20 Start the engine and run it at 2000 to 2500 rpm until the cooling fan switches on. Continue running the engine at between 2000 and 2500 rpm for a further 2 minutes.

21 Stop the engine, and allow it to cool, then recheck the coolant level with reference to *Weekly checks*. Top-up the level if necessary and refit the expansion tank filler cap.

### Antifreeze mixture

22 Always use an ethylene-glycol based antifreeze which is suitable for use in mixed-metal cooling systems. **Note:** *Vauxhall/ Opel recommend the use of silicate-free 'red' coolant (93 170 402)*. The quantity of antifreeze and level of protection is given in the Specifications.

23 Before adding antifreeze, the cooling system should be completely drained, preferably flushed, and all hoses checked for condition and security.

24 After filling with antifreeze, a label should be attached to the expansion tank, stating the type and concentration of antifreeze used, and the date installed. Any subsequent topping-up should be made with the same type and concentration of antifreeze.

25 Do not use engine antifreeze in the windscreen/tailgate washer system, as it will cause damage to the vehicle paintwork. A screenwash additive should be added to the washer system in the quantities stated on the bottle.

### 27 Exhaust emission check

1 The exhaust emission check is carried out initially after 3 years, then every 2 years, however, on vehicles which are subject to intensive use (eg, taxis/hire cars/ambulances) it must be carried out annually. The check involves checking the engine management system operation by plugging an electronic tester into the system diagnostic socket to check the electronic control unit (ECU) memory for faults (see Chapter 4A).

2 In reality, if the vehicle is running correctly and the engine management warning light in the instrument panel is functioning normally, then this check need not be carried out.

# Every 40 000 miles or 4 years

**28.2  Disconnect the wiring connector from the airflow meter**

**28.3a  Undo the retaining screws . . .**

### 28 Air cleaner element renewal

1 The air cleaner is located in the front right-hand corner of the engine compartment.

2 Disconnect the wiring connector from the side of the airflow meter **(see illustration)**.

3 Undo the screws and lift off the air cleaner cover, then lift out the filter element **(see illustrations)**.

4 Wipe out the casing and the cover.

5 Fit the new filter, noting that the rubber

**28.3b . . . lift off the air cleaner cover . . .**

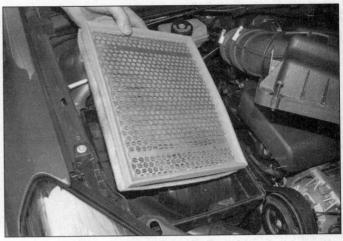

**28.3c . . . then lift out the filter element**

locating flange should be uppermost, and secure the cover with the screws.

**6** Reconnect the airflow meter wiring connector.

## 29 Spark plug renewal

**1** The correct functioning of the spark plugs is vital for the correct running and efficiency of the engine. It is essential that the plugs fitted are appropriate for the engine; suitable types are specified at the beginning of this Chapter, or in the vehicle's Owner's Handbook. If the correct type is used and the engine is in good condition, the spark plugs should not need attention between scheduled renewal intervals. Spark plug cleaning is rarely necessary, and should not be attempted unless specialised equipment is available, as damage can easily be caused to the firing ends.

**2** Where applicable, remove the engine top cover after removing the oil filler cap. Refit the cap.

**3** Remove the ignition module from the spark plugs with reference to Chapter 5B.

**4** It is advisable to remove the dirt from the spark plug recesses using a clean brush, vacuum cleaner or compressed air before removing the plugs, to prevent dirt dropping into the cylinders.

**5** Unscrew the spark plugs from the cylinder head using a spark plug spanner, suitable box spanner or a deep socket and extension bar **(see illustrations)**. Keep the socket aligned with the spark plug – if it is forcibly moved to one side, the ceramic insulator may be broken off.

**6** Examination of the spark plugs will give a good indication of the condition of the engine. As each plug is removed, examine it as follows. If the insulator nose of the spark plug is clean and white, with no deposits, this is indicative of a weak mixture or too hot a plug (a hot plug transfers heat away from the electrode slowly, a cold plug transfers heat away quickly).

**7** If the tip and insulator nose are covered with hard black-looking deposits, then this is indicative that the mixture is too rich. Should the plug be black and oily, then it is likely that the engine is fairly worn, as well as the mixture being too rich.

**8** If the insulator nose is covered with light tan to greyish-brown deposits, then the mixture is correct and it is likely that the engine is in good condition.

**9** The spark plug electrode gap is of considerable importance. If the gap is too large or too small, the size of the spark and its efficiency will be seriously impaired and it will not perform correctly under all engine speed and load conditions. For the best results, the spark plug gap should be set in accordance with the Specifications at the beginning of this Chapter.

**10** To set the gap, measure it with a feeler blade or spark plug gap gauge and then carefully bend the outer plug electrode until the correct gap is achieved. The centre electrode should never be bent, as this may crack the insulator and cause plug failure, if nothing worse. If using feeler blades, the gap is correct when the appropriate-size blade is a firm sliding fit **(see illustrations)**.

**11** Special spark plug electrode gap adjusting tools are available from most motor

**29.5a Unscrew the spark plugs . . .**

**29.5b . . . and remove them**

**29.10a Measuring a spark plug electrode gap using a feeler blade**

**29.10b Measuring a spark plug electrode gap using a wire gauge**

**HAYNES HINT**

*It's often difficult to insert spark plugs into their holes without cross-threading them. To avoid this possibility, fit a short piece of rubber hose over the end of the spark plug. The flexible hose acts as a universal joint, to help align the plug with the plug hole. Should the plug begin to cross-thread, the hose will slip on the spark plug, preventing thread damage.*

accessory shops, or from some spark plug manufacturers.

**12** Before fitting the spark plugs, check that the threaded connector sleeves on the top of the plug are tight, and that the plug exterior surfaces and threads are clean.

**13** Screw in the spark plugs by hand where possible, then tighten them to the specified torque. Take extra care to enter the plug threads correctly, as the cylinder head is of light alloy construction **(see Haynes Hint)**.

**14** On completion, refit the ignition module as described in Chapter 5B then, where applicable, refit the engine top cover.

**30 Timing belt, tensioner and idler pulley renewal – 1.6 and 1.8 litre engines**

Refer to the procedures contained in the relevant Part of Chapter 2.

**31 Automatic transmission fluid renewal**

Refer to the procedures contained in Chapter 7B.

# Every 100 000 miles or 10 years

**32 Valve clearance check and adjustment – 1.6 litre and 1.8 litre Z18XER engines**

Refer to the procedures contained in the relevant Part of Chapter 2.

# Chapter 2 Part A:
# 1.4 litre engine in-car repair procedures

## Contents

## Degrees of difficulty

| **Easy,** suitable for novice with little experience | **Fairly easy,** suitable for beginner with some experience | **Fairly difficult,** suitable for competent DIY mechanic | **Difficult,** suitable for experienced DIY mechanic | **Very difficult,** suitable for expert DIY or professional |
|---|---|---|---|---|

## Specifications

### General

| | |
|---|---|
| Engine type | Four-cylinder, in-line, water-cooled. Double overhead camshafts, chain-driven, acting on rocker arms and hydraulic valve lifters |
| Manufacturer's engine codes* | Z14XEP and Z14XEL |
| Bore | 73.40 mm |
| Stroke | 80.60 mm |
| Capacity | 1364 cc |
| Firing order | 1-3-4-2 (No 1 cylinder at timing chain end of engine) |
| Direction of crankshaft rotation | Clockwise (viewed from timing chain end of engine) |
| Compression ratio | 10.5:1 |

*For details of engine code location, see 'Vehicle identification' in the Reference Chapter.*

### Compression pressures

| | |
|---|---|
| Maximum difference between any two cylinders | 1 bar |

### Lubrication system

| | |
|---|---|
| Minimum oil pressure at 80°C | 1.5 bars at idle speed |
| Oil pump type | Gear-type, driven directly from crankshaft |
| Gear-to-housing clearance (endfloat) | 0.020 to 0.065 mm |

## Torque wrench settings

| | Nm | lbf ft |
|---|---|---|
| Air conditioning compressor to cylinder block | 20 | 15 |
| Auxiliary drivebelt tensioner to cylinder block: | | |
|   M8 bolt | 20 | 15 |
|   M10 bolt | 55 | 41 |
| Big-end bearing cap bolts*: | | |
|   Stage 1 | 13 | 10 |
|   Stage 2 | Angle-tighten a further 60° | |
|   Stage 3 | Angle-tighten a further 15° | |
| Camshaft bearing cap bolts | 8 | 6 |
| Camshaft sprocket bolt*: | | |
|   Stage 1 | 50 | 37 |
|   Stage 2 | Angle-tighten a further 60° | |
| Coolant pump pulley bolts | 20 | 15 |
| Crankshaft pulley hub-to-crankshaft bolt*: | | |
|   Stage 1 | 150 | 111 |
|   Stage 2 | Angle-tighten a further 45° | |
| Cylinder block baseplate to cylinder block*: | | |
|   M6 bolts: | | |
|     Stage 1 | 10 | 7 |
|     Stage 2 | Angle-tighten a further 60° | |
|   M8 bolts: | | |
|     Stage 1 | 25 | 18 |
|     Stage 2 | Angle-tighten a further 60° | |
| Cylinder block closure bolt (for TDC setting tool) | 60 | 44 |
| Cylinder head bolts*: | | |
|   Stage 1 | 25 | 18 |
|   Stage 2 | Angle-tighten a further 60° | |
|   Stage 3 | Angle-tighten a further 60° | |
|   Stage 4 | Angle-tighten a further 60° | |
| Engine mountings: | | |
|   Front mounting/torque link: | | |
|     Mounting-to-transmission bolts | 80 | 59 |
|     Mounting to subframe | 55 | 41 |
|   Left-hand mounting: | | |
|     Mounting-to-body bolts | 20 | 15 |
|     Mounting bracket to transmission bracket | 55 | 41 |
|     Rubber mounting through-bolt | 55 | 41 |
|     Transmission bracket to transmission | 35 | 26 |
|   Rear mounting/torque link: | | |
|     Mounting-to-bracket bolts | 55 | 41 |
|     Mounting-to-subframe bolts | 55 | 41 |
|     Bracket-to-transmission bolts | 80 | 59 |
|   Right-hand mounting: | | |
|     Engine bracket-to-engine bolts | 60 | 44 |
|     Mounting-to-body bolts | 35 | 26 |
|     Mounting-to-engine bracket bolts | 55 | 41 |
|     Rubber mounting through-bolt | 55 | 41 |
| Engine-to-transmission bolts | 60 | 44 |
| Exhaust front pipe-to-manifold nuts | 20 | 15 |
| Exhaust manifold securing nuts* | 20 | 15 |
| Exhaust manifold-to-support bracket bolts | 8 | 6 |
| Flywheel bolts*: | | |
|   Stage 1 | 35 | 26 |
|   Stage 2 | Angle-tighten a further 30° | |
| Fuel feed and return hose unions | 15 | 11 |
| Inlet manifold support bracket to cylinder block | 20 | 15 |
| Oil filter housing cap to filter housing | 10 | 7 |
| Oil filter housing to cylinder block | 20 | 15 |
| Sump to cylinder block baseplate/timing cover | 10 | 7 |
| Sump to transmission | 40 | 30 |
| Timing chain tension rail pivot bolt | 20 | 15 |
| Timing chain tensioner closure bolt (for locking pin access) | 50 | 37 |
| Timing cover bolts: | | |
|   M10 | 35 | 26 |
|   M6 | 8 | 6 |
| Timing cover oil fill channel closure plug | 50 | 37 |

* Use new fasteners.

## 1  General information

### How to use this Chapter

This Part of Chapter 2 describes the repair procedures which can reasonably be carried out on the engine while it remains in the vehicle. If the engine has been removed from the vehicle and is being dismantled as described in Chapter 2D, any preliminary dismantling procedures can be ignored.

Note that, while it may be possible physically to overhaul items such as the piston/connecting rod assemblies while the engine is in the vehicle, such tasks are not usually carried out as separate operations, and usually require the execution of several additional procedures (not to mention the cleaning of components and of oilways); for this reason, all such tasks are classed as major overhaul procedures, and are described in Chapter 2D.

Chapter 2D describes the removal of the engine/transmission unit from the vehicle, and the full overhaul procedures which can then be carried out.

### Engine description

The engine is of four-cylinder in-line type, with double overhead camshafts (DOHC). The engine is mounted transversely at the front of the vehicle.

The power unit is known as a 'Twinport' engine due to the design of the inlet manifold and cylinder head combustion chambers. Vacuum operated flap valves located in the inlet manifold are opened or closed according to engine operating conditions, to create a variable venturi manifold arrangement. This system has significant advantages in terms of engine power, fuel economy and reduced exhaust emissions.

The crankshaft runs in five shell-type main bearings with crankshaft endfloat being controlled by thrustwashers which are an integral part of No 4 main bearing shells.

The connecting rods are attached to the crankshaft by horizontally-split shell-type big-end bearings. The pistons are attached to the connecting rods by gudgeon pins, which are an interference fit in the connecting rod small-end bores. The aluminium-alloy pistons are fitted with three piston rings – two compression rings and an oil control ring.

The camshafts are driven from the crankshaft by a hydraulically tensioned timing chain. Each cylinder has four valves (two inlet and two exhaust), operated via rocker arms which are supported at their pivot ends by hydraulic self-adjusting valve lifters (tappets). One camshaft operates the inlet valves, and the other operates the exhaust valves.

The inlet and exhaust valves are each closed by a single valve spring, and operate in guides pressed into the cylinder head.

A rotor-type oil pump is located in the timing cover attached to the cylinder block, and is driven directly from the crankshaft.

The coolant pump is located externally on the timing cover, and is driven by the auxiliary drivebelt.

### Operations with engine in car

The following operations can be carried out without having to remove the engine from the vehicle.
a) Removal and refitting of the cylinder head.
b) Removal and refitting of the timing cover.
c) Removal and refitting of the timing chain, tensioner and sprockets.
d) Removal and refitting of the camshafts.
e) Removal and refitting of the sump.
f) Removal and refitting of the big-end bearings, connecting rods, and pistons*.
g) Removal and refitting of the oil pump.
h) Renewal of the crankshaft oil seals.
i) Renewal of the engine mountings.
j) Removal and refitting of the flywheel.
* Although the operation marked with an asterisk can be carried out with the engine in the vehicle (after removal of the sump), it is preferable for the engine to be removed, in the interests of cleanliness and improved access. For this reason, the procedure is described in Chapter 2D.

## 2  Compression test – general information

1 When engine performance is down, or if misfiring occurs which cannot be attributed to the ignition or fuel systems, a compression test can provide diagnostic clues as to the engine's condition. If the test is performed regularly, it can give warning of trouble before any other symptoms become apparent.

2 Due to the electronic throttle control system used on these engines, a compression test can only be carried out with the engine management electronic control unit connected to Vauxhall/Opel diagnostic test equipment, or a compatible alternative unit. Without the test equipment, the throttle valve cannot be opened (as there is no accelerator cable) and the test will be inconclusive. Note that even with the accelerator pedal fully-depressed, the engine management ECU will only control the throttle valve position when the engine is actually running. The test equipment independently actuates the throttle valve (irrespective of ECU commands) and opens the throttle valve fully.

3 As the equipment needed for the compression test is unlikely to be available to the home mechanic, it is recommended that the test is performed by a Vauxhall/Opel dealer, or suitably-equipped garage.

## 3  Camshaft cover – removal and refitting

Note: A new camshaft cover rubber seal will be required for refitting, and a suitable silicone sealant will be required to seal the timing cover-to-cylinder head upper joint.

### Removal

1 Disconnect the battery negative terminal (refer to *Disconnecting the battery* in the Reference Chapter).

2 Disconnect the wiring connectors at the airflow meter, coolant temperature sensor, camshaft position sensor and oil pressure switch **(see illustrations)**.

3.2a  Disconnect the wiring connectors at the airflow meter . . .

3.2b  . . . the coolant temperature sensor (A) and camshaft position sensor (B) . . .

3.2c  . . . and at the oil pressure switch

3.3 Lift the wiring harness trough from the camshaft cover and move it to one side

3.4 Breather hoses on the rear of the camshaft cover

3.7 Lift the camshaft cover up and off the cylinder head

3.9a If necessary, tap the bolts out of the camshaft cover . . .

3.9b . . . and fit new seals to the bolts

3.10 Fit a new rubber seal to the camshaft cover ensuring that it is correctly located in the cover groove

3 Lift the wiring harness trough from the camshaft cover and move it to one side (see illustration).

4 Disconnect the two breather hoses at the rear of the camshaft cover (see illustration).

5 Remove the ignition module from the centre of the camshaft cover as described in Chapter 5B.

6 Progressively slacken the camshaft cover retaining bolts until they are all fully unscrewed. Note that the bolts are captive and will remain in place in the cover as it is removed.

7 Lift the camshaft cover up and off the cylinder head (see illustration).

### Refitting

8 Remove the old seal from the camshaft cover, then examine the inside of the cover for a build-up of oil sludge or any other contamination, and if necessary clean the cover with paraffin, or a water-soluble solvent. Dry the cover thoroughly before refitting.

3.11 Cut off any projecting timing cover gasket using a sharp knife

9 Check the condition of the rubber seals on the camshaft cover retaining bolts. If the seals are in any way damaged or deformed, carefully tap the bolts out of the camshaft cover using a soft-faced mallet and fit new seals to the bolts (see illustrations).

10 Fit a new rubber seal to the cover ensuring that it is correctly located in the camshaft cover groove (see illustration).

11 Inspect the joint between the timing cover and cylinder head, and cut off any projecting timing cover gasket using a sharp knife (see illustration).

12 Thoroughly clean the mating faces of the camshaft cover and cylinder head.

13 Apply a 2 mm diameter bead of silicone sealant to the joint between the timing cover and cylinder head on each side (see illustration).

14 Locate the camshaft cover on the cylinder head and screw in the retaining bolts.

3.13 Apply a bead of silicone sealant to the joint between the timing cover and cylinder head on each side

Progressively and evenly tighten the retaining bolts securely.

15 Refit the ignition module from the centre of the camshaft cover as described in Chapter 5B.

16 Reconnect the two breather hoses to the right-hand rear of the camshaft cover.

17 Locate the wiring harness trough in the camshaft cover slots then reconnect the airflow meter, coolant temperature sensor, camshaft position sensor and oil pressure switch wiring connectors.

18 Reconnect the battery negative terminal on completion.

## 4 Valve timing – checking and adjustment

**Note:** *Certain special tools will be required for this operation. Read through the entire procedure to familiarise yourself with the work involved, then either obtain the manufacturer's special tools, or use the alternatives described. New gaskets and sealing rings will also be required for all disturbed components.*

### Checking

1 Disconnect the battery negative terminal (refer to *Disconnecting the battery* in the Reference Chapter).

2 Remove the air cleaner assembly as described in Chapter 4A.

3 Remove the camshaft cover as described in Section 3.

4 Firmly apply the handbrake, then jack up

**4.6 Turn the crankshaft until the TDC notch (A) on the pulley is located just before the cast lug (B) on the timing cover**

**4.7 With No 1 piston on the compression stroke, the camshaft lobes for No 1 cylinder should be pointing outwards**

the front of the car and support it securely on axle stands (see *Jacking and vehicle support*). Remove the right-hand front roadwheel and the wheel arch liner lower cover for access to the crankshaft pulley.

**5** On models with air conditioning, release the tension on the auxiliary drivebelt and lock the tensioner in the released position as described in the auxiliary drivebelt renewal procedure in Chapter 1. Note that it is not necessary to completely remove the drivebelt, as this would entail removal of the right-hand engine mounting bracket. With the drivebelt tension released, slip the belt off the compressor pulley. Unbolt the compressor from the cylinder block, release the refrigerant lines from their brackets and support the compressor clear of the engine. **Do not** disconnect the refrigerant lines from the compressor.

**6** Using a socket or spanner on the crankshaft pulley hub bolt, turn the crankshaft in the normal direction of rotation (clockwise as viewed from the right-hand side of the car) until the TDC notch on the crankshaft pulley is located just before the cast lug on the timing cover **(see illustration)**.

**7** Check that No 1 piston is on the compression stroke by observing No 1 cylinder camshaft lobes. All four lobes should be pointing outwards (away from the engine) **(see illustration)**. If they are not, No 1 piston is on the exhaust stroke and the crankshaft should be turned through a further full turn, stopping once again just before the TDC notch aligns with the lug on the timing cover.

**8** Undo the closure bolt from the crankshaft TDC position setting hole. The plug is located on the front facing side of the cylinder block baseplate, adjacent to the timing cover joint. Note that a new closure bolt sealing ring will be required for refitting.

**9** If the Vauxhall TDC positioning pin KM-952 is available, insert the tool into the TDC position setting hole. Slowly turn the crankshaft in the normal direction of rotation until the tool engages with the TDC slot in the crankshaft, and moves fully in, up to its stop.

**Tool Tip 1: A commercially-available clutch aligning tool can be used as a TDC positioning tool.**

**10** In the absence of the Vauxhall tool, a typical commercially-available clutch aligning tool of the type having interchangeable cones and collars of various diameters can be used as an alternative **(see Tool Tip 1)**. Assemble the tool so that the end collar (the part that normally engages with the crankshaft spigot bearing) is of 12 mm diameter, and the sliding cone (the part that normally engages with the clutch disc hub) is of 17.5 mm diameter. Insert the tool into the TDC position setting hole, and slowly turn the crankshaft in the normal direction of rotation until the end collar engages with the TDC slot in the crankshaft web. Push the cone fully into the setting hole as far as it will go, and

**4.10b Clutch aligning tool in position in the TDC setting hole**

**4.10a The end of the tool must engage with the slot in the crankshaft web (arrowed) – shown with engine partially dismantled**

the crankshaft should now be locked in the TDC position **(see illustrations)**.

**11** If the Vauxhall camshaft setting tool KM-953 is available, insert the tool into the slots in the left-hand end of the camshafts. Ensure that the tool is inserted fully, up to its stop, to lock both camshafts.

**12** In the absence of the Vauxhall tool, a camshaft setting tool can be made out of 5 mm thick flat steel strip, approximately 20 mm wide and long enough to engage both camshaft slots. Insert the setting tool into the camshaft slots to lock the camshafts in the TDC position **(see illustration)**. Note that a ready-made equivalent is available from tool stockists.

**4.12 Camshaft setting tool (arrowed) made from steel strip and inserted into the camshaft slots**

**4.15a Vauxhall/Opel camshaft sensor phase disc positioning tool (KM-954)**

**4.15b Home-made cardboard alternative camshaft sensor phase disc positioning tool in place**

**Tool Tip 2: A home-made camshaft sensor phase disc positioning tool can be fabricated using the dimensions shown.**

**4.18 Unscrew the timing chain tensioner closure plug from the timing cover**

**4.19 Use a spanner on the flats of the inlet camshaft to take up any slack in the timing chain**

**4.20a Insert a 2 mm diameter roll-pin, approximately 30 mm long, through the closure plug aperture . . .**

**4.20b . . . and into the hole on the tensioner body (arrowed)**

**13** If it is not possible to insert the camshaft setting tool, then the valve timing must be adjusted as described in paragraphs 17 to 35 below.

**14** If all is satisfactory so far, the position of the camshaft position sensor phase disc on the inlet camshaft should be checked. This check entails the use of Vauxhall camshaft sensor phase disc positioning tool KM-954. If this tool is not available, an alternative can be fabricated as follows.

**15** The Vauxhall positioning tool (KM-954) is a relatively substantial die-casting, the purpose of which is to check the position of the phase disc, and also to hold the phase disc in the correct position on the camshaft sprocket if adjustment is required. During the workshop procedures undertaken for the preparation of this manual, we discovered that a tool made from stiff cardboard (such that used for the cover of a Haynes manual) worked just as well as the factory tool **(see illustrations and Tool Tip 2)**.

**16** Using the Vauxhall positioning tool, or the home-made alternative, check to see if the tool will engage with the phase disc on the camshaft, and also seat squarely on the timing cover surface. If it does, proceed to paragraph 31. If adjustment is required, proceed as follows.

### Adjustment

**Note:** *New camshaft sprocket retaining bolts will be required for this operation.*

**17** Remove the camshaft sensor phase disc positioning tool, and the tool used to lock the camshafts in position.

**18** Unscrew the timing chain tensioner closure plug from the timing cover, located just below the heater hose union on the coolant pump. Note that a new closure bolt sealing ring will be required for refitting **(see illustration)**.

**19** Using a suitable spanner engaged with the flats provided on the inlet camshaft, apply tension in a clockwise direction (as viewed from the right-hand side of the car) to the camshaft, to take up any slack in the timing chain **(see illustration)**. This will push the timing chain tensioner plunger fully into its bore.

**20** Hold the camshaft in this position and retain the tensioner plunger in the released position by inserting a 2 mm diameter roll-pin, approximately 30 mm long, through the closure plug aperture and into the hole on the tensioner body **(see illustrations)**.

**21** Slacken and remove the sprocket retaining bolts for both camshafts, using a spanner to counter-hold each camshaft as the bolts are slackened.

**22** Fit the new bolts to both camshaft sprockets and tighten them finger-tight only at this stage. Check that the phase disc on the inlet camshaft can still be turned.

**23** Again, using the spanner on the camshaft flats, turn the camshafts slightly, as necessary, until the camshaft setting tool can be reinserted into the slots in the ends of the camshafts.

**24** Remove the roll-pin used to hold the timing chain tensioner plunger in the retracted position.

**25** Turn the camshaft sensor phase disc slightly, as necessary, and locate the Vauxhall positioning tool (KM-954), or the home-made alternative over the disc and in contact with the timing cover. If the Vauxhall tool is being used, bolt it into position on the timing cover.

**26** Tighten the camshaft sprocket retaining bolts to 10 Nm (7 lbf ft). The inlet camshaft sprocket bolts should be tightened first. Note that this is just an initial torque loading to hold the sprockets and the phase disc in position when the setting tools are removed.

**27** Remove the crankshaft, camshaft and phase disc setting tools, then tighten the camshaft sprocket retaining bolts to the specified torque in the stages given in the Specifications. The inlet camshaft sprocket bolts should be tightened first. Counter-hold the camshafts using the spanner on the camshaft flats as the sprocket bolts are tightened.

**28** Turn the crankshaft through two complete revolutions, stopping just before the TDC notch on the crankshaft pulley aligns with the cast lug on the timing cover **(see illustration 4.6)**. Check that all four lobes for No 1 cylinder are pointing outwards (away from the engine).

**29** Slowly turn the crankshaft further until the TDC position setting tool can once again be inserted to lock the crankshaft.

**30** It should now be possible to re-insert the camshaft setting tool into the slots in the camshafts, and to fit the camshaft sensor phase disc setting tool over the disc. If this is not possible repeat the entire adjustment procedure.

**31** If all is satisfactory, remove all the setting/aligning tools and refit the timing chain tensioner and cylinder block closure bolts using new sealing rings. Tighten both closure bolts to the specified torque.

**32** On models with air conditioning, refit the compressor to the cylinder block and tighten the mounting bolts to the specified torque. Refit the refrigerant lines to their relevant clips or brackets, then refit the auxiliary drivebelt as described in Chapter 1.

**33** Refit the wheel arch liner lower cover and the roadwheel. Tighten the roadwheel bolts to the specified torque, then lower the vehicle to the ground.

**34** Refit the camshaft cover as described in Section 3.

**35** Refit the air cleaner assembly as described in Chapter 4A, then reconnect the battery negative terminal.

## 5 Crankshaft pulley – removal and refitting

### Removal

**1** Firmly apply the handbrake, then jack up the front of the car and support it securely on

axle stands (see *Jacking and vehicle support*). Remove the right-hand roadwheel and the wheel arch liner lower cover.

**2** Release the tension on the auxiliary drivebelt and lock the tensioner in the released position as described in the auxiliary drivebelt renewal procedure in Chapter 1. Note that it is not necessary to completely remove the drivebelt, as this would entail removal of the right-hand engine mounting bracket.

**3** With the drivebelt tension released, slip the belt off the crankshaft pulley.

**4** Using quick-drying paint, or similar, make an alignment mark between the crankshaft pulley and the pulley hub. It should only be possible to refit the pulley in one position, but it is advisable to make an alignment mark anyway.

**5** Unscrew the six crankshaft pulley retaining bolts and remove the pulley from the hub **(see illustration)**. If necessary, prevent the crankshaft from turning as the pulley bolts are slackened using a spanner or socket on the pulley hub bolt.

### Refitting

**6** Align the marks made on removal and locate the pulley on the hub.

**7** Refit the six retaining bolts and progressively tighten them securely.

**8** Refit the auxiliary drivebelt over the crankshaft pulley and ensure that it is correctly seated in the other pulleys.

**9** Unlock the auxiliary drivebelt tensioner as described in Chapter 1 to retension the drivebelt.

**10** Refit the wheel arch liner lower cover and the roadwheel and tighten the wheel bolts to the specified torque.

**11** Lower the car to the ground.

## 6 Timing cover and chain – removal and refitting

**Note:** *The special tools described in Section 4 will also be required for this operation. Read through the entire procedure and also the procedures contained in Section 4 to familiarise yourself with the work involved, then either obtain the manufacturer's special tools, or use the alternatives described. New gaskets and sealing rings will also be required for all disturbed components, together with new camshaft sprocket retaining bolts. A tube of silicone sealant will be needed to seal the joint between the cylinder block and cylinder head.*

### Removal

**1** Disconnect the battery negative terminal (refer to *Disconnecting the battery* in the Reference Chapter).

**2** Apply the handbrake, then jack up the front of the vehicle and support it on axle stands (see *Jacking and vehicle support*). Remove the right-hand roadwheel.

**5.5 Undo the six bolts and remove the crankshaft pulley from the pulley hub**

**3** Drain the cooling system as described in Chapter 1. Tighten the drain plug after draining the system.

**4** Remove the air cleaner assembly as described in Chapter 4A.

**5** At the right-hand end of the engine, loosen the clip and disconnect the throttle housing preheater hose from the thermostat housing.

**6** Loosen the clip and disconnect the heater feed hose from the coolant pump.

**7** Disconnect the wiring from the oil pressure switch, coolant temperature sensor and camshaft position sensor, then unclip the wiring conduit and move it to one side.

**8** Loosen the clips and disconnect the radiator upper hose from the radiator and thermostat housing.

**9** Loosen the clip and disconnect the radiator lower hose from the coolant pump **(see illustration)**.

**10** Remove the ignition module as described in Chapter 5B.

**11** Disconnect the crankcase ventilation hose from the camshaft cover.

**12** Progressively slacken the camshaft cover retaining bolts until they are all fully unscrewed. Note that the bolts are captive and will remain in place in the cover as it is removed. Lift the camshaft cover up and off the cylinder head.

**13** Remove the wheel arch liner lower cover from under the right-hand wheel arch.

**14** Position a container beneath the engine sump, then unscrew the drain plug and drain the engine oil. Clean, refit and tighten the drain plug on completion.

**15** Refer to Chapter 4A, and disconnect the wiring from the oxygen sensor on the

**6.9 Radiator lower hose on the coolant pump**

**6.17 The coolant pump pulley retaining bolts**

catalytic converter, then unbolt the exhaust front pipe from the exhaust manifold, taking care to support the flexible section. **Note:** *Angular movement in excess of 10° can cause permanent damage to the flexible section.*

16  Release the mounting rubbers and support the front of the exhaust pipe to one side.

17  Slacken, but do not remove, the three coolant pump pulley retaining bolts **(see illustration)**.

18  On models without air conditioning, turn the auxiliary drivebelt tensioner pulley bolt clockwise then insert a suitable pin through the spring centre shaft to lock the spring in its compressed state. Note the routing of the drivebelt, then remove it from the pulleys – mark the drivebelt for fitted direction. **Note:** *The drivebelt cannot be removed completely until the right-hand engine mounting has been removed.* Unscrew the auxiliary drivebelt tensioner lower mounting bolt and the tensioner roller upper pivot bolt. Remove the tensioner from the timing cover.

19  On models with air conditioning, turn the auxiliary drivebelt tensioner pulley bolt clockwise to tension the spring, then insert a suitable pin through the hole in the tensioner body and into the hole in the timing cover to lock the spring. Note the routing of the drivebelt, then remove it from the pulleys – mark the drivebelt for fitted direction. **Note:** *The drivebelt cannot be removed completely until the right-hand engine mounting has been removed.* Turn the tensioner pulley bolt clockwise again and remove the locking pin, then gradually release the tensioner until it is

**6.31 Slacken the crankshaft pulley hub retaining bolt (arrowed)**

fully released. Unbolt the tensioner from the timing cover.

20  Remove the alternator as described in Chapter 5A.

21  Remove the sump as described in Section 11.

22  The engine must now be supported while the right-hand engine mounting is removed. To do this, use a hoist attached to the top of the engine, or make up a wooden frame to locate on the crankcase and use a trolley jack.

23  Remove the right-hand engine mounting bracket with reference to Section 15, then remove the auxiliary drivebelt.

24  Fully unscrew the bolts and remove the coolant pump pulley from its drive flange.

25  On models with air conditioning, unbolt the compressor from the cylinder block, release the refrigerant lines from their brackets and support the compressor clear of the engine. **Do not** disconnect the refrigerant lines from the compressor.

26  Undo the three bolts securing the thermostat housing cover to the coolant pump. Remove the sealing ring from the housing cover noting that a new one will be required for refitting.

27  Using a socket or spanner on the crankshaft pulley hub bolt, turn the crankshaft in the normal direction of rotation (clockwise as viewed from the right-hand side of the car) until the TDC notch on the crankshaft pulley is located just before the cast lug on the timing cover **(see illustration 4.6)**.

28  Check that No 1 piston is on the compression stroke by observing No 1 cylinder camshaft lobes. All four lobes should be pointing outwards (away from the engine). If they are not, No 1 piston is on the exhaust stroke and the crankshaft should be turned through a further full turn, stopping once again just before the TDC notch aligns with the lug on the timing cover.

29  Using quick-drying paint, or similar, make an alignment mark between the crankshaft pulley and the pulley hub. It should only be possible to refit the pulley in one position, but it is advisable to make an alignment mark anyway.

30  Unscrew the six crankshaft pulley retaining bolts and remove the pulley from the hub. If necessary, prevent the crankshaft from turning as the pulley bolts are slackened, using a spanner or socket on the pulley hub bolt.

31  Using a suitable socket, initially slacken (but do not remove) the crankshaft pulley hub retaining bolt **(see illustration)**. The crankshaft can be prevented from turning as the bolt is slackened, using Vauxhall special tool KM-956 or a similar tool which will engage with the flats on each side of the pulley hub. Alternatively, remove the starter motor, and lock the flywheel ring gear teeth using a suitable hooked tool bolted to the bellhousing.

32  Undo the closure bolt from the crankshaft TDC position setting hole. The plug is located on the front facing side of the cylinder block baseplate, adjacent to the timing cover joint.

Note that a new closure bolt sealing ring will be required for refitting.

33  Temporarily place the crankshaft pulley back on the hub and check that the TDC notch is still positioned just before the lug on the timing cover.

34  Slowly turn the crankshaft in the normal direction of rotation until the TDC positioning pin (or suitable alternative) described in Section 4, engages with the TDC slot in the crankshaft.

35  Remove the crankshaft pulley, if still in place, and check that the punch mark on the pulley hub is in the 11 o'clock position.

36  Insert the camshaft setting tool described in Section 4 into the slots in the ends of the camshafts.

37  Unscrew the coolant pump retaining bolts, noting the locations of the three short bolts. The short bolts secure the pump to the timing cover, and the long bolts secure the pump and the timing cover to the cylinder block and cylinder head.

38  Withdraw the coolant pump from the timing cover, noting that it may be necessary to tap the pump lightly with a soft-faced mallet to free it from the locating dowels.

39  Recover the pump sealing ring/gasket noting that a new one must be used for refitting.

40  Unscrew the previously-slackened crankshaft pulley hub retaining bolt and remove the hub from the crankshaft. Note that a new bolt will be required for refitting.

41  Undo the timing cover retaining bolts and remove the timing cover from the engine. The cover will be initially tight as it is located on dowels and secured by sealant. If necessary, gently tap it off using a soft-faced mallet.

42  Fully push back the timing chain tensioner plunger and secure it in the released position by inserting a 2 mm diameter roll-pin, approximately 30 mm long, in the hole on the tensioner body **(see illustration)**.

43  Undo the two bolts and remove the timing chain sliding rail from the top of the cylinder head **(see illustration)**.

44  Undo the two bolts and remove the timing chain (front) guide rail from the cylinder block **(see illustration)**.

45  Undo the lower pivot bolt and remove the

**6.42 Push back the timing chain tensioner plunger and secure it in the released position with a 2 mm diameter roll-pin**

**6.43 Undo the two bolts (arrowed) and remove the timing chain sliding rail from the cylinder head**

**6.44 Undo the two bolts (arrowed) and remove the timing chain guide rail from the cylinder block**

**6.45 Undo the lower pivot bolt and remove the timing chain tension rail from the cylinder block**

timing chain (rear) tension rail from the cylinder block **(see illustration)**.

**46** Lift the timing chain off the sprockets and remove the chain, then remove the drive sprocket from the crankshaft **(see illustrations)**.

**47** Remove the composite gasket from the cylinder block baseplate, cylinder block, and cylinder head, using a plastic spatula if necessary to release the sealant **(see illustration)**. Note that if the cylinder head has ever been previously removed, the gasket will be a two-piece type, with a split at the cylinder head-to cylinder block joint. A new gasket will be required for refitting.

**48** Thoroughly clean the timing cover and remove all traces of gasket and sealant from all the mating surfaces. Similarly clean the cylinder block baseplate, cylinder block and cylinder head mating surfaces. Ensure that all traces of old sealant are removed, particularly from the area of the cylinder head-to-cylinder block joint.

**49** Inspect the timing chain, sprockets, sliding rail, guide rail and tension rail for any sign of wear or deformation, and renew any suspect components as necessary. Renew the crankshaft timing chain end oil seal in the timing cover as a matter of course using the procedures described in Section 13.

**50** It is advisable to check the condition of the timing chain tensioner at this stage, as described in Section 7.

**51** Obtain all new gaskets and components as necessary ready for refitting.

**6.46a Lift the timing chain off the sprockets and remove the chain . . .**

### Refitting

**52** Commence refitting by inserting a new coolant pump gasket or rubber seal into the timing cover.

**53** Check that the locating dowels are in place, and that the mating surfaces are clean and dry, then locate the pump in position on the timing cover.

**54** Refit the three coolant pump pulley short retaining bolts, ensuring that the bolts are fitted to their correct locations (refer to Chapter 3 if necessary). Tighten the bolts to the specified torque.

**55** Apply a 2 mm diameter bead of silicone sealant to the joint between the cylinder block and cylinder head on each side **(see illustration)**. The bead should be long enough to fill the joint in the area covered by the timing cover gasket. Similarly, apply silicone sealant

**6.46b . . . then remove the drive sprocket from the crankshaft**

to the joint between the cylinder block and baseplate.

**56** Ensure that the locating dowels are in position, then locate the new timing cover gasket in place on the cylinder head, cylinder block and baseplate.

**57** Slide the timing chain drive sprocket onto the crankshaft with the markings facing outwards **(see illustration)**.

**58** Engage the timing chain with the drive sprocket then, keeping it tight on the exhaust camshaft side, feed the chain up and over the camshaft sprockets **(see illustration)**.

**59** Place the timing chain tension rail in position, refit the lower pivot bolt and tighten the bolt to the specified torque.

**60** Attach the timing chain guide rail to the cylinder block and secure with the two bolts tightened securely.

**61** Refit the timing chain sliding rail to the

**6.47 Remove the timing cover composite gasket from the cylinder block baseplate, cylinder block and cylinder head**

**6.55 Apply a 2 mm diameter bead of silicone sealant to the joint between the cylinder block and cylinder head on each side**

**6.57 Slide the timing chain drive sprocket onto the crankshaft with the markings facing outwards**

**6.58  Keeping the timing chain tight on the exhaust camshaft side, locate the chain over the sprockets**

**6.66  Lubricate the crankshaft pulley hub, then refit the hub to the crankshaft**

**6.67a  Screw in the new pulley hub retaining bolt . . .**

**6.67b  . . . tighten it to the specified torque . . .**

**6.67c  . . . then through the specified angle in the stages given in the Specifications**

cylinder head and secure with the two bolts tightened securely.

**62** Remove the roll-pin used to secure the timing chain tensioner plunger in the released position.

**63** Locate the timing cover in position and refit all the retaining bolts, finger-tight only at this stage. Now tighten all the bolts to the specified torque, starting with the bolts around the coolant pump first, followed by the bolts around the periphery of the cover.

**64** Refit the sump as described in Section 11.

**65** Remove the position setting tools used to lock the crankshaft and camshafts in the TDC position.

**66** Lubricate the crankshaft pulley hub with engine oil, then refit the hub to the crankshaft, ensuring that the punch mark on the hub is in the 11 o'clock position **(see illustration)**.

**67** Screw in the new pulley hub retaining bolt and tighten it to the specified torque, in the stages given in the Specifications **(see illustrations)**. Prevent crankshaft rotation as the bolt is tightened, using the method employed for removal.

**68** Refit the crankshaft pulley to the pulley hub, with the marks made on removal aligned, and tighten the six bolts securely.

**69** Turn the crankshaft through two complete revolutions, stopping just before the TDC notch on the crankshaft pulley aligns with the cast lug on the timing cover. Check that all four lobes for No 1 cylinder are pointing outwards (away from the engine).

**70** Slowly turn the crankshaft further until the TDC position setting tool can once again be inserted to lock the crankshaft.

**71** It should now be possible to re-insert the camshaft setting tool into the slots in the camshafts. If the setting tool cannot be inserted, carry out the valve timing adjustment procedures contained in Section 4.

**72** If all is satisfactory, remove all the setting/aligning tools and refit the closure bolt to the cylinder block using a new sealing ring. Tighten the closure bolt to the specified torque.

**73** Refit the coolant pump pulley and tighten the three bolts to the specified torque. To prevent the pulley turning as the bolts are tightened, hold the pulley using a screwdriver engaged with one of the bolts and the pump centre spindle. Alternatively, wait until the auxiliary drivebelt has been refitted and tighten the bolts then.

**74** Ensure that the mating surfaces are clean, then fit a new sealing ring to the thermostat housing cover. Refit the cover to the coolant pump and tighten the bolts securely.

**75** On models with air conditioning, refit the compressor to the cylinder block and tighten the mounting bolts to the specified torque. Refit the refrigerant lines to their relevant clips or brackets.

**76** Refit the alternator as described in Chapter 5A.

**77** Refit the auxiliary drivebelt tensioner and tighten the mounting bolts to the specified torque.

**78** Rotate the tensioner pulley bolt clockwise as for removal, refit the auxiliary drivebelt as previously noted and release the tensioner.

**79** Refit the right-hand engine mounting bracket with reference to Section 15.

**80** Refit the exhaust front pipe and oxygen sensor with reference to Chapter 4A.

**81** Refill the engine with fresh oil with reference to Chapter 1.

**82** Refit the wheel arch liner lower cover.

**83** Refit the camshaft cover and reconnect the crankcase ventilation hose as described in Section 3.

**84** Refit the ignition module and cover.

**85** Reconnect the radiator top and bottom hoses and heater hose to their respective connections.

**86** Reconnect the wiring to the oil pressure switch, coolant temperature sensor and camshaft position sensor, then clip the wiring conduit in position.

**87** Reconnect the throttle housing preheater hose and tighten the clip.

**88** Refit the air cleaner assembly as described in Chapter 4A.

**89** Refill the cooling system as described in Chapter 1, then reconnect the battery negative terminal.

**90** Refit the roadwheel and lower the vehicle to the ground.

---

**7  Timing chain tensioner –** removal, inspection and refitting

### Removal

**1** Remove the timing cover as described in Section 6.

**2** Undo the two tensioner retaining bolts and remove the tensioner from the cylinder head **(see illustration)**.

**3** Extract the roll-pin used to retain the

**7.2  Undo the two retaining bolts and remove the timing chain tensioner from the cylinder head**

**7.3a Extract the roll-pin used to retain the tensioner plunger in the retracted position . . .**

**7.3b . . . and withdraw the tensioner plunger and spring**

**7.6 Timing chain tensioner plunger fully retracted and locked with the roll-pin**

tensioner plunger in the retracted position and withdraw the tensioner plunger and spring **(see illustrations)**.

### Inspection

4 Examine the components for any sign of wear, deformation or damage and, if evident, renew the complete tensioner assembly.

### Refitting

5 Lubricate the tensioner spring and plunger, then insert the spring, followed by the plunger into the tensioner body.

6 Fully compress the tensioner plunger and reinsert the retaining roll-pin **(see illustration)**.

7 Refit the tensioner assembly to the cylinder head and tighten the retaining bolts securely.

---

## 8 Camshaft sprockets – removal and refitting

**Note:** *The special tools described in Section 4 will also be required for this operation. Read through the entire procedure and also the procedures contained in Section 4 to familiarise yourself with the work involved, then either obtain the manufacturer's special tools, or use the alternatives described. New gaskets and sealing rings will also be required for all disturbed components, together with new camshaft sprocket retaining bolts.*

### Removal

1 Disconnect the battery negative terminal (refer to *Disconnecting the battery* in the Reference Chapter).

2 Remove the air cleaner assembly as described in Chapter 4A.

3 Disconnect the wiring from the oil pressure switch, coolant temperature sensor and camshaft position sensor, then unclip the wiring conduit and move it to one side.

4 Remove the ignition module as described in Chapter 5B.

5 Disconnect the crankcase ventilation hoses from the camshaft cover.

6 Progressively slacken the camshaft cover retaining bolts until they are all fully unscrewed. Note that the bolts are captive and will remain in place in the cover as it is removed. Lift the camshaft cover up and off the cylinder head.

7 Firmly apply the handbrake, then jack up the front of the car and support it securely on axle stands (see *Jacking and vehicle support*). Remove the right-hand front roadwheel and the wheel arch liner lower cover for access to the crankshaft pulley.

8 On models with air conditioning, release the tension on the auxiliary drivebelt and lock the tensioner in the released position as described in the auxiliary drivebelt renewal procedure in Chapter 1. Note that it is not necessary to completely remove the drivebelt, as this entails removal of the right-hand engine mounting bracket. With the drivebelt tension released, slip the belt off the compressor pulley. Unbolt the compressor from the cylinder block, release the refrigerant lines from their brackets and support the compressor clear of the engine. **Do not** disconnect the refrigerant lines from the compressor.

9 Using a socket or spanner on the crankshaft pulley hub bolt, turn the crankshaft in the normal direction of rotation (clockwise as viewed from the right-hand side of the car) until the TDC notch on the crankshaft pulley is located just before the cast lug on the timing cover **(see illustration 4.6)**.

10 Check that No 1 piston is on the compression stroke by observing No 1 cylinder camshaft lobes. All four lobes should be pointing outwards (away from the engine). If they are not, No 1 piston is on the exhaust stroke and the crankshaft should be turned through a further full turn, stopping once again just before the TDC notch aligns with the lug on the timing cover.

11 Unscrew the timing chain tensioner closure bolt from the front of the timing cover, below the heater hose union on the coolant pump. Note that a new closure bolt sealing ring will be required for refitting.

12 Obtain a suitable roll-pin or similar of 2 mm diameter and approximately 30 mm long to use as a timing chain tensioner locking tool.

13 Using a suitable spanner engaged with the flats provided on the inlet camshaft, apply tension in a clockwise direction (as viewed from the right-hand side of the car) to the camshaft, to take up any slack in the timing chain. This will push the timing chain tensioner plunger fully into its bore.

14 Hold the camshaft in this position and

retain the tensioner plunger in the released position by inserting the roll-pin through the closure plug aperture and into the hole on the tensioner body.

15 Undo the two bolts and remove the timing chain sliding rail from the top of the cylinder head.

16 Slacken the sprocket retaining bolts for both camshafts, using the spanner to counter-hold each camshaft as the bolts are slackened **(see illustration)**. Remove the bolt for the sprocket(s) being removed together with the camshaft position sensor phase disc, if removing the inlet camshaft. Withdraw the relevant sprocket(s) from the camshaft(s), disengage the timing chain and remove the sprocket(s) from the engine.

### Refitting

17 Engage the sprocket(s) with the timing chain and locate the sprocket(s) on the camshaft(s). Fit the new retaining bolt(s) together with the phase disc, if working on the inlet camshaft. Note that new retaining bolts must be fitted to **both** sprockets, even if only one sprocket was removed. Tighten the bolts finger-tight only at this stage and check that the phase disc on the inlet camshaft can still be turned.

18 Refit the timing chain sliding rail to the top of the cylinder head and secure with the two bolts tightened securely.

19 Using the spanner on the camshaft flats, turn the camshafts slightly, as necessary, until the camshaft setting tool described in Section 4 can be inserted into the slots in the ends of the camshafts.

**8.16 Slacken the camshaft sprocket retaining bolts using a spanner to counter-hold each camshaft as the bolts are slackened**

**9.2 Camshaft bearing cap identification numbers (arrowed)**

**9.4 Lift off the camshaft bearing caps, keeping them in order – shown with cylinder head removed**

**9.5 Lift the camshafts from their locations in the cylinder head – shown with cylinder head removed**

**20** Turn the camshaft sensor phase disc as necessary until the phase disc positioning tool (or suitable alternative) described in Section 4 can be located over the phase disc. If the Vauxhall tool is being used, bolt it to the top of the timing cover. If the alternative tool described is being used, ensure that its base is in contact with the timing cover.

**21** Remove the roll-pin used to hold the timing chain tensioner plunger in the retracted position.

**22** Undo the closure bolt from the crankshaft TDC position setting hole. The plug is located on the front facing side of the cylinder block baseplate, adjacent to the timing cover joint. Note that a new closure bolt sealing ring will be required for refitting.

**23** Slowly turn the crankshaft in the normal direction of rotation until the TDC positioning pin (or suitable alternative), described in Section 4, engages with the TDC slot in the crankshaft.

**24** Tighten the camshaft sprocket retaining bolts to 10 Nm (7 lbf ft). Note that this is just an initial torque loading to hold the sprockets and the phase disc in position when the setting tools are removed.

**25** Remove the crankshaft, camshaft and phase disc setting tools, then tighten the camshaft sprocket retaining bolts to the specified torque in the stages given in the Specifications. Counter-hold the camshafts using the spanner on the camshaft flats as the sprocket bolts are tightened.

**26** Turn the crankshaft through two complete revolutions, stopping just before the TDC notch on the crankshaft pulley aligns with the cast lug on the timing cover. Check that

all four lobes for No 1 cylinder are pointing outwards (away from the engine).

**27** Slowly turn the crankshaft further until the TDC position setting tool can once again be inserted to lock the crankshaft.

**28** It should now be possible to re-insert the camshaft setting tool into the slots in the camshafts, and to fit the camshaft sensor phase disc setting tool over the disc. If this is not possible carry out the valve timing adjustment procedure contained in Section 4.

**29** If all is satisfactory, remove all the setting/aligning tools and refit the timing chain tensioner and cylinder block closure bolts using new sealing rings. Tighten both closure bolts to the specified torque.

**30** On models with air conditioning, refit the compressor to the cylinder block and tighten the mounting bolts to the specified torque. Refit the refrigerant lines to their relevant clips or brackets, then refit the auxiliary drivebelt as described in Chapter 1.

**31** Refit the wheel arch liner lower cover and the roadwheel. Tighten the roadwheel bolts to the specified torque, then lower the vehicle to the ground.

**32** Refit the camshaft cover as described in Section 3.

**33** Refit the ignition module and cover, and reconnect the wiring.

**34** Reconnect the wiring to the oil pressure switch, coolant temperature sensor and camshaft position sensor, then clip the wiring conduit into position.

**35** Refit the air cleaner assembly as described in Chapter 4A, then reconnect the battery negative terminal.

**9.6a Withdraw each rocker arm . . .**

**9.6b . . . and hydraulic tappet in turn, and place them in their respective containers – shown with cylinder head removed**

## 9  Camshafts, hydraulic tappets and rocker arms – removal and refitting

### Removal

**1** Remove the camshaft sprocket(s) as described in Section 8.

**2** Observe the identification numbers and markings on the camshaft bearing caps **(see illustration)**. On the project car used during the compilation of this manual, the bearing caps with odd numbers were fitted to the exhaust camshaft, and the caps with the even numbers were fitted to the inlet camshaft. However, this may not be the case on other engines. Also, as it is possible to fit the caps either way round, it will be necessary to mark the caps with quick-drying paint, or identify them in some way, so that they can be refitted in exactly the same position. On the project car, all the numbers could be read the correct way up, when viewed from the exhaust camshaft side of the engine. Again, this may not always be the case.

**3** With the bearing caps correctly identified, and working in a spiral pattern from the outside to the inside, initially slacken the bearing cap bolts, one at a time, by half a turn. When all the bolts have been initially slackened, repeat the procedure, slackening the bolts by a further half a turn. Continue until all the bolts have been fully-slackened. The camshaft will rise up under the action of the valve springs as the bolts are slackened. Ensure that the camshaft rises uniformly and does not jam in its bearings.

**4** When all the bolts have been slackened, remove the bolts and lift off the bearing caps, keeping them in order according to the identification method decided on **(see illustration)**.

**5** Note the installed position of the camshafts before removal – the cam lobes for No 1 cylinder should be pointing outwards (ie, away from the centre). Carefully lift the camshafts from their locations in the cylinder head. If both camshafts are removed, identify them as exhaust and inlet **(see illustration)**.

**6** Obtain sixteen small, clean plastic containers, and number them inlet 1 to 8 and exhaust 1 to 8; alternatively, divide a larger container into sixteen compartments and number each compartment accordingly. Withdraw each rocker arm and hydraulic tappet in turn, and place them in their respective container **(see illustrations)**. Do not interchange the rocker arms and tappets, or the rate of wear will be much increased.

### Inspection

**7** Examine the camshaft bearing surfaces and cam lobes for signs of wear ridges and scoring. Renew the camshaft if any of these conditions are apparent. Examine the condition of the bearing surfaces, both on the camshaft journals and in the cylinder head/bearing caps. If the head bearing surfaces are worn excessively, the cylinder head will need to be renewed.

**8** Examine the rocker arm and hydraulic tappet bearing surfaces for wear ridges and scoring. Renew any rocker arm or tappet on which these conditions are apparent.

**9** If either camshaft is being renewed, it will be necessary to renew all the rocker arms and tappets for that particular camshaft also.

### Refitting

**10** Before refitting, thoroughly clean all the components and the cylinder head and bearing cap journals.

**11** Liberally oil the cylinder head hydraulic tappet bores and the tappets. Carefully refit the tappets to the cylinder head, ensuring that each tappet is refitted to its original bore.

**12** Lay each rocker arm in position over its respective tappet.

**13** Liberally oil the camshaft bearings in the cylinder head and the camshaft lobes, then place the camshafts in the cylinder head. Turn the camshafts so that the cam lobes for No 1 cylinder are pointing outwards as noted during removal.

**14** Refit all the bearing caps to their respective locations ensuring they are fitted the correct way round as noted during removal.

**15** Working in a spiral pattern from the inside to the outside, initially tighten the bearing cap bolts, one at a time, by half a turn. When all the bolts have been initially tightened, repeat the procedure, tightening the bolts by a further half a turn. Continue until all the bearing caps are in contact with the cylinder head and the bolts are lightly tightened.

**16** Again, working in a spiral pattern from inside to outside, tighten all the bolts to the specified torque.

**17** Refit the camshaft sprockets as described in Section 8.

### 10  Cylinder head –
### removal and refitting

**Note 1:** *The engine must be cold when removing the cylinder head. A new cylinder head gasket, timing cover gasket, cylinder head bolts, camshaft sprocket bolts together with seals and sealing rings will be required for refitting. A suitable sealant will also be needed to seal the timing cover-to-cylinder block joint.* **Note 2:** *The special tools described in Section 4 will also be required for this operation. Read through the entire procedure and also the procedures contained in Section 4 to familiarise yourself with the work involved, then either obtain the manufacturer's special tools, or use the alternatives described.*

### Removal

**1** Apply the handbrake, then jack up the front of the vehicle and support it on axle stands (see *Jacking and vehicle support*). Remove the right-hand roadwheel.

**2** Disconnect the battery negative terminal (refer to *Disconnecting the battery* in the Reference Chapter).

**3** Drain the cooling system as described in Chapter 1.

**4** Remove the air cleaner assembly as described in Chapter 4A. Also remove the air inlet duct from the front of the engine compartment by unscrewing the single bolt.

**5** Remove the throttle housing as described in Chapter 4A.

**6** Disconnect the heater feed hose from the coolant pump and position it to one side.

**7** Disconnect the brake servo vacuum line from the inlet manifold. Where applicable, also disconnect the evaporative system hose from the manifold.

**8** Where applicable, undo the two bolts and remove the cover over the fuel rail. Similarly, undo the two bolts and release the wiring harness support bracket from the rear of the inlet manifold.

**9** From under the car, undo the bolt securing the support bracket to the base of the inlet manifold. Slacken the bolt securing the bracket to the cylinder block and twist the bracket to one side **(see illustration)**.

**10** Disconnect the heater return hose from the EGR coolant flange, and unclip the wiring harness.

**11** Depressurise the fuel system as described in Chapter 4A, then disconnect the fuel feed and return hoses from the fuel rail, noting their locations to aid refitting. Be prepared for fuel spillage, and take adequate precautions. Clamp or plug the open ends of the hoses, to minimise further fuel loss.

**12** Disconnect the wiring from the following components:

a) *Oil pressure switch.*
b) *Coolant temperature sensor.*
c) *Camshaft position sensor.*
d) *Fuel injectors.*
e) *Throttle valve adjuster.*
f) *Engine electronic control unit (LH end of engine).*
g) *Wiring combination plug (LH end of engine).*
h) *EGR valve.*

**13** Release the ignition module cover from the centre of the camshaft cover and remove it toward the transmission end of the engine.

Disconnect the wiring plug from the left-hand end of the module.

**14** Disconnect the earth cables from the electronic control unit bracket.

**15** Undo the two bolts, one at each end, securing the plastic fuel injector wiring trough to the top of the fuel rail. Note that these bolts also secure the fuel rail to the inlet manifold. With the injector wiring disconnected, lift the wiring trough up and off the injectors. Place the trough to one side.

**16** Remove the wheel arch liner lower cover from under the right-hand wheel arch.

**17** Refer to Chapter 4A, and disconnect the wiring from the oxygen sensor in the exhaust front pipe, then unbolt the front pipe from the exhaust manifold, taking care to support the flexible section. **Note:** *Angular movement in excess of 10° can cause permanent damage to the flexible section.*

**18** Release the mounting rubbers and support the front of the exhaust pipe to one side.

**19** Slacken, but do not remove, the three coolant pump pulley retaining bolts.

**20** Unscrew the nuts and disconnect the wiring from the starter motor. Also, release the cable ties.

**21** Unbolt the two wiring harness brackets from the inlet manifold.

**22** On models without air conditioning, turn the auxiliary drivebelt tensioner pulley bolt clockwise then insert a suitable pin through the spring centre shaft to lock the spring in its compressed state. Note the routing of the drivebelt, then remove it from the pulleys – mark the drivebelt for fitted direction. **Note:** *The drivebelt cannot be removed completely until the right-hand engine mounting has been removed.* Unscrew the auxiliary drivebelt tensioner lower mounting bolt and the tensioner roller upper pivot bolt. Remove the tensioner from the timing cover.

**23** On models with air conditioning, turn the auxiliary drivebelt tensioner pulley bolt clockwise to tension the spring, then insert a suitable pin through the hole in the tensioner body and into the hole in the timing cover to lock the spring. Note the routing of the drivebelt, then remove it from the pulleys – mark the drivebelt for fitted direction. **Note:** *The drivebelt cannot be removed completely*

**10.9 Undo the bolt (arrowed) securing the support bracket to the base of the inlet manifold**

**10.28 Undo the two bolts (arrowed) and remove the exhaust manifold heat shield**

**10.30 Undo the three bolts and remove the oil filter housing from the cylinder block**

*until the right-hand engine mounting has been removed.* Turn the tensioner pulley bolt clockwise again and remove the locking pin, then gradually release the tensioner until it is fully released. Unbolt the tensioner from the timing cover.

24 Undo the bolt securing the oil dipstick guide tube to the exhaust manifold and withdraw the dipstick and guide tube from the cylinder block baseplate. To do this, turn the guide tube forward. Suitably cover or plug the guide tube aperture in the cylinder block baseplate to prevent dirt ingress.

25 Disconnect the wiring from the oxygen sensor on the exhaust manifold at the left-hand front of the engine, then unscrew the sensor from the manifold. Refer to Chapter 4A if necessary.

26 Unbolt the left-hand engine lifting eye from the cylinder head, complete with attached wiring harness.

27 On models with air conditioning, unbolt the compressor from the cylinder block, release the refrigerant lines from their brackets and

support the compressor clear of the engine. **Do not** disconnect the refrigerant lines from the compressor.

28 On early models, unbolt the exhaust manifold heat shield **(see illustration)**. On all models, unscrew the mounting nuts and lower support bracket bolts (where fitted) and withdraw the exhaust manifold from the cylinder head. Recover the gasket.

29 Remove the oil filter from the filter housing as described in Chapter 1. Remove as much of the oil remaining in the filter housing as possible using clean rags.

30 Undo the three bolts and remove the oil filter housing from the cylinder block **(see illustration)**. Place absorbent rags below the housing as it is removed to catch any remaining oil. Recover the filter housing seal noting that a new seal will be required for refitting.

31 Loosen the clips and disconnect the radiator upper hose from the radiator and thermostat housing.

32 The engine must now be supported while

the right-hand engine mounting is removed. To do this, use a hoist attached to the top of the engine, or make up a wooden frame to locate beneath the sump and use a trolley jack.

33 Remove the right-hand engine mounting bracket with reference to Section 15, then remove the auxiliary drivebelt.

34 Fully unscrew the bolts and remove the coolant pump pulley from its drive flange.

35 Undo the three bolts securing the thermostat housing cover to the coolant pump. Remove the sealing ring from the housing cover noting that a new one will be required for refitting.

36 Undo the bolts securing the coolant pump and timing cover to the cylinder head **(see illustration)**. Note that it is not necessary to remove all the coolant pump bolts as three are shorter than the rest, and only secure the pump to the timing cover.

37 Remove the camshaft cover as described in Section 3.

38 Using a socket or spanner on the crankshaft pulley hub bolt, turn the crankshaft in the normal direction of rotation (clockwise as viewed from the right-hand side of the car) until the TDC notch on the crankshaft pulley is located just before the cast lug on the timing cover (see Section 4).

39 Check that No 1 piston is on the compression stroke by observing No 1 cylinder camshaft lobes. All four lobes should be pointing outwards (away from the engine). If they are not, No 1 piston is on the exhaust stroke and the crankshaft should be turned through a further full turn, stopping once again just before the TDC notch aligns with the lug on the timing cover.

40 Undo the closure bolt from the crankshaft TDC position setting hole. The plug is located on the front facing side of the cylinder block baseplate, adjacent to the timing cover joint. Note that a new closure bolt sealing ring will be required for refitting.

41 Slowly turn the crankshaft in the normal direction of rotation until the TDC positioning pin (or suitable alternative), described in Section 4, engages with the TDC slot in the crankshaft.

42 Obtain a suitable roll-pin, or similar, of 2 mm diameter and approximately 30 mm long, to use as a timing chain tensioner locking tool.

43 Using a suitable spanner engaged with the flats provided on the inlet camshaft, apply tension in a clockwise direction (as viewed from the right-hand side of the car) to the camshaft, to take up any slack in the timing chain. This will push the timing chain tensioner plunger fully into its bore.

44 Hold the camshaft in this position and retain the tensioner plunger in the released position by inserting the roll-pin through the closure plug aperture and into the hole on the tensioner body.

45 Undo the two bolts and remove the timing chain sliding rail from the top of the cylinder head.

46 Slacken the sprocket retaining bolts for

**10.36 Undo the bolts (1) securing the coolant pump, and the bolts (arrowed) securing the timing cover to the cylinder head**

H32571

both camshafts, using the spanner to counter-hold each camshaft as the bolts are slackened. Remove both sprocket bolts together with the camshaft position sensor phase disc from the inlet camshaft. Ease the sprockets and chain off the camshafts and rest the sprockets on the top of the timing cover.

**47** Undo the retaining bolt and remove the camshaft position sensor from the front of the timing cover.

**48** Working in the specified sequence, progressively slacken the cylinder head retaining bolts half a turn at a time until all the bolts are loose **(see illustration)**. Remove the bolts from their locations noting that new bolts will be required for refitting.

**49** Slightly raise the cylinder head so it just clears the cylinder block face and move the head toward the transmission end of the engine. The head will be initially tight due to the sealant on the timing cover gasket and head gasket. Note that the locating dowel holes on the cylinder head are elongated to allow the head to move sideways slightly.

**50** As soon as sufficient clearance exists, lift the cylinder head up and off the cylinder block. At the same time, release the timing chain guide rail from the peg on the cylinder head, and guide the chain tensioner clear of the tensioning rail. Check that the tensioner locking pin is not dislodged as the cylinder head is lifted up. Place the cylinder head on wooden blocks after removal to avoid damage to the valves. Recover the cylinder head gasket.

### Preparation for refitting

**51** The mating faces of the cylinder head and cylinder block must be perfectly clean before refitting the head. Scouring agents are available for this purpose, but acceptable results can be achieved by using a hard plastic or wood scraper to remove all traces of gasket and carbon. The same method can be used to clean the piston crowns. Take particular care to avoid scoring or gouging the cylinder head mating surfaces during the cleaning operations, as aluminium alloy is easily damaged. Make sure that the carbon is not allowed to enter the oil and water passages – this is particularly important for the lubrication system, as carbon could block the oil supply

**10.48 Cylinder head bolt slackening sequence**

to the engine's components. Using adhesive tape and paper, seal the water, oil and bolt holes in the cylinder block. To prevent carbon entering the gap between the pistons and bores, smear a little grease in the gap. After cleaning each piston, use a small brush to remove all traces of grease and carbon from the gap, then wipe away the remainder with a clean rag.

**52** Check the mating surfaces of the cylinder block and the cylinder head for nicks, deep scratches and other damage. If slight, they may be removed carefully with a file, but if excessive, machining may be the only alternative to renewal. If warpage of the cylinder head gasket surface is suspected, use a straight-edge to check it for distortion. Refer to Part D of this Chapter if necessary.

**53** Thoroughly clean the threads of the cylinder head bolt holes in the cylinder block. Ensure that the bolts run freely in their threads, and that all traces of oil and water are removed from each bolt hole.

**54** Using a sharp knife, partially cut through the timing cover gasket flush with the top of the cylinder block. Release the gasket from the timing cover and bend it in half to break it off at the cut line. Remove the upper part of the gasket, and thoroughly clean the mating surface, paying particular attention to the cylinder block edge where it contacts the timing cover.

**55** Before refitting the cylinder head, using

the spanner on the camshaft flats, turn the camshafts slightly, as necessary, until the camshaft setting tool described in Section 4 can be inserted into the slots in the ends of the camshafts **(see illustration)**. With the tool in position, the camshaft lobes for No 1 cylinder should be pointing outward.

### Refitting

**56** Prior to locating the cylinder head gasket on the cylinder block, cut off the two protruding tabs at the timing cover end of the gasket, flush with the gasket edge.

**57** Apply a 2 mm diameter bead of silicone sealant to the joint between the cylinder block and the timing cover on each side.

**58** Check that the locating dowels are in position in the cylinder block, then lay the new gasket on the block face, with the words OBEN/TOP uppermost **(see illustration)**. Push the gasket hard up against the timing cover so that it engages with the sealant.

**59** Position the new timing cover gasket upper part on the timing cover, so that its lower ends engage with the sealant. Temporarily insert the left- and right-hand upper timing cover mounting bolts to locate the gasket in the correct position.

**60** Apply a further 2 mm diameter bead of silicone sealant to the joint between the cylinder block and the timing cover on each side.

**61** Carefully lower the cylinder head into position on the gasket, guiding the chain tensioner past the tensioning rail and guiding the tensioner locking pin into the timing cover access hole. Check also that the timing chain guide rail engages with cylinder head peg.

**62** Once the head is seated on its dowels, tap it towards the timing cover with a rubber mallet.

**63** Refit the three lower timing cover retaining bolts (one at each side, and one below the coolant pump). Tighten the three bolts to the specified torque.

**64** Remove the camshaft setting tool from the camshaft slots.

**65** Fit the new cylinder head retaining bolts and screw in the bolts until they contact the cylinder head. Working in the reverse order to the loosening sequence shown earlier in this Section, tighten the cylinder head bolts

**10.55 Before refitting the cylinder head, insert the camshaft setting tool (arrowed) into the slots in the ends of the camshafts**

**10.58 Position the cylinder head gasket on the block with the words OBEN/TOP uppermost**

**10.65a Tighten the cylinder head bolts to the Stage 1 torque setting using a torque wrench**

to the Stage one torque setting given in the Specifications, using a torque wrench. Again working in the correct order, tighten all the bolts through the Stage two angle using an angle measuring gauge **(see illustrations)**. Repeat for Stage three and Stage four.

66 Slacken the three previously-fitted bolts securing the timing cover to the cylinder head.

67 Refit the bolts around the coolant pump and tighten them securely.

68 Refit the remaining timing cover retaining bolts and tighten them to the specified torque.

69 Using the spanner on the camshaft flats, turn the camshafts slightly, as necessary, until the camshaft setting tool can once again be inserted into the camshaft slots.

70 Engage the camshaft sprockets with their respective camshafts, and fit the new retaining bolts together with the phase disc on the inlet camshaft. Tighten the bolts finger-tight only at this stage and check that the phase disc on the inlet camshaft can still be turned.

71 Refit the timing chain sliding rail to the top of the cylinder head and secure with the two bolts tightened securely.

72 Remove the roll-pin used to hold the timing chain tensioner plunger in the retracted position.

73 Turn the camshaft sensor phase disc as necessary until the phase disc positioning tool (or suitable alternative), described in Section 4, can be located over the phase disc. If the Vauxhall/Opel tool is being used, bolt it to the top of the timing cover. If the alternative tool described is being used, ensure that its base is in contact with the timing cover.

74 Tighten the camshaft sprocket retaining bolts to 10 Nm (7 lbf ft). Note that this is just an initial torque loading to hold the sprockets and the phase disc in position when the setting tools are removed. Tighten the inlet camshaft sprocket bolt first, followed by the exhaust camshaft sprocket bolt.

75 Remove the crankshaft, camshaft and phase disc setting tools, then tighten the camshaft sprocket retaining bolts to the specified torque in the stages given in the Specifications. Counter-hold the camshafts using the spanner on the camshaft flats as the sprocket bolts are tightened.

76 Turn the crankshaft through two complete revolutions, stopping just before the TDC notch on the crankshaft pulley aligns with the cast lug on the timing cover. Check that all four lobes for No 1 cylinder are pointing outwards (away from the engine).

77 Slowly turn the crankshaft further until the TDC position setting tool can once again be inserted to lock the crankshaft.

78 It should now be possible to re-insert the camshaft setting tool into the slots in the camshafts, and to fit the camshaft sensor phase disc setting tool over the disc. If this is not possible carry out the valve timing adjustment procedure contained in Section 4.

79 If all is satisfactory, remove all the setting/

**10.65b Tighten the cylinder head bolts through the Stage two, three and four angles using an angle tightening gauge**

aligning tools and refit the timing chain tensioner and cylinder block closure bolts using new sealing rings. Tighten both closure bolts to the specified torque.

80 Refit the camshaft position sensor using a new sealing ring and tighten the retaining bolt securely.

81 Refit the camshaft cover as described in Section 3.

82 Ensure that the mating surfaces are clean, then fit a new sealing ring to the thermostat housing cover. Refit the cover to the coolant pump and tighten the bolts securely.

83 Refit the coolant pump pulley and tighten the three bolts to the specified torque. To prevent the pulley turning as the bolts are tightened, hold the pulley using a screwdriver engaged with one of the bolts and the pump centre spindle. Alternatively, wait until the auxiliary drivebelt has been refitted and tighten the bolts then.

84 Refit the right-hand engine mounting bracket together with the auxiliary drivebelt with reference to Section 15. Remove the hoist or trolley jack supporting the engine.

85 Reconnect the radiator top hose and tighten the clips.

86 Thoroughly clean the mating surfaces of the oil filter housing and cylinder block, and refit the housing using a new seal. Refit and tighten the retaining bolts to the specified torque.

87 Fit a new sealing O-ring to the oil filter housing cap, then clip the new oil filter element to the cap.

88 Fit the cap and filter element assembly to the oil filter housing and screw the cap into position. Finally, tighten the cap to the specified torque.

89 Refit the exhaust manifold, together with a new gasket, and tighten the mounting nuts and support bracket bolts (where fitted) to the specified torque. On early models, refit the exhaust manifold heat shield.

90 On models with air conditioning, refit the compressor to the cylinder block and tighten the mounting bolts to the specified torque. Refit the refrigerant lines to their relevant clips or brackets.

91 Refit the left-hand engine lifting eye to the cylinder head and tighten the bolts securely. Attach the wiring harness.

92 Refer to Chapter 4A and refit the oxygen

sensor to the exhaust manifold. Reconnect the wiring.

93 Renew the oil dipstick guide tube O-rings and lubricate the O-rings with petroleum jelly. Insert the guide tube into the cylinder block baseplate then secure the tube to the exhaust manifold with the retaining bolt.

94 Refit the auxiliary drivebelt tensioner and tighten the mounting bolts to the specified torque.

95 Rotate the tensioner pulley bolt clockwise as for removal, refit the auxiliary drivebelt as previously noted and release the tensioner.

96 Refit the wiring harness brackets to the inlet manifold.

97 Reconnect the wiring to the starter motor and tighten the nuts. Secure the cable with ties.

98 Reconnect the exhaust front pipe to the exhaust manifold using a new flange gasket. Tighten the pipe-to-manifold nuts to the specified torque. Refit the mounting rubbers, then reconnect the oxygen sensor wiring.

99 Refit the auxiliary drivebelt cover under the right-hand wheel arch.

100 Refit the injector wiring and trough to the top of the fuel rail.

101 Reconnect the earth cables to the electronic control unit bracket.

102 Refit the ignition module with reference to Chapter 5B, and reconnect the wiring.

103 Reconnect the wiring to the following components:

a) Oil pressure switch.
b) Coolant temperature sensor.
c) Camshaft position sensor.
d) Fuel injectors.
e) Throttle valve adjuster.
f) Engine electronic control unit (LH end of engine).
g) Wiring combination plug (LH end of engine).
h) EGR valve.

104 Reconnect the fuel feed and return hoses to the fuel rail.

105 Disconnect the heater return hose to the EGR coolant flange, and secure the wiring harness.

106 Refit and tighten the bolt securing the support bracket to the base of the inlet manifold.

107 Refit the wiring harness support bracket to the rear of the inlet manifold.

108 Reconnect the brake servo vacuum line to the inlet manifold.

109 Where applicable, refit the cover over the fuel rail.

110 Reconnect the heater feed hose to the coolant pump and tighten the clip.

111 Refit the throttle housing as described in Chapter 4A.

112 Refit the air cleaner assembly with reference to Chapter 4A. Also refit the air inlet duct to the front of the engine compartment.

113 Reconnect the battery negative terminal.

114 Refill the cooling system and top-up the engine oil with reference to Chapter 1.

115 Refit the roadwheel then lower the vehicle to the ground.

**11.7a Undo the bolts (arrowed) . . .**

**11.7b . . . remove the oil pick-up pipe . . .**

**11.7c . . . and recover the O-ring from the flange**

## 11 Sump and oil pick-up pipe – removal and refitting

**Note:** *A new sump gasket must be used on refitting. If the oil pick-up pipe is removed, a new O-ring should be used on refitting.*

### Removal

**1** Firmly apply the handbrake, then jack up the front of the car and support it securely on axle stands (see *Jacking and vehicle support*). Remove the right-hand roadwheel.

**2** Drain the engine oil, with reference to Chapter 1, then refit and tighten the sump drain plug.

**3** Refer to Chapter 4A, and disconnect the wiring from the oxygen sensor, then unbolt the exhaust front pipe from the exhaust manifold, taking care to support the flexible section. **Note:** *Angular movement in excess of 10° can cause permanent damage to the flexible section.* Release the mounting rubbers and support the front of the exhaust pipe to one side to allow removal of the sump.

**4** Remove the wheel arch liner lower cover from under the right-hand wheel arch.

**5** Undo the bolts securing the sump to the cylinder block baseplate, timing cover and transmission bellhousing, then withdraw the sump. If necessary, tap the sump with a soft-faced mallet to free it from its location – do not lever between the sump and cylinder block baseplate mating faces. Recover the gasket.

**6** To remove the oil baffle plate, undo the retaining bolts and remove the baffle plate from the cylinder block baseplate.

**7** If desired, the oil pick-up pipe can be removed from the sump by unscrewing the two support bracket retaining bolts and the two bolts securing the flange to the end face of the sump. Lift out the pick-up pipe and recover the O-ring from the flange **(see illustrations)**. Note that a new O-ring will be required for refitting.

### Refitting

**8** Thoroughly clean the inside and outside of the sump ensuring that all traces of old gasket are removed from the mating face. Also clean the cylinder block baseplate mating face to remove all traces of old gasket.

**9** If the oil pick-up pipe has been removed, fit a new O-ring to the flange, then refit the pipe to the sump. Refit the flange bolts and support bracket bolts, then tighten the flange bolts securely. Tighten the support bracket bolts securely.

**10** If removed, refit the oil baffle plate and secure with the retaining bolts tightened securely.

**11** Apply a 2 mm diameter bead of silicone sealant to the joint between the timing cover and cylinder block, on each side. Place a new gasket on the sump, then locate the sump on the cylinder block baseplate **(see illustrations)**. Refit the securing bolts and tighten them finger-tight at this stage.

**12** If the engine has been removed from the car and separated from the transmission, use a straight-edge to check that the transmission mating face is aligned with the cylinder block baseplate mating face **(see illustration)**.

**13** Tighten the bolts securing the sump to the cylinder block baseplate and timing cover progressively and securely. Now tighten the bolts securing the sump to the transmission bellhousing to the specified torque.

**14** Refit the lower cover under the right-hand wheel arch.

**15** Reconnect the exhaust system front pipe to the manifold as described in Chapter 4A. Also, reconnect the wiring to the oxygen sensor.

**16** Refit the roadwheel, then lower the car to the ground and refill the engine with oil as described in Chapter 1.

## 12 Oil pump – removal, inspection and refitting

**Note:** *A new pressure relief valve cap sealing ring and new oil fill channel closure plug sealing ring will be required for refitting.*

### Removal

**1** Remove the timing cover and chain as described in Section 6.

**2** Remove the securing screws/bolts and withdraw the oil pump cover from the rear of the timing cover **(see illustration)**.

**11.11a Apply a 2 mm diameter bead of silicone sealant to the joint between the timing cover and cylinder block on each side . . .**

**11.11b . . . then place a new gasket on the sump and locate the sump on the cylinder block baseplate – shown with engine removed**

**11.12 If the engine has been separated from the transmission, use a straight-edge to check the transmission mating face alignment when refitting the sump**

**12.2 Remove the securing screws and withdraw the oil pump cover from the rear of the timing cover**

**12.4a Unscrew the oil pressure relief valve cap and sealing ring . . .**

**12.4b . . . then withdraw the spring and plastic pin . . .**

**12.4c . . . and the plunger**

**12.6 Check the oil pump gear endfloat using a straight-edge and feeler gauge**

**3** Remove the inner and outer rotor from the timing cover and wipe them clean. Also clean the rotor location in the timing cover.
**4** The oil pressure relief valve components can also be removed from the timing cover by unscrewing the cap. Withdraw the cap and sealing ring, the spring and plastic pin, and the plunger **(see illustrations)**.

### Inspection

**5** Locate the inner and outer rotor back in the timing cover, noting that the chamfer on the outer rotor outside diameter must face the timing cover.
**6** Check the clearance between the end faces of the gears and the housing (endfloat) using a straight-edge and a feeler gauge **(see illustration)**.
**7** If the clearance is outside the specified limits, renew the components as necessary.
**8** Examine the pressure relief valve spring and plunger, and renew if any sign of damage or wear is evident.
**9** Ensure that the rotor location in the interior of the timing cover is scrupulously clean before commencing reassembly.

### Refitting

**10** Thoroughly clean the pressure relief valve components, and lubricate them with clean engine oil before refitting. Insert the plunger, the spring and plastic pin, then refit the cap using a new sealing ring. Tighten the cap securely.
**11** Ensure that the gears are clean, then lubricate them with clean engine oil, and refit them to the pump body. Ensure that the

chamfer on the outer rotor outside diameter faces the timing cover.
**12** Ensure that the mating faces of the rear cover and the pump housing are clean, then refit the rear cover. Refit and tighten the securing screws securely.
**13** Fit a new crankshaft oil seal to the timing cover as described in Section 13.
**14** Refit the timing chain and cover to the engine as described in Section 6.
**15** After refitting the timing cover, unscrew the oil fill channel closure bolt from the lower front facing side of the timing cover. Using a pump type oil can filled with clean engine oil, insert the oil can spout into the oil channel, so that the spout pushes back the internal ball valve. Prime the pump by filling it with oil until the oil runs out of the fill channel. Refit the closure plug using a new sealing ring and tighten it to the specified torque.

### 13 Crankshaft oil seals – renewal

#### Timing chain end oil seal

**Note:** A new crankshaft pulley hub retaining bolt will be required for refitting.
**1** Disconnect the battery negative terminal (refer to Disconnecting the battery in the Reference Chapter).
**2** Remove the air cleaner assembly as described in Chapter 4A.
**3** Firmly apply the handbrake, then jack up the front of the car and support it securely on

axle stands (see Jacking and vehicle support). Remove the right-hand front roadwheel and the wheel arch liner lower cover for access to the crankshaft pulley.
**4** Release the tension on the auxiliary drivebelt and lock the tensioner in the released position as described in the auxiliary drivebelt renewal procedure in Chapter 1. Note that it is not necessary to completely remove the drivebelt, as this would entail removal of the right-hand engine mounting bracket. With the drivebelt tension released, slip the belt off the crankshaft pulley.
**5** Using a socket or spanner on the crankshaft pulley hub bolt, turn the crankshaft in the normal direction of rotation (clockwise as viewed from the right-hand side of the car) until the TDC notch on the crankshaft pulley is located just before the cast lug on the timing cover (see illustration 4.6).
**6** Using quick-drying paint, or similar, make an alignment mark between the crankshaft pulley and the pulley hub. It should only be possible to refit the pulley in one position, but it is advisable to make an alignment mark anyway.
**7** Unscrew the six crankshaft pulley retaining bolts and remove the pulley from the hub. If necessary, prevent the crankshaft from turning as the pulley bolts are slackened, using a spanner or socket on the pulley hub bolt.
**8** Using a suitable socket, slacken the crankshaft pulley hub retaining bolt. The crankshaft can be prevented from turning as the bolt is slackened, using Vauxhall special tool KM-956 or a similar tool which will engage with the flats on each side of the pulley hub. Alternatively, remove the starter motor, and lock the flywheel ring gear teeth using a suitable hooked tool bolted to the bellhousing.
**9** Unscrew the slackened crankshaft pulley hub retaining bolt and remove the hub from the crankshaft. Note that a new bolt will be required for refitting.
**10** The seal can now be carefully prised out with a screwdriver or similar hooked tool (see illustration).
**11** Clean the oil seal seat with a wooden or plastic scraper.
**12** Tap the new seal into position until it is flush with the outer face of the timing cover,

using a suitable socket or tube, or a wooden block **(see illustration)**.

**13** Refit the crankshaft pulley hub to the crankshaft, ensuring that the punch mark on the pulley hub is in the 11 o'clock position.

**14** Screw in the new pulley hub retaining bolt and tighten it to the specified torque, in the stages given in the Specifications. Prevent crankshaft rotation as the bolt is tightened, using the method employed for removal.

**15** Refit the crankshaft pulley to the pulley hub, with the marks made on removal aligned, and tighten the six bolts securely.

**16** Refit the auxiliary drivebelt as described in Chapter 1.

**17** Refit the air cleaner assembly as described in Chapter 4A.

**18** Refit the wheel arch liner lower cover and roadwheel, tightening the wheel bolts to the specified torque.

**19** Lower the car to the ground, then reconnect the battery negative terminal.

### Transmission end oil seal

**20** Remove the flywheel as described in Section 14.

**21** Carefully prise out the old seal from its location using a screwdriver or similar hooked tool.

**22** Clean the oil seal seat with a wooden or plastic scraper.

**23** Carefully locate the new seal over the crankshaft and into the recess in the cylinder block and baseplate **(see illustration)**.

**24** Tap the seal into position using a suitable socket or tube, or a wooden block, until it is flush with the outer faces of the cylinder block and baseplate **(see illustration)**.

**25** Refit the flywheel as described in Section 14.

### 14 Flywheel –
removal, inspection and refitting

**Note:** *New flywheel securing bolts must be used on refitting.*

### Removal

**1** Remove the transmission as described in Chapter 7A or 7C, as applicable.

**2** Remove the clutch assembly as described in Chapter 6.

**13.10  Carefully prise out the crankshaft oil seal from the timing cover – shown with timing cover removed**

**13.23  Locate the seal over the crankshaft and into the recess – shown with engine removed**

**3** Although the flywheel bolt holes are offset so that the flywheel can only be fitted in one position, it will make refitting easier if alignment marks are made between the flywheel and the end of the crankshaft.

**4** Prevent the flywheel from turning by jamming the ring gear teeth using a suitable tool **(see illustration)**.

**5** Unscrew the securing bolts, and remove the flywheel **(see illustration)**.

**Caution: Take care, as the flywheel is heavy.**

### Inspection

**6** Examine the flywheel for wear or chipping of the ring gear teeth. Renewal of the ring gear is possible but is not a task for the home mechanic; renewal requires the new ring gear to be heated (up to 180° to 230ºC) to allow it to be fitted.

**7** Examine the flywheel for scoring of the

**13.12  Tap the new seal into position until it is flush with the outer face of the timing cover – shown with timing cover removed**

**13.24  Tap the seal into position until it is flush – shown with engine removed**

clutch face. If the clutch face is scored, the flywheel may be surface-ground, but renewal is preferable.

**8** If there is any doubt about the condition of the flywheel, seek the advice of a Vauxhall/Opel dealer or engine reconditioning specialist. They will be able to advise if it is possible to recondition it or whether renewal is necessary.

### Refitting

**9** Offer the flywheel to the end of the crankshaft, and align the previously-made marks on the flywheel and crankshaft.

**10** Coat the threads of the new flywheel bolts with thread-locking compound (note that new bolts may be supplied ready-coated), then fit the bolts and tighten them to the specified torque, whilst preventing the flywheel from turning as during removal **(see illustrations)**.

**14.4  If the engine is removed, lock the flywheel with a suitable tool**

**14.5  Unscrew the securing bolts, and remove the flywheel – shown with engine removed**

**14.10a  Tighten the flywheel bolts to the specified torque using a torque wrench . . .**

**14.10b . . . then through the specified angle using an angle tightening gauge**

11 Refit the clutch as described in Chapter 6, then refit the transmission as described in Chapter 7A or 7C, as applicable.

## 15 Engine/transmission mountings –
inhibition and renewal

### Inspection

1 To improve access, firmly apply the handbrake, then jack up the front of the vehicle and support it on axle stands (see *Jacking and vehicle support*).
2 Check the mounting blocks (rubbers) to see if they are cracked, hardened or separated from the metal at any point. Renew the mounting block if any such damage or deterioration is evident.
3 Check that all the mounting securing nuts and bolts are securely tightened, using a torque wrench to check if possible.
4 Using a large screwdriver, or a similar tool, check for wear in the mounting blocks by carefully levering against them to check for free play. Where this is not possible, enlist the aid of an assistant to move the engine/

transmission unit back-and-forth, and from side-to-side, while you observe the mountings. While some free play is to be expected, even from new components, excessive wear should be obvious. If excessive free play is found, check first to see that the securing nuts and bolts are correctly tightened, then renew any worn components as described in the following paragraphs.

### Renewal

**Note:** *Before slackening any of the engine mounting bolts/nuts, the relative positions of the mountings to their various brackets should be marked to ensure correct alignment upon refitting.*

### Right-hand mounting

5 With reference to Chapter 4A, remove the air cleaner housing.
6 Support the weight of the engine using a trolley jack with a block of wood placed on its head.
7 Remove the three bolts securing the right-hand engine mounting to the engine mounting support bracket **(see illustration)**.
8 Undo the bolts securing the mounting to the body, and withdraw the bracket with the mounting. If necessary, the engine mounting bracket may be unbolted from the cylinder block.
9 If required, the mounting can be separated by undoing the single bolt in the centre of the rubber element.
10 Refitting is a reversal of removal. Tighten the bolts to the specified torque.

### Left-hand mounting

11 Remove the battery and battery tray as described in Chapter 5A.
12 Support the weight of the transmission using a trolley jack with a block of wood placed on its head.
13 Unscrew the three bolts securing the mounting bracket to the transmission

bracket, and the three bolts securing the transmission bracket to the transmission **(see illustration)**.
14 Undo the four bolts securing the mounting to the body, slightly lower the engine, then remove the mounting assembly from the car **(see illustration)**.
15 If necessary, undo the through-bolt and separate the rubber mounting from the mounting bracket.
16 Refitting is a reversal of removal. Ensure all bolts are tightened to their specified torques.

### Front mounting/torque link

17 Firmly apply the handbrake, then jack up the front of the car and support it securely on axle stands (see *Jacking and vehicle support*).
18 Support the weight of the engine/transmission using a trolley jack with a block of wood placed on its head.
19 Slacken and remove the nut and washer securing the mounting to the subframe, then withdraw the bolt **(see illustration)**.
20 Undo the two bolts securing the mounting bracket to the transmission, then manoeuvre the mounting and bracket out of position.
21 Refitting is a reversal of removal. Ensure all bolts/nuts are tightened to their specified torques.

### Rear mounting/torque link

22 Firmly apply the handbrake, then jack up the front of the car and support it securely on axle stands (see *Jacking and vehicle support*).
23 Support the weight of the engine/transmission using a trolley jack with a block of wood placed on its head. Position the jack underneath the transmission and raise the transmission slightly to remove all load from the rear mounting.
24 Slacken and remove the two bolts securing the rear mounting to the subframe, and the nut securing the mounting to the transmission bracket, then manoeuvre the

**15.7 Right-hand engine mounting-to-engine bracket bolts (A) and mounting-to-body bolts (B)**

**15.13 Left-hand engine mounting bracket and transmission bracket bolts (arrowed)**

**15.14 Undo the four bolts and remove the left-hand mounting from the body**

**15.19 Front engine mounting/torque link-to-subframe nut/bolt (arrowed)**

**15.24 Rear engine mounting/torque link retaining bolts and nut (arrowed)**

assembly out from underneath the vehicle **(see illustration)**.

**25** On refitting, manoeuvre the mounting into position and refit the bolts/nuts securing

it to the subframe. Ensure that the mounting is correctly engaged with the transmission bracket and fit the mounting-to-bracket retaining nut. Tighten the mounting bolts/

nuts to their specified torque settings. Remove the jack from underneath the engine/ transmission.

**26** Lower the vehicle to the ground.

# Notes

# Chapter 2 Part B:
# 1.6 litre engine in-car repair procedures

## Contents

## Degrees of difficulty

| **Easy,** suitable for novice with little experience 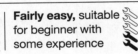 | **Fairly easy,** suitable for beginner with some experience | **Fairly difficult,** suitable for competent DIY mechanic | **Difficult,** suitable for experienced DIY mechanic | **Very difficult,** suitable for expert DIY or professional |
|---|---|---|---|---|

## Specifications

### General

| | |
|---|---|
| Engine type. . . . . . . . . . . . . . . . . . . . . . . . . . . . . . . . . . . . . . . . . . . . . . . | Four-cylinder, in-line, water-cooled. Double overhead camshafts, belt-driven |
| Manufacturer's engine code* . . . . . . . . . . . . . . . . . . . . . . . . . . . . . . . . | Z16XEP |
| Bore . . . . . . . . . . . . . . . . . . . . . . . . . . . . . . . . . . . . . . . . . . . . . . . . . . | 79.0 mm |
| Stroke. . . . . . . . . . . . . . . . . . . . . . . . . . . . . . . . . . . . . . . . . . . . . . . . . . | 81.5 mm |
| Capacity . . . . . . . . . . . . . . . . . . . . . . . . . . . . . . . . . . . . . . . . . . . . . . . | 1598 cc |
| Compression ratio . . . . . . . . . . . . . . . . . . . . . . . . . . . . . . . . . . . . . . . | 10.5:1 |
| Firing order . . . . . . . . . . . . . . . . . . . . . . . . . . . . . . . . . . . . . . . . . . . . . | 1-3-4-2 (No 1 cylinder at timing belt end) |
| Direction of crankshaft rotation . . . . . . . . . . . . . . . . . . . . . . . . . . . . . | Clockwise (viewed from timing belt end of engine) |

*\* For details of engine code location, see 'Vehicle identification' in the Reference Chapter.*

### Compression pressures

| | |
|---|---|
| Maximum difference between any two cylinders. . . . . . . . . . . . . . . . . . | 1 bar |

### Valve clearances

| | |
|---|---|
| Engine cold: | |
|    Inlet. . . . . . . . . . . . . . . . . . . . . . . . . . . . . . . . . . . . . . . . . . . . . . . . | 0.21 to 0.29 mm |
|    Exhaust. . . . . . . . . . . . . . . . . . . . . . . . . . . . . . . . . . . . . . . . . . . . . | 0.26 to 0.35 mm |

### Lubrication system

| | |
|---|---|
| Minimum oil pressure at 80°C . . . . . . . . . . . . . . . . . . . . . . . . . . . . . . | 1.3 bar at idle speed |
| Oil pump type. . . . . . . . . . . . . . . . . . . . . . . . . . . . . . . . . . . . . . . . . . . | Rotor-type, driven directly from crankshaft |
| Rotor-to-housing clearance (endfloat) . . . . . . . . . . . . . . . . . . . . . . . . | 0.020 to 0.058 mm |

## Torque wrench settings

| | Nm | lbf ft |
|---|---|---|
| Auxiliary drivebelt tensioner retaining bolt . . . . . . . . . . . . . . . . . . . . . . . | 50 | 37 |
| Camshaft bearing cap bolts. . . . . . . . . . . . . . . . . . . . . . . . . . . . . . . . . . . | 8 | 6 |
| Camshaft cover bolts . . . . . . . . . . . . . . . . . . . . . . . . . . . . . . . . . . . . . . | 8 | 6 |
| Camshaft sprocket bolt*: | | |
|   Stage 1 . . . . . . . . . . . . . . . . . . . . . . . . . . . . . . . . . . . . . . . . . . | 50 | 37 |
|   Stage 2 . . . . . . . . . . . . . . . . . . . . . . . . . . . . . . . . . . . . . . . . . . | Angle-tighten a further 60° | |
|   Stage 3 . . . . . . . . . . . . . . . . . . . . . . . . . . . . . . . . . . . . . . . . . . | Angle-tighten a further 15° | |
| Connecting rod big-end bearing cap bolt*: | | |
|   M9 bolts: | | |
|     Stage 1 . . . . . . . . . . . . . . . . . . . . . . . . . . . . . . . . . . . . | 35 | 26 |
|     Stage 2 . . . . . . . . . . . . . . . . . . . . . . . . . . . . . . . . . . . . | Angle-tighten a further 45° | |
|     Stage 3 . . . . . . . . . . . . . . . . . . . . . . . . . . . . . . . . . . . . | Angle-tighten a further 15° | |
|   M8 bolts: | | |
|     Stage 1 . . . . . . . . . . . . . . . . . . . . . . . . . . . . . . . . . . . . | 25 | 18 |
|     Stage 2 . . . . . . . . . . . . . . . . . . . . . . . . . . . . . . . . . . . . | Angle-tighten a further 30° | |
|     Stage 3 . . . . . . . . . . . . . . . . . . . . . . . . . . . . . . . . . . . . | Angle-tighten a further 15° | |
| Coolant pipe flange to coolant pump. . . . . . . . . . . . . . . . . . . . . . . . . . . . | 10 | 7 |
| Crankshaft pulley bolt*: | | |
|   Stage 1 . . . . . . . . . . . . . . . . . . . . . . . . . . . . . . . . . . . . . . . . . . | 95 | 70 |
|   Stage 2 . . . . . . . . . . . . . . . . . . . . . . . . . . . . . . . . . . . . . . . . . . | Angle-tighten a further 30° | |
|   Stage 3 . . . . . . . . . . . . . . . . . . . . . . . . . . . . . . . . . . . . . . . . . . | Angle-tighten a further 15° | |
| Cylinder head bolts*: | | |
|   Stage 1 . . . . . . . . . . . . . . . . . . . . . . . . . . . . . . . . . . . . . . . . . . | 25 | 18 |
|   Stage 2 . . . . . . . . . . . . . . . . . . . . . . . . . . . . . . . . . . . . . . . . . . | Angle-tighten a further 90° | |
|   Stage 3 . . . . . . . . . . . . . . . . . . . . . . . . . . . . . . . . . . . . . . . . . . | Angle-tighten a further 90° | |
|   Stage 4 . . . . . . . . . . . . . . . . . . . . . . . . . . . . . . . . . . . . . . . . . . | Angle-tighten a further 90° | |
|   Stage 5 . . . . . . . . . . . . . . . . . . . . . . . . . . . . . . . . . . . . . . . . . . | Angle-tighten a further 45° | |
| Engine mountings: | | |
|   Front mounting/torque link: | | |
|     Mounting-to-transmission bolts . . . . . . . . . . . . . . . . . . . . . . . | 80 | 59 |
|     Mounting to subframe . . . . . . . . . . . . . . . . . . . . . . . . . . . . | 55 | 41 |
|   Left-hand mounting: | | |
|     Mounting-to-body bolts . . . . . . . . . . . . . . . . . . . . . . . . . . . . | 20 | 15 |
|     Mounting bracket to transmission bracket. . . . . . . . . . . . . . . . | 55 | 41 |
|     Rubber mounting through-bolt. . . . . . . . . . . . . . . . . . . . . . . . | 55 | 41 |
|     Transmission bracket to transmission . . . . . . . . . . . . . . . . . . | 35 | 26 |
|   Rear mounting/torque link: | | |
|     Mounting-to-bracket bolts . . . . . . . . . . . . . . . . . . . . . . . . . . | 55 | 41 |
|     Mounting-to-subframe bolts. . . . . . . . . . . . . . . . . . . . . . . . . | 55 | 41 |
|     Bracket-to-transmission bolts . . . . . . . . . . . . . . . . . . . . . . . | 80 | 59 |
|   Right-hand mounting: | | |
|     Engine bracket-to-engine bolts: | | |
|       Cylinder head bolt. . . . . . . . . . . . . . . . . . . . . . . . . . . | 18 | 13 |
|       Cylinder block bolts . . . . . . . . . . . . . . . . . . . . . . . . . | 20 | 15 |
|     Mounting-to-body bolts . . . . . . . . . . . . . . . . . . . . . . . . . . . . | 35 | 26 |
|     Mounting-to-engine bracket bolts . . . . . . . . . . . . . . . . . . . . | 55 | 41 |
|     Rubber mounting through-bolt. . . . . . . . . . . . . . . . . . . . . . . . | 55 | 41 |
| Engine-to-transmission bolts . . . . . . . . . . . . . . . . . . . . . . . . . . . . . . . . | 60 | 44 |
| Flywheel bolts*: | | |
|   Stage 1 . . . . . . . . . . . . . . . . . . . . . . . . . . . . . . . . . . . . . . . . . . | 35 | 26 |
|   Stage 2 . . . . . . . . . . . . . . . . . . . . . . . . . . . . . . . . . . . . . . . . . . | Angle-tighten a further 30° | |
|   Stage 3 . . . . . . . . . . . . . . . . . . . . . . . . . . . . . . . . . . . . . . . . . . | Angle-tighten a further 15° | |
| Main bearing cap bolts*: | | |
|   Stage 1 . . . . . . . . . . . . . . . . . . . . . . . . . . . . . . . . . . . . . . . . . . | 50 | 37 |
|   Stage 2 . . . . . . . . . . . . . . . . . . . . . . . . . . . . . . . . . . . . . . . . . . | Angle-tighten a further 45° | |
|   Stage 3 . . . . . . . . . . . . . . . . . . . . . . . . . . . . . . . . . . . . . . . . . . | Angle-tighten a further 15° | |
| Oil pump: | | |
|   Retaining bolts . . . . . . . . . . . . . . . . . . . . . . . . . . . . . . . . . . . . . | 20 | 15 |
|   Pump cover screws . . . . . . . . . . . . . . . . . . . . . . . . . . . . . . . . . . | 8 | 6 |
|   Oil pressure relief valve cap . . . . . . . . . . . . . . . . . . . . . . . . . . . . | 15 | 11 |
| Oil pump pick-up/strainer and baffle plate bolts . . . . . . . . . . . . . . . . . . | 8 | 6 |
| Roadwheel bolts. . . . . . . . . . . . . . . . . . . . . . . . . . . . . . . . . . . . . . . . . . | 110 | 81 |
| Sump bolts: | | |
|   Sump-to-cylinder block/oil pump bolts . . . . . . . . . . . . . . . . . . . . | 10 | 7 |
|   Sump flange-to-transmission bolts . . . . . . . . . . . . . . . . . . . . . . . | 40 | 30 |
| Timing belt cover bolts. . . . . . . . . . . . . . . . . . . . . . . . . . . . . . . . . . . . . | 6 | 4 |
| Timing belt idler pulley bolt . . . . . . . . . . . . . . . . . . . . . . . . . . . . . . . . . | 25 | 18 |
| Timing belt tensioner bolt* . . . . . . . . . . . . . . . . . . . . . . . . . . . . . . . . . . | 20 | 15 |

*Use new fasteners*

## 1 General information

### How to use this Chapter

This Part of Chapter 2 describes the repair procedures which can reasonably be carried out on the engine while it remains in the vehicle. If the engine has been removed from the vehicle and is being dismantled as described in Chapter 2D, any preliminary dismantling procedures can be ignored.

Note that, while it may be possible physically to overhaul items such as the piston/connecting rod assemblies while the engine is in the vehicle, such tasks are not usually carried out as separate operations, and usually require the execution of several additional procedures (not to mention the cleaning of components and of oil ways); for this reason, all such tasks are classed as major overhaul procedures, and are described in Chapter 2D.

Chapter 2D describes the removal of the engine/transmission unit from the vehicle, and the full overhaul procedures which can then be carried out.

### Engine description

The engine is of four-cylinder in-line type, with double overhead camshafts (DOHC). The engine is mounted transversely at the front of the vehicle.

The power unit is known as a 'Twinport' engine due to the design of the inlet manifold and cylinder head combustion chambers. Vacuum operated flap valves located in the inlet manifold are opened or closed according to engine operating conditions, to create a variable venturi manifold arrangement. This system has significant advantages in terms of engine power, fuel economy and reduced exhaust emissions.

The crankshaft is supported within the cylinder block on five shell-type main bearings. Thrustwashers are fitted to number 3 main bearing, to control crankshaft endfloat.

The connecting rods are attached to the crankshaft by horizontally-split shell-type big-end bearings, and to the pistons by interference-fit gudgeon pins. The aluminium alloy pistons are of the slipper type, and are fitted with three piston rings, comprising two compression rings and a scraper-type oil control ring.

The camshafts run directly in the cylinder head, and are driven by the crankshaft via a toothed composite rubber timing belt. The camshafts operate each valve via a camshaft follower. One camshaft operates the inlet valves, and the other operates the exhaust valves. The camshaft followers are available in various thicknesses to facilitate valve clearance adjustment.

Lubrication is by pressure-feed from a rotor-type oil pump, which is mounted on the right-hand end of the crankshaft. The pump draws oil through a strainer located in the sump, and then forces it through an externally mounted full-flow oil filter. The oil flows into galleries in the cylinder block/crankcase, from where it is distributed to the crankshaft (main bearings) and camshafts. The big-end bearings are supplied with oil via internal drillings in the crankshaft, while the camshaft bearings also receive a pressurised supply. The camshaft lobes and valves are lubricated by splash, as are all other engine components.

A semi-closed crankcase ventilation system is employed; crankcase fumes are drawn from cylinder head cover, and passed via a hose to the inlet manifold.

The coolant pump is located externally on the engine, and is driven by the auxiliary drivebelt.

### Operations with engine in car

The following operations can be carried out without having to remove the engine from the car.

a) Removal and refitting of the camshaft cover.
b) Adjustment of the valve clearances.
c) Removal and refitting of the cylinder head.
d) Removal and refitting of the timing belt, tensioner and sprockets.
e) Renewal of the camshaft oil seals.
f) Removal and refitting of the camshafts and followers.
g) Removal and refitting of the sump.
h) Removal and refitting of the connecting rods and pistons*.
i) Removal and refitting of the oil pump.
j) Renewal of the crankshaft oil seals.
k) Renewal of the engine mountings.
l) Removal and refitting of the flywheel.

* Although the operation marked with an asterisk can be carried out with the engine in the car (after removal of the sump), it is preferable for the engine to be removed, in the interests of cleanliness and improved access. For this reason, the procedure is described in Chapter 2D.

## 2 Compression test – general information

1 When engine performance is down, or if misfiring occurs which cannot be attributed to the ignition or fuel systems, a compression test can provide diagnostic clues as to the engine's condition. If the test is performed regularly, it can give warning of trouble before any other symptoms become apparent.
2 Due to the electronic throttle control system used on these engines, a compression test can only be carried out with the engine management electronic control unit connected to Vauxhall/Opel diagnostic test equipment, or a compatible alternative unit. Without the test equipment, the throttle valve cannot be opened (as there is no accelerator cable) and the test will be inconclusive. Note that even with the accelerator pedal fully depressed, the engine management ECU will only control the throttle valve position when the engine is actually running. The test equipment independently actuates the throttle valve (irrespective of ECU commands) and opens the throttle valve fully.
3 As the equipment needed for the compression test is unlikely to be available to the home mechanic, it is recommended that the test is performed by a Vauxhall/Opel dealer, or suitably-equipped garage.

## 3 Top dead centre (TDC) for No 1 piston – locating

1 Top dead centre (TDC) is the highest point in the cylinder that a piston reaches as the crankshaft turns. Each piston reaches TDC at the end of the compression stroke, and again at the end of the exhaust stroke. For the purpose of timing the engine, TDC refers to the position of No 1 piston at the end of its compression stroke. No 1 piston and cylinder are at the timing belt end of the engine.
2 Disconnect the battery negative terminal (refer to *Disconnecting the battery* in the Reference Chapter). If necessary, remove all the spark plugs as described in Chapter 1 to enable the engine to be easily turned over.
3 Remove the timing belt upper cover as described in Section 6.
4 Apply the handbrake, then jack up the front of the vehicle and support it on axle stands (see *Jacking and vehicle support*). Remove the right-hand front roadwheel, then remove the wheel arch liner inner cover for access to the crankshaft pulley.
5 Using a socket and extension bar on the crankshaft pulley bolt, rotate the crankshaft until the timing marks on the camshaft sprockets are facing towards each other, and an imaginary straight line can be drawn through the camshaft sprocket bolts and the timing marks. With the camshaft sprocket marks correctly positioned, align the notch on the crankshaft pulley rim with the mark at the base of the timing belt lower cover (see illustrations). The engine is now positioned with No 1 piston at TDC on its compression stroke.

3.5a Align the camshaft timing marks . . .

**3.5b . . . and the notch on the crankshaft pulley rim with the mark at the base of the timing belt lower cover (arrowed)**

**6** If the crankshaft pulley and lower timing belt cover have been removed, the timing mark on the crankshaft sprocket can be used instead of the mark on the pulley. The mark on the crankshaft sprocket must align with the corresponding mark on the oil pump housing.

## 4  Camshaft cover – removal and refitting

### Removal

**1** Remove the air cleaner assembly and intake ducts as described in Chapter 4A.
**2** Remove the ignition module from the spark plugs as described in Chapter 5B.
**3** Remove the timing belt upper cover as described in Section 6.
**4** Release the fitting and disconnect the breather hose from the camshaft cover.
**5** Unclip the wiring harness trough from the vicinity of the camshaft cover and move it to one side.
**6** Unscrew the three camshaft cover retaining bolts at the timing belt end of the cover. Pull the captive bolts upward from the cover as far as possible and retain them in this position with adhesive tape.
**7** Unscrew the remaining six bolts securing the camshaft cover to the cylinder head.
**8** Lift the camshaft cover away from the cylinder head and recover the rubber seal. Examine the seal for signs of wear or damage and renew if necessary.

**5.3 Engage a strip of metal with the flywheel ring gear teeth through the access slot (arrowed) to lock the flywheel**

**4.11 Locate the rubber seal into the grooves of the camshaft cover, ensuring that it is fully seated**

### Refitting

**9** Ensure that the camshaft cover grove and rubber seal are clean and dry with all traces of oil removed. If necessary, de-grease the seal and cover groove with brake cleaner or a similar product.
**10** Clean the mating surface of the cylinder head and the area around the camshaft bearing caps at the timing belt end, ensuring that all traces of oil are removed.
**11** Locate the rubber seal into the grooves of the camshaft cover, ensuring that it is fully seated, with no chance of it falling out as the cover is fitted (see illustration).
**12** Carefully manoeuvre the camshaft cover into position, taking great care to ensure the seal remains correctly seated. Locate the flywheel end of the camshaft cover on the cylinder head, then carefully bring the timing belt end of the cover down onto the head.
**13** Remove the adhesive tape from the three timing belt end retaining bolts. Screw in all the cover retaining bolts and tighten them to the specified torque, working in a spiral pattern from the centre outwards.
**14** Clip the wiring harness trough back into position, then reconnect the engine breather hose.
**15** Refit the timing belt upper cover as described in Section 6.
**16** Refit the ignition module to the spark plugs as described in Chapter 5B.
**17** Refit the air cleaner assembly and intake ducts as described in Chapter 4A.

**5.5 Align the pulley cut-out with the raised notch**

## 5  Crankshaft pulley – removal and refitting

**Note:** *A new pulley retaining bolt will be required on refitting.*

### Removal

**1** Firmly apply the handbrake, then jack up the front of the car and support it securely on axle stands (see *Jacking and vehicle support*). Remove the right-hand roadwheel, then remove the wheel arch liner inner cover for access to the crankshaft pulley.
**2** Remove the auxiliary drivebelt as described in Chapter 1. Prior to removal, mark the direction of rotation on the belt to ensure the belt is refitted the same way around.
**3** Slacken the crankshaft pulley retaining bolt. To prevent crankshaft rotation, have an assistant select top gear and apply the brakes firmly. Alternatively engage a strip of metal with the flywheel ring gear teeth through the access slot located just above the front engine mounting/torque link (see illustration).
**4** Unscrew the retaining bolt and washer and remove the crankshaft pulley from the end of the crankshaft.

### Refitting

**5** Refit the crankshaft pulley, aligning the pulley cut-out with the raised notch on the timing belt sprocket, then fit the washer and new retaining bolt (see illustration).
**6** Lock the crankshaft by the method used on removal, and tighten the pulley retaining bolt to the specified Stage 1 torque setting, then angle-tighten the bolt through the specified Stage 2 angle, using a socket and extension bar, and finally through the specified Stage 3 angle. It is recommended that an angle-measuring gauge is used during the final stages of the tightening, to ensure accuracy. If a gauge is not available, use white paint to make alignment marks between the bolt head and pulley prior to tightening; the marks can then be used to check that the bolt has been rotated through the correct angle.
**7** Refit the auxiliary drivebelt as described in Chapter 1 using the mark made prior to removal to ensure the belt is fitted the correct way around.
**8** Refit the wheel arch liner inner cover and the roadwheel. Lower the car to the ground and tighten the wheel bolts to the specified torque.

## 6  Timing belt covers – removal and refitting

### Upper cover

**1** Remove the air cleaner assembly and intake ducts as described in Chapter 4A.
**2** Undo the two retaining bolts then unclip

the upper cover from the rear cover and remove it from the engine compartment (see illustration).

3 Refitting is the reverse of removal, tightening the cover retaining bolts to the specified torque.

### Lower cover

4 Remove the upper cover as described in paragraphs 1 and 2.
5 Remove the crankshaft pulley as described in Section 5.
6 Undo the retaining bolt and remove the auxiliary drivebelt tensioner (see illustration).
7 Undo the four retaining bolts then manoeuvre the lower cover off the engine.
8 Refitting is the reverse of removal, tightening the cover retaining bolts and auxiliary drivebelt tensioner bolt to the specified torque.

### Rear cover

9 Remove the timing belt as described in Section 7.
10 Remove the camshaft sprockets, crankshaft sprocket, timing belt tensioner and idler pulley as described in Section 8.
11 Unclip the wiring harness from the cover, then undo the four bolts securing the cover to the cylinder head. Remove the camshaft sensor from the cover by turning it slightly, then remove the cover from the cylinder head.
12 Refitting is the reverse of removal, tightening the cover retaining bolts to the specified torque.

**6.2  Timing belt upper cover retaining bolts (arrowed)**

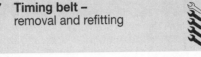

### 7  Timing belt – removal and refitting

**Note:** *The timing belt must be removed and refitted with the engine cold.*

### Removal

1 Position No 1 cylinder at TDC on its compression stroke as described in Section 3.
2 Remove the timing belt lower cover as described in Section 6.
3 Check that the timing marks on the camshaft sprockets are still correctly aligned and facing towards each other, and the timing mark on the crankshaft sprocket is aligned with the corresponding mark on the oil pump housing (see illustration).

**6.6  Auxiliary drivebelt tensioner retaining bolt (arrowed)**

4 Remove the right-hand engine mounting as described in Section 17, then undo the three retaining bolts and remove the mounting bracket bolted to the cylinder block.
5 Using an Allen key inserted in the slot on the face of the timing belt tensioner, rotate the tensioner clockwise to relieve the tension in the timing belt. Insert a small drill bit or similar into the slot on the inner edge of the tensioner body to lock the tensioner in the released position.
6 Slide the timing belt from its sprockets and remove it from the engine (see illustration). If the belt is to be re-used, use white paint or similar to mark the direction of rotation on the belt. **Do not** rotate the crankshaft or camshafts until the timing belt has been refitted.
7 Check the timing belt carefully for any signs of uneven wear, splitting or oil contamination, and renew it if there is the slightest doubt about its condition. If the engine is undergoing an overhaul and is approaching the specified interval for belt renewal (see Chapter 1) renew the belt as a matter of course, regardless of its apparent condition. If signs of oil contamination are found, trace the source of the oil leak and rectify it, then wash down the engine timing belt area and all related components to remove all traces of oil.

### Refitting

8 On reassembly, thoroughly clean the timing belt sprockets and tensioner/idler pulleys.
9 Check that the camshaft and crankshaft sprocket timing marks are still correctly aligned as described in paragraph 3.

**7.3  Camshaft and crankshaft timing marks**

1  Camshaft sprocket timing marks adjacent and aligned
2  Crankshaft sprocket timing mark aligned with mark on oil pump housing

**7.6  Removing the timing belt**

10 Fit the timing belt over the crankshaft and camshaft sprockets and around the idler pulley, ensuring that the belt front run is taut (ie, all slack is on the tensioner side of the belt), then fit the belt over the tensioner pulley. Do not twist the belt sharply while refitting it. Ensure that the belt teeth are correctly seated centrally in the sprockets, and that the timing marks remain in alignment. If a used belt is being refitted, ensure that the arrow mark made on removal points in the normal direction of rotation, as before.

11 Using the Allen key, turn the tensioner clockwise slightly and remove the drill bit or similar tool used to lock the tensioner. Slowly release the tensioner and allow it to turn anti-clockwise and automatically tension the timing belt.

12 Check the sprocket timing marks are still correctly aligned. If adjustment is necessary, release the tensioner again then disengage the belt from the sprockets and make any necessary adjustments.

13 Using a socket on the temporarily refitted crankshaft pulley bolt, rotate the crankshaft smoothly through two complete turns (720°) in the normal direction of rotation to settle the timing belt in position.

14 Set the crankshaft back in the timing position and check that all the sprocket timing marks are still correctly aligned. If this is not the case, repeat the timing belt refitting procedure.

15 If everything is satisfactory, refit the engine mounting bracket, tightening the three retaining bolts to the specified torque.

16 Refit the right-hand engine mounting as described in Section 17, then refit the timing belt covers as described in Section 6.

17 Refit the crankshaft pulley as described in Section 5.

---

## 8 Timing belt sprockets, tensioner and idler pulley – removal and refitting

### Camshaft sprockets

**Note:** *New sprocket retaining bolt(s) will be required for refitting.*

#### Removal

1 Remove the timing belt as described in Section 7.

2 Turn the crankshaft 60° anti-clockwise away from TDC, to move the pistons away from the valves in the cylinder head. This is purely a precaution to prevent valve-to-piston contact if the camshafts are inadvertently rotated during the sprocket bolt removal/refitting procedure.

3 The camshaft sprocket must be prevented from turning as the sprocket bolt is unscrewed. Vauxhall/Opel special tools KM-6347 and KM-956-1 are available for this purpose, however a home-made tool can easily be fabricated (see **Tool Tip**).

4 Hold the sprocket with the tool, then unscrew the retaining bolt and washer and remove the sprocket from the end of the camshaft. If the sprocket locating pin is a loose fit in the camshaft end, remove it and store it with the sprocket for safe-keeping.

5 If necessary, remove the remaining sprocket using the same method. The inlet and exhaust sprockets are different; the exhaust camshaft sprocket can be easily identified by the lugs which activate the camshaft position sensor.

#### Refitting

6 Prior to refitting check the oil seal(s) for signs of damage or leakage. If necessary, renew as described in Section 9.

7 Ensure the locating pin is in position in the camshaft end.

8 Refit the sprocket to the camshaft end, aligning its cut-out with the locating pin, and fit the washer and new retaining bolt. If both sprockets have been removed, ensure each sprocket is fitted to the correct shaft; the exhaust camshaft sprocket can be identified by the lugs on the sprocket outer face which trigger the camshaft position sensor.

9 Retain the sprocket by the method used on removal, and tighten the pulley retaining bolt to the specified Stage 1 torque setting then angle-tighten the bolt through the specified Stage 2 angle, using a socket and extension bar, and finally through the specified Stage 3 angle. It is recommended that an angle-measuring gauge is used during the final stages of the tightening, to ensure accuracy. If a gauge is not available, use white paint to make alignment marks between the bolt head and pulley prior to tightening; the marks can then be used to check that the bolt has been rotated through the correct angle.

10 Carefully rotate the crankshaft 60° clockwise until the mark on the crankshaft sprocket aligns with the mark at the base of the oil pump housing, then refit the timing belt as described in Section 7.

*Make up a sprocket-holding tool using two lengths of steel strip (one long, the other short), and three nuts and bolts; one nut and bolt forms the pivot of a forked tool, with the remaining two nuts and bolts at the tips of the 'forks' to engage with the sprocket spokes.*

### Crankshaft sprocket

#### Removal

11 Remove the timing belt as described in Section 7.

12 Slide the sprocket off from the end of the crankshaft, noting which way around it is fitted.

#### Refitting

13 Align the sprocket locating key with the crankshaft groove then slide the sprocket into position

14 Refit the timing belt as described in Section 7.

### Tensioner assembly

**Note:** *A new tensioner retaining bolt will be required for refitting.*

#### Removal

15 Remove the timing belt as described in Section 7.

16 Slacken and remove the central retaining bolt and remove the tensioner assembly from the engine.

#### Refitting

17 Clean the tensioner retaining bolt threads in the oil pump housing, ensuring that all traces of sealant, oil or grease are removed.

18 Fit the tensioner to the engine, making sure that the lug on the backplate is correctly located in the oil pump housing hole. On later models, also ensure that the projecting end of the tensioner spring engages with the slot on the oil pump housing. Ensure the tensioner is correctly seated then refit the new retaining bolt and tighten it to the specified torque.

19 Refit the timing belt as described in Section 7.

### Idler pulley

#### Removal

20 Remove the timing belt as described in Section 7.

21 Slacken and remove the retaining bolt and remove the idler pulley from the engine.

#### Refitting

22 Clean the idler pulley retaining bolt threads in the oil pump housing, ensuring that all traces of sealant, oil or grease are removed.

23 Refit the idler pulley and tighten the retaining bolt to the specified torque.

24 Refit the timing belt as described in Section 7.

---

## 9 Camshaft oil seals – renewal

1 Remove the relevant camshaft sprocket as described in Section 8.

2 Carefully punch or drill two small holes opposite each other in the oil seal. Screw a self-tapping screw into each, and pull on the

screws with pliers to extract the seal (see illustration).

**3** Clean the seal housing, and polish off any burrs or raised edges which may have caused the seal to fail in the first place.

**4** Press the new seal into position using a suitable tubular drift (such as a socket) which bears only on the hard outer edge of the seal (see illustration). Take care not to damage the seal lips during fitting; note that the seal lips should face inwards.

**5** Refit the camshaft sprocket as described in Section 8.

### 10 Valve clearances – checking and adjustment

#### Checking

**1** The importance of having the valve clearances correctly adjusted cannot be overstressed, as they vitally affect the performance of the engine. The engine must be cold for the check to be accurate. The clearances are checked as follows.

**2** Apply the handbrake, then jack up the front of the car and support it on axle stands. Remove the right-hand front roadwheel then remove the wheel arch liner inner cover for access to the crankshaft pulley.

**3** Remove the camshaft cover as described in Section 4.

**4** Position No 1 cylinder at TDC on its compression stroke as described in Section 3.

**5** With the engine at TDC on compression for No 1 cylinder, the inlet camshaft lobes for No 2 cylinder and the exhaust camshaft lobes for No 3 cylinder are pointing upwards and slightly towards the centre. This indicates that these valves are completely closed, and the clearances can be checked.

**6** On a piece of paper, draw the outline of the engine with the cylinders numbered from the timing belt end. Show the position of each valve, together with the required valve clearance (see Specifications).

**7** With the cam lobes positioned as described in paragraph 5, using feeler blades, measure the clearance between the base of both No 2 cylinder inlet cam lobes and No 3 cylinder exhaust cam lobes and their followers. Record the clearances on the paper (see illustrations).

**8** Rotate the crankshaft pulley in the normal direction of rotation through a half a turn (180°) to position No 1 cylinder inlet camshaft lobes and No 4 cylinder exhaust camshaft lobes pointing upwards and slightly towards the centre. Measure the clearance between the base of the camshaft lobes and their followers and record the clearances on the paper.

**9** Rotate the crankshaft pulley through a half a turn (180°) to position No 3 cylinder inlet camshaft lobes and No 2 cylinder exhaust camshaft lobes pointing upwards and slightly

**9.2 Camshaft oil seal removal method**

towards the centre. Measure the clearance between the base of the camshaft lobes and their followers and record the clearances on the paper.

**10** Rotate the crankshaft pulley through a half a turn (180°) to position No 4 cylinder inlet camshaft lobes and No 1 cylinder exhaust camshaft lobes pointing upwards and slightly towards the centre. Measure the clearance between the base of the camshaft lobes and their followers and record the clearances on the paper.

**11** If all the clearances are correct, refit the camshaft cover (see Section 4), then refit the wheel arch liner inner cover and the roadwheel. Lower the vehicle to the ground and tighten the wheel bolts to the specified torque. If any clearance measured is not correct, adjustment must be carried out as described in the following paragraphs.

#### Adjustment

**12** If adjustment is necessary, remove the relevant camshaft(s) and camshaft followers as described in Section 11.

**13** Clean the followers of the valves that require clearance adjustment and note the thickness marking on the follower. The thickness marking is stamped on the underside of each follower. For example, a 3.20 mm thick follower will have a 20 thickness marking, a 3.21 mm thick follower will have a 21 thickness marking, etc.

**14** Add the measured clearance of the valve to the thickness of the original follower then subtract the required valve clearance from this

**10.7a Using feeler blades, measure the inlet valve clearances . . .**

**9.4 Refit the camshaft oil seal with a tool that bears only on the hard outer edge of the seal**

figure. This will give you the thickness of the follower required. For example:

| | |
|---|---|
| Clearance measured of inlet valve | 0.31 mm |
| Plus thickness of the original follower | 3.20 mm |
| Equals | 3.51 mm |
| Minus clearance required | 0.25 mm |
| Thickness of follower required | 3.26 mm |

**15** Repeat this procedure on the remaining valves which require adjustment, then obtain the correct thickness of follower(s) required.

**16** Refit the camshaft followers and the relevant camshaft(s) as described in Section 11. Rotate the crankshaft a few times to settle all the components, then recheck the valve clearances before refitting the camshaft cover (Section 4).

**17** Refit the wheel arch liner inner cover and roadwheel then lower the vehicle to the ground and tighten the wheel bolts to the specified torque.

### 11 Camshaft and followers – removal, inspection and refitting

**Note:** *New timing belt end oil seals, and a tube of suitable sealant will be required when refitting.*

#### Removal

**1** Remove the camshaft cover as described in Section 4.

**2** Remove the timing belt as described in Section 7.

**3** Remove the camshaft sprockets as described in Section 8.

**10.7b . . . and the exhaust valve clearances**

**11.4a Camshaft bearing cap numbering sequence (No 1 at timing belt end)**

4 Starting on the inlet camshaft, working in a spiral pattern from the outside inwards, slacken the camshaft bearing cap retaining bolts by half a turn at a time, to relieve the pressure of the valve springs on the bearing caps gradually and evenly **(the reverse of illustration 11.15)**. Once the valve spring pressure has been relieved, the bolts can be fully unscrewed and removed along with the caps; the bearing caps are numbered inlet camshaft 1 to 5, exhaust camshaft 6 to 10 (or 6 to 0) to ensure the caps are correctly positioned on refitting **(see illustrations)**. Take care not to lose the locating dowels (where fitted).

*Caution: If the bearing cap bolts are carelessly slackened, the bearing caps might break. If any bearing cap breaks*

**11.7 Use a valve lapping tool to remove the cam followers**

**11.13 Apply a smear of sealant to the right-hand bearing caps**

**11.4b Camshaft bearing cap numbers (arrowed – inlet camshaft shown)**

*then the complete cylinder head assembly must be renewed; the bearing caps are matched to the head and are not available separately.*

5 Lift the camshaft out of the cylinder head and slide off the oil seal.

6 Repeat the operations described in paragraphs 4 and 5 and remove the exhaust camshaft.

7 Obtain sixteen small, clean plastic containers, and label them for identification. Alternatively, divide a larger container into compartments. Using a rubber sucker tool, lift the followers out from the top of the cylinder head and store each one in its respective fitted position **(see illustration)**.

### Inspection

8 Examine the camshaft bearing surfaces and cam lobes for signs of wear ridges and scoring. Renew the camshaft if any of these conditions are apparent. Examine the condition of the bearing surfaces both on the camshaft journals and in the cylinder head. If the head bearing surfaces are worn excessively, the cylinder head will need to be renewed.

9 Examine the follower bearing surfaces which contact the camshaft lobes for wear ridges and scoring. Check the followers and

their bores in the cylinder head for signs of wear or damage. If any follower is thought to be faulty or is visibly worn it should be renewed.

### Refitting

10 Where removed, lubricate the followers with clean engine oil and carefully insert each one into its original location in the cylinder head.

11 Lubricate the camshaft followers with molybdenum disulphide paste (or clean engine oil) then lay the camshafts in position.

12 Ensure the mating surfaces of the bearing caps and cylinder head are clean and dry and lubricate the camshaft journals and lobes with clean engine oil.

13 Apply a smear of sealant to the mating surfaces of both the inlet (No 1) and exhaust (No 6) camshaft right-hand bearing caps **(see illustration)**.

14 Ensure the locating dowels (where fitted) are in position then refit the camshaft bearing caps and the retaining bolts in their original locations on the cylinder head.

15 Working on the inlet camshaft, tighten the bearing cap bolts by hand only then, working in a spiral pattern from the centre outwards, tighten the bolts by half a turn at a time to gradually impose the pressure of the valve springs on the bearing caps **(see illustration)**. Repeat this sequence until all bearing caps are in contact with the cylinder head then go around and tighten the camshaft bearing cap bolts to the specified torque.

*Caution: If the bearing cap bolts are carelessly tightened, the bearing caps might break. If any bearing cap breaks then the complete cylinder head assembly must be renewed; the bearing caps are matched to the head and are not available separately.*

16 Tighten the exhaust camshaft bearing cap bolts as described in paragraph 15.

**11.15 Camshaft bearing cap tightening sequence (exhaust camshaft shown – inlet identical)**

**17** Fit new camshaft oil seals as described in Section 9.

**18** Refit the camshaft sprockets as described in Section 8.

**19** Align all the sprocket timing marks to bring the camshafts and crankshaft back to TDC then refit the timing belt as described in Section 7.

**20** Refit the camshaft cover as described in Section 4.

## 12 Cylinder head – removal and refitting

**Note:** *The engine must be cold when removing the cylinder head. A new cylinder head gasket and new cylinder head bolts must be used on refitting.*

### Removal

**1** Depressurise the fuel system as described in Chapter 4A.

**2** Disconnect the battery negative terminal (refer to *Disconnecting the battery* in the Reference Chapter).

**3** Apply the handbrake, then jack up the front of the vehicle and support it on axle stands (see *Jacking and vehicle support*). Remove the right-hand front roadwheel and the wheel arch liner inner cover for access to the right-hand side of the engine.

**4** Drain the cooling system as described in Chapter 1.

**5** Remove the camshaft cover as described in Section 4.

**6** Remove the spark plugs as described in Chapter 1.

**7** Remove the timing belt as described in Section 7.

**8** Remove the camshaft sprockets, timing belt tensioner, and the timing belt idler roller, as described in Section 8.

**9** Remove the rear timing belt cover with reference to Section 6.

**10** Refer to Chapter 4A and unbolt the exhaust front pipe from the exhaust manifold, taking care to support the flexible section. **Note:** *Angular movement in excess of 10° can cause permanent damage to the flexible section.* Release the mounting rubbers and support the front of the exhaust pipe to one side.

**11** Disconnect the wiring connectors from the following components:

  a) *Crankshaft speed/position sensor.*
  b) *Camshaft sensor.*
  c) *Oil pressure switch.*
  d) *Thermostat.*
  e) *Coolant temperature sensor.*
  f) *EGR valve.*

**12** Release the cable ties and place the wiring loom to one side.

**13** Remove the inlet and exhaust manifolds as described in Chapter 4A.

**14** Undo the five bolts and remove the metal coolant pipe from the coolant pump and thermostat housing.

**15** Referring to Chapter 3, disconnect the coolant hoses from the heater matrix unions on the engine compartment bulkhead.

**16** Loosen the clips and remove the coolant hose from the radiator and thermostat housing.

**17** Make a final check to ensure that all relevant hoses, pipes and wires have been disconnected.

**18** Working in sequence, progressively loosen the cylinder head bolts **(see illustration)**. First loosen all the bolts by quarter of a turn, then loosen all the bolts by half a turn, then finally slacken all the bolts fully and withdraw them from the cylinder head. Recover the washers (where fitted).

**19** Lift the cylinder head from the cylinder block. If necessary, tap the cylinder head gently with a soft-faced mallet to free it from the block, but **do not** lever at the mating faces. Note that the cylinder head is located on dowels.

**20** Recover the cylinder head gasket, and discard it.

### Preparation for refitting

**21** The mating faces of the cylinder head and block must be perfectly clean before refitting the head. Use a scraper to remove all traces of gasket and carbon, and also clean the tops of the pistons. Take particular care with the aluminium surfaces, as the soft metal is damaged easily. Also, make sure that debris is not allowed to enter the oil and water channels – this is particularly important for the oil circuit, as carbon could block the oil supply to the camshaft or crankshaft bearings. Using adhesive tape and paper, seal the water, oil and bolt holes in the cylinder block. To prevent carbon entering the gap between the pistons and bores, smear a little grease in the gap. After cleaning the piston, rotate the crankshaft so that the piston moves down the bore, then wipe out the grease and carbon with a cloth rag. Clean the other piston crowns in the same way.

**22** Check the block and head for nicks, deep scratches and other damage. If slight, they may be removed carefully with a file. More serious damage may be repaired by machining, but this is a specialist job.

**23** If warpage of the cylinder head is suspected, use a straight-edge to check it for distortion. Refer to Chapter 2D if necessary.

**24** Ensure that the cylinder head bolt holes in the crankcase are clean and free of oil. Syringe or soak up any oil left in the bolt holes. This is most important in order that the correct bolt tightening torque can be applied and to prevent the possibility of the block being cracked by hydraulic pressure when the bolts are tightened.

**25** Renew the cylinder head bolts regardless of their apparent condition.

### Refitting

**26** Ensure that the two locating dowels are in position at each end of the cylinder block/crankcase surface.

**27** Fit the new cylinder head gasket to the

**12.18 Cylinder head bolt loosening sequence**

**12.27 Ensure the head gasket is fitted with its OBEN/TOP marking uppermost**

block, making sure it is fitted with the correct way up with its OBEN/TOP mark uppermost **(see illustration)**.

**28** Carefully refit the cylinder head, locating it on the dowels.

**29** Fit the washers (where applicable) to the new cylinder head bolts then carefully insert them into position **(do not drop)**, tightening them finger-tight only at this stage.

**30** Working progressively and in sequence, first tighten all the cylinder head bolts to the Stage 1 torque setting **(see illustrations)**.

**31** Once all bolts have been tightened to the Stage 1 torque, again working in sequence, tighten each bolt through its specified Stage 2 angle, using a socket and extension bar. It is recommended that an angle-measuring gauge is used during this stage of the tightening, to ensure accuracy **(see illustration)**.

**32** Working in the specified sequence, go around again and tighten all bolts through the specified Stage 3 angle.

**33** Working again in the specified sequence, go around and tighten all bolts through the specified Stage 4 angle.

**34** Finally go around in the specified sequence again and tighten all bolts through the specified Stage 5 angle.

**35** Using new gaskets, refit the metal coolant pipe to the coolant pump and thermostat housing, tightening the bolts securely.

**36** Reconnect the coolant hose to the radiator and thermostat housing.

**37** Reconnect the coolant hoses to the heater matrix unions on the engine compartment bulkhead.

**38** Refit the inlet and exhaust manifolds as described in Chapter 4A.

**39** Reconnect the wiring to the components listed in paragraph 11, then secure the wiring with cable ties.

**40** Refer to Chapter 4A and refit the exhaust front pipe to the exhaust manifold. Refit the mounting rubbers.

**41** Refit the rear timing belt cover with reference to Section 6.

**42** Refit the camshaft sprockets, timing belt tensioner, and the timing belt idler roller, with reference to Section 8.

**43** Refit the timing belt as described in Section 7.

**44** Refit the spark plugs as described in Chapter 1.

**45** Refit the camshaft cover as described in Section 4.

**46** Refit the wheel arch liner inner cover and front roadwheel, then lower the vehicle to the ground.

**47** Reconnect the battery negative terminal.

**48** Check that all relevant hoses, pipes and wires, etc, have been reconnected. Check the security of the fuel hose connections.

**49** Refill and bleed the cooling system with reference to Chapter 1.

**50** When the engine is started, check for signs of oil or coolant leakage.

**12.30a Cylinder head bolt tightening sequence**

**12.30b Tighten the cylinder head bolts to the specified Stage 1 torque setting . . .**

**12.31 . . . and then through the various specified angles as described in the text**

## 13 Sump – removal and refitting

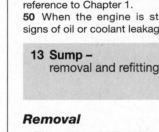

### Removal

**1** Disconnect the battery negative terminal (refer to *Disconnecting the battery* in the Reference Chapter).

**2** Apply the handbrake, then jack up the front of the vehicle and support it on axle stands (see *Jacking and vehicle support*). Remove the right-hand front roadwheel and the wheel arch liner inner cover for access to the right-hand side of the engine.

**3** Drain the engine oil as described in Chapter 1, then fit a new sealing washer and refit the drain plug, tightening it to the specified torque (Chapter 1).

**4** Remove the exhaust system as described in Chapter 4A.

**5** Disconnect the wiring connector from the oil level sensor.

**6** Undo the retaining bolt and remove the oil dipstick guide tube.

**13.14 Apply sealant to the oil pump and main bearing cap joints (arrowed) before the sump is refitted**

**14.7 Remove the securing screws and withdraw the oil pump cover from the rear of the housing**

**7** Slacken and remove the bolts securing the sump flange to the transmission housing.

**8** On early models, remove the rubber plugs from the transmission end of the sump flange to gain access to the sump end retaining bolts.

**9** Progressively slacken and remove the bolts securing the sump to the base of the cylinder block/oil pump. Using a wide-bladed scraper or similar tool inserted between the sump and cylinder block, carefully break the joint, then remove the sump from under the car.

**10** While the sump is removed, take the opportunity to check the oil pump pick-up/strainer for signs of clogging or splitting. To gain access, undo the two bolts and remove the baffle plate from the sump. Unbolt the pick-up/strainer flange and strainer base and remove it from the sump along with its sealing ring. The strainer can then be cleaned easily in solvent or renewed.

### Refitting

**11** Thoroughly clean the sump, baffle plate and pick-up/strainer, then remove all traces of sealer and oil from the mating surfaces of the sump and cylinder block and (where removed) the pick-up/strainer. Also remove all traces of locking compound from the pick-up bolts (where removed).

**12** Position a new gasket/seal on the oil pump pick-up/strainer flange and fit the strainer. Refit the flange and base retaining bolts and tighten to the specified torque.

**13** Ensure the sump and cylinder block mating surfaces are clean and dry and remove all traces of locking compound from the sump bolts.

**14** Apply a smear of suitable sealant (available from Vauxhall/Opel dealers) to the areas of the cylinder block mating surface around the areas of the of the oil pump housing and main bearing cap joints **(see illustration)**.

**15** Apply a bead of suitable sealant (available from Vauxhall/Opel dealers) approximately 2.5 mm thick to the sealing surface of the sump. Around the No 5 main bearing cap area, increase the thickness of the bead to 3.5 mm.

**16** Offer up the sump, and loosely refit all the retaining bolts. Working out from the centre in a diagonal sequence, progressively tighten the bolts securing the sump to the cylinder block/oil pump to their specified torque setting.

**17** Tighten the bolts securing the sump flange to the transmission housing to their specified torque settings. Refit the rubber plugs to the sump flange cut-outs (where fitted).

**18** Refit the oil dipstick guide tube.

**19** Refit the exhaust system (see Chapter 4A) and reconnect the oil level sender wiring connector.

**20** Refit the wheel arch liner inner cover and front roadwheel, then lower the vehicle to the ground. Fill the engine with fresh oil, with reference to Chapter 1.

## 14 Oil pump – removal, overhaul and refitting

### Removal

**1** Remove the alternator as described in Chapter 5A.

**14.9a Unscrew the oil pressure relief valve cap . . .**

**2** Remove the timing belt as described in Section 7.

**3** Remove the timing belt tensioner and Idler pulley as described in Section 8.

**4** Remove the sump as described in Section 13.

**5** Undo the two bolts securing the metal coolant pipe to the rear of the coolant pump.

**6** Slacken and remove the eight retaining bolts (noting their different lengths) then slide the oil pump housing assembly off of the end of the crankshaft, taking great care not to lose the locating dowels. Remove the housing gasket and discard it.

### Overhaul

**7** Remove the securing screws/bolts and withdraw the oil pump cover from the rear of the oil pump housing **(see illustration)**.

**8** Remove the inner and outer rotor from the pump housing, noting which way round they are fitted, and wipe them clean. Also clean the rotor location in the oil pump housing.

**9** The oil pressure relief valve components can also be removed from the oil pump housing by unscrewing the cap. Withdraw the cap, spring and plunger **(see illustrations)**.

**10** Locate the inner and outer rotor back in the oil pump housing, ensuring they are fitted the right way round as noted during removal.

**14.9b . . . then withdraw the spring . . .**

**14.9c ... and the plunger**

**11** Check the clearance between the end faces of the rotors and the housing (endfloat) using a straight-edge and a feeler gauge **(see illustration)**.

**12** If the clearance is outside the specified limits, renew the components as necessary.

**13** Examine the pressure relief valve spring and plunger, and renew if any sign of damage or wear is evident.

**14** Ensure that the rotor location in the interior of the oil pump housing is scrupulously clean before commencing reassembly.

**15** Thoroughly clean the pressure relief valve components, and lubricate them with clean engine oil before refitting. Insert the plunger and spring, then refit the cap and tighten to the specified torque.

**16** Ensure that the rotors are clean, then lubricate them with clean engine oil, and refit them to the pump body ensuring they are fitted the right way round as noted during removal.

**17** Wipe clean the mating faces of the rear cover and the pump housing, then refit the rear cover. Refit and tighten the securing screws securely. Prime the oil pump by filling it with clean engine oil whilst rotating the inner rotor

### Refitting

**18** Prior to refitting, carefully lever out the crankshaft oil seal using a flat-bladed screwdriver. Fit the new oil seal, ensuring its sealing lip is facing inwards, and press it

squarely into the housing using a tubular drift which bears only on the hard outer edge of the seal. Press the seal into position so that it is flush with the housing.

**19** Ensure the mating surfaces of the oil pump housing and cylinder block are clean and dry and the locating dowels are in position.

**20** Fit a new gasket to the cylinder block.

**21** Carefully manoeuvre the oil pump into position and engage the inner rotor with the crankshaft end. Locate the pump on the dowels, taking great care not damage the oil seal lip.

**22** Refit the pump housing retaining bolts in their original locations and tighten them to the specified torque.

**23** Using a new gasket, refit the metal coolant pipe flange to the coolant pump and tighten the retaining bolts to the specified torque.

**24** Refit the sump as described in Section 13.

**25** Refit the timing belt tensioner and idler pulley, then refit the timing belt as described in Sections 8 and 7.

**26** Refit the alternator as described in Chapter 5A.

**27** On completion, fit a new oil filter and fill the engine with clean oil as described in Chapter 1.

## 15 Crankshaft oil seals – renewal

### Right-hand (timing belt end)

**1** Remove the crankshaft sprocket as described in Section 8.

**2** Carefully punch or drill two small holes opposite each other in the oil seal. Screw a self-tapping screw into each and pull on the screws with pliers to extract the seal **(see illustration)**.

*Caution: Great care must be taken to avoid damage to the oil pump*

**3** Clean the seal housing and polish off any burrs or raised edges which may have caused the seal to fail in the first place.

**4** Carefully ease the new seal into position on the end of the crankshaft. Press the seal

**14.11 Check the oil pump rotor endfloat using a straight-edge and feeler gauge**

squarely into position until it is flush with the housing. If necessary, a suitable tubular drift, such as a socket, which bears only on the hard outer edge of the seal can be used to tap the seal into position **(see illustration)**. Take great care not to damage the seal lips during fitting and ensure that the seal lips face inwards.

**5** Wash off any traces of oil, then refit the crankshaft sprocket as described in Section 8.

### Left-hand (flywheel end)

**6** Remove the flywheel as described in Section 16.

**7** Renew the seal as described in paragraphs 2 to 4 **(see illustration)**.

**8** Refit the flywheel as described in Section 16.

## 16 Flywheel – removal, inspection and refitting

Refer to Chapter 2A, Section 14.

## 17 Engine/transmission mountings – inspection and renewal

Refer to Chapter 2A, Section 15, but observe the different torque wrench settings given in the Specifications of this Chapter for the right-hand mounting engine bracket.

**15.2 Removing the crankshaft oil seal**

**15.4 Fitting a new crankshaft oil seal**

**15.7 Left-hand crankshaft oil seal – transmission and flywheel removed**

# Chapter 2 Part C:
# 1.8 litre engine in-car repair procedures

## Contents

## Degrees of difficulty

| | | | | |
|---|---|---|---|---|
| **Easy,** suitable for novice with little experience | **Fairly easy,** suitable for beginner with some experience | **Fairly difficult,** suitable for competent DIY mechanic | **Difficult,** suitable for experienced DIY mechanic | **Very difficult,** suitable for expert DIY or professional |

## Specifications

### General

| | |
|---|---|
| Engine type | Four-cylinder, in-line, water-cooled. Double overhead camshafts, belt-driven |
| Manufacturer's engine code* | Z18XE and Z18XER |
| Bore | 80.5 mm |
| Stroke | 88.2 mm |
| Capacity | 1796 cc |
| Compression ratio | 10.5:1 |
| Firing order | 1-3-4-2 (No 1 cylinder at timing belt end) |
| Direction of crankshaft rotation | Clockwise (viewed from timing belt end of engine) |

*\* For details of engine code location, see 'Vehicle identification' in the Reference Chapter.*

### Compression pressures

| | |
|---|---|
| Maximum difference between any two cylinders | 1 bar |

### Valve clearances (Z18XER engines)

Engine cold:

| | |
|---|---|
| Inlet | 0.21 to 0.29 mm |
| Exhaust | 0.27 to 0.35 mm |

### Lubrication system

| | |
|---|---|
| Minimum oil pressure at 80°C | 1.3 bar at idle speed |
| Oil pump type | Rotor-type, driven directly from crankshaft |

Rotor-to-housing clearance (endfloat):

| | |
|---|---|
| Z18XE engines | 0.03 to 0.10 mm |
| Z18XER engines | 0.02 to 0.058 mm |

## Torque wrench settings

| | Nm | lbf ft |
|---|---|---|
| **Z18XE engines** | | |
| Auxiliary drivebelt tensioner bolt | 35 | 26 |
| Camshaft bearing cap bolts | 8 | 6 |
| Camshaft cover bolts | 8 | 6 |
| Camshaft sprocket bolt*: | | |
|   Stage 1 | 50 | 37 |
|   Stage 2 | Angle-tighten a further 60° | |
|   Stage 3 | Angle-tighten a further 15° | |
| Connecting rod big-end bearing cap bolt*: | | |
|   Stage 1 | 25 | 18 |
|   Stage 2 | Angle-tighten a further 30° | |
| Crankshaft pulley bolt*: | | |
|   Stage 1 | 95 | 70 |
|   Stage 2 | Angle-tighten a further 45° | |
|   Stage 3 | Angle-tighten a further 15° | |
| Crankshaft sensor mounting bracket bolt | 8 | 6 |
| Cylinder head bolts*: | | |
|   Stage 1 | 25 | 18 |
|   Stage 2 | Angle-tighten a further 90° | |
|   Stage 3 | Angle-tighten a further 90° | |
|   Stage 4 | Angle-tighten a further 90° | |
|   Stage 5 | Angle-tighten a further 45° | |
| Driveplate bolts* | 60 | 44 |
| Engine mountings: | | |
|   Front mounting/torque link: | | |
|     Mounting-to-transmission bolts | 80 | 59 |
|     Mounting to subframe | 55 | 41 |
|   Left-hand mounting: | | |
|     Mounting-to-body bolts | 20 | 15 |
|     Mounting bracket to transmission bracket | 55 | 41 |
|     Rubber mounting through-bolt | 55 | 41 |
|     Transmission bracket to transmission | 35 | 26 |
|   Rear mounting/torque link: | | |
|     Mounting-to-bracket bolts | 55 | 41 |
|     Mounting-to-subframe bolts | 55 | 41 |
|     Bracket-to-transmission bolts | 80 | 59 |
|   Right-hand mounting: | | |
|     Engine bracket-to-engine bolts*: | | |
|       Stage 1 | 65 | 48 |
|       Stage 2 | Angle-tighten a further 45° | |
|       Stage 3 | Angle-tighten a further 15° | |
|     Mounting-to-body bolts | 35 | 26 |
|     Mounting-to-engine bracket bolts | 55 | 41 |
|     Rubber mounting through-bolt | 55 | 41 |
| Engine-to-transmission bolts | 60 | 44 |
| Flywheel bolts*: | | |
|   Stage 1 | 35 | 26 |
|   Stage 2 | Angle-tighten a further 30° | |
|   Stage 3 | Angle-tighten a further 15° | |
| Main bearing cap bolts*: | | |
|   Stage 1 | 50 | 37 |
|   Stage 2 | Angle-tighten a further 45° | |
|   Stage 3 | Angle-tighten a further 15° | |
| Oil pump: | | |
|   Retaining bolts | 10 | 17 |
|   Pump cover screws | 6 | 4 |
|   Oil pressure relief valve bolt | 50 | 37 |
| Oil pump pick-up/strainer and baffle plate bolts | 8 | 6 |
| Roadwheel bolts | 110 | 81 |
| Sump bolts: | | |
|   Sump-to-cylinder block/oil pump bolts | 10 | 7 |
|   Sump flange-to-transmission bolts | 40 | 30 |
| Timing belt cover bolts | 6 | 4 |
| Timing belt idler pulley bolt | 25 | 18 |
| Timing belt tensioner bolt | 20 | 15 |

* Use new fasteners

## Torque wrench settings (continued)

| | Nm | lbf ft |
|---|---|---|
| **Z18XER engines** | | |
| Auxiliary drivebelt tensioner bolt* | 50 | 37 |
| Camshaft bearing cap bolts | 8 | 6 |
| Camshaft bearing support bolts | 8 | 6 |
| Camshaft cover bolts | 8 | 6 |
| Camshaft sprocket closure bolt | 30 | 22 |
| Camshaft sprocket retaining bolt*: | | |
| Stage 1 | 65 | 48 |
| Stage 2 | Angle-tighten a further 120° | |
| Stage 3 | Angle-tighten a further 15° | |
| Connecting rod big-end bearing cap bolt*: | | |
| Stage 1 | 35 | 26 |
| Stage 2 | Angle-tighten a further 45° | |
| Stage 3 | Angle-tighten a further 15° | |
| Crankshaft pulley bolt*: | | |
| Stage 1 | 95 | 70 |
| Stage 2 | Angle-tighten a further 30° | |
| Stage 3 | Angle-tighten a further 15° | |
| Cylinder head bolts*: | | |
| Stage 1 | 25 | 18 |
| Stage 2 | Angle-tighten a further 90° | |
| Stage 3 | Angle-tighten a further 90° | |
| Stage 4 | Angle-tighten a further 90° | |
| Stage 5 | Angle-tighten a further 45° | |
| Engine mountings: | | |
| Front mounting/torque link: | | |
| Mounting-to-transmission bolts | 80 | 59 |
| Mounting to subframe | 55 | 41 |
| Left-hand mounting: | | |
| Mounting-to-body bolts | 55 | 41 |
| Mounting bracket to transmission bracket | 55 | 41 |
| Rubber mounting through-bolt | 55 | 41 |
| Transmission bracket to transmission | 35 | 26 |
| Rear mounting/torque link: | | |
| Mounting-to-bracket bolts | 55 | 41 |
| Mounting-to-subframe bolts | 55 | 41 |
| Bracket-to-transmission bolts | 80 | 59 |
| Right-hand mounting: | | |
| Engine bracket-to-engine bolts | 55 | 41 |
| Mounting-to-body bolts | 35 | 26 |
| Mounting-to-engine bracket bolts | 55 | 41 |
| Rubber mounting through-bolt | 55 | 41 |
| Engine-to-transmission bolts | 60 | 44 |
| Exhaust front pipe-to-manifold nuts | 20 | 15 |
| Flywheel bolts*: | | |
| Stage 1 | 35 | 26 |
| Stage 2 | Angle-tighten a further 30° | |
| Stage 3 | Angle-tighten a further 15° | |
| Main bearing cap bolts*: | | |
| Stage 1 | 50 | 37 |
| Stage 2 | Angle-tighten a further 45° | |
| Stage 3 | Angle-tighten a further 15° | |
| Oil pump: | | |
| Retaining bolts | 20 | 15 |
| Pump cover screws | 8 | 6 |
| Oil pressure relief valve cap | 20 | 15 |
| Oil pump pick-up/strainer and baffle plate bolts | 8 | 6 |
| Roadwheel bolts | 110 | 81 |
| Sump bolts: | | |
| Sump-to-cylinder block/oil pump bolts | 10 | 7 |
| Sump flange-to-transmission bolts | 40 | 30 |
| Timing belt cover bolts | 6 | 4 |
| Timing belt idler pulley bolt* | 25 | 18 |
| Timing belt tensioner bolt* | 20 | 15 |
| VVT oil control valve bolts | 6 | 4 |

* Use new fasteners

## 1  General information

### How to use this Chapter

This Part of Chapter 2 describes the repair procedures which can reasonably be carried out on the engine while it remains in the vehicle. If the engine has been removed from the vehicle and is being dismantled as described in Chapter 2D, any preliminary dismantling procedures can be ignored.

Note that, while it may be possible physically to overhaul items such as the piston/connecting rod assemblies while the engine is in the vehicle, such tasks are not usually carried out as separate operations, and usually require the execution of several additional procedures (not to mention the cleaning of components and of oilways); for this reason, all such tasks are classed as major overhaul procedures, and are described in Chapter 2D.

Chapter 2D describes the removal of the engine/transmission unit from the vehicle, and the full overhaul procedures which can then be carried out.

### Engine description

The engine is a double overhead camshaft, four-cylinder, in-line unit, mounted transversely at the front of the car, with the transmission attached to its left-hand end.

The crankshaft is supported within the cylinder block on five shell-type main bearings. Thrustwashers are fitted to number 3 main bearing, to control crankshaft endfloat.

The connecting rods are attached to the crankshaft by horizontally-split shell-type big-end bearings, and to the pistons by interference-fit gudgeon pins. The aluminium alloy pistons are of the slipper type, and are fitted with three piston rings, comprising two compression rings and a scraper-type oil control ring.

The camshafts run directly in the cylinder head, and are driven by the crankshaft via a toothed composite rubber timing belt (which also drives the coolant pump on Z18XE engines). One camshaft operates the inlet valves, and the other operates the exhaust valves.

On Z18XE engines, the camshafts operate each valve via a hydraulic self-adjusting camshaft follower. On Z18XER engines, the camshafts operate each valve via a solid camshaft follower. The camshaft followers are available in various thicknesses to facilitate valve clearance adjustment.

On Z18XER engines, a variable valve timing (VVT) system is employed. The VVT system allows the inlet and exhaust camshaft timing to be varied under the control of the engine management system, to boost both low-speed torque and top-end power, as well as reducing exhaust emissions. The VVT camshaft adjuster is integral with each camshaft timing belt sprocket, and is supplied with two pressurised oil feeds through passages in the camshaft itself. Two electro-magnetic oil control valves, one for each camshaft and operated by the engine management system, are fitted to the cylinder head, and are used to supply the pressurised oil to each camshaft adjuster through the two oil feeds. Each adjuster contains two chambers – depending on which of the two oil feeds is enabled by the control valve, the oil pressure will turn the camshaft clockwise (advance) or anti-clockwise (retard) to adjust the valve timing as required. If pressure is removed from both feeds, this induces a timing 'hold' condition. Thus the valve timing is infinitely variable within a given range.

Lubrication is by pressure-feed from a rotor-type oil pump, which is mounted on the right-hand end of the crankshaft. The pump draws oil through a strainer located in the sump, and then forces it through an externally mounted full-flow oil filter. The oil flows into galleries in the cylinder block/crankcase, from where it is distributed to the crankshaft (main bearings) and camshafts. The big-end bearings are supplied with oil via internal drillings in the crankshaft, while the camshaft bearings also receive a pressurised supply. The camshaft lobes and valves are lubricated by splash, as are all other engine components.

A semi-closed crankcase ventilation system is employed; crankcase fumes are drawn from camshaft cover, and passed via a hose to the inlet manifold.

### Operations with engine in car

The following operations can be carried out without having to remove the engine from the car.

a) Removal and refitting of the camshaft cover.
b) Adjustment of the valve clearances (Z18XER engines).
c) Removal and refitting of the VVT oil control valves (Z18XER engines).
d) Removal and refitting of the cylinder head.
e) Removal and refitting of the timing belt, tensioner and sprockets.
f) Renewal of the camshaft oil seals.
g) Removal and refitting of the camshafts and followers.
h) Removal and refitting of the sump.
i) Removal and refitting of the connecting rods and pistons*.
j) Removal and refitting of the oil pump.
k) Renewal of the crankshaft oil seals.
l) Renewal of the engine mountings.
m) Removal and refitting of the flywheel/driveplate.

* Although the operation marked with an asterisk can be carried out with the engine in the car (after removal of the sump), it is preferable for the engine to be removed, in the interests of cleanliness and improved access. For this reason, the procedure is described in Chapter 2D.

## 2  Compression test – general information

1 When engine performance is down, or if misfiring occurs which cannot be attributed to the ignition or fuel systems, a compression test can provide diagnostic clues as to the engine's condition. If the test is performed regularly, it can give warning of trouble before any other symptoms become apparent.

2 Due to the electronic throttle control system used on these engines, a compression test can only be carried out with the engine management electronic control unit connected to Vauxhall/Opel diagnostic test equipment, or a compatible alternative unit. Without the test equipment, the throttle valve cannot be opened (as there is no accelerator cable) and the test will be inconclusive. Note that even with the accelerator pedal fully depressed, the engine management ECU will only control the throttle valve position when the engine is actually running. The test equipment independently actuates the throttle valve (irrespective of ECU commands) and opens the throttle valve fully.

3 As the equipment needed for the compression test is unlikely to be available to the home mechanic, it is recommended that the test is performed by a Vauxhall/Opel dealer, or suitably-equipped garage.

## 3  Top dead centre (TDC) for No 1 piston – locating

1 Top dead centre (TDC) is the highest point in the cylinder that a piston reaches as the crankshaft turns. Each piston reaches TDC at the end of the compression stroke, and again at the end of the exhaust stroke. For the purpose of timing the engine, TDC refers to the position of No 1 piston at the end of its compression stroke. No 1 piston and cylinder are at the timing belt end of the engine.

2 Disconnect the battery negative terminal (refer to *Disconnecting the battery* in the Reference Chapter). If necessary, remove all the spark plugs as described in Chapter 1 to enable the engine to be easily turned over.

3 Remove the timing belt upper cover as described in Section 6.

4 Apply the handbrake, then jack up the front of the vehicle and support it on axle stands (see *Jacking and vehicle support*). Remove the right-hand front roadwheel, then remove the wheel arch liner inner cover for access to the crankshaft pulley.

5 Using a socket and extension bar on the crankshaft pulley bolt, rotate the crankshaft until the timing marks on the camshaft sprockets are facing towards each other, and an imaginary straight line can be

3.5a Align the camshaft timing marks . . .

3.5b . . . and the notch on the crankshaft pulley rim with the mark on the timing belt lower cover – Z18XE engines

3.5c Align the camshaft timing marks (arrowed) . . .

drawn through the camshaft sprocket bolts and the timing marks. With the camshaft sprocket marks correctly positioned, align the notch on the crankshaft pulley rim with the mark on the timing belt lower cover (see illustrations). The engine is now positioned with No 1 piston at TDC on its compression stroke.

6 If the crankshaft pulley and lower timing belt cover have been removed, the timing mark on the crankshaft sprocket can be used instead of the mark on the pulley. The mark on the crankshaft sprocket must align with the corresponding mark on the timing belt rear cover, or oil pump housing (see illustration).

3.5d . . . and the notch on the crankshaft pulley rim with the mark on the timing belt lower cover (arrowed) – Z18XER engines

3.6 Crankshaft sprocket timing mark (A) aligned with mark (B) on timing belt rear cover (crankshaft pulley removed)

## 4 Camshaft cover – removal and refitting

### Z18XE engines

#### Removal

1 Remove the oil filler cap, then undo the retaining screws, and remove the plastic cover from the top of the engine. Refit the oil filler cap.

2 Remove the ignition module from the spark plugs with reference to Chapter 5B.

3 Slacken the retaining clips and disconnect the breather hoses from the left-hand rear of the cover (see illustration).

4 Disconnect the wiring plug from the coolant temperature sensor and camshaft sensor, then release the wiring harness from the camshaft cover.

5 Disconnect the coolant pipe from the thermostat housing. Unbolt the retaining bracket from the camshaft cover and inlet manifold, release the retaining clips and move the pipe to one side. Be prepared for coolant spillage.

6 Unclip the oxygen sensor wiring from the camshaft cover.

7 Evenly and progressively slacken and remove the camshaft cover retaining bolts.

8 Lift the camshaft cover away from the cylinder head and recover the rubber seal. Examine the seal for signs of wear or damage and renew if necessary.

#### Refitting

9 Ensure the cover and cylinder head surfaces are clean and dry then fit the rubber seal securely to the cover groove (see illustration).

10 Apply a smear of suitable sealant to areas of the cylinder head surface around the right-hand end inlet and exhaust camshaft bearing caps.

11 Carefully manoeuvre the camshaft cover into position, taking great care to ensure the seal remains correctly seated. Refit the cover retaining bolts and tighten the retaining bolts to the specified torque, working in a spiral pattern from the centre outwards.

12 Reconnect the coolant pipe to the thermostat housing, making sure it is secured by the retaining bracket on the camshaft cover and inlet manifold.

4.3 Disconnect the breather hoses from the camshaft cover – Z18XE engines

13 Refit the wiring plugs to the coolant temperature sensor and camshaft sensor. Clip the oxygen sensor wiring back into position in the camshaft cover.

14 Reconnect the breather hoses, securing them in position with the retaining clips.

15 Refit the ignition module with reference to Chapter 5B.

16 Refit the engine cover, then top-up the cooling system as described in Chapter 1.

### Z18XER engines

#### Removal

17 Remove the ignition module from the spark plugs as described in Chapter 5B.

18 Lift the wiring harness up and out of the support on the right-hand end of the camshaft cover (see illustration).

4.9 Carefully fit the camshaft cover seal – Z18XE engines

**4.18 Lift the wiring harness out of the support on the camshaft cover – Z18XER engines**

**4.19 Unclip the wiring harness trough from the rear of the camshaft cover – Z18XER engines**

## 5 Crankshaft pulley – removal and refitting

**Note:** *A new pulley retaining bolt will be required on refitting.*

### Removal

1 Firmly apply the handbrake, then jack up the front of the car and support it securely on axle stands (see *Jacking and vehicle support*). Remove the right-hand roadwheel, then remove the wheel arch liner inner cover for access to the crankshaft pulley.

2 Remove the auxiliary drivebelt as described in Chapter 1. Prior to removal, mark the direction of rotation on the belt to ensure the belt is refitted the same way around.

3 Slacken the crankshaft pulley retaining bolt. To prevent crankshaft rotation, have an assistant select top gear and apply the brakes firmly. Alternatively, on Z18XER engines, engage a strip of metal with the flywheel ring gear teeth through the access slot located just above the front engine mounting/torque link **(see illustration)**.

4 Unscrew the retaining bolt and washer and remove the crankshaft pulley from the end of the crankshaft.

**4.20 Pull out the retaining wire clip and disconnect the breather hose from the camshaft cover – Z18XER engines**

19 Unclip the wiring harness trough from the rear of the camshaft cover **(see illustration)**.

20 Pull out the retaining wire clip and disconnect the breather hose from the camshaft cover **(see illustration)**.

21 Unscrew the eleven bolts securing the camshaft cover to the cylinder head.

22 Lift the camshaft cover away from the cylinder head and recover the rubber seal. Examine the seal for signs of wear or damage and renew if necessary.

### Refitting

23 Ensure that the camshaft cover grove and rubber seal are clean and dry with all traces of oil removed. If necessary, de-grease the seal and cover groove with brake cleaner or a similar product.

24 Clean the mating surface of the cylinder

**4.25 Locate the rubber seal into the grooves of the camshaft cover – Z18XER engines**

head and the area around the camshaft bearing caps at the timing belt end, ensuring that all traces of oil are removed.

25 Locate the rubber seal into the grooves of the camshaft cover, ensuring that it is fully seated, with no chance of it falling out as the cover is fitted **(see illustration)**.

26 Carefully manoeuvre the camshaft cover into position, taking great care to ensure the seal remains correctly seated. Screw in all the cover retaining bolts and tighten them to the specified torque, working in a spiral pattern from the centre outwards.

27 Reconnect the engine breather hose, then clip the wiring harness trough back into position. Engage the wiring harness with the support on cover.

28 Refit the ignition module to the spark plugs as described in Chapter 5B.

### Refitting

5 Refit the crankshaft pulley, aligning the pulley cut-out with the raised notch on the timing belt sprocket, then fit the washer and new retaining bolt **(see illustration)**.

6 Lock the crankshaft by the method used on removal, and tighten the pulley retaining bolt to the specified Stage 1 torque setting, then angle-tighten the bolt through the specified Stage 2 angle, using a socket and extension bar, and finally through the specified Stage 3 angle. It is recommended that an angle-measuring gauge is used during the final stages of the tightening, to ensure accuracy. If a gauge is not available, use white paint to make alignment marks between the bolt head and pulley prior to tightening; the marks can then be used to check that the bolt has been rotated through the correct angle.

7 Refit the auxiliary drivebelt as described in Chapter 1 using the mark made prior to removal to ensure the belt is fitted the correct way around.

8 Refit the wheel arch liner inner cover and the roadwheel. Lower the car to the ground and tighten the wheel bolts to the specified torque.

## 6 Timing belt covers – removal and refitting

**5.3 Engage a strip of metal with the flywheel ring gear teeth through the access slot (arrowed) – Z18XER engines**

**5.5 Align the pulley cut-out with the raised notch**

### Z18XE engines

#### Upper cover

1 Remove the oil filler cap, then undo the

**6.3  Undo the three screws and remove the timing belt upper cover – Z18XE engines**

retaining screws, and remove the plastic cover from the top of the engine. Refit the oil filler cap.

2  Remove the air cleaner assembly and intake ducts as described in Chapter 4A.

3  Undo the three retaining screws then unclip the upper cover from the rear cover and remove it from the engine compartment **(see illustration)**.

4  Refitting is the reverse of removal, tighten the retaining bolts to the specified torque.

### Lower cover

5  Remove the upper cover as described in paragraphs 1 to 3.

6  Remove the crankshaft pulley as described in Section 5.

7  Undo the retaining bolt and remove the auxiliary drivebelt tensioner **(see illustration)**.

8  Undo the retaining bolt then unclip the lower cover from the rear cover and manoeuvre it out of position **(see illustration)**.

9  Refitting is the reverse of removal, clip the cover into position and tighten the cover bolts and auxiliary drivebelt tensioner bolt to the specified torque.

### Rear cover

10  Remove the timing belt as described in Section 7.

11  Remove the camshaft sprockets, crankshaft sprocket, timing belt tensioner, front idler pulley and the rear idler pulley as described in Section 8.

12  Slacken and remove the three retaining bolts, and withdraw the engine mounting bracket bolted to the cylinder block **(see illustration)**.

13  Undo the four retaining bolts and remove the rear cover upwards and away from the engine **(see illustration)**.

14  Refitting is the reverse of removal. Refit and tighten the cover bolts to the specified torque.

## Z18XER engines

### Upper cover

15  Remove the air cleaner assembly and intake ducts as described in Chapter 4A.

16  Undo the two retaining bolts then withdraw the upper cover from the rear cover and remove it from the engine compartment **(see illustration)**.

**6.7  Remove the auxiliary drivebelt tensioner – Z18XE engines**

17  Refitting is the reverse of removal, tightening the cover retaining bolts to the specified torque.

### Lower cover

18  Remove the crankshaft pulley as described in Section 5.

19  Undo the retaining bolt and remove the auxiliary drivebelt tensioner **(see illustration)**.

20  Undo the four retaining bolts then manoeuvre the lower cover off the engine.

21  Refitting is the reverse of removal, tightening the cover retaining bolts and auxiliary drivebelt tensioner bolt to the specified torque.

### Centre cover

22  Remove the upper and lower covers as described previously.

23  Remove the right-hand engine mounting

**6.12  Engine mounting bracket-to-cylinder block retaining bolts – Z18XE engines**

**6.16  Undo the two retaining bolts (arrowed) and withdraw the upper cover from the rear cover – Z18XER engines**

H32265

**6.8  Timing belt lower cover retaining bolt – Z18XE engines**

as described in Section 18, then undo the three retaining bolts and remove the mounting bracket bolted to the cylinder block.

24  Release the two clips securing the centre cover to the rear cover and manoeuvre the centre cover off the engine.

25  Refitting is the reverse of removal, tightening the engine mounting bracket retaining bolts to the specified torque.

**6.13  Lift the rear cover away from the engine – Z18XE engines**

**6.19  Undo the retaining bolt and remove the auxiliary drivebelt tensioner – Z18XER engines**

**7.3 Unbolt the camshaft sensor and position it clear of the timing belt – Z18XE engines**

**7.5 Slacken the timing belt tensioner bolt (1) and rotate the tensioner clockwise using an Allen key in the arm cut-out (2) – Z18XE engines**

### Rear cover

**26** Remove the timing belt as described in Section 7.

**27** Remove the camshaft sprockets, crankshaft sprocket, timing belt tensioner and idler pulley as described in Section 8.

**28** Unclip the wiring harness from the cover, then undo the four retaining bolts and manoeuvre the rear cover off the engine.

**29** Refitting is the reverse of removal, tightening the cover retaining bolts to the specified torque.

### 7 Timing belt – removal and refitting

**Note:** *The timing belt must be removed and refitted with the engine cold.*

### Z18XE engines

#### Removal

**1** Position No 1 cylinder at TDC on its compression stroke as described in Section 3.

**2** Remove the timing belt lower cover as described in Section 6.

**3** Check that the timing marks on the camshaft sprockets are still correctly aligned and facing towards each other and the crankshaft

**7.6 Removing the timing belt – Z18XE engines**

sprocket timing mark is aligned with the mark on the rear timing belt cover (see Section 3). Undo the two bolts securing the camshaft sensor to the cylinder head and position it clear of the engine **(see illustration)**.

**4** Remove the right-hand engine mounting as described in Section 18.

**5** Slacken the timing belt tensioner bolt. Using an Allen key, rotate the tensioner arm clockwise to its stop, to relieve the tension in the timing belt, hold it in position and securely tighten the retaining bolt **(see illustration)**.

**6** Slide the timing belt from its sprockets and remove it from the engine **(see illustration)**. If the belt is to be re-used, use white paint or similar to mark the direction of rotation on the belt. **Do not** rotate the crankshaft or camshafts until the timing belt has been refitted.

**7** Check the timing belt carefully for any signs of uneven wear, splitting or oil contamination, and renew it if there is the slightest doubt about its condition. If the engine is undergoing an overhaul and is approaching the specified interval for belt renewal (see Chapter 1) renew the belt as a matter of course, regardless of its apparent condition. If signs of oil contamination are found, trace the source of the oil leak and rectify it, then wash down the engine timing belt area and all related components to remove all traces of oil.

#### Refitting

**8** On reassembly, thoroughly clean the timing belt sprockets and tensioner/idler pulleys.

**9** Check that the camshaft and crankshaft sprocket timing marks are still correctly aligned as described in Section 3.

**10** Fit the timing belt over the crankshaft and camshaft sprockets and around the idler pulleys, ensuring that the belt front run is taut (ie, all slack is on the tensioner side of the belt), then fit the belt over the coolant pump sprocket and tensioner pulley. Do not twist the belt sharply while refitting it. Ensure that the belt teeth are correctly seated centrally in the sprockets, and that the timing marks remain in alignment. If a used belt is being refitted,

ensure that the arrow mark made on removal points in the normal direction of rotation, as before.

**11** Slacken the timing belt tensioner bolt to release the tensioner spring. Rotate the tensioner arm anti-clockwise until the tensioner pointer is positioned just before the left stop, without exerting any excess strain on the belt. Hold the tensioner in position and securely tighten its retaining bolt.

**12** Check the sprocket timing marks are still correctly aligned. If adjustment is necessary, release the tensioner again then disengage the belt from the sprockets and make any necessary adjustments.

**13** Using a socket on the crankshaft pulley bolt, rotate the crankshaft smoothly through two complete turns (720°) in the normal direction of rotation to settle the timing belt in position.

**14** Check that both the camshaft and crankshaft sprocket timing marks are correctly realigned then slacken the tensioner bolt again.

**15** If a new timing belt is being fitted, adjust the tensioner so that the pointer is aligned with the cut-out on the backplate **(see illustration)**. Hold the tensioner in the correct position and tighten its retaining bolt to the specified torque. Rotate the crankshaft smoothly through another two complete turns in the normal direction of rotation, to bring the sprocket timing marks back into alignment. Check that the tensioner pointer is still aligned with the backplate cut-out.

**16** If the original belt is being refitted, adjust the tensioner so that the pointer is positioned 4 mm to the left of the cut-out on the backplate **(see illustration 7.15)**. Hold the tensioner in the correct position and tighten its retaining bolt to the specified torque. Rotate the crankshaft smoothly through another two complete turns in the normal direction of rotation, to bring the sprocket timing marks back into alignment. Check that the tensioner pointer is still correctly positioned in relation to the backplate cut-out.

**17** If the tensioner pointer is not correctly positioned in relation to the backplate, repeat the procedure in paragraph 15 (new belt) or 16 (original belt) (as applicable).

**18** Once the tensioner pointer and backplate remain correctly aligned, refit the camshaft sensor, then refit the timing belt covers as described in Section 6.

**19** Refit the right-hand engine mounting as described in Section 18, then refit the crankshaft pulley as described in Section 5.

### Z18XER engines

#### Removal

**20** Position No 1 cylinder at TDC on its compression stroke as described in Section 3.

**21** Remove the timing belt lower and centre covers as described in Section 6.

**22** Check that the timing marks on the camshaft sprockets are still correctly aligned and facing towards each other, and the timing mark on the crankshaft sprocket is aligned with the corresponding mark on the oil pump housing (Section 3).

**23** Using an Allen key inserted in the slot on the face of the timing belt tensioner, rotate the tensioner clockwise to relieve the tension in the timing belt. Insert a small drill bit or similar into the slot on the inner edge of the tensioner body to lock the tensioner in the released position.

**24** Slide the timing belt from its sprockets and remove it from the engine. If the belt is to be re-used, use white paint or similar to mark the direction of rotation on the belt. **Do not** rotate the crankshaft or camshafts until the timing belt has been refitted.

**25** Check the timing belt carefully for any signs of uneven wear, splitting or oil contamination, and renew it if there is the slightest doubt about its condition. If the engine is undergoing an overhaul and is approaching the specified interval for belt renewal (see Chapter 1) renew the belt as a matter of course, regardless of its apparent condition. If signs of oil contamination are found, trace the source of the oil leak and rectify it, then wash down the engine timing belt area and all related components to remove all traces of oil.

#### Refitting

**26** On reassembly, thoroughly clean the timing belt sprockets and tensioner/idler pulleys.

**27** Check that the camshaft and crankshaft sprocket timing marks are still correctly aligned as described in Section 3.

**28** Fit the timing belt over the crankshaft and camshaft sprockets and around the idler pulley, ensuring that the belt front run is taut (ie, all slack is on the tensioner side of the belt), then fit the belt over the tensioner pulley. Do not twist the belt sharply while refitting it. Ensure that the belt teeth are correctly seated centrally in the sprockets, and that the timing marks remain in alignment. If a used belt is being refitted, ensure that the arrow mark made on removal points in the normal direction of rotation, as before.

**7.15 Align the pointer (1) with the relevant mark on the tensioner backplate (2) – Z18XE engines**

**29** Using the Allen key, turn the tensioner clockwise slightly and remove the drill bit or similar tool used to lock the tensioner. Slowly release the tensioner and allow it to turn anticlockwise and automatically tension the timing belt.

**30** Check the sprocket timing marks are still correctly aligned. If adjustment is necessary, release the tensioner again then disengage the belt from the sprockets and make any necessary adjustments.

**31** Using a socket on the temporarily refitted crankshaft pulley bolt, rotate the crankshaft smoothly through two complete turns (720°) in the normal direction of rotation to settle the timing belt in position.

**32** Set the crankshaft back in the timing position and check that all the sprocket timing marks are still correctly aligned. If this

**8.3 Counter-holding the inlet camshaft using a spanner on the flats in front of No 1 cam lobe – Z18XE engines**

is not the case, repeat the timing belt refitting procedure.

**33** If everything is satisfactory, refit the timing belt covers as described in Section 6.

### 8 Timing belt sprockets, tensioner and idler pulleys – removal and refitting

### Z18XE engines

#### Camshaft sprockets

**Note:** *New sprocket retaining bolt(s) will be required for refitting.*

**1** Remove the camshaft cover as described in Section 4.

**2** Remove the timing belt as described in Section 7.

**3** The camshaft must be prevented from turning as the sprocket bolt is unscrewed, and this can be achieved in one of two ways as follows.

a) *Make up a sprocket-holding tool using two lengths of steel strip (one long, the other short), and three nuts and bolts; one nut and bolt forms the pivot of a forked tool, with the remaining two nuts and bolts at the tips of the 'forks' to engage with the sprocket holes.*

b) *Hold the camshaft with an open-ended spanner on the flats provided (see illustration).*

**4** Unscrew the retaining bolt and washer and remove the sprocket from the end of the camshaft. If the sprocket locating pin is a loose fit in the camshaft end, remove it and store it with the sprocket for safe-keeping.

**5** If necessary, remove the remaining sprocket using the same method. The inlet and exhaust sprockets are different; the exhaust camshaft sprocket can be easily identified by the lugs which activate the camshaft position sensor.

**6** Prior to refitting check the oil seal(s) for signs of damage or leakage. If necessary, renew as described in Section 10.

**7** Ensure the locating pin is in position in the camshaft end.

**8** Refit the sprocket to the camshaft end, aligning its cut-out with the locating pin, and fit the washer and new retaining bolt **(see illustration)**. If both sprockets have been

**8.8 Ensure the camshaft sprocket cut-out (arrowed) is correctly engaged with the locating pin – Z18XE engines**

**8.13 Refit the crankshaft sprocket with the locating flange and pulley locating lug outermost – Z18XE engines**

**8.17 Engage the tensioner backplate lug with the locating hole in the oil pump housing – Z18XE engines**

**8.20 Idler pulley retaining bolt – Z18XE engines**

removed, ensure each sprocket is fitted to the correct shaft; the exhaust camshaft sprocket can be identified by the lugs on the sprocket outer face which trigger the camshaft position sensor.

**9** Retain the sprocket by the method used on removal, and tighten the sprocket retaining bolt to the specified Stage 1 torque setting then angle-tighten the bolt through the specified Stage 2 angle, using a socket and extension bar, and finally through the specified Stage 3 angle. It is recommended that an angle-measuring gauge is used during the final stages of the tightening, to ensure accuracy. If a gauge is not available, use white paint to make alignment marks between the bolt head and sprocket prior to tightening; the marks can then be used to check that the bolt has been rotated through the correct angle.

**10** Refit the timing belt as described in Section 7, then refit the camshaft cover as described in Section 4.

### Crankshaft sprocket

**11** Remove the timing belt as described in Section 7.

**12** Slide the sprocket off from the end of the crankshaft, noting which way around it is fitted.

**13** Align the sprocket locating key with the crankshaft groove then slide the sprocket into position, making sure its timing mark is facing outwards **(see illustration)**.

**TOOL TiP**

*A camshaft locking tool can be made from a steel strip approximately 4.5 mm thick, with two slots filed in the strip to clear the camshaft sensor trigger lugs.*

**14** Refit the timing belt as described in Section 7.

### Tensioner assembly

**15** Remove the timing belt as described in Section 7.

**16** Slacken and remove the retaining bolt and remove the tensioner assembly from the engine.

**17** Fit the tensioner to the engine, making sure that the lug on the backplate is correctly located in the oil pump housing hole **(see illustration)**. Ensure the tensioner is correctly seated then refit the retaining bolt. Using an Allen key, rotate the tensioner arm clockwise to its stop then securely tighten the retaining bolt.

**18** Refit the timing belt as described in Section 7.

### Idler pulleys

**19** Remove the timing belt as described in Section 7.

**20** Slacken and remove the retaining bolt(s) and remove the idler pulley(s) from the engine **(see illustration)**.

**21** Refit the idler pulley(s) and tighten the retaining bolt(s) to the specified torque.

**22** Refit the timing belt as described in Section 7.

### Z18XER engines

#### Camshaft sprockets

**Note 1:** *Vauxhall/Opel special tools KM-6340 and KM-6628 or suitable alternatives will be required for this procedure.*

**8.25 Insert the tool into the ends of the camshafts to lock the camshafts in the TDC position – Z18XER engines**

**Note 2:** *New sprocket retaining bolt(s) and a new sprocket closure bolt seal will be required for refitting.*

**23** Remove the camshaft cover as described in Section 4.

**24** Remove the timing belt as described in Section 7.

**25** Insert Vauxhall/Opel special tool KM-6628 into the slots on the end of the camshafts to lock the camshafts in the TDC position. In the absence of the special tool, a suitable alternative can be fabricated from a steel strip **(see Tool Tip and illustration)**. It may be necessary to turn the camshafts slightly using an open-ended spanner on the flats provided, to allow the tool to fully engage with the slots.

**26** Unscrew the closure bolt from the relevant camshaft sprocket **(see illustration)**. Note that a new closure bolt seal will be required for refitting.

**27** Hold the camshaft using an open-ended spanner on the flats provided, and unscrew the camshaft sprocket retaining bolt. Withdraw the sprocket from the end of the camshaft.

**28** If necessary, remove the remaining sprocket using the same method.

**29** Prior to refitting check the oil seal(s) for signs of damage or leakage. If necessary, renew as described in Section 10.

**30** Refit the sprocket to the camshaft end and fit the new retaining bolt. Tighten the bolt finger-tight only at this stage. If both sprockets have been removed, ensure each sprocket is fitted to the correct shaft; the exhaust camshaft sprocket has the timing belt guide

**8.26 Camshaft sprocket closure bolts (arrowed) – Z18XER engines**

flange on its inner face and the inlet sprocket has the guide flange on its outer face.

**31** Turn the camshaft sprocket(s) until the timing marks are facing towards each other and aligned. It will now be necessary to retain the sprockets in the timing position while the sprocket retaining bolt is tightened. Engage Vauxhall/Opel special tool KM-6340 or a suitable alternative with the teeth on both sprockets, to lock the sprockets together.

**32** With the camshafts and sprockets locked in the timing position with the special tools, hold the camshaft using an open-ended spanner on the flats provided and tighten the sprocket retaining bolt to the specified Stage 1 torque setting. Now angle-tighten the bolt through the specified Stage 2 angle, using a socket and extension bar, and finally through the specified Stage 3 angle. It is recommended that an angle-measuring gauge is used during the final stages of the tightening, to ensure accuracy. If a gauge is not available, use white paint to make alignment marks between the bolt head and sprocket prior to tightening; the marks can then be used to check that the bolt has been rotated through the correct angle.

**33** Fit a new seal to the camshaft sprocket closure bolt, then refit the closure bolt and tighten to the specified torque.

**34** Remove the special tools, then refit the timing belt as described in Section 7, and the camshaft cover as described in Section 4.

### Crankshaft sprocket

**35** Remove the timing belt as described in Section 7.

**36** Slide the sprocket off from the end of the crankshaft, noting which way around it is fitted.

**37** Align the sprocket locating key with the crankshaft groove then slide the sprocket into position, making sure its timing mark is facing outwards.

**38** Refit the timing belt as described in Section 7.

### Tensioner assembly

**Note:** *A new tensioner retaining bolt will be required for refitting.*

**39** Remove the timing belt as described in Section 7.

**40** Slacken and remove the retaining bolt and remove the tensioner assembly from the engine.

**41** Clean the tensioner retaining bolt threads in the oil pump housing, ensuring that all traces of sealant, oil or grease are removed.

**42** Fit the tensioner to the engine, making sure that the lug on the backplate is correctly located in the oil pump housing hole. On later models, also ensure that the projecting end of the tensioner spring engages with the slot on the oil pump housing. Ensure the tensioner is correctly seated then refit the new retaining bolt and tighten it to the specified torque.

**43** Refit the timing belt as described in Section 7.

**9.2  Disconnect the wiring connector (arrowed) from the VVT oil control valve**

### Idler pulley

**Note:** *A idler pulley retaining bolt will be required for refitting.*

**44** Remove the timing belt as described in Section 7.

**45** Slacken and remove the retaining bolt and remove the idler pulley from the engine.

**46** Refit the idler pulley and tighten the new retaining bolt to the specified torque.

**47** Refit the timing belt as described in Section 7.

## 9  VVT oil control valves (Z18XER engines) – removal and refitting

### *Removal*

**1** The VVT oil control valves are fitted to the camshaft bearing support, adjacent to the camshaft sprockets. Two oil control valves are used, one for each camshaft.

**2** Disconnect the wiring connector from the relevant oil control valve **(see illustration)**.

**3** Undo the retaining bolt located below the valve, and withdraw the valve from the camshaft bearing support. Be prepared for oil spillage.

### *Refitting*

**4** Lubricate the valve sealing rings with clean engine oil and insert the valve into the camshaft bearing support.

**5** Refit and tighten the retaining bolt and reconnect the wiring connector.

**10.2  Camshaft oil seal removal method**

**6** On completion, check and if necessary top-up the engine oil as described in *Weekly checks*.

## 10  Camshaft oil seals – renewal

**1** Remove the relevant camshaft sprocket as described in Section 8.

**2** Carefully punch or drill two small holes opposite each other in the oil seal. Screw a self-tapping screw into each, and pull on the screws with pliers to extract the seal **(see illustration)**.

**3** Clean the seal housing, and polish off any burrs or raised edges which may have caused the seal to fail in the first place.

**4** Press the new seal into position using a suitable tubular drift (such as a socket) which bears only on the hard outer edge of the seal **(see illustration)**. Take care not to damage the seal lips during fitting; note that the seal lips should face inwards.

**5** Refit the camshaft sprocket as described in Section 8.

## 11  Valve clearances (Z18XER engines) – checking and adjustment

**Note:** *Z18XE engines are equipped with hydraulic self-adjusting camshaft followers and valve clearance adjustment is not required.*

### *Checking*

**1** The importance of having the valve clearances correctly adjusted cannot be overstressed, as they vitally affect the performance of the engine. The engine must be cold for the check to be accurate. The clearances are checked as follows.

**2** Firmly apply the handbrake, then jack up the front of the car and support it securely on axle stands (see *Jacking and vehicle support*). Remove the right-hand front roadwheel then remove the wheel arch liner inner cover for access to the crankshaft pulley.

**3** Remove the camshaft cover as described in Section 4.

**10.4  Using the old camshaft sprocket bolt and a socket to fit the new camshaft oil seal**

**11.7a  Using feeler blades, measure the clearance between the base of both No 2 cylinder inlet cam lobes . . .**

**11.7b  . . . and No 3 cylinder exhaust cam lobes and their followers**

**4** Position No 1 cylinder at TDC on its compression stroke as described in Section 3.

**5** With the engine at TDC on compression for No 1 cylinder, the inlet camshaft lobes for No 2 cylinder and the exhaust camshaft lobes for No 3 cylinder are pointing upwards and slightly towards the centre. This indicates that these valves are completely closed, and the clearances can be checked.

**6** On a piece of paper, draw the outline of the engine with the cylinders numbered from the timing belt end. Show the position of each valve, together with the required valve clearance (see Specifications).

**7** With the cam lobes positioned as described in paragraph 5, using feeler blades, measure the clearance between the base of both No 2 cylinder inlet cam lobes and No 3 cylinder exhaust cam lobes and their followers. Record the clearances on the paper **(see illustrations)**.

**8** Rotate the crankshaft pulley in the normal direction of rotation through a half a turn (180°) to position No 1 cylinder inlet camshaft lobes and No 4 cylinder exhaust camshaft lobes pointing upwards and slightly towards the centre. Measure the clearance between the base of the camshaft lobes and their followers and record the clearances on the paper.

**9** Rotate the crankshaft pulley through a half a turn (180°) to position No 3 cylinder inlet

camshaft lobes and No 2 cylinder exhaust camshaft lobes pointing upwards and slightly towards the centre. Measure the clearance between the base of the camshaft lobes and their followers and record the clearances on the paper.

**10** Rotate the crankshaft pulley through a half a turn (180°) to position No 4 cylinder inlet camshaft lobes and No 1 cylinder exhaust camshaft lobes pointing upwards and slightly towards the centre. Measure the clearance between the base of the camshaft lobes and their followers and record the clearances on the paper.

**11** If all the clearances are correct, refit the camshaft cover (see Section 4), then refit the wheel arch liner inner cover and the roadwheel. Lower the vehicle to the ground and tighten the wheel bolts to the specified torque. If any clearance measured is not correct, adjustment must be carried out as described in the following paragraphs.

### Adjustment

**12** If adjustment is necessary, remove the relevant camshaft(s) and camshaft followers as described in Section 12.

**13** Clean the followers of the valves that require clearance adjustment and note the thickness marking on the follower. The thickness marking is stamped on the underside of each follower. For example, a 3.20 mm thick follower will have a 20 thickness marking, a 3.21 mm thick follower will have a 21 thickness marking, etc.

**12.4b  Camshaft bearing cap numbers (exhaust camshaft shown) – Z18XE engines**

**14** Add the measured clearance of the valve to the thickness of the original follower then subtract the required valve clearance from this figure. This will give you the thickness of the follower required. For example:

| | |
|---|---|
| Clearance measured of inlet valve | 0.31 mm |
| Plus thickness of the original follower | 3.20 mm |
| Equals | 3.51 mm |
| Minus clearance required | 0.25 mm |
| Thickness of follower required | 3.26 mm |

**15** Repeat this procedure on the remaining valves which require adjustment, then obtain the correct thickness of follower(s) required.

**16** Refit the camshaft followers and the relevant camshaft(s) as described in Section 12. Rotate the crankshaft a few times to settle all the components, then recheck the valve clearances before refitting the camshaft cover (Section 4).

**17** Refit the wheel arch liner inner cover and roadwheel then lower the vehicle to the ground and tighten the wheel bolts to the specified torque.

---

**12  Camshaft and followers –**
**removal, inspection and refitting**

**Note:** *New timing belt end oil seals, and a tube of suitable sealant will be required when refitting.*

### Z18XE engines

#### Removal

**1** Remove the timing belt as described in Section 7.

**2** Remove the camshaft sprockets as described in Section 8.

**3** Remove the timing belt rear cover as described in Section 6.

**4** Starting on the inlet camshaft, working in a spiral pattern from the outside inwards, slacken the camshaft bearing cap retaining bolts by half a turn at a time, to relieve the pressure of the valve springs on the bearing caps gradually and evenly **(the reverse of illustration 12.16)**. Once the valve spring pressure has been relieved, the bolts can be fully unscrewed and removed along with the caps; the bearing caps and the cylinder head locations are numbered (inlet camshaft 1 to 5, exhaust camshaft 6 to 10) to ensure the caps are correctly positioned on refitting **(see illustrations)**. Take care not to lose the locating dowels (where fitted).

*Caution: If the bearing cap bolts are carelessly slackened, the bearing caps might break. If any bearing cap breaks then the complete cylinder head assembly must be renewed; the bearing caps are matched to the head and are not available separately.*

**5** Lift the camshaft out of the cylinder head and slide off the oil seal.

**6** Repeat the operations described in paragraphs 4 and 5 and remove the exhaust camshaft.

**7** Obtain sixteen small, clean plastic containers, and label them for identification.

**12.4a  Camshaft bearing cap numbering sequence (No 1 at timing belt end) – Z18XE engines**

Alternatively, divide a larger container into compartments. Using a rubber sucker tool, lift the followers out from the top of the cylinder head and store each one in its respective fitted position (see illustration). Note: *Store all the followers the correct way up, with the oil groove at the bottom, to prevent the oil draining from the hydraulic valve adjustment mechanisms.*

### Inspection

**8** Examine the camshaft bearing surfaces and cam lobes for signs of wear ridges and scoring. Renew the camshaft if any of these conditions are apparent. Examine the condition of the bearing surfaces both on the camshaft journals and in the cylinder head. If the head bearing surfaces are worn excessively, the cylinder head will need to be renewed.

**9** Examine the follower bearing surfaces which contact the camshaft lobes for wear ridges and scoring. Check the followers and their bores in the cylinder head for signs of wear or damage. If any follower is thought to be faulty or is visibly worn it should be renewed.

### Refitting

**10** Commence refitting by turning the crankshaft anti-clockwise by 60°. This will position Nos 1 and 4 pistons a third of the way down the bore, and prevent any chance of the valves touching the piston crowns as the camshafts are being fitted. This could happen if any of the cam followers have excessive oil in them before the pressure of the valve springs forces it out.

**11** Where removed, lubricate the followers with clean engine oil and carefully insert each one into its original location in the cylinder head.

**12** Lubricate the camshaft followers with molybdenum disulphide paste (or clean engine oil) then lay the camshafts in position.

**13** Ensure the mating surfaces of the bearing caps and cylinder head are clean and dry and lubricate the camshaft journals and lobes with clean engine oil.

**14** Apply a smear of sealant to the mating surfaces of both the inlet (No 1) and exhaust (No 6) camshaft right-hand bearing caps (see illustration).

**15** Ensure the locating dowels (where fitted) are in position then refit the camshaft bearing caps and the retaining bolts in their original locations on the cylinder head. The caps are numbered (inlet camshaft 1 to 5, exhaust camshaft 6 to 10) from the timing belt end, and the corresponding numbers are marked on the cylinder head upper surface. All bearing cap numbers should be the right way up when viewed from the front of the engine.

**16** Working on the inlet camshaft, tighten the bearing cap bolts by hand only then, working in a spiral pattern from the centre outwards, tighten the bolts by half a turn at a time to gradually impose the pressure of the valve springs on the bearing caps (see illustration). Repeat this sequence until all bearing caps

**12.7 Remove the followers from the cylinder head, and store with the oil groove (arrowed) at the bottom – Z18XE engines**

are in contact with the cylinder head then go around and tighten the camshaft bearing cap bolts to the specified torque.

*Caution: If the bearing cap bolts are carelessly tightened, the bearing caps might break. If any bearing cap breaks then the complete cylinder head assembly must be renewed; the bearing caps are matched to the head and are not available separately.*

**17** Tighten the exhaust camshaft bearing cap bolts as described in paragraph 16.

**18** Fit new camshaft oil seals as described in Section 10.

**19** Refit and tighten the timing belt rear cover bolts.

**20** Refit the camshaft sprockets as described in Section 8.

**21** Align all the sprocket timing marks to bring the camshafts and crankshaft back to TDC then refit the timing belt as described in Section 7.

### Z18XER engines

#### Removal

**22** Remove the camshaft cover as described in Section 4.

**12.14 Apply a smear of sealant to the right-hand bearing caps – Z18XE engines**

**23** Remove the timing belt as described in Section 7.

**24** Remove the camshaft sprockets as described in Section 8.

**25** Remove the timing belt rear cover as described in Section 6.

**26** Remove the special tool used to lock the camshafts in the TDC position.

**27** Disconnect the wiring connector at the inlet camshaft and exhaust camshaft VVT oil control valves (see illustration 9.2).

**28** Undo the four bolts securing the camshaft bearing support at the timing belt end of the engine (see illustration). Undo the two outer bolts first, followed by the two inner bolts. Using a plastic mallet, gently tap the bearing support free and remove it from the cylinder head.

**29** Starting on the inlet camshaft, working in a spiral pattern from the outside inwards, slacken the camshaft bearing cap retaining bolts by half a turn at a time, to relieve the pressure of the valve springs on the bearing caps gradually and evenly (the reverse of illustration 12.40). Once the valve spring pressure has been relieved, the bolts can be fully unscrewed and removed along with the

H.28124

**12.16 Camshaft bearing cap tightening sequence (exhaust camshaft shown – inlet identical) – Z18XE engines**

**12.28 Camshaft bearing support retaining bolts (arrowed) – Z18XER engines**

**12.29 Camshaft bearing cap numbers (inlet camshaft shown) – Z18XER engines**

**12.32 Use a valve lapping tool to remove the cam followers – Z18XER engines**

caps; the bearing caps are numbered inlet camshaft 2 to 5, exhaust camshaft 6 to 9 to ensure the caps are correctly positioned on refitting **(see illustration)**. Take care not to loose the locating dowels (where fitted).

*Caution: If the bearing cap bolts are carelessly slackened, the bearing caps might break. If any bearing cap breaks then the complete cylinder head assembly must be renewed; the bearing caps are matched to the head and are not available separately.*

**30** Lift the camshaft out of the cylinder head and slide off the oil seal.

**31** Repeat the operations described in paragraphs 29 and 30 and remove the exhaust camshaft.

**32** Obtain sixteen small, clean plastic containers, and label them for identification. Alternatively, divide a larger container into compartments. Using a rubber sucker tool, lift the followers out from the top of the cylinder head and store each one in its respective fitted position **(see illustration)**.

### Inspection

**33** Refer to the information contained in paragraphs 8 and 9.

### Refitting

**34** Commence refitting by turning the crankshaft anti-clockwise by 60°. This will position Nos 1 and 4 pistons a third of the way down the bore, and prevent any chance of the valves touching the piston crowns as the camshafts are being fitted.

**35** Thoroughly clean the mating surfaces of

**12.40 Camshaft bearing cap tightening sequence (inlet camshaft shown – exhaust identical) – Z18XER engines**

the camshaft bearing support and cylinder head, ensuring all traces of old sealant are removed.

**36** Where removed, lubricate the followers with clean engine oil and carefully insert each one into its original location in the cylinder head.

**37** Lubricate the camshaft followers with molybdenum disulphide paste (or clean engine oil) then lay the camshafts in position.

**38** Ensure the mating surfaces of the bearing caps and cylinder head are clean and dry and lubricate the camshaft journals and lobes with clean engine oil.

**39** Ensure the locating dowels (where fitted) are in position then refit camshaft bearing caps 2 to 9 and the retaining bolts in their original locations on the cylinder head.

**40** Working on the inlet camshaft, tighten the bearing cap bolts by hand only then, working in a spiral pattern from the centre outwards, tighten the bolts by half a turn at a time to gradually impose the pressure of the valve springs on the bearing caps **(see illustration)**. Repeat this sequence until all bearing caps are in contact with the cylinder head then go around and tighten the camshaft bearing cap bolts to the specified torque.

*Caution: If the bearing cap bolts are carelessly tightened, the bearing caps might break. If any bearing cap breaks then the complete cylinder head assembly must be renewed; the bearing caps are matched to the head and are not available separately.*

**41** Tighten the exhaust camshaft bearing cap bolts as described in paragraph 40.

**42** Apply a smear of sealant to the mating surface of the camshaft bearing support, ensuring that the oil grooves remain free of sealant. Do not apply sealant to the area immediately adjacent to the bearing surface on the inside of the oil groove.

**43** Place the camshaft bearing support in position and refit the four retaining bolts. Tighten the bolts to the specified torque, starting with the two inner bolts, then the two outer bolts.

**44** If new components have been fitted, the valve clearances should now be checked and, if necessary adjusted, before proceeding with the refitting procedure. Temporarily refit the camshaft sprockets and secure with their

retaining bolts, to allow the camshafts to be turned for the check. Refer to the procedure contained in Section 11, but as the timing belt is not fitted, check the clearances of each camshaft individually. Use the sprocket retaining bolt to turn the camshafts as necessary until the cam lobes for each pair of valves are pointing upward, away from the valves.

**45** Once the valve clearances have been checked and if necessary adjusted, position the camshafts so that their timing slots are parallel with the cylinder head surface and refit the locking tool to the slots. Undo the retaining bolts and remove the camshaft sprockets.

**46** Reconnect the wiring connector at the inlet camshaft and exhaust camshaft VVT oil control valves.

**47** Refit the timing belt rear cover as described in Section 6.

**48** Fit new camshaft oil seals as described in Section 9.

**49** Refit the camshaft sprockets as described in Section 8.

**50** Align all the sprocket timing marks to bring the camshafts and crankshaft back to TDC then refit the timing belt as described in Section 7.

**51** Refit the camshaft cover as described in Section 4.

---

## 13 Cylinder head – removal and refitting

**Note:** *The engine must be cold when removing the cylinder head. A new cylinder head gasket and new cylinder head bolts must be used on refitting.*

### Removal

**1** Depressurise the fuel system as described in Chapter 4A.

**2** Disconnect the battery negative terminal (refer to *Disconnecting the battery* in the Reference Chapter).

**3** Apply the handbrake, then jack up the front of the vehicle and support it on axle stands (see *Jacking and vehicle support*). Remove the right-hand front roadwheel and the wheel arch liner inner cover for access to the right-hand side of the engine.

**4** Drain the cooling system as described in Chapter 1.

**5** Remove the spark plugs as described in Chapter 1.

**6** Remove the camshaft cover as described in Section 4.

**7** Remove the timing belt as described in Section 7.

**8** Remove the camshaft sprockets, timing belt tensioner, and the timing belt idler pulleys, as described in Section 8.

**9** Remove the rear timing belt cover with reference to Section 6.

**10** Refer to Chapter 4A and unbolt the exhaust front pipe from the exhaust manifold, taking care to support the flexible section. **Note:** *Angular movement in excess of 10° can cause permanent damage to the flexible section.* Release the mounting rubbers and support the front of the exhaust pipe to one side.

**11** Disconnect the engine management wiring loom from the following, noting its routing:
 a) *Crankshaft speed/position sensor.*
 b) *Oil pressure switch.*
 c) *Oil level sensor.*

**12** Release the cable ties and place the wiring loom to one side.

**13** On Z18XE engines, unscrew the securing bolts, and remove the upper alternator mounting bracket. Pivot the alternator rearwards away from the manifold as far as it will go.

**14** Remove the inlet and exhaust manifolds as described in Chapter 4A.

**15** Referring to Chapter 3, unclip the coolant hoses from the heater matrix unions on the engine compartment bulkhead to drain the coolant from the cylinder block. Once the flow of coolant has stopped, reconnect both hoses and mop-up any spilt coolant.

**16** Loosen the clips and remove the upper hose from the radiator and thermostat housing.

**17** Loosen the clips and disconnect the heater hoses from the left-hand end of the cylinder head or thermostat housing.

**18** Undo the bolt and free the oil dipstick guide tube from the cylinder head.

**19** Make a final check to ensure that all relevant hoses, pipes and wires have been disconnected.

**20** Working in sequence, progressively loosen the cylinder head bolts **(see illustration)**. First loosen all the bolts by quarter of a turn, then loosen all the bolts by half a turn, then finally slacken all the bolts fully and withdraw them from the cylinder head. Recover the washers.

**21** Lift the cylinder head from the cylinder block. If necessary, tap the cylinder head gently with a soft-faced mallet to free it from the block, but **do not** lever at the mating faces. Note that the cylinder head is located on dowels.

**22** Recover the cylinder head gasket, and discard it.

### Preparation for refitting

**23** The mating faces of the cylinder head and

**13.20 Cylinder head bolt loosening sequence**

block must be perfectly clean before refitting the head. Use a scraper to remove all traces of gasket and carbon, and also clean the tops of the pistons. Take particular care with the aluminium surfaces, as the soft metal is damaged easily. Also, make sure that debris is not allowed to enter the oil and water channels – this is particularly important for the oil circuit, as carbon could block the oil supply to the camshaft or crankshaft bearings. Using adhesive tape and paper, seal the water, oil and bolt holes in the cylinder block. To prevent carbon entering the gap between the pistons and bores, smear a little grease in the gap. After cleaning the piston, rotate the crankshaft so that the piston moves down the bore, then wipe out the grease and carbon with a cloth rag. Clean the other piston crowns in the same way.

**24** Check the block and head for nicks, deep scratches and other damage. If slight, they may be removed carefully with a file. More serious damage may be repaired by machining, but this is a specialist job.

**25** If warpage of the cylinder head is suspected, use a straight-edge to check it for distortion. Refer to Chapter 2D if necessary.

**26** Ensure that the cylinder head bolt holes in the crankcase are clean and free of oil. Syringe or soak up any oil left in the bolt holes. This is most important in order that the correct bolt tightening torque can be applied and to prevent the possibility of the block being cracked by hydraulic pressure when the bolts are tightened.

**27** Renew the cylinder head bolts regardless of their apparent condition.

### Refitting

**28** Ensure that the two locating dowels are in position at each end of the cylinder block/crankcase surface.

**29** Fit the new cylinder head gasket to the block, making sure it is fitted with the correct way up with its OBEN/TOP mark uppermost **(see illustration)**.

**30** Carefully refit the cylinder head, locating it on the dowels.

**31** Fit the washers to the new cylinder head bolts then carefully insert them into position **(do not drop)**, tightening them finger-tight only at this stage.

**32** Working progressively and in sequence, first tighten all the cylinder head bolts to the Stage 1 torque setting **(see illustrations)**.

**33** Once all bolts have been tightened to the Stage 1 torque, again working in sequence, tighten each bolt through its specified Stage 2 angle, using a socket and extension bar. It is recommended that an angle-measuring gauge

**13.29 Ensure the head gasket is fitted with its OBEN/TOP marking uppermost**

**13.32a  Cylinder head bolt tightening sequence**

**13.32b  Tighten the cylinder head bolts to the specified Stage 1 torque setting . . .**

**13.33  . . . and then through the various specified angles as described in the text**

is used during this stage of the tightening, to ensure accuracy **(see illustration)**.

**34** Working in the specified sequence, go around again and tighten all bolts through the specified Stage 3 angle.

**35** Working again in the specified sequence, go around and tighten all bolts through the specified Stage 4 angle.

**36** Finally go around in the specified sequence again and tighten all bolts through the specified Stage 5 angle.

**37** Refit the exhaust manifold as described in Chapter 4A.

**38** Reconnect the heater hoses to the left-hand end of the cylinder head or thermostat housing and tighten the clips.

**39** Refit the upper hose to the radiator and thermostat housing and tighten the clips.

**40** Refit the inlet manifold as described in Chapter 4A.

**41** Where applicable, refit the alternator upper mounting bracket and tighten the bolts.

**42** Reconnect the wiring to the components listed in paragraph 11, then secure the wiring with cable ties.

**43** Refer to Chapter 4A and refit the exhaust front pipe to the exhaust manifold. Refit the mounting rubbers.

**44** Refit the rear timing belt cover with reference to Section 6.

**45** Refit the camshaft sprockets, timing belt tensioner, and the timing belt idler pulleys, with reference to Section 8.

**46** Refit the timing belt as described in Section 7.

**47** Refit the spark plugs as described in Chapter 1.

**48** Refit the camshaft cover as described in Section 4.

**49** Refit the wheel arch liner inner cover and front roadwheel, then lower the vehicle to the ground.

**50** Reconnect the battery negative terminal.

**51** Check that all relevant hoses, pipes and wires, etc, have been reconnected. Check the security of the fuel hose connections.

**52** Refill and bleed the cooling system with reference to Chapter 1.

**53** When the engine is started, check for signs of oil or coolant leakage.

## 14 Sump – removal and refitting

### Removal

**1** Disconnect the battery negative terminal (refer to *Disconnecting the battery* in the Reference Chapter).

**2** Apply the handbrake, then jack up the front of the vehicle and support it on axle stands (see *Jacking and vehicle support*). Remove the right-hand front roadwheel and the wheel arch liner inner cover for access to the right-hand side of the engine.

**3** Drain the engine oil, then fit a new sealing washer and refit the drain plug, tightening it to the specified torque (Chapter 1).

**4** Remove the exhaust system as described in Chapter 4A.

**5** Disconnect the wiring connector from the oil level sensor.

**6** On Z18XER engines, undo the retaining bolt and remove the oil dipstick guide tube.

**7** Slacken and remove the bolts securing the sump flange to the transmission housing.

**8** On Z18XE engines, remove the rubber plugs from the transmission end of the sump flange to gain access to the sump end retaining bolts.

**9** Progressively slacken and remove the bolts securing the sump to the base of the cylinder block/oil pump. Using a wide-bladed scraper or similar tool inserted between the sump and cylinder block, carefully break the joint, then remove the sump from under the car.

**10** While the sump is removed, take the opportunity to check the oil pump pick-up/strainer for signs of clogging or splitting. On Z18XE engines, unbolt the pick-up/strainer and remove it from the engine along with its sealing ring. On Z18XER engines, undo the two bolts and remove the baffle plate from the sump. Unbolt the pick-up/strainer flange and strainer base and remove it from the sump along with its sealing ring. The strainer can then be cleaned easily in solvent or renewed.

### Refitting

**11** Thoroughly clean the sump, baffle plate and pick-up/strainer, then remove all traces of sealer and oil from the mating surfaces of the sump and cylinder block and (where removed) the pick-up/strainer. Also remove all traces of locking compound from the pick-up bolts (where removed).

**12** On Z18XE engines, where necessary, position a new gasket/seal on top of the oil pump pick-up/strainer and fit the strainer **(see**

**14.12 Fit new seal/gasket to the oil pump pick-up pipe – Z18XE engines**

**illustration).** Apply locking compound to the threads of the retaining bolts then fit the bolts and tighten to the specified torque.

**13** On Z18XER engines, where necessary, position a new gasket/seal on the oil pump pick-up/strainer flange and fit the strainer. Refit the flange and base retaining bolts and tighten to the specified torque.

**14** Ensure the sump and cylinder block mating surfaces are clean and dry and remove all traces of locking compound from the sump bolts.

**15** Apply a smear of suitable sealant (available form Vauxhall/Opel dealers) to the areas of the cylinder block mating surface around the areas of the of the oil pump housing and main bearing cap joints **(see illustration)**.

**16** Apply a bead of suitable sealant (available from Vauxhall/Opel dealers) approximately 2.5 mm thick to the sealing surface of the sump. Around the No 5 main bearing cap area, increase the thickness of the bead to 3.5 mm **(see illustration)**.

**17** Offer up the sump, and loosely refit all the retaining bolts. Working out from the centre in a diagonal sequence, progressively tighten the bolts securing the sump to the cylinder block/ oil pump to their specified torque setting.

**18** Tighten the bolts securing the sump flange to the transmission housing to their specified torque settings. Where fitted, refit the rubber plugs to the sump flange cut-outs.

**19** Refit the exhaust system (see Chapter 4A) and reconnect the oil level sensor wiring connector.

**14.15 Apply sealant to the oil pump and main bearing cap joints (arrowed) before the sump is refitted**

**20** Refit the wheel arch liner inner cover and front roadwheel, then lower the vehicle to the ground. Fill the engine with fresh oil, with reference to Chapter 1.

---

### 15 Oil pump – removal, overhaul and refitting

#### Z18XE engines

**Note:** *The pressure relief valve can be removed with pump in position on the engine unit, although on some models it will be necessary to unbolt the mounting bracket assembly from the block to allow the valve to be removed.*

#### Removal

**1** Remove the timing belt as described in Section 7.

**2** Remove the rear timing belt cover as described in Section 6.

**3** Remove the sump and oil pump pick-up/ strainer as described in Section 14.

**4** Disconnect the wiring connector from the oil pressure switch.

**5** Slacken and remove the retaining bolts then slide the oil pump housing assembly off of the end of the crankshaft, taking great care not to lose the locating dowels.

**6** Remove the housing gasket and discard it.

#### Overhaul

**7** Undo the retaining screws and lift off the pump cover from the rear of the housing.

**8** Check the inner and outer rotors for identification dots indicating which way round they are fitted. If no marks are visible, use a suitable marker pen to mark the surface of both the pump inner and outer rotors.

**9** Lift out the inner and outer rotors from the pump housing **(see illustration)**.

**10** Unscrew the oil pressure relief valve bolt from the front of the housing and withdraw the spring and plunger from the housing, noting which way around the plunger is fitted. Remove the sealing washer from the valve bolt **(see illustration)**.

**11** Clean the components, and carefully examine the rotors, pump body and relief valve plunger for any signs of scoring or wear. Renew any component which shows signs of wear or damage; if the rotors or pump housing

**14.16 Apply a 2.5mm thick bead of sealant to the sump sealing surface – increase the thickness to 3.5mm around the No 5 main bearing cap area**

**15.9 Removal of the pump outer rotor – outer face identification punch mark arrowed – Z18XE engines**

**15.10 Oil pressure relief valve components – Z18XE engines**

1  *Plunger*  3  *Sealing washer*
2  *Spring*  4  *Valve bolt*

**15.12 Using a straight-edge and feeler blade to measure rotor endfloat – Z18XE engines**

**15.14 Fitting a new crankshaft oil seal to the oil pump housing – Z18XE engines**

**15.17 Take care not to damage the oil seal on the crankshaft lip (1) and engage the inner rotor with the crankshaft flats (2) – Z18XE engines**

are marked then the complete pump assembly should be renewed.

**12** If the components appear serviceable, measure the rotor endfloat using feeler blades, and check the flatness of the end cover **(see illustration)**. If the clearances exceed the specified tolerances the pump must be renewed.

**13** If the pump is satisfactory, reassemble the components in the reverse order of removal, noting the following:

a) *Ensure both rotors are fitted the correct way around.*

b) *Fit a new sealing ring to the pressure relief valve bolt and tighten the bolt to the specified torque.*

c) *Apply a little locking compound to the threads, and tighten the pump cover screws to the specified torque.*

d) *On completion prime the oil pump by filling it with clean engine oil whilst rotating the inner rotor.*

### Refitting

**14** Prior to refitting, carefully lever out the crankshaft oil seal using a flat-bladed screwdriver. Fit the new oil seal, ensuring its sealing lip is facing inwards, and press it squarely into the housing using a tubular drift which bears only on the hard outer edge of the seal **(see illustration)**. Press the seal into position so that it is flush with the housing.

**15** Ensure the mating surfaces of the oil pump and cylinder block are clean and dry and the locating dowels are in position.

**16** Fit a new gasket to the cylinder block.

**17** Carefully manoeuvre the oil pump into position and engage the inner rotor with the crankshaft end **(see illustration)**. Locate the pump on the dowels, taking great care not to damage the oil seal lip.

**18** Refit the pump housing retaining bolts in their original locations and tighten them to the specified torque.

**19** Reconnect the oil pressure sensor wiring connector.

**20** Refit the oil pump pick-up/strainer and sump as described in Section 14.

**21** Refit the rear timing belt cover to the engine, tightening its retaining bolts to the specified torque.

**22** Refit the timing belt sprockets, idler pulleys and tensioner then refit the belt as described in Sections 8 and 7.

**23** On completion, fit a new oil filter and fill the engine with clean oil as described in Chapter 1.

## Z18XER engines

### Removal

**24** Drain the cooling system as described in Chapter 1.

**25** Remove the alternator as described in Chapter 5A.

**26** Remove the exhaust manifold as described in Chapter 4A.

**27** Remove the timing belt as described in Section 7.

**28** Remove the timing belt tensioner and idler pulley, and the crankshaft sprocket as described in Section 8.

**29** Remove the sump as described in Section 14.

**30** Release the clamp and disconnect the coolant hose from the coolant pump.

**31** Undo the two bolts securing the upper metal coolant pipe to the rear of the coolant pump.

**32** Undo the support bracket bolt securing the lower metal coolant pipe to the oil filter housing.

**33** Slacken and remove the eight retaining bolts (noting their different lengths) then slide the oil pump housing assembly off of the end of the crankshaft, taking great care not to lose the locating dowels. Remove the housing gasket and discard it.

**34** Remove the metal coolant pipes and renew the four seals.

### Overhaul

**35** Remove the securing screws/bolts and withdraw the oil pump cover from the rear of the oil pump housing **(see illustration)**.

**36** Remove the inner and outer rotor from the pump housing, noting which way round they are fitted, and wipe them clean. Also clean the rotor location in the oil pump housing.

**37** The oil pressure relief valve components can also be removed from the oil pump housing by unscrewing the cap. Withdraw the cap, spring and plunger **(see illustrations)**.

**38** Locate the inner and outer rotor back in the oil pump housing, ensuring they are fitted the right way round as noted during removal.

**39** Check the clearance between the end

**15.35 Remove the securing screws and withdraw the oil pump cover from the rear of the housing – Z18XER engines**

**15.37a Unscrew the oil pressure relief valve cap . . .**

**15.37b . . . then withdraw the spring . . .**

faces of the rotors and the housing (endfloat) using a straight-edge and a feeler gauge **(see illustration)**.

**40** If the clearance is outside the specified limits, renew the components as necessary.

**41** Examine the pressure relief valve spring and plunger, and renew if any sign of damage or wear is evident.

**42** Ensure that the rotor location in the interior of the oil pump housing is scrupulously clean before commencing reassembly.

**43** Thoroughly clean the pressure relief valve components, and lubricate them with clean engine oil before refitting. Insert the plunger and spring, then refit the cap and tighten to the specified torque.

**44** Ensure that the rotors are clean, then lubricate them with clean engine oil, and refit them to the pump body ensuring they are fitted the right way round as noted during removal.

**45** Wipe clean the mating faces of the rear cover and the pump housing, then refit the rear cover. Refit and tighten the securing screws securely. Prime the oil pump by filling it with clean engine oil whilst rotating the inner rotor

### Refitting

**46** Prior to refitting, carefully lever out the crankshaft oil seal using a flat-bladed screwdriver. Fit the new oil seal, ensuring its sealing lip is facing inwards, and press it squarely into the housing using a tubular drift which bears only on the hard outer edge of the seal. Press the seal into position so that it is flush with the housing.

**47** Refit the two previously removed metal coolant pipes.

**48** Ensure the mating surfaces of the oil pump housing and cylinder block are clean and dry and the locating dowels are in position.

**49** Fit a new gasket to the cylinder block.

**50** Carefully manoeuvre the oil pump into position and engage the inner rotor with the crankshaft end. Engage the coolant pipes, then locate the pump on the dowels, taking great care not to damage the oil seal lip.

**51** Refit the pump housing retaining bolts in their original locations and tighten them to the specified torque.

**52** Refit the metal coolant pipe retaining bolts and tighten securely.

**15.37c . . . and the plunger – Z18XER engines**

**53** Reconnect the coolant hose to the pump and secure with the retaining clip.

**54** Refit the sump as described in Section 14.

**55** Refit the timing belt tensioner and idler pulley and the crankshaft sprocket, then refit the timing belt as described in Sections 8 and 7.

**56** Refit the exhaust manifold as described in Chapter 4A.

**57** Refit the alternator as described in Chapter 5A.

**58** On completion, refer to Chapter 1 and fit a new oil filter and fill the engine with clean oil, then refill the cooling system.

## 16 Crankshaft oil seals – renewal

### Right-hand (timing belt end)

**1** Remove the crankshaft sprocket as described in Section 8.

**2** Carefully punch or drill two small holes opposite each other in the oil seal. Screw a self-tapping screw into each and pull on the screws with pliers to extract the seal **(see illustration)**.

**Caution: Great care must be taken to avoid damage to the oil pump.**

**3** Clean the seal housing and polish off any burrs or raised edges which may have caused the seal to fail in the first place.

**4** Ease the new seal into position on the end of the crankshaft. Press the seal squarely into position until it is flush with the housing.

**15.39 Check the oil pump rotor endfloat using a straight-edge and feeler gauge – Z18XER engines**

If necessary, a suitable tubular drift, such as a socket, which bears only on the hard outer edge of the seal can be used to tap the seal into position **(see illustration)**. Take great care not to damage the seal lips during fitting and ensure that the seal lips face inwards.

**5** Wash off any traces of oil, then refit the crankshaft sprocket as described in Section 8.

### Left-hand (flywheel/driveplate end)

**6** Remove the flywheel/driveplate as described in Section 17.

**7** Renew the seal as described in paragraphs 2 to 4 **(see illustration)**.

**8** Refit the flywheel as described in Section 17.

## 17 Flywheel/driveplate – removal, inspection and refitting

**Note:** *New flywheel/driveplate retaining bolts will be required on refitting.*

### Removal

#### Manual transmission models

**1** Remove the transmission as described in Chapter 7A then remove the clutch assembly as described in Chapter 6.

**2** Prevent the flywheel from turning by locking the ring gear teeth with a similar arrangement to that shown **(see illustration)**. Alternatively, bolt a strap between the flywheel and the cylinder block/crankcase.

**16.2 Removing the crankshaft oil seal**

**16.4 Fitting a new crankshaft oil seal**

**16.7 Left-hand crankshaft oil seal – transmission and flywheel removed**

**17.2  Prevent the flywheel from turning by locking the ring gear teeth with a suitable tool**

**17.10a  Tighten the flywheel bolts to the specified torque using a torque wrench . . .**

**17.10b  . . . then through the specified angle using an angle tightening gauge**

Make alignment marks between the flywheel and crankshaft using paint or a suitable marker pen.

3  Slacken and remove the retaining bolts and remove the flywheel. Do not drop it, as it is very heavy.

### Automatic transmission models

4  Remove the transmission as described in Chapter 7B then remove the driveplate as described in paragraphs 2 and 3.

### Inspection

5  On manual transmission models, examine the flywheel for scoring of the clutch face. If the clutch face is scored, the flywheel may be surface-ground, but renewal is preferable.

6  On automatic transmission models closely examine the driveplate and ring gear teeth for signs of wear or damage and check the driveplate surface for any signs of cracks.

7  If there is any doubt about the condition of the flywheel/driveplate, seek the advice of a Vauxhall/Opel dealer or engine reconditioning specialist. They will be able to advise if it is possible to recondition it or whether renewal is necessary.

### Refitting

#### Manual transmission models

8  Clean the mating surfaces of the flywheel and crankshaft.

9  Apply a drop of locking compound to each of the new retaining bolt threads then offer up the flywheel, if the original is being refitted align the marks made prior to removal. Screw in the retaining bolts.

10  Lock the flywheel by the method used on removal, and tighten the retaining bolts to the specified Stage 1 torque setting then angle-tighten the bolts through the specified Stage 2 angle, using a socket and extension bar, and finally through the specified Stage 3 angle. It is recommended that an angle-measuring gauge is used during the final stages of the tightening, to ensure accuracy **(see illustrations)**. If a gauge is not available, use white paint to make alignment marks between the bolt head and flywheel prior to tightening; the marks can then be used to check that the bolt has been rotated through the correct angle.

11  Refit the clutch as described in Chapter 6

then remove the locking tool, and refit the transmission as described in Chapter 7A.

#### Automatic transmission models

12  Clean the mating surfaces of the drive-plate and crankshaft and remove all traces of locking compound from the driveplate retaining bolt threads.

13  Apply a drop of locking compound to each of the new retaining bolt threads then offer up the driveplate, if the original is being refitted align the marks made prior to removal. Screw in the retaining bolts.

14  Lock the driveplate by the method used on removal, and tighten the retaining bolts to the specified torque.

15  Remove the locking tool and refit the transmission as described in Chapter 7B.

### 18  Engine/transmission mountings – inspection and renewal

Refer to Chapter 2A, Section 15, but observe the different torque wrench settings given in the Specifications of this Chapter.

# Chapter 2  Part D:
# Engine removal and overhaul procedures

## Contents

## Degrees of difficulty

| | | | | |
|---|---|---|---|---|
| **Easy,** suitable for novice with little experience  | **Fairly easy,** suitable for beginner with some experience | **Fairly difficult,** suitable for competent DIY mechanic | **Difficult,** suitable for experienced DIY mechanic | **Very difficult,** suitable for expert DIY or professional  |

## Specifications

### Engine identification

**Engine type**

1.4 litre (1364 cc) DOHC 16-valve engine . . . . . . . . . . . . . . . . . . . . .
1.6 litre (1598 cc) DOHC 16-valve engine . . . . . . . . . . . . . . . . . . . . .
1.8 litre (1796 cc) DOHC 16-valve engine . . . . . . . . . . . . . . . . . . . . .

**Manufacturer's engine code***

Z14XEP and Z14XEL
Z16XEP
Z18XE and Z18XER (VVT engine)

* For details of engine code location, see 'Vehicle identification' in the Reference Chapter.

## 1.4 litre engines (Z14XEP and Z14XEL)

### Cylinder head

| | |
|---|---|
| Maximum gasket face distortion | 0.025 mm |
| Cylinder head height | 126.0 mm |
| Valve seat angle in cylinder head | 90° 30' |
| Valve seat width in cylinder head: | |
| Inlet valve | 1.00 to 1.40 mm |
| Exhaust valve | 1.40 to 1.80 mm |

### Valves and guides

| | Inlet | Exhaust |
|---|---|---|
| Stem diameter (standard) | 4.955 to 4.970 mm | 4.945 to 4.960 mm |
| Valve head diameter | 27.900 to 28.100 mm | 24.900 to 25.100 mm |
| Valve length (standard) | 93.65 to 94.05 mm | 93.65 to 94.05 mm |
| Maximum permissible valve stem play in guide | 0.021 to 0.052 mm | 0.031 to 0.062 mm |
| Valve clearances | Automatic adjustment by hydraulic cam followers | |

### Cylinder block

| | |
|---|---|
| Maximum gasket face distortion | 0.05 mm |
| Cylinder bore diameter | 73.385 to 73.415 mm (nominal) |
| Maximum cylinder bore ovality and taper | 0.013 mm |

### Crankshaft and bearings

| | |
|---|---|
| Number of main bearings | 5 |
| Main bearing journal diameter: | |
| Standard size | 50.004 to 50.017 mm (nominal) |
| Big-end bearing journal diameter: | |
| Standard size | 42.971 to 42.987 mm (nominal) |
| Crankshaft endfloat | 0.100 to 0.200 mm |

### Pistons

| | |
|---|---|
| Piston diameter | 73.345 to 73.375 mm (nominal) |

### Piston rings

| | |
|---|---|
| Number of rings (per piston) | 2 compression, 1 oil control |
| Ring end gap: | |
| Compression | 0.30 to 0.45 mm |
| Oil control | 0.25 to 0.75 mm |

### Torque wrench settings

Refer to Chapter 2A Specifications

## 1.6 litre engines (Z16XEP)

**Note:** *Where specifications are given as N/A, no information was available at the time of writing. Refer to your Vauxhall/Opel dealer for the latest information available.*

### Cylinder head

| | |
|---|---|
| Maximum gasket face distortion | 0.05 mm |
| Cylinder head height | N/A |
| Valve seat angle in cylinder head | 90° 30' |
| Valve seat width in cylinder head: | |
| Inlet valve | 1.0 to 1.4 mm |
| Exhaust valve | 1.4 to 1.8 mm |

### Valves and guides

| | Inlet | Exhaust |
|---|---|---|
| Stem diameter (standard) | 4.955 to 4.970 mm | 4.935 to 4.950 mm |
| Valve head diameter | 30.70 to 30.80 mm | 27.10 to 27.20 mm |
| Valve length (standard) | 117.10 to 117.30 mm | 116.16 to 116.36 mm |
| Maximum permissible valve stem play in guide | 0.030 to 0.061 mm | 0.050 to 0.081 mm |
| Valve clearances (cold) | 0.21 to 0.29 mm | 0.26 to 0.35 mm |

### Cylinder block

| | |
|---|---|
| Maximum gasket face distortion | 0.05 mm |
| Cylinder bore diameter | 78.992 to 79.058 mm (nominal) |
| Maximum cylinder bore ovality and taper | 0.013 mm |

### Crankshaft and bearings

| | |
|---|---|
| Number of main bearings | 5 |
| Main bearing journal diameter: | |
| Standard size | 54.980 to 54.997 mm |
| Big-end bearing journal diameter: | |
| Standard size | 42.971 to 42.987 mm |
| Crankshaft endfloat | 0.100 to 0.202 mm |

## 1.6 litre engines (Z16XEP) (continued)

### Pistons
Piston diameter . . . . . . . . . . . . . . . . . . . . . . . . . . . . . . . . . . . . . . . . . .  78.833 to 78.847 mm (nominal)

### Piston rings
Number of rings (per piston) . . . . . . . . . . . . . . . . . . . . . . . . . . . . . .  2 compression, 1 oil control

Ring end gap:

    Compression . . . . . . . . . . . . . . . . . . . . . . . . . . . . . . . . . . . . . . . . .  0.25 to 0.50 mm

    Oil control . . . . . . . . . . . . . . . . . . . . . . . . . . . . . . . . . . . . . . . . . . . .  0.25 to 0.75 mm

### Torque wrench settings
Refer to Chapter 2B Specifications

## 1.8 litre engines (Z18XE)

### Cylinder head
Maximum gasket face distortion . . . . . . . . . . . . . . . . . . . . . . . . . . .  0.05 mm

Cylinder head height . . . . . . . . . . . . . . . . . . . . . . . . . . . . . . . . . . . .  135.85 to 136.00 mm

Valve seat angle in cylinder head . . . . . . . . . . . . . . . . . . . . . . . . . .  90° 30'

Valve seat width in cylinder head:

    Inlet valve . . . . . . . . . . . . . . . . . . . . . . . . . . . . . . . . . . . . . . . . . . .  1.0 to 1.4 mm

    Exhaust valve . . . . . . . . . . . . . . . . . . . . . . . . . . . . . . . . . . . . . . . .  1.4 to 1.8 mm

### Valves and guides

| | Inlet | Exhaust |
|---|---|---|
| Stem diameter (standard) . . . . . . . . . . . . . . . . . . . . . . . . . . . . . . . . | 4.955 to 4.970 mm | 4.935 to 4.950 mm |
| Valve head diameter . . . . . . . . . . . . . . . . . . . . . . . . . . . . . . . . . . . . | 31.10 to 31.30 mm | 27.40 to 27.60 mm |
| Valve length (standard) . . . . . . . . . . . . . . . . . . . . . . . . . . . . . . . . . | 101.20 to 101.60 mm | 100.56 to 100.96 mm |
| Maximum permissible valve stem play in guide . . . . . . . . . . . . . . . | 0.030 to 0.057 mm | 0.050 to 0.077 mm |
| Valve clearances . . . . . . . . . . . . . . . . . . . . . . . . . . . . . . . . . . . . . . | Automatic adjustment by hydraulic cam followers | |

### Cylinder block
Maximum gasket face distortion . . . . . . . . . . . . . . . . . . . . . . . . . . .  0.05 mm

Cylinder bore diameter . . . . . . . . . . . . . . . . . . . . . . . . . . . . . . . . . .  80.485 to 80.555 mm (nominal)

Maximum cylinder bore ovality and taper . . . . . . . . . . . . . . . . . . . .  0.013 mm

### Crankshaft and bearings
Number of main bearings . . . . . . . . . . . . . . . . . . . . . . . . . . . . . . . .  5

Main bearing journal diameter:

    Standard size . . . . . . . . . . . . . . . . . . . . . . . . . . . . . . . . . . . . . . . .  54.980 to 54.997 mm

Big-end bearing journal diameter:

    Standard size . . . . . . . . . . . . . . . . . . . . . . . . . . . . . . . . . . . . . . . .  42.971 to 42.987 mm

Crankshaft endfloat . . . . . . . . . . . . . . . . . . . . . . . . . . . . . . . . . . . .  0.100 to 0.202 mm

### Pistons
Piston diameter . . . . . . . . . . . . . . . . . . . . . . . . . . . . . . . . . . . . . . . . .  80.455 to 80.525 mm (nominal)

### Piston rings
Number of rings (per piston) . . . . . . . . . . . . . . . . . . . . . . . . . . . . . .  2 compression, 1 oil control

Ring end gap:

    Compression . . . . . . . . . . . . . . . . . . . . . . . . . . . . . . . . . . . . . . . . .  0.30 to 0.50 mm

    Oil control . . . . . . . . . . . . . . . . . . . . . . . . . . . . . . . . . . . . . . . . . . . .  0.40 to 1.40 mm

### Torque wrench settings
Refer to Chapter 2C Specifications

## 1.8 litre engines (Z18XER)

**Note:** *Where specifications are given as N/A, no information was available at the time of writing. Refer to your Vauxhall/Opel dealer for the latest information available.*

### Cylinder head
Maximum gasket face distortion . . . . . . . . . . . . . . . . . . . . . . . . . . .  0.05 mm

Cylinder head height . . . . . . . . . . . . . . . . . . . . . . . . . . . . . . . . . . . .  N/A

Valve seat angle in cylinder head . . . . . . . . . . . . . . . . . . . . . . . . . .  90° 30'

Valve seat width in cylinder head:

    Inlet . . . . . . . . . . . . . . . . . . . . . . . . . . . . . . . . . . . . . . . . . . . . . . . .  1.0 to 1.4 mm

    Exhaust . . . . . . . . . . . . . . . . . . . . . . . . . . . . . . . . . . . . . . . . . . . . .  1.4 to 1.8 mm

### Valves and guides

| | Inlet | Exhaust |
|---|---|---|
| Stem diameter (standard) . . . . . . . . . . . . . . . . . . . . . . . . . . . . . . . . | 4.955 to 4.970 mm | 4.935 to 4.950 mm |
| Valve head diameter . . . . . . . . . . . . . . . . . . . . . . . . . . . . . . . . . . . . | 30.70 to 30.80 mm | 27.10 to 27.20 mm |
| Valve length (standard) . . . . . . . . . . . . . . . . . . . . . . . . . . . . . . . . . | 117.10 to 117.30 mm | 116.16 to 116.36 mm |
| Maximum permissible valve stem play in guide . . . . . . . . . . . . . . . | 0.030 to 0.061 mm | 0.050 to 0.081 mm |
| Valve clearances (cold) . . . . . . . . . . . . . . . . . . . . . . . . . . . . . . . . . | 0.21 to 0.29 mm | 0.27 to 0.35 mm |

## 1.8 litre engines (Z18XER) (continued)

**Cylinder block**

| | |
|---|---|
| Maximum gasket face distortion . . . . . . . . . . . . . . . . . . . . . . . . . . . . | 0.05 mm |
| Cylinder bore diameter. . . . . . . . . . . . . . . . . . . . . . . . . . . . . . . . . . . . . | 80.492 to 80.558 mm (nominal) |
| Maximum cylinder bore ovality and taper . . . . . . . . . . . . . . . . . . . | 0.013 mm |

**Crankshaft and bearings**

| | |
|---|---|
| Number of main bearings. . . . . . . . . . . . . . . . . . . . . . . . . . . . . . . . . . | 5 |
| Main bearing journal diameter: | |
|    Standard size . . . . . . . . . . . . . . . . . . . . . . . . . . . . . . . . . . . . . . . | 54.980 to 54.997 mm |
| Big-end bearing journal diameter: | |
|    Standard size . . . . . . . . . . . . . . . . . . . . . . . . . . . . . . . . . . . . . . . | 42.971 to 42.987 mm |
| Crankshaft endfloat . . . . . . . . . . . . . . . . . . . . . . . . . . . . . . . . . . . . . | 0.100 to 0.202 mm |

**Pistons**

| | |
|---|---|
| Piston diameter . . . . . . . . . . . . . . . . . . . . . . . . . . . . . . . . . . . . . . . . . | 80.455 to 80.515 mm (nominal) |

**Piston rings**

| | |
|---|---|
| Number of rings (per piston). . . . . . . . . . . . . . . . . . . . . . . . . . . . . . | 2 compression, 1 oil control |
| Ring end gap: | |
|    Top compression . . . . . . . . . . . . . . . . . . . . . . . . . . . . . . . . . . . . | 0.20 to 0.40 mm |
|    Second compression . . . . . . . . . . . . . . . . . . . . . . . . . . . . . . . . . | 0.40 to 0.60 mm |
|    Oil control. . . . . . . . . . . . . . . . . . . . . . . . . . . . . . . . . . . . . . . . . . | 0.25 to 0.75 mm |

**Torque wrench settings**
Refer to Chapter 2C Specifications

## 1 General information

Included in this Part of Chapter 2 are details of removing the engine/transmission from the car and general overhaul procedures for the cylinder head, cylinder block/crankcase and all other engine internal components.

The information given ranges from advice concerning preparation for an overhaul and the purchase of parts, to detailed step-by-step procedures covering removal, inspection, renovation and refitting of engine internal components.

After Section 5, all instructions are based on the assumption that the engine has been removed from the car. For information concerning in-car engine repair, as well as the removal and refitting of those external components necessary for full overhaul, refer to Part A, B or C of this Chapter (as applicable) and to Section 5. Ignore any preliminary dismantling operations described in Part A, B or C that are no longer relevant once the engine has been removed from the car.

Apart from torque wrench settings, which are given at the beginning of Part A, B or C (as applicable), all specifications relating to engine overhaul are at the beginning of this Part of Chapter 2.

## 2 Engine overhaul – general information

It is not always easy to determine when, or if, an engine should be completely overhauled, as a number of factors must be considered.

High mileage is not necessarily an indication that an overhaul is needed, while low mileage does not preclude the need for an overhaul. Frequency of servicing is probably the most important consideration. An engine which has had regular and frequent oil and filter changes, as well as other required maintenance, should give many thousands of miles of reliable service. Conversely, a neglected engine may require an overhaul very early in its life.

Excessive oil consumption is an indication that piston rings, valve seals and/or valve guides are in need of attention. Make sure that oil leaks are not responsible before deciding that the rings and/or guides are worn. Have a compression test performed (refer to Part A, B or C of this Chapter, to determine the likely cause of the problem.

Check the oil pressure with a gauge fitted in place of the oil pressure switch, and compare it with that specified. If it is extremely low, the main and big-end bearings, and/or the oil pump, are probably worn out.

Loss of power, rough running, knocking or metallic engine noises, excessive valve gear noise, and high fuel consumption may also point to the need for an overhaul, especially if they are all present at the same time. If a complete service does not cure the situation, major mechanical work is the only solution.

A full engine overhaul involves restoring all internal parts to the specification of a new engine. During a complete overhaul, the pistons and the piston rings are renewed, and the cylinder bores are reconditioned. New main and big-end bearings are generally fitted; if necessary, the crankshaft may be reground, to compensate for wear in the journals. The valves are also serviced as well, since they are usually in less-than-perfect condition at this point. Always pay careful attention to the

condition of the oil pump when overhauling the engine, and renew it if there is any doubt as to its serviceability. The end result should be an as-new engine that will give many trouble-free miles.

Critical cooling system components such as the hoses, thermostat and coolant pump should be renewed when an engine is overhauled. The radiator should also be checked carefully, to ensure that it is not clogged or leaking.

Before beginning the engine overhaul, read through the entire procedure, to familiarise yourself with the scope and requirements of the job. Check on the availability of parts and make sure that any necessary special tools and equipment are obtained in advance. Most work can be done with typical hand tools, although a number of precision measuring tools are required for inspecting parts to determine if they must be renewed.

The services provided by an engineering machine shop or engine reconditioning specialist will almost certainly be required, particularly if major repairs such as crankshaft regrinding or cylinder reboring are necessary. Apart from carrying out machining operations, these establishments will normally handle the inspection of parts, offer advice concerning reconditioning or renewal and supply new components such as pistons, piston rings and bearing shells. It is recommended that the establishment used is a member of the Federation of Engine Re-Manufacturers, or a similar society.

Always wait until the engine has been completely dismantled, and until all components (especially the cylinder block/crankcase and the crankshaft) have been inspected, before deciding what service and repair operations must be performed by an engineering works. The condition of these components will be the major factor to consider when determining whether to overhaul the original engine, or to buy a reconditioned unit. Do not, therefore, purchase parts or have overhaul work done on other components until they have been thoroughly inspected. As a general rule, time is the primary cost of an overhaul, so it does not pay to fit worn or sub-standard parts.

As a final note, to ensure maximum life and minimum trouble from a reconditioned engine, everything must be assembled with care, in a spotlessly-clean environment.

## 3  Engine removal – methods and precautions

If you have decided that the engine must be removed for overhaul or major repair work, several preliminary steps should be taken.

Engine/transmission removal is extremely complicated and involved on these vehicles. It must be stated that unless the vehicle can be positioned on a ramp, or raised and supported on axle stands over an inspection pit, it will be very difficult to carry out the work involved.

Cleaning the engine compartment and engine/transmission before beginning the removal procedure will help keep tools clean and organised.

An engine hoist will also be necessary. Make sure the equipment is rated in excess of the combined weight of the engine and transmission. Safety is of primary importance, considering the potential hazards involved in removing the engine/transmission from the car.

The help of an assistant is essential. Apart from the safety aspects involved, there are many instances when one person cannot simultaneously perform all of the operations required during engine/transmission removal.

Plan the operation ahead of time. Before starting work, arrange for the hire of or obtain all of the tools and equipment you will need. Some of the equipment necessary to perform engine/transmission removal and installation safely (in addition to an engine hoist) is as follows: a heavy duty trolley jack, complete sets of spanners and sockets as described in the rear of this manual, wooden blocks, and plenty of rags and cleaning solvent for mopping-up spilled oil, coolant and fuel. If the hoist must be hired, make sure that you arrange for it in advance, and perform all of the operations possible without it beforehand. This will save you money and time.

Plan for the car to be out of use for quite a while. An engineering machine shop or engine reconditioning specialist will be required to perform some of the work which cannot be accomplished without special equipment. These places often have a busy schedule, so it would be a good idea to consult them before removing the engine, in order to accurately

estimate the amount of time required to rebuild or repair components that may need work.

During the engine/transmission removal procedure, it is advisable to make notes of the locations of all brackets, cable ties, earthing points, etc, as well as how the wiring harnesses, hoses and electrical connections are attached and routed around the engine and engine compartment. An effective way of doing this is to take a series of photographs of the various components before they are disconnected or removed; the resulting photographs will prove invaluable when the engine/transmission is refitted.

Always be extremely careful when removing and refitting the engine/transmission. Serious injury can result from careless actions. Plan ahead and take your time, and a job of this nature, although major, can be accomplished successfully.

On all Astra models, the engine must be removed complete with the transmission as an assembly. There is insufficient clearance in the engine compartment to remove the engine leaving the transmission in the vehicle. The assembly is removed by raising the front of the vehicle, and lowering the assembly from the engine compartment.

## 4  Engine and transmission unit – removal, separation and refitting

**Note 1:** *The engine can be removed from the car only as a complete unit with the transmission; the two are then separated for overhaul. The engine/transmission unit is lowered out of position, and withdrawn from under the vehicle. Bearing this in mind, and also bearing in mind the information contained in Section 3, ensure the vehicle is raised sufficiently so that there is enough clearance between the front of the vehicle and the floor to allow the engine/transmission unit to be slid out once it has been lowered out of position.*
**Note 2:** *Such is the complexity of the power unit arrangement on these vehicles, and the variations that may be encountered according to model and optional equipment fitted, that the following should be regarded as a guide to the work involved, rather than a step-by-step procedure. Where differences are encountered, or additional component disconnection or removal is necessary, make notes of the work involved as an aid to refitting.*

### Removal

**1** On models equipped with air conditioning, have the air conditioning system fully discharged by an air conditioning specialist.
**2** Position the vehicle as described in Section 3, paragraph 2, and remove both front road-wheels. Also remove the right-hand wheel arch liner inner cover.
**3** Remove the bonnet and the front bumper as described in Chapter 11.

**4** Where fitted, remove the plastic cover from the top of the engine.
**5** Remove the battery and battery tray as described in Chapter 5A.
**6** Undo the retaining nuts, remove the bolts and disconnect the positive and negative secondary leads from the main battery positive and negative terminals.
**7** Carry out the following operations as described in Chapter 1:
  a) *Drain the engine oil.*
  b) *Drain the cooling system.*
  c) *Remove the auxiliary drivebelt.*
**8** Remove the air cleaner assembly and intake ducts as described in Chapter 4A.
**9** Disconnect the main wiring harness connector situated in front of the battery location.
**10** Disconnect the wiring connector(s) from the engine management ECU.
**11** Undo the nut securing the earth lead to the stud in front of the battery box location.
**12** Disconnect the wiring block connector from the cooling fan module. Release the wiring harness from the retaining clips so that it is free to be removed with the engine.
**13** On models with Easytronic transmission, disconnect the transmission wiring harness connectors, and release the harness from the transmission.
**14** Disconnect the wiring connector from the reversing light switch on the transmission.
**15** Remove the air conditioning system compressor as described in Chapter 3.
**16** Depressurise the fuel system with reference to Chapter 4A, then disconnect the fuel supply pipe from the fuel rail and support bracket. Be prepared for fuel spillage, and take adequate precautions. Clamp or plug the open unions, to minimise further fuel loss.
**17** Disconnect the brake vacuum servo hose, and fuel evaporation purge hose.
**18** Loosen the clips and remove the upper and lower radiator hoses.
**19** Release the retaining clips and disconnect the coolant hoses at the cooling system expansion tank. Disconnect the wiring connector then remove the expansion tank from its mounting bracket.
**20** Release the quick-release connectors by sliding them forward, and disconnect the two heater hoses from the heater matrix pipe stubs.
**21** On automatic transmission models, use a forked tool or flat-bladed screwdriver, and carefully lever the gear selector inner cable end fitting off the balljoint on the selector lever position switch. Pull back the retaining sleeve and detach the outer cable from the mounting bracket on the transmission.
**22** Drain the manual transmission oil or automatic transmission fluid as described in Chapter 7A or 7B, as applicable.
**23** Remove both driveshafts as described in Chapter 8.
**24** Position the steering with the front road-wheels straight-ahead, and lock the steering by removing the ignition key.

**4.26a Prise out the clip securing the clutch hydraulic hose to the end fitting on the transmission bellhousing . . .**

**4.26b . . . then detach the hose from the end fitting**

**25** On standard manual transmission models (not Easytronic), remove the filler cap from the brake/clutch fluid reservoir on the bulkhead, then tighten it onto a piece of polythene. This will reduce the loss of fluid when the clutch hydraulic hose is disconnected. Alternatively, fit a hose clamp to the flexible hose next to the clutch hydraulic connection on the transmission housing.

**26** Place some cloth rags beneath the hose, then prise out the retaining clip securing the clutch hydraulic hose to the end fitting on top of the transmission bellhousing. Detach the hose from the end fitting **(see illustrations)**. Gently squeeze the two legs of the retaining clip together and re-insert the retaining clip back into position in the end fitting. Discard the sealing ring from the hose end; a new sealing ring must be used on refitting. Plug/cover both the end fitting and hose end to minimise fluid loss and prevent the entry of dirt into the hydraulic system. **Note:** *Whilst the hose is disconnected, do not depress the clutch pedal.*

**27** On automatic transmission models, unscrew the central retaining bolt (or nut) and detach the fluid cooler pipes from the transmission. Suitably cover the pipe ends and plug the transmission orifices to prevent dirt entry.

**28** Attach a suitable hoist and lifting tackle to the engine lifting brackets on the cylinder head, and support the weight of the engine/transmission.

**29** Remove the front subframe as described in Chapter 10.

**30** Mark the position of the three bolts securing the right-hand engine mounting bracket to the engine bracket and undo the bolts **(see illustration)**. **Note:** *There is no need to remove the mounting, since the engine/transmission is lowered from the engine compartment.*

**31** Mark the position of the three bolts securing the left-hand engine mounting to the transmission bracket **(see illustration)**.

**32** Make a final check to ensure that all relevant pipes, hoses, wires, etc, have been disconnected, and that they are positioned clear of the engine and transmission.

**33** With the help of an assistant, carefully lower the engine/transmission assembly to the ground. Make sure that the surrounding components in the engine compartment are not damaged. Ideally, the assembly should be lowered onto a trolley jack or low platform with castors, so that it can easily be withdrawn from under the car.

**34** Ensure that the assembly is adequately supported, then disconnect the engine hoist and lifting tackle, and withdraw the engine/transmission assembly from under the front of the vehicle.

**35** Clean away any external dirt using paraffin or a water-soluble solvent and a stiff brush.

**36** Refer to the procedures contained in Chapter 7A or 7B, and unbolt the transmission from the engine. Carefully withdraw the transmission from the engine. On manual transmission models, ensure that its weight is not allowed to hang on the input shaft while

engaged with the clutch friction disc. On automatic transmission models, ensure that the torque converter is removed together with the transmission so that it remains engaged with the oil pump. Note that the transmission locates on dowels positioned in the rear of the cylinder block.

### Refitting

**37** With reference to Chapter 7A or 7B, refit the transmission to the engine and tighten the bolts to the specified torque.

**38** With the front of the vehicle raised and supported on axle stands, move the engine/transmission assembly under the vehicle, ensuring that the assembly is adequately supported.

**39** Reconnect the hoist and lifting tackle to the engine lifting brackets, and carefully raise the engine/transmission assembly up into the engine compartment with the help of an assistant.

**40** Reconnect the right- and left-hand engine/transmission mountings and tighten the bolts to the specified torque given in Chapter 2A, 2B or 2C, as applicable. Ensure that the marks made on removal are correctly aligned when tightening the retaining bolts.

**41** Refit the front subframe as described in Chapter 10.

**42** Disconnect the hoist and lifting tackle from the engine lifting brackets.

**43** Refit the driveshafts as described in Chapter 8.

**44** On manual transmission models, refill the transmission with correct quantity and type of oil, as described in Chapter 7A.

**45** On automatic transmission models, reconnect the fluid cooler pipes together with new O-ring seals to the transmission.

**46** On manual transmission models, reconnect and bleed the clutch hydraulic connection at the transmission with reference to Chapter 6.

**47** On automatic transmission models, refit the gearchange selector outer cable to the mounting bracket on the transmission. Engage the inner cable end fitting with the selector lever balljoint, squeezing them together with pliers if necessary.

**48** Push the heater hoses back onto the matrix pipe stubs. Ensure that the quick-release connectors securely lock the hoses in position.

**49** Refit the cooling system expansion tank, and reconnect the wiring connector and the coolant hoses.

**50** Reconnect the upper and lower radiator hoses.

**51** Reconnect the brake vacuum servo hose, and fuel evaporation purge hose and fuel supply pipe.

**52** Refit the air conditioning system compressor as described in Chapter 3, then refit the auxiliary drivebelt as described in Chapter 1.

**53** Reconnect the wiring block connector to the cooling fan module.

**54** Reconnect the earth lead to the stud in

**4.30 Right-hand engine mounting bracket-to-engine bracket retaining bolts (arrowed)**

**4.31 Left-hand engine mounting-to-transmission bracket retaining bolts (arrowed)**

front of the battery tray location and secure with the retaining nut.

**55** Reconnect the main wiring harness connector situated in front of the battery location.

**56** Reconnect the wiring connector(s) from the engine management ECU.

**57** On models with Easytronic transmission, reconnect the transmission wiring harness connectors, and secure the harness to the transmission.

**58** Reconnect the reversing light switch wiring connector.

**59** Refit the air cleaner assembly and intake ducts as described in Chapter 4A.

**60** Refit the battery tray and battery as described in Chapter 5A.

**61** Refit the bonnet and the front bumper as described in Chapter 11.

**62** Refit the right-hand wheel arch liner inner cover and both front roadwheels, then lower the vehicle to the ground.

**63** Make a final check to ensure that all relevant hoses, pipes and wires have been correctly reconnected.

**64** Refill the engine with oil with reference to Chapter 1.

**65** On automatic transmission models, refill the transmission with correct quantity and type of fluid, as described in Chapter 7B.

**66** Refill and bleed the cooling system with reference to Chapter 1.

**67** On models equipped with air conditioning, have the air conditioning system evacuated, charged and leak-tested by the specialist who discharged it.

## 5 Engine overhaul – dismantling sequence

**1** It is much easier to dismantle and work on the engine if it is mounted on a portable engine stand. These stands can often be hired from a tool hire shop. Before the engine is mounted on a stand, the flywheel/driveplate should be removed, so that the stand bolts can be tightened into the end of the cylinder block/crankcase.

**2** If a stand is not available, it is possible to dismantle the engine with it blocked up on a sturdy workbench, or on the floor. Be extra careful not to tip or drop the engine when working without a stand.

**3** If you are going to obtain a reconditioned engine, all the external components must be removed first, to be transferred to the new engine (just as they will if you are doing a complete engine overhaul yourself). These components include the following:

a) *Engine wiring harness and supports.*
b) *Alternator and air conditioning compressor mounting brackets (as applicable).*
c) *Coolant pump (where applicable) and inlet/outlet housings.*
d) *Dipstick tube.*

e) *Fuel system components.*
f) *All electrical switches and sensors.*
g) *Inlet and exhaust manifolds.*
h) *Oil filter and oil cooler/heat exchanger.*
i) *Flywheel/driveplate.*

**Note:** *When removing the external components from the engine, pay close attention to details that may be helpful or important during refitting. Note the fitted position of gaskets, seals, spacers, pins, washers, bolts, and other small items.*

**4** If you are obtaining a 'short' engine (which consists of the engine cylinder block/crankcase, crankshaft, pistons and connecting rods all assembled), then the cylinder head, sump, oil pump, and timing belt/chains (as applicable) will have to be removed also.

**5** If you are planning a complete overhaul, the engine can be dismantled, and the internal components removed, in the order given below.

a) *Inlet and exhaust manifolds (see Chapter 4A).*
b) *Timing belt, sprockets, tensioner and idler pulleys (see Chapter 2B or 2C).*
c) *Coolant pump (see Chapter 3).*
d) *Cylinder head (see Chapter 2A, 2B or 2C).*
e) *Flywheel/driveplate (see Chapter 2A, 2B or 2C).*
f) *Sump (see Chapter 2A, 2B or 2C).*
g) *Oil pump (see Chapter 2A, 2B or 2C).*
h) *Timing chain and sprockets (see Chapter 2A).*
i) *Pistons/connecting rod assemblies (see Section 9).*
j) *Crankshaft (see Section 10).*

**6** Before beginning the dismantling and overhaul procedures, make sure that you have all of the correct tools necessary. See *Tools and working facilities* for further information.

## 6 Cylinder head – dismantling

**Note:** *New and reconditioned cylinder heads are available from the manufacturer, and from engine overhaul specialists. Due to the fact that some specialist tools are required for the dismantling and inspection procedures, and new components may not be readily available, it may be more practical and economical for the home mechanic to purchase a reconditioned head rather than to dismantle, inspect and recondition the original head. A valve spring compressor tool will be required for this operation.*

**1** With the cylinder head removed as described in the relevant Part of this Chapter, clean away all external dirt, and remove the following components as applicable, if not already done:

a) *Manifolds (see Chapter 4A).*
b) *Spark plugs (see Chapter 1).*
c) *Camshafts and and associated valve train components (see Chapter 2A, 2B or 2C).*

**6.2 Using a valve spring compressor, compress the valve spring to relieve the pressure on the collets**

d) *Cooling system components (see Chapter 3).*
e) *Engine lifting brackets.*

**2** To remove a valve, fit a valve spring compressor tool. Ensure that the arms of the compressor tool are securely positioned on the head of the valve and the spring cap **(see illustration)**. The valves are deeply-recessed on most engines, and a suitable extension piece may be required for the spring compressor.

**3** Compress the valve spring to relieve the pressure of the spring cap acting on the collets.

> **HAYNES HiNT** *If the spring cap sticks to the valve stem, support the compressor tool, and give the end a light tap with a soft-faced mallet to help free the spring cap.*

**4** Extract the two split collets by hooking them out using a small screwdriver, then slowly release the compressor tool **(see illustration)**.

**5** Remove the valve spring cap and the spring, then withdraw the valve through the combustion chamber. Using pliers, remove the valve stem oil seal, which also incorporates the spring seat on most engines **(see illustrations)**. If the spring seat is not part of the valve stem oil seal, hook it out using a small screwdriver.

**6** Repeat the procedure for the remaining valves, keeping all components in strict order

**6.4 Extract the two split collets by hooking them out using a small screwdriver**

6.5a Remove the valve spring cap . . .

6.5b . . . and the spring . . .

6.5c . . . then withdraw the valve through the combustion chamber

6.5d Using pliers, remove the valve stem oil seal, which also incorporates the spring seat on most engines

6.6 Place each valve assembly in a labelled polythene bag or similar container

so that they can be refitted in their original positions, unless all the components are to be renewed. If the components are to be kept and used again, place each valve assembly in a labelled polythene bag or a similar small container (see illustration). Note that as with cylinder numbering, the valves are normally numbered from the timing chain (or timing belt) end of the engine. Make sure that the valve components are identified as inlet and exhaust, as well as numbered.

## 7 Cylinder head and valves – cleaning and inspection

1 Thorough cleaning of the cylinder head and valve components, followed by a detailed inspection, will enable you to decide how much valve service work must be carried out during the engine overhaul. **Note:** *If the engine has been severely overheated, it is best to assume that the cylinder head is warped – check carefully for signs of this.*

### Cleaning

2 Scrape away all traces of old gasket material from the cylinder head.
3 Scrape away the carbon from the combustion chambers and ports, then wash the cylinder head thoroughly with paraffin or a suitable solvent.
4 Scrape off any heavy carbon deposits that may have formed on the valves, then use a power-operated wire brush to remove deposits from the valve heads and stems.

### Inspection

**Note:** *Be sure to perform all the following inspection procedures before concluding*

that the services of a machine shop or engine overhaul specialist are required. Make a list of all items that require attention.

### Cylinder head

5 Inspect the head very carefully for cracks, evidence of coolant leakage, and other damage. If cracks are found, a new cylinder head should be obtained.
6 Use a straight-edge and feeler gauge blade to check that the cylinder head surface is not distorted (see illustration). If it is, it may be possible to resurface it, provided that the cylinder head is not reduced to less than the minimum specified height.
7 Examine the valve seats in each of the combustion chambers. If they are severely pitted, cracked or burned, then they will need to be recut by an engine overhaul specialist. If they are only slightly pitted, this can be removed by grinding-in the valve heads and seats with fine valve-grinding compound, as described below.
8 If the valve guides are worn, indicated by a side-to-side motion of the valve, oversize valve guides are available, and valves with oversize stems can be fitted. This work is best carried out by an engine overhaul specialist. A dial gauge may be used to determine whether the amount of side play of a valve exceeds the specified maximum.
9 Check the tappet bores in the cylinder head for wear. If excessive wear is evident, the cylinder head must be renewed. Also check the tappet oil holes in the cylinder head for obstructions.

### Valves

10 Examine the head of each valve for pitting, burning, cracks and general wear, and check the valve stem for scoring and wear ridges. Rotate the valve, and check for any obvious indication that it is bent. Look for pitting and excessive wear on the tip of each valve stem. Renew any valve that shows any such signs of wear or damage.
11 If the valve appears satisfactory at this stage, measure the valve stem diameter at several points using a micrometer (see illustration). Any significant difference in the readings obtained indicates wear of the valve stem. Should any of these conditions be apparent, the valve(s) must be renewed.

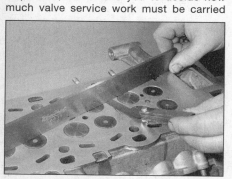

7.6 Using a straight-edge and feeler gauge to check cylinder head surface distortion

7.11 Using a micrometer to measure valve stem diameter

**12** If the valves are in satisfactory condition, they should be ground (lapped) into their respective seats, to ensure a smooth gas-tight seal. If the seat is only lightly pitted, or if it has been recut, fine grinding compound **only** should be used to produce the required finish. Coarse valve-grinding compound should **not** be used unless a seat is badly burned or deeply pitted; if this is the case, the cylinder head and valves should be inspected by an expert to decide whether seat recutting, or even the renewal of the valve or seat insert, is required.

**13** Valve grinding is carried out as follows. Place the cylinder head upside-down on a bench, with a block of wood at each end to give clearance for the valve stems.

**14** Smear a trace of the appropriate grade of valve-grinding compound on the seat face, and press a suction grinding tool onto the valve head. With a semi-rotary action, grind the valve head to its seat, lifting the valve occasionally to redistribute the grinding compound **(see illustration)**. A light spring placed under the valve head will greatly ease this operation.

**15** If coarse grinding compound is being used, work only until a dull, matt even surface is produced on both the valve seat and the valve, then wipe off the used compound and repeat the process with fine compound. When

**7.14  Grinding-in a valve**

a smooth unbroken ring of light grey matt finish is produced on both the valve and seat, the grinding operation is complete. **Do not** grind in the valves any further than absolutely necessary, or the seat will be prematurely sunk into the cylinder head.

**16** When all the valves have been ground-in, carefully wash off all traces of grinding compound using paraffin or a suitable solvent before reassembly of the cylinder head.

**Valve components**

**17** Examine the valve springs for signs of damage and discoloration; if possible; also compare the existing spring free length with new components.

**18** Stand each spring on a flat surface, and check it for squareness. If any of the springs are damaged, distorted or have lost their tension, obtain a complete new set of springs.

**8  Cylinder head –**
  reassembly

**1** Lubricate the stems of the valves, and insert them into their original locations **(see illustration)**. If new valves are being fitted, insert them into the locations to which they have been ground.

**2** Working on the first valve, refit the spring seat if it is not an integral part of the valve stem oil seal. Dip the new valve stem seal in fresh engine oil, then carefully locate it over the valve and onto the guide. Take care not to damage the seal as it is passed over the valve stem. Use a suitable socket or metal tube to press the seal firmly onto the guide. **Note:** *If genuine seals are being fitted, use the oil seal protector which is supplied with the seals; the protector fits over the valve stem and prevents the oil seal lip being damaged on the valve* **(see illustrations)**.

**3** Locate the spring on the seat and fit the spring cap **(see illustration)**.

**8.1  Lubricate the valve stem with engine oil and insert the valve into the correct guide**

**8.2a  Fit the spring seat . . .**

**8.2b  . . . then fit the seal protector (where supplied) to the valve . . .**

**8.2c  . . . and install the new valve stem oil seal . . .**

**8.2d  . . . pressing it onto the valve guide with a suitable socket**

**8.3 Refit the valve spring and fit the spring cap**

**8.4 Compress the valve and locate the collets in the recess on the valve stem**

*Use a little dab of grease to hold the collets in position on the valve stem while the spring compressor is released.*

**4** Compress the valve spring, and locate the split collets in the recess in the valve stem **(see illustration and Haynes Hint)**. Release the compressor, then repeat the procedure on the remaining valves.

**5** With all the valves installed, support the cylinder head on blocks on the bench and, using a hammer and interposed block of wood, tap the end of each valve stem to settle the components.

**6** Refit the components removed in Section 6, paragraph 1.

### 9 Pistons/connecting rods – removal

**Note :** *New connecting rod big-end cap bolts will be needed on refitting.*

**1** Referring to the relevant Part of this Chapter, remove the cylinder head and sump. Where fitted, unbolt the pick-up/strainer from the base of the oil pump and the oil baffle plate from the cylinder block baseplate **(see illustration)**.

**2** If there is a pronounced wear ridge at the top of any bore, it may be necessary to remove it with a scraper or ridge reamer, to avoid piston damage during removal. Such a ridge indicates excessive wear of the cylinder bore.

**3** If the connecting rods and big-end caps are not marked to indicate their positions in the cylinder block (ie, marked with cylinder numbers), suitably mark both the rod and

cap with quick-drying paint or similar. Note which side of the engine the marks face and accurately record this also. There may not be any other way of identifying which way round the cap fits on the rod when refitting.

**4** Turn the crankshaft to bring pistons 1 and 4 to BDC (bottom dead centre).

**5** Unscrew the bolts from No 1 piston big-end bearing cap, then take off the cap and recover the bottom half-bearing shell **(see illustration)**. If the bearing shells are to be re-used, tape the cap and the shell together.

***Caution: On some engines, the connecting rod/bearing cap mating surfaces are not machined flat; the big-end bearing caps are 'cracked' off from the rod during production and left untouched to ensure the cap and rod mate perfectly. Where this type of connecting rod is fitted, great care must be taken to ensure the mating surfaces of the cap and rod are not marked or damaged in anyway. Any damage to the mating surfaces will adversely affect the strength of the connecting rod and could lead to premature failure.***

**6** Using a hammer handle, push the piston up through the bore, and remove it from the top of the cylinder block **(see illustration)**. Recover the bearing shell, and tape it to the connecting rod for safe-keeping.

**7** Loosely refit the big-end cap to the connecting rod, and secure with the nuts/bolts – this will help to keep the components in their correct order.

**8** Remove No 4 piston assembly in the same way.

**9** Turn the crankshaft through 180° to bring pistons 2 and 3 to BDC, and remove them in the same way.

### 10 Crankshaft – removal

### 1.4 litre engines

**Note:** *New cylinder block baseplate retaining bolts will be required for refitting.*

**1** Remove the flywheel as described in Chapter 2A.

**2** Remove the pistons and connecting rods, as described in Section 9. If no work is to be done on the pistons and connecting rods, unbolt the caps and push the pistons far enough up the bores that the connecting rods are positioned clear of the crankshaft journals.

**3** Invert the engine so that the crankshaft is uppermost.

**4** Before removing the crankshaft, check the endfloat using a dial gauge in contact with the end of the crankshaft. Push the crankshaft fully one way, and then zero the gauge. Push the crankshaft fully the other way, and check the endfloat **(see illustration)**. The result should be compared with the specified limit,

**9.1 Undo the bolts and remove the oil baffle plate from the cylinder block baseplate – 1.4 litre engines**

**9.5 Unscrew the big-end cap bolts from the first connecting rod, and remove the cap**

**9.6 Push the piston/rod assembly up and out of the top of the cylinder bore**

and will give an indication as to the size of the main bearing shell thrust journal width which will be required for reassembly.

**5** If a dial gauge is not available, a feeler gauge can be used to measure crankshaft endfloat. Push the crankshaft fully towards one end of the crankcase, and insert a feeler gauge between the thrust flange of the main bearing shell and the machined surface of the crankshaft web **(see illustration)**. Before measuring, ensure that the crankshaft is fully forced towards one end of the crankcase, to give the widest possible gap at the measuring location. **Note:** *Measure at the bearing with the thrustwasher (see Section 17).*

**6** Working in a diagonal sequence, progressively slacken the outer (M6) bolts securing the cylinder block baseplate to the cylinder block.

**7** When all the outer bolts have been slackened, repeat the procedure on the inner (M8) retaining bolts.

**8** Remove all the bolts and lift the cylinder block baseplate off the cylinder block **(see illustration)**. If the baseplate is initially tight to remove, carefully tap it free using a soft-faced mallet.

**9** As the baseplate is withdrawn check that the lower main bearing shells come away with the baseplate. If they remain on the crankshaft journals, lift them off and refit them to their respective locations in the baseplate.

**10** Lift the crankshaft from the cylinder block and remove the crankshaft oil seal.

**11** Extract the upper bearing shells, and identify them for position if they are to be re-used.

### 1.6 and 1.8 litre engines

**Note:** *New main bearing cap bolts will be required on refitting.*

**12** Working as described in Part B or C of this Chapter, remove the flywheel/driveplate and the oil pump.

**13** Remove the piston and connecting rod assemblies as described in Section 9. If no work is to be done on the pistons and connecting rods, unbolt the caps and push the pistons far enough up the bores that the connecting rods are positioned clear of the crankshaft journals.

**14** Before removing the crankshaft, check the endfloat as described previously in paragraphs 4 and 5.

**15** The main bearing caps should be numbered 1 to 5 from the timing belt end of the engine and all identification numbers should be the right way up when read from the rear of the cylinder block **(see illustration)**. If the bearing caps are not marked, using a hammer and punch or a suitable marker pen, number the caps from 1 to 5 from the timing belt end of the engine and mark each cap to indicate its correct fitted direction to avoid confusion on refitting.

**16** Working in a diagonal sequence, evenly and progressively slacken the ten main bearing cap retaining bolts by half a turn at a

**10.4  Check the crankshaft endfloat using a dial gauge . . .**

**10.8  Lift the cylinder block baseplate off the cylinder block – 1.4 litre engines**

time until all bolts are loose. Remove all the bolts.

**17** Carefully remove each cap from the cylinder block, ensuring that the lower main bearing shell remains in position in the cap.

**18** Carefully lift out the crankshaft, taking care not to displace the upper main bearing shells **(see illustration)**. Remove the oil seal and discard it.

**19** Recover the upper bearing shells from the cylinder block, and tape them to their respective caps for safe-keeping.

 **11  Cylinder block –**
   **cleaning and inspection**

### Cleaning

**1** For complete cleaning, remove all external components (senders, sensors, brackets, oil pipes, coolant pipes, etc) from the cylinder block.

**2** Scrape all traces of gasket and/or sealant from the cylinder block and lower baseplate (where applicable), taking particular care not to damage the cylinder head and sump mating faces.

**3** Remove all oil gallery plugs, where fitted. The plugs are usually very tight – they may have to be drilled out and the holes retapped. Use new plugs when the engine is reassembled.

**4** If the block and baseplate (where applicable) are extremely dirty, they should be steam-cleaned.

**10.5  . . . or a feeler gauge**

**10.15  Main bearing cap identification markings (arrowed) – 1.6 and 1.8 litre engines**

**5** If the components have been steam-cleaned, clean all oil holes and oil galleries one more time on completion. Flush all internal passages with warm water until the water runs clear. Dry the block and, where necessary, the lower casing thoroughly and wipe all machined surfaces with a light oil. If you have access to compressed air, use it to speed-up the drying process, and to blow out all the oil holes and galleries.

⚠️ *Warning: Wear eye protection when using compressed air.*

**6** If the block and baseplate are relatively clean, an adequate cleaning job can be achieved with hot soapy water and a stiff brush. Take plenty of time, and do a thorough job. Regardless of the cleaning method used, be sure to clean all oil holes and galleries very

**10.18  Removing the crankshaft – 1.6 and 1.8 litre engines**

**12.2 Using a feeler blade to remove a piston ring**

thoroughly, dry everything completely, and coat all cast-iron machined surfaces with light oil.

**7** The threaded holes in the cylinder block must be clean, to ensure accurate torque readings when tightening fixings during reassembly. Run the correct-size tap (which can be determined from the size of the relevant bolt) into each of the holes to remove rust, corrosion, thread sealant or other contamination, and to restore damaged threads. If possible, use compressed air to clear the holes of debris produced by this operation. Do not forget to clean the threads of all bolts and nuts which are to be re-used, as well.

**8** Where applicable, apply suitable sealant to the new oil gallery plugs, and insert them into the relevant holes in the cylinder block. Tighten the plugs securely.

**9** If the engine is to be left dismantled for some time, cover the cylinder block with a large plastic bag to keep it clean and prevent corrosion. Where applicable, refit the lower casing and tighten the bolts finger-tight.

*Inspection*

**10** Visually check the block for cracks, rust and corrosion. Look for stripped threads in the threaded holes. It's also a good idea to have the block checked for hidden cracks by an engine reconditioning specialist that has the equipment to do this type of work, especially if the vehicle had a history of overheating or using coolant. If defects are found, have the block repaired, if possible, or renewed.

**13.8 Transfer the crankshaft speed/ position sensor pulse pick-up ring to the new crankshaft**

**11** If in any doubt as to the condition of the cylinder block, have it inspected and measured by an engine reconditioning specialist. If the bores are worn or damaged, they will be able to carry out any necessary reboring (where possible), and supply appropriate oversized pistons, etc.

## 12 Pistons/connecting rods – inspection

**1** Before the inspection process can begin, the piston/connecting rod assemblies must be cleaned, and the original piston rings removed from the pistons. **Note:** *Always use new piston rings when the engine is reassembled.*

**2** Carefully expand the old rings over the top of the pistons. The use of two or three old feeler gauges will be helpful in preventing the rings dropping into empty grooves **(see illustration)**.

**3** Scrape away all traces of carbon from the top of the piston. A hand-held wire brush, or a piece of fine emery cloth, can be used once the majority of the deposits have been scraped away.

**4** Remove the carbon from the ring grooves in the piston, using an old ring. Break the ring in half to do this (be careful not to cut your fingers – piston rings are sharp). Be very careful to remove only the carbon deposits – do not remove any metal, and do not nick or scratch the sides of the ring grooves.

**5** Once the deposits have been removed, clean the piston/connecting rod assembly with paraffin or a suitable solvent, and dry thoroughly. Make sure that the oil return holes in the ring grooves are clear.

**6** If the pistons and cylinder bores are not damaged or worn excessively, and if the cylinder block does not need to be rebored, the original pistons can be refitted. Normal piston wear shows up as even vertical wear on the piston thrust surfaces, and slight looseness of the top ring in its groove. New piston rings should always be used when the engine is reassembled.

**7** Carefully inspect each piston for cracks around the skirt, at the gudgeon pin bosses, and at the piston ring lands (between the ring grooves).

**8** Look for scoring and scuffing on the thrust faces of the piston skirt, holes in the piston crown, and burned areas at the edge of the crown. If the skirt is scored or scuffed, the engine may have been suffering from overheating, and/or abnormal combustion ('pinking') which caused excessively-high operating temperatures. The cooling and lubrication systems should be checked thoroughly. A hole in the piston crown, or burned areas at the edge of the piston crown indicates that abnormal combustion (pre-ignition, 'pinking', knocking or detonation) has been occurring. If any of the above problems exist, the causes must be

investigated and corrected, or the damage will occur again.

**9** Corrosion of the piston, in the form of pitting, indicates that coolant has been leaking into the combustion chamber and/ or the crankcase. Again, the cause must be corrected, or the problem may persist in the rebuilt engine.

**10** If in any doubt as to the condition of the pistons and connecting rods, have them inspected and measured by an engine reconditioning specialist. If new parts are required, they will be able to supply and fit appropriate-sized pistons/rings, and rebore (where possible) or hone the cylinder block.

## 13 Crankshaft – inspection

**1** Clean the crankshaft using paraffin or a suitable solvent, and dry it, preferably with compressed air if available. Be sure to clean the oil holes with a pipe cleaner or similar probe, to ensure that they are not obstructed.

> ⚠️ **Warning: Wear eye protection when using compressed air.**

**2** Check the main and big-end bearing journals for uneven wear, scoring, pitting and cracking.

**3** Big-end bearing wear is accompanied by distinct metallic knocking when the engine is running (particularly noticeable when the engine is pulling from low revs), and some loss of oil pressure.

**4** Main bearing wear is accompanied by severe engine vibration and rumble – getting progressively worse as engine revs increase – and again by loss of oil pressure.

**5** Check the bearing journal for roughness by running a finger lightly over the bearing surface. Any roughness (which will be accompanied by obvious bearing wear) indicates that the crankshaft requires regrinding.

**6** Have the crankshaft journals measured by an engine reconditioning specialist. If the crankshaft is worn or damaged, they may be able to regrind the journals and supply suitable undersize bearing shells. If no undersize shells are available and the crankshaft has worn beyond the specified limits, it will have to be renewed. Consult your Vauxhall/Opel dealer or engine reconditioning specialist for further information on parts availability.

**7** If the crankshaft has been reground, check for burrs around the crankshaft oil holes (the holes are usually chamfered, so burrs should not be a problem unless regrinding has been carried out carelessly). Remove any burrs with a fine file or scraper, and thoroughly clean the oil holes as described previously.

**8** If a new crankshaft is to be fitted, undo the screws securing the crankshaft speed/position sensor pulse pick-up ring to the crankshaft, and transfer the ring to the new crankshaft **(see illustration)**.

## 14 Main and big-end bearings – inspection

1 Even though the main and big-end bearings should be renewed during the engine overhaul, the old bearings should be retained for close examination, as they may reveal valuable information about the condition of the engine.
2 Bearing failure occurs because of lack of lubrication, the presence of dirt or other foreign particles, overloading the engine, or corrosion **(see illustration)**. If a bearing fails, the cause must be found and eliminated before the engine is reassembled, to prevent the failure from happening again.
3 To examine the bearing shells, remove them from the cylinder block, the main bearing caps or cylinder block lower casing, the connecting rods and the big-end bearing caps, and lay them out on a clean surface in the same order as they were fitted to the engine. This will enable any bearing problems to be matched with the corresponding crankshaft journal.
4 Dirt and other foreign particles can enter the engine in a variety of ways. Contamination may be left in the engine during assembly, or it may pass through filters or the crankcase ventilation system. Normal engine wear produces small particles of metal, which can eventually cause problems. If particles find their way into the lubrication system, it is likely that they will eventually be carried to the bearings. Whatever the source, these foreign particles often end up embedded in the soft bearing material, and are easily recognised. Large particles will not embed in the bearing, and will score or gouge the bearing and journal. To prevent possible contamination, clean all parts thoroughly, and keep everything spotlessly-clean during engine assembly. Once the engine has been installed in the vehicle, ensure that engine oil and filter changes are carried out at the recommended intervals.
5 Lack of lubrication (or lubrication breakdown) has a number of interrelated causes. Excessive heat (which thins the oil), overloading (which squeezes the oil from the bearing face), and oil leakage (from excessive bearing clearances, worn oil pump or high engine speeds) all contribute to lubrication breakdown. Blocked oil passages, which may be the result of misaligned oil holes in a bearing shell, will also starve a bearing of oil and destroy it. When lack of lubrication is the cause of bearing failure, the bearing material is wiped or extruded from the steel backing of the bearing. Temperatures may increase to the point where the steel backing turns blue from overheating.
6 Driving habits can have a definite effect on bearing life. Full-throttle, low-speed operation (labouring the engine) puts very high loads on bearings, which tends to squeeze out the oil film. These loads cause the bearings to flex, which produces fine cracks in the bearing face (fatigue failure). Eventually the bearing

material will loosen in places, and tear away from the steel backing. Regular short journeys can lead to corrosion of bearings, because insufficient engine heat is produced to drive off the condensed water and corrosive gases which form inside the engine. These products collect in the engine oil, forming acid and sludge. As the oil is carried to the bearings, the acid attacks and corrodes the bearing material.
7 Incorrect bearing installation during engine assembly will also lead to bearing failure. Tight-fitting bearings leave insufficient bearing lubrication clearance, and will result in oil starvation. Dirt or foreign particles trapped behind a bearing shell results in high spots on the bearing which can lead to failure.
8 *Do not* touch any shell's bearing surface with your fingers during reassembly; there is a risk of scratching the delicate surface, or of depositing particles of dirt on it.
9 As mentioned at the beginning of this Section, the bearing shells should be renewed as a matter of course during engine overhaul; to do otherwise is false economy.

**14.2 Typical bearing failures**

## 15 Engine overhaul – reassembly sequence

1 Before reassembly begins, ensure that all necessary new parts have been obtained (particularly gaskets, and various bolts which must be renewed), and that all the tools required are available. Read through the entire procedure to familiarise yourself with the work involved, and to ensure that all items necessary for reassembly of the engine are to hand. In addition to all normal tools and materials, a thread-locking compound will be required. A tube of suitable sealant will be required to seal certain joint faces which are not fitted with gaskets.
2 In order to save time and avoid problems, engine reassembly can be carried out in the following order:
 a) *Piston rings (see Section 16).*
 b) *Crankshaft (see Section 17).*
 c) *Piston/connecting rod assemblies (see Section 18).*
 d) *Timing chain and sprockets (see Chapter 2A).*
 e) *Oil pump (see Chapter 2A, 2B or 2C).*
 f) *Sump (see Chapter 2A, 2B or 2C).*
 g) *Flywheel/driveplate (see Chapter 2A, 2B or 2C).*
 h) *Cylinder head (see Chapter 2A, 2B or 2C).*
 i) *Coolant pump (see Chapter 3).*
 j) *Timing belt, sprockets and tensioner (see Chapter 2B or 2C).*
 k) *Inlet and exhaust manifolds (see Chapter 4A).*
3 At this stage, all engine components should be absolutely clean and dry, with all faults repaired. The components should be laid out (or in individual containers) on a completely clean work surface.

## 16 Piston rings – refitting

1 Before refitting the new piston rings, the ring end gaps must be checked as follows.
2 Lay out the piston/connecting rod assemblies and the new piston ring sets, so that the ring sets will be matched with the same piston and cylinder during the end gap measurement and subsequent engine reassembly.
3 Insert the top ring into the first cylinder, and push it down the bore slightly using the top of the piston. This will ensure that the ring remains square with the cylinder walls. Push the ring down into the bore until it is positioned 15 to 20 mm down from the top edge of the bore, then withdraw the piston.
4 Measure the end gap using feeler gauges, and compare the measurements with the figures given in the Specifications **(see illustration)**.
5 If the gap is too small (unlikely if genuine Vauxhall/Opel parts are used), it must be

**16.4 Measuring a piston ring end gap using a feeler gauge**

**16.9 Fitting the oil control spreader ring**

enlarged or the ring ends may contact each other during engine operation, causing serious damage. Ideally, new piston rings providing the correct end gap should be fitted, but as a last resort, the end gap can be increased by filing the ring ends very carefully with a fine file. Mount the file in a vice equipped with soft jaws, slip the ring over the file with the ends contacting the file face, and slowly move the ring to remove material from the ends – take care, as piston rings are sharp, and are easily broken.

6 With new piston rings, it is unlikely that the end gap will be too large. If they are too large, check that you have the correct rings for your engine and for the particular cylinder bore size.

7 Repeat the checking procedure for each ring in the first cylinder, and then for the rings in the remaining cylinders. Remember to keep rings, pistons and cylinders matched up.

**17.6 Fitting a main bearing shell to the cylinder block**

**17.10 Lubricate the bearing shells in the baseplate – 1.4 litre engines**

8 Once the ring end gaps have been checked and if necessary corrected, the rings can be fitted to the pistons.

9 The oil control ring (lowest one on the piston) is composed of three sections, and should be installed first. Fit the lower steel ring, then the spreader ring, followed by the upper steel ring **(see illustration)**.

10 With the oil control ring components installed, the second (middle) ring can be fitted. It is usually stamped with a mark (TOP) which must face up, towards the top of the piston. **Note:** *Always follow the instructions supplied with the new piston ring sets – different manufacturers may specify different procedures. Do not mix up the top and middle rings, as they have different cross-sections.* Using two or three old feeler blades, as for removal of the old rings, carefully slip the ring into place in the middle groove.

11 Fit the top ring in the same manner, ensuring that, where applicable, the mark on the ring is facing up. If a stepped ring is being fitted, fit the ring with the smaller diameter of the step uppermost.

12 Repeat the procedure for the remaining pistons and rings.

## 17 Crankshaft – refitting

**Note:** *It is recommended that new main bearing shells are fitted regardless of the condition of the original ones.*

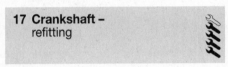

**17.7 Liberally lubricate each bearing shell in the cylinder block then lower the crankshaft into position – 1.4 litre engines**

**17.11 Apply a 2 mm diameter bead of silicone sealant to the outside of the groove in the baseplate – 1.4 litre engines**

1 Refitting the crankshaft is the first step in the engine reassembly procedure. It is assumed at this point that the cylinder block, baseplate (where applicable) and crankshaft have been cleaned, inspected and repaired or reconditioned as necessary.

2 Position the cylinder block with the sump/baseplate mating face uppermost.

3 Clean the bearing shells and the bearing recesses in both the cylinder block and the baseplate/caps. If new shells are being fitted, ensure that all traces of the protective grease are cleaned off using paraffin. Wipe the shells dry with a clean lint-free cloth.

4 Note that the crankshaft endfloat is controlled by thrustwashers located on one of the main bearing shells. The thrustwashers may be separate or incorporated into, or attached to, the bearing shells themselves.

5 If the original bearing shells are being re-used, they must be refitted to their original locations in the block and baseplate, or caps.

6 Fit the upper main bearing shells in place in the cylinder block, ensuring that the tab on each shell engages in the notch in the cylinder block **(see illustration)**. Where separate thrustwashers are fitted, use a little grease to stick them to each side of their respective bearing upper location; ensure that the oilway grooves on each thrustwasher face outwards (away from the block).

### 1.4 litre engines

**Note:** *New cylinder block baseplate bolts must be used when refitting the crankshaft. A tube of sealant (Loctite 5900 or equivalent) will be required when fitting the baseplate to the cylinder block.*

7 Liberally lubricate each bearing shell in the cylinder block, and lower the crankshaft into position **(see illustration)**.

8 If necessary, seat the crankshaft using light taps from a soft-faced mallet on the crankshaft balance webs.

9 Fit the bearing shells in the baseplate.

10 Lubricate the crankshaft journals, and the bearing shells in the baseplate **(see illustration)**.

11 Ensure that the cylinder block and baseplate mating surfaces are clean and dry, then apply a 2 mm diameter bead of sealant to the outside of the groove (not in the groove itself) in the baseplate **(see illustration)**.

12 Locate the baseplate over the crankshaft and onto the cylinder block.

13 Fit the new baseplate retaining bolts, then working progressively and in a diagonal sequence, tighten the inner (M8) bolts to the specified torque, then through the specified angle, in the two stages given in the Specifications. Now similarly tighten the outer (M6) retaining bolts **(see illustrations)**.

14 Check that the crankshaft is free to rotate smoothly; if excessive pressure is required to turn the crankshaft, investigate the cause before proceeding further.

15 Check the crankshaft endfloat with reference to Section 10.

**17.13a  Fit the new baseplate inner bolts . . .**

**17.13b  . . . and outer bolts – 1.4 litre engines**

**17.13c  Tighten the inner bolts to the specified Stage 1 torque setting using a torque wrench . . .**

**17.13d  . . . then through the specified Stage 2 angle using an angle tightening gauge – 1.4 litre engines**

**17.13e  Similarly tighten the outer bolts to the specified torque . . .**

**17.13f  . . . and through the specified angle – 1.4 litre engines**

16  Refit the pistons and connecting rods as described in Section 18.

17  Referring to Part A of this Chapter, fit a new left-hand crankshaft oil seal, then refit the flywheel, timing chain and cover components, sump and cylinder head.

### 1.6 and 1.8 litre engines

**Note:** *New main bearing cap bolts must be used when refitting the crankshaft. A tube of suitable sealant will be required when fitting the main bearing cap to the cylinder block.*

18  Liberally lubricate each bearing shell in the cylinder block, and lower the crankshaft into position **(see illustration)**.

19  If necessary, seat the crankshaft using light taps from a soft-faced mallet on the crankshaft balance webs.

20  Fit the bearing shells into the bearing caps.

21  Lubricate the bearing shells in the bearing caps, and the crankshaft journals, then fit Nos 2, 3 and 4 bearing caps, and tighten the new bolts as far as possible by hand **(see illustration)**.

22  Ensure the No 5 bearing cap is clean and dry then fill the groove on each side of the cap with sealing compound (Vauxhall/Opel recommend the use of sealant, part No 90485251, available from your dealer) **(see illustration)**. Fit the bearing cap to the engine, ensuring it is fitted the correct way around, and tighten the new bolts as far as possible by hand.

23  Working in a diagonal sequence from the centre outwards, tighten the main bearing cap bolts to the specified Stage 1 torque setting **(see illustration)**.

24  Once all bolts are tightened to the specified Stage 1 torque, go around again and tighten all bolts through the specified Stage 2 angle then go around for once more and tighten all bolts through the specified Stage 3 angle. It is recommended that an

angle-measuring gauge is used during the final stages of the tightening, to ensure accuracy **(see illustration)**. If a gauge is not available, use white paint to make alignment marks between the bolt head and cap prior to tightening; the marks can then be used to

**17.18  Lubricate the upper bearing shells with clean engine oil then fit the crankshaft – 1.6 and 1.8 litre engines**

**17.21  Lubricate the crankshaft journals then refit bearing caps Nos 1 to 4 – 1.6 and 1.8 litre engines**

**17.22  Fill the side grooves of the No 5 bearing cap with sealant prior to refitting it to the engine – 1.6 and 1.8 litre engines**

**17.23  Tighten the bolts to the specified Stage 1 torque setting . . .**

**17.24 ... and then through the specified Stages 2 and 3 angles – 1.6 and 1.8 litre engines**

**18.2 Fit the bearing shells making sure their tabs are correctly located in the connecting rod/cap groove (arrowed)**

**18.3 Lubricate the piston rings with clean engine oil**

check that the bolt has been rotated through the correct angle.

**25** Once all the bolts have been tightened, inject more sealant down the grooves in the rear main bearing cap until sealant is seen to be escaping through the joints. Once you are sure the cap grooves are full of sealant, wipe off all excess sealant using a clean cloth.

**26** Check that the crankshaft is free to rotate smoothly; if excessive pressure is required to turn the crankshaft, investigate the cause before proceeding further.

**18.4 Piston ring end gap positions – petrol engines**

I  *Top and second compression rings*
II  *Oil control ring side rails*

**27** Check the crankshaft endfloat with reference to Section 10.

**28** Refit the piston connecting rod assemblies to the crankshaft as described in Section 18.

**29** Referring to Part B or C of this Chapter, fit a new left-hand crankshaft oil seal, then refit the oil pump, sump, flywheel/driveplate, cylinder head, timing belt sprocket(s) and fit a new timing belt.

## 18 Pistons/connecting rods – refitting

**Note:** *It is recommended that new big-end bearing shells are fitted regardless of the condition of the original ones. New big-end bearing cap bolts will also be required.*

**1** Clean the backs of the big-end bearing shells and the recesses in the connecting rods and big-end caps. If new shells are being fitted, ensure that all traces of the protective grease are cleaned off using paraffin. Wipe the shells, caps and connecting rods dry with a lint-free cloth.

**2** Press the bearing shells into their locations, ensuring that the tab on each shell engages in the notch in the connecting rod and cap **(see illustration)**. If there is no tab on the bearing shell (and no notch in the rod or cap) position the shell equidistant from each side of the rod and cap. If the original bearing shells are being used ensure they are refitted in their original locations.

**3** Lubricate the bores, the pistons and piston rings then lay out each piston/connecting rod assembly in its respective position **(see illustration)**.

**4** Lubricate No 1 piston and piston rings, and check that the ring gaps are correctly positioned. The gaps in the upper and lower steel rings of the oil control ring should be offset by 25 to 50 mm to the right and left of the spreader ring gap. The two upper compression ring gaps should be offset by 180° to each other **(see illustration)**.

**5** Liberally lubricate the cylinder bore with clean engine oil.

**6** Fit a ring compressor to No 1 piston, then insert the piston and connecting rod into the cylinder bore so that the base of the compressor stands on the block. With the crankshaft big-end bearing journal positioned at its lowest point, tap the piston carefully into the cylinder bore with the wooden handle of a hammer, and at the same time guide the connecting rod onto the bearing journal. Note that the arrow or notch on the piston crown must point towards the timing chain/belt end of the engine **(see illustrations)**.

**7** Liberally lubricate the bearing journals and bearing shells, and fit the bearing cap in its original location.

**8** Screw in the new bearing cap retaining bolts then tighten the bolts to the Stage 1 torque setting, then tighten all bolts through the specified angles.

**9** Refit the remaining three piston and connecting rod assemblies in the same way.

**18.6a Ensure the piston ring end gaps are correctly spaced then fit the ring compressor**

**18.6b Ensuring the arrow on the piston crown (circled) is pointing towards the timing belt/chain end of the engine**

**18.6c Tap the piston gently into the bore using handle of a hammer**

**10** Rotate the crankshaft, and check that it turns freely, with no signs of binding or tight spots.

**11** Refit the oil pump pick-up/strainer, sump and the cylinder head as described in Part A, B or C (as applicable) of this Chapter.

## 19 Engine –
### initial start-up after overhaul

**1** With the engine refitted in the vehicle, double-check the engine oil and coolant levels. Make a final check that everything has been reconnected, and that there are no tools or rags left in the engine compartment.

**2** Start the engine, noting that this may take a little longer than usual. Make sure that the oil pressure warning light goes out.

**3** While the engine is idling, check for fuel, water and oil leaks. Don't be alarmed if there are some odd smells and smoke from parts getting hot and burning off oil deposits.

**4** Assuming all is well, run the engine until it reaches normal operating temperature, then switch off the engine.

**5** After a few minutes, recheck the oil and coolant levels as described in *Weekly checks*, and top-up as necessary.

**6** Note that there is no need to retighten the cylinder head bolts once the engine has first run after reassembly.

**7** If new pistons, rings or crankshaft bearings have been fitted, the engine must be treated as new, and run-in for the first 600 miles. *Do not* operate the engine at full-throttle, or allow it to labour at low engine speeds in any gear. It is recommended that the oil and filter be changed at the end of this period.

**Notes**

# Chapter 3
# Cooling, heating and air conditioning systems

## Contents

## Degrees of difficulty

| **Easy,** suitable for novice with little experience  | **Fairly easy,** suitable for beginner with some experience | **Fairly difficult,** suitable for competent DIY mechanic | **Difficult,** suitable for experienced DIY mechanic | **Very difficult,** suitable for expert DIY or professional  |
| --- | --- | --- | --- | --- |

## Specifications

### Thermostat

Opening temperature:
| | |
| --- | --- |
| 1.4 litre engines . . . . . . . . . . . . . . . . . . . . . . . . . . . . . . . . . . . . . . | 92°C |
| 1.6 and 1.8 litre engines: | |
|    With wax thermostat. . . . . . . . . . . . . . . . . . . . . . . . . . . . . . . . . | 90°C |
|    With electric thermostat . . . . . . . . . . . . . . . . . . . . . . . . . . . . . . | 105°C |

### Air conditioning compressor

| | |
| --- | --- |
| Lubricant capacity . . . . . . . . . . . . . . . . . . . . . . . . . . . . . . . . . . . . . | 150 cc |
| Lubricant type (synthetic PAG fluid) . . . . . . . . . . . . . . . . . . . . . . . . | Vauxhall part number 90 509 933/19 49 873 |

### Torque wrench settings

| | Nm | lbf ft |
| --- | --- | --- |
| Air conditioning compressor mounting bolts . . . . . . . . . . . . . . . . . . . . | 25 | 18 |
| Air conditioning refrigerant pipe block connections. . . . . . . . . . . . . . . . | 20 | 15 |
| Coolant pump pulley bolts. . . . . . . . . . . . . . . . . . . . . . . . . . . . . . . . . . | 20 | 15 |
| Coolant pump retaining bolts. . . . . . . . . . . . . . . . . . . . . . . . . . . . . . . . | 8 | 6 |
| Coolant temperature sensor. . . . . . . . . . . . . . . . . . . . . . . . . . . . . . . . . | 20 | 15 |
| Radiator mounting brackets to subframe. . . . . . . . . . . . . . . . . . . . . . . . | 15 | 11 |
| Thermostat housing/cover: | | |
|   1.4 and 1.6 litre engines . . . . . . . . . . . . . . . . . . . . . . . . . . . . . . . . | 8 | 6 |
|   1.8 litre engines: | | |
|     Z18XE engines . . . . . . . . . . . . . . . . . . . . . . . . . . . . . . . . . . . . . . | 20 | 15 |
|     Z18XER engines . . . . . . . . . . . . . . . . . . . . . . . . . . . . . . . . . . . . . | 8 | 6 |

## 1  General information and precautions

### General information

The cooling system is of pressurised type, comprising a coolant pump, a crossflow radiator, electric cooling fan, and thermostat.

On all except 1.8 litre Z18XE engines, the coolant pump is driven by the auxiliary drivebelt. On 1.8 litre Z18XE engines, the coolant pump is driven by the timing belt.

The system functions as follows. Cold coolant from the radiator passes through the bottom hose to the coolant pump, where it is pumped around the cylinder block, head passages and heater matrix. After cooling the cylinder bores, combustion surfaces and valve seats, the coolant reaches the underside of the thermostat, which is initially closed. The coolant passes through the heater, and is returned to the coolant pump.

When the engine is cold, the coolant circulates only through the cylinder block, cylinder head and heater. When the coolant reaches a predetermined temperature, the thermostat opens and the coolant also passes through to the radiator. As the coolant circulates through the radiator, it is cooled by the inrush of air when the car is in forward motion. Airflow is supplemented by the action of the electric cooling fan when necessary. Once the coolant has passed through the radiator, and has cooled, the cycle is repeated.

On 1.6 litre and 1.8 litre Z18XER engines, an electrically assisted thermostat is fitted. Engine coolant temperature is monitored by the engine management system electronic control unit, via the coolant temperature sensor. In conjunction with information received from various other engine sensors, the thermostat opening temperature can controlled according to engine speed and load. During normal engine operation the thermostat operates conventionally. Under conditions of high engine speed and load, an electric heating element within the thermostat is energised, to cause the thermostat to open at a lower temperature (typically 90°).

The electric cooling fan, mounted on the rear of the radiator, is controlled by the engine management system electronic control unit, in conjunction with a cooling fan module. At a predetermined coolant temperature, the fan is actuated.

An expansion tank is fitted to the left-hand side of the engine compartment to accommodate expansion of the coolant when hot. The expansion tank is connected to the top of the radiator and to the thermostat housing.

### Precautions

 *Warning: Do not attempt to remove the expansion tank filler cap, or disturb any part of the* cooling system, while the engine is hot; there is a high risk of scalding. If the cap must be removed before the engine and radiator have fully cooled (even though this is not recommended) the pressure in the cooling system must first be relieved. Cover the cap with a thick layer of cloth, to avoid scalding, and slowly unscrew the filler cap until a hissing sound can be heard. When the hissing has stopped, indicating that the pressure has reduced, slowly unscrew the filler cap until it can be removed; if more hissing sounds are heard, wait until they have stopped before unscrewing the cap completely. At all times, keep well away from the filler cap opening.

 *Warning: Do not allow antifreeze to come into contact with the skin, or with the painted surfaces of the vehicle. Rinse off spills immediately, with plenty of water. Never leave antifreeze lying around in an open container, or in a puddle on the driveway or garage floor. Children and pets are attracted by its sweet smell, but antifreeze can be fatal if ingested.*

 *Warning: If the engine is hot, the electric cooling fan may start rotating even if the engine is not running; be careful to keep hands, hair and loose clothing well clear when working in the engine compartment.*

*Warning: Refer to Section 10 for precautions to be observed when working on models equipped with air conditioning.*

## 2  Cooling system hoses – disconnection and renewal

*Note: Refer to the warnings given in Section 1 of this Chapter before proceeding. Do not attempt to disconnect any hose while the system is still hot.*

**1** If the checks described in Chapter 1 reveal a faulty hose, it must be renewed as follows.

**2** First drain the cooling system (see Chapter 1). If the coolant is not due for renewal, it may be re-used if it is collected in a clean container.

**3** Before disconnecting a hose, first note its routing in the engine compartment, and

**3.6 Disconnect the cooling fan wiring harness connector from the base of the fan housing**

whether it is secured by any additional retaining clips or cable ties. Use a pair of pliers to release the clamp-type clips, or a screwdriver to slacken the screw-type clips, then move the clips along the hose, clear of the relevant inlet/outlet union. Carefully work the hose free.

**4** Note that the radiator inlet and outlet unions are fragile; do not use excessive force when attempting to remove the hoses. If a hose proves to be difficult to remove, try to release it by rotating the hose ends before attempting to free it.

**5** When fitting a hose, first slide the clips onto the hose, then work the hose into position. If clamp-type clips were originally fitted, it is a good idea to use screw-type clips when refitting the hose. If the hose is stiff, use a little soapy water (washing-up liquid is ideal) as a lubricant, or soften the hose by soaking it in hot water.

**6** Work the hose into position, checking that it is correctly routed and secured. Slide each clip along the hose until it passes over the flared end of the relevant inlet/outlet union, before tightening the clips securely.

**7** Refill the cooling system with reference to Chapter 1.

**8** Check thoroughly for leaks as soon as possible after disturbing any part of the cooling system.

## 3  Radiator – removal, inspection and refitting

### Removal

**1** Remove the battery and battery tray as described in Chapter 5A.

**2** Where fitted, remove the plastic cover from the top of the engine.

**3** Apply the handbrake, then jack up the front of the vehicle and support it on axle stands (see *Jacking and vehicle support*).

**4** Remove the front bumper as described in Chapter 11.

**5** Drain the cooling system as described in Chapter 1.

**6** Disconnect the cooling fan wiring harness connector from the base of the fan housing **(see illustration)**. Free the wiring harness from the cable ties.

**7** Where fitted, disconnect the wiring connector at the second coolant temperature sensor located at the base of the radiator right-hand tank.

**8** On models with air conditioning, open the retaining clip and detach the air conditioning refrigerant pipe from the right-hand side of the radiator. Release the air conditioning compressor wiring harness from the retaining clip.

**9** Release the clamp and disconnect the bottom hose from the radiator.

**10** Retain the radiator in position by inserting a drill bit or similar, through the holes provided

3.10 Insert a drill bit (arrowed) or similar, through the holes provided on the radiator mounting brackets (shown with radiator removed)

3.11a Undo the two bolts (arrowed) each side . . .

on each of the radiator upper mounting brackets **(see illustration)**.

**11** Undo the two bolts each side securing the radiator left-hand and right-hand mounting brackets to the subframe. Remove the brackets, noting their orientation **(see illustrations)**.

**12** Release the clamps and disconnect the top hose and expansion tank hose from the right-hand side of the radiator.

**13** Undo the bolt each side securing the fan housing to the top of the radiator **(see illustrations)**.

**14** On models with automatic transmission, detach the protective ring (where fitted) over the fluid cooler pipe unions at the radiator. Using a small screwdriver, release the quick-release fitting retaining lugs and disconnect the fitting from the radiator. Suitably cover the open unions after disconnection.

**15** On models with air conditioning, secure the condenser to the bonnet crossmember with cable ties. Undo the upper and lower bolts securing the right-hand side of the condenser to the radiator **(see illustrations)**. Similarly undo the upper bolt and two lower bolts securing the condenser to the radiator.

**16** Remove the drill bits, or similar tools used to retain the radiator in position and carefully lower the radiator out from under the car.

## Inspection

**17** If the radiator has been removed due to suspected blockage, reverse-flush it as described in Chapter 1.

**18** Clean dirt and debris from the radiator fins, using an airline (in which case, wear eye protection) or a soft brush.

***Caution: Be careful, as the fins are easily damaged, and are sharp.***

**19** If necessary, a radiator specialist can perform a 'flow test' on the radiator, to establish whether an internal blockage exists.

**20** A leaking radiator must be referred to a specialist for permanent repair. Do not attempt to weld or solder a leaking radiator.

**21** In an emergency, minor leaks from the radiator can be cured by using a suitable radiator sealant (in accordance with its manufacturer's instructions) with the radiator fitted in the vehicle.

**22** Inspect the radiator mounting rubbers, and renew them if necessary.

## Refitting

**23** Refitting is a reversal of removal, bearing in mind the following points.

a) *Ensure that all hoses are correctly reconnected, and their retaining clips securely tightened.*

b) *On completion, refill the cooling system as described in Chapter 1.*

c) *On models with automatic transmission,*

3.11b . . . and remove the radiator mounting brackets, noting their orientation

3.13a Undo the fan housing right-hand mounting bolt (arrowed) . . .

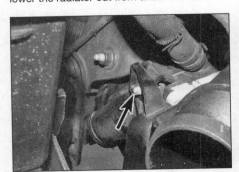

3.13b . . . and left-hand mounting bolt (arrowed)

3.15a Condenser right-hand upper retaining bolt (arrowed) . . .

3.15b . . . and right-hand lower retaining bolt (arrowed)

**4.2 Release the clip (arrowed) and disconnect the hose from the thermostat housing cover – 1.4 litre engines**

**4.3 Remove the thermostat housing cover from the coolant pump – 1.4 litre engines**

check and if necessary top-up the automatic transmission fluid level with reference to the 'Transmission fluid – draining and refilling' procedures contained in Chapter 7B.

## 4 Thermostat – removal and refitting

### Removal

#### 1.4 litre engines

**1** Drain the cooling system (see Chapter 1).
**2** Slacken the retaining clip, and disconnect the coolant hose from the thermostat housing cover **(see illustration)**.
**3** Slacken and remove the three retaining bolts, and remove the thermostat housing cover **(see illustration)**. Note that the thermostat is an integral part of the housing cover, and cannot be renewed separately.
**4** Remove the sealing ring from the housing cover and discard it; a new one should be used on refitting **(see illustration)**. Thoroughly clean the housing contact surfaces.

#### 1.6 litre engines

**5** Drain the cooling system (see Chapter 1).

**4.4 Remove the sealing ring from the thermostat cover – 1.4 litre engines**

**6** Loosen the clip and disconnect the radiator hose from the thermostat housing cover.
**7** Undo the three bolts and free the heat shield from the exhaust manifold.
**8** Disconnect the thermostat wiring connector.
**9** Unscrew the four bolts and remove the thermostat cover from the housing. Note that the thermostat is an integral part of the housing cover, and cannot be renewed separately.
**10** Remove the sealing ring from the housing cover and discard it; a new one should be used on refitting. Thoroughly clean the housing contact surfaces.

#### 1.8 litre Z18XE engines

**11** Drain the cooling system (see Chapter 1).
**12** Loosen the clips and disconnect the radiator hose and throttle housing coolant hose from the thermostat housing cover.
**13** Disconnect the wiring connector from the coolant temperature sensor on the housing.
**14** Unbolt and remove the housing cover from the cylinder head, then remove the gasket and discard it; a new one should be used on refitting. Note that the thermostat is an integral part of the housing cover, and cannot be renewed separately. Thoroughly clean the housing contact surfaces.

#### 1.8 litre Z18XER engines

**15** Drain the cooling system (see Chapter 1).

**5.6 Manoeuvre the fan housing assembly up and out of the engine compartment**

**16** Undo the retaining nut and detach the wiring harness bracket from the thermostat housing.
**17** Disconnect the thermostat wiring connector.
**18** Loosen the clips and disconnect the radiator hose from the thermostat housing.
**19** Unscrew the four bolts and remove the thermostat cover from the housing. Note that the thermostat is an integral part of the housing cover, and cannot be renewed separately.
**20** Remove the sealing ring from the housing cover and discard it; a new one should be used on refitting. Thoroughly clean the housing contact surfaces.

### Refitting

**21** Refitting is a reversal of removal, but fit a new gasket/seal and tighten the retaining bolts to the specified torque. Refill the cooling system as described in Chapter 1.

## 5 Electric cooling fan – removal and refitting

⚠ *Warning: If the engine is hot, the cooling fan may start up at any time. Take extra precautions when working in the vicinity of the fan.*

### Removal

**1** Where fitted, remove the plastic cover from the top of the engine.
**2** Unclip the radiator top hose and the coolant hoses(s) from the fan housing.
**3** Disconnect the cooling fan wiring harness connector from the base of the fan housing **(see illustration 3.6)**. Free the wiring harness from the cable ties.
**4** Detach the air cleaner intake from the duct on the bonnet crossmember. Undo the two retaining bolts, slide the intake duct sideways and remove it from the crossmember.
**5** Undo the bolt each side securing the

**5.7  Undo the three bolts (arrowed) and lift off the fan**

**5.8a  Undo the bolt (arrowed) securing the fan motor resistor to the housing . . .**

**5.8b  . . . then undo the three bolts (arrowed) and remove the motor from the housing**

fan housing to the top of the radiator (**see illustrations 3.11a and 3.11b**).

6  Lift the fan housing from the lower guides on the radiator and manoeuvre the assembly up and out of the engine compartment (**see illustration**).

7  To remove the fan motor, undo the three bolts and lift off the fan (**see illustration**).

8  Undo the bolt securing the fan motor resistor to the housing, then undo the three bolts and remove the motor from the housing (**see illustrations**).

### Refitting

9  Refitting is a reversal of removal.

### 6  Coolant temperature sensor – testing, removal and refitting

### Testing

1  Testing of the coolant temperature sensor must be entrusted to a Vauxhall/Opel dealer, who will have the necessary specialist diagnostic equipment.

### Removal

2  Partially drain the cooling system with reference to Chapter 1. Alternatively, it is possible to change the sensor quickly with minimal loss of coolant by first releasing any pressure from the cooling system. With the engine cold, temporarily remove the expansion tank cap.

3  Where fitted, remove the plastic cover over the top of the engine.

#### 1.4 litre engines

4  The coolant temperature sensor is located at the top of the coolant pump housing (**see illustration**).

5  Disconnect the wiring from the temperature sensor, then unscrew and remove it from the coolant pump. If the cooling system has not been drained, either insert the new sensor or fit a blanking plug to prevent further loss of coolant.

#### 1.6 litre engines

6  The coolant temperature sensor is located in the thermostat housing at the left-hand end of the cylinder head.

7  Remove the battery and battery tray as described in Chapter 5A.

8  Disconnect the wiring from the temperature sensor, then unscrew and remove it from the thermostat housing. If the cooling system has not been drained, either insert the new sensor or fit a blanking plug to prevent further loss of coolant.

#### 1.8 litre Z18XE engines

9  Remove the thermostat as described in Section 4.

10  Unscrew the sensor and remove it from the thermostat housing.

#### 1.8 litre Z18XER engines

11  The coolant temperature sensor is located in the thermostat housing at the left-hand end of the cylinder head.

12  Disconnect the wiring from the temperature sensor, then unlock the retaining clamp and remove it from the thermostat housing (**see illustration**). If the cooling system has not

been drained, either insert the new sensor or fit a blanking plug to prevent further loss of coolant.

### Refitting

13  Fit the new sensor using a reversal of the removal procedure and using a new seal (where applicable). Tighten the sensor to the specified torque and refill the cooling system with reference to Chapter 1.

### 7  Coolant pump – removal and refitting

### Removal

#### 1.4 litre engines

1  Disconnect the battery negative terminal (refer to *Disconnecting the battery* in the Reference Chapter).

2  Remove the air cleaner assembly and air intake ducts as described in Chapter 4A.

3  Slacken the three coolant pump pulley retaining bolts (**see illustration**).

4  Remove the auxiliary drivebelt as described in Chapter 1.

5  Drain the cooling system as described in Chapter 1.

6  Support the engine and remove the right-hand engine mounting as described in Chapter 2A.

7  Unscrew the previously-slackened coolant pump pulley bolts and withdraw the pulley from the pump.

**6.4  Coolant temperature sensor location (arrowed) – 1.4 litre engines**

**6.12  Coolant temperature sensor location (arrowed) – 1.8 litre Z18XER engines**

**7.3  Slacken the three coolant pump pulley retaining bolts (arrowed) – 1.4 litre engines**

**7.9a Release the clips (arrowed) and disconnect the hoses from the front . . .**

**8** Disconnect the coolant temperature sensor wiring connector.

**9** Release the retaining clips and disconnect the hoses from the coolant pump and thermostat housing **(see illustrations)**.

**10** Unscrew the coolant pump retaining bolts, noting the locations of the three short bolts **(see illustration)**. The short bolts secure the pump to the timing cover, and the long bolts secure the pump and the timing cover to the cylinder block and cylinder head.

**11** Withdraw the coolant pump from the timing cover, noting that it may be necessary to tap the pump lightly with a soft-faced hammer to free it from the locating dowels. **Note:** *Coolant which is trapped in the cylinder block will leak out when the pump is removed.*

**12** Recover the pump sealing ring/gasket, and discard it; a new one must be used on refitting **(see illustration)**.

**13** Note that it is not possible to overhaul the pump. If it is faulty, the unit must be renewed complete.

**14** If the pump is being renewed, remove the thermostat (referring to the procedure in Section 4) and temperature sensor then transfer them to the new pump.

### 1.6 litre engines

**15** Disconnect the battery negative terminal (refer to *Disconnecting the battery* in the Reference Chapter).

**16** Remove the air cleaner assembly and air intake ducts as described in Chapter 4A.

**17** Slacken the three coolant pump pulley retaining bolts.

**7.10 Coolant pump short retaining bolt locations (arrowed) – 1.4 litre engine shown with timing cover removed**

**7.9b . . . and rear (arrowed) of the coolant pump housing – 1.4 litre engines**

**18** Remove the auxiliary drivebelt as described in Chapter 1.

**19** Drain the cooling system as described in Chapter 1.

**20** Unscrew the previously-slackened coolant pump pulley retaining bolts and remove the pulley from the pump flange.

**21** Undo the five retaining bolts and remove the pump from the oil pump housing.

**22** Note that it is not possible to overhaul the pump. If it is faulty, the unit must be renewed complete.

### 1.8 litre Z18XE engines

**23** Disconnect the battery negative terminal (refer to *Disconnecting the battery* in the Reference Chapter).

**24** Remove the plastic cover from the top of the engine.

**25** Drain the cooling system as described in Chapter 1.

**26** Remove the timing belt and timing belt rear cover as described in Chapter 2C. **Note:** *The timing belt must not come into contact with coolant.*

**27** Unscrew and remove the three coolant pump securing bolts **(see illustration)**.

**28** Withdraw the coolant pump from the cylinder block, noting that it may be necessary to tap the pump lightly with a soft-faced mallet to free it from the cylinder block.

**29** Recover the pump sealing ring, and discard it; a new one must be used on refitting.

**30** Note that it is not possible to overhaul the pump. If it is faulty, the unit must be renewed complete.

**7.12 Remove the sealing ring or gasket from the timing cover – 1.4 litre engine shown with timing cover removed**

### 1.8 litre Z18XER engines

**31** Disconnect the battery negative terminal (refer to *Disconnecting the battery* in the Reference Chapter).

**32** Remove the air cleaner assembly and air intake ducts as described in Chapter 4A.

**33** Slacken the three coolant pump pulley retaining bolts.

**34** Remove the auxiliary drivebelt as described in Chapter 1.

**35** Drain the cooling system as described in Chapter 1.

**36** Unscrew the previously-slackened coolant pump pulley retaining bolts and remove the pulley from the pump flange.

**37** Undo the five retaining bolts and remove the pump from the oil pump housing.

**38** Note that it is not possible to overhaul the pump. If it is faulty, the unit must be renewed complete.

### Refitting

**39** Refitting is a reversal of the removal procedure, bearing in mind the following points:

a) Ensure that the pump and cylinder block mating surfaces are clean and dry, and fit a new sealing ring/gasket to the pump.

b) On 1.8 litre Z18XE engines, ensure that the lug on the oil pump housing engages with the groove in the coolant pump flange.

c) Tighten all retaining bolts to the specified torque.

d) On 1.8 litre Z18XE engines, refit the timing belt rear cover and timing belt as described in Chapter 2C.

e) Refill the cooling system and refit the auxiliary drivebelt as described in Chapter 1.

## 8 Heating and ventilation system – general information

The heater/ventilation system consists of a four-speed blower motor (housed behind the facia), face-level vents in the centre and at each end of the facia, and air ducts to the front and rear footwells.

The heater controls are located in the centre of the facia, and the controls operate

**7.27 Unscrew and remove the three coolant pump securing bolts – 1.8 litre Z18XE engines**

flap valves to deflect and mix the air flowing through the various parts of the heater/ventilation system. The flap valves are contained in the air distribution housing, which acts as a central distribution unit, passing air to the various ducts and vents.

Cold air enters the system through the grille at the rear of the engine compartment. A pollen filter is fitted to the ventilation intake, to filter out dust, soot, pollen and spores from the air entering the vehicle.

The air (boosted by the blower fan if required) then flows through the various ducts, according to the settings of the controls. Stale air is expelled through ducts at the rear of the vehicle. If warm air is required, the cold air is passed through the heater matrix, which is heated by the engine coolant.

A recirculation switch enables the outside air supply to be closed off, while the air inside the vehicle is recirculated. This can be useful to prevent unpleasant odours entering from outside the vehicle, but should only be used briefly, as the recirculated air inside the vehicle will soon deteriorate.

**9.2 Undo the two screws and remove the facia lower panel below the glovebox**

**9.3 Remove the passenger's side footwell air duct**

**9.5a Undo the five retaining bolts (arrowed) . . .**

**9.5b . . . and remove the blower motor from the recirculating air valve housing**

## 9 Heater/ventilation system components – removal and refitting

### Heater blower motor

#### Removal

1 Remove the glovebox as described in Chapter 11.
2 Undo the two screws and remove the facia lower panel below the glovebox (see illustration).
3 Release the expanding rivet and remove the passenger's side footwell air duct (see illustration).
4 Trace the wiring from the blower motor up to the resistor and disconnect the two wires at the resistor.
5 Undo the five bolts securing the blower

motor housing to the base of the recirculating air valve housing and remove the blower motor down and out from under the facia (see illustrations).

#### Refitting

6 Refitting is a reversal of removal.

### Heater blower motor resistor

#### Removal

7 Remove the glovebox as described in Chapter 11.
8 Carefully prise free the blower motor resistor from the air distribution housing (see illustration).

9 Disconnect the main wiring connector and the two heater blower motor wiring connectors and remove the resistor (see illustration).

#### Refitting

10 Refitting is a reversal of removal.

### Recirculating air valve housing

#### Removal

11 Remove the heater blower motor as described previously.
12 Remove the water deflector at the base of the windscreen as described in Chapter 11.
13 Working in the water deflector aperture,

**9.8 Heater blower motor resistor location (arrowed)**

**9.9 Disconnect the main wiring connector (A) and the two heater blower motor wiring connectors (B)**

**9.13 Undo the bolt (arrowed) securing the top of the recirculating air valve housing to the bulkhead**

**9.14 Undo the two retaining bolts (arrowed) and lower the housing from its location**

**9.15 Disconnect the wiring connector from the servo motor, then manoeuvre the housing out from under the facia**

undo the four screws and remove the recirculating air valve housing grille. With the grille removed, undo the bolt now exposed securing the top of the air valve housing to the bulkhead (see illustration).

14 Undo the two retaining bolts and lower the housing from its location (see illustration).

15 Disconnect the wiring connector from the recirculating air valve servo motor, then manoeuvre the housing out from under the facia (see illustration).

**Refitting**

16 Refitting is a reversal of removal, ensuring that the housing seals correctly seated.

**9.18 Recirculating air valve servo motor retaining bolts (arrowed)**

### Recirculating air valve servo motor

**Removal**

17 Remove the recirculating air valve housing as described previously.

18 Undo the three retaining bolts and remove the motor from the housing (see illustration).

**Refitting**

19 Refitting is a reversal of removal.

### Mixed air valve servo motor

**Removal**

20 Remove the glovebox as described in Chapter 11.

21 Undo the two screws and remove the facia lower panel below the glovebox (see illustration 9.2).

22 Release the expanding rivet and remove the passenger's side footwell air duct (see illustration 9.3).

23 Disconnect the wiring connector, then undo the three bolts and remove the servo motor from the side of the air distribution housing (see illustration).

**Refitting**

24 Refitting is a reversal of removal.

### Heater matrix

**Removal**

25 Remove the centre console as described in Chapter 11.

26 Working in the engine compartment, use two hose clamps to clamp the hoses leading to the heater matrix. The hoses are located on the bulkhead, just above the steering gear. Alternatively, drain the cooling system completely as described in Chapter 1.

27 Release the quick-release connectors by sliding them forward, and disconnect the two heater hoses from the heater matrix pipe stubs (see illustration).

28 Remove the water deflector at the base of the windscreen as described in Chapter 11.

29 Working in the water deflector aperture, undo the four screws and remove the recirculating air valve housing grille. With the grille removed, undo the bolt now exposed securing the top of the air valve housing to the bulkhead (see illustration 9.13).

30 Remove the engine/transmission rear mounting/torque link and transmission bracket, as described in the relevant Part of Chapter 2, for access to the heater matrix condensation drain tube.

31 From under the car, unclip and carefully move aside the fuel and brake pipes in the area of the matrix condensation drain tube, then undo the two bolts securing the drain tube to the bulkhead (see illustration).

**9.23 Mixed air valve servo motor wiring connector (A) and retaining bolts (B)**

**9.27 Release the quick-release connectors (arrowed) and disconnect the heater hoses from the matrix pipe stubs**

**9.31 Undo the two bolts (arrowed) securing the heater matrix condensation drain tube to the bulkhead**

**9.32a Undo the two bolts (arrowed) adjacent to the heater hoses . . .**

**9.32b . . . the bolt (arrowed) behind the refrigerant pipe . . .**

**9.32c . . . and the bolt (arrowed) adjacent to the wiper linkage securing the air distribution housing to the bulkhead**

**9.34a Undo the bolts (arrowed) on each side . . .**

**9.34b . . . and the bolts (arrowed) at the front securing the heater matrix lower cover panel to the air distribution housing**

**32** Working in the engine compartment, undo the four bolts securing the air distribution housing to the bulkhead (see illustrations).

**33** From inside the car, undo the bolts and remove the facia lower centre support brackets.

**34** Undo the eight bolts securing the heater matrix lower cover panel to the air distribution housing. Lift the air distribution housing as far as clearance will allow and withdraw the lower cover panel (see illustrations).

**35** Be prepared for coolant spillage as the matrix is removed and place some cloths or absorbent material over the carpet. Pull the heater matrix from its location and remove it from the car (see illustration).

### Refitting

**36** Refitting is a reversal of removal, bearing in mind the following:

a) *Push the heater hoses back onto the matrix pipe stubs, ensuring that the quick-release connectors securely lock the hoses in position.*

b) *Refit the engine/transmission rear mounting/torque link and transmission bracket, as described in the relavant Part of Chapter 2.*

c) *If the cooling system was completely drained, refill as described in Chapter 1. If the heater hoses were clamped prior to removal, top-up the cooling system as described in 'Weekly checks'.*

### Heater control assembly

#### Removal

**37** Remove the radio/cassette/CD player as described in Chapter 12.

**38** Lift up the two upper retaining catches and withdraw the heater control assembly from the facia. Disconnect the two wiring connectors and remove the unit from the car (see illustrations).

**9.34c Lift the air distribution housing as far as clearance will allow and withdraw the lower cover panel**

**9.38a Lift up the two retaining catches (arrowed) and withdraw the heater control assembly from the facia**

### Refitting

**39** Refitting is a reversal of removal.

### *Air distribution housing*

**Note:** *On models with air conditioning, it is*

**9.35 Pull the heater matrix from its location and remove it from the car**

**9.38b Disconnect the two wiring connectors and remove the unit from the car**

**9.41 Undo the bolt (arrowed) securing the refrigerant pipe block connection to the expansion valve**

**10.6 Air conditioning system high-pressure service port (arrowed) . . .**

not possible to remove the air distribution housing without opening the refrigerant circuit (see Sections 10 and 11). Have the refrigerant discharged at a dealer service department or an automotive air conditioning repair facility before proceeding.

### Removal

**40** Drain the cooling system as described in Chapter 1.

**41** On models with air conditioning, undo the bolt securing the refrigerant pipe block connection to the expansion valve and withdraw the refrigerant pipes from the valve **(see illustration)**. Note that new seals for the refrigerant pipes will be required for refitting. Suitably plug or cover the disconnected pipes.

**42** Refit the bolt used to secure the refrigerant pipe block connection to the expansion valve and draw off the expansion valve.

**43** Remove the expansion valve retaining plate.

**44** Remove the engine/transmission rear mounting/torque link and transmission bracket, as described in the relevant Part of Chapter 2, for access to the heater matrix condensation drain tube.

**45** From under the car, unclip and carefully move aside the fuel and brake pipes in the area of the matrix condensation drain tube, then undo the two bolts securing the drain tube to the bulkhead **(see illustration 9.31)**.

**46** Working in the engine compartment, use two hose clamps to clamp the hoses leading to the heater matrix. The hoses are located on the bulkhead, just above the steering gear. Alternatively, drain the cooling system completely as described in Chapter 1.

**47** Release the quick-release connectors by sliding them forward, and disconnect the two heater hoses from the heater matrix pipe stubs **(see illustration 9.27)**.

**48** Remove the complete facia assembly and the facia crossmember as described in Chapter 11.

**49** Remove the passenger's airbag as described in Chapter 12.

**50** Remove the water deflector at the base of the windscreen as described in Chapter 11.

**51** Working in the water deflector aperture, undo the four screws and remove the recirculating air valve housing grille. With the grille removed, undo the bolt now exposed securing the top of the air valve housing to the bulkhead **(see illustration 9.13)**.

**52** Working in the engine compartment, undo the four bolts securing the air distribution housing to the bulkhead **(see illustrations 9.32a to 9.32c)**.

**53** From inside the car, undo the bolts and remove the facia lower centre support brackets.

**54** Disconnect the wiring connectors at the heater blower motor resistor.

**55** Carefully withdraw the air distribution housing from the bulkhead. **Note:** *Keep the matrix unions uppermost as the housing is removed, to prevent coolant spillage.* Mop-up any spilt coolant immediately, and wipe the affected area with a damp cloth to prevent staining.

### Refitting

**56** Refitting is the reverse of removal. On completion, refill the cooling system as described in Chapter 1. On models with air conditioning, have the system evacuated, charged and leak-tested by the specialist who discharged it.

## 10 Air conditioning system – general information and precautions

### General information

**1** Air conditioning is standard on top of the range models, and optional on certain other models. It enables the temperature of incoming air to be lowered, and also dehumidifies the air, which makes for rapid demisting and increased comfort.

**2** The cooling side of the system works in the same way as a domestic refrigerator. Refrigerant gas is drawn into a belt-driven compressor, and passes into a condenser mounted in front of the radiator, where it loses heat and becomes liquid. The liquid

passes through an expansion valve to an evaporator, where it changes from liquid under high pressure to gas under low pressure. This change is accompanied by a drop in temperature, which cools the evaporator. The refrigerant returns to the compressor, and the cycle begins again.

**3** Air blown through the evaporator passes to the heater assembly, where it is mixed with hot air blown through the heater matrix, to achieve the desired temperature in the passenger compartment.

**4** The heating side of the system works in the same way as on models without air conditioning (see Section 8).

**5** The operation of the system is controlled electronically. Any problems with the system should be referred to a Vauxhall/Opel dealer or an air conditioning specialist.

### Air conditioning service ports

**Note:** *The air conditioning service port location varies slightly according to model. The following is a general description of service port location.*

**6** The high-pressure service port is the larger of the two service port connections and is located in front of the radiator. Remove the radiator grille as described in Chapter 11 for access **(see illustration)**.

**7** The low-pressure service port is located at the rear right-hand side of the engine compartment **(see illustration)**.

**10.7 . . . and low-pressure service port (arrowed)**

## Precautions

**8** It is necessary to observe special precautions whenever dealing with any part of the system, its associated components, and any items which necessitate disconnection of the system.

⚠ *Warning: The refrigeration circuit contains a liquid refrigerant. This refrigerant is potentially dangerous, and should only be handled by qualified persons. If it is splashed onto the skin, it can cause frostbite. It is not itself poisonous, but in the presence of a naked flame it forms a poisonous gas; inhalation of the vapour through a lighted cigarette could prove fatal. Uncontrolled discharging of the refrigerant is dangerous, and potentially damaging to the environment. Do not disconnect any part of the system unless it has been discharged by a Vauxhall/Opel dealer or an air conditioning specialist. Caution: Do not operate the air conditioning system if it is known to be short of refrigerant, as this may damage the compressor.*

## 11 Air conditioning system components – removal and refitting

⚠ *Warning: The air conditioning system is under high pressure. Do not loosen any fittings or remove any components until after the system has been discharged. Air conditioning refrigerant should be properly discharged into an approved type of container at a dealer service department or an automotive air conditioning repair facility capable of handling R134a refrigerant. Cap or plug the pipe lines as soon as they are disconnected, to prevent the entry of moisture. Always wear eye protection when disconnecting air conditioning system fittings.*

**Note:** *This Section refers to the components of the air conditioning system itself – refer to Sections 8 and 9 for details of components common to the heating/ventilation system.*

## Compressor

### Removal

**1** Have the refrigerant discharged at a dealer service department or an automotive air conditioning repair facility.
**2** Disconnect the battery negative terminal (refer to *Disconnecting the battery* in the Reference Chapter).
**3** Firmly apply the handbrake, then jack up the front of the car and support it securely on axle stands (see *Jacking and vehicle support*).
**4** Remove the auxiliary drivebelt as described in Chapter 1.
**5** With the system discharged, undo the retaining bolt(s) and disconnect the refrigerant pipes from the compressor. Discard the O-ring seals – new ones must be used when refitting.

Suitably cap the open fittings immediately to keep moisture and contamination out of the system.
**6** Disconnect the compressor wiring connector.
**7** Unbolt the compressor from the cylinder block/crankcase/sump, then withdraw the compressor from the vehicle.

### Refitting

**8** Refit the compressor in the reverse order of removal; renew all seals disturbed.
**9** If you are installing a new compressor, refer to the compressor manufacturer's instructions for adding refrigerant oil to the system.
**10** Have the system evacuated, charged and leak-tested by the specialist that discharged it.
**11** After installing a new compressor, always observe the following running-in procedure:
  *1) Open all instrument panel air outlet flaps.*
  *2) Start vehicle engine and stabilise idle speed for approximately 5 seconds.*
  *3) Switch fan to maximum speed.*
  *4) Switch on the air conditioning and let it run for at least 2 minutes without interruption at engine speed under 1500 rpm.*

## Evaporator

### Removal

**12** Have the refrigerant discharged at a dealer service department or an automotive air conditioning repair facility.
**13** Remove the recirculating air valve housing as described in Section 9.
**14** From within the engine compartment, undo the bolt securing the refrigerant pipe block connection to the expansion valve and withdraw the refrigerant pipes from the valve **(see illustration 9.41)**. Note that new seals for the refrigerant pipes will be required for refitting. Suitably plug or cover the disconnected pipes.
**15** Refit the bolt used to secure the refrigerant pipe block connection to the expansion valve and draw off the expansion valve.
**16** Remove the expansion valve retaining plate.
**17** Remove the pollen filter as described in Chapter 1.
**18** On models equipped with a radio/glovebox cooling tube, unclip and remove the tube.
**19** Using a sharp knife cut off the evaporator cover on the air distribution housing, working in the groove around the periphery of the cover **(see illustration)**. Note that a new cover will be required for refitting.
**20** Carefully withdraw the evaporator from the side of the air distribution housing.

### Refitting

**21** Slide the evaporator in place in the air distribution housing.
**22** Using a sharp knife, cut off the two internal webs in the new evaporator cover.
**23** On models equipped with a radio/glovebox cooling tube, lay the old evaporator cover on the new cover and mark the position of the

**11.19 Cut off the evaporator cover on the air distribution housing, working in the groove around the cover periphery**

cooling tube hole. Cut a cooling tube hole in the new cover using a suitable knife or tank cutter. Using suitable adhesive (Vauxhall/Opel part No 93160951) glue the radio/glovebox cooling tube in place on both sides.
**24** Fit the new evaporator cover to the air distribution housing and secure with four screws in the holes provided on the air distribution housing.
**25** The remainder of refitting is the reverse of removal ensuring that all disturbed pipe seals are renewed.
**26** Have the system evacuated, charged and leak-tested by the specialist who discharged it.

## Auxiliary cooling fan

### Removal

**27** Disconnect the battery negative terminal (refer to *Disconnecting the battery* in the Reference Chapter).
**28** Apply the handbrake, then jack up the front of the vehicle and support it on axle stands (see *Jacking and vehicle support*).
**29** Remove the front bumper as described in Chapter 11.
**30** Unclip the relays, then release the cable ties securing the wiring harness to the auxiliary cooling fan housing **(see illustration)**.
**31** Release and disconnect the wiring harness connector at the base of the fan housing.
**32** Undo the two upper retaining nuts, then lift the fan and housing up and off the condenser **(see illustration)**. Remove the fan and housing from under the car.

**11.30 Unclip the relays from the auxiliary cooling fan housing**

**11.32  Undo the two upper retaining nuts (arrowed), then lift the fan and housing up and off the condenser**

**11.39a  Undo the upper retaining bolt (arrowed) . . .**

**11.39b  . . . and lower retaining bolt (arrowed) and disconnect the refrigerant pipe connector blocks from the condenser**

### Refitting

33  Refitting is the reverse of removal.

## *Condenser*

### Removal

34  Have the refrigerant discharged at a dealer service department or an automotive air conditioning repair facility.

35  Disconnect the battery negative terminal (refer to *Disconnecting the battery* in the Reference Chapter).

36  Apply the handbrake, then jack up the front of the vehicle and support it on axle stands (see *Jacking and vehicle support*).

37  Remove the front bumper as described in Chapter 11.

38  Remove the auxiliary cooling fan as described previously in this Section.

39  Undo the retaining bolts and disconnect the upper and lower refrigerant pipe connector blocks from the right-hand side of the condenser **(see illustrations)**. Discard the seals – new ones must be used when refitting. Suitably cap the open fittings immediately to keep moisture and contamination out of the system.

40  Disconnect the wiring connector from the pressure sensor on the right-hand side of the condenser.

41  Undo the four bolts securing the condenser to the radiator. Carefully lower the condenser and remove it from under the car.

### Refitting

42  Refitting is the reverse of removal ensuring that all disturbed pipe seals are renewed.

43  Have the system evacuated, charged and leak-tested by the specialist who discharged it.

# Chapter 4 Part A:
# Fuel and exhaust systems

## Contents

## Degrees of difficulty

| | | | | |
|---|---|---|---|---|
| **Easy,** suitable for novice with little experience | **Fairly easy,** suitable for beginner with some experience | **Fairly difficult,** suitable for competent DIY mechanic | **Difficult,** suitable for experienced DIY mechanic | **Very difficult,** suitable for expert DIY or professional |

## Specifications

### System type

| | |
|---|---|
| 1.4 litre engines . . . . . . . . . . . . . . . . . . . . . . . . . . . . . . . . . . . . . . . . . . . . | Bosch Motronic ME 7.6.1/2 sequential multipoint fuel injection |
| 1.6 litre engines . . . . . . . . . . . . . . . . . . . . . . . . . . . . . . . . . . . . . . . . . . . . | Multec-S sequential multipoint fuel injection |
| 1.8 litre engines: | |
|    Z18XE . . . . . . . . . . . . . . . . . . . . . . . . . . . . . . . . . . . . . . . . . . . . . . . | Simtec 71.5 sequential multipoint fuel injection |
|    Z18XER . . . . . . . . . . . . . . . . . . . . . . . . . . . . . . . . . . . . . . . . . . . . . . . | Simtec 75.1 sequential multipoint fuel injection |

### Fuel system data

| | |
|---|---|
| Fuel supply pump type . . . . . . . . . . . . . . . . . . . . . . . . . . . . . . . . . . . . . . | Electric, immersed in tank |
| Fuel pump regulated constant pressure . . . . . . . . . . . . . . . . . . . . . . . . | 3.8 bar |
| Specified idle speed . . . . . . . . . . . . . . . . . . . . . . . . . . . . . . . . . . . . . . . | Not adjustable – controlled by ECU |
| Idle mixture CO content . . . . . . . . . . . . . . . . . . . . . . . . . . . . . . . . . . . . | Not adjustable – controlled by ECU |

## Torque wrench settings

| | Nm | lbf ft |
|---|---|---|
| Accelerator pedal position sensor nuts . . . . . . . . . . . . . . . . . . . . . . . | 12 | 9 |
| Camshaft sensor retaining bolt . . . . . . . . . . . . . . . . . . . . . . . . . . . . . | 6 | 4 |
| Crankshaft speed/position sensor retaining bolt: | | |
|    1.4 litre engines . . . . . . . . . . . . . . . . . . . . . . . . . . . . . . . . . . . . . | 8 | 6 |
|    1.6 litre engines . . . . . . . . . . . . . . . . . . . . . . . . . . . . . . . . . . . . . | 10 | 7 |
|    1.8 litre engines: | | |
|       Z18XE . . . . . . . . . . . . . . . . . . . . . . . . . . . . . . . . . . . . . . . . . . | 8 | 6 |
|       Z18XER . . . . . . . . . . . . . . . . . . . . . . . . . . . . . . . . . . . . . . . . | 5 | 3 |
| Exhaust front pipe to manifold* . . . . . . . . . . . . . . . . . . . . . . . . . . . . | 20 | 15 |
| Exhaust manifold securing nuts*: | | |
|    1.4 litre engines . . . . . . . . . . . . . . . . . . . . . . . . . . . . . . . . . . . . . | 20 | 15 |
|    1.6 litre engines . . . . . . . . . . . . . . . . . . . . . . . . . . . . . . . . . . . . . | 15 | 11 |
|    1.8 litre engines: | | |
|       Z18XE . . . . . . . . . . . . . . . . . . . . . . . . . . . . . . . . . . . . . . . . . . | 12 | 9 |
|       Z18XER . . . . . . . . . . . . . . . . . . . . . . . . . . . . . . . . . . . . . . . . | 20 | 15 |
| Exhaust system clamp bolts . . . . . . . . . . . . . . . . . . . . . . . . . . . . . . | 50 | 37 |
| Fuel tank retaining strap bolts . . . . . . . . . . . . . . . . . . . . . . . . . . . . . | 23 | 17 |
| Inlet manifold retaining bolts/nuts | | |
|    1.4 litre engines . . . . . . . . . . . . . . . . . . . . . . . . . . . . . . . . . . . . . | 10 | 7 |
|    1.6 litre engines . . . . . . . . . . . . . . . . . . . . . . . . . . . . . . . . . . . . . | 8 | 6 |
|    1.8 litre Z18XE engines: | | |
|       Manifold to cylinder head . . . . . . . . . . . . . . . . . . . . . . . . . . . . | 20 | 15 |
|       Support bracket to manifold . . . . . . . . . . . . . . . . . . . . . . . . . . | 20 | 15 |
|       Support bracket to cylinder block . . . . . . . . . . . . . . . . . . . . . . | 35 | 26 |
|    1.8 litre Z18XER engines . . . . . . . . . . . . . . . . . . . . . . . . . . . . . . | 20 | 15 |
| Knock sensor . . . . . . . . . . . . . . . . . . . . . . . . . . . . . . . . . . . . . . . . . . | 20 | 15 |
| Manifold pressure sensor bolt . . . . . . . . . . . . . . . . . . . . . . . . . . . . . | 8 | 6 |
| Throttle housing retaining bolts . . . . . . . . . . . . . . . . . . . . . . . . . . . . | 8 | 6 |

*\* Use new fasteners*

## 1 General information and precautions

### General information

The fuel supply system consists of a fuel tank (which is mounted under the rear of the car, with an electric fuel pump immersed in it), and fuel feed lines. The fuel pump supplies fuel to the fuel rail, which acts as a reservoir for the fuel injectors which inject fuel into the inlet tracts. The fuel pressure regulator is located on the fuel pump module in the fuel tank.

The electronic control unit controls both the fuel injection system and the ignition system, integrating the two into a complete engine management system. Refer to Section 10 for further information on the operation of the fuel system and to Chapter 5B for details of the ignition side of the system.

1.4, 1.6 and 1.8 litre Z18XE engines utilise a 'Twinport' inlet manifold configuration. Vacuum operated flap valves located in the inlet manifold are opened or closed according to engine operating conditions, to create a variable venturi manifold arrangement. This layout has significant advantages in terms of engine power, fuel economy and reduced exhaust emissions. 1.8 litre Z18XER engines utilise a similar arrangement, but a switching drum operated by an electric motor is used instead of flap valves, to create the variable venturi manifold arrangement.

The exhaust manifold incorporates an integral catalytic converter to reduce harmful exhaust gas emissions. The remaining exhaust system is in three sections. Further details can be found in Section 20 and in Part B of this Chapter, along with details of the other emission control systems and components.

### Precautions

**Note:** *Refer to Part B of this Chapter for general information and precautions relating to the catalytic converter.*

Before disconnecting any fuel lines, or working on any part of the fuel system, the system must be depressurised as described in Section 5.

Care must be taken when disconnecting the fuel lines. When disconnecting a fuel union or hose, loosen the union or clamp screw slowly, to avoid sudden uncontrolled fuel spillage. Take adequate fire precautions.

When working on fuel system components, scrupulous cleanliness must be observed, and care must be taken not to introduce any foreign matter into fuel lines or components.

After carrying out any work involving disconnection of fuel lines, it is advisable to check the connections for leaks; pressurise the system by switching the ignition on and off several times.

Electronic control units are very sensitive components, and certain precautions must be taken to avoid damage to these units as follows.

a) *When carrying out welding operations on the vehicle using electric welding equipment, the battery and alternator should be disconnected.*

b) *Although the underbonnet-mounted control units will tolerate normal underbonnet conditions, they can be adversely affected by excess heat or moisture. If using welding equipment or pressure-washing equipment in the vicinity of an electronic control unit, take care not to direct heat, or jets of water or steam, at the unit. If this cannot be avoided, remove the control unit from the vehicle, and protect its wiring plug with a plastic bag.*

c) *Before disconnecting any wiring, or removing components, always ensure that the ignition is switched off.*

d) *After working on fuel injection/engine management system components, ensure that all wiring is correctly reconnected before reconnecting the battery or switching on the ignition.*

⚠️ **Warning: Many of the procedures in this Chapter require the removal of fuel lines and connections, which may result in some fuel spillage. Before carrying out any operation on the fuel system, refer to the precautions given in 'Safety first!' at the beginning of this manual, and follow them implicitly. Petrol is a highly-dangerous and volatile liquid, and the precautions necessary when handling it cannot be overstressed.**

**Note:** *Residual pressure will remain in the fuel lines long after the vehicle was last used. Before disconnecting any fuel line, first depressurise the fuel system as described in Section 5.*

**2.1 Disconnect the wiring connector from the side of the airflow meter**

**2.2 Slacken the clamp screw (arrowed) and lift the intake duct from the throttle housing**

**2.3 Undo the retaining bolt (arrowed) and release the air cleaner housing mounting bracket**

## 2 Air cleaner assembly and intake ducts – removal and refitting

### Removal

**1** Disconnect the wiring connector from the side of the airflow meter **(see illustration)**.
**2** Slacken the clamp screw and lift the intake duct from the throttle housing **(see illustration)**. Where applicable, release the clip and disconnect the crankcase ventilation hose from the duct.
**3** Undo the retaining bolt and release the mounting bracket at the rear of the air cleaner housing **(see illustration)**.
**4** Detach the air intake duct at the front of the air cleaner housing **(see illustration)**.
**5** Lift the housing upwards at the rear, then disengage the front mounting rubber from the body bracket.
**6** When sufficient clearance exists, release the retaining clip and disconnect the water drain tube from the base of the air cleaner housing **(see illustration)**. Remove the assembly from the engine compartment.
**7** To remove the intake pipe from the crossmember, undo the retaining screws, and slide the intake pipe to one side to release it from the radiator crossmember.

### Refitting

**8** Refitting is the reverse of removal, making sure all the air intake ducts are securely reconnected.

## 3 Accelerator pedal/position sensor – removal and refitting

### Removal

**1** Disconnect the battery negative terminal (refer to *Disconnecting the battery* in the Reference Chapter).
**2** Undo the two screws and remove the facia lower panel on the driver's side.
**3** Working in the driver's footwell under the facia, disconnect the wiring connector from the top of the accelerator pedal/position sensor **(see illustration)**.

**2.4 Detach the air intake duct at the front of the air cleaner housing**

**4** Unscrew the three mounting nuts, and withdraw the sensor from the bulkhead.

### Refitting

**5** Refitting is a reversal of removal.

## 4 Unleaded petrol – general information and usage

**Note:** *The information given in this Chapter is correct at the time of writing. If updated information is thought to be required, check with a Vauxhall/Opel dealer. If travelling abroad, consult one of the motoring organisations (or a similar authority) for advice on the fuel available.*

All models are designed to run on fuel with a minimum octane rating of 95 RON. However, if

**3.3 Disconnect the wiring connector (arrowed) from the accelerator pedal/position sensor**

**2.6 Release the clip and disconnect the water drain tube from the base of the air cleaner housing**

unavailable, 91 octane may be used although a reduction in engine power and torque will be noticed.

All models have a catalytic converter, and so must be run on unleaded fuel **only**. Under no circumstances should leaded fuel or LRP be used, as this will damage the converter.

Super unleaded petrol (98 octane) can also be used in all models if wished, though there is no advantage in doing so.

## 5 Fuel injection system – depressurisation

 *Warning: Refer to the warning note in Section 1 before proceeding. The following procedure will merely relieve the pressure in the fuel system – remember that fuel will still be present in the system components, and take precautions accordingly before disconnecting any of them.*

**1** The fuel system referred to in this Section is defined as the tank-mounted fuel pump, the fuel injectors, and the metal pipes and flexible hoses of the fuel lines between these components. All these contain fuel which will be under pressure while the engine is running, and/or while the ignition is switched on. The pressure will remain for some time after the ignition has been switched off, and it must be relieved in a controlled fashion when any of these components are disturbed for servicing work.

**5.3 Fuel pressure connection valve (arrowed) on the fuel rail**

**2** Where fitted, remove the plastic cover over the top of the engine.

**3** Locate the fuel pressure connection valve which is fitted to the fuel rail. On 1.8 litre Z18XER engines it can be found on the top, left-hand end of the fuel rail **(see illustration)**. On all other engines, the valve is located at the top right-hand end of the fuel rail.

**4** Unscrew the cap from the valve and position a container beneath the valve. Hold a wad of rag over the valve and relieve the pressure in the fuel system by depressing the valve core with a suitable screwdriver. Be prepared for the squirt of fuel as the valve core is depressed and catch it with the rag. Hold the valve core down until no more fuel is expelled from the valve.

**5** Once all pressure is relieved, securely refit the valve cap.

## 6 Fuel gauge sender unit – removal and refitting

**Note 1:** *Vauxhall/Opel special tool KM-797 (or suitable alternative) will be required to remove and refit the fuel pump cover locking ring, and special tool KM-6391 (or suitable alternative) will be required to remove the in-tank module from the fuel tank.*

**Note 2:** *A new fuel pump cover sealing ring will be required on refitting.*

**Note 3:** *The fuel tank should be as empty as possible when carrying out this procedure.*

### Removal

**1** Disconnect the battery negative terminal (refer to *Disconnecting the battery* in the Reference Chapter).

**2** Remove the rear seat cushion as described in Chapter 11.

**3** Lift up the sound insulation reveal the fuel tank access cover.

**4** Using a screwdriver, carefully prise the plastic access cover from the floor **(see illustration)**.

**5** Disconnect the wiring connector from the fuel supply pump cover, and tape the connector to the vehicle body, to prevent it disappearing behind the tank **(see illustration)**.

**6** Compress the clips located on each side of the fuel hose end fitting and ease the fitting off of its union. Plug the hose end to minimise fuel loss.

**7** Using the Vauxhall/Opel special tool, unscrew the locking ring and remove it from the tank **(see illustration)**.

**8** Make identification marks on the fuel pump cover and the body to ensure that the cover is refitted in its original position. There may be an arrow stamped on the cover; if so note its direction.

**9** Carefully lift the fuel pump cover away from tank and remove the cover sealing ring **(see illustration)**.

**10** Disconnect the wiring connector(s) from the underside of the fuel pump cover **(see illustration)**.

**11** Depress the retaining tabs and lift the fuel pump out of the in-tank module **(see illustration)**. Place the assembly to one side.

**12** To remove the in-tank module (containing the gauge sender unit) from the fuel tank, Vauxhall/Opel special tool KM-6391, or a suitable alternative will be required. The special tool consists of four metal strips that are inserted down the sides of the in-tank module, to release the module from the four tabs of the mounting bracket, which remains in the tank. In the absence of the special tool a suitable alternative can be easily made **(see Tool Tip)**.

**13** Carefully insert the four tools down through the slots on the side of the in-tank module until they engage and release the four retaining tabs in the tank mounting bracket **(see illustrations)**. Move the float arm on the sender unit slightly when inserting the tool adjacent to the sender unit.

**14** Once the tabs in the tank mounting bracket are released, carefully lift the in-tank

**6.4 Carefully prise the plastic access cover from the floor**

**6.5 Disconnect the wiring connector (arrowed) from the fuel supply pump cover**

**6.7 Unscrew the locking ring and remove it from the tank**

**6.9 Lift the fuel pump cover away from tank and remove the cover sealing ring**

**6.10 Disconnect the wiring connector(s) from the underside of the fuel pump cover**

**6.11 Depress the retaining tabs and lift the fuel pump out of the in-tank module**

**TOOL TiP**

*An in-tank module removal tool can be made from 3 mm thick steel strip, approximately 150 mm long and 26 mm wide. Cut or file a 12 mm slot in one end of the tool and put a slight bend in the tool at the other end, approximately 100 mm from the slotted end. Note that 4 of these tools will be required to remove the module.*

6.13a Carefully insert the removal tools down through the slots on the side of the in-tank module . . .

6.13b . . . push the tools down into the slots . . .

6.13c . . . until they release the four retaining tabs (arrowed) in the tank mounting bracket (shown with in-tank module removed)

6.14 With the tabs in the mounting bracket released, lift the in-tank module up and out of the fuel tank

module up and out of the fuel tank (see illustration).

15 With the assembly on the bench, release the two retaining tabs and lift the fuel gauge sender unit up and out of the in-tank module (see illustrations).

### Refitting

16 Refit the gauge sender unit to the in-tank module ensuring that the retaining tabs positively engage.

17 Manoeuvre the in-tank module carefully in through the tank aperture and push it down onto the retaining tabs of the tank mounting bracket. Ensure that the retaining tabs audibly engage with the module.

18 Locate the fuel pump or fuel filter into the in-tank module and engage the retaining tabs.

19 Reconnect the wiring connector(s) to the fuel pump cover, and place a new sealing ring in position on the tank. Locate the cover on the tank and align the marks, or direction arrow in the position noted during removal.

20 Refit the locking ring and tighten it with the special tool until it locks in place.

21 Reconnect the fuel hoses to the pump cover, using the marks made on removal, then reconnect the wiring connector.

22 Reconnect the battery then start the engine and check for fuel leaks. If all is well, refit the access cover and sound insulation, then refit the seat cushion.

### 7 Fuel pump –
removal and refitting

1 The fuel pump is located in the in-tank module in the fuel tank. The removal and refitting procedures are the same as for the fuel gauge sender unit described in Section 6. The pump is integral with the in-tank module and cannot be renewed separately.

### 8 Fuel tank –
removal and refitting

**Note 1:** *Refer to the information contained in Section 1 before proceeding.*

**Note 2:** *The fuel tank should be as empty as possible when carrying out this procedure.*

### Removal

1 Depressurise the fuel system as described in Section 5, then disconnect the battery negative terminal (refer to *Disconnecting the battery* in the Reference Chapter).

2 Before removing the fuel tank, all fuel must be drained from the tank. Since a fuel tank drain plug is not provided, it is therefore preferable to carry out the removal operation

6.15a Release the two retaining tabs . . .

6.15b . . . and lift the fuel gauge sender unit up and out of the in-tank module

when the tank is nearly empty. The remaining fuel can then be syphoned or hand-pumped from the tank.

3 Remove the exhaust system and relevant heat shield(s) as described in Section 20.

4 Disconnect the wiring for the gauge sender unit and fuel pump at the underbody connector adjacent to the fuel tank. Unclip the wiring harness from the retaining clips.

5 Disconnect the fuel lines at the underbody quick-release connectors on the left-hand side of the tank. Be prepared for some loss of fuel. A Vauxhall/Opel special tool is available to release the fuel line connectors, but provided care is taken, the connectors can be released using a pair of long-nosed pliers, or a similar tool, to depress the retaining tangs. Suitably plug the disconnected fuel and vent hoses to prevent entry of dust and dirt.

**8.6 Unclip the handbrake cables from the fuel tank retaining straps (arrowed)**

**6** Unclip the handbrake cables from the fuel tank and fuel tank retaining straps **(see illustration)**.

**7** Open the fuel filler flap and unscrew the filler cap. Remove the rubber cover from around the filler neck aperture, then unscrew the retaining bolt securing the filler neck to the body. Refit the filler cap.

**8** Remove the right-hand rear roadwheel, then unscrew the two bolts and two nuts and remove the wheel arch liner.

**9** Place a suitable container under the tank, then release the retaining clamp and disconnect the fuel filler pipe connection hose from the fuel tank. Collect the escaping fuel in the container.

**10** Undo the bolt securing the filler pipe to the underbody on the right-hand side.

**11** Unscrew the retaining bolt and detach the fuel moisture separator from the top of the fuel filler pipe.

**12** Support the weight of the fuel tank on a jack with interposed block of wood.

**13** Undo the four bolts and remove the two securing straps from the fuel tank.

**14** Slowly lower the tank while at the same time guiding the filler pipe over the rear axle.

**15** Continue to lower the tank until it can be removed from under the vehicle.

**16** If necessary, remove the fuel lines and vent hoses, heat shield and wiring from the tank for transfer to the new tank. This will entail cutting off the cable ties and cutting the vent hose end fittings with a sharp knife to allow removal from the tank connections. New hoses will be required for refitting as the end fittings will be destroyed during removal. Take

**9.3 Disconnect the wiring connector from the throttle housing**

care when doing this not to damage the tank connections.

**17** If the tank contains sediment or water, it may cleaned out with two or three rinses of clean fuel. Remove the fuel gauge sender unit as described in Sections 6. Shake the tank vigorously, and change the fuel as necessary to remove all contamination from the tank.

**18** Any repairs to the fuel tank should be carried out by a professional. Do not under any circumstances attempt any form of DIY repair to a fuel tank.

**Refitting**

**19** Refitting is the reverse of the removal procedure, noting the following points:

a) *When lifting the tank back into position, take care to ensure that none of the hoses become trapped between the tank and vehicle body. Refit the retaining straps and tighten the bolts securely.*

b) *Ensure all pipes and hoses are correctly routed and all hoses unions are securely joined.*

c) *On completion, refill the tank with a small amount of fuel, and check for signs of leakage prior to taking the vehicle out on the road.*

## 9 Throttle housing – removal and refitting

**Removal**

**1** Disconnect the battery negative terminal (refer to *Disconnecting the battery* in the Reference Chapter).

**2** Remove the air cleaner assembly and intake ducts as described in Section 2.

**3** Disconnect the wiring connector from the throttle housing **(see illustration)**.

**4** Partially drain the cooling system as described in Chapter 1 (drain enough coolant to empty the coolant expansion tank).

**5** Release the retaining clips and disconnect the two coolant hoses from the rear of the throttle housing.

**6** On 1.8 litre engines, release the retaining clips and disconnect the crankcase ventilation hose and, where fitted, the evaporative emission system hose from the throttle housing.

**9.7 Throttle housing retaining bolts (arrowed)**

**7** Undo the four bolts and lift the throttle housing off the inlet manifold **(see illustration)**. Recover the gasket.

**8** It is not possible to obtain the throttle valve control motor or throttle valve position sensor separately, so if either is faulty, the complete throttle housing must be renewed.

**Refitting**

**9** Refitting is a reversal of removal, but thoroughly clean the mating faces and use a new gasket. Tighten the bolts progressively to the specified torque. Top-up the coolant level as described in *Weekly checks*. Finally, switch on the ignition for 30 seconds without starting the engine to allow ECU matching.

## 10 Fuel injection systems – general information

The fuel injection system is integrated with the emissions control system and ignition system to form a combined engine management system under the control of one electronic control unit (ECU).

All the systems operate in a similar manner and comply with the latest emission control standards. The fuel injection side of the systems operate as follows. Refer to Chapter 4B for information on the emissions control systems, and to Chapter 5B for information on the ignition system.

Fuel is supplied from the rear-mounted tank, via a pressure regulator to the fuel rail. The fuel rail acts as a reservoir for the fuel injectors, which inject fuel into the cylinder inlet tracts, upstream of the inlet valves. The systems are of the 'sequential' injection type, which means that each of the four fuel injectors is triggered individually, just before the inlet valve on the relevant cylinder opens.

The duration of the electrical pulses to the fuel injectors determines the quantity of fuel injected. The pulse duration is computed by the ECU on the basis of information received from the following sensors:

a) *Accelerator pedal position sensor – informs the ECU of accelerator pedal position, and the rate of throttle opening/ closing.*

b) *Throttle potentiometer (integral with the throttle housing) – informs the ECU of the throttle position, and confirms the signals received from the accelerator pedal position sensor.*

c) *Coolant temperature sensor – informs the ECU of engine temperature.*

d) *Airflow meter (incorporating inlet air temperature sensor) – informs the ECU of the load on the engine (expressed in terms of the mass of air passing from the air cleaner to the throttle housing).*

e) *Oxygen sensors (two) – inform the ECU of the oxygen content of the exhaust gases (explained in greater detail in Part B of this Chapter).*

f) Manifold pressure sensor (1.6 litre engines) – informs the ECU of the engine load by monitoring the pressure in the inlet manifold.

g) Crankshaft speed/position sensor – informs the ECU of the crankshaft speed and position.

h) Camshaft sensor (two sensors on 1.8 litre Z18XER engines) – inform the ECU of speed and position of the camshaft(s).

i) Knock sensor – informs the ECU when pre-ignition ('pinking') is occurring.

j) ABS control unit – informs the ECU of the vehicle speed, based on wheel speed sensor signals (explained in greater detail in Chapter 9).

The signals from the various sensors are processed by the ECU, and the optimum fuelling and ignition settings are selected for the prevailing engine operating conditions.

Idle speed and throttle position is controlled by the throttle valve control motor, which is an integral part of the throttle housing. The motor is controlled by the ECU, in conjunction with signals received from the accelerator pedal position sensor.

A catalytic converter is incorporated in the exhaust manifold, to reduce harmful exhaust gas emissions. Details of this and other emissions control system equipment are given in Chapter 4B.

If certain sensors fail, and send abnormal signals to the ECU, the ECU has a back-up programme. In this event, the abnormal signals are ignored, and a pre-programmed value is substituted for the sensor signal, allowing the engine to continue running, albeit at reduced efficiency. If the ECU enters its back-up mode, a warning light on the instrument panel will illuminate, and a fault code will be stored in the ECU memory. This fault code can be read using suitable specialist test equipment.

## 11 Fuel injection system components – testing

**1** If a fault appears in the engine management system, first ensure that all the system wiring connectors are securely connected and free of corrosion. Ensure that the fault is not due to poor maintenance; ie, check that the air cleaner filter element is clean, the spark plugs are in good condition and correctly gapped, the cylinder compression pressures are correct and that the engine breather hoses are clear and undamaged, referring to Chapters 1, 2A, 2B and 2C for further information.

**2** If these checks fail to reveal the cause of the problem, the vehicle should be taken to a Vauxhall/Opel dealer or suitably-equipped engine management diagnostic specialist for testing.

**3** A diagnostic socket is located in the centre console, to which a fault code reader or other suitable test equipment can be connected. Unclip and remove the trim panel beneath the handbrake lever for access (see illustrations).

**11.3a Unclip and remove the trim panel beneath the handbrake lever . . .**

By using the code reader or test equipment, the engine management ECU (and the various other vehicle system ECUs) can be interrogated, and any stored fault codes can be retrieved. This will allow the fault to be quickly and simply traced, alleviating the need to test all the system components individually, which is a time-consuming operation that carries a risk of damaging the ECU.

## 12 Bosch Motronic injection system components – removal and refitting

### Airflow meter

#### Removal

**1** Disconnect the wiring connector from the airflow meter at the right-hand rear corner of the engine compartment (see illustration).

**2** Slacken the retaining clamps and remove the airflow meter from the air intake ducts.

#### Refitting

**3** Refitting is a reversal of removal, but ensure that the arrow on the airflow meter body points toward the throttle housing when fitted.

### Fuel injectors and fuel rail

**Note:** Refer to the precautions given in Section 1 before proceeding. The seals at both ends of the fuel injectors must be renewed on refitting.

#### Removal

**4** Disconnect the battery negative terminal (refer to Disconnecting the battery in the Reference Chapter).

**12.1 Disconnect the wiring connector from the airflow meter**

**11.3b . . . for access to the diagnostic socket (arrowed)**

**5** Depressurise the fuel system as described in Section 5.

**6** Remove the throttle housing as described in Section 9, however, it is not necessary to drain the cooling system, as the housing can be placed to one side with the hoses still attached.

**7** Loosen the clip and disconnect the engine breather hose from the camshaft cover.

**8** Undo the two screws and remove the cover over the fuel rail (where fitted).

**9** Disconnect the wiring connector from each fuel injector (see illustration).

**10** Disconnect the fuel feed hose quick-release connector at the fuel rail. Be prepared for some loss of fuel. A Vauxhall/ Opel special tool is available to release the connector, but provided care is taken, it can be released using a pair of long-nosed pliers, or a similar tool, to depress the retaining tangs. Clamp or plug the open end of the hose, to prevent dirt ingress and further fuel spillage.

**11** Unscrew the mounting bolts, then lift the fuel rail complete with the injectors off of the inlet manifold.

**12** To remove an injector from the fuel rail, prise out the metal securing clip using a screwdriver or a pair of pliers, and pull the injector from the fuel rail. Remove and discard the injector sealing rings; new ones must be fitted on refitting.

**13** Overhaul of the fuel injectors is not possible, as no spares are available. If faulty, an injector must be renewed.

#### Refitting

**14** Before refitting, clean thoroughly the

**12.9 Fuel injector wiring connectors (arrowed)**

**12.15 Fit new O-rings (arrowed) to the fuel injectors before refitting**

mating surfaces of the throttle housing and inlet manifold.

**15** Commence refitting by fitting new O-ring seals to both ends of the fuel injectors **(see illustration)**. Coat the seals with a thin layer of petroleum jelly before fitting.

**16** Refitting is a reversal of removal, bearing in mind the following points:

a) *When refitting the injectors to the fuel rail, note that the groove in the metal securing clip must engage with the lug on the injector body.*

b) *Make sure that the quick-release connector audibly engages on the fuel rail.*

c) *Refit the throttle housing as described in Section 9.*

d) *Ensure that all wiring connectors are securely reconnected, and that the wiring is secured in the relevant clips and brackets.*

### Crankshaft speed/position sensor

**Note:** *A new O-ring seal must be used on refitting.*

#### Removal

**17** The crankshaft speed/position sensor is located at the rear left-hand end of the cylinder block baseplate, below the starter motor **(see illustration)**.

**18** Apply the handbrake, then jack up the front of the vehicle and support it on axle stands (see *Jacking and vehicle support*).

**19** Disconnect the sensor wiring connector, then undo the retaining bolt and withdraw the sensor from the cylinder block baseplate.

#### Refitting

**20** Refitting is a reversal of removal, but ensure that the mating surfaces of the sensor and baseplate are clean and fit a new O-ring seal to the sensor before refitting. Tighten the bolt to the specified torque.

### Camshaft sensor

#### Removal

**21** The camshaft position sensor is located on the timing cover, on the inlet camshaft side.

**22** Disconnect the sensor wiring connector.

**23** Undo the retaining bolt and withdraw the sensor from the timing cover.

**12.17 Crankshaft speed/position sensor location**

#### Refitting

**24** Refitting is a reversal of removal, but ensure that the mating surfaces of the sensor and timing cover are clean before fitting.

### Coolant temperature sensor

**25** Refer to Chapter 3 for removal and refitting details.

### Knock sensor

#### Removal

**26** The knock sensor is located on the rear of the cylinder block, just above the starter motor.

**27** Apply the handbrake, then jack up the front of the vehicle and support it on axle stands (see *Jacking and vehicle support*).

**28** On the left-hand side of the engine, disconnect the wiring connectors for the engine ECU by releasing them in the direction of the arrow marked on the connector.

**29** Unscrew the bolt securing the earth wire to the cylinder head, then unbolt and remove the ECU.

**30** Reach up behind the engine and disconnect the wiring from the knock sensor.

**31** Note its position, then unscrew the bolt and remove the knock sensor from the block.

#### Refitting

**32** Clean the contact surfaces of the sensor and block. Also clean the threads of the sensor mounting bolt.

**33** Locate the sensor on the block and insert the mounting bolt. Position the sensor as previously noted, then tighten the bolt to the

**12.38 Disconnect the wiring connectors from the electronic control unit. Note the location of the earth lead (arrowed)**

specified torque. Note that the torque setting is critical for the sensor to function correctly.

**34** Reconnect the wiring, then refit the engine ECU together with its wiring and earth wire.

**35** Lower the vehicle to the ground and reconnect the battery.

### Electronic control unit (ECU)

#### Removal

**36** The engine management ECU is located on the rear, left-hand side of the engine.

**37** Disconnect the battery negative terminal (refer to *Disconnecting the battery* in the Reference Chapter).

**38** Lift up the locking bars and disconnect the two wiring connectors at the ECU by releasing them in the direction of the arrow marked on the connector **(see illustration)**.

**39** Unscrew the bolt securing the earth wire to the cylinder head, then unbolt and remove the unit.

#### Refitting

**40** Refitting is a reversal of removal.

### Oxygen sensors

**41** Refer to Chapter 4B for removal and refitting details.

## 13 Multec-S injection system components – removal and refitting

### Airflow meter

#### Removal

**1** Disconnect the wiring connector from the airflow meter at the right-hand rear corner of the engine compartment **(see illustration 12.1)**.

**2** Slacken the retaining clamps and remove the airflow meter from the air intake ducts.

#### Refitting

**3** Refitting is a reversal of removal, but ensure that the arrow on the airflow meter body points toward the throttle housing when fitted.

### Fuel injectors and fuel rail

**Note:** *Refer to the precautions given in Section 1 before proceeding. The seals at both ends of the fuel injectors must be renewed on refitting.*

#### Removal

**4** Disconnect the battery negative terminal (refer to *Disconnecting the battery* in the Reference Chapter).

**5** Remove the air cleaner assembly and air intake duct as described in Section 2.

**6** Depressurise the fuel system as described in Section 5.

**7** Disconnect the fuel feed hose quick-release connector at the fuel rail. Be prepared for some loss of fuel. A Vauxhall/Opel special tool is available to release the connector, but provided care is taken, it can be released using a pair of long-nosed pliers, or a similar tool, to depress the retaining tangs. Clamp or plug the open end of the hose, to prevent dirt ingress and further fuel spillage.

8 Lift up the locking bars and disconnect the two wiring connectors from the ECU.

9 Disconnect the wiring connector from the throttle housing.

10 Undo the bolt securing the earth lead to the top of the ECU, then undo the three retaining bolts and remove the ECU from the inlet manifold.

11 Disconnect the wiring connector from the manifold pressure sensor on the side of the inlet manifold.

12 Release the two clips and move the wiring harness clear of the fuel rail.

13 Disconnect the wiring connector from each fuel injector.

14 Unscrew the two mounting bolts, then lift the fuel rail complete with the injectors off of the inlet manifold.

15 To remove an injector from the fuel rail, prise out the metal securing clip using a screwdriver or a pair of pliers, and pull the injector from the fuel rail. Remove and discard the injector sealing rings; new ones must be fitted on refitting.

16 Overhaul of the fuel injectors is not possible, as no spares are available. If faulty, an injector must be renewed.

### Refitting

17 Before refitting, clean thoroughly the mating surfaces of the throttle housing and inlet manifold.

18 Commence refitting by fitting new O-ring seals to both ends of the fuel injectors. Coat the seals with a thin layer of petroleum jelly before fitting.

19 Refitting is a reversal of removal, bearing in mind the following points:

a) When refitting the injectors to the fuel rail, note that the groove in the metal securing clip must engage with the lug on the injector body.

b) Make sure that the quick-release connector audibly engages on the fuel rail.

c) Ensure that all wiring connectors are securely reconnected, and that the wiring is secured in the relevant clips and brackets.

### Crankshaft speed/position sensor

**Note:** A new O-ring seal must be used on refitting.

### Removal

20 The crankshaft sensor is mounted on the front of the cylinder block below the oil filter.

21 Firmly apply the handbrake, then jack up the front of the car and support it securely on axle stands (see Jacking and vehicle support).

22 Disconnect the wiring connector, then unscrew the retaining bolt and remove the sensor from the front of the cylinder block. Discard the sealing ring, a new one should be used on refitting.

### Refitting

23 Refitting is a reversal of removal using a

new sealing ring and tightening the sensor bolt to the specified torque.

### Camshaft sensor

### Removal

24 The camshaft position sensor is located behind the timing belt rear cover, on the exhaust camshaft side.

25 Remove the air cleaner assembly and intake duct as described in Section 2.

26 Undo the two retaining bolts then unclip and remove the timing belt upper cover from the rear cover.

27 Disconnect the camshaft sensor wiring connector.

28 Using a spanner or socket on the crankshaft pulley retaining bolt, turn the crankshaft until the camshaft sensor retaining bolt is accessible through the spokes in the exhaust camshaft sprocket.

29 Undo the sensor retaining bolt, then turn the sensor and remove it from the rear of the timing belt cover.

### Refitting

30 Refitting is a reversal of removal, tightening the sensor retaining bolt to the specified torque.

### Coolant temperature sensor

31 Refer to Chapter 3 for removal and refitting details.

### Manifold pressure sensor

### Removal

32 Remove the engine management ECU as described later in this Section.

33 Disconnect the pressure sensor wiring connector.

34 Undo the sensor retaining bolt, then remove the sensor from the inlet manifold.

### Refitting

35 Refitting is a reversal of removal, tightening the sensor retaining bolt to the specified torque.

### Knock sensor

### Removal

36 The knock sensor is located on the rear of the cylinder block, just above the starter motor.

37 Apply the handbrake, then jack up the front of the vehicle and support it on axle stands (see Jacking and vehicle support).

38 Release the vacuum hose from the inlet manifold support bracket, then undo the two bolts and remove the support from the cylinder block and manifold.

39 Disconnect the wiring connector from the knock sensor.

40 Note its position, then unscrew the bolt and remove the knock sensor from the block.

### Refitting

41 Clean the contact surfaces of the sensor and block. Also clean the threads of the sensor mounting bolt.

42 Locate the sensor on the block and insert the mounting bolt. Position the sensor as previously noted, then tighten the bolt to the specified torque. Note that the torque setting is critical for the sensor to function correctly.

43 Refit the inlet manifold support bracket and attach the vacuum hose, then lower the vehicle to the ground.

### Electronic control unit (ECU)

**Note:** If a new ECU is to be fitted, this work must be entrusted to a Vauxhall/Opel dealer or suitably-equipped specialist as it is necessary to programme the new ECU after installation. This work requires the use of dedicated Vauxhall/Opel diagnostic equipment or a compatible alternative.

### Removal

44 The engine management ECU is located on the left-hand side of the inlet manifold.

45 Disconnect the battery negative terminal (refer to Disconnecting the battery in the Reference Chapter).

46 Lift up the locking bars and disconnect the two wiring connectors from the ECU.

47 Undo the bolt securing the earth lead to the top of the ECU, then undo the three retaining bolts and remove the ECU from the inlet manifold.

### Refitting

48 Refitting is a reversal of removal.

### Oxygen sensors

49 Refer to Chapter 4B for removal and refitting details.

## 14 Simtec 71.5 injection system components – removal and refitting

### Airflow meter

### Removal

1 Disconnect the wiring from the airflow meter at the right-hand rear corner of the engine compartment (see illustration 12.1).

2 Slacken the retaining clamps and remove the airflow meter from the air intake ducts.

### Refitting

3 Refitting is a reversal of removal, but ensure that the arrow on the airflow meter body points toward the throttle housing when fitted.

### Fuel injectors and fuel rail

**Note:** Refer to the precautions given in Section 1 before proceeding. The seals at both ends of the fuel injectors must be renewed on refitting.

### Removal

4 Disconnect the battery negative terminal (refer to Disconnecting the battery in the Reference Chapter).

5 Remove the plastic cover over the top of the engine.

6 Depressurise the fuel system as described in Section 5.

**14.30 Undo the two retaining bolts and remove the sensor from the cylinder head**

7 Remove the air cleaner assembly and intake duct as described in Section 2.

8 Firmly apply the handbrake, then jack up the front of the car and support it securely on axle stands (see *Jacking and vehicle support*).

9 From under the rear of the engine, disconnect the wiring connectors for the oxygen sensor and oil pressure switch. Release the wiring harness from its clips.

10 From under the front of the engine disconnect the wiring connectors at the oil level sensor and crankshaft sensor. Release the wiring harness from its clips.

11 Working from above, disconnect the camshaft sensor wiring connector, then undo the nut and disconnect the earth lead from the alternator.

12 Release the clip and disconnect the remaining crankcase ventilation hose from the camshaft cover.

13 Undo the union nut securing the fuel feed hose to the pipe on the fuel rail. Be prepared for some loss of fuel. Suitably cover or plug the open unions, to prevent dirt ingress and further fuel spillage.

14 Disconnect the wiring connectors from the following components, labelling each connector to avoid confusion when refitting:
 a) Fuel injectors.
 b) Air conditioning compressor.
 c) Coolant temperature sensor.
 d) Air conditioning pressure switch.
 e) Throttle housing.
 f) Engine management ECU.
 g) Knock sensor.
 h) EGR valve.
 i) Ignition module.

**14.35 Undo the retaining bolt and release the knock sensor from the cylinder block**

 j) Oxygen sensor.
 k) Wiring harness block connector.

15 Detach the knock sensor wiring harness plug bracket and the earth lead.

16 Release the wiring harness cable ties and unscrew the bolt securing the plastic wiring trough to the engine lifting eye. Lift up the disconnected harness and place it to one side.

17 Unscrew the two mounting bolts, then lift the fuel rail complete with the injectors off of the inlet manifold.

18 To remove an injector from the fuel rail, prise out the metal securing clip using a screwdriver or a pair of pliers, and pull the injector from the fuel rail. Remove and discard the injector sealing rings; new ones must be fitted on refitting.

19 Overhaul of the fuel injectors is not possible, as no spares are available. If faulty, an injector must be renewed.

### Refitting

20 Commence refitting by fitting new O-ring seals to both ends of the fuel injectors. Coat the seals with a thin layer of petroleum jelly before fitting.

21 Refitting is a reversal of removal, bearing in mind the following points:
 a) *When refitting the injectors to the fuel rail, note that the groove in the metal securing clip must engage with the lug on the injector body.*
 b) *Make sure that the quick-release connector audibly engages on the fuel rail.*
 c) *Ensure that all wiring connectors are securely reconnected, and that the wiring is secured in the relevant clips and brackets.*

## Crankshaft speed/position sensor

**Note:** *A new O-ring seal must be used on refitting.*

### Removal

22 The crankshaft sensor is mounted on the front of the cylinder block below the oil filter.

23 Firmly apply the handbrake, then jack up the front of the car and support it securely on axle stands (see *Jacking and vehicle support*).

24 Disconnect the wiring connector, then unscrew the retaining bolt and remove the sensor from the front of the cylinder block. Discard the sealing ring, a new one should be used on refitting.

### Refitting

25 Refitting is a reversal of removal using a new sealing ring and tightening the sensor bolt to the specified torque.

## Camshaft sensor

### Removal

26 Remove the plastic cover over the top of the engine.

27 Remove the air cleaner assembly and intake duct as described in Section 2.

28 Undo the three retaining screws, then unclip the timing belt upper cover from the rear cover and remove it from the engine compartment.

29 Disconnect the camshaft sensor wiring connector, then unclip the wiring harness.

30 Undo the two retaining bolts and remove the sensor from the cylinder head **(see illustration)**.

### Refitting

31 Refitting is the reverse of removal, tightening the sensor retaining bolts to the specified torque.

## Coolant temperature sensor

32 Refer to Section 6 of Chapter 3.

## Knock sensor

### Removal

33 The knock sensor is located on the rear of the cylinder block, just above the starter motor.

34 Apply the handbrake, then jack up the front of the vehicle and support it on axle stands (see *Jacking and vehicle support*).

35 Undo the retaining bolt securing the knock sensor to the cylinder block and release the sensor from its location **(see illustration)**.

36 Trace the wiring back to the knock sensor wiring connector. Disconnect the connector, release the wiring harness and remove the sensor.

### Refitting

37 On refitting, ensure the mating surfaces are clean and dry then fit the sensor and tighten its retaining bolt to the specified torque. Note that the torque setting is critical for the sensor to function correctly. Ensure the wiring is correctly routed and securely reconnected.

## Electronic control unit (ECU)

**Note:** *If a new ECU is to be fitted, this work must be entrusted to a Vauxhall/Opel dealer or suitably-equipped specialist as it is necessary to programme the new ECU after installation. This work requires the use of dedicated Vauxhall/Opel diagnostic equipment or a compatible alternative.*

### Removal

38 The ECU is located on the left-hand side of the inlet manifold.

39 Disconnect the battery negative terminal (refer to *Disconnecting the battery* in the Reference Chapter).

40 Remove the plastic cover over the top of the engine.

41 Lift up the locking bars and disconnect the two ECU wiring connectors.

42 Disconnect the knock sensor wiring connector and unclip the connector from the support bracket.

43 Undo the retaining bolt and detach the earth lead and knock sensor wiring support bracket from the ECU.

44 Undo the three retaining bolts and remove the ECU from the engine.

### Refitting

45 Refitting is a reversal of removal.

## Oxygen sensors

46 Refer to Section 2 of Chapter 4B.

## 15 Simtec 75.1 injection system components – removal and refitting

### Airflow meter

#### Removal

1 Disconnect the wiring connector from the airflow meter at the right-hand rear corner of the engine compartment (**see illustration**).
2 Slacken the retaining clamps and remove the airflow meter from the air intake ducts.

#### Refitting

3 Refitting is a reversal of removal, but ensure that the arrow on the airflow meter body points toward the throttle housing when fitted.

### Fuel injectors and fuel rail

**Note:** *Refer to the precautions given in Section 1 before proceeding. The seals at both ends of the fuel injectors must be renewed on refitting.*

#### Removal

4 Disconnect the battery negative terminal (refer to *Disconnecting the battery* in the Reference Chapter).
5 Depressurise the fuel system as described in Section 5.
6 Remove the air cleaner assembly and intake duct as described in Section 2.
7 Unclip the wiring harness trough from the rear of the camshaft cover (**see illustration**).
8 Pull out the retaining wire clip and disconnect the breather hose from the camshaft cover (**see illustration**).
9 Disconnect the wiring connectors from the following components, labelling each connector to avoid confusion when refitting:
  a) Engine management ECU.
  b) Evaporative emission control system purge valve.
  c) Throttle housing.
  d) Inlet camshaft VVT oil control valve.
  e) Fuel injectors.
10 Unclip the wiring harness from the support brackets and move the harness to one side.
11 Disconnect the fuel feed hose quick-release connector at the fuel rail (**see illustration**). Be prepared for some loss of fuel.

**15.1 Disconnect the wiring connector from the airflow meter**

A Vauxhall/Opel special tool is available to release the connector, but provided care is taken, it can be released using a pair of long-nosed pliers, or a similar tool, to depress the retaining tangs. Clamp or plug the open end of the hose, to prevent dirt ingress and further fuel spillage.

12 Unscrew the two mounting bolts, then lift the fuel rail complete with the injectors off of the inlet manifold.
13 To remove an injector from the fuel rail, prise out the metal securing clip using a screwdriver or a pair of pliers, and pull the injector from the fuel rail. Remove and discard the injector sealing rings; new ones must be fitted on refitting.
14 Overhaul of the fuel injectors is not possible, as no spares are available. If faulty, an injector must be renewed.

#### Refitting

15 Commence refitting by fitting new O-ring seals to both ends of the fuel injectors. Coat the seals with a thin layer of petroleum jelly before fitting.
16 Refitting is a reversal of removal, bearing in mind the following points:
  a) *When refitting the injectors to the fuel rail, note that the groove in the metal securing clip must engage with the lug on the injector body.*
  b) *Make sure that the quick-release connector audibly engages on the fuel rail.*
  c) *Ensure that all wiring connectors are securely reconnected, and that the wiring is secured in the relevant clips and brackets.*

**15.7 Unclip the wiring harness trough from the rear of the camshaft cover**

### Crankshaft speed/position sensor

**Note:** *A new O-ring seal must be used on refitting.*

#### Removal

17 The crankshaft speed/position sensor is located at the rear left-hand end of the cylinder block, below the starter motor
18 Apply the handbrake, then jack up the front of the vehicle and support it on axle stands (see *Jacking and vehicle support*).
19 Remove the starter motor as described in Chapter 5A.
20 Disconnect the sensor wiring connector, then undo the retaining bolt and withdraw the sensor from the cylinder block.

#### Refitting

21 Refitting is a reversal of removal, but ensure that the mating surfaces of the sensor and baseplate are clean and fit a new O-ring seal to the sensor before refitting. Tighten the bolt to the specified torque.

### Camshaft sensor

#### Removal

22 Two sensors are fitted, one for each camshaft. Both sensors are located at the left-hand end of the cylinder head.
23 Disconnect the wiring connector from the relevant sensor (**see illustration**). If removing the exhaust camshaft sensor, unclip the oxygen sensor wiring harness from the support bracket.
24 Undo the retaining bolt and remove the sensor from the cylinder head.

**15.8 Pull out the retaining wire clip and disconnect the breather hose from the camshaft cover**

**15.11 Disconnect the fuel feed hose quick-release connector (arrowed) at the fuel rail**

**15.23 Disconnect the wiring connector (arrowed) from the camshaft sensor (exhaust sensor shown)**

### Refitting

25 Refitting is a reversal of removal, tightening the sensor retaining bolt to the specified torque.

### Coolant temperature sensor

26 Refer to Section 6 of Chapter 3.

### Knock sensor

#### Removal

27 The knock sensor is located on the rear of the cylinder block, just above the starter motor.
28 Apply the handbrake, then jack up the front of the vehicle and support it on axle stands (see *Jacking and vehicle support*).
29 Disconnect the oxygen sensor wiring connector, then unclip the connector from the support bracket.
30 Unscrew the two retaining bolts and remove the inlet manifold support bracket.
31 Disconnect the knock sensor wiring connector, then unscrew the retaining bolt and remove the sensor from the cylinder block.

#### Refitting

32 Clean the contact surfaces of the sensor and block. Also clean the threads of the sensor mounting bolt.
33 Locate the sensor on the block and insert the mounting bolt. Tighten the bolt to the specified torque. Note that the torque setting is critical for the sensor to function correctly.
34 Refit the inlet manifold support bracket and oxygen sensor wiring connector, then lower the vehicle to the ground.

### Electronic control unit (ECU)

**Note:** *If a new ECU is to be fitted, this work must be entrusted to a Vauxhall/Opel dealer or suitably-equipped specialist as it is necessary to programme the new ECU after installation. This work requires the use of dedicated Vauxhall/Opel diagnostic equipment or a compatible alternative.*

#### Removal

35 The ECU is located on the left-hand side of the inlet manifold.

36 Disconnect the battery negative terminal (refer to *Disconnecting the battery* in the Reference Chapter).
37 Lift up the locking bars and disconnect the two ECU wiring connectors **(see illustration)**.
38 Undo the retaining bolt and detach the earth lead from the ECU.
39 Undo the four retaining bolts and remove the ECU from the engine.

#### Refitting

40 Refitting is a reversal of removal.

### Oxygen sensors

41 Refer to Section 2 of Chapter 4B.

## 16 Inlet manifold (1.4 litre engines) – removal and refitting

### Removal

1 Apply the handbrake, then jack up the front of the vehicle and support it on axle stands (see *Jacking and vehicle support*).
2 Disconnect the battery negative terminal (refer to *Disconnecting the battery* in the Reference Chapter).
3 Drain the cooling system as described in Chapter 1.
4 Remove the throttle housing as described in Section 9.
5 Disconnect the evaporative emission control system hose from the inlet manifold.
6 Depressurise the fuel system as described in Section 5.
7 Disconnect the fuel supply line from the fuel rail and release it from the support clip. A quick-release connector is fitted and Vauxhall technicians use a special tool to release it, however, provided care is taken, the connector can be released using a pair of long-nosed pliers, or a similar tool, to depress the retaining tangs.
8 Disconnect the crankcase ventilation hose from the camshaft cover, and the brake servo vacuum line from the inlet manifold.

9 Undo the two screws and remove the cover over the fuel rail.
10 Disconnect the wiring from the injectors and engine ECU, also unbolt the earth cable and unclip the wiring conduit. Place the wiring harness to one side.
11 Unbolt the EGR valve pipe from the EGR valve housing and position to one side. Discard the gasket; a new one must be used for refitting.
12 Disconnect the wiring connector from the evaporative emission control system purge valve.
13 Unscrew the nuts and withdraw the inlet manifold from the cylinder head. Discard the seals; new ones must be used for refitting.

### Refitting

14 Thoroughly clean the mating face of the inlet manifold and cylinder head, then locate the new rubber seals in the grooves in the manifold mating face **(see illustration)**.
15 Locate the inlet manifold over the cylinder head studs and secure with the nuts tightened progressively and securely.
16 Refit the EGR valve pipe together with a new gasket, and tighten the bolts securely.
17 Reconnect the wiring connector to the evaporative emission control system purge valve.
18 Reconnect the wiring to the injectors and engine ECU, and tighten the earth cable bolt.
19 Reconnect the brake servo vacuum line and crankcase ventilation hose.
20 Reconnect the fuel supply line to the fuel rail, making sure that an audible click is heard as it engages.
21 Reconnect the fuel evaporation system hose to the inlet manifold.
22 Refit the throttle housing with reference to Section 9.
23 Refit the cover over the fuel rail.
24 Lower the vehicle to the ground and reconnect the battery negative terminal.
25 Refill the cooling system with reference to Chapter 1.

**15.37 Lift up the locking bars and disconnect the two ECU wiring connectors**

**16.14 Fit new individual rubber seals to the grooves in the inlet manifold**

## 17 Inlet manifold (1.6 litre engines) – removal and refitting

### Removal

**1** Apply the handbrake, then jack up the front of the vehicle and support it on axle stands (see *Jacking and vehicle support*).

**2** Disconnect the battery negative terminal (refer to *Disconnecting the battery* in the Reference Chapter).

**3** Drain the cooling system as described in Chapter 1.

**4** Release the vacuum hose from the inlet manifold support bracket, then undo the two bolts and remove the support from the cylinder block and manifold.

**5** Disconnect the wiring connector from the evaporative emission control system purge valve. Release the quick-release connector and disconnect the hose from the valve.

**6** Remove the air cleaner assembly and air intake duct as described in Section 2.

**7** Depressurise the fuel system as described in Section 5.

**8** Disconnect the fuel supply line from the fuel rail and release it from the support clip. A quick-release connector is fitted and Vauxhall technicians use a special tool to release it, however, provided care is taken, the connector can be released using a pair of long-nosed pliers, or a similar tool, to depress the retaining tangs.

**9** Release the clips and disconnect the coolant hose from the throttle housing and thermostat housing.

**10** Remove the engine management ECU from the inlet manifold as described in Section 13.

**11** Disconnect the wiring connectors from the inlet manifold pressure sensor and throttle housing.

**12** Disconnect the brake servo vacuum hose from the inlet manifold.

**13** Unclip the wiring harness trough from the rear of the camshaft cover. Release the harness from the two support clips and move the harness to one side.

**14** Pull out the retaining wire clip and disconnect the breather hose from the camshaft cover.

**15** Unscrew the five bolts and withdraw the inlet manifold from the cylinder head. Discard the seals; new ones must be used for refitting.

### Refitting

**16** Thoroughly clean the mating face of the inlet manifold and cylinder head, then locate the new rubber seals in the grooves in the manifold mating face.

**17** Locate the inlet manifold in position on the cylinder head and secure with the bolts tightened progressively and securely.

**18** Reconnect the breather hose to the camshaft cover, then clip the wiring harness trough back in position. Secure the harness with the support clips.

**19** Reconnect the brake servo vacuum hose to the inlet manifold.

**20** Reconnect the wiring connectors to the inlet manifold pressure sensor and throttle housing.

**21** Refit the engine management ECU as described in Section 13.

**22** Reconnect the coolant hose to the throttle housing and thermostat housing.

**23** Reconnect the fuel supply line to the fuel rail, making sure that an audible click is heard as it engages.

**24** Refit the air cleaner assembly and air intake duct as described in Section 2.

**25** Reconnect the wiring connector and vapour hose to the emission control system purge valve.

**26** Refit the inlet manifold support bracket and attach the vacuum hose.

**27** Lower the vehicle to the ground and reconnect the battery negative terminal.

**28** Refill the cooling system with reference to Chapter 1.

## 18 Inlet manifold (1.8 litre engines) – removal and refitting

### Z18XE engines

#### Removal

**1** Disconnect the battery negative terminal (refer to *Disconnecting the battery* in the Reference Chapter).

**2** Remove the plastic cover over the top of the engine.

**3** Drain the cooling system as described in Chapter 1.

**4** Remove the air cleaner assembly and air intake duct as described in Section 2.

**5** Depressurise the fuel system as described in Section 5.

**6** Remove the auxiliary drivebelt as described in Chapter 1.

**7** Remove the alternator as described in Chapter 5A.

**8** Undo the two bolts and remove the inlet manifold support bracket.

**9** Disconnect the engine breather hose from the camshaft cover.

**10** Release the quick-release connector and disconnect the evaporative emission control system hose from the throttle housing.

**11** Release the retaining clips and disconnect the two coolant hoses from the throttle housing. Undo the two bolts securing the throttle housing coolant pipe to the inlet manifold and camshaft cover.

**12** Disconnect the brake servo vacuum hose from the inlet manifold.

**13** Disconnect the wiring connectors from the following components, labelling each connector to avoid confusion when refitting:

   a) *Throttle housing.*
   b) *Evaporative emission control system purge valve.*
   c) *Camshaft sensor.*

   d) *Manifold switchover flap solenoid valve.*
   e) *Oxygen sensor.*
   f) *Coolant temperature sensor.*

**14** Lift up the locking bars and disconnect the two ECU wiring connectors.

**15** Disconnect the knock sensor wiring connector and unclip the connector from the support bracket.

**16** Undo the retaining bolt and detach the earth lead and knock sensor wiring support bracket from the ECU.

**17** Undo the retaining bolts and remove the left-hand and right-hand engine lifting brackets from the cylinder head.

**18** Disconnect the wiring connectors from the four fuel injectors, then move the wiring harness trough to one side.

**19** Undo the union nut securing the fuel feed hose to the pipe on the fuel rail. Be prepared for some loss of fuel. Suitably cover or plug the open unions, to prevent dirt ingress and further fuel spillage.

**20** Referring to Chapter 3, release the quick-release fitting and disconnect the upper coolant hose from the heater matrix union on the engine compartment bulkhead.

**21** Slacken and remove the seven retaining nuts and manoeuvre the manifold assembly away from the cylinder head. Remove the gasket and discard it. **Note:** *The manifold assembly must be treated as a sealed unit; do not attempt to dismantle it as no components, other than the switchover diaphragm and solenoid, are available separately.*

#### Refitting

**22** Refitting is the reverse of removal noting the following.

   a) *Prior to refitting, check the manifold studs and renew any that are worn or damaged.*
   b) *Ensure the manifold and cylinder head mating surfaces are clean and dry and fit the new gasket. Refit the manifold and tighten the retaining nuts evenly and progressively to the specified torque.*
   c) *Ensure that all relevant hoses are reconnected to their original positions, and are securely held (where necessary) by their retaining clips.*
   d) *On completion, refill the cooling system as described in Chapter 1.*

### Z18XER engines

#### Removal

**23** Disconnect the battery negative terminal (refer to *Disconnecting the battery* in the Reference Chapter).

**24** Firmly apply the handbrake, then jack up the front of the car and support it securely on axle stands (see *Jacking and vehicle support*).

**25** Drain the cooling system as described in Chapter 1.

**26** Remove the air cleaner assembly and air intake duct as described in Section 2.

**27** Depressurise the fuel system as described in Section 5.

**28** Remove the throttle housing as described in Section 9.

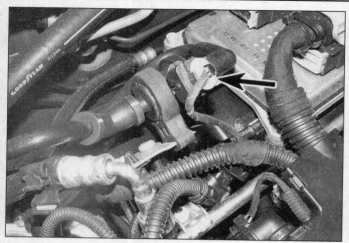

**18.32 Disconnect the wiring connector (arrowed) from the evaporative emission control system purge valve**

**18.38 Disconnect the wiring harness block connector on the left-hand side of the inlet manifold**

**29** From under the car, disconnect the oxygen sensor wiring connector, then unclip the connector from the support bracket.

**30** Unscrew the two retaining bolts and remove the inlet manifold support bracket.

**31** Unclip the wiring harness from the base of the inlet manifold.

**32** Disconnect the wiring connector from the evaporative emission control system purge valve (**see illustration**).

**33** Slide the purge valve rubber mounting off the mounting bracket, then disconnect the vapour hose from the inlet manifold. Place the valve to one side.

**34** Unclip the wiring harness trough from the rear of the camshaft cover (**see illustration 15.7**).

**35** Pull out the retaining wire clip and disconnect the breather hose from the camshaft cover (**see illustration 15.8**).

**36** Remove the engine management ECU as described in Section 15.

**37** Disconnect the wiring connectors from the inlet camshaft VVT oil control valve and the four fuel injectors. Release the wiring harness from the support brackets and place it to one side.

**38** Disconnect the wiring harness block connector on the left-hand side of the inlet manifold (**see illustration**).

**39** Release the throttle housing coolant hoses from their clips and supports on the inlet manifold and disconnect the hoses from the coolant expansion tank and thermostat housing. Move the hoses to one side.

**40** Disconnect the wiring connectors at the manifold switchover valve diaphragm and solenoid.

**41** Undo the retaining bolt and detach the wiring harness support bracket from the engine lifting bracket.

**42** Disconnect the quick-release fitting and detach the brake servo vacuum hose from the inlet manifold.

**43** Slacken and remove the seven retaining bolts and manoeuvre the manifold assembly

away from the cylinder head. Remove the gasket and discard it. **Note:** *The manifold assembly must be treated as a sealed unit; do not attempt to dismantle it as no components, other than the switchover diaphragm and solenoid, are available separately.*

**Refitting**

**44** Refitting is the reverse of removal noting the following.

 a) *Ensure the manifold and cylinder head mating surfaces are clean and dry and fit the new gasket. Refit the manifold and tighten the retaining bolts evenly and progressively to the specified torque.*

 b) *Ensure that all relevant hoses are reconnected to their original positions, and are securely held (where necessary) by their retaining clips.*

 c) *On completion, refill the cooling system as described in Chapter 1.*

## 19 Exhaust manifold – removal and refitting

### 1.4 litre engines

**Note 1:** *New manifold and exhaust front pipe retaining nuts, a new manifold gasket, exhaust*

**19.8 Remove the engine lifting brackets from the front of the cylinder head**

front pipe gasket and oil dipstick guide tube O-rings must be used on refitting.

**Note 2:** *Either a cast iron, or a pressed steel manifold may be fitted according to engine type. The following procedures are applicable to both types, but the pressed steel manifold does not have a separate heat shield.*

**Removal**

**1** Apply the handbrake, then jack up the front of the vehicle and support it on axle stands (see *Jacking and vehicle support*).

**2** Disconnect the battery negative lead (refer to *Disconnecting the battery* in the Reference Chapter).

**3** On models with air conditioning, unbolt the compressor from the front of the engine with reference to Chapter 3, and support it to one side. **Do not** disconnect the refrigerant lines from the compressor.

**4** Disconnect the wiring from the oxygen sensor, then unbolt the exhaust front pipe from the exhaust manifold, taking care to support the flexible section. **Note:** *Angular movement in excess of 10° can cause permanent damage to the flexible section.* Recover the gasket.

**5** Release the mounting rubbers and support the front of the exhaust pipe to one side.

**6** Where applicable, undo the two lower exhaust manifold support bolts.

**7** Remove the oxygen sensor from the exhaust manifold as described in Chapter 4B.

**8** Unbolt the engine lifting brackets from the cylinder head (**see illustration**).

**9** Unbolt and remove the oil dipstick guide tube, and withdraw it from the baseplate. Remove and discard the O-ring seals.

**10** Where necessary, detach the two coolant hoses from the cooling fan shroud.

**11** Unbolt the heat shield (where fitted), then undo the retaining nuts and withdraw the exhaust manifold upwards from the cylinder head studs (**see illustrations**). Recover the gasket.

**Refitting**

**12** Thoroughly clean the mating face of the

**19.11a Remove the exhaust manifold heat shield . . .**

**19.11b . . . then undo the exhaust manifold retaining nuts . . .**

**19.11c . . . and withdraw the manifold from the cylinder head studs**

exhaust manifold and cylinder head, then locate a new gasket over the studs.

**13** Locate the exhaust manifold over the cylinder head studs and secure with the (new) nuts tightened progressively to the specified torque.

**14** Refit the heat shield and tighten the retaining bolts.

**15** Fit the new O-ring seals to the oil dipstick guide tube, then insert the tube in the baseplate. Insert and tighten the retaining bolt.

**16** Refit the engine lifting brackets and securely tighten the bolts.

**17** Refer to Chapter 4B and refit the oxygen sensor to the manifold. Tighten to the specified torque.

**18** Where applicable, refit the two lower exhaust manifold support bolts.

**19** Refit the exhaust front pipe to the manifold together with a new gasket, then tighten the (new) nuts to the specified torque. Reconnect the oxygen sensor wiring connector.

**20** On air conditioning models, refit the compressor to the front of the engine with reference to Chapter 3.

**21** Lower the vehicle to the ground, then reconnect the battery negative lead.

## 1.6 litre engines

**Note:** *New manifold and exhaust front pipe retaining nuts, a new manifold gasket and exhaust front pipe gasket must be used on refitting.*

### Removal

**22** Apply the handbrake, then jack up the front of the vehicle and support it on axle stands (see *Jacking and vehicle support*).

**23** Disconnect the battery negative lead (refer to *Disconnecting the battery* in the Reference Chapter).

**24** Disconnect the wiring from the oxygen sensor, then unbolt the exhaust front pipe from the exhaust manifold, taking care to support the flexible section. **Note:** *Angular movement in excess of 10° can cause permanent damage to the flexible section.* Recover the gasket.

**25** Release the mounting rubbers and support the front of the exhaust pipe to one side.

**26** Undo the two lower exhaust manifold support bolts.

**27** On engines with an oil pressure switch

fitted to the cylinder head, remove the switch as described in Chapter 5A.

**28** Remove the oxygen sensor from the exhaust manifold as described in Chapter 4B.

**29** Unbolt the engine lifting bracket from the cylinder head.

**30** Undo the three bolts and remove the heat shield from the exhaust manifold.

**31** Undo the eleven retaining nuts and withdraw the exhaust manifold from the cylinder head studs. Recover the gasket.

### Refitting

**32** Thoroughly clean the mating face of the exhaust manifold and cylinder head, then locate a new gasket over the studs.

**33** Locate the exhaust manifold over the cylinder head studs and secure with the (new) nuts tightened progressively to the specified torque.

**34** Refit the heat shield and tighten the retaining bolts.

**35** Refit the engine lifting bracket and securely tighten the bolt.

**36** Refer to Chapter 4B and refit the oxygen sensor to the manifold. Tighten to the specified torque.

**37** Where applicable, refit the oil pressure switch to the cylinder head as described in Chapter 5A.

**38** Refit the two lower exhaust manifold support bolts.

**39** Refit the exhaust front pipe to the manifold together with a new gasket, then tighten the (new) nuts to the specified torque. Reconnect the oxygen sensor wiring connector.

**40** Lower the vehicle to the ground, then reconnect the battery negative lead.

## 1.8 litre Z18XE engines

**Note:** *New manifold and exhaust front pipe retaining nuts, a new manifold gasket, exhaust front pipe gasket and oil dipstick guide tube O-rings must be used on refitting.*

### Removal

**41** Disconnect the battery negative terminal (refer to *Disconnecting the battery* in the Reference Chapter).

**42** Remove the plastic cover over the top of the engine.

**43** Apply the handbrake, then jack up the front of the vehicle and support it on axle stands (see *Jacking and vehicle support*).

**44** Disconnect the wiring from the oxygen

sensor, then unbolt the exhaust front pipe from the exhaust manifold, taking care to support the flexible section. **Note:** *Angular movement in excess of 10° can cause permanent damage to the flexible section.* Recover the gasket.

**45** Release the mounting rubbers and support the front of the exhaust pipe to one side.

**46** Trace the wiring back from the manifold oxygen sensor and disconnect its wiring connector. Free the wiring from all the necessary clips and ties so the sensor is free to be removed with the manifold.

**47** Undo the three retaining bolts and remove the heat shield from the manifold.

**48** Unbolt the engine lifting bracket from the exhaust manifold.

**49** Unbolt and remove the oil dipstick guide tube, and withdraw it from the cylinder block. Remove and discard the O-ring seals.

**50** Slacken and remove the ten retaining nuts, and manoeuvre the manifold out of the engine compartment. Recover the gasket.

### Refitting

**51** Examine all the exhaust manifold studs for signs of damage and corrosion; remove all traces of corrosion, and repair or renew any damaged studs.

**52** Ensure that the manifold and cylinder head sealing faces are clean and flat, and fit the new gasket.

**53** Refit the manifold then fit the new retaining nuts and tighten them progressively, in a diagonal sequence, to the specified torque.

**54** Align the heat shield with the manifold, and tighten the bolts securely.

**55** Reconnect the exhaust front pipe, using a new gasket. Tighten the new nuts to the specified torque. Reconnect the oxygen sensor wiring connector.

**56** Reconnect the exhaust manifold oxygen sensor wiring connector making sure the wiring is correctly routed and retained by all the necessary clips.

**57** Refit the engine cover.

**58** Lower the vehicle to the ground, then reconnect the battery negative lead.

## 1.8 litre Z18XER engines

**Note:** *New manifold and exhaust front pipe retaining nuts, a new manifold gasket, exhaust front pipe gasket and oil dipstick guide tube O-rings must be used on refitting.*

## Removal

**59** Disconnect the battery negative terminal (refer to *Disconnecting the battery* in the Reference Chapter).

**60** Remove the air cleaner assembly and air intake ducts as described in Section 2.

**61** Unbolt and remove the oil dipstick guide tube, and withdraw it from the cylinder block. Remove and discard the O-ring seals.

**62** Trace the wiring back from the manifold oxygen sensor and disconnect its wiring connector. Free the wiring from the support bracket so the sensor is free to be removed with the manifold.

**63** Apply the handbrake, then jack up the front of the vehicle and support it on axle stands (see *Jacking and vehicle support*).

**64** Disconnect the wiring from the oxygen sensor, then unbolt the exhaust front pipe from the exhaust manifold, taking care to support the flexible section. **Note:** *Angular movement in excess of 10° can cause permanent damage to the flexible section.* Recover the gasket.

**65** Release the mounting rubbers and support the front of the exhaust pipe to one side.

**66** Undo the two lower bolts securing the heat shield to the exhaust manifold.

**67** Undo the two bolts securing the manifold to the lower support bracket, and the two bolts securing the support bracket to the cylinder block. Remove the bracket.

**68** On models with air conditioning, unbolt the compressor from the front of the engine with reference to Chapter 3, and support it to one side. **Do not** disconnect the refrigerant lines from the compressor.

**69** Unbolt the two engine lifting brackets from the exhaust manifold.

**70** Undo the bolt securing the wiring harness support bracket, then remove the bracket and the exhaust manifold heat shield.

**71** Slacken and remove the nine retaining nuts, and manoeuvre the manifold out of the engine compartment. Recover the gasket.

## Refitting

**72** Examine all the exhaust manifold studs for signs of damage and corrosion; remove all traces of corrosion, and repair or renew any damaged studs.

**73** Ensure that the manifold and cylinder head sealing faces are clean and flat, and fit the new gasket.

**20.7 Exhaust front pipe-to-catalytic converter/exhaust manifold joint**

**74** Refit the manifold then fit the new retaining nuts and tighten them progressively, in a diagonal sequence, to the specified torque.

**75** Align the heat shield with the manifold, then refit the wiring harness support bracket and tighten the retaining bolt securely.

**76** On air conditioning models, refit the compressor with reference to Chapter 3.

**77** Refit the lower support bracket to the cylinder block and manifold and tighten the retaining bolts securely.

**78** Refit and tighten the two lower bolts securing the heat shield to the exhaust manifold.

**79** Reconnect the exhaust front pipe, using a new gasket. Tighten the new nuts to the specified torque. Reconnect the oxygen sensor wiring connector.

**80** Reconnect the exhaust manifold oxygen sensor wiring connector making sure the wiring is correctly routed and retained by the support bracket.

**81** Fit the new O-ring seals to the oil dipstick guide tube, then insert the tube in the cylinder block. Insert and tighten the retaining bolt.

**82** Refit the air cleaner assembly and air intake ducts as described in Section 2.

**83** Lower the vehicle to the ground, then reconnect the battery negative lead.

### 20 Exhaust system – general information, removal and refitting

## General information

**1** The exhaust system consists of three main sections comprising a front pipe including the oxygen sensor (catalytic converter control), an intermediate pipe incorporating the front silencer and a tailpipe incorporating the rear silencer.

**2** The front pipe is attached to the exhaust manifold (catalytic converter) by a flange joint secured by nuts. All other exhaust sections are joined by overlap joints which are secured by clamps.

**3** The front pipe is fitted with a flexible section to allow for exhaust system movement and the system is suspended throughout its entire length by rubber mountings.

## Removal

**4** To remove the various parts of the system, first jack up the front or rear of the car, and support it on axle stands. Alternatively, position the car over an inspection pit, or on car ramps.

### Front pipe and intermediate pipe

**Note:** *The front pipe and intermediate pipe are removed from the car together as an assembly, then separated after removal.*

**5** Remove the tailpipe as described later in this Section.

**6** Trace the wiring back from the oxygen sensor, noting its correct routing, and disconnect its wiring connector. Free the wiring from its retaining clips so the sensor is free to be removed with the front pipe.

**7** Undo the three nuts securing the front pipe to the exhaust manifold, then free the front pipe from the manifold and recover the gasket **(see illustration)**. While doing this, take care to support the flexible section. **Note:** *Angular movement in excess of 10° can cause permanent damage to the flexible section.*

**8** Spray some penetrating oil over the exhaust rubber mounting blocks so that the mounting blocks will slide easily on the exhaust and underbody hangers.

**9** Slide the front pipe rubber mounting blocks as far forward as possible. Move the exhaust system to the rear and disengage the front pipe hangers from the mounting blocks.

**10** Move the exhaust system forward and disengage the intermediate pipe hangers from the rubber mounting blocks. Lower the front pipe and intermediate pipe to the ground and slide them out from under the car.

**11** Loosen the clamp securing the front pipe to the intermediate pipe. Support the front pipe and slide out the intermediate pipe. If the intermediate pipe is rusted onto the front pipe, apply liberal amounts of penetrating oil and tap around the joint with a hammer to free it. Twist the intermediate pipe in both directions until free.

### Tailpipe

**12** Loosen the clamp securing the tail pipe to the intermediate pipe.

**13** Unhook the tailpipe from its rubber mountings and slide the tailpipe from the intermediate pipe. If the tailpipe is rusted onto the intermediate pipe, apply liberal amounts of penetrating oil and tap around the joint with a hammer to free it. Twist the tailpipe in both directions until free.

### Heat shield(s)

**14** The heat shields are secured to the underside of the body by various nuts and bolts. Each shield can be removed once the relevant exhaust section has been removed. If a shield is being removed to gain access to a component located behind it, it may prove sufficient in some cases to remove the retaining nuts and/or bolts, and simply lower the shield, without disturbing the exhaust system.

### Refitting

**15** Each section is refitted by reversing the removal sequence, noting the following points:

a) *Ensure that all traces of corrosion have been removed from the system joints.*

b) *When refitting the front pipe to the exhaust manifold flange joint, use a new gasket and new retaining nuts, and tighten the nuts to the specified torque.*

c) *Inspect the rubber mountings for signs of damage or deterioration, and renew as necessary.*

d) *Prior to tightening the exhaust system fasteners, ensure that all rubber mountings are correctly located, and that there is adequate clearance between the exhaust system and vehicle underbody.*

# Chapter 4 Part B:
# Emissions control systems

## Contents

## Degrees of difficulty

| | | | | |
|---|---|---|---|---|
| **Easy,** suitable for novice with little experience  | **Fairly easy,** suitable for beginner with some experience | **Fairly difficult,** suitable for competent DIY mechanic | **Difficult,** suitable for experienced DIY mechanic | **Very difficult,** suitable for expert DIY or professional |

## Specifications

| Torque wrench settings | Nm | lbf ft |
|---|---|---|
| Oxygen sensor (catalytic converter control) | 40 | 30 |
| Oxygen sensor (mixture regulation): | | |
| 1.4 litre engines | 40 | 30 |
| 1.6 litre engines | 30 | 22 |
| 1.8 litre engines: | | |
| Z18XE | 30 | 22 |
| Z18XER | 40 | 30 |

### 1 General information and precautions

**1** All models use unleaded petrol and have various features built into the fuel/exhaust system to help minimise harmful emissions. All models are equipped with a crankcase emission control system, an evaporative emission control system and a catalytic converter. Additionally, all except 1.8 litre Z18XER engine models are equipped with an exhaust gas recirculation (EGR) system to keep exhaust gas emissions down to a minimum.

**2** The emission control systems function as follows.

### Crankcase emissions control

**3** To reduce the emission of unburned hydrocarbons from the crankcase into the atmosphere, the engine is sealed and the blow-by gases and oil vapour are drawn from the camshaft cover into the inlet manifold to be burned by the engine during normal combustion.

**4** The gases are forced out of the crankcase by the relatively higher crankcase pressure; if the engine is worn, the raised crankcase pressure (due to increased blow-by) will cause some of the flow to return under all manifold conditions.

### Exhaust emission control

**5** To minimise the amount of pollutants which escape into the atmosphere, all models are fitted with a catalytic converter which is integral with the exhaust manifold. The system is of the closed-loop type, in which oxygen sensors in the exhaust system provide the engine management system ECU with constant feedback, enabling the ECU to adjust the mixture to provide the best possible conditions for the converter to operate.

**6** On all engines covered by this manual, there are two heated oxygen sensors fitted to the exhaust system. The sensor on the top of the exhaust manifold/catalytic converter determines the residual oxygen content of the exhaust gases for mixture correction. The sensor in the exhaust front pipe (after the catalytic converter) monitors the function of the catalytic converter to give the driver a warning signal if there is a fault.

**7** The oxygen sensor's tip is sensitive to oxygen and sends the ECU a varying voltage signal depending on the amount of oxygen in the exhaust gases. Peak conversion efficiency of all major pollutants occurs if the intake air/fuel mixture is maintained at the chemically-correct ratio for the complete combustion of petrol of 14.7 parts (by weight) of air to 1 part of fuel (the 'stoichiometric' ratio). The sensor output voltage alters in a large step at this point, the ECU using the signal change as a reference point and correcting the intake air/fuel mixture accordingly by altering the fuel injector pulse width.

### Fuel evaporation emission control

**8** To minimise the escape into the atmosphere of unburned hydrocarbons, a fuel evaporation emission control system is fitted. The fuel tank filler cap is sealed and a charcoal canister is mounted behind the right-hand front wing. The canister collects the petrol vapours generated in the tank when the car is parked and stores them until they can be cleared from the canister (under the control of the engine management system ECU) via the purge valve into the inlet manifold to be burned by the engine during normal combustion.

**9** To ensure that the engine runs correctly when it is cold and/or idling and to protect the catalytic converter from the effects of an over-rich mixture, the purge control valve is not opened by the ECU until the engine has warmed-up, and the engine is under load; the valve solenoid is then modulated on and off to allow the stored vapour to pass into the inlet manifold.

### Exhaust gas recirculation system

**10** This system is designed to recirculate small quantities of exhaust gas into the inlet manifold, and therefore into the combustion process. This reduces the level of unburnt hydrocarbons present in the exhaust gas before it reaches the catalytic converter. The system is controlled by the engine management ECU, using the information from its various sensors, via the electrically-operated EGR solenoid valve mounted on a housing bolted to the left-hand end of the cylinder head.

**2.3 Disconnect the charcoal canister quick-release connectors**

**2.7 Withdraw the canister, together with the vapour hoses from the inner wing**

## 2 Emissions control systems – testing and component renewal

### Crankcase emission control

1 The components of this system require no attention other than to check that the hose(s) are clear and undamaged at regular intervals.

### Evaporative emission control

#### Testing

2 If the system is thought to be faulty, disconnect the hoses from the charcoal canister and purge control valve and check that they are clear by blowing through them. Full testing of the system can only be carried out using specialist electronic equipment which is connected to the engine management system diagnostic wiring connector (see Chapter 4A). If the purge control valve or charcoal canister are thought to be faulty, they must be renewed.

#### Charcoal canister renewal

3 At the right-hand rear corner of the engine compartment, disconnect the quick-release connectors connecting the charcoal canister to the inlet manifold and fuel vapour hose

(see illustration). A Vauxhall/Opel special tool is available to release the connectors, but provided care is taken, the connectors can be released using a pair of long-nosed pliers, or a similar tool, to depress the retaining tangs.

4 Apply the handbrake, then jack up the front of the vehicle and support it on axle stands (see Jacking and vehicle support). Remove the right-hand front roadwheel.

5 Remove the wheel arch liner for access to the charcoal canister which is located on the inner wing.

6 Unbolt the charcoal canister from the mounting bracket.

7 Withdraw the canister, together with the vapour hoses from the inner wing (see illustration).

8 Refitting is a reversal of the removal procedure. Make sure the hoses are correctly and securely reconnected.

#### Purge valve renewal

9 On 1.4, 1.6 and 1.8 litre Z18XER engines, the purge valve is mounted on the inlet manifold (see illustration). On 1.8 litre Z18XE engines, the valve is mounted on the alternator.

10 Disconnect the wiring from the purge valve.

11 Release the purge valve from its mounting bracket, or undo the bracket retaining bolt, as applicable.

12 Disconnect the vapour hoses and remove the purge valve.

13 Refitting is a reversal of the removal procedure, ensuring the valve is fitted the correct way around and the hoses are securely connected. Check the hoses carefully for cracking and damage, and where evident, renew them. **Note:** A cracked ventilation hose is potentially a fire hazard.

### Exhaust emission control

#### Testing

14 The performance of the catalytic converter can be checked only by measuring the exhaust gases using a good-quality, carefully-calibrated exhaust gas analyser.

15 If the CO level at the tailpipe is too high, the vehicle should be taken to a Vauxhall/Opel dealer so that the complete fuel injection and ignition systems, including the oxygen sensors, can be thoroughly checked using the special diagnostic equipment. Once these have been checked and are known to be free from faults, the fault must be in the catalytic converter, which must be renewed.

#### Catalytic converter renewal

16 The catalytic converter is an integral part of the exhaust manifold, and the removal and refitting procedure is described in Chapter 4A.

#### Oxygen sensor (mixture regulation) renewal

*Caution: The sensor will be very hot if the engine has been running within 10 or 15 minutes.*

17 The mixture regulation oxygen sensor is located on the exhaust manifold (see illustration). First, trace the wiring back from the sensor to the connector on the left-hand side of the cylinder head and disconnect it. Release the wiring from the clip.

18 Unscrew the sensor from the exhaust manifold. Ideally, a special 'split' socket should be used, as this will locate over the sensor wiring.

**2.9 Typical purge valve location (arrowed)**

**2.17 Mixture regulation oxygen sensor (arrowed)**

**2.22 Catalytic converter control oxygen sensor (arrowed)**

**2.29 EGR valve location (arrowed) – 1.4 litre engines**

**2.32 Disconnecting the wiring from the EGR valve – 1.4 litre engines**

19 Clean the threads of the sensor then coat them with Vauxhall/Opel special grease for oxygen sensors. If a new sensor is being fitted, it will be supplied with the threads already coated with the special grease to prevent it seizing in the manifold.

20 Screw the sensor into the exhaust manifold and tighten to the specified torque.

21 Reconnect the wiring and clip it in place.

### Oxygen sensor (catalytic converter control) renewal

*Caution: The sensor will be very hot if the engine has been running within 10 or 15 minutes.*

22 The catalytic converter control oxygen sensor is located in the exhaust front pipe, just behind the flexible section **(see illustration)**. First, apply the handbrake, then jack up the front of the vehicle and support it on axle stands (see *Jacking and vehicle support*).

23 Trace the wiring back from the sensor to the connector above the right-hand driveshaft, and disconnect it. Release the wiring from the clips.

24 Unscrew the sensor from the exhaust front pipe. Ideally, a special 'split' socket should be used, as this will locate over the sensor wiring.

25 Clean the threads of the sensor then coat

them with Vauxhall/Opel special grease for oxygen sensors. If a new sensor is being fitted, it will be supplied with the threads already coated with the special grease to prevent it seizing in the pipe.

26 Screw the sensor into the exhaust front pipe and tighten to the specified torque.

27 Reconnect the wiring and clip it in place.

### Exhaust gas recirculation system

#### Testing

28 Comprehensive testing of the system can only be carried out using specialist electronic equipment which is connected to the engine management system diagnostic wiring connector (see Chapter 4A). If the EGR valve is thought to be faulty, it must be renewed.

#### EGR valve renewal – 1.4 litre engines

29 The exhaust gas recirculation valve is bolted to the left-hand end of the cylinder head **(see illustration)**. First drain the cooling system as described in Chapter 1.

30 Remove the battery and battery tray as described in Chapter 5A.

31 Release the plastic locking clip and lift the coolant expansion tank out of its mounting bracket. Place the tank to one side.

32 Disconnect the wiring connector from the EGR valve and ignition module **(see illustration)**.

33 Undo the retaining bolt and remove the left-hand engine lifting bracket.

34 Disconnect the oxygen sensor wiring connector.

35 Undo the two retaining bolts and detach the wiring harness support bracket.

36 Disconnect the two wiring harness connectors from the engine management ECU.

37 Release the clip and disconnect the coolant hose from the EGR valve **(see illustration)**.

38 Unscrew the bolts securing the EGR pipe to the EGR valve **(see illustration)**. Recover the gasket and seal.

39 Unbolt the EGR valve/housing from the cylinder block and recover the gasket **(see illustration)**.

40 Refitting is a reversal of removal, but clean the mating surfaces, fit new gaskets, and tighten all bolts securely. Refill the cooling system with reference to Chapter 1.

#### EGR valve renewal – 1.6 litre engines

41 The exhaust gas recirculation valve is an integral part of the coolant housing attached to the left-hand end of the cylinder head. First drain the cooling system as described in Chapter 1.

**2.37 EGR valve coolant hose (1), wiring plug (2) and coolant temperature sensor wiring connector (3) – 1.4 litre engines**

**2.38 EGR pipe-to-EGR valve housing securing bolts (arrowed) – 1.4 litre engines**

**2.39 EGR valve housing securing bolts (arrowed) – 1.4 litre engines**

**42** Remove the battery and battery tray as described in Chapter 5A.

**43** Disconnect the wiring connectors at the thermostat, coolant temperature sensor and EGR valve.

**44** Release the retaining clips and disconnect the four coolant hoses from the coolant housing.

**45** Undo the two bolts and detach the oxygen sensor wiring harness support bracket.

**46** Undo the two bolts and remove the coolant pipe from the front of the coolant housing.

**47** Undo the four bolts and remove the coolant housing from the cylinder head. Recover the gasket.

**48** Refitting is a reversal of removal, but clean the mating surfaces, fit new gaskets, and tighten all bolts securely. Refill the cooling system with reference to Chapter 1.

### EGR valve renewal – 1.8 litre Z18XE engines

**49** Ensure the ignition is switched off then disconnect the wiring connector from the EGR valve which mounted at the left-hand end of the cylinder head.

**50** Undo the mounting bolts and remove the valve from its location. Recover the gasket.

**51** Refitting is the reverse of removal using a new gasket and tightening the valve bolts securely.

---

**3 Catalytic converter – general information and precautions**

The catalytic converter is a reliable and simple device which needs no maintenance in itself, but there are some facts of which an owner should be aware if the converter is to function properly for its full service life.

a) DO NOT use leaded petrol or LRP – the lead will coat the precious metals and reduce their efficiency, and will eventually destroy the converter.

b) Always keep the ignition and fuel systems well-maintained in accordance with the manufacturer's schedule.

c) If the engine develops a misfire, do not drive the car at all (or at least as little as possible) until the fault is cured.

d) DO NOT push- or tow-start the car.

e) Remember that the catalytic converter is FRAGILE – do not strike it with tools during servicing work.

f) The catalytic converter, used on a well-maintained and well-driven car, should last for between 50 000 and 100 000 miles – if the converter is no longer effective it must be renewed.

# Chapter 5 Part A:
## Starting and charging systems

## Contents

## Degrees of difficulty

| Easy, suitable for novice with little experience | Fairly easy, suitable for beginner with some experience | Fairly difficult, suitable for competent DIY mechanic | Difficult, suitable for experienced DIY mechanic | Very difficult, suitable for expert DIY or professional |
|---|---|---|---|---|

## Specifications

### General
Electrical system type . . . . . . . . . . . . . . . . . . . . . . . . . . . . . . . . . . . . .     12 volt negative earth

### Battery
Type . . . . . . . . . . . . . . . . . . . . . . . . . . . . . . . . . . . . . . . . . . . . . . . . . . . .     Lead-acid, 'maintenance-free' (sealed for life)
Charge condition:
  Poor . . . . . . . . . . . . . . . . . . . . . . . . . . . . . . . . . . . . . . . . . . . . . . . . .     12.5 volts
  Normal . . . . . . . . . . . . . . . . . . . . . . . . . . . . . . . . . . . . . . . . . . . . . . .     12.6 volts
  Good . . . . . . . . . . . . . . . . . . . . . . . . . . . . . . . . . . . . . . . . . . . . . . . . .     12.7 volts

## Torque wrench settings

| | Nm | lbf ft |
|---|---|---|
| Alternator: | | |
| 1.4 and 1.6 litre engines: | | |
| Alternator to mounting bracket | 35 | 26 |
| 1.8 litre engines: | | |
| Alternator mounting bracket to cylinder block | 35 | 26 |
| Alternator to mounting bracket: | | |
| Lower mounting bolt | 35 | 26 |
| Upper mounting bolt | 20 | 15 |
| Auxiliary drivebelt tensioner: | | |
| 1.4 litre engines: | | |
| M8 bolt | 20 | 15 |
| M10 bolt | 55 | 41 |
| 1.6 litre engines | 50 | 37 |
| 1.8 litre engines: | | |
| Z18XE | 35 | 26 |
| Z18XER | 50 | 37 |
| Oil level sensor: | | |
| 1.6 litre engines | 8 | 6 |
| 1.8 litre engines: | | |
| Z18XE | 18 | 13 |
| Z18XER | 8 | 6 |
| Oil pressure warning light switch: | | |
| 1.4 and 1.6 litre engines | 20 | 15 |
| 1.8 litre engines: | | |
| Z18XE | 30 | 22 |
| Z18XER | 20 | 15 |
| Roadwheel bolts | 110 | 81 |
| Starter motor: | | |
| 1.4 litre engines: | | |
| Starter motor mounting bolts | 25 | 18 |
| 1.6 litre engines: | | |
| Starter motor mounting bolts | 25 | 18 |
| Inlet manifold support bracket bolts | 8 | 6 |
| 1.8 litre Z18XE engines: | | |
| Inlet manifold support bracket to cylinder block | 35 | 26 |
| Inlet manifold support bracket to manifold | 20 | 15 |
| Starter motor mounting bolt | 25 | 18 |
| Starter motor mounting nut | 40 | 30 |
| 1.8 litre Z18XER engines: | | |
| Inlet manifold support bracket bolts | 8 | 6 |
| Starter motor mounting bolt | 25 | 18 |
| Starter motor mounting nut | 40 | 30 |

## 1  General information, precautions and battery disconnection

### General information

The engine electrical system consists mainly of the charging and starting systems. Because of their engine-related functions, these components are covered separately from the body electrical devices such as the lights, instruments, etc (which are covered in Chapter 12). Refer to Part B for information on the ignition system.

The electrical system is of 12 volt negative earth type.

The battery is of the maintenance-free (sealed for life) type, and is charged by the alternator, which is belt-driven from the crankshaft pulley.

The starter motor is of pre-engaged type incorporating an integral solenoid. On starting, the solenoid moves the drive pinion into engagement with the flywheel/driveplate ring gear before the starter motor is energised. Once the engine has started, a one-way clutch prevents the motor armature being driven by the engine until the pinion disengages.

Further details of the various systems are given in the relevant Sections of this Chapter. While some repair procedures are given, the usual course of action is to renew the component concerned.

### Precautions

It is necessary to take extra care when working on the electrical system to avoid damage to semi-conductor devices (diodes and transistors), and to avoid the risk of personal injury. In addition to the precautions given in *Safety first!* at the beginning of this manual, observe the following when working on the system:

• Always remove rings, watches, etc, before working on the electrical system. Even with the battery disconnected, capacitive discharge could occur if a component's live terminal is earthed through a metal object. This could cause a shock or nasty burn.

• Do not reverse the battery connections. Components such as the alternator, electronic control units, or any other components having semi-conductor circuitry could be irreparably damaged.

• If the engine is being started using jump leads and a slave battery, connect the batteries positive-to-positive and negative-to-negative (see *Jump starting*). This also applies when connecting a battery charger but in this case both of the battery terminals should first be disconnected.

• Never disconnect the battery terminals, the alternator, any electrical wiring or any test instruments when the engine is running.

• Do not allow the engine to turn the alternator when the alternator is not connected.

• Never test for alternator output by flashing the output lead to earth.

• Never use an ohmmeter of the type incorporating a hand-cranked generator for circuit or continuity testing.
• Always ensure that the battery negative lead is disconnected when working on the electrical system.
• Before using electric-arc welding equipment on the car, disconnect the battery, alternator and components such as the fuel injection/ignition electronic control unit to protect them from the risk of damage.

## Battery disconnection

Refer to the precautions listed in *Disconnecting the battery* in the Reference Chapter.

### 2 Electrical fault finding – general information

Refer to Chapter 12.

### 3 Battery – testing and charging

## Testing

### Traditional and low maintenance battery

**1** If the vehicle covers a small annual mileage, it is worthwhile checking the specific gravity of the electrolyte every three months to determine the state of charge of the battery. Use a hydrometer to make the check and compare the results with the following table. Note that the specific gravity readings assume an electrolyte temperature of 15°C; for every 10°C below 15°C subtract 0.007. For every 10°C above 15°C add 0.007.

| | Ambient temperature: | |
| | above 25°C | below 25°C |
| Fully-charged | 1.210 to 1.230 | 1.270 to 1.290 |
| 70% charged | 1.170 to 1.190 | 1.230 to 1.250 |
| Discharged | 1.050 to 1.070 | 1.110 to 1.130 |

**2** If the battery condition is suspect, first check the specific gravity of electrolyte in each cell. A variation of 0.040 or more between any cells indicates loss of electrolyte or deterioration of the internal plates.
**3** If the specific gravity variation is 0.040 or more, the battery should be renewed. If the cell variation is satisfactory but the battery is discharged, it should be charged as described later in this Section.

### Maintenance-free battery

**4** Where a 'sealed for life' maintenance-free battery is fitted, topping-up and testing of the electrolyte in each cell is not possible. The condition of the battery can therefore only be tested using a battery condition indicator or a voltmeter.
**5** Some models are fitted with a maintenance-free battery with a built-in 'magic-eye' charge condition indicator. The indicator is located in the top of the battery casing, and indicates the condition of the battery from its colour **(see illustration)**. If the indicator shows green, then the battery is in a good state of charge. If the indicator turns darker, eventually to black, then the battery requires charging, as described later in this Section. If the indicator shows clear/yellow, then the electrolyte level in the battery is too low to allow further use, and the battery should be renewed. Do not attempt to charge, load or jump start a battery when the indicator shows clear/yellow.

### All battery types

**6** If testing the battery using a voltmeter, connect the voltmeter across the battery and compare the result with those given in the Specifications under 'charge condition'. The test is only accurate if the battery has not been subjected to any kind of charge for the previous six hours. If this is not the case, switch on the headlights for 30 seconds, then wait four to five minutes before testing the battery after switching off the headlights. All other electrical circuits must be switched off, so check that the doors and tailgate are fully shut when making the test.
**7** If the voltage reading is less than 12.2 volts, then the battery is discharged, whilst a reading of 12.2 to 12.4 volts indicates a partially-discharged condition.
**8** If the battery is to be charged, remove it from the vehicle (Section 4) and charge it as described later in this Section.

## Charging

**Note:** *The following is intended as a guide only. Always refer to the manufacturer's recommendations (often printed on a label attached to the battery) before charging a battery.*

### Traditional and low maintenance battery

**9** Charge the battery at a rate of 3.5 to 4 amps and continue to charge the battery at this rate until no further rise in specific gravity is noted over a four hour period.
**10** Alternatively, a trickle charger charging at the rate of 1.5 amps can safely be used overnight.
**11** Specially rapid 'boost' charges which are claimed to restore the power of the battery in 1 to 2 hours are not recommended, as they can cause serious damage to the battery plates through overheating.
**12** While charging the battery, note that the temperature of the electrolyte should never exceed 38°C.

### Maintenance-free battery

**13** This battery type takes considerably longer to fully recharge than the standard type, the time taken being dependent on the extent of discharge, but it will take anything up to three days.
**14** A constant voltage type charger is required, to be set, when connected, to 13.9 to 14.9 volts

**3.5 Battery condition indicator (arrowed)**

with a charger current below 25 amps. Using this method, the battery should be usable within three hours, giving a voltage reading of 12.5 volts, but this is for a partially-discharged battery and, as mentioned, full charging can take considerably longer.
**15** If the battery is to be charged from a fully-discharged state (condition reading less than 12.2 volts), have it recharged by your Vauxhall/Opel dealer or local automotive electrician, as the charge rate is higher and constant supervision during charging is necessary.

### 4 Battery and battery tray – removal and refitting

**Note:** *Refer to 'Disconnecting the battery' in the Reference Chapter before proceeding.*

## Battery

### Removal

**1** The battery is located at the front, left-hand side of the engine compartment.
**2** Disconnect the lead at the negative (–) terminal by unscrewing the retaining nut and removing the terminal clamp **(see illustration)**. Note that the battery negative (–) and positive (+) terminal connections are stamped on the battery case.
**3** Disconnect the lead at the positive (+) terminal by lifting the plastic terminal cover, unscrewing the retaining nut and removing the terminal clamp. If necessary, the auxiliary lead may also be unbolted from the terminal.

**4.2 Unscrew the battery negative (–) terminal retaining nut, then lift the terminal clamp off the battery post**

**4.4 Unscrew the bolt and remove the battery retaining clamp**

**4.10a Undo the three retaining bolts (arrowed) . . .**

**4.10b . . . and remove the battery tray from the engine compartment**

**4** On the inner side of the battery, unscrew the bolt and remove the retaining clamp (see illustration).

**5** Carefully lift the battery from its location and remove it from the car. Make sure the battery is kept upright at all times.

### Refitting

**Note:** *As a precaution before refitting the battery, check that all doors are unlocked.*

**6** Refitting is a reversal of removal, but smear petroleum jelly on the terminals after reconnecting the leads to reduce corrosion, and always reconnect the positive lead first, followed by the negative lead.

### *Battery tray*

#### Removal

**7** Remove the battery as described previously.

**8** Release the wiring harness cable ties from the battery tray and move the harness to one side.

**9** Unclip the coolant hose and release it from the battery tray.

**10** Undo the three retaining bolts and remove the battery tray from the engine compartment (see illustrations).

#### Refitting

**11** Refitting is a reversal of removal.

---

### 5 Charging system – testing

**Note:** *Refer to the precautions given in 'Safety*

**7.5 Auxiliary drivebelt tensioner mounting bolts – 1.4 litre engines**

first!' and in Section 1 of this Chapter before starting work.

**1** If the ignition no-charge warning light fails to illuminate when the ignition is switched on, first check the alternator wiring connections for security. If satisfactory, check the condition of all related fuses, fusible links, wiring connections and earthing points. If this fails to reveal the fault, the vehicle should be taken to a Vauxhall/Opel dealer or auto-electrician, as further testing entails the use of specialist diagnostic equipment.

**2** If the ignition warning light illuminates when the engine is running, stop the engine and check the condition of the auxiliary drivebelt (see Chapter 1) and the security of the alternator wiring connections. If satisfactory, have the alternator checked by a Vauxhall/Opel dealer or auto-electrician.

**3** If the alternator output is suspect even though the warning light functions correctly, the regulated voltage may be checked as follows.

**4** Connect a voltmeter across the battery terminals, and start the engine.

**5** Increase the engine speed until the voltmeter reading remains steady; the reading should be approximately 12 to 13 volts, and no more than 14 volts.

**6** Switch on as many electrical accessories (eg, the headlights, heated rear window and heater blower) as possible, and check that the alternator maintains the regulated voltage at around 13.5 to 14.5 volts.

**7** If the regulated voltage is not as stated, the fault may be due to worn brushes, weak brush springs, a faulty voltage regulator, a faulty

**7.9 Auxiliary drivebelt tensioner mounting bolt (arrowed) – 1.6 and 1.8 litre engines**

diode, a severed phase winding, or worn or damaged slip-rings. The alternator should be renewed or taken to a Vauxhall/Opel dealer or auto-electrician for testing and repair.

---

### 6 Auxiliary drivebelt – removal and refitting

Refer to Chapter 1.

### 7 Auxiliary drivebelt tensioner – removal and refitting

### *Removal*

#### 1.4 litre engines

**1** Firmly apply the handbrake, then jack up the front of the car and support it securely on axle stands (see *Jacking and vehicle support*). Remove the right-hand front roadwheel.

**2** Remove the air cleaner assembly and air intake duct as described in Chapter 4A.

**3** Remove the auxiliary drivebelt as described in Chapter 1.

**4** Remove the right-hand engine mounting and engine mounting bracket as described in Chapter 2A.

**5** Unscrew the upper and lower mounting bolts and withdraw the tensioner pulley and spring assembly (see illustration).

#### 1.6 and 1.8 litre engines

**6** Firmly apply the handbrake, then jack up the front of the car and support it securely on axle stands (see *Jacking and vehicle support*). Remove the right-hand front roadwheel.

**7** Remove the air cleaner assembly and air intake duct as described in Chapter 4A.

**8** Remove the auxiliary drivebelt as described in Chapter 1.

**9** Undo the central mounting bolt, and remove the tensioner assembly from the engine (see illustration).

### *Refitting*

#### 1.4 litre engines

**10** Place the tensioner assembly in position, then refit and tighten the mounting bolts to the specified torque.

**11** Refit the right-hand engine mounting bracket and engine mounting as described in Chapter 2A.
**12** Refit the auxiliary drivebelt as described in Chapter 1.
**13** Refit the air cleaner assembly and air intake duct as described in Chapter 4A.
**14** Refit the roadwheel then lower the car to the ground. Tighten the roadwheel bolts to the specified torque.

### 1.6 and 1.8 litre engines

**15** Place the tensioner assembly in position ensuring that on 1.8 litre Z18XE engines, the locating pegs on the tensioner mounting surface engage correctly with the corresponding holes in the mounting bracket. Tighten the tensioner central mounting bolt to the specified torque.
**16** Refit the auxiliary drivebelt as described in Chapter 1.
**17** Refit the air cleaner assembly and air intake duct as described in Chapter 4A.
**18** Refit the roadwheel then lower the car to the ground. Tighten the roadwheel bolts to the specified torque.

### 8 Alternator – removal and refitting

## Removal

### 1.4 litre engines

**1** Disconnect the battery negative terminal (refer to *Disconnecting the battery* in the Reference Chapter).
**2** Firmly apply the handbrake, then jack up the front of the car and support it securely on axle stands (see *Jacking and vehicle support*). Remove the right-hand front roadwheel.
**3** Remove the air cleaner assembly and air intake duct as described in Chapter 4A.
**4** Remove the auxiliary drivebelt as described in Chapter 1.
**5** Undo the auxiliary drivebelt tensioner lower mounting bolt and pivot the tensioner away from the alternator.
**6** Unscrew the nuts and disconnect the two wires from the rear of the alternator.
**7** Unscrew the upper and lower mounting bolts/nuts and withdraw the alternator downwards from the block **(see illustration)**.

### 1.6 litre engines

**8** Disconnect the battery negative terminal (refer to *Disconnecting the battery* in the Reference Chapter).
**9** Firmly apply the handbrake, then jack up the front of the car and support it securely on axle stands (see *Jacking and vehicle support*). Remove the right-hand front roadwheel.
**10** Remove the air cleaner assembly and air intake duct as described in Chapter 4A.
**11** Disconnect the wiring connector and the operating rod from the port deactivation vacuum valve on the inlet manifold. Unscrew

**8.7 Alternator upper and lower mounting bolts/nuts (arrowed) – 1.4 litre engines**

the two mounting bolts and move the valve to one side.
**12** Remove the auxiliary drivebelt as described in Chapter 1.
**13** Unscrew the nuts and disconnect the two wires from the rear of the alternator.
**14** Unscrew the upper and lower mounting bolts and withdraw the alternator upwards from the block.

### 1.8 litre Z18XE engines

**15** Disconnect the battery negative terminal (refer to *Disconnecting the battery* in the Reference Chapter).
**16** Firmly apply the handbrake, then jack up the front of the car and support it securely on axle stands (see *Jacking and vehicle support*). Remove the right-hand front roadwheel.
**17** Remove the air cleaner assembly and air intake duct as described in Chapter 4A.
**18** Remove the auxiliary drivebelt as described in Chapter 1.
**19** Disconnect the camshaft sensor wiring connector and unclip the wiring from the support bracket.
**20** Undo the central mounting bolt, and remove the auxiliary drivebelt tensioner assembly from the engine **(see illustration 7.9)**.
**21** Remove the upper alternator mounting bolt.
**22** Slacken the alternator lower mounting bolt, and swing the alternator to the rear.
**23** Disconnect the oil pressure switch wiring connector and move the cable to one side.
**24** Release the wiring harness and cables from the clips on the alternator mounting bracket.
**25** Remove the rubber covers (where fitted)

**8.26 Alternator mounting bracket bolts (arrowed) – 1.8 litre Z18XE engines**

from the alternator terminals, then unscrew the retaining nuts and disconnect the wiring from the rear of the alternator.
**26** Slacken and remove the bolts securing the alternator mounting bracket to the cylinder block, then manoeuvre the alternator and bracket assembly upwards and out of position **(see illustration)**.
**27** Undo the bolt securing the alternator to its mounting bracket and separate the two components **(see illustration)**.

### 1.8 litre Z18XER engines

**28** Disconnect the battery negative terminal (refer to *Disconnecting the battery* in the Reference Chapter).
**29** Firmly apply the handbrake, then jack up the front of the car and support it securely on axle stands (see *Jacking and vehicle support*). Remove the right-hand front roadwheel.
**30** Remove the auxiliary drivebelt as described in Chapter 1.
**31** Unscrew the nuts and disconnect the two wires from the rear of the alternator.
**32** Unscrew the upper and lower mounting bolts and withdraw the alternator upwards from the block.

## Refitting

### 1.4 litre engines

**33** Manoeuvre the alternator into position and refit the retaining bolts and nuts. Tighten the nuts to the specified torque.
**34** Reconnect the wiring to the alternator terminals and tighten the retaining nuts securely.
**35** Reposition the auxiliary drivebelt tensioner, then insert the lower mounting bolt and tighten it to the specified torque.
**36** Refit the auxiliary drivebelt as described in Chapter 1.
**37** Refit the air cleaner assembly and air intake duct as described in Chapter 4A.
**38** Refit the roadwheel then lower the car to the ground. Tighten the roadwheel bolts to the specified torque.
**39** On completion, reconnect the battery negative terminal.

### 1.6 litre engines

**40** Manoeuvre the alternator into position and refit the upper and lower mounting bolts. Tighten the bolts to the specified torque.

**8.27 Undo the bolt securing the alternator to its mounting bracket and separate the two components – 1.8 litre Z18XE engines**

**41** Reconnect the wiring to the alternator terminals and tighten the retaining nuts securely.

**42** Refit the auxiliary drivebelt as described in Chapter 1.

**43** Locate the port deactivation vacuum valve back into position and secure with the two mounting bolts securely tightened. Reconnect the wiring connector and the operating rod to the valve.

**44** Refit the air cleaner assembly and air intake duct as described in Chapter 4A.

**45** Refit the roadwheel then lower the car to the ground. Tighten the roadwheel bolts to the specified torque.

**46** On completion, reconnect the battery negative terminal.

### 1.8 litre Z18XE engines

**47** Refit the mounting bracket to the alternator and secure with the mounting bolt, tightened finger-tight only at this stage.

**48** Manoeuvre the alternator and mounting bracket assembly into position and refit the mounting bracket retaining bolts. Tighten the bolts to the specified torque.

**49** Reconnect the wiring to the alternator terminals and tighten the retaining nuts securely. Where applicable, refit the rubber covers to the alternator terminals.

**50** Reconnect the wiring to the oil pressure switch, then secure the wiring harness and cables to the alternator mounting bracket.

**51** Refit the alternator upper mounting bolt, then tighten the upper and lower mounting bolts to the specified torque.

**52** Place the auxiliary drivebelt tensioner assembly in position ensuring that the locating pegs on the tensioner mounting surface engage correctly with the corresponding holes in the mounting bracket. Tighten the tensioner central mounting bolt to the specified torque.

**53** Reconnect the camshaft sensor wiring and clip the wiring into the support bracket.

**54** Refit the auxiliary drivebelt as described in Chapter 1.

**55** Refit the air cleaner assembly and air intake duct as described in Chapter 4A.

**56** Refit the roadwheel then lower the car to the ground. Tighten the roadwheel bolts to the specified torque.

**57** On completion, reconnect the battery negative terminal.

### 1.8 litre Z18XER engines

**58** Manoeuvre the alternator into position and refit the upper and lower mounting bolts. Tighten the bolts to the specified torque.

**59** Reconnect the wiring to the alternator terminals and tighten the retaining nuts securely.

**60** Refit the auxiliary drivebelt as described in Chapter 1.

**61** Refit the roadwheel then lower the car to the ground. Tighten the roadwheel bolts to the specified torque.

**62** On completion, reconnect the battery negative terminal.

## 9 Alternator – testing and overhaul

If the alternator is thought to be suspect, it should be removed from the vehicle and taken to an auto-electrician for testing. Most auto-electricians will be able to supply and fit brushes at a reasonable cost. However, check on the cost of repairs before proceeding as it may prove more economical to obtain a new or exchange alternator.

## 10 Starting system – testing

**Note:** *Refer to the precautions given in 'Safety first!' and in Section 1 of this Chapter before starting work.*

**1** If the starter motor fails to operate during the normal starting procedure, the possible causes are as follows:

a) *The engine immobiliser is faulty.*

b) *The battery is faulty.*

b) *The electrical connections between the switch, solenoid, battery and starter motor are somewhere failing to pass the necessary current from the battery through the starter to earth.*

c) *The solenoid is faulty.*

d) *The starter motor is mechanically or electrically defective.*

**2** To check the battery, switch on the headlights. If they dim after a few seconds, this indicates that the battery is discharged – recharge (see Section 3) or renew the battery. If the headlights glow brightly, operate the starter switch while watching the headlights. If they dim, then this indicates that current is reaching the starter motor, therefore the fault must lie in the starter motor. If the lights continue to glow brightly (and no clicking sound can be heard from the starter motor solenoid), this indicates that there is a fault in the circuit or solenoid – see the following paragraphs. If the starter motor turns slowly when operated, but the battery is in good condition, then this indicates either

**11.3 Battery positive cable connection on the starter motor (arrowed) – 1.4 litre engines**

that the starter motor is faulty, or there is considerable resistance somewhere in the circuit.

**3** If a fault in the circuit is suspected, disconnect the battery leads (including the earth connection to the body), the starter/solenoid wiring and the engine/transmission earth strap. Thoroughly clean the connections, and reconnect the leads and wiring. Use a voltmeter or test light to check that full battery voltage is available at the battery positive lead connection to the solenoid. Smear petroleum jelly around the battery terminals to prevent corrosion – corroded connections are among the most frequent causes of electrical system faults.

**4** If the battery and all connections are in good condition, check the circuit by disconnecting the ignition switch supply wire from the solenoid terminal. Connect a voltmeter or test lamp between the wire end and a good earth (such as the battery negative terminal), and check that the wire is live when the ignition switch is turned to the 'start' position, or the 'start/stop' button is depressed. If it is, then the circuit is sound – if not the circuit wiring can be checked as described in Chapter 12.

**5** The solenoid contacts can be checked by connecting a voltmeter or test light between the battery positive feed connection on the starter side of the solenoid and earth. When the ignition switch is turned to the 'start' position, or the 'start/stop' button is depressed, there should be a reading or lighted bulb, as applicable. If there is no reading or lighted bulb, the solenoid is faulty and should be renewed.

**6** If the circuit and solenoid are proved sound, the fault must lie in the starter motor. In this event, it may be possible to have the starter motor overhauled by a specialist, but check on the cost of spares before proceeding, as it may prove more economical to obtain a new or exchange motor.

## 11 Starter motor – removal and refitting

### Removal

#### 1.4 litre engines

**1** Disconnect the battery negative terminal (refer to *Disconnecting the battery* in the Reference Chapter).

**2** Apply the handbrake, then jack up the front of the vehicle and support it on axle stands (see *Jacking and vehicle support*).

**3** Unscrew the two nuts and disconnect the battery positive cable and the starter trigger wire from the starter **(see illustration)**.

**4** Unscrew the nut and disconnect the earth cable from the starter mounting bolt.

**5** Unscrew the two mounting bolts and withdraw the starter motor from the engine.

**14.1 Oil pressure warning light switch location (arrowed) – 1.4 litre engines**

**14.9 Oil pressure warning light switch location (arrowed) – 1.8 litre Z18XE engines**

### 1.6 litre engines

**6** Disconnect the battery negative terminal (refer to *Disconnecting the battery* in the Reference Chapter).

**7** Apply the handbrake, then jack up the front of the vehicle and support it on axle stands (see *Jacking and vehicle support*).

**8** Detach the vacuum hose from the inlet manifold support bracket, then undo the two bolts and remove the support bracket.

**9** Unscrew the two nuts and disconnect the battery positive cable and the starter trigger wire from the starter.

**10** Unscrew the nut and disconnect the earth cable from the starter mounting bolt.

**11** Unscrew the two mounting bolts and withdraw the starter motor from the engine.

### 1.8 litre engines

**12** Disconnect the battery negative terminal (refer to *Disconnecting the battery* in the Reference Chapter).

**13** Firmly apply the handbrake, then jack up the front of the car and support it securely on axle stands (see *Jacking and vehicle support*).

**14** Unscrew the two retaining bolts and remove the support bracket from the underside of the inlet manifold. Where applicable, disconnect the oxygen sensor wiring at the cable connector on the manifold support bracket.

**15** Unscrew the two retaining nuts and disconnect the wiring from the starter motor solenoid.

**16** Unscrew the retaining nut and disconnect the earth lead from the starter motor mounting bolt.

**17** Unscrew the starter motor mounting nut and mounting bolt then manoeuvre the starter motor out from underneath the engine.

### Refitting

**18** Refitting is a reversal of removal tightening the retaining nuts/bolts to the specified torque. Ensure all wiring is correctly routed and its retaining nuts are securely tightened.

## 12 Starter motor – testing and overhaul

If the starter motor is thought to be suspect, it should be removed from the vehicle and taken to an auto-electrician for testing. Most auto-electricians will be able to supply and fit brushes at a reasonable cost. However, check on the cost of repairs before proceeding as it may prove more economical to obtain a new or exchange motor.

## 13 Ignition switch – removal and refitting

The switch is integral with the steering column lock, and removal and refitting is described in Chapter 10.

## 14 Oil pressure warning light switch – removal and refitting

### Removal

#### 1.4 litre engines

**1** The oil pressure warning light switch is screwed into the front right-hand side of the cylinder head **(see illustration)**.

**2** Pull back the cover and disconnect the wiring from the switch.

**3** Place some cloth rags beneath the switch, then unscrew the switch from the block. Be prepared for oil spillage, and if the switch is to be left removed from the engine for any length of time, plug the switch aperture.

#### 1.6 litre engines

**4** On early engines two oil pressure warning light switches are fitted; one screwed into the front of the cylinder head, and one screwed into the front of the cylinder block. On later engines, only the cylinder block switched is used.

**5** To remove the cylinder head switch, undo the cable tie and detach the heat protection sheath. Disconnect the wiring connector then unscrew the switch and recover the sealing washer. If the switch is to be left removed from the engine for any length of time, plug the switch aperture.

**6** To remove the cylinder block switch, firmly apply the handbrake, then jack up the front of the car and support it securely on axle stands (see *Jacking and vehicle support*). Disconnect the wiring connector then unscrew the switch and recover the sealing washer. Be prepared for oil spillage, and if the switch is to be left removed from the engine for any length of time, plug the switch aperture.

#### 1.8 litre Z18XE engines

**7** The oil pressure warning light switch is screwed into the rear of the oil pump housing which is located on the right-hand end of the engine, on the end of the crankshaft.

**8** Firmly apply the handbrake, then jack up the front of the car and support it securely on axle stands (see *Jacking and vehicle support*).

**9** Disconnect the wiring connector then unscrew the switch and recover the sealing washer. Be prepared for oil spillage, and if the switch is to be left removed from the engine for any length of time, plug the switch aperture **(see illustration)**.

#### 1.8 litre Z18XER engines

**10** The oil pressure warning light switch is screwed into the front of the cylinder block.

**11** Firmly apply the handbrake, then jack up the front of the car and support it securely on axle stands (see *Jacking and vehicle support*).

**12** On models equipped with air conditioning, refer to Chapter 3 and unbolt the air conditioning compressor from the cylinder block **without disconnecting the refrigerant lines**. Support the compressor to one side for access to the oil pressure warning light switch.

**15.2 Slide off the retaining clip (arrowed) and free the sensor wiring connector from the sump – 1.6 and 1.8 litre Z18XER engines**

**15.3 Undo the retaining bolts and remove the oil baffle plate – 1.6 and 1.8 litre Z18XER engines**

**15.4 Undo the retaining bolts (arrowed) and remove the oil level sensor from the sump**

**15.9 Remove the oil level sensor and remove the seal – 1.8 litre Z18XE engines**

**13** Disconnect the wiring connector then unscrew the switch and recover the sealing washer. Be prepared for oil spillage, and if the switch is to be left removed from the engine for any length of time, plug the switch aperture.

### Refitting

**14** Examine the sealing washer (where fitted) for signs of damage or deterioration and if necessary renew.
**15** Refit the switch and washer (where fitted), tightening it to the specified torque, and reconnect the wiring connector.
**16** Where applicable, refit the air conditioning compressor as described in Chapter 3.
**17** Lower the vehicle to the ground then check and, if necessary, top-up the engine oil as described in *Weekly checks*.

## 15 Oil level sensor – removal and refitting

**Note:** *An oil level sensor is not fitted to 1.4 litre engines.*

### Removal

#### 1.6 litre and 1.8 litre Z18XER engines

**1** The oil level sensor is located inside the sump which must first be removed (see Chapter 2B or 2C).
**2** With the sump removed, slide off the retaining clip and free the sensor wiring connector from the sump **(see illustration)**.
**3** Undo the retaining bolts and remove the oil baffle plate from inside the sump **(see illustration)**.
**4** Note the correct routing of the wiring then undo the retaining bolts and remove the sensor assembly from the sump **(see illustration)**. Check the wiring connector seal for signs or damage and renew if necessary.

#### 1.8 litre Z18XE engines

**5** The oil level sensor is located on the front face of the engine sump.
**6** Firmly apply the handbrake, then jack up the front of the car and support it securely on axle stands (see *Jacking and vehicle support*).
**7** Drain the engine oil into a clean container then refit the drain plug and tighten it to the specified torque (see Chapter 1).

**8** Disconnect the wiring connector from the sensor.
**9** Unscrew the retaining bolts then ease the sensor out from the sump and remove it along with its sealing ring/washer. Discard the sealing ring/washer, a new one should be used on refitting **(see illustration)**.

### Refitting

#### 1.6 litre and 1.8 litre Z18XER engines

**10** Prior to refitting remove all traces of locking compound from the sensor retaining bolt and sump threads. Apply a drop of fresh locking compound to the bolt threads and lubricate the wiring connector seal with a smear of engine oil.
**11** Fit the sensor, making sure the wiring is correctly routed, and securely tighten its retaining bolts. Ease the wiring connector through the sump, taking care not to damage its seal, and secure it in position with the retaining clip.
**12** Ensure the sensor is correctly refitted then refit the oil baffle plate.
**13** Refit the sump as described in Chapter 2B or 2C.

#### 1.8 litre Z18XE engines

**14** Refitting is the reverse of removal ensuring the wiring is correctly routed and securely reconnected. On completion refill the engine with oil (see Chapter 1).

# Chapter 5 Part B:
# Ignition system

## Contents

## Degrees of difficulty

| | | | | |
|---|---|---|---|---|
| **Easy,** suitable for novice with little experience | **Fairly easy,** suitable for beginner with some experience | **Fairly difficult,** suitable for competent DIY mechanic | **Difficult,** suitable for experienced DIY mechanic | **Very difficult,** suitable for expert DIY or professional |

## Specifications

### General

| | |
|---|---|
| System type . . . . . . . . . . . . . . . . . . . . . . . . . . . . . . . . . . . . . . . . . . | Distributorless ignition system |
| System application: | |
|   1.4 litre engines . . . . . . . . . . . . . . . . . . . . . . . . . . . . . . . . . . . . . | Bosch Motronic ME 7.6.1/2 |
|   1.6 litre engines . . . . . . . . . . . . . . . . . . . . . . . . . . . . . . . . . . . . . | GM Multec-S |
|   1.8 litre engines: | |
|     Z18XE . . . . . . . . . . . . . . . . . . . . . . . . . . . . . . . . . . . . . . . . . . | Simtec 71.5 |
|     Z18XER . . . . . . . . . . . . . . . . . . . . . . . . . . . . . . . . . . . . . . . . . | Simtec 75.1 |
| Location of No 1 cylinder . . . . . . . . . . . . . . . . . . . . . . . . . . . . . . . | Timing chain/timing belt end of engine |
| Firing order . . . . . . . . . . . . . . . . . . . . . . . . . . . . . . . . . . . . . . . . . . | 1-3-4-2 |

| Torque wrench setting | Nm | lbf ft |
|---|---|---|
| Ignition module retaining bolts. . . . . . . . . . . . . . . . . . . . . . . . . . . . | 8 | 6 |

---

## 1  Ignition system – general information

The ignition system is integrated with the fuel injection system to form a combined engine management system under the control of one electronic control unit (ECU) – see Chapter 4A for further information. The ignition side of the system is of the distributorless type, and consists of the ignition module and the knock sensor.

The ignition module consists of four ignition coils, one per cylinder, in one casing mounted directly above the spark plugs. This module eliminates the need for any HT leads as the coils locate directly onto the relevant spark plug. The ECU uses its inputs from the various sensors to calculate the required ignition advance setting and coil charging time.

The knock sensor is mounted onto the cylinder block and informs the ECU when the engine is 'pinking' under load. The sensor is sensitive to vibration and detects the knocking which occurs when the engine starts to 'pink' (pre-ignite). The knock sensor sends an electrical signal to the ECU which in turn retards the ignition advance setting until the 'pinking' ceases.

The ignition systems fitted to the engines covered by this manual all operate in a similar fashion under the overall control of the engine management ECU. The systems comprise various sensors (whose inputs also provide data to control the fuel injection system), and the ECU, in addition to the ignition module and spark plugs. Further details of the system sensors and the ECU are given in Chapter 4A.

The ECU selects the optimum ignition advance setting based on the information received from the various sensors, and fires the relevant ignition coil accordingly. The degree of advance can thus be constantly varied to suit the prevailing engine operating conditions.

 *Warning: Due to the high voltages produced by the electronic ignition system, extreme care must be taken when working on the system with the ignition switched on. Persons with surgically-implanted cardiac pacemaker devices should keep well clear of the ignition circuits, components and test equipment.*

**2.2a  Unclip and remove the trim panel beneath the handbrake lever . . .**

**2.2b  . . . for access to the diagnostic socket (arrowed)**

## 2  Ignition system – testing

**1** If a fault appears in the engine management system, first ensure that all the system wiring connectors are securely connected and free of corrosion. Ensure that the fault is not due to poor maintenance; ie, check that the air cleaner filter element is clean, the spark plugs are in good condition and correctly gapped, the cylinder compression pressures are correct and that the engine breather hoses are clear and undamaged, referring to Chapters 1, 2A, 2B and 2C for further information.

**2** If these checks fail to reveal the cause of the problem, the vehicle should be taken to a suitably-equipped Vauxhall/Opel dealer or engine management diagnostic specialist for testing. A diagnostic socket is located in the centre console, to which a fault code reader or other suitable test equipment can be connected **(see illustrations)**. By using the code reader or test equipment, the engine management ECU can be interrogated, and any stored fault codes can be retrieved. This will allow the fault to be quickly and simply traced, alleviating the need to test all the system components individually, which is a time-consuming operation that carries a risk of damaging the ECU.

**3** The only ignition system checks which can be carried out by the home mechanic are those described in Chapter 1 relating to the spark plugs. If necessary, the system wiring and wiring connectors can be checked as described in Chapter 12, ensuring that the ECU wiring connector(s) have first been disconnected.

## 3  Ignition module – removal and refitting

### Removal

**1** On 1.8 litre Z18XE engines, remove the oil filler cap and unscrew the two bolts securing the plastic cover over the top of the engine. Lift off the cover and refit the oil filler cap.

**2** On 1.6 litre and 1.8 litre Z18XER engines, unclip the wiring trough from the left-hand end of the cylinder head.

**3** The ignition module is mounted at the top of the engine, between the inlet and exhaust camshaft casings. Disconnect the wiring connector at the left-hand end of the module **(see illustration)**.

**4** On all except 1.8 litre Z18XE engines, remove the cover from the ignition module by sliding it towards the transmission and lifting off **(see illustration)**.

**5** Undo the two retaining bolts, and lift the module up and out of position **(see illustration)**. If the module proves reluctant to separate from the spark plugs, insert two long 8 mm bolts into the threaded holes in the top of the module, and pull up on the bolts to free the module from the plugs.

**6** With the module removed, check the condition of the sealing grommets and renew if necessary **(see illustration)**.

### Refitting

**7** Refitting is the reversal of removal, tightening the retaining bolts to the specified torque.

**3.3  Disconnect the wiring connector from the module**

**3.4  Remove the ignition module cover by sliding it towards the transmission and lifting off**

## 4  Ignition timing – checking and adjustment

Due to the nature of the ignition system, the ignition timing is constantly being monitored and adjusted by the engine management ECU.

The only way in which the ignition timing can be checked is by using specialist diagnostic test equipment, connected to the engine management system diagnostic socket. No adjustment of the ignition timing is possible. Should the ignition timing be incorrect, then a fault is likely to be present in the engine management system.

## 5  Knock sensor – removal and refitting

Refer to the procedures contained in Chapter 4A.

**3.5  Undo the two retaining bolts, and lift the module up and out of position**

**3.6  Check the condition of the sealing grommets and renew if necessary**

# Chapter 6
# Clutch

## Contents

## Degrees of difficulty

| | | | | |
|---|---|---|---|---|
| **Easy,** suitable for novice with little experience | **Fairly easy,** suitable for beginner with some experience | **Fairly difficult,** suitable for competent DIY mechanic | **Difficult,** suitable for experienced DIY mechanic | **Very difficult,** suitable for expert DIY or professional |

## Specifications

Type . . . . . . . . . . . . . . . . . . . . . . . . . . . . . . . . . . . . . . . . . . . .   Single dry plate with diaphragm spring, hydraulically-operated

### Friction disc
Diameter:
    1.4 and 1.6 litre engines:
        Standard transmission . . . . . . . . . . . . . . . . . . . . . . . . . . . .   200 mm
        Easytronic transmission . . . . . . . . . . . . . . . . . . . . . . . . . . .   205 mm
    1.8 litre engines . . . . . . . . . . . . . . . . . . . . . . . . . . . . . . . . . .   205 mm
New lining thickness. . . . . . . . . . . . . . . . . . . . . . . . . . . . . . . . .   7.65 mm

### Torque wrench settings

| | Nm | lbf ft |
|---|---|---|
| ABS hydraulic modulator mounting bracket bolts | 20 | 15 |
| Clutch master cylinder retaining nuts* | 20 | 15 |
| Clutch pedal bracket nut/bolts* | 20 | 15 |
| Pressure plate retaining bolts: | | |
|   M7 bolts | 15 | 11 |
|   M8 bolts | 28 | 21 |
| Release cylinder mounting bolts | 5 | 4 |

\* Use new fastenings

## 1  General information

The clutch consists of a friction disc, a pressure plate assembly, and the hydraulic release cylinder (which incorporates the release bearing); all of these components are contained in the large cast-aluminium alloy bellhousing, sandwiched between the engine and the transmission.

The friction disc is fitted between the engine flywheel and the clutch pressure plate, and is allowed to slide on the transmission input shaft splines.

The pressure plate assembly is bolted to the engine flywheel. When the engine is running, drive is transmitted from the crankshaft, via the flywheel, to the friction disc (these components being clamped securely together by the pressure plate assembly) and from the friction disc to the transmission input shaft.

To interrupt the drive, the spring pressure must be relaxed. This is achieved using a hydraulic release mechanism which consists of the master cylinder, the release cylinder and the pipe/hose linking the two components. Depressing the pedal pushes on the master cylinder pushrod which hydraulically forces the release cylinder piston against the pressure plate spring fingers. This causes the springs to deform and releases the clamping force on the friction disc.

The clutch is self-adjusting and requires no manual adjustment.

### Semi-automatic clutch

Models equipped with the Easytronic MTA (Manual Transmission with Automatic shift), are fitted with a semi-automatic clutch. The clutch may be operated either fully-automatically or semi-automatically by means of the gear selector lever. There is no conventional clutch pedal fitted.

The Easytronic system essentially consists of a conventional manual gearbox and clutch fitted with electrical and hydraulic controls, the clutch being operated by a clutch module attached to the side of the transmission casing. Refer to Chapter 7C for more information. The clutch component removal and refitting procedures are included in this Chapter as they are very similar to those for the standard manual transmission.

## 2 Clutch hydraulic system – bleeding

**Note:** *On models equipped with the Easytronic transmission, the following manual method of bleeding the clutch is not possible since the hydraulic control unit is integral with the transmission. On these models, bleeding is carried out using the Vauxhall/Opel TECH2 diagnostic instrument, therefore this work should be entrusted to a Vauxhall/Opel dealer.*

⚠️ *Warning: Hydraulic fluid is poisonous; wash off immediately and thoroughly in the case of skin contact, and seek immediate medical advice if any fluid is swallowed or gets into the eyes. Certain types of hydraulic fluid are flammable, and may ignite when allowed into contact with hot components; when servicing any hydraulic system, it is safest to assume that the fluid is flammable, and to take precautions against the risk of fire as though it is petrol that is being handled. Hydraulic fluid is also an effective paint stripper, and will attack plastics; if any is spilt, it should be washed off immediately, using copious quantities of fresh water. Finally, it is hygroscopic (it absorbs moisture from the air) – old fluid may be contaminated and unfit for further use. When topping-up or renewing the fluid, always use the recommended type, and ensure that it comes from a freshly-opened sealed container.*

### General information

**1** The correct operation of any hydraulic system is only possible after removing all air from the components and circuit; this is achieved by bleeding the system.

**2** The manufacturer's stipulate that the system must be initially bled by the 'back-bleeding' method using Vauxhall/Opel special bleeding equipment. This entails connecting a pressure bleeding unit containing fresh brake fluid to the release cylinder bleed screw, with a collecting vessel connected to the brake fluid master cylinder reservoir. The pressure bleeding unit is then switched on, the bleed screw is opened and hydraulic fluid is delivered under pressure,

**2.8 Clutch bleed screw (arrowed)**

backwards, to be expelled from the reservoir into the collecting vessel. Final bleeding is then carried out in the conventional way.

**3** In practice, this method would normally only be required if new hydraulic components have been fitted, or if the system has been completely drained of hydraulic fluid. If the system has only been disconnected to allow component removal and refitting procedures to be carried out, such as removal and refitting of the transmission (for example for clutch renewal) or engine removal and refitting, then it is quite likely that normal bleeding will be sufficient.

**4** Our advice would therefore be as follows:

a) *If the hydraulic system has only been partially disconnected, try bleeding by the conventional methods described in paragraphs 10 to 15, or 16 to 19.*

b) *If the hydraulic system has been completely drained and new components have been fitted, try bleeding by using the pressure bleeding method described in paragraphs 20 to 22.*

c) *If the above methods fail to produce a firm pedal on completion, it will be necessary to 'back-bleed' the system using Vauxhall/Opel bleeding equipment, or suitable alternative equipment as described in paragraphs 23 to 28.*

**5** During the bleeding procedure, add only clean, unused hydraulic fluid of the recommended type; never re-use fluid that has already been bled from the system. Ensure that sufficient fluid is available before starting work.

**6** If there is any possibility of incorrect fluid being already in the system, the hydraulic circuit must be flushed completely with uncontaminated, correct fluid.

**7** If hydraulic fluid has been lost from the system, or air has entered because of a leak, ensure that the fault is cured before continuing further.

**8** The bleed screw is located in the hose end fitting which is situated on the top of the transmission housing **(see illustration)**. On some models access to the bleed screw is limited and it may be necessary to jack up the front of the vehicle and support it on axle stands so that the screw can be reached from below, or remove the battery and battery tray as described in Chapter 5A, so that the screw can be reached from above.

**9** Check that all pipes and hoses are secure, unions tight and the bleed screw is closed. Clean any dirt from around the bleed screw.

### Bleeding procedure

#### Conventional method

**10** Collect a clean glass jar, a suitable length of plastic or rubber tubing which is a tight fit over the bleed screw, and a ring spanner to fit the screw. The help of an assistant will also be required.

**11** Unscrew the master cylinder fluid reservoir cap (the clutch shares the same fluid reservoir

as the braking system), and top the master cylinder reservoir up to the upper (MAX) level line. Ensure that the fluid level is maintained at least above the lower level line in the reservoir throughout the procedure.

**12** Remove the dust cap from the bleed screw. Fit the spanner and tube to the screw, place the other end of the tube in the jar, and pour in sufficient fluid to cover the end of the tube.

**13** Have the assistant fully depress the clutch pedal several times to build-up pressure, then maintain it on the final downstroke.

**14** While pedal pressure is maintained, unscrew the bleed screw (approximately one turn) and allow the compressed fluid and air to flow into the jar. The assistant should maintain pedal pressure and should not release it until instructed to do so. When the flow stops, tighten the bleed screw again, have the assistant release the pedal slowly, and recheck the reservoir fluid level.

**15** Repeat the steps given in paragraphs 13 and 14 until the fluid emerging from the bleed screw is free from air bubbles. If the master cylinder has been drained and refilled allow approximately five seconds between cycles for the master cylinder passages to refill.

#### Using a one-way valve kit

**16** As their name implies, these kits consist of a length of tubing with a one-way valve fitted, to prevent expelled air and fluid being drawn back into the system; some kits include a translucent container, which can be positioned so that the air bubbles can be more easily seen flowing from the end of the tube.

**17** The kit is connected to the bleed screw, which is then opened.

**18** The user returns to the driver's seat, depresses the clutch pedal with a smooth, steady stroke, and slowly releases it; this is repeated until the expelled fluid is clear of air bubbles.

**19** Note that these kits simplify work so much that it is easy to forget the clutch fluid reservoir level; ensure that this is maintained at least above the lower level line at all times.

#### Pressure-bleeding method

**20** These kits are usually operated by the reservoir of pressurised air contained in the spare tyre. However, note that it will probably be necessary to reduce the pressure to a lower level than normal; refer to the instructions supplied with the kit.

**21** By connecting a pressurised, fluid-filled container to the clutch fluid reservoir, bleeding can be carried out simply by opening the bleed screw and allowing the fluid to flow out until no more air bubbles can be seen in the expelled fluid.

**22** This method has the advantage that the large reservoir of fluid provides an additional safeguard against air being drawn into the system during bleeding.

#### 'Back-bleeding' method

**23** The following procedure describes the bleeding method using Vauxhall/Opel equipment. Alternative equipment is available and should be used in accordance with the maker's instructions.

**24** Connect the pressure hose (MKM-6174-1) to the bleed screw located in the hose end fitting situated on the top of the transmission housing **(see illustration 2.8)**. Connect the other end of the hose to a suitable pressure bleeding device set to operate at approximately 2.0 bar.

**25** Attach the cap (MKM-6174-2) to the master cylinder reservoir, and place the hose in a collecting vessel.

**26** Switch on the pressure bleeding equipment, open the bleed screw, and allow fresh hydraulic fluid to flow from the pressure bleeding unit, through the system and out through the top of the reservoir and into the collecting vessel. When fluid, free from air bubbles appears in the reservoir, close the bleed screw and switch off the bleeding equipment.

**27** Disconnect the bleeding equipment from the bleed screw and reservoir.

**28** Carry out a final conventional bleeding procedure as described in paragraphs 10 to 15, or 16 to 19.

### All methods

**29** When bleeding is complete, no more bubbles appear and correct pedal feel is restored, tighten the bleed screw securely (do not overtighten). Remove the tube and spanner, and wash off any spilt fluid. Refit the dust cap to the bleed screw.

**30** Check the hydraulic fluid level in the master cylinder reservoir, and top-up if necessary (see *Weekly checks*).

**31** Discard any hydraulic fluid that has been bled from the system; it will not be fit for re-use.

**32** Check the operation of the clutch pedal. If the clutch is still not operating correctly, air must still be present in the system, and further bleeding is required. Failure to bleed satisfactorily after a reasonable repetition of the bleeding procedure may be due to worn master cylinder/release cylinder seals.

---

### 3  Master cylinder – removal and refitting

**Note 1:** *New master cylinder retaining nuts will be required for refitting.*
**Note 2:** *This procedure does not apply to models fitted with the Easytronic transmission.*

### Removal

#### Right-hand drive models

**1** Unscrew the brake/clutch hydraulic fluid reservoir filler cap, and top-up the reservoir to the MAX mark (see *Weekly checks*). Place a piece of polythene over the filler neck, and secure the polythene with the filler cap. This will minimise brake fluid loss during subsequent operations.

**3.3 Extract the retaining clip (arrowed) and disconnect the hydraulic pipe from the master cylinder connector**

**2** Remove all traces of dirt from the outside of the master cylinder and the brake/clutch hydraulic fluid reservoir, then position some cloth beneath the cylinder to catch any spilt fluid.

**3** Extract the retaining clip and disconnect the hydraulic pipe from the connector on the end of the master cylinder **(see illustration)**. Plug the pipe end and master cylinder port to minimise fluid loss and prevent the entry of dirt. Gently squeeze the two legs of the retaining clip together, and re-insert the clip into the master cylinder connector.

**4** Release the retaining clip (where fitted) and disconnect the fluid supply hose from the brake/clutch hydraulic fluid reservoir **(see illustration)**.

**5** From inside the car, remove the lower facia panel on the driver's side as described in Chapter 11.

**6** Disconnect the return spring from the clutch pedal, then slide off the spring clip and withdraw the clevis pin securing the master cylinder pushrod to the clutch pedal.

**7** Unscrew the two nuts securing the master cylinder to the pedal support bracket, then return to the engine compartment and remove the master cylinder from the vehicle. If the master cylinder is faulty it must be renewed; overhaul of the unit is not possible.

#### Left-hand drive models

**8** Remove the battery and battery tray as described in Chapter 5A.

**9** Lift the coolant expansion tank up and out of its mounting bracket and place it to one side.

**10** Undo the two upper bolts and one lower bolt securing the ABS hydraulic modulator mounting bracket to the bulkhead and body. Taking great care not to strain the hydraulic brake pipes, carefully move the assembly to one side as far as the brake pipes will allow and support it in this position.

**11** Continue with the removal procedure as described in paragraphs 1 to 7.

### Refitting

#### Right-hand drive models

**12** Manoeuvre the master cylinder into position whilst ensuring that the pushrod aligns correctly with the pedal. Fit two new

**3.4 Disconnect the fluid supply hose (arrowed) from the reservoir**

master cylinder retaining nuts and tighten them to the specified torque.

**13** Refit the master cylinder pushrod-to-clutch pedal clevis pin, and secure it in position with the spring clip.

**14** Refit the return spring to the clutch pedal.

**15** Refit the lower facia panel on the driver's side as described in Chapter 11.

**16** Connect the fluid supply hose to the brake/clutch hydraulic fluid reservoir and, where applicable, secure with the retaining clip.

**17** Press the hydraulic pipe back into the connector on the end of the master cylinder ensuring that the pipe audibly engages and is securely retained.

**18** Bleed the clutch hydraulic system as described in Section 2.

#### Left-hand drive models

**19** Carry out the operations described in paragraphs 12 to 17.

**20** Carefully locate the ABS hydraulic modulator mounting bracket back into position and secure with the three bolts, tightened to the specified torque.

**21** Refit the coolant expansion back into its mounting bracket.

**22** Refit the battery tray and battery described in Chapter 5A.

**23** Bleed the clutch hydraulic system as described in Section 2.

---

### 4  Release cylinder – removal and refitting

**Note 1:** *Due to the amount of work necessary to remove and refit clutch components, it is usually considered good practice to renew the clutch friction disc, pressure plate assembly and release cylinder as a matched set, even if only one of these is actually worn enough to require renewal. It is also worth considering the renewal of the clutch components on a preventative basis if the engine and/or transmission have been removed for some other reason.*
**Note 2:** *Refer to the warning concerning the dangers of asbestos dust at the beginning of Section 6.*

**4.2 Clutch release cylinder hydraulic pipe union nut (arrowed)**

**Note 3:** *On models equipped with the Easytronic transmission, Vauxhall/Opel TECH2 diagnostic equipment will be required to bleed the clutch hydraulic system and carry out a clutch Contact Point Determination program. If this equipment is not available, the following procedure should be entrusted to a Vauxhall/Opel dealer.*

### Removal

1 Unless the complete engine/transmission unit is to be removed from the car and separated for major overhaul (see the relevant Part of Chapter 2), the clutch release cylinder can be reached by removing the transmission only, as described in Chapter 7A or 7C.
2 Wipe clean the outside of the release cylinder then slacken the union nut and disconnect the hydraulic pipe **(see illustration)**. Wipe up any spilt fluid with a clean cloth.
3 Unscrew the three retaining bolts and slide the release cylinder off from the transmission input shaft **(see illustration)**. Remove the sealing ring which is fitted between the cylinder and transmission housing and discard it; a new one must be used on refitting. Whilst the cylinder is removed, take care not to allow any debris to enter the transmission unit.
4 The release cylinder is a sealed unit and cannot be overhauled. If the cylinder seals are leaking or the release bearing is noisy or rough in operation, then the complete unit must be renewed.
5 To remove the hydraulic pipe, extract the retaining clip and remove the hydraulic hose end fitting from the fastening sleeve on top of the transmission housing **(see illustration)**.

**4.5 Extract the retaining clip (arrowed) and remove the hydraulic hose end fitting from the fastening sleeve**

**4.3 Clutch release cylinder retaining bolts (arrowed)**

Gently squeeze the legs of the retaining clip together and re-insert the clip back into position in the end fitting.
6 Using a small screwdriver, carefully spread the retaining lugs of the fastening sleeve to release the hydraulic pipe connection, and remove the pipe from inside the transmission housing. Check the condition of the sealing ring on the hydraulic pipe and renew if necessary.
7 If required, the fastening sleeve can be removed by squeezing the lower retaining lugs together with pointed-nose pliers, then withdrawing the sleeve upwards and out of the transmission. Note that if the fastening sleeve is removed, a new one must be obtained for refitting.

### Refitting

8 Ensure the release cylinder and transmission mating surfaces are clean and dry and fit the new sealing ring to the transmission recess.
9 Lubricate the release cylinder seal with a smear of transmission oil then carefully ease the cylinder along the input shaft and into position. **Note:** *Vauxhall/Opel technicians use a special tapered sleeve on the input shaft to prevent damage to the seal. If necessary, wrap suitable tape around the end of the shaft.* Ensure the sealing ring is still correctly seated in its groove then refit the release cylinder retaining bolts and tighten them to the specified torque.
10 If removed, fit the new fastening sleeve, engaging the lug on the sleeve with the cut-out in the housing **(see illustration)**. Ensure that the sleeve can be felt to positively lock in position.

**4.10 Make sure the lug (arrowed) on the fastening sleeve is located correctly in the transmission housing**

11 Insert the hydraulic pipe into the fastening sleeve until the end fitting can be felt to positively lock in position.
12 Reconnect the hydraulic pipe to the release cylinder, tightening its union nut securely.
13 Refit the hydraulic hose end fitting to the fastening sleeve ensuring that it is positively retained by its clip.
14 Refit the transmission unit as described in Chapter 7A or 7C.
15 On models equipped with a conventional transmission, bleed the clutch hydraulic system as described in Section 2.
16 On models equipped with the Easytronic transmission, bleed the clutch hydraulic system and carry out a clutch Contact Point Determination program using Vauxhall/Opel TECH2 diagnostic equipment.

## 5 Clutch pedal – removal and refitting

**Note:** *New master cylinder retaining nuts and pedal bracket retaining nut/bolts will be required for refitting.*

### Removal

1 Remove the lower facia panel on the driver's side, and the steering column lower shroud, as described in Chapter 11.
2 Where fitted (according to model), remove the clutch switch from the pedal bracket.
3 Disconnect the return spring from the clutch pedal, then slide off the spring clip and withdraw the clevis pin securing the master cylinder pushrod to the clutch pedal.
4 Unscrew the upper nut (right-hand drive models), or the two upper bolts (left-hand drive models), securing the pedal bracket to the facia crossmember.
5 Unscrew the two nuts securing the clutch master cylinder to the pedal bracket, then carefully withdraw the clutch pedal and bracket from inside the vehicle. Make sure that all wiring is moved to one side as the pedal and bracket are removed.
6 Check the pedal and bracket for excessive wear and damage. It is not possible to renew the pedal pivot bushes separately, so if they are worn, the complete assembly must be renewed.

### Refitting

7 Manoeuvre the pedal and bracket assembly into position, making sure that the surrounding wiring is not trapped. Screw on the new retaining nuts/bolts, including those for the master cylinder, and tighten to the specified torque.
8 Refit the master cylinder pushrod-to-clutch pedal clevis pin, and secure it in position with the spring clip.
9 Refit the return spring to the clutch pedal then, where applicable, refit the clutch switch.
10 Refit the steering column lower shroud and the lower facia panel as described in Chapter 11.

## 6 Clutch assembly –
removal, inspection and refitting

**Warning: Dust created by clutch wear and deposited on the clutch components may contain asbestos, which is a health hazard. DO NOT blow it out with compressed air, or inhale any of it. DO NOT use petrol or petroleum-based solvents to clean off the dust. Brake system cleaner or methylated spirit should be used to flush the dust into a suitable receptacle. After the clutch components are wiped clean with rags, dispose of the contaminated rags and cleaner in a sealed, marked container.**

**Note 1:** *To prevent possible damage to the ends of the pressure plate diaphragm spring fingers, Vauxhall/Opel recommend the use of a special jig (KM-6263) to remove the clutch assembly, however, with care it is possible to carry out the work without the jig.*

**Note 2:** *On models equipped with the Easytronic transmission, Vauxhall/Opel TECH2 diagnostic equipment will be required to carry out a clutch Contact Point Determination program after the transmission has been refitted. If this equipment is not available, the following procedure should be entrusted to a Vauxhall/Opel dealer.*

### Removal

**1** Unless the complete engine/transmission unit is to be removed from the car and separated for major overhaul (see the relevant Part of Chapter 2), the clutch can be reached by removing the transmission as described in Chapter 7A or 7C.

**2** Before disturbing the clutch, use chalk or a marker pen to mark the relationship of the pressure plate assembly to the flywheel.

**3** At this stage, Vauxhall/Opel technicians fit the special jig KM-6263 to the engine and compress the diaphragm spring fingers until the friction disc is released **(see illustrations)**. The pressure plate mounting bolts are then unscrewed, and the jig spindle backed off.

**4** If the jig is not available, progressively unscrew the pressure plate retaining bolts in diagonal sequence by half a turn at a time, until spring pressure is released and the bolts can be unscrewed by hand.

**5** Remove the pressure plate assembly and collect the friction disc, noting which way round the disc is fitted. It is recommended that new pressure plate retaining bolts are obtained.

### Inspection

**Note:** *Due to the amount of work necessary to remove and refit clutch components, it is usually considered good practice to renew the clutch friction disc, pressure plate assembly and release cylinder as a matched set, even if only one of these is actually worn enough to require renewal. It is also worth considering the renewal of the clutch components on a preventative basis if the engine and/or transmission have been removed for some other reason.*

**6** When cleaning clutch components, read first the warning at the beginning of this Section; remove dust using a clean, dry cloth, and working in a well-ventilated atmosphere.

**7** Check the friction disc facings for signs of wear, damage or oil contamination. If the friction material is cracked, burnt, scored or damaged, or if it is contaminated with oil or grease (shown by shiny black patches), the friction disc must be renewed.

**8** If the friction material is still serviceable, check that the centre boss splines are unworn, that the torsion springs are in good condition and securely fastened, and that all the rivets are tight. If any wear or damage is found, the friction disc must be renewed.

**9** If the friction material is fouled with oil, this must be due to an oil leak from the crankshaft oil seal, from the sump-to-cylinder block joint, or from the release cylinder assembly (either the main seal or the sealing ring). Renew the crankshaft oil seal or repair the sump joint as described in the appropriate Part of Chapter 2, before installing the new friction disc. The clutch release cylinder is covered in Section 4.

**10** Check the pressure plate assembly for obvious signs of wear or damage; shake it to check for loose rivets, or worn or damaged fulcrum rings, and check that the drive straps securing the pressure plate to the cover do not show signs of overheating (such as a deep yellow or blue discoloration). If the diaphragm spring is worn or damaged, or if its pressure is in any way suspect, the pressure plate assembly should be renewed.

**11** Examine the machined bearing surfaces

**6.3a Vauxhall special jig KM-6263 for removing the clutch pressure plate and friction disc**

*1, 3 and 6*   *Bolts securing the jig to the engine*
*2 and 5*   *Bolts for adjusting the jig to the centre of the crankshaft*

**6.3b Thrust piece (1) in contact with the diaphragm spring fingers (3) of the pressure plate (2)**

**6.15 Mount a large bolt and washer into a vice, then fit the pressure plate over it**

**6.16 Fit large washers and a nut to the bolt and hand-tighten**

**6.17a Tighten the nut until the spring adjuster is free to turn . . .**

**6.17b . . . then open up the jaws of suitable pliers to compress the springs**

of the pressure plate and of the flywheel; they should be clean, completely flat, and free from scratches or scoring. If either is discoloured from excessive heat, or shows signs of cracks, it should be renewed – although minor damage of this nature can sometimes be polished away using emery paper.

12 Check that the release cylinder bearing rotates smoothly and easily, with no sign of noise or roughness. Also check that the surface itself is smooth and unworn, with no signs of cracks, pitting or scoring. If there is any doubt about its condition, the clutch release cylinder should be renewed (it is not possible to renew the bearing separately).

**6.21 The lettering 'transmission side' or 'Getriebeseite' on the friction disc must point towards the transmission**

### Refitting

13 On models equipped with the Easytronic transmission, the clutch pressure plate is unusual, as there is a pre-adjustment mechanism to compensate for wear in the friction disc (this is termed by Vauxhall/Opel as a self-adjusting clutch (SAC), which is slightly ambiguous as all clutches fitted to these models are essentially self-adjusting). However, this mechanism must be reset before refitting the pressure plate. A new plate may be supplied preset, in which case this procedure can be ignored.

14 A large diameter bolt (M14 at least) long enough to pass through the pressure plate, a matching nut, and several large diameter washers, will be needed for this procedure. Mount the bolt head in the jaws of a sturdy bench vice, with one large washer fitted.

15 Offer the plate over the bolt, friction disc surface facing down, and locate it centrally over the bolt and washer – the washer should bear on the centre hub **(see illustration)**.

16 Fit several further large washers over the bolt, so that they bear on the ends of the spring fingers, then add the nut and tighten by hand to locate the washers **(see illustration)**.

17 The purpose of the procedure is to turn the plate's internal adjuster disc so that the three small coil springs visible on the plate's outer surface are fully compressed. Tighten the nut just fitted until the adjuster disc is free to turn. Using a pair of thin-nosed, or circlip pliers, in one of the three windows in the top surface, open the jaws of the pliers to turn the adjuster disc anti-clockwise, so that the springs are fully compressed **(see illustrations)**.

18 Hold the pliers in this position, then unscrew the centre nut. Once the nut is released, the adjuster disc will be gripped in position, and the pliers can be removed. Take the pressure plate from the vice, and it is ready to fit.

19 On reassembly, ensure that the friction surfaces of the flywheel and pressure plate are completely clean, smooth, and free from oil or grease. Use solvent to remove any protective grease from new components.

20 Lightly grease the teeth of the friction disc hub with high melting-point grease. Do not apply too much, otherwise it may eventually contaminate the friction disc linings.

### Using the Vauxhall jig

21 Fit the special Vauxhall guide bush to the centre of the crankshaft, and locate the friction disc on it, making sure that the lettering 'transmission side' or 'Getriebeseite' points towards the transmission **(see illustration)**.

22 Locate the pressure plate on the special centring pins on the flywheel, then compress the diaphragm spring fingers with the jig, until the friction disc is in full contact with the flywheel.

23 Insert new pressure plate retaining bolts, and progressively tighten them to the specified torque. If necessary, hold the flywheel stationary while tightening the bolts, using a screwdriver engaged with the teeth of the starter ring gear.

24 Back off the jig spindle so that the diaphragm spring forces the pressure plate against the friction disc and flywheel, then remove the jig and guide bush from the engine.

25 Refit the transmission as described in Chapter 7A or 7C.

**Without using the Vauxhall jig**

**26** Locate the friction disc on the flywheel, making sure that the lettering 'transmission side' or 'Getriebeseite' points towards the transmission **(see illustration 6.21)**.

**27** Refit the pressure plate assembly, aligning the marks made on dismantling (if the original pressure plate is re-used). Fit new pressure plate bolts, but tighten them only finger-tight so that the friction disc can still be moved **(see illustration)**.

**28** The friction disc must now be centralised so that, when the transmission is refitted, its input shaft will pass through the splines at the centre of the friction disc.

**29** Centralisation can be achieved by passing a screwdriver or other long bar through the friction disc and into the hole in the crankshaft. The friction disc can then be moved around until it is centred on the crankshaft hole.

**6.27 Fit the pressure plate assembly over the friction disc**

Alternatively, a clutch-aligning tool can be used to eliminate the guesswork; these can be obtained from most accessory shops **(see illustration)**.

**30** When the friction disc is centralised,

**6.29 Centralise the friction disc using a clutch aligning tool or similar**

tighten the pressure plate bolts evenly and in a diagonal sequence to the specified torque setting.

**31** Refit the transmission as described in Chapter 7A or 7C.

# Notes

# Chapter 7 Part A:
# Manual transmission

## Contents

## Degrees of difficulty

| **Easy,** suitable for novice with little experience | **Fairly easy,** suitable for beginner with some experience | **Fairly difficult,** suitable for competent DIY mechanic | **Difficult,** suitable for experienced DIY mechanic | **Very difficult,** suitable for expert DIY or professional |
|---|---|---|---|---|

## Specifications

### General

| | |
|---|---|
| Type . . . . . . . . . . . . . . . . . . . . . . . . . . . . . . . . . . . . . . . . . . . . . . . . . | Five forward speeds and reverse. Synchromesh on all forward speeds |
| Manufacturer's designation: | |
|    1.4 litre models . . . . . . . . . . . . . . . . . . . . . . . . . . . . . . . . . . . . . . . | F13 |
|    1.6 and 1.8 litre models . . . . . . . . . . . . . . . . . . . . . . . . . . . . . . . | F17+ |

### Gear ratios

| | **F13 transmissions** | **F17+ transmissions** |
|---|---|---|
| 1st . . . . . . . . . . . . . . . . . . . . . . . . . . . . . . . . . . . . . . . . . . . | 3.72:1 | 3.72:1 |
| 2nd . . . . . . . . . . . . . . . . . . . . . . . . . . . . . . . . . . . . . . . . . . . | 2.13:1 | 2.13:1 |
| 3rd . . . . . . . . . . . . . . . . . . . . . . . . . . . . . . . . . . . . . . . . . . . | 1.41:1 | 1.41:1 |
| 4th . . . . . . . . . . . . . . . . . . . . . . . . . . . . . . . . . . . . . . . . . . . | 1.12:1 | 1.12:1 |
| 5th . . . . . . . . . . . . . . . . . . . . . . . . . . . . . . . . . . . . . . . . . . . | 0.89:1 | 0.89:1 |
| Reverse . . . . . . . . . . . . . . . . . . . . . . . . . . . . . . . . . . . . . . . | 3.30:1 | 3.30:1 |

### Final drive ratios

| | |
|---|---|
| F13 transmissions . . . . . . . . . . . . . . . . . . . . . . . . . . . . . . . . | 4.18:1 |
| F17+ transmissions . . . . . . . . . . . . . . . . . . . . . . . . . . . . . . . | 3.94:1 |

### Lubrication

| | |
|---|---|
| Lubricant type . . . . . . . . . . . . . . . . . . . . . . . . . . . . . . . . . . . | See *Lubricants and fluids* on page 0•18 |
| Lubricant capacity . . . . . . . . . . . . . . . . . . . . . . . . . . . . . . . . | See Chapter 1 |

### Torque wrench settings

| | **Nm** | **lbf ft** |
|---|---|---|
| Differential lower cover plate bolts: | | |
|    Alloy plate . . . . . . . . . . . . . . . . . . . . . . . . . . . . . . . . . . . . | 18 | 13 |
|    Steel plate . . . . . . . . . . . . . . . . . . . . . . . . . . . . . . . . . . . . | 30 | 22 |
| Engine/transmission mountings . . . . . . . . . . . . . . . . . . . . . | See the relevant Part of Chapter 2 | |
| Gearchange mechanism selector rod clamp bolt: | | |
|    Stage 1 . . . . . . . . . . . . . . . . . . . . . . . . . . . . . . . . . . . . . . | 12 | 9 |
|    Stage 2 . . . . . . . . . . . . . . . . . . . . . . . . . . . . . . . . . . . . . . | Angle-tighten a further 225° | |
| Reversing light switch . . . . . . . . . . . . . . . . . . . . . . . . . . . . . | 20 | 15 |
| Roadwheel bolts . . . . . . . . . . . . . . . . . . . . . . . . . . . . . . . . . | 110 | 81 |
| Transmission oil level plug: | | |
|    Stage 1 . . . . . . . . . . . . . . . . . . . . . . . . . . . . . . . . . . . . . . | 4 | 3 |
|    Stage 2 . . . . . . . . . . . . . . . . . . . . . . . . . . . . . . . . . . . . . . | Angle-tighten a further 45° to 135° | |
| Transmission-to-engine bolts . . . . . . . . . . . . . . . . . . . . . . . | See the relevant Part of Chapter 2 | |

**2.5 Differential cover plate securing bolts (arrowed)**

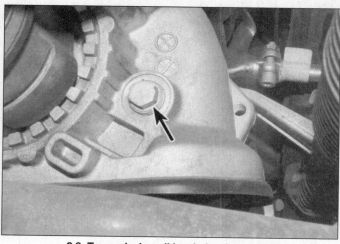

**2.8 Transmission oil level plug (arrowed)**

## 1  General information

The transmission is contained in a cast-aluminium alloy casing bolted to the engine's left-hand end, and consists of the gearbox and final drive differential – often called a transaxle.

Drive is transmitted from the crankshaft via the clutch to the input shaft, which has a splined extension to accept the clutch friction disc, and rotates in sealed ball-bearings. From the input shaft, drive is transmitted to the output shaft, which rotates in a roller bearing at its right-hand end, and a sealed ball-bearing at its left-hand end. From the output shaft, the drive is transmitted to the differential crownwheel, which rotates with the differential case and planetary gears, thus driving the sun gears and driveshafts. The rotation of the planetary gears on their shaft allows the inner roadwheel to rotate at a slower speed than the outer roadwheel when the car is cornering.

The input and output shafts are arranged side-by-side, parallel to the crankshaft and driveshafts, so that their gear pinion teeth are in constant mesh. In the neutral position, the output shaft gear pinions rotate freely, so that drive cannot be transmitted to the crownwheel.

Gear selection is via a floor-mounted lever and a rod-operated selector linkage mechanism. The selector linkage cause the appropriate selector fork to move its respective synchro-sleeve along the shaft, to lock the gear pinion to the synchro-hub. Since the synchro-hubs are splined to the output shaft, this locks the pinion to the shaft, so that drive can be transmitted. To ensure that gearchanging can be made quickly and quietly, a synchromesh system is fitted to all forward gears, consisting of baulk rings and spring-loaded fingers, as well as the gear

pinions and synchro-hubs. The synchromesh cones are formed on the mating faces of the baulk rings and gear pinions.

## 2  Transmission oil – draining and refilling

1 This operation is much more efficient if the car is first taken on a journey of sufficient length to warm the engine/transmission up to normal operating temperature.
*Caution: If the procedure is to be carried out on a hot transmission unit, take care not to burn yourself on the hot exhaust or the transmission/engine unit.*
2 Position the vehicle over an inspection pit, on vehicle ramps, or jack it up and support it securely on axle stands (see *Jacking and vehicle support*), but make sure that it is level. Where fitted, remove the clips and bolts and remove the undertray from beneath the engine.

### Draining

**Note:** *A new differential lower cover plate gasket will be required for this operation.*
3 Since the transmission oil is not renewed as part of the manufacturer's maintenance

**2.9 Fill the transmission through the reversing light switch aperture**

schedule, no drain plug is fitted to the transmission. If for any reason the transmission needs to be drained, the only way of doing so is to remove the differential lower cover plate.
4 Wipe clean the area around the differential lower cover plate and position a suitable container underneath the cover plate.
5 Evenly and progressively slacken and remove the retaining bolts then withdraw the cover plate and allow the transmission oil to drain into the container **(see illustration)**. Remove the gasket and discard it; a new one should be used on refitting.
6 Allow the oil to drain completely into the container. If the oil is hot, take precautions against scalding. Remove all traces of dirt and oil from the cover plate and transmission mating surfaces and wipe clean the inside of the cover plate.
7 Once the oil has finished draining, ensure the mating surfaces are clean and dry then refit the cover plate to the transmission unit, complete with a new gasket. Refit the retaining bolts and evenly and progressively tighten them to the specified torque.

### Refilling

8 Wipe clean the area around the level plug. The level plug is located behind the driveshaft inner joint on the left-hand side of the transmission **(see illustration)**. Unscrew the plug and clean it.
9 The transmission is refilled via the reversing light switch aperture **(see illustration)**. Wipe clean the area around the reversing light switch, and remove the switch as described in Section 6. Refill the transmission with the specified grade of oil given in *Lubricants and fluids*, until it reaches the bottom of the level plug aperture. Allow any excess oil to drain, then refit and tighten the level plug to the specified torque.
10 Refit the reversing light switch with reference to Section 6, then lower the vehicle to the ground.

**3.4 Gearchange selector rod clamp bolt and nut (arrowed)**

**3.5 Unclip and remove the access panel in the centre console**

**3.6 Carefully prise up and remove the ashtray from the centre console**

## 3 Gearchange linkage/mechanism – adjustment

**Note:** *A 5 mm drill or metal rod will be required to carry out this procedure.*

1 Adjustment of the gearchange linkage/mechanism should only be needed if the mechanism has been disconnected or removed. The mechanism is adjusted at the clamp bolt which secures the selector rod to the transmission linkage at the rear of the engine compartment. Access is best from under the vehicle.

2 Remove the battery and battery tray as described in Chapter 5A.

3 Apply the handbrake, then jack up the front of the vehicle and support it on axle stands (see *Jacking and vehicle support*). Remove the engine undertray where fitted.

4 Slacken the gearchange selector rod clamp bolt which is situated at the front of the rod (see illustration). Do not remove the bolt completely.

5 From inside the vehicle, unclip and remove the access panel in the centre console, beneath the handbrake lever (see illustration).

6 Using a small screwdriver, carefully prise up the right-hand side of the ashtray, withdraw the ashtray from the centre console and disconnect the wiring connector (see illustration).

7 Undo the two screws securing the rear of the gear lever gaiter trim panel to the centre console. Lift the panel up at the rear and disengage it from the centre console at the front (see illustrations). Fold the gaiter up the gear lever for access to the gear lever base.

8 Push the gear lever to the left in neutral, then insert a 5 mm drill or metal rod through the special hole in the lever base to lock it in the adjusting position (see illustration).

9 Working in the engine compartment, with the selector mechanism in neutral, turn the selector shaft anti-clockwise against the spring pressure towards the third gear position, and lock the selector mechanism by pressing in the spring-loaded locking pin which is located on the top of the transmission unit (see illustration). Ensure that the locking pin is pressed fully in so that the spring is completely compressed.

**3.7a Undo the two screws (arrowed) securing the gear lever gaiter trim panel to the centre console . . .**

10 With both the lever and transmission locked in position, tighten the selector rod clamp bolt to the specified Stage 1 torque, then through the Stage 2 angle.

11 Remove the locking rod from the gear lever and check the operation of the gearchange mechanism; the transmission locking pin will automatically release when the lever is moved into the reverse position.

12 Ensure the transmission locking pin has released, then refit the engine undertray (where necessary) and lower the vehicle to the ground.

13 Refit the battery tray and battery as described in Chapter 5A.

14 Check that all gears can be engaged easily, first with the engine off, then with the engine running and the clutch disengaged.

15 On completion, refit the gear lever gaiter trim panel, ashtray, and access panel to the centre console.

**3.8 Insert a 5 mm drill or punch through the lever base and into the locating hole**

**3.7b . . . then lift the panel up and disengage it from the centre console at the front**

## 4 Gearchange linkage/mechanism – removal and refitting

1 The gearchange mechanism consists of the gear lever housing and selector rod, and the linkage assembly on the transmission. The lever housing and selector rod, and the linkage assembly can be removed separately.

### Gear lever housing and selector rod

#### Removal

2 Apply the handbrake, then jack up the front of the vehicle and support it on axle stands (see *Jacking and vehicle support*). Where fitted, remove the engine undertray.

3 Reach up behind the transmission and

**3.9 Lock the selector mechanism by pressing in the spring-loaded locking pin (arrowed)**

**4.11 Gearchange universal joint removal**

*Arrow shows position of hollow pin retaining spring*

slacken the gearchange selector rod clamp bolt which is situated at the front of the rod **(see illustration 3.4)**. Do not remove the bolt completely. Push the selector rod rearwards and separate it from the shift guide.

**4** Prise the gaiter from the bulkhead and withdraw from the selector rod.

**5** Remove the centre console as described in Chapter 11.

**6** Unscrew the four bolts, then withdraw the gear lever housing and selector rod assembly from the vehicle.

**Refitting**

**7** Refitting is a reversal of removal, tightening the housing mounting bolts securely. Adjust the linkage as described in Section 3 before refitting the centre console.

### Linkage assembly

**Removal**

**8** Apply the handbrake, then jack up the front of the vehicle and support it on axle stands (see *Jacking and vehicle support*). Where fitted, remove the engine undertray.

**5.4 Prising out a driveshaft oil seal**

**9** Reach up behind the transmission and slacken the gearchange selector rod clamp bolt which is situated at the front of the rod **(see illustration 3.4)**. Do not remove the bolt completely. Push the selector rod rearwards and separate it from the shift guide.

**10** Remove the two clips and disconnect the linkage from the shift guide brackets.

**11** Depress the retaining spring and lever out the pin. Detach the universal joint from the shift rod **(see illustration)**.

**12** Withdraw the linkage assembly upwards and out of position.

**Refitting**

**13** Refitting is a reversal of removal, but adjust the linkage as described in Section 3.

| 5 | Oil seals –<br>renewal |
|---|---|

### Driveshaft oil seals

**1** Firmly apply the handbrake, then jack up

**5.5 Fitting a new driveshaft oil seal using a socket as a tubular drift**

the front of the car and support it securely on axle stands (see *Jacking and vehicle support*).

**2** Drain the transmission oil as described in Section 2.

**3** Remove the driveshaft/intermediate shaft as described in Chapter 8.

**4** Note the correct fitted depth of the seal in its housing then carefully prise it out of position using a large flat-bladed screwdriver **(see illustration)**.

**5** Remove all traces of dirt from the area around the oil seal aperture, then apply a smear of grease to the outer lip of the new oil seal. Ensure the seal is correctly positioned, with its sealing lip facing inwards, and tap it squarely into position, using a suitable tubular drift (such as a socket) which bears only on the hard outer edge of the seal **(see illustration)**. Ensure the seal is fitted at the same depth in its housing that the original was.

**6** Refit the driveshaft/intermediate shaft as described in Chapter 8.

**7** Refill the transmission with the specified type and amount of oil, as described in Section 2.

### Input shaft oil seal

**8** The input shaft oil seal is an integral part of the clutch release cylinder; if the seal is leaking the complete release cylinder assembly must be renewed. Before condemning the release cylinder, check that the leak is not coming from the sealing ring which is fitted between the cylinder and the transmission housing; the sealing ring can be renewed once the release cylinder assembly has been removed. Refer to Chapter 6 for removal and refitting details.

### Selector rod oil seal

**9** Renewal of the selector rod oil seal requires the selector mechanism cover to be unbolted from the transmission and dismantled. This task is considered to be beyond the scope of the DIY mechanic, and should therefore be entrusted to a Vauxhall/Opel dealer or transmission specialist.

| 6 | Reversing light switch –<br>testing, removal and refitting |  |
|---|---|---|

### Testing

**1** The reversing light circuit is controlled by a plunger-type switch screwed into the top of the transmission towards the front of the housing.

**2** If a fault develops in the circuit, first ensure that the circuit fuse has not blown and that the reversing light bulbs are sound.

**3** To test the switch, disconnect the wiring connector **(see illustration)**. Use a multimeter (set to the resistance function) or a battery-and-bulb test circuit to check that there is continuity between the switch terminals only when reverse gear is selected. If this is not the case, and there are no obvious breaks or other damage to the wires, the switch is faulty, and must be renewed.

### Removal

**4** Disconnect the wiring connector, then unscrew the switch and remove it from the transmission casing along with its sealing washer **(see illustration)**.

### Refitting

**5** Fit a new sealing washer to the switch, then screw it back into position in the top of the transmission housing and tighten it to the specified torque. Reconnect the wiring connector, then test the operation of the circuit.

**7 Transmission –** removal and refitting

### Removal

**1** Apply the handbrake, then jack up the front of the vehicle and support it on axle stands (see *Jacking and vehicle support*). Allow sufficient working room to remove the transmission from under the left-hand side of the engine compartment. Remove both front roadwheels then, where necessary, undo the retaining clips/screws and remove the engine undertray. Also remove the engine top cover where fitted.

**2** Remove the battery and battery tray as described in Chapter 5A.

**3** Drain the transmission oil as described in Section 2.

**4** Disconnect the wiring connector from the reversing light switch and free the wiring from the transmission unit and retaining brackets.

**5** Remove the filler cap from the brake/clutch fluid reservoir on the bulkhead, then tighten it onto a piece of polythene. This will reduce the loss of fluid when the clutch hydraulic hose is disconnected. Alternatively, fit a hose clamp to the flexible hose next to the clutch hydraulic connection on the transmission housing.

**6** Place some cloth rags beneath the hose, then prise out the retaining clip securing the clutch hydraulic pipe/hose end fitting to the top of the transmission bellhousing and detach the end fitting from the transmission **(see illustration)**. Gently squeeze the two legs of the retaining clip together and re-insert the retaining clip back into position in the end fitting. Discard the sealing ring from the pipe end; a new sealing ring must be used on refitting. Plug/cover both the union and pipe ends to minimise fluid loss and prevent the entry of dirt into the hydraulic system. **Note:** *Whilst the hose/pipe is disconnected, do not depress the clutch pedal.*

**7** Refer to Section 4 and disconnect the gearchange/selector rod from the transmission.

**8** Disconnect the inner ends of both driveshafts/intermediate shaft from the differential as described in Chapter 8. There is no need to disconnect the driveshafts from the swivel

**6.3 Disconnecting the wiring from the reversing light switch**

hub. Support the driveshafts by suspending them with wire or string – do not allow the driveshafts to hang down under their own weight, or the joints may be damaged.

**9** Remove the front subframe assembly as described in Chapter 10, ensuring that the engine unit is securely supported by connecting a hoist to the engine assembly. If available, the type of support bar which locates in the engine compartment side channels is to be preferred.

**10** Unscrew and remove the upper bolts securing the transmission to the rear of the engine. Where necessary, pull up the coolant hoses and secure them away from the transmission using plastic cable ties.

**11** Place a jack with a block of wood beneath the transmission, and raise the jack to take the weight of the transmission.

**12** Unbolt the left-hand engine/transmission mounting bracket from the transmission with reference to the relevant Part of Chapter 2.

**13** Lower the left-hand side of the engine/transmission making sure that the coolant hoses and wiring harnesses are not stretched.

**14** Slacken and remove the remaining bolts securing the transmission to the engine and sump flange. Note the correct fitted positions of each bolt, and the relevant brackets, as they are removed to use as a reference on refitting. Make a final check that all components have been disconnected, and are positioned clear of the transmission so that they will not hinder the removal procedure.

**15** With the bolts removed, move the trolley jack and transmission, to free it from its locating dowels. Once the transmission is free, lower the jack and manoeuvre the unit out from under the car. Remove the locating dowels from the transmission or engine if they are loose, and keep them in a safe place.

### Refitting

**16** The transmission is refitted by a reversal of the removal procedure, bearing in mind the following points.

a) Ensure the locating dowels are correctly positioned prior to installation.

b) Tighten all nuts and bolts to the specified torque (where given).

c) Renew the driveshaft oil seals (see Section 5) before refitting the driveshafts/intermediate shaft.

**6.4 Removing the reversing light switch and sealing washer**

d) Refit the front subframe assembly as described in Chapter 10.

e) Fit a new sealing ring to the clutch hydraulic hose before clipping the hose into the end fitting. Ensure the hose is securely retained by its clip then bleed the hydraulic system as described in Chapter 6.

f) Refill the transmission with the specified type and quantity of oil, as described in Section 2.

g) On completion, adjust the gearchange linkage/mechanism as described in Section 3.

**8 Transmission overhaul –** general information

**1** Overhauling a manual transmission unit is a difficult and involved job for the DIY home mechanic. In addition to dismantling and reassembling many small parts, clearances must be precisely measured and, if necessary, changed by selecting shims and spacers. Internal transmission components are also often difficult to obtain, and in many instances, extremely expensive. Because of this, if the transmission develops a fault or becomes noisy, the best course of action is to have the unit overhauled by a specialist repairer, or to obtain an exchange reconditioned unit.

**2** Nevertheless, it is not impossible for the more experienced mechanic to overhaul the transmission, provided the special tools are available, and the job is done in a deliberate

**7.6 Prise out the clip to disconnect the clutch hydraulic hose from the release cylinder pipe**

step-by-step manner, so that nothing is overlooked.

**3** The tools necessary for an overhaul include internal and external circlip pliers, bearing pullers, a slide hammer, a set of pin punches, a dial test indicator, and possibly a hydraulic press. In addition, a large, sturdy workbench and a vice will be required.

**4** During dismantling of the transmission, make careful notes of how each component is fitted, to make reassembly easier and more accurate.

**5** Before dismantling the transmission, it will help if you have some idea what area is malfunctioning. Certain problems can be closely related to specific areas in the transmission, which can make component examination and renewal easier. Refer to the *Fault finding* Section of this manual for more information.

### 9  Transmission oil level check

**1** Position the vehicle over an inspection pit, on vehicle ramps, or jack it up and support it securely on axle stands (see *Jacking and vehicle support*), but make sure that it is level. The oil must be checked before the car is driven, or at least 5 minutes after the engine has been switched off. If the oil is checked immediately after driving the car, some of the oil will remain distributed around the transmission components, resulting in an inaccurate level reading.

**2** Where fitted, undo the retaining clips/screws and remove the engine undertray.

**3** Wipe clean the area around the level plug.

The level plug is located behind the driveshaft inner joint on the left-hand side of the transmission **(see illustration 2.8)**. Unscrew the plug and clean it.

**4** The oil level should reach the lower edge of the level plug aperture. If topping-up is necessary, wipe clean the area around the reversing light switch, and remove the switch as described in Section 6.

**5** Add the specified grade of oil given in *Lubricants and fluids*, through the reversing light switch aperture, until it reaches the bottom of the level plug aperture. Allow any excess oil to drain, then refit and tighten the level plug to the specified torque.

**6** Refit the reversing light switch with reference to Section 6.

**7** Where applicable, refit the engine undertray, then lower the vehicle to the ground.

# Chapter 7 Part B:
# Automatic transmission

## Contents

## Degrees of difficulty

| | | | | |
|---|---|---|---|---|
| **Easy,** suitable for novice with little experience  | **Fairly easy,** suitable for beginner with some experience  | **Fairly difficult,** suitable for competent DIY mechanic  | **Difficult,** suitable for experienced DIY mechanic  | **Very difficult,** suitable for expert DIY or professional  |

## Specifications

### General

Type . . . . . . . . . . . . . . . . . . . . . . . . . . . . . . . . . . . . . . . . . . . . . . . . . Four forward and one reverse speed electronically-controlled automatic with three driving modes (economy, sport and winter)

Manufacturer's designation . . . . . . . . . . . . . . . . . . . . . . . . . . . . . . . AF17

### Lubrication

Fluid type . . . . . . . . . . . . . . . . . . . . . . . . . . . . . . . . . . . . . . . . . . . . . See *Lubricants and fluids* on page 0•18
Fluid capacity . . . . . . . . . . . . . . . . . . . . . . . . . . . . . . . . . . . . . . . . . See Specifications, Chapter 1

### Torque wrench settings

| | Nm | lbf ft |
|---|---|---|
| Drain plug. . . . . . . . . . . . . . . . . . . . . . . . . . . . . . . . . . . . . . . . . . . . | 35 | 26 |
| Engine/transmission mountings. . . . . . . . . . . . . . . . . . . . . . . . . . . | See Chapter 2C | |
| Input shaft speed sensor bolt. . . . . . . . . . . . . . . . . . . . . . . . . . . . . | 5 | 4 |
| Output shaft speed sensor bolt . . . . . . . . . . . . . . . . . . . . . . . . . . . | 5 | 4 |
| Roadwheel bolts. . . . . . . . . . . . . . . . . . . . . . . . . . . . . . . . . . . . . . . | 110 | 81 |
| Starter inhibitor/reversing light switch bolts . . . . . . . . . . . . . . . . . | 25 | 18 |
| Torque converter-to-driveplate bolts*: | | |
|   Stage 1 . . . . . . . . . . . . . . . . . . . . . . . . . . . . . . . . . . . . . . . . . . . . | 20 | 15 |
|   Stage 2 . . . . . . . . . . . . . . . . . . . . . . . . . . . . . . . . . . . . . . . . . . . . | 45 | 33 |
|   Stage 3 . . . . . . . . . . . . . . . . . . . . . . . . . . . . . . . . . . . . . . . . . . . . | Angle-tighten a further 30° | |
| Transmission selector shaft nuts: | | |
|   Main (starter/reversing light switch) nut . . . . . . . . . . . . . . . . . . | 8 | 6 |
|   Selector lever nut . . . . . . . . . . . . . . . . . . . . . . . . . . . . . . . . . . . . | 16 | 12 |
| Transmission-to-engine bolts. . . . . . . . . . . . . . . . . . . . . . . . . . . . . | See Chapter 2C | |

* Use new bolts

**2.3 Automatic transmission drain plug (1)**

# 1 General information

1.8 litre models are available with the option of a four-speed, electronically-controlled automatic transmission, consisting of a torque converter, an epicyclic geartrain, and hydraulically-operated clutches and brakes. The unit is controlled by an electronic control unit (ECU) via four electrically-operated solenoid valves. The transmission unit has three driving modes: economy, sport and winter.

The economy mode is the standard mode for driving in which the transmission shifts up at relatively low engine speeds to combine reasonable performance with economy. If the transmission unit is switched into sport mode, using the button on the facia, the transmission shifts up only at high engine speeds, giving improved acceleration and overtaking performance. When the transmission is in sport mode, the indicator light in the instrument panel is illuminated. If the transmission is switched into winter mode, using the button on the selector lever indicator panel, the transmission will select third gear as the vehicle pulls away from a standing start;

**3.4 Release the selector outer cable by lifting the locking clip (1)**

this helps to maintain traction on very slippery surfaces.

The torque converter provides a fluid coupling between engine and transmission, which acts as an automatic clutch, and also provides a degree of torque multiplication when accelerating.

The epicyclic geartrain provides either of the four forward or one reverse gear ratios, according to which of its component parts are held stationary or allowed to turn. The components of the geartrain are held or released by brakes and clutches which are activated by the control unit. A fluid pump within the transmission provides the necessary hydraulic pressure to operate the brakes and clutches.

Driver control of the transmission is by a seven-position selector lever. The drive D position, allows automatic changing throughout the range of all four gear ratios. An automatic kickdown facility shifts the transmission down a gear if the accelerator pedal is fully depressed. The transmission also has three hold positions, 1 means only the first gear ratio can be selected, 2 allows both the first and second gear ratios position to be automatically selected and 3 allows automatic changing between the first three gear ratios. These hold positions are useful for providing engine braking when travelling down steep gradients. Note, however, that the transmission should never be shifted down a position at high engine speeds.

Due to the complexity of the automatic transmission, any repair or overhaul work must be left to a Vauxhall/Opel dealer with the necessary special equipment for fault diagnosis and repair. The contents of the following Sections are therefore confined to supplying general information, and any service information and instructions that can be used by the owner.

# 2 Automatic transmission fluid – draining and refilling

## Draining

**1** This operation is much quicker and more efficient if the vehicle is first taken on a journey of sufficient length to warm the engine/transmission up to normal operating temperature.

**2** Park the vehicle on level ground, switch off the ignition, and apply the handbrake firmly. For improved access, jack up the front of the car and support it securely on axle stands (see *Jacking and vehicle support*). Where fitted, remove the clips and bolts and remove the undertray from beneath the engine.

**3** Withdraw the dipstick, then position a container under the drain plug at the rear right-hand side of the transmission, below the driveshaft. Unscrew the plug and remove it along with its sealing washer **(see illustration)**.

**4** Allow the fluid to drain completely into the container. If the fluid is hot, take precautions against scalding.

**5** When the fluid has finished draining, clean the drain plug threads and those of the transmission casing, fit a new sealing washer and refit the drain plug, tightening it to the specified torque wrench setting. Where applicable, refit the engine undertray and lower the vehicle to the ground.

## Refilling

**6** Refilling the transmission is an awkward operation, adding the specified type and amount of fluid to the transmission a little at a time via the dipstick tube. Use a funnel with a fine mesh gauze, to avoid spillage, and to ensure that no foreign matter enters the transmission. Allow plenty of time for the fluid level to settle properly.

**7** Start the engine, and allow it to idle for a few minutes whilst moving the selector lever through its various positions. Switch off the engine and add sufficient fluid to bring the level up to the lower mark on the dipstick. Take the car on a short run to fully distribute the new fluid around the transmission, then recheck the fluid level as described in Chapter 1 with the transmission at normal operating temperature.

# 3 Selector cable – adjustment

**Note:** *If the battery is disconnected with the selector lever in the P (park) position, the lever will be locked in position. To manually release the lever, carefully detach the selector lever gaiter from the selector lever cover and slide it up the lever. Using a flat-bladed screwdriver, push the yellow emergency release lever, located at the front right- or left-hand side of the selector housing, forward whilst moving the selector lever to the N (neutral) position.*

**1** Operate the selector lever throughout its entire range and check that the transmission engages the correct gear indicated on the selector lever position indicator. If adjustment is necessary, continue as follows.

**2** Position the selector lever in the P (Park) position.

**3** To gain access to the transmission end of the selector cable, remove the battery and battery tray as described in Chapter 5A.

**4** Locate the selector cable mounting bracket on the top of the transmission unit and release the outer cable by carefully lifting the locking clip in the cable end fitting **(see illustration)**.

**5** Ensure that the selector lever is locked in the P position and move the lever on the transmission selector mechanism fully forwards so that the transmission is also positioned in the Park position **(see illustration)**. With both the selector lever and transmission correctly positioned, lock the cable adjuster in position by pushing the locking clip firmly down until it clicks in position.

**6** Refit the battery tray and battery then check the operation of the selector lever and, if necessary, repeat the adjustment procedure.

## 4 Selector cable – removal and refitting

### Removal

**1** Remove the centre console as described in Chapter 11 then position the selector lever in the P (Park) position.

**2** Using a flat-bladed screwdriver, carefully lever off the selector cable end fitting balljoint from the base of the lever. Slide out the retaining clip and release the cable from the front of the lever mounting plate (see illustration).

**3** To gain access to the transmission end of the selector cable, remove the battery and battery tray as described in Chapter 5A.

**4** Slide off the retaining clip (where fitted) then carefully unclip the selector cable end fitting from the transmission lever. Unclip the outer cable from its mounting bracket.

**5** Work back along the cable, noting its correct routing, and free it from all the relevant retaining clips. Ensure that the rubber cable grommet stays in the bulkhead.

**6** Examine the cable, looking for worn end fittings or a damaged outer casing, and for signs of fraying of the inner cable. Check the cable's operation; the inner cable should move smoothly and easily through the outer casing. Remember that a cable that appears serviceable when tested off the car may well be much heavier in operation when curved into its working position. Renew the cable if it shows any signs of excessive wear or any damage.

### Refitting

**7** Manoeuvre the cable into position, ensuring it is correctly routed and pass it through the bulkhead. Ensure the cable passes through the selector lever mounting plate. In order to allow the cable to pass easily through the bulkhead, lubricate the grommet with a little soap solution.

**8** Pass the transmission end of the cable through its mounting bracket and clip the outer cable securely in position. Align the inner cable end fitting with the transmission lever then clip it on the lever and (where necessary) secure it in position with the retaining clip.

**9** From inside the vehicle, secure the outer cable in position with the retaining clip, and clip the inner cable end fitting securely onto the selector lever balljoint.

**10** Adjust the selector cable as described in Section 3.

**11** Refit the centre console, as described in Chapter 11, and refit all components removed to gain access to the transmission end of the cable.

## 5 Selector lever assembly – removal and refitting

### Removal

**1** Remove the centre console, as described in Chapter 11, then position the selector lever in the P (Park) position.

**2** Using a flat-bladed screwdriver, carefully lever off the selector cable end fitting balljoint from the base of the lever. Slide out the retaining clip and release the cable from the front of the lever mounting plate (see illustration 4.2).

**3** Disconnect the wiring connector at the front of the selector lever assembly.

**4** Slacken and remove the four mounting bolts then manoeuvre the lever assembly out of position.

### Refitting

**5** Where necessary, reassemble the lever and mounting plate and insert the pivot crank. Ensure the crank is correctly engaged with the selector lever then refit the washer and tighten its retaining nut to the specified torque. Clip the indicator panel onto the mounting plate then check the operation of the lever before refitting it to the car.

**6** Manoeuvre the lever assembly into position, engage it with the selector cable. Refit the retaining bolts and tighten them securely.

**7** Secure the outer cable in position with the retaining clip and securely clip the cable end fitting onto the selector lever crank balljoint.

**8** Ensuring the wiring is correctly routed and reconnect the wiring connector.

**9** Adjust the selector cable, as described in Section 3, then refit the centre console as described in Chapter 11.

## 6 Oil seals – renewal

### Driveshaft oil seals

**1** Refer to Chapter 7A.

### Torque converter oil seal

**2** Remove the transmission as described in Section 9.

**3** Carefully slide the torque converter off of the transmission shaft whilst being prepared for fluid spillage.

**4** Note the correct fitted position of the seal in the oil pump housing then carefully lever the seal out of position taking care not to mark the housing or input shaft.

**5** Remove all traces of dirt from the area around the oil seal aperture then press the new seal into position, ensuring its sealing lip is facing inwards.

**6** Lubricate the seal with clean transmission fluid then carefully ease the torque converter into position.

**7** Refit the transmission (see Section 9).

**3.5 Move the transmission selector (1) fully forwards so that it is in the P position (2)**

**4.2 Remove the retaining clip (1) then lever the selector cable (2) off the selector lever balljoint (3)**

**8.15 Unclip and remove the access panel in the centre console, beneath the handbrake lever**

## 7 Fluid cooler –
general information

1 The transmission fluid cooler is an integral part of the radiator assembly. Refer to Chapter 3 for removal and refitting details, if the cooler is damaged the complete radiator assembly must be renewed.

## 8 Transmission control system electrical components –
removal and refitting

### Starter inhibitor/ reversing light switch

#### Adjustment

1 Adjustment of the switch entails the use of Vauxhall/Opel special tool KM-962, which is then connected to the starter inhibitor/ reversing light switch wiring connector on the transmission. The tool contains a series of LEDs (light emitting diodes), that illuminate in sequence, with the ignition switched on, as each selector position is engaged. If the LEDs do not illuminate correctly in each selector lever position, the position switch securing bolts must be slackened and the switch repositioned accordingly. As accurate

**8.28 Transmission output shaft sensor (1) and input shaft speed sensor (2) locations**

adjustment of the position switch can only be carried out using this tool, the work should be entrusted to a Vauxhall/Opel dealer.

#### Removal

**Note:** *It will be necessary to have the adjustment of the switch carried out by a Vauxhall/Opel dealer on completion (see adjustment above). Bearing this in mind, it may be beneficial to have the complete operation (removal, refitting and adjustment) carried out by the dealer at the same time.*

2 Position the selector lever in the N (Neutral) position.
3 To gain access to the switch, remove the battery and battery tray as described in Chapter 5A.
4 Slide off the retaining clip (where fitted) then carefully unclip the selector cable end fitting from the transmission lever. Unscrew the retaining nut and remove the lever from the transmission selector shaft.
5 Trace the wiring back from the switch and disconnect it at the wiring connector. Unlock the wiring plug by pulling the lock clip away from the main body of the plug.
6 Bend back the lockwasher then slacken and remove the main nut and washer(s) from the transmission selector shaft.
7 Mark the position of the switch in relation to the transmission, then slacken and remove the switch and wiring retaining plate bolts. Manoeuvre the switch assembly upwards and away from the transmission unit.

#### Refitting

8 Prior to refitting, first make sure that the transmission selector shaft is still in the N (Neutral) position. If there is any doubt, engage the selector lever with the transmission shaft and move the lever fully forwards (to the P position) then move it two notches backwards.
9 Locate the switch on the transmission shaft in the previously-noted position, then refit the wiring retaining plate. Refit the retaining bolts, tightening them to the specified torque.
10 Refit the washer(s) and main nut to the selector shaft. Tighten the nut to the specified torque setting and secure it in position by bending up the locking washer against one of its flats.
11 Reconnect the wiring connector, ensuring that the wiring is correctly routed.
12 Refit the selector lever to the shaft and tighten its retaining nut to the specified torque. Clip the selector cable end fitting securely onto the lever balljoint.
13 Refit the battery tray and battery and check the operation of the switch. If necessary, have a Vauxhall/Opel dealer adjust the switch.

### Sport mode switch

14 The sport mode switch is an integral part of the facia centre switch panel and cannot be individually removed. If the switch is faulty, the complete switch panel must be renewed. Removal and refitting procedures for the facia centre switch panel are contained in Chapter 12.

### Winter mode switch

#### Removal

15 From inside the vehicle, unclip and remove the access panel in the centre console, beneath the handbrake lever **(see illustration)**.
16 Using a small screwdriver, carefully prise up the right-hand side of the ashtray, withdraw the ashtray from the centre console and disconnect the wiring connector.
17 Carefully detach the selector lever gaiter from the selector lever cover and slide it up the lever
18 Undo the two screws securing the rear of the selector lever cover to the centre console. Lift the cover up at the rear and disengage it from the centre console at the front. Disconnect the two wiring connectors, carefully feed the gaiter through the cover and remove the cover.
19 Unclip the winter mode switch from the underside of the selector lever cover and remove the switch from the cover.

#### Refitting

20 Refitting is the reverse of removal, ensuring the wiring is correctly routed.

### Selector lever position indicator

#### Removal

21 Remove the selector lever cover as described previously in paragraphs 15 to 18.
22 Unclip the selector lever position indicator from the underside of the selector lever cover and remove the indicator from the cover.

#### Refitting

23 Refitting is the reverse of removal.

### Electronic control unit (ECU)

#### Removal

24 The ECU is located in front of the centre console, and clipped into a bracket on the heater distribution housing. Prior to removal, disconnect the battery negative terminal (refer to *Disconnecting the battery* in the Reference Chapter).
25 Remove the centre console as described in Chapter 11, and the left-hand central air distribution duct.
26 Unclip the ECU bracket from the heater distribution housing, and pull out to one side. If the wiring harness prevents the ECU from being moved to one side, cut the cable ties securing the harness in place. Disconnect the ECU wiring plug, and if necessary, unclip the ECU from the bracket.

#### Refitting

27 Refitting is the reverse of removal, ensuring that the wiring is securely reconnected.

### Input and output shaft speed sensors

#### Removal

28 The speed sensors are fitted to the top-rear of the transmission unit. The output shaft speed sensor is the uppermost of the two sensors **(see illustration)**.

**29** Firmly apply the handbrake, jack up the front of the car and support it securely on axle stands (see *Jacking and vehicle support*). Remove the left-front roadwheel.

**30** Disconnect the wiring connector and wipe clean the area around the relevant sensor.

**31** Undo the retaining bolt and remove the sensor from the transmission. Remove the sealing ring from the sensor and discard it, a new one should be used on refitting.

### Refitting

**32** Fit the new sealing ring to the sensor groove and lubricate it with a smear of trans-mission fluid.

**33** Ease the sensor into position then refit the retaining bolt and tighten it to the specified torque setting. Reconnect the wiring connector.

**34** Refit the left-front roadwheel, and lower the vehicle to the ground.

### 9  Automatic transmission – removal and refitting

**Note:** *New torque converter-to-driveplate bolts and fluid cooler union sealing rings will be required on refitting.*

### Removal

**1** Apply the handbrake, place the selector lever in the N (Neutral) position. then jack up the front of the vehicle and support it on axle stands (see *Jacking and vehicle support*). Allow sufficient working room to remove the transmission from under the left-hand side of the engine compartment. Remove both front roadwheels then, where necessary, undo the retaining clips/screws and remove the engine undertray. Also remove the engine top cover where fitted.

**2** Drain the transmission fluid as described in Section 2, then refit the drain plug and tighten it to the specified torque.

**3** Remove the battery and battery tray as described in Chapter 5A.

**4** Remove the exhaust system as described in Chapter 4A.

**5** Disconnect the inner ends of both drive-shafts/intermediate shaft from the differential as described in Chapter 8. There is no need to disconnect the driveshafts from the swivel hub. Support the driveshafts by suspending them with wire or string – do not allow the driveshafts to hang down under their own weight, or the joints may be damaged.

**6** Remove the front subframe assembly as described in Chapter 10, ensuring that the engine unit is securely supported by connecting a hoist to the engine assembly. If available, the type of support bar which locates in the engine compartment side channels is to be preferred.

**7** Slide off the retaining clip (where fitted) then carefully unclip the selector cable end fitting from the transmission lever. Unclip the outer cable from its mounting bracket and position the cable clear of the transmission unit.

**8** Undo the retaining bolt and remove the automatic transmission fluid filler pipe/dipstick tube – recover the sealing ring.

**9** Trace the wiring back from the transmission switches and sensors and disconnect the various connectors by lifting their retaining clips. Release the main wiring harness from any clips or ties securing it to the transmission unit.

**10** Remove the fastening bolts for the

**9.14 Remove the three bolts securing the right-hand engine mounting**

selector outer cable retaining bracket/wiring harness bracket, and withdraw the bracket.

**11** Disconnect the breather hose (where fitted) from the top of the transmission unit.

**12** Remove the air cleaner housing and air intake duct (see Chapter 4A).

**13** Place a jack with a block of wood beneath the transmission, and raise the jack to take the weight of the transmission.

**14** Mark the bolt positions for correct refitting, then slacken and remove the three bolts securing the right-hand engine mounting to the bracket bolted to the end of the cylinder block **(see illustration)**.

**15** Mark the bolt positions for correct refitting, then unscrew the bolts securing the left-hand engine/transmission mounting and bracket to the transmission casing **(see illustration)**.

**16** Make identification marks between the oil cooler hoses and their unions on the front of the transmission housing. Using a flat-bladed screwdriver, prise out the retaining clips from each hose end fitting and detach both hoses from the transmission **(see illustration)**. Clip

H32271

**9.15 Left-hand transmission mounting bracket**

1  *Bracket-to-mounting bolts*    2  *Bracket-to-transmission bolts*

**9.16 Transmission fluid cooler hose connections**

1  *Hose end fitting*    2  *Retaining clip*    3  *Transmission union*

**9.23 Check that the torque converter is fully entered**

1 Straight-edge
2 Vernier calipers on bolt hole

3 Torque converter centre stub

the retaining clips back into position in the end fittings and discard the sealing rings; new sealing rings must be used on refitting. Plug/cover both the union and hose ends to prevent the entry of dirt.

**17** Undo the two retaining bolts and remove the engine/transmission front mounting/torque link from the front of the transmission housing.

**18** By manipulating the engine hoist and the jack under the transmission, lower the engine/transmission approximately 50 mm. Ensure that the various coolant hoses and wiring harnesses are not stretched.

**19** Remove the rubber cover(s) from the cylinder block/sump flange to gain access to the torque converter retaining bolts. Slacken and remove the visible bolt(s) then, using a socket and extension bar to rotate the crankshaft pulley, undo the remaining bolts securing the torque converter to the driveplate as they become accessible. There are three bolts in total. Discard the bolts, new ones must be used on refitting.

**20** To ensure that the torque converter does not fall out as the transmission is removed, slide the converter along the shaft and fully into the transmission housing.

**21** With the jack positioned beneath the transmission taking the weight, slacken and remove the upper and lower bolts securing the

transmission housing to the engine. Note the correct fitted positions of each bolt, and the necessary brackets, as they are removed to use as a reference on refitting. Do not overlook the bolts securing the engine oil sump to the transmission casing. Make a final check that all components have been disconnected, and are positioned clear of the transmission so that they will not hinder the removal procedure.

**22** With all the bolts removed, move the trolley jack and transmission to free it from its locating dowels. Once the transmission is free, lower the jack and manoeuvre the unit out from under the car, taking care to ensure that the torque converter does not fall off. Remove the locating dowels from the transmission or engine if they are loose, and keep them in a safe place.

## Refitting

**23** The transmission is refitted by a reversal of the removal procedure, bearing in mind the following points.

a) Prior to refitting, remove all traces of old locking compound from the torque converter threads by running a tap of the correct thread diameter and pitch down the holes. In the absence of a suitable tap, use one of the old bolts with slots cut in its threads.

b) Prior to refitting, ensure the engine/transmission locating dowels are correctly positioned and apply a smear of molybdenum disulphide grease to the torque converter locating pin and its centring bush in the crankshaft end.

c) Check that the torque converter is fully entered inside the transmission bellhousing by measuring the distance from the flange to the bolt holes in the torque converter, using a straight-edge and vernier calipers **(see illustration)**. The distance must measure approximately 12.0 mm.

d) Once the transmission and engine are correctly joined, refit the securing bolts, tightening them to the specified torque setting.

e) Fit the new torque converter-to-driveplate bolts and tighten them lightly only to start then go around and tighten them to the specified torque setting in a diagonal sequence.

f) Tighten all nuts and bolts to the specified torque (where given).

g) Renew the driveshaft oil seals (see Chapter 7A) and refit the driveshafts/intermediate shaft to the transmission as described in Chapter 8.

h) Fit new sealing rings to the fluid cooler hose unions and ensure both unions are securely retained by their clips.

i) Fit a new sealing ring to the fluid filler pipe/dipstick guide tube.

j) On completion, refill the transmission with the specified type and quantity of fluid as described in Section 2 and adjust the selector cable as described in Section 3.

## 10 Automatic transmission overhaul – general information

**1** In the event of a fault occurring with the transmission, it is first necessary to determine whether it is of a mechanical, electrical or hydraulic nature, and to do this, special test equipment is required. It is therefore essential to have the work carried out by a Vauxhall/Opel dealer or specialist if a transmission fault is suspected.

**2** Do not remove the transmission from the car for possible repair before professional fault diagnosis has been carried out, since most tests require the transmission to be in the vehicle.

# Chapter 7 Part C:
## Easytronic transmission

## Contents

## Degrees of difficulty

| | | | | |
|---|---|---|---|---|
| **Easy,** suitable for novice with little experience | **Fairly easy,** suitable for beginner with some experience | **Fairly difficult,** suitable for competent DIY mechanic | **Difficult,** suitable for experienced DIY mechanic | **Very difficult,** suitable for expert DIY or professional |

## Specifications

### General
Type . . . . . . . . . . . . . . . . . . . . . . . . . . . . . . . . . . . . . . . . . . . . . . . . . Five forward speeds and one reverse, automatic or manual selection. Integral differential

Manufacturer's designation:
1.4 litre engines . . . . . . . . . . . . . . . . . . . . . . . . . . . . . . . . . . . . . . . F13 MTA
1.6 litre engines . . . . . . . . . . . . . . . . . . . . . . . . . . . . . . . . . . . . . . . F17+ MTA

### Gear ratios

| | F13 MTA transmissions | F17+ MTA transmissions |
|---|---|---|
| 1st | 3.72:1 | 3.72:1 |
| 2nd | 1.96:1 | 2.13:1 |
| 3rd | 1.30:1 | 1.41:1 |
| 4th | 0.94:1 | 1.12:1 |
| 5th | 0.76:1 | 0.89:1 |
| Reverse | 3.30:1 | 3.30:1 |

### Final drive ratios
F13 MTA transmissions . . . . . . . . . . . . . . . . . . . . . . . . . . . . . . . . . . 4.18:1
F17+ MTA transmissions . . . . . . . . . . . . . . . . . . . . . . . . . . . . . . . . 3.94:1

### Torque wrench settings

| | Nm | lbf ft |
|---|---|---|
| Differential lower cover plate bolts: | | |
| Alloy plate | 18 | 13 |
| Steel plate | 30 | 22 |
| Clutch module with MTA control unit | 11 | 8 |
| Engine/transmission mountings | See Chapter 2A or 2B | |
| Transmission oil filler/level plug: | | |
| Stage 1 | 4 | 3 |
| Stage 2 | Angle-tighten a further 45° to 135° | |
| Transmission shift module | 11 | 8 |
| Transmission-to-engine bolts | See Chapter 2A or 2B | |

J44733

**1.1 Easytronic (MTA) transmission**

1 *Transmission shift module*
2 *Wiring harness*
3 *Hydraulic fluid reservoir*
4 *Clutch control module*
5 *Hydraulic supply line to clutch control module*
6 *Wiring harness for clutch control module*
7 *Hydraulic pressure line to clutch release cylinder*

## 1 General information

**1** The Easytronic MTA transmission (Manual Transmission Automatic-shift) is essentially a conventional manual transmission with the addition of a clutch module and shift module, used in conjunction with a self-adjusting clutch plate **(see illustration)**.
**2** The description of the MTA transmission is basically as for the manual transmission given in Chapter 7A, but with an electronically-operated hydraulic clutch control module and gear selection module. The transmission can be switched between fully automatic and manual mode, even while driving.
**3** The clutch control module incorporates its own master cylinder and pushrod, which is operated electrically by a worm gear.
**4** The gear selection module is fitted with a shifting motor and a selector motor, which together position the selector lever to move the selector forks in the transmission. It is located in exactly the same position as the gear selection cover fitted to the conventional manual transmission.
**5** Since the transmission is electronically-controlled, in the event of a problem, in the first instance the vehicle should be taken to a Vauxhall/Opel dealer or diagnostic specialist who will have the TECH2 diagnostic equipment (or equivalent) necessary to pin-point the faulty area. Note also that if the transmission assembly, shift module or clutch module are renewed, the vehicle must be taken to a Vauxhall/Opel dealer or diagnostic specialist in order to have the fault memory erased and new parameters programmed into the ECU.

## 2 Transmission oil – draining and refilling

**1** This operation is much more efficient if the car is first taken on a journey of sufficient length to warm the engine/transmission up to normal operating temperature.
*Caution: If the procedure is to be carried out on a hot transmission unit, take care not to burn yourself on the hot exhaust or the transmission/engine unit.*
**2** Position the vehicle over an inspection pit, on vehicle ramps, or jack it up and support it securely on axle stands (see *Jacking and vehicle support*), but make sure that it is level. Where fitted, remove the clips and bolts and remove the undertray from beneath the engine.

### Draining

**Note:** *A new differential lower cover plate gasket will be required for this operation.*
**3** Since the transmission oil is not renewed as part of the manufacturer's maintenance schedule, no drain plug is fitted to the transmission. If for any reason the transmission needs to be drained, the only way of doing so is to remove the differential lower cover plate.
**4** Wipe clean the area around the differential lower cover plate and position a suitable container underneath the cover plate.
**5** Evenly and progressively slacken and remove the retaining bolts then withdraw the cover plate and allow the transmission oil to drain into the container **(see illustration)**.

**2.5 Differential cover plate securing bolts (arrowed)**

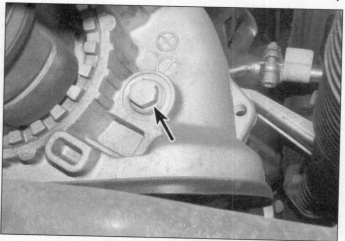

**2.8 Transmission oil filler/level plug (arrowed)**

Remove the gasket and discard it; a new one should be used on refitting.

**6** Allow the oil to drain completely into the container. If the oil is hot, take precautions against scalding. Remove all traces of dirt and oil from the cover plate and transmission mating surfaces and wipe clean the inside of the cover plate.

**7** Once the oil has finished draining, ensure the mating surfaces are clean and dry then refit the cover plate to the transmission unit, complete with a new gasket. Refit the retaining bolts and evenly and progressively tighten them to the specified torque.

### Refilling

**8** Wipe clean the area around the filler/level plug. The filler/level plug is located behind the driveshaft inner joint on the left-hand side of the transmission (**see illustration**). Unscrew the plug and clean it.

**9** Refill the transmission via the filler/level plug orifice with the specified type of oil until it begins to trickle out of the orifice. Once the oil level is correct, refit the filler/level plug and tighten to the specified torque.

**10** Refit the engine undertray (where fitted) and lower the vehicle to the ground.

### 3  Selector lever assembly – removal and refitting

#### Removal

**1** Remove the centre console as described in Chapter 11.

**2** Disconnect the wiring from the selector lever.

**3** Unscrew the mounting bolts and withdraw the selector lever assembly from the floor.

#### Refitting

**4** Refitting is a reversal of removal.

### 4  Transmission shift module – removal and refitting

#### Removal

**1** Switch on the ignition, then depress the footbrake pedal and move the selector lever to position N. Switch off the ignition.

**2** Remove the battery and battery tray as described in Chapter 5A.

**3** Disconnect the two wiring plugs and release the harness from the support cable ties on the top of the transmission.

**4** Unbolt and remove the transmission shift module from the top of the transmission. To do this, lift it and tilt it slightly forwards before removing. Recover the gasket.

**5** If the module cannot be removed because of internal jamming, unbolt the selector motor followed by the shifting motor (**see illustration**), and use a screwdriver to move

**4.5  Shift motor (1) and selector motor (2) on the transmission shift module**

the selector lever to its neutral position first. The selector motor is the uppermost unit.
**Note:** *The manufacturers recommend that the shift module assembly is never re-used if dismantled.*

### Refitting

**6** Clean the gasket faces of the module and transmission, and obtain a new gasket.

**7** Make sure that the selector lever is in neutral, by checking that the mark on the segment is aligned with the pinion tooth. Check also that the lever is fully extended so that the annular groove is visible. The shift forks in the transmission must also be in neutral – use a screwdriver to move them if necessary (**see illustrations**).

**8** Refit the shift module together with a new gasket, then insert the bolts and tighten to the specified torque.

**9** Reconnect the wiring and secure with new cable ties.

**10** Refit the battery tray and battery as described in Chapter 5A.

**11** Finally, it may be necessary to have a Vauxhall/Opel dealer or diagnostic specialist

**4.7b  Groove (3) visible when the shift module is in neutral**

**4.7c  Using a screwdriver to move the transmission shift forks into neutral**

reprogramme all volatile control unit memories. If a new control unit has been fitted, a Vauxhall/Opel dealer or diagnostic specialist must programme the unit specifically for the model to which it is fitted.

### 5  Clutch module with MTA control unit – removal and refitting

**Note:** *Bleeding the module is carried out using the Vauxhall/Opel TECH2 diagnostic instrument, therefore this work should be entrusted to a Vauxhall/Opel dealer or diagnostic specialist.*

### Removal

**1** Apply the handbrake, then jack up the front of the vehicle and support it on axle stands (see *Jacking and vehicle support*). Where necessary, remove the engine undertray.

**2** Disconnect the wiring from the Easytronic transmission and release it from the cable tie supports.

**4.7a  Neutral mark (1) and shift lever shaft (2) on the transmission shift module**

**3** Place a suitable container beneath the front of the transmission to catch spilt hydraulic fluid.

**4** Fit a hose clamp to the hydraulic hose leading from the hydraulic fluid reservoir to the clutch control unit, then disconnect the hose.

**5** Disconnect the hydraulic quick-release pressure hose from the clutch control unit.

**6** Unscrew the mounting bolts and remove the clutch module with MTA control unit from the transmission.

### Refitting

**7** Refitting is a reversal of removal, but tighten the mounting bolts to the specified torque. Make sure that the quick-release pressure hose is fully engaged – it must make an audible sound. Bleed the hydraulic circuit. Finally, it may be necessary to reprogramme all volatile control unit memories. If a new control unit has been fitted, a Vauxhall/Opel dealer or diagnostic specialist must programme the unit specifically for the model to which it is fitted.

## 6  Driveshaft oil seals – renewal

**1** Apply the handbrake, then jack up the front of the vehicle and support it on axle stands (see *Jacking and vehicle support*). Remove the relevant front roadwheel.

**2** Drain the transmission oil as described in Section 2 or be prepared for oil loss as the seal is changed.

**3** Disconnect the inner end of the relevant driveshaft from the differential as described in Chapter 8. There is no need to disconnect the driveshaft from the swivel hub. Support the driveshaft by suspending it with wire or string – do not allow the driveshaft to hang down under its own weight, or the joints may be damaged.

**4** Prise the now-exposed oil seal from the differential housing, using a screwdriver or similar instrument.

**5** Smear the sealing lip of the new oil seal with a little transmission oil, then using a metal tube or socket of suitable diameter, drive the new seal into the differential casing until the outer surface of the seal is flush with the outer surface of the differential casing.

**6** Reconnect the driveshaft to the differential as described in Chapter 8.

**7** Refill or top-up the transmission oil level with reference to Section 2.

## 7  Easytronic transmission – removal and refitting

### Removal

**1** Apply the handbrake, then jack up the front of the vehicle and support it on axle stands (see *Jacking and vehicle support*). Allow sufficient working room to remove the transmission from under the left-hand side of the engine compartment. Remove both front roadwheels then, where necessary, undo the retaining clips/screws and remove the engine undertray. Also remove the engine top cover where fitted.

**2** Remove the battery and battery tray as described in Chapter 5A.

**3** Drain the transmission oil as described in Section 2 or be prepared for oil loss as the transmission is removed.

**4** Attach a suitable hoist and lifting tackle to the lifting bracket(s) located on the left-hand side of the cylinder head, and support the weight of the engine/transmission.

**5** Refer to Chapter 10 and remove the front subframe.

**6** Disconnect the inner ends of both driveshafts from the differential as described in Chapter 8. There is no need to disconnect the driveshafts from the swivel hub. Support the driveshafts by suspending them with wire or string – do not allow the driveshafts to hang down under their own weight, or the joints may be damaged.

**7** Disconnect the wiring from the transmission clutch and shift modules, and release the wiring from the support cables.

**8** Place a jack with a block of wood beneath the transmission, and raise the jack to take the weight of the transmission.

**9** Unbolt the left-hand engine/transmission mounting bracket from the transmission with reference to Chapter 2A or 2B.

**10** Lower the engine and transmission by approximately 5o mm making sure that the coolant hoses and wiring harnesses are not stretched.

**11** Unscrew and remove the upper bolts securing the transmission to the rear of the engine. Where necessary, pull up the coolant hoses and secure them away from the transmission using plastic cable ties.

**12** Slacken and remove the remaining bolts securing the transmission to the engine and sump flange. Note the correct fitted positions of each bolt, and the relevant brackets, as they are removed to use as a reference on refitting. Make a final check that all components have been disconnected, and are positioned clear of the transmission so that they will not hinder the removal procedure.

**13** With the bolts removed, move the trolley jack and transmission to free it from its locating dowels. Once the transmission is free, lower the jack and manoeuvre the unit out from under the car. Remove the locating dowels from the transmission or engine if they are loose, and keep them in a safe place.

### Refitting

**14** The transmission is refitted by a reversal of the removal procedure, bearing in mind the following points.

a) Tighten all nuts and bolts to the specified torque (where given).

b) Renew the driveshaft oil seals (see Section 6) before refitting the driveshafts.

c) Refit the front subframe assembly with reference to Chapter 10.

d) Refill or top-up the transmission with the specified type and quantity of oil, as described in Section 2.

e) Finally, it may be necessary to have a dealer or diagnostic specialist reprogramme all volatile control unit memories.

## 8  Easytronic transmission overhaul – general information

In the event of a fault occurring on the transmission, it is first necessary to determine whether it is of an electrical, mechanical or hydraulic nature, and to achieve this, special test equipment is required. It is therefore essential to have the work carried out by a Vauxhall/Opel dealer if a transmission fault is suspected.

Do not remove the transmission from the car for possible repair before professional fault diagnosis has been carried out, since most tests require the transmission to be in the vehicle.

# Chapter 8
# Driveshafts

## Contents

## Degrees of difficulty

| Easy, suitable for novice with little experience | Fairly easy, suitable for beginner with some experience | Fairly difficult, suitable for competent DIY mechanic | Difficult, suitable for experienced DIY mechanic | Very difficult, suitable for expert DIY or professional |
|---|---|---|---|---|

## Specifications

**General**

Driveshaft type . . . . . . . . . . . . . . . . . . . . . . . . . . . . . . . . . . . . . . . . . . . . Solid steel shafts with inner and outer constant velocity (CV) joints

**Lubrication (overhaul only – see text)**

Lubricant type/specification. . . . . . . . . . . . . . . . . . . . . . . . . . . . . . . . Use only special grease supplied in sachets with gaiter kits – joints are otherwise pre-packed with grease and sealed

**Torque wrench settings**

| | Nm | lbf ft |
|---|---|---|
| Anti-roll bar connecting link retaining nut* | 55 | 41 |
| Driveshaft retaining nut*: | | |
| Stage 1 | 150 | 111 |
| Stage 2 | Slacken the nut by 45° | |
| Stage 3 | 250 | 185 |
| Lower arm balljoint clamp bolt nut* | 50 | 37 |
| Roadwheels | 110 | 81 |
| Track rod end to swivel hub*: | | |
| Stage 1 | 30 | 22 |
| Stage 2 | Angle-tighten a further 90° | |
| Stage 3 | Angle-tighten a further 15° | |

*Use new nuts/bolts*

### 1 General information

Drive is transmitted from the differential to the front wheels by means of two, unequal-length driveshafts.

Both driveshafts are splined at their outer ends to accept the wheel hubs, and are threaded so that each hub can be fastened by a large nut. The inner end of each driveshaft is splined to accept the intermediate shaft or differential sun gear and is held in place by an internal circlip.

Constant velocity (CV) joints are fitted to each end of the driveshafts, to ensure the smooth and efficient transmission of drive at all the angles possible as the roadwheels move up-and-down with the suspension, and as they turn from side-to-side under steering. Both inner and outer constant velocity joints are of the ball-and-cage type.

**TOOL TIP**

*A tool to hold the wheel hub stationary whilst the driveshaft retaining nut is slackened can be fabricated from two lengths of steel strip (one long, one short) and a nut an bolt; the nut and bolt forming the pivot of a forked tool.*

## 2 Driveshaft –
removal and refitting

**Note:** *A new driveshaft retaining nut, inner joint circlip, lower arm balljoint clamp bolt and nut, anti-roll bar connecting link retaining nut and a new track rod end retaining nut will be needed for refitting. The driveshaft outer joint splines may be a tight fit in the hub and it is possible that a puller/extractor will be required to draw the hub assembly off the driveshaft during removal.*

**2.6 Unscrew the retaining nut and withdraw the clamp bolt from the swivel hub**

**2.8 Push down the lower suspension arm to free the balljoint from the swivel hub**

**2.4 Unscrew the retaining nut, then use a balljoint separator tool to remove the track rod end from the swivel hub**

### Removal

**1** Firmly apply the handbrake, then jack up the front of the car and support it securely on axle stands (see *Jacking and vehicle support*). Remove the relevant front roadwheel.

**2** To prevent rotation of the wheel hub as the driveshaft retaining nut is slackened, make up a holding tool and bolt the tool to the wheel hub using two wheel bolts **(see Tool Tip)**.

**3** With the holding tool in place, slacken and remove the driveshaft retaining nut using a socket and long bar. Where necessary, support the socket on an axle stand to prevent it slipping off the nut. This nut is very tight; make sure that there is no risk of pulling the car off the axle stands as the nut is slackened.

**4** Unscrew the nut securing the track rod end to the steering arm on the swivel hub, then use a balljoint separator tool to remove the track rod end **(see illustration)**.

**2.7 Use a chisel or screwdriver as a wedge to expand the lower portion of the swivel hub**

**2.9a Use a soft-faced hammer to drive the driveshaft from the hub splines . . .**

**2.5 Unscrew the nut securing the connecting link to the anti-roll bar, while holding the link stub with a further spanner**

**5** Unscrew and remove the nut securing the anti-roll bar connecting link to the suspension strut, while holding the link stub on the flats provided with a further spanner **(see illustration)**. Release the link from the strut and move it to one side.

**6** Unscrew the nut and remove the clamp bolt securing the front suspension lower arm to the swivel hub. Note that the bolt head faces the front of the vehicle **(see illustration)**.

**7** Use a chisel or screwdriver as a wedge to expand the lower portion of the swivel hub **(see illustration)**.

**8** Using a lever, push down on the suspension lower arm to free the balljoint from the swivel hub, then move the swivel hub to one side and release the arm, taking care not to damage the balljoint rubber boot **(see illustration)**. It is advisable to place a protective cover over the rubber boot such as the plastic cap from an aerosol can, suitably cut to fit.

**9** The hub must now be freed from the end of the driveshaft. It may be possible to pull the hub off the driveshaft, but if the end of the driveshaft is tight in the hub, temporarily refit the driveshaft retaining nut to protect the driveshaft threads, then tap the end of the driveshaft with a soft-faced hammer while pulling outwards on the swivel hub **(see illustrations)**. Alternatively, use a suitable puller to press the driveshaft through the hub.

**10** With the driveshaft detached from the swivel hub, tie the suspension strut to one side and support the driveshaft on an axle stand.

**11** Place a suitable container beneath the

**2.9b . . . then pull the swivel hub outwards**

differential, to collect escaping transmission oil/fluid when the driveshaft is withdrawn.

**12** Using a stout bar, release the inner end of the driveshaft from the differential. Lever between the constant velocity joint and differential housing to release the driveshaft retaining circlip **(see illustration)**.

**13** Withdraw the driveshaft, ensuring that the constant velocity joints are not placed under excessive strain, and remove the driveshaft from beneath the vehicle. Whilst the driveshaft is removed, plug or tape over the differential aperture to prevent dirt entry.

*Caution: Do not allow the vehicle to rest on its wheels with one or both driveshafts removed, as damage to the wheel bearings(s) may result. If the vehicle must be moved on its wheels, clamp the wheel bearings using spacers and a long threaded rod to take the place of the driveshaft.*

### Refitting

**14** Before refitting the driveshaft, examine the oil seal in the transmission housing and renew it if necessary as described in the relevant Part of Chapter 7.

**15** Remove the circlip from the end of the driveshaft inner joint splines and discard it. Fit a new circlip, making sure it is correctly located in the groove.

**16** Thoroughly clean the driveshaft splines and the apertures in the transmission and hub assembly. Apply a thin film of grease to the oil seal lips, and to the driveshaft splines and shoulders. Check that all gaiter clips are securely fastened.

**17** Offer up the driveshaft, and engage the inner joint splines with those of the differential sun gear, taking care not to damage the oil seal. Push the joint fully into position, then check that the circlip is correctly located and securely holds the joint in position. If necessary, use a soft-faced mallet or drift to drive the driveshaft inner joint fully into position.

**18** Align the outer constant velocity joint splines with those of the hub, and slide the joint back into position in the hub.

**19** Using a lever, push down on the lower suspension arm, then relocate the balljoint and release the arm. Make sure that the balljoint stub is fully entered in the swivel hub.

**20** Insert a new lower arm balljoint clamp bolt

**2.12 Using a stout bar, release the inner end of the driveshaft from the differential or intermediate shaft**

with its head facing the front of the vehicle, fit a new retaining nut and tighten the nut to the specified torque.

**21** Refit the track rod end to the steering arm on the swivel hub and tighten the new nut to the specified torque in the stages given.

**22** Locate the anti-roll bar connecting link on the suspension strut, fit a new retaining nut and tighten the nut to the specified torque.

**23** Lubricate the inner face and threads of the new driveshaft retaining nut with clean engine oil, and refit it to the end of the driveshaft. Use the method employed on removal to prevent the hub from rotating, and tighten the driveshaft retaining nut to the specified torque in the stages given in the Specifications. Check that the hub rotates freely.

**24** Where fitted, tap a new driveshaft retaining nut dust cap into position.

**25** Where applicable, refit the engine undertray.

**26** Refit the roadwheel, lower the vehicle to the ground and tighten the roadwheel bolts to the specified torque.

**27** Check and if necessary top-up the transmission oil/fluid level, using the information given in the relevant Part of Chapter 7.

### 3 Driveshaft joint gaiters – renewal

## *Outer CV joint*

**1** Remove the driveshaft from the car as described in Section 2, then secure the shaft in a vice equipped with soft jaws.

**2** Release the rubber gaiter inner and outer retaining clips by cutting through them using a junior hacksaw **(see illustration)**. Spread the clips and remove them from the gaiter.

**3** Slide the rubber gaiter down the shaft to expose the CV joint or, alternatively, cut the gaiter open using a suitable knife and remove it from the driveshaft **(see illustration)**.

**4** Using old rags, clean away as much of the old grease as possible from the CV joint. It is advisable to wear disposable rubber gloves during this operation.

**5** The outer CV joint will be retained on the driveshaft either by an external snap-ring, or by an internal circlip **(see illustration)**. If an external snap-ring is fitted, use circlip pliers to expand the snap-ring as the CV joint is removed.

**6** Using a mallet, sharply strike the edge of the outer joint to drive it off the end of the shaft **(see illustrations)**.

**3.2 Release the rubber gaiter retaining clips by cutting through them using a hacksaw**

**3.3 Cut the gaiter open using a suitable knife and remove it from the driveshaft**

**3.5 Outer CV joint snap-ring (arrowed)**

**3.6a Sharply strike the edge of the outer joint to drive it off the end of the shaft**

**3.6b If an external snap-ring is fitted, use circlip pliers to expand the snap-ring as the joint is removed**

3.7  Removing the circlip from the groove in the driveshaft splines

3.12  Components required for driveshaft gaiter renewal

3.13  Slide the new rubber gaiter and retaining clips onto the driveshaft

3.14a  Fit a new snap-ring to the constant velocity joint . . .

3.14b  . . . or a new circlip to the groove in the driveshaft

3.15  Pack the joint with the grease supplied in the repair kit

**7** Once the joint has been removed, extract the snap-ring from the joint, or remove the circlip from the groove in the driveshaft splines **(see illustration)**. A new snap-ring or circlip must be fitted on reassembly.

**8** If still in place, withdraw the rubber gaiter from the driveshaft.

**9** With the CV joint removed from the driveshaft, wipe away the remaining grease (do not use any solvent) to allow the joint components to be inspected.

**10** Move the inner splined driving member from side-to-side, to expose each ball in turn at the top of its track. Examine the balls for cracks, flat spots, or signs of surface pitting.

**11** Inspect the ball tracks on the inner and outer members. If the tracks have widened, the balls will no longer be a tight fit. At the same time, check the ball cage windows for wear or cracking between the windows.

**12** If on inspection any of the constant

velocity joint components are found to be worn or damaged, it will be necessary to renew the complete joint assembly. If the joint is in satisfactory condition, obtain a repair kit consisting of a new gaiter and retaining clips, a constant velocity joint snap-ring or circlip, and the correct type and quantity of grease **(see illustration)**.

**13** Slide the new rubber gaiter and retaining clips onto the driveshaft **(see illustration)**.

**14** Fit a new snap-ring to the constant velocity joint, or a new circlip to the groove in the driveshaft, as applicable **(see illustrations)**.

**15** Pack the joint with the grease supplied in the repair kit **(see illustration)**. Work the grease well into the bearing tracks whilst twisting the joint, and fill the rubber gaiter with any excess.

**16** Screw on the driveshaft retaining nut two or three turns to protect the threads, then engage the joint with the driveshaft splines. Tap the

joint onto the driveshaft until the snap-ring or circlip engages in its groove **(see illustration)**. Make sure that the joint is securely retained, by pulling on the joint, not the shaft.

**17** Ease the gaiter over the joint, and ensure that the gaiter lips are correctly located in the grooves on both the driveshaft and constant velocity joint. Lift the outer sealing lip of the gaiter, to equalise air pressure within the gaiter.

**18** Pull the large gaiter retaining clip as tight as possible, and locate the hooks on the clip in their slots. Remove any slack in the gaiter retaining clip by carefully compressing the raised section of the clip. In the absence of the special tool, a pair of side-cutters may be used. Secure the small retaining clip using the same procedure **(see illustrations)**.

**19** Check that the constant velocity joint moves freely in all directions, then refit the driveshaft to the car as described in Section 2.

3.16  Tap the joint onto the driveshaft until the snap-ring or circlip engages in its groove

3.18a  Secure the large gaiter retaining clip in position by compressing the raised section of the clip

3.18b  The small inner retaining clip is secured in the same way

**3.21a Remove the circlip from the groove in the inner CV joint splines . . .**

**3.21b . . . then, where fitted, slide off the rubber dust cover**

**3.22 Cut off the rubber gaiter retaining clips, then slide the gaiter down the shaft**

**3.24 Clean away as much of the old grease as possible from the CV joint**

**3.25a Expand the joint retaining snap-ring using circlip pliers . . .**

**3.25b . . . then remove the joint by tapping it off the driveshaft with a hammer and punch**

### Inner CV joint

**20** Remove the driveshaft from the car as described in Section 2, then secure the shaft in a vice equipped with soft jaws.

**21** Remove the circlip from the groove in the CV joint splines then, where fitted, slide off the rubber dust cover (see illustrations). Note that a new circlip must be fitted on reassembly.

**22** Release the rubber gaiter inner and outer retaining clips by cutting through them using a junior hacksaw (see illustration). Spread the clips and remove them from the gaiter.

**23** Slide the rubber gaiter down the shaft to expose the CV joint.

**24** Using old rags, clean away as much of the old grease as possible from the CV joint (see illustration). It is advisable to wear disposable rubber gloves during this operation.

**25** Expand the CV joint retaining snap-ring using circlip pliers, then remove the joint by

tapping it off the driveshaft with a hammer and punch in contact with the joint inner member (see illustrations).

**26** Once the joint has been removed, extract the snap-ring noting that a new one must be fitted on reassembly.

**27** Withdraw the rubber gaiter from the driveshaft.

**28** With the CV joint removed from the driveshaft, wipe away the remaining grease (do not use any solvent) and inspect the joint components as described previously in paragraphs 10 and 11.

**29** If on inspection any of the constant velocity joint components are found to be worn or damaged, it will be necessary to renew the complete joint assembly. If the joint is in satisfactory condition, obtain a repair kit consisting of a new gaiter and retaining clips, a constant velocity joint snap-ring and circlip, and the correct type and quantity of grease.

**30** Slide the new rubber gaiter and retaining clips onto the driveshaft (see illustration).

**31** Fit a new snap-ring to the constant velocity joint, then engage the joint with the driveshaft splines. Tap the joint onto the driveshaft until the snap-ring engages in its groove (see illustration). Make sure that the joint is securely retained, by pulling on the joint, not the shaft.

**32** Pack the joint with the grease supplied in the repair kit (see illustration). Work the grease well into the bearing tracks whilst twisting the joint, and fill the rubber gaiter with any excess.

**33** Ease the gaiter over the joint, and ensure that the gaiter lips are correctly located in the grooves on both the driveshaft and constant velocity joint. Lift the outer sealing lip of the gaiter, to equalise air pressure within the gaiter.

**34** Pull the large gaiter retaining clip as tight

**3.30 Slide the new rubber gaiter and retaining clips onto the driveshaft**

**3.31 Tap the joint onto the driveshaft until the snap-ring engages in its groove**

**3.32 Pack the joint with the grease supplied in the repair kit**

**3.34a Secure the large gaiter retaining clip in position by compressing the raised section of the clip**

**3.34b The small inner retaining clip is secured in the same way**

as possible, and locate the hooks on the clip in their slots. Remove any slack in the gaiter retaining clip by carefully compressing the raised section of the clip. In the absence of the special tool, a pair of side-cutters may be used. Secure the small retaining clip using the same procedure **(see illustrations)**.

**35** Where applicable, slide the rubber dust cover onto the CV joint, then fit a new circlip to the groove in the joint splines.

**36** Check that the constant velocity joint moves freely in all directions, then refit the driveshaft to the car as described in Section 2.

## 4 Driveshaft overhaul – general information

**1** If any of the checks described in Chapter 1 reveal possible wear in any driveshaft joint, carry out the following procedures to identify the source of the problem.

**2** Firmly apply the handbrake, then jack up the front of the vehicle and support it securely on axle stands (see *Jacking and vehicle support*).

**3** Referring to the information contained in Section 2, make up a tool to hold the wheel hub, and bolt the tool to the hub. Use a torque wrench to check that the driveshaft retaining nut is securely fastened, then repeat this check on the remaining driveshaft nut.

**4** Road test the vehicle, and listen for a metallic clicking from the front as the vehicle is driven slowly in a circle on full-lock. If a clicking noise is heard, this indicates wear in the outer constant velocity joint.

**5** If vibration, consistent with roadspeed, is felt through the car when accelerating, there is a possibility of wear in the inner constant velocity joints.

**6** To check the joints for wear, remove the driveshafts, then dismantle them as described in Section 3; if any wear or free play is found, the affected joint must be renewed.

# Chapter 9
# Braking system

## Contents

## Degrees of difficulty

| Easy, suitable for novice with little experience | Fairly easy, suitable for beginner with some experience | Fairly difficult, suitable for competent DIY mechanic | Difficult, suitable for experienced DIY mechanic | Very difficult, suitable for expert DIY or professional |
|---|---|---|---|---|

## Specifications

### Front brakes
| | |
|---|---|
| Type ......... | Ventilated disc, with single-piston sliding caliper |
| Disc diameter ......... | 280.0 mm |
| Disc thickness: | |
| New ......... | 25.0 mm |
| Minimum ......... | 22.0 mm |
| Maximum disc run-out ......... | 0.11 mm |
| Brake pad friction material minimum thickness ......... | 2.0 mm |
| Brake caliper piston diameter ......... | 57.0 mm |

### Rear disc brakes
| | |
|---|---|
| Type ......... | Solid disc, with single-piston sliding caliper |
| Disc diameter ......... | 264.0 mm |
| Disc thickness: | |
| New ......... | 10.0 mm |
| Minimum ......... | 8.0 mm |
| Maximum disc run-out ......... | 0.13 mm |
| Brake pad friction material minimum thickness ......... | 2.0 mm |
| Brake caliper piston diameter ......... | 38.0 mm |

### Rear drum brakes
| | |
|---|---|
| Type ......... | Single leading shoe |
| Drum diameter (inner): | |
| New ......... | 230.0 mm |
| Maximum ......... | 231.0 mm |
| Maximum drum out-of-round ......... | 0.05 mm |
| Brake shoe friction material minimum thickness ......... | 1.0 mm |

### ABS system type
| | |
|---|---|
| Standard ABS system ......... | ATE Mk 70 |
| ABS with traction control and electronic stability programme ......... | ATE Mk 60 ESP |

## Torque wrench settings

| | Nm | lbf ft |
|---|---|---|
| ABS hydraulic modulator mounting bracket bolts . . . . . . . . . . . . . . . . . | 20 | 15 |
| ABS hydraulic modulator to mounting bracket . . . . . . . . . . . . . . . . . | 8 | 6 |
| Air conditioning refrigerant pipe block connection . . . . . . . . . . . . . . . | 20 | 15 |
| Brake caliper bleed screws . . . . . . . . . . . . . . . . . . . . . . . . . . . . . . | 6 | 4 |
| Brake caliper guide bolts: | | |
|    Front caliper . . . . . . . . . . . . . . . . . . . . . . . . . . . . . . . . . . . . | 28 | 21 |
|    Rear caliper . . . . . . . . . . . . . . . . . . . . . . . . . . . . . . . . . . . . | 25 | 18 |
| Brake caliper mounting bracket bolts . . . . . . . . . . . . . . . . . . . . . | 100 | 74 |
| Brake fluid pipe unions. . . . . . . . . . . . . . . . . . . . . . . . . . . . . . . . . | 14 | 10 |
| Brake hydraulic hose banjo union bolts . . . . . . . . . . . . . . . . . . . . . | 40 | 30 |
| Brake pedal mounting bracket bolts/nuts . . . . . . . . . . . . . . . . . . . | 20 | 15 |
| Handbrake lever retaining nuts . . . . . . . . . . . . . . . . . . . . . . . . . . . | 10 | 7 |
| Master cylinder retaining nuts . . . . . . . . . . . . . . . . . . . . . . . . . . . | 15 | 11 |
| Roadwheel bolts. . . . . . . . . . . . . . . . . . . . . . . . . . . . . . . . . . . . . | 110 | 81 |
| Vacuum servo unit mounting nuts . . . . . . . . . . . . . . . . . . . . . . . . | 20 | 15 |
| Wheel cylinder retaining bolts . . . . . . . . . . . . . . . . . . . . . . . . . . . | 10 | 7 |

* Use new fasteners

## 1 General information

The braking system is of servo-assisted, dual-circuit hydraulic type split diagonally. The arrangement of the hydraulic system is such that each circuit operates one front and one rear brake from a tandem master cylinder. Under normal circumstances, both circuits operate in unison. However, in the event of hydraulic failure in one circuit, full braking force will still be available at two wheels.

All models are fitted with front disc brakes and rear disc or drum brakes. The disc brakes are actuated by single-piston sliding type calipers, which ensure that equal pressure is applied to each disc pad.

The rear drum brakes incorporate leading and trailing shoes, which are actuated by twin-piston wheel cylinders. A self-adjust mechanism is incorporated to automatically compensate for brake shoe wear. As the brake shoe linings wear, the footbrake operation automatically operates the adjuster mechanism, which effectively lengthens the shoe strut, and repositions the brake shoes to maintain the lining-to-drum clearance.

An Anti-lock Braking System (ABS) is fitted as standard equipment to all vehicles covered in this manual. On higher specification models, the ABS may also incorporate traction control or an electronic stability programme. Refer to Section 20 for further information on ABS operation.

The, cable-operated handbrake provides an independent mechanical means of rear brake application.

⚠️ *Warning: When servicing any part of the system, work carefully and methodically; also observe cleanliness when overhauling any part of the hydraulic system. Always renew components (in axle sets, where applicable) if in doubt about their condition, and use only genuine Vauxhall/Opel parts, or at least those of known good quality. Note the warnings given in 'Safety first!' and at relevant points in this Chapter concerning the dangers of asbestos dust and hydraulic fluid.*

## 2 Hydraulic system – bleeding

⚠️ *Warning: Hydraulic fluid is poisonous; wash off immediately and thoroughly in the case of skin contact, and seek immediate medical advice if any fluid is swallowed or gets into the eyes. Certain types of hydraulic fluid are inflammable, and may ignite when allowed into contact with hot components; when servicing any hydraulic system, it is safest to assume that the fluid is inflammable, and to take precautions against the risk of fire as though it is petrol that is being handled. Hydraulic fluid is also an effective paint stripper, and will attack plastics; if any is spilt, it should be washed off immediately, using copious quantities of fresh water. Finally, it is hygroscopic (it absorbs moisture from the air) – old fluid may be contaminated and unfit for further use. When topping-up or renewing the fluid, always use the recommended type, and ensure that it comes from a freshly-opened sealed container.*

### General

1 The correct operation of any hydraulic system is only possible after removing all air from the components and circuit; this is achieved by bleeding the system.

2 During the bleeding procedure, add only clean, unused hydraulic fluid of the recommended type; never re-use fluid that has already been bled from the system. Ensure that sufficient fluid is available before starting work.

3 If there is any possibility of incorrect fluid being already in the system, the brake components and circuit must be flushed completely with uncontaminated, correct fluid, and new seals should be fitted to the various components.

4 If hydraulic fluid has been lost from the system, or air has entered because of a leak, ensure that the fault is cured before proceeding further.

5 Park the vehicle over an inspection pit or on car ramps. Alternatively, apply the handbrake then jack up the front and rear of the vehicle and support it on axle stands (see *Jacking and vehicle support*). For improved access with the vehicle jacked up, remove the roadwheels.

6 Check that all pipes and hoses are secure, unions tight and bleed screws closed. Clean any dirt from around the bleed screws.

7 Unscrew the master cylinder reservoir cap, and top the master cylinder reservoir up to the MAX level line; refit the cap loosely, and remember to maintain the fluid level at least above the MIN level line throughout the procedure, otherwise there is a risk of further air entering the system.

8 There is a number of one-man, do-it-yourself brake bleeding kits currently available from motor accessory shops. It is recommended that one of these kits is used whenever possible, as they greatly simplify the bleeding operation, and also reduce the risk of expelled air and fluid being drawn back into the system. If such a kit is not available, the basic (two-man) method must be used, which is described in detail below.

*Caution: Vauxhall recommend using a pressure bleeding kit for this operation (see paragraphs 24 to 27).*

9 If a kit is to be used, prepare the vehicle as described previously, and follow the kit manufacturer's instructions, as the procedure may vary slightly according to the type being used; generally, they are as outlined below in the relevant sub-section.

10 Whichever method is used, the same sequence should be followed (paragraphs 11 and 12) to ensure the removal of all air from the system.

### Bleeding sequence

11 If the system has been only partially disconnected, and suitable precautions were taken to minimise fluid loss, it should only be necessary to bleed that part of the system (ie, the primary or secondary circuit). If the master cylinder or main brake lines have been disconnected, then the complete system must be bled.

**12** If the complete system is to be bled, then it should be done in the following sequence:

### Right-hand drive models

a) Left-hand rear brake.
b) Right-hand rear brake.
c) Left-hand front brake.
d) Right-hand front brake.

### Left-hand drive models

a) Right-hand rear brake.
b) Left-hand rear brake.
c) Right-hand front brake.
d) Left-hand front brake.

## Bleeding

### Basic (two-man) method

**13** Collect together a clean glass jar, a suitable length of plastic or rubber tubing which is a tight fit over the bleed screw, and a ring spanner to fit the screw. The help of an assistant will also be required.

**14** Remove the dust cap from the first bleed screw in the sequence **(see illustrations)**. Fit the spanner and tube to the screw, place the other end of the tube in the jar, and pour in sufficient fluid to cover the end of the tube.

**15** Ensure that the master cylinder reservoir fluid level is maintained at least above the MIN level line throughout the procedure.

**16** Have the assistant fully depress the brake pedal several times to build-up pressure, then maintain it on the final downstroke.

**17** While pedal pressure is maintained, unscrew the bleed screw (approximately one turn) and allow the compressed fluid and air to flow into the jar. The assistant should maintain pedal pressure, following it down to the floor if necessary, and should not release it until instructed to do so. When the flow stops, tighten the bleed screw again, have the assistant release the pedal slowly, and recheck the reservoir fluid level.

**18** Repeat the steps given in paragraphs 16 and 17 until the fluid emerging from the bleed screw is free from air bubbles. If the master cylinder has been drained and refilled, and air is being bled from the first screw in the sequence, allow approximately five seconds between cycles for the master cylinder passages to refill.

**19** When no more air bubbles appear, securely tighten the bleed screw, remove the tube and spanner, and refit the dust cap. Do not overtighten the bleed screw.

**20** Repeat the procedure on the remaining screws in the sequence, until all air is removed from the system and the brake pedal feels firm again.

### Using a one-way valve kit

**21** As the name implies, these kits consist of a length of tubing with a one-way valve fitted, to prevent expelled air and fluid being drawn back into the system; some kits include a translucent container, which can be positioned so that the air bubbles can be more easily seen flowing from the end of the tube.

**22** The kit is connected to the bleed screw, which is then opened. The user returns to the

2.14a  **Remove the dust caps from the front . . .**

driver's seat, depresses the brake pedal with a smooth, steady stroke, and slowly releases it; this is repeated until the expelled fluid is clear of air bubbles.

**23** Note that these kits simplify work so much that it is easy to forget the master cylinder reservoir fluid level; ensure that this is maintained at least above the MIN level line at all times.

### Using a pressure-bleeding kit

**24** These kits are usually operated by a reservoir of pressurised air contained in the spare tyre. However, note that it will probably be necessary to reduce the pressure to a lower level than normal; refer to the instructions supplied with the kit.

**25** By connecting a pressurised, fluid-filled container to the master cylinder reservoir, bleeding can be carried out simply by opening each screw in turn (in the specified sequence), and allowing the fluid to flow out until no more air bubbles can be seen in the expelled fluid.

**26** This method has the advantage that the large reservoir of fluid provides an additional safeguard against air being drawn into the system during bleeding.

**27** Pressure-bleeding is particularly effective when bleeding 'difficult' systems, or when bleeding the complete system at the time of routine fluid renewal.

### All methods

**28** When bleeding is complete, and firm pedal feel is restored, wash off any spilt fluid, securely tighten the bleed screws, and refit the dust caps.

**29** Check the hydraulic fluid level in the master cylinder reservoir, and top-up if necessary (see *Weekly checks*).

3.2a  **Pull out the spring clip . . .**

2.14b  **. . . and rear bleed screws**

**30** Discard any hydraulic fluid that has been bled from the system; it will not be fit for re-use.

**31** Check the feel of the brake pedal. If it feels at all spongy, air must still be present in the system, and further bleeding is required. Failure to bleed satisfactorily after a reasonable repetition of the bleeding procedure may be due to worn master cylinder seals.

## 3  Hydraulic pipes and hoses – renewal

**Note:** *Before starting work, refer to the note at the beginning of Section 2 concerning the dangers of hydraulic fluid.*

**1** If any pipe or hose is to be renewed, minimise fluid loss by first removing the master cylinder reservoir cap and screwing it down onto a piece of polythene. Alternatively, flexible hoses can be sealed, if required, using a proprietary brake hose clamp. Metal brake pipe unions can be plugged (if care is taken not to allow dirt into the system) or capped immediately they are disconnected. Place a wad of rag under any union that is to be disconnected, to catch any spilt fluid.

**2** If a flexible hose is to be disconnected, unscrew the brake pipe union nut before removing the spring clip which secures the hose to its mounting bracket. Where applicable, unscrew the banjo union bolt securing the hose to the caliper and recover the copper washers. When removing the front flexible hose, pull out the spring clip and disconnect it from the strut **(see illustrations)**.

3.2b  **. . . and disconnect the hydraulic hose from the strut bracket**

**3** To unscrew union nuts, it is preferable to obtain a brake pipe spanner of the correct size; these are available from most motor accessory shops. Failing this, a close-fitting open-ended spanner will be required, though if the nuts are tight or corroded, their flats may be rounded-off if the spanner slips. In such a case, a self-locking wrench is often the only way to unscrew a stubborn union, but it follows that the pipe and the damaged nuts must be renewed on reassembly. Always clean a union and surrounding area before disconnecting it. If disconnecting a component with more than one union, make a careful note of the connections before disturbing any of them.

**4** If a brake pipe is to be renewed, it can be obtained, cut to length and with the union nuts and end flares in place, from Vauxhall/Opel dealers. All that is then necessary is to bend

it to shape, following the line of the original, before fitting it to the car. Alternatively, most motor accessory shops can make up brake pipes from kits, but this requires very careful measurement of the original, to ensure that the new one is of the correct length. The safest answer is usually to take the original to the shop as a pattern.

**5** On refitting, do not overtighten the union nuts.

**6** When refitting hoses to the calipers, always use new copper washers and tighten the banjo union bolts to the specified torque. Make sure that the hoses are positioned so that they will not touch surrounding bodywork or the roadwheels.

**7** Ensure that the pipes and hoses are correctly routed, with no kinks, and that they are secured in the clips or brackets provided.

After fitting, remove the polythene from the reservoir, and bleed the hydraulic system as described in Section 2. Wash off any spilt fluid, and check carefully for fluid leaks.

## 4  Front brake pads – renewal

> **Warning: Renew BOTH sets of front brake pads at the same time – NEVER renew the pads on only one wheel, as uneven braking may result. Note that the dust created by wear of the pads may contain asbestos, which is a health hazard. Never blow it out with compressed air, and do not inhale any of it. An approved filtering mask should be worn when working on the brakes. DO NOT use petroleum-based solvents to clean brake parts – use brake cleaner or methylated spirit only.**

**1** Apply the handbrake, then jack up the front of the vehicle and support it on axle stands (see *Jacking and vehicle support*). Remove the front roadwheels.

**2** Follow the accompanying photos **(illustrations 4.2a to 4.2y)** for the actual pad renewal procedure, bearing in mind the additional points listed below. Be sure to stay in order and read the caption under each illustration. Note that if the old pads are to be refitted, ensure that they are identified so that they can be returned to their original positions.

**4.2a  Push in the caliper piston by levering the caliper body towards the outside of the vehicle**

**4.2b  Unclip the wiring guide from the brake hose. Where fitted, detach the pad wear warning indicator wire from the inner pad**

**4.2c  Release the legs of the retaining spring from the caliper body . . .**

**4.2d  . . . then remove the spring from the caliper mounting bracket**

**4.2e  Remove the dust caps from the upper and lower guide bolts**

**4.2f  Unscrew the upper guide bolt . . .**

**4.2g  . . . and remove it from the caliper**

**4.2h  Similarly unscrew the lower guide bolt and remove it from the caliper**

4.2i Lift the caliper and brake pads off the mounting bracket

4.2j Remove the outer pad from the caliper body . . .

4.2k . . . and the inner pad from the caliper piston, noting that it is retained by a spring clip attached to the pad backing plate

4.2l Measure the thickness of the pad friction material. If any are worn down to the specified minimum, or fouled with oil or grease, all four pads must be renewed

4.2m Brush the dust and dirt from the caliper piston and mounting bracket

4.2n Apply a little high melting-point copper brake grease to the pad backing plate contact areas on the mounting bracket

4.2o If new pads are to be fitted, before refitting the caliper, push back the caliper piston whilst opening the bleed screw. This is to prevent any dirt/debris being forced back up the hydraulic circuit in the ABS modulator

4.2p The brake pads are 'handed' for each side. Make sure the arrow on the backing plate points in the direction of forward rotation of the brake disc

4.2q Fit the inner pad to the caliper, ensuring that its clip is correctly located in the caliper piston

4.2r Fit the outer pad to the caliper mounting bracket, ensuring that its friction material is facing the brake disc

4.2s Slide the caliper into position in the mounting bracket

4.2t Fit the guide bolts . . .

4.2u . . . tighten the guide bolts to the specified torque . . .

4.2v . . . then refit the dust caps

4.2w Locate the retaining spring legs into the holes in the caliper . . .

4.2x . . . then hold the legs in place and locate the spring behind the lugs on the mounting bracket

4.2y Clip the wiring guide back onto the brake hose. Where fitted, attach the pad wear warning indicator wire to the inner pad

3 After removing the caliper from the mounting bracket, support it on top of the brake disc. Do not allow the caliper to hang unsupported on the flexible brake hose.

4 If the original brake pads are still serviceable, carefully clean them using a clean, fine wire brush or similar, paying particular attention to the sides and back of the metal backing plate. Clean out the grooves in the friction material, and pick out any large embedded particles of dirt or debris. Carefully clean the pad locations in the caliper body/mounting bracket.

5 Prior to fitting the pads, check that the guide bolts are a snug fit in the caliper mounting bracket. Inspect the dust seal around the piston for damage, and the piston for evidence of fluid leaks, corrosion or damage. If attention to any of these components is necessary, refer to Section 7.

6 If new brake pads are to be fitted, the caliper piston must be pushed back into the cylinder to allow for the extra pad thickness. Either use a G-clamp or similar tool, or use suitable pieces of wood as levers. Clamp off the flexible brake hose leading to the caliper then connect a brake bleeding kit to the caliper bleed screw. Open the bleed screw as the piston is retracted, the surplus brake fluid will then be collected in the bleed kit vessel (see illustration 4.2o). Close the bleed screw just before the caliper piston is pushed fully into the caliper. This should ensure no air enters the hydraulic system.

*Caution: The ABS unit contains hydraulic components that are very sensitive to impurities in the brake fluid. Even the smallest particles can cause the system to fail through blockage. The pad retraction method described here prevents any debris in the brake fluid expelled from the caliper*

*from being passed back to the ABS hydraulic unit, as well as preventing any chance of damage to the master cylinder seals.*

7 With the brake pads installed, depress the brake pedal repeatedly, until normal (non-assisted) pedal pressure is restored, and the pads are pressed into firm contact with the brake disc.

8 Repeat the above procedure on the remaining front brake caliper.

9 Refit the roadwheels, then lower the vehicle to the ground and tighten the roadwheel bolts to the specified torque setting.

10 Check the hydraulic fluid level as described in *Weekly checks*.

*Caution: New pads will not give full braking efficiency until they have bedded-in. Be prepared for this, and avoid hard braking as far as possible for the first hundred miles or so after pad renewal.*

## 5 Rear brake pads – renewal

⚠ *Warning: Renew BOTH sets of rear brake pads at the same time – NEVER renew the pads on only one wheel, as uneven braking may result. Note that the dust created by wear of the pads may contain asbestos, which is a health hazard. Never blow it out with compressed air, and do not inhale any of it. An approved filtering mask should be worn when working on the brakes. DO NOT use petroleum-based solvents to clean brake parts – use brake cleaner or methylated spirit only.*

1 Chock the front wheels then jack up the rear of the car and securely support it on axle stands (see *Jacking and vehicle support*). Remove the rear roadwheels.

2 Slacken the handbrake cable adjuster at the handbrake lever as described in Section 17, paragraphs 11 to 13.

3 Follow the accompanying photos (illustrations 5.3a to 5.3u) for the actual pad renewal procedure, bearing in mind the additional points listed below. Be sure to stay in order and read the caption under each illustration. Note that if the old pads are to be refitted, ensure that they are identified so that they can be returned to their original positions.

5.3a Using a screwdriver, push the handbrake operating lever downwards, and detach the cable end fitting from the lever

5.3b Prise out the handbrake outer cable retaining clip . . .

5.3c ... and withdraw the handbrake cable from the caliper bracket

5.3d Unscrew the upper guide pin bolt while counter-holding the guide pin with a second spanner

5.3e Unscrew the lower guide pin bolt in the same way

5.3f Lift the caliper off the mounting bracket and suspend it from a suitable place under the wheel arch using a cable tie or similar

5.3g Remove the inner pad ...

5.3h ... and outer pad from the caliper mounting bracket

5.3i Remove the lower guide plate ...

5.3j ... and upper guide plate from the caliper mounting bracket

5.3k Measure the thickness of the pad friction material. If any are worn down to the specified minimum, or fouled with oil or grease, all four pads must be renewed

5.3l Using a caliper retracting tool to retract the piston as far as the stop

5.3m Once the piston is fully retracted, unscrew it slightly until the next piston cut-out (arrowed) is visible through the front of the caliper

5.3n Brush the dust and dirt from the caliper, piston and mounting bracket, then fit the lower guide plate ...

5.3o . . . and upper guide plate to the caliper mounting bracket

5.3p Apply a little high melting-point copper brake grease to the pad backing plate contact areas on the guide plates

5.3q If present remove the protective film from the pad backing plate, then fit the inner pad to the caliper mounting bracket . . .

5.3r . . . followed by the outer pad

5.3s Slide the caliper into position in the mounting bracket

5.3t Refit the upper and lower guide pin bolts and tighten them to the specified torque

5.3u Refit the handbrake cable to the mounting bracket and secure with the retaining clip, then reconnect the cable end to the caliper lever

**4** If the original brake pads are still serviceable, carefully clean them using a clean, fine wire brush or similar, paying particular attention to the sides and back of the metal backing plate. Clean out the grooves in the friction material, and pick out any large embedded particles of dirt or debris. Carefully clean the pad locations in the caliper body/mounting bracket.

**5** Prior to fitting the pads, check that the guide pins are a snug fit in the caliper mounting bracket. Brush the dust and dirt from the caliper and piston, but do not inhale it, as it is injurious to health. Inspect the dust seal around the piston for damage, and the piston for evidence of fluid leaks, corrosion or damage. If attention to any of these components is necessary, refer to Section 8.

**6** If new brake pads are to be fitted, it will be necessary to retract the piston fully into

the caliper bore by rotating it in a clockwise direction. This can be achieved by using sturdy circlip pliers, noting that as well as being turned, the piston has to be pressed in very firmly. Special tools are readily available to achieve this with less effort. While the caliper is being retracted, clamp off the flexible brake hose leading to the caliper then connect a brake bleeding kit to the caliper bleed screw. Open the bleed screw as the piston is retracted, the surplus brake fluid will then be collected in the bleed kit vessel (**see illustration 5.3l**). Close the bleed screw just before the caliper piston is pushed fully into the caliper. This should ensure no air enters the hydraulic system.

*Caution: The ABS unit contains hydraulic components that are very sensitive to impurities in the brake fluid. Even the smallest particles can cause the system to fail through blockage. The pad retraction method described here prevents any debris in the brake fluid expelled from the caliper from being passed back to the ABS hydraulic unit, as well as preventing any chance of damage to the master cylinder seals.*

**7** With the brake pads installed, depress the brake pedal repeatedly, until normal (non-assisted) pedal pressure is restored, and the pads are pressed into firm contact with the brake disc.

**8** Repeat the above procedure on the remaining rear brake caliper.

**9** Adjust the handbrake cable as described in Chapter 1 after fitting both sets of brake pads.

**10** Refit the roadwheels, then lower the vehicle to the ground and tighten the roadwheel bolts to the specified torque setting.

**11** Check the hydraulic fluid level as described in *Weekly checks*.

*Caution: New pads will not give full braking efficiency until they have bedded-in. Be prepared for this, and avoid hard braking as far as possible for the first hundred miles or so after pad renewal.*

**6 Front/rear brake disc –** inspection, removal and refitting

**Note:** *Before starting work, refer to the warning at the beginning of Section 4 or 5 concerning the dangers of asbestos dust. If either disc requires renewal, both should be renewed at the same time together with new pads, to ensure even and consistent braking.*

### Inspection

**1** Remove the wheel trim, then loosen the roadwheel bolts. If checking a front disc, apply the handbrake, and if checking a rear disc, chock the front wheels and release the handbrake, then jack up the relevant end of the vehicle and support on axle stands (see *Jacking and vehicle support*). Remove the roadwheel.

**2** Check that the brake disc securing screw is tight, then fit a spacer approximately 10.0 mm thick to one of the roadwheel bolts, and refit and tighten the bolt in the hole opposite the disc securing screw.

**6.9a Unclip the ABS wheel speed sensor wiring guide from the brake hydraulic hose . . .**

**6.9b . . . pull out the spring clip . . .**

**6.9c . . . and disconnect the hydraulic hose from the strut bracket**

**3** Rotate the brake disc, and examine it for deep scoring or grooving. Light scoring is normal, but if excessive, the disc should be removed and either renewed or machined (within the specified limits) by an engineering works. The minimum thickness is given in the Specifications at the start of this Chapter.

**4** Using a dial gauge, or a flat metal block and feeler blades, check that the disc run-out does not exceed the figure given in the Specifications. Measure the run-out 10.0 mm in from the outer edge of the disc.

**5** If the disc run-out is excessive, remove the disc as described later, and check that the disc-to-hub surfaces are perfectly clean. Refit the disc and check the run-out again.

**6** If the run-out is still excessive, the disc should be renewed.

**7** To remove a disc, proceed as follows.

### Front disc

#### Removal

**8** Remove the roadwheel bolt and spacer used when checking the disc.

**9** Unclip the ABS wheel speed sensor wiring guide from the brake hydraulic hose, then extract the retaining clip and release the hydraulic hose from the suspension strut (see illustrations).

**10** Unbolt and remove the front brake caliper, complete with disc pads and mounting bracket, and suspend it from the coil spring using a cable tie (see illustrations).

**11** Remove the securing screw and withdraw the disc from the hub (see illustrations).

#### Refitting

**12** Refit the disc, making sure that the mating faces of the disc and hub are perfectly clean, and apply a little locking fluid to the threads of the securing screw.

**13** Refit the caliper mounting bracket, complete with caliper and pads, and tighten the bolts to the specified torque.

### Rear disc

#### Removal

**14** Where applicable, remove the roadwheel bolt and spacer used when checking the disc.

**15** Remove the rear brake pads as described in Section 5.

**6.10a Unbolt and remove the front brake caliper complete with disc pads and mounting bracket . . .**

**6.10b . . . and suspend it from the coil spring using a cable tie**

**16** Undo the two bolts securing the caliper mounting bracket to the hub carrier and remove the mounting bracket.

**17** Remove the securing screw and withdraw the disc from the hub (see illustrations).

#### Refitting

**18** Refit the disc, making sure that the mating faces of the disc and hub are perfectly clean, and apply a little locking fluid to the threads of the securing screw.

**6.11a Remove the securing screw . . .**

**6.11b . . . and withdraw the disc from the hub**

**6.17a Remove the securing screw (arrowed)**

**6.17b . . . and withdraw the disc from the hub**

**7.7 Removing the piston seal from the caliper body**

**19** Refit the caliper mounting bracket and tighten the bolts to the specified torque.
**20** Refit the brake pads as described in Section 5.

## 7 Front brake caliper –
removal, overhaul and refitting

**Note:** *New brake hose copper washers will be required when refitting. Before starting work, refer to the note at the beginning of Section 2 concerning the dangers of hydraulic fluid, and to the warning at the beginning of Section 4 concerning the dangers of asbestos dust.*

### Removal

**1** Apply the handbrake, then jack up the front of the vehicle and support it on axle stands (see *Jacking and vehicle support*). Remove the roadwheel.
**2** Minimise fluid loss by first removing the master cylinder reservoir cap and screwing it down onto a piece of polythene. Alternatively, use a brake hose clamp to clamp the flexible hose leading to the brake caliper.
**3** Clean the area around the caliper brake hose union. Unscrew and remove the union bolt, and recover the copper sealing washer from each side of the hose union. Discard the washers; new ones must be used on refitting. Plug the hose end and caliper hole, to minimise fluid loss and prevent the ingress of dust and dirt into the hydraulic system.
**4** Remove the brake pads as described in Section 4, then remove the caliper from the vehicle.

**8.3 Rear caliper brake hose union bolt (arrowed)**

### Overhaul

**5** With the caliper on the bench, wipe it clean with a cloth rag.
**6** Withdraw the partially-ejected piston from the caliper body, and remove the dust seal. The piston can be withdrawn by hand, or if necessary pushed out by applying compressed air to the brake hose union hole. Only low pressure should be required, such as is generated by a foot pump.
**7** Using a small screwdriver, carefully remove the piston seal from the groove in the caliper, taking care not to mark the bore **(see illustration)**.
**8** Carefully press the guide bushes out of the caliper body.
**9** Thoroughly clean all components, using only methylated spirit or clean hydraulic fluid. Never use mineral-based solvents such as petrol or paraffin, which will attack the rubber components of the hydraulic system. Dry the components using compressed air or a clean, lint-free cloth. If available, use compressed air to blow clear the fluid passages.

>  **Warning: Wear eye protection when using compressed air.**

**10** Check all components, and renew any that are worn or damaged. If the piston and/or cylinder bore are scratched excessively, renew the complete caliper body. Similarly check the condition of the guide bushes and bolts; both bushes and bolts should be undamaged and (when cleaned) a reasonably tight sliding fit. If there is any doubt about the condition of any component, renew it.
**11** If the caliper is fit for further use, obtain the necessary components from your Vauxhall/Opel dealer. Renew the caliper seals and dust covers as a matter of course; these should never be re-used.
**12** On reassembly, ensure that all components are absolutely clean and dry.
**13** Dip the piston and the new piston seal in clean hydraulic fluid, and smear clean fluid on the cylinder bore surface.
**14** Locate the new seal in the cylinder bore groove, using only the fingers to manipulate it into position.
**15** Fit the new dust seal to the piston, then insert the piston into the cylinder bore using a twisting motion to ensure it enters the seal correctly. Locate the dust seal in the body groove, and push the piston fully into the caliper bore.
**16** Insert the guide bushes into position in the caliper body.

### Refitting

**17** Refit the brake pads as described in Section 4, together with the caliper which at this stage will not have the hose attached.
**18** Position a new copper sealing washer on each side of the hose union, and connect the brake hose to the caliper. Ensure that the hose is correctly positioned against the caliper body lug, then install the union bolt and tighten it to the specified torque setting.

**19** Remove the brake hose clamp or polythene, and bleed the hydraulic system as described in Section 2. Note that, providing the precautions described were taken to minimise brake fluid loss, it should only be necessary to bleed the relevant front brake circuit.
**20** Refit the roadwheel, then lower the vehicle to the ground and tighten the roadwheel bolts to the specified torque.

## 8 Rear brake caliper –
removal, overhaul and refitting

**Note 1:** *Before starting work, refer to the note at the beginning of Section 2 concerning the dangers of hydraulic fluid, and to the warning at the beginning of Section 5 concerning the dangers of asbestos dust.*
**Note 2:** *Due to the integral handbrake operating mechanism incorporated in the caliper piston, it is not possible to fully dismantle the caliper. Only the guide bushes and dust seal can be individually renewed. Check the availability of parts before proceeding.*

### Removal

**1** Chock the front wheels, then jack up the rear of the vehicle and support on axle stands (see *Jacking and vehicle support*). Remove the roadwheel.
**2** Minimise fluid loss by first removing the master cylinder reservoir cap and screwing it down onto a piece of polythene. Alternatively, use a brake hose clamp to clamp the flexible hose leading to the brake caliper.
**3** Clean the area around the caliper brake hose union. Unscrew and remove the union bolt, and recover the copper sealing washer from each side of the hose union **(see illustration)**. Discard the washers; new ones must be used on refitting. Plug the hose end and caliper hole, to minimise fluid loss and prevent the ingress of dust and dirt into the hydraulic system.
**4** Remove the brake pads as described in Section 5, then remove the caliper from the vehicle.

### Overhaul

**5** With the caliper on the bench, wipe it clean with a cloth rag.
**6** Using a small screwdriver, carefully prise out the dust seal from the caliper, taking care not to damage the piston.
**7** Carefully press the guide bushes out of the caliper body.
**8** Further dismantling of the caliper is not possible as individual parts are not available separately.
**9** Thoroughly clean all components, using only methylated spirit or clean hydraulic fluid. Dry the components using a clean, lint-free cloth.
**10** Check the condition of the exposed portion of the caliper piston. If the piston and/

or cylinder bore are scratched excessively or corroded, renew the complete caliper body. Similarly check the condition of the guide bushes and pins; both bushes and pins should be undamaged and (when cleaned) a reasonably tight sliding fit. If there is any doubt about the condition of any component, renew it.

**11** If the caliper is fit for further use, obtain the necessary components from your Vauxhall/Opel dealer. Renew the caliper dust cover as a matter of course; it should never be re-used.

**12** Fit the new dust seal to the piston, then locate the dust seal in the caliper body groove.

**13** Insert the guide bushes into position in the caliper body.

### Refitting

**14** Refit the brake pads as described in Section 5, together with the caliper which at this stage will not have the hose attached.

**15** Position a new copper sealing washer on each side of the hose union, and connect the brake hose to the caliper. Ensure that the hose is correctly positioned against the caliper body lug, then install the union bolt and tighten it to the specified torque setting.

**16** Remove the brake hose clamp or polythene, and bleed the hydraulic system as described in Section 2. Note that, providing

the precautions described were taken to minimise brake fluid loss, it should only be necessary to bleed the relevant front brake circuit.

**17** Refit the roadwheel, then lower the vehicle to the ground and tighten the roadwheel bolts to the specified torque.

### 9  Rear brake drum – removal, inspection and refitting

**Note:** *Before starting work, refer to the warning at the beginning of Section 5 concerning the dangers of asbestos dust. A new hub nut and dust cap will be required on refitting.*

### Removal

**1** Chock the front wheels then jack up the rear of the car and securely support it on axle stands (see *Jacking and vehicle support*). Remove the appropriate rear wheel and release the handbrake.

**2** Undo the brake drum retaining screw and withdraw the brake drum **(see illustrations)**. It may be difficult to remove the drum, due to the brake shoes binding on the inner circumference of the drum. If the brake shoes are binding, first check that the handbrake is fully released, then proceed as follows.

**3** Referring to Section 17 for further information, fully slacken the handbrake cable adjuster nut to obtain maximum free play in the cable.

**4** Remove the plug from the inspection hole in the brake backplate, and push the handbrake operating lever outwards away from the brake shoe. This will release the handbrake lever stop-peg from the edge of the brake shoe, and further collapse the shoes **(see illustrations)**. The brake drum can then be withdrawn from the stub axle.

### Inspection

**Note:** *If either drum requires renewal, BOTH should be renewed at the same time, to ensure even and consistent braking.*

**5** Working carefully, remove all traces of brake dust from the drum, but *avoid inhaling the dust, as it is a health-hazard.*

**6** Scrub clean the outside of the drum, and check it for obvious signs of wear or damage (such as cracks around the roadwheel bolt holes); renew the drum if necessary.

**7** Examine the inside of the drum carefully. Light scoring of the friction surface is normal, but if heavy scoring is found, the drum must be renewed. It is usual to find a lip on the drum's inboard edge which consists of a mixture of rust and brake dust; this should be scraped away, to leave a smooth surface which can be

9.2a  Undo the brake drum retaining screw . . .

9.2b  . . . and withdraw the brake drum

9.4a  Remove the rubber plug (arrowed) from the brake backplate . . .

9.4b  . . . release the handbrake lever stop-peg by inserting a screwdriver in through the hole in the rear of the backplate . . .

9.4c  . . . and use a screwdriver (A) to push the handbrake lever away from the brake shoe in the direction of arrow (B) – shown with drum removed

**9.10 Prior to refitting the drum, check that the handbrake lever is correctly positioned on the shoe**

polished with fine (120- to 150-grade) emery paper. If, however, the lip is due to the friction surface being recessed by excessive wear, then the drum must be renewed.

8 If the drum is thought to be excessively worn, or oval, its internal diameter must be measured at several points using an internal micrometer. Take measurements in pairs, the second at right-angles to the first, and compare the two to check for signs of ovality. Provided that it does not enlarge the drum to beyond the specified maximum diameter, it may be possible to have the drum refinished by skimming or grinding; if this is not possible, then the drums on both sides must be renewed. Note that if the drum is to be skimmed, both drums must be refinished, to maintain a consistent internal diameter on both sides.

## Refitting

9 If a new brake drum is to be installed, use a suitable solvent to remove any preservative coating that may have been applied to its interior. Note that it may also be necessary to shorten the adjuster strut length by rotating the strut wheel, to allow the new drum to pass over the brake shoes.

10 Ensure that the handbrake lever stop-peg is correctly repositioned against the edge of the brake shoe web (see illustration).

11 Slide the drum into position, refit the retaining screw and tighten the screw securely.

12 With the handbrake fully released, adjust the lining-to-drum clearance by repeatedly depressing the brake pedal 20 to 25 times. Whilst depressing the pedal, have an assistant listen to the rear drums, to check that the adjuster strut is functioning correctly; if so, a clicking sound will be emitted by the strut as the pedal is depressed.

13 With the lining-to-drum clearance set, check and, if necessary, adjust the handbrake as described in Chapter 1.

14 Refit the roadwheel, then lower the vehicle to the ground and tighten the roadwheel bolts to the specified torque setting.

## 10 Rear brake shoes – renewal

⚠️ *Warning: Brake shoes must be renewed on BOTH rear wheels at the same time – NEVER renew the shoes on only one wheel, as uneven braking may result. The dust created as the shoes wear may contain asbestos, which is a health hazard. Never blow it out with compressed air, and don't inhale any of it. An approved filtering mask should be worn when working on the brakes. DO NOT use petroleum-based solvents to clean brake parts – use brake cleaner or methylated spirit only.*

1 Remove the brake drum as described in Section 9.

2 Working carefully and taking the necessary precautions, remove all traces of brake dust from the brake drum, backplate and shoes.

3 Follow the accompanying photos (illustrations 10.3a to 10.3w) for the actual brake shoe renewal procedure, bearing in mind the additional points listed below. Be sure to stay in order and read the caption under each illustration.

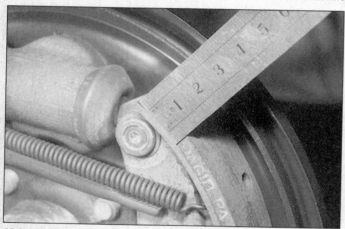

**10.3a Measure the thickness of the brake shoe friction material at several points. If any are worn down to the specified minimum, or fouled with oil or grease, all four shoes must be renewed**

**10.3b Prior to disturbing the shoes, note the correct fitted locations of all components, paying particular attention to the adjuster strut components**

**10.3c Unhook the upper return spring, and remove it from the brake shoes**

**10.3d Prise the adjusting lever retaining spring out of the leading brake shoe . . .**

**10.3e . . . then remove the return spring . . .**

10.3f . . . and the adjusting lever

10.3g Prise the brake shoes apart and remove the adjuster strut

10.3h Remove the leading shoe retainer spring cup by depressing and turning it through 90°. With the cup removed, lift off the spring and withdraw the retainer pin

10.3i Remove the leading shoe from the backplate and unhook the return spring

10.3j Remove the trailing shoe retainer spring cup then lift off the spring and withdraw the retainer pin

10.3k Remove the trailing shoe from the backplate and unhook the handbrake cable

10.3l Use a cable tie or elastic band to retain the wheel cylinder pistons

10.3m The left-hand adjuster strut assembly is marked L (arrowed)

10.3n Dismantle and clean the adjuster strut and apply a smear of silicone-based grease to the adjuster threads

10.3o It may be necessary to transfer the adjusting lever pivot pin and clip (arrowed) from the original shoes to the new ones

10.3p With the brake shoes removed, check the wheel cylinder for hydraulic fluid leaks

10.3q Thoroughly clean the backplate, then apply a smear of high-temperature brake grease to the contact surfaces (arrowed)

10.3r  Locate the handbrake cable under the clip (arrowed), then engage the trailing shoe with the cable. Locate the shoe on the backplate and secure with the retainer pin, spring and cup

10.3s  Connect the lower return spring to both shoes (arrowed), then locate the leading shoe on the backplate and secure with the retainer pin, spring and cup

10.3t  Refit the adjuster strut, noting that the shorter part of the fork (arrowed) must be to the front of the shoe

10.3u  Refit the adjusting lever and retaining spring . . .

10.3v  . . . then refit the return spring, making sure that the spring is correctly engaged in the correct hole (arrowed)

10.3w  Cut the plastic cable tie from the wheel cylinder after fitting the brake shoes

**4** If both brake assemblies are dismantled at the same time, take care not to mix up the components. Note that the left-hand and right-hand adjuster components are marked as such; the threaded rod is marked L or R, and the other 'handed' components are colour-coded black for the left-hand side, and silver for the right-hand side.

**5** If a new handbrake operating lever was not supplied with the new shoes (where applicable), transfer the lever from the old shoes. The lever may be secured with a pin and circlip, or by a rivet, which will have to be

drilled out. It may also be necessary to transfer the adjusting lever pivot pin and clip from the original front shoe to the new shoe.

**6** Prior to refitting the adjuster strut, screw the wheel fully onto the forked end of the adjuster, so that the adjuster strut is set to its shortest possible length. Back the wheel off a half a turn, and check that it is free to rotate easily.

**7** On completion, ensure that the handbrake operating lever stop peg is correctly positioned against the edge of the shoe web, then refit the brake drum as described in Section 9.

**8** Repeat the operation on the remaining brake.

**9** Once both sets of rear shoes have been renewed, with the handbrake fully released, adjust the lining-to-drum clearance by repeatedly depressing the brake pedal 20 to 25 times. Whilst depressing the pedal, have an assistant listen to the rear drums, to check that the adjuster strut is functioning correctly; if so, a clicking sound will be emitted by the strut as the pedal is depressed.

**10** Check and, if necessary, adjust the handbrake as described in Chapter 1.

**11** Refit the roadwheels, then lower the vehicle to the ground and tighten the roadwheel bolts to the specified torque setting.

**12** Check the hydraulic fluid level as described in *Weekly checks*.

*Caution: New brake shoes will not give full braking efficiency until they have bedded-in. Be prepared for this, and avoid hard braking as far as possible for the first hundred miles or so after shoe renewal.*

## 11  Rear wheel cylinder – removal, overhaul and refitting

*Note: Before starting work, refer to the warning at the beginning of Section 2 concerning the dangers of hydraulic fluid, and to the warning at the beginning of Section 5 concerning the dangers of asbestos dust.*

### Removal

**1** Remove the brake drum as described in Section 9.

**2** Using pliers, carefully unhook the upper brake shoe return spring, and remove it from both brake shoes **(see illustration 10.3c)**. Pull the upper ends of the shoes away from the wheel cylinder to disengage them from the pistons.

**3** Minimise fluid loss by first removing the

**11.4 Brake pipe union nut (A) and wheel cylinder retaining bolt (B)**

H.28158

**11.7 Exploded view of a rear brake wheel cylinder**

master cylinder reservoir cap, then tightening it down onto a piece of polythene to obtain an airtight seal. Alternatively, use a brake hose clamp, a G-clamp or a similar tool to clamp the flexible hose at the nearest convenient point to the wheel cylinder.

**4** Wipe away all traces of dirt around the brake pipe union at the rear of the wheel cylinder, and unscrew the union nut. Carefully ease the pipe out of the wheel cylinder, and plug or tape over its end to prevent dirt entry. Wipe off any spilt fluid immediately **(see illustration)**.

**5** Unscrew the wheel cylinder retaining bolt from the rear of the backplate **(see illustration 11.4)**, and remove the cylinder, taking great care not to allow surplus hydraulic fluid to contaminate the brake shoe linings.

### Overhaul

**Note:** *Before starting work, check with your local dealer for the availability of parts to overhaul the wheel cylinder.*

**6** Brush the dirt and dust from the wheel cylinder, but take care not to inhale it.

**7** Pull the rubber dust seals from the ends of the cylinder body **(see illustration)**.

**8** The pistons will normally be ejected by the pressure of the coil spring, but if they are not, tap the end of the cylinder body on a piece of wood, or apply low air pressure (eg, from a foot pump) to the hydraulic fluid union hole to eject the pistons from their bores.

**9** Inspect the surfaces of the pistons and their bores in the cylinder body for scoring, or evidence of metal-to-metal contact. If evident, renew the complete wheel cylinder assembly.

**10** If the pistons and bores are in good condition, discard the seals and obtain a repair kit, which will contain all the necessary renewable items.

**11** Lubricate the piston seals with clean brake fluid, and insert them into the cylinder bores, with the spring between them, using finger pressure only.

**12** Dip the pistons in clean brake fluid, and insert them into the cylinder bores.

**13** Fit the dust seals, and check that the pistons can move freely in their bores.

### Refitting

**14** Ensure that the backplate and wheel cylinder mating surfaces are clean, then spread the brake shoes and manoeuvre the wheel cylinder into position.

**15** Engage the brake pipe, and screw in the union nut two or three turns to ensure that the thread has started.

**16** Insert the wheel cylinder retaining bolt, and tighten it to the specified torque setting. Now tighten the brake pipe union nut to the specified torque.

**17** Remove the clamp from the flexible brake hose, or the polythene from the master cylinder reservoir (as applicable).

**18** Ensure that the brake shoes are correctly located against the cylinder pistons, then carefully refit the brake shoe upper return spring, using a screwdriver to stretch the spring into position.

**19** Refit the brake drum as described in Section 9.

**20** Bleed the brake hydraulic system as described in Section 2. Providing suitable precautions were taken to minimise loss of fluid, it should only be necessary to bleed the relevant rear brake.

**12.3 Disconnect the clutch hydraulic pipe (arrowed) from the fluid reservoir**

## 12 Master cylinder – removal, overhaul and refitting

**Note:** *Before starting work, refer to the warning at the beginning of Section 2 concerning the dangers of hydraulic fluid.*

### Removal

**1** Remove the master cylinder reservoir cap, and syphon the hydraulic fluid from the reservoir. **Note:** *Do not syphon the fluid by mouth, as it is poisonous; use a syringe or an old hydrometer.* Alternatively, open any convenient bleed screw in the system, and gently pump the brake pedal to expel the fluid through a plastic tube connected to the screw (see Section 2).

**2** Disconnect the wiring connector from the brake fluid level sensor at the base of the reservoir.

**3** On models with manual transmission, release the clip and disconnect the clutch hydraulic pipe from the fluid reservoir **(see illustration)**. Tape over or plug the outlet.

**4** Place cloth rags beneath the fluid reservoir then undo the reservoir retaining bolt and carefully prise the reservoir from the top of the master cylinder and remove it from the engine compartment. If necessary, prise the reservoir seals from the top of the cylinder.

**5** Place cloth rags beneath the master cylinder to collect escaping brake fluid. Identify the brake lines for position, then unscrew the union nuts and move the lines to one side. Tape over or plug the line outlets.

**6** Unscrew the mounting nuts and withdraw the master cylinder from the vacuum servo unit **(see illustration)**. Take care not to spill fluid on the vehicle paintwork.

### Overhaul

**7** At the time of writing, master cylinder overhaul is not possible as no spares are available.

**12.6 Master cylinder mounting nuts (arrowed)**

**8** The only parts available individually are the fluid reservoir and its mounting seals and the filler cap.

**9** If the master cylinder is worn excessively, it must be renewed.

**10** Remove the reservoir seals from the master cylinder body and obtain new seals for reassembly.

**11** Lubricate the new seals with clean brake hydraulic fluid and push the new seals into position.

### Refitting

**12** Fit the master cylinder to the servo unit, ensuring that the servo unit pushrod enters the master cylinder piston centrally. Fit the retaining nuts and tighten them to the specified torque setting.

**13** Refit the brake lines and tighten the union nuts securely.

**14** On manual transmission models, reconnect the clutch hydraulic pipe.

**15** Reconnect the wiring connector to the brake fluid level sensor.

**16** Remove the reservoir filler cap and polythene, then top-up the reservoir with fresh hydraulic fluid to the MAX mark (see *Weekly checks*).

**17** Bleed the hydraulic systems as described in Section 2 and Chapter 6 then refit the filler cap. Thoroughly check the operation of the brakes and clutch before using the vehicle on the road.

## 13 Brake pedal –
removal and refitting

### Removal

**1** Remove the lower trim panel beneath the facia on the driver's side as described in Chapter 11.

**2** Release the two retaining clips and remove the facia lower panel above the pedals.

**3** Release the expanding rivet and remove the driver's side footwell air duct.

**4** Disconnect the wiring connector at the stop-light switch and release the wiring harness from the support clips.

**5** Unhook the return spring from the brake

**13.5 Unhook the pedal return spring (A) then slide off the spring clip (B) and withdraw the clevis pin**

pedal, then slide off the spring clip, and withdraw the clevis pin securing the pedal to the servo unit pushrod **(see illustration)**.

**6** On left-hand drive models, remove the steering column intermediate shaft as described in Chapter 10.

**7** Undo the six mounting bracket retaining nuts (right-hand drive models) or the four nuts and two bolts (left-hand drive models) and remove the pedal and support bracket assembly from the vehicle.

**8** Check the pedal and bracket for excessive wear and damage. It is not possible to renew the pedal pivot bushes separately, so if they are worn, the complete assembly must be renewed.

### Refitting

**9** Manoeuvre the pedal and support bracket assembly into place making sure the brake servo pushrod fits correctly over the brake pedal.

**10** Refit the pedal mounting bracket bolts/nuts and tighten to the specified torque.

**11** Align the pedal hole with the pushrod end, and insert the clevis pin. Secure the pin in position with the spring clip.

**12** Refit the return spring to the brake pedal.

**13** Reconnect the stop-light switch wiring connector.

**14** On left-hand drive models, refit the steering column intermediate shaft as described in Chapter 10.

**15** Refit the driver's side footwell air duct, then refit the facia trim panels as described in Chapter 11.

**14.6 Undo the bolt (arrowed) and withdraw the refrigerant pipes from the expansion valve**

## 14 Vacuum servo unit –
testing, removal and refitting

### Testing

**1** To test the operation of the servo unit, with the engine off, depress the footbrake several times to exhaust the vacuum. Now start the engine, keeping the pedal firmly depressed. As the engine starts, there should be a noticeable 'give' in the brake pedal as the vacuum builds-up. Allow the engine to run for at least two minutes, then switch it off. The brake pedal should now feel normal, but further applications should result in the pedal feeling firmer, the pedal stroke decreasing with each application.

**2** If the servo does not operate as described, first inspect the servo unit check valve as described in Section 15.

**3** If the servo unit still fails to operate satisfactorily, the fault lies within the unit itself. Repairs to the unit are not possible; if faulty, the servo unit must be renewed.

### Removal

#### Right-hand drive models

**Note:** *On models equipped with air conditioning, refer to the air conditioning system precautionary information contained in Chapter 3.*

**4** On models equipped with air conditioning, have the refrigerant discharged at a dealer service department or an automotive air conditioning repair facility.

**5** Remove the windscreen wiper motor and linkage as described in Chapter 12.

**6** On models equipped with air conditioning, undo the bolt securing the refrigerant pipe block connection to the expansion valve and withdraw the refrigerant pipes from the valve **(see illustration)**. Note that new seals for the refrigerant pipes will be required for refitting. Suitably plug or cover the disconnected pipes.

**7** On models equipped with air conditioning, unscrew the retaining nut, release the two clips and free the refrigerant pipes from the vicinity of the servo unit.

**8** Remove the master cylinder as described in Section 12.

**9** Carefully ease the vacuum hose out of the servo unit, taking care not to displace the sealing grommet **(see illustration)**.

**10** Remove the lower trim panel beneath the facia on the driver's side as described in Chapter 11.

**11** Release the two retaining clips and remove the facia lower panel above the pedals.

**12** Release the expanding rivet and remove the driver's side footwell air duct.

**13** Unhook the return spring from the brake pedal, then slide off the spring clip, and withdraw the clevis pin securing the pedal to the servo unit pushrod **(see illustration 13.5)**.

**14** Slacken and remove the two diagonally opposite nuts securing the servo unit to the pedal mounting bracket.

**15** Return to the engine compartment, and lift the servo unit out of position.

### Left-hand drive models

**16** Remove the battery and battery tray as described in Chapter 5A.

**17** Release the locking clip, then lift up the cooling system expansion tank and remove it from the mounting bracket. Place the tank to one side.

**18** Remove the ABS hydraulic modulator as described in Section 21, then undo the three retaining bolts and remove the modulator mounting bracket.

**19** Remove the master cylinder as described in Section 12.

**20** Carefully ease the vacuum hose out of the servo unit, taking care not to displace the sealing grommet.

**21** Remove the lower trim panel beneath the facia on the driver's side as described in Chapter 11.

**22** Release the two retaining clips and remove the facia lower panel above the pedals.

**23** Release the expanding rivet and remove the driver's side footwell air duct.

**24** Unhook the return spring from the brake pedal, then slide off the spring clip, and withdraw the clevis pin securing the pedal to the servo unit pushrod **(see illustration 13.5)**.

**25** Slacken and remove the two diagonally opposite nuts securing the servo unit to the pedal mounting bracket.

**26** Return to the engine compartment, and lift the servo unit out of position.

### Refitting

#### Right-hand drive models

**27** Locate the vacuum servo unit in position on the bulkhead ensuring that the servo unit pushrod locates correctly around the brake pedal. Refit the two nuts and tighten them to the specified torque.

**28** Apply a smear of multi-purpose grease to the clevis pin then align the servo unit pushrod with the brake pedal hole and insert the pin. Secure the pin in position with the retaining clip, making sure it is correctly located in the groove.

**29** Refit the driver's side footwell air duct, then refit the facia trim panels as described in Chapter 11.

**30** Refit the vacuum hose to the servo grommet, ensuring that the hose is correctly seated.

**31** Refit the brake master cylinder as described in Section 12.

**32** On models equipped with air conditioning, resecure the refrigerant pipes in the vicinity of the servo unit.

**33** On models equipped with air conditioning, refit the refrigerant pipe block connection to the expansion valve using new seals and secure with the retaining bolt, tightened to the specified torque.

**14.9 Carefully ease the vacuum hose (arrowed) out of the servo unit rubber grommet**

**34** Refit the windscreen wiper motor and linkage as described in Chapter 12.

**35** On models with air conditioning, on completion, have the system evacuated, charged and leak-tested by the specialist who discharged it.

### Left-hand drive models

**36** Locate the vacuum servo unit in position on the bulkhead ensuring that the servo unit pushrod locates correctly around the brake pedal. Refit the two nuts and tighten them to the specified torque.

**37** Apply a smear of multi-purpose grease to the clevis pin then align the servo unit pushrod with the brake pedal hole and insert the pin. Secure the pin in position with the retaining clip, making sure it is correctly located in the groove.

**38** Refit the driver's side footwell air duct, then refit the facia trim panels as described in Chapter 11.

**39** Refit the vacuum hose to the servo grommet, ensuring that the hose is correctly seated.

**40** Refit the brake master cylinder as described in Section 12, but don't bleed the hydraulic circuits at this stage.

**41** Refit the ABS hydraulic modulator mounting bracket, then refit the hydraulic modulator as described in Section 21.

**42** Refit the cooling system expansion tank and secure with the locking clip.

**43** Refit the battery and battery tray as described in Chapter 5A.

**44** Remove the master cylinder reservoir filler

**16.4 Disconnect the wiring connector (arrowed) from the handbrake lever warning light switch**

cap and polythene, then top-up the reservoir with fresh hydraulic fluid to the MAX mark (see *Weekly checks*).

**46** Bleed the hydraulic systems as described in Section 2 and Chapter 6 then refit the filler cap. Thoroughly check the operation of the brakes and clutch before using the vehicle on the road.

## 15 Vacuum servo unit check valve and hose – removal, testing and refitting

### Removal

**1** Carefully ease the vacuum hose out of the servo unit, taking care not to displace the sealing grommet **(see illustration 14.9)**.

**2** Where fitted, remove the plastic cover over the top of the engine.

**3** Disconnect the hose fitting from the inlet manifold.

**4** Unclip the vacuum hose from its supports on the bulkhead and engine, then remove the hose and check valve from the car.

### Testing

**5** Examine the check valve and hose for signs of damage, and renew if necessary. The valve may be tested by blowing through it in both directions. Air should flow through the valve in one direction only – when blown through from the servo unit end. If air flows in both directions, or not at all, renew the valve and hose as an assembly.

**6** Examine the servo unit rubber sealing grommet for signs of damage or deterioration, and renew as necessary.

### Refitting

**7** Refitting is a reversal of removal ensuring that the quick-release connector (where fitted) audibly locks in position, and that the hose is correctly seated in the servo grommet.

**8** On completion, start the engine and check that there are no air leaks.

## 16 Handbrake lever – removal and refitting

### Removal

**1** Disconnect the battery negative terminal (refer to *Disconnecting the battery* in the Reference Chapter).

**2** Remove the centre console as described in Chapter 11.

**3** Ensure that the handbrake lever is released (off).

**4** Disconnect the wiring connector from the handbrake lever warning light switch **(see illustration)**.

**5** Disconnect the two wiring connectors at the airbag ECU located at the rear of the handbrake lever. Unclip the wiring harness from both sides of the handbrake lever frame.

6 Undo the handbrake cable adjuster nut and release the cable from the handbrake lever (see illustration).
7 Undo the three retaining nuts and remove the handbrake lever assembly from inside the car.

### Refitting

8 Refitting is the reverse of removal, but adjust the handbrake as described in Chapter 1, and refit the centre console as described in Chapter 11.

## 17 Handbrake cables – removal and refitting

### Removal

1 The handbrake cable consists of two sections, a short front (primary) section which connects the lever to the compensator plate, and the main cables (secondary) section which links the compensator plate to the rear brakes. Each section can be removed individually as follows.

### Primary (front) cable

2 Chock the front wheels then jack up the rear of the car and securely support it on axle stands (see *Jacking and vehicle support*). Ensure that the handbrake lever is released (off).
3 Remove the centre console as described in Chapter 11.
4 Undo the handbrake cable adjuster nut and

16.6 Undo the handbrake cable adjuster nut (arrowed) and release the cable from the handbrake lever

release the cable from the handbrake lever (see illustration 16.6).
5 Release the cable from the guide on the mounting plate where necessary.
6 Remove the exhaust front pipe and intermediate pipe with reference to Chapter 4A.
7 Unscrew the nuts and remove the exhaust heat shield from the underbody.
8 Detach the front cable from the compensator plate by twisting it through 90°.
9 Release the grommet from the lever mounting plate, and withdraw the front cable from inside the vehicle. Remove the grommet from the cable.

### Secondary (main) cable

**Note:** *The secondary cables are supplied as one part, together with the compensator plate.*
10 Chock the front wheels then jack up the rear of the car and securely support it on axle stands (see *Jacking and vehicle support*). Remove both rear roadwheels.

17.11 Unclip and remove the centre console access panel

17.12 Unclip the cover from around the handbrake lever

17.14 Push the handbrake operating lever on the brake caliper downwards, and detach the cable end fitting from the lever

17.15a Prise out the handbrake outer cable retaining clip . . .

11 From inside the vehicle, unclip and remove the access panel in the centre console, beneath the handbrake lever (see illustration).
12 Unclip the cover from around the handbrake lever (see illustration).
13 Move the handbrake lever to the fully released position, then turn the cable adjuster nut anti-clockwise to remove all tension from the cables (see illustration 16.6).
14 On models with rear disc brakes, working on each side in turn, use a screwdriver to push the handbrake operating lever on the brake caliper downwards, and detach the cable end fitting from the lever (see illustration).
15 On models with rear disc brakes, prise out the handbrake outer cable retaining clip and withdraw the handbrake cable from the caliper bracket (see illustrations).
16 On models with rear drum brakes, disconnect the handbrake cable end fitting from the trailing brake shoe with reference to Section 10. Prise out the handbrake outer cable retaining clip and withdraw the handbrake cable from the brake backplate.
17 Remove the exhaust front pipe and intermediate pipe with reference to Chapter 4A.
18 Unscrew the nuts and remove the exhaust heat shield from the underbody.
19 Detach the front cable from the compensator plate by twisting it through 90°.
20 Release the main cable sections from the supports on the rear axle and fuel tank, and withdraw the cable from under the vehicle.

### Refitting

21 Refitting is a reversal of the removal procedure, but adjust the handbrake as described in Chapter 1. Where applicable, make sure that the fitting on the rear of the front cable locates correctly in the compensator plate. Also make sure that the protective sleeve on the front cable is firmly located over the bead next to the compensator plate.

## 18 Stop-light switch – removal, refitting and adjustment

### Removal

1 The stop-light switch is located on the brake pedal bracket in the driver's footwell.

17.15b . . . and withdraw the handbrake cable from the caliper bracket

**2** Remove the lower trim panel beneath the facia on the driver's side as described in Chapter 11.

**3** Release the two retaining clips and remove the facia lower panel above the pedals.

**4** Release the expanding rivet and remove the driver's side footwell air duct.

**5** Disconnect the wiring connector at the stop-light switch.

**6** Push the brake pedal down, pull out the brake switch actuating pin, then unclip the locking sleeve from around the actuating pin **(see illustrations)**.

**7** Release the securing clips and pull the switch to disengage it from the pedal mounting bracket.

### Refitting and adjustment

**8** With the actuating pin pulled out, and the locking sleeve unclipped, refit the switch to the pedal bracket.

**9** Secure the switch with the locking sleeve.

**10** Release the brake pedal and the pedal will automatically adjust the position of the actuating pin.

**11** Reconnect the wiring connector, then refit the facia footwell trim panel as described in Chapter 11.

### 19 Handbrake warning light switch – removal and refitting

### Removal

**1** Remove the centre console as described in Chapter 11.

**2** Disconnect the wiring connector from the warning light switch on the side of the handbrake lever **(see illustration 16.4)**.

**3** Unscrew the mounting bolt and remove the switch from the handbrake lever bracket.

### Refitting

**4** Refitting is a reversal of removal.

### 20 Anti-lock braking and traction control systems – general information

ABS is fitted as standard to all models. On higher specification models, the ABS may also incorporate traction control or an electronic stability programme as additional safety features.

The ABS system comprises a hydraulic modulator and electronic control unit together with four wheel speed sensors. The hydraulic modulator contains the electronic control unit (ECU), the hydraulic solenoid valves (one set for each brake) and the electrically-driven pump. The purpose of the system is to prevent the wheel(s) locking during heavy braking. This is achieved by automatic release of the brake on the relevant wheel, followed by re-application of the brake.

The solenoid valves are controlled by the

**18.6a Pull out the centre actuating pin arrowed (switch removed for clarity) . . .**

ECU, which itself receives signals from the four wheel speed sensors which monitor the speed of rotation of each wheel. By comparing these signals, the ECU can determine the speed at which the vehicle is travelling. It can then use this speed to determine when a wheel is decelerating at an abnormal rate, compared to the speed of the vehicle, and therefore predicts when a wheel is about to lock. During normal operation, the system functions in the same way as a conventional braking system.

If the ECU senses that a wheel is about to lock, it operates the relevant solenoid valve(s) in the hydraulic unit, which then isolates from the master cylinder the relevant brake(s) on the wheel(s) which is/are about to lock, effectively sealing-in the hydraulic pressure.

If the speed of rotation of the wheel continues to decrease at an abnormal rate, the ECU operates the electrically-driven pump which pumps the hydraulic fluid back into the master cylinder, releasing the brake. Once the speed of rotation of the wheel returns to an acceptable rate, the pump stops, and the solenoid valves switch again, allowing the hydraulic master cylinder pressure to return to the caliper, which then re-applies the brake. This cycle can be carried out many times a second.

The action of the solenoid valves and return pump creates pulses in the hydraulic circuit. When the ABS system is functioning, these pulses can be felt through the brake pedal.

On models with traction control, the ABS hydraulic modulator incorporates an additional set of solenoid valves which operate the traction control system. The system operates at speeds up to approximately 30 mph using the signals supplied by the wheel speed sensors. If the ECU senses that a driving wheel is about to lose traction, it prevents this by momentarily applying the relevant front brake. The ABS ECU also communicates with the engine management ECU during traction control operation. In severe cases of traction loss the engine management ECU will reduce engine power to assist with traction recovery.

The electronic stability programme (ESP) is a further development of ABS and traction control. Using additional sensors to monitor steering wheel position, vehicle yaw rate, acceleration and deceleration, in conjunction with the ABS sensors, the ECU can intervene

**18.6b . . . and unclip the locking sleeve**

under conditions of vehicle instability. Using the signals from the various sensors, the ECU can determine driver intent (steering wheel position, throttle position, vehicle speed and engine speed). From the sensor inputs from the wheel speed sensors, yaw rate sensors and acceleration sensors the ECU can calculate whether the vehicle is responding to driver input, or whether an unstable driving situation is occurring. If instability is detected, the ECU will intervene by applying or releasing the relevant front or rear brake, in conjunction with a power reduction, until vehicle stability returns.

The operation of the ABS, traction control and stability programmes is entirely dependent on electrical signals. To prevent the system responding to any inaccurate signals, a built-in safety circuit monitors all signals received by the ECU. If an inaccurate signal or low battery voltage is detected, the system is automatically shut down, and the relevant warning light on the instrument panel is illuminated, to inform the driver that the system is not operational. Normal braking is still available, however.

If a fault develops in the ABS/traction control/ESP system, the vehicle must be taken to a Vauxhall/Opel dealer for fault diagnosis and repair.

### 21 Anti-lock braking and traction control system components – removal and refitting

**Note 1:** *Faults on the ABS system can only be diagnosed using Vauxhall/Opel diagnostic equipment or compatible alternative equipment.*
**Note 2:** *Before starting work, refer to the note at the beginning of Section 2 concerning the dangers of hydraulic fluid.*

### Hydraulic modulator and ECU

**1** Remove the battery and battery tray as described in Chapter 5A.

**2** Release the locking clip, then lift up the cooling system expansion tank and remove it from the mounting bracket. Place the tank to one side.

**3** Minimise fluid loss by first removing the master cylinder reservoir cap and screwing it down onto a piece of polythene.

**21.4 Disconnect the wiring harness plug (arrowed) from the ECU**

**4** Pull out the locking bar and disconnect the wiring harness plug from the ECU **(see illustration)**.

**5** Note and record the fitted position of the brake pipes at the modulator, then unscrew the union nuts and release the pipes. As a precaution, place absorbent rags beneath the brake pipe unions when unscrewing them. Suitably plug or cap the disconnected unions to prevent dirt entry and fluid loss.

**6** Unscrew the three retaining bolts and remove the hydraulic modulator from the mounting bracket.

**7** Refitting is the reverse of the removal procedure, noting the following points:

a) *Tighten the modulator retaining bolts to the specified torque.*

b) *Refit the brake pipes to their respective locations, and tighten the union nuts to the specified torque.*

c) *Ensure that the wiring is correctly routed, and that the ECU wiring harness plug is firmly pressed into position and secured with the locking bar.*

d) *Refit the battery tray and battery as described in Chapter 5A.*

e) *On completion, bleed the complete hydraulic system as described in Section 2. Ensure that the system is bled in the correct order, to prevent air entering the modulator return pump.*

## Electronic control unit (ECU)

**Note:** *At the time of writing, no information was available for removal and refitting of the ECU on systems incorporating an electronic stability programme (ESP). This work should therefore be entrusted to a Vauxhall/Opel dealer.*

**8** Remove the hydraulic modulator from the car as described previously in this Section.

**9** Undo the three retaining bolts and carefully withdraw the ECU from the base of the hydraulic modulator. Note that new retaining bolts will be required for refitting.

**10** Carefully remove the eight sealing rings from the modulator valves and obtain new sealing rings for refitting.

**11** Locate the new sealing rings over the solenoid valves, then carefully place the ECU in position, keeping it square and level.

**12** Fit the three new retaining bolts and tighten securely.

**13** On completion, refit the hydraulic modulator as described previously in this Section.

## Wheel speed sensors

**14** The front and rear wheel speed sensors are an integral part of the hub bearings and cannot be separated.

**15** Refer to Chapter 10 for front and rear hub bearing removal and refitting procedures.

# Chapter 10
# Suspension and steering

## Contents

## Degrees of difficulty

| | | | | |
|---|---|---|---|---|
| **Easy,** suitable for novice with little experience | **Fairly easy,** suitable for beginner with some experience | **Fairly difficult,** suitable for competent DIY mechanic | **Difficult,** suitable for experienced DIY mechanic | **Very difficult,** suitable for expert DIY or professional |

## Specifications

**Front suspension**

Type . . . . . . . . . . . . . . . . . . . . . . . . . . . . . . . . . . . . . . . . Independent, with MacPherson struts, gas-filled shock absorbers and anti-roll bar

**Rear suspension**

Type . . . . . . . . . . . . . . . . . . . . . . . . . . . . . . . . . . . . . . . . Semi-independent torsion beam, with trailing arms, coil springs and telescopic shock absorbers

**Steering**

Type . . . . . . . . . . . . . . . . . . . . . . . . . . . . . . . . . . . . . . . . Rack and pinion with electro-hydraulic power steering (EHPS)

**Front and rear hub bearings**

Bearing play (maximum). . . . . . . . . . . . . . . . . . . . . . . . . . . . 0.1 mm
Bearing radial run-out. . . . . . . . . . . . . . . . . . . . . . . . . . . . . . 0.04 mm
Bearing lateral run-out . . . . . . . . . . . . . . . . . . . . . . . . . . . . . 0.05 mm

## Torque wrench settings

| | Nm | lbf ft |
|---|---|---|
| **Front suspension** | | |
| Anti-roll bar connecting link retaining nut* . . . . . . . . . . . . . . . . . . . . . | 55 | 41 |
| Anti-roll bar to subframe. . . . . . . . . . . . . . . . . . . . . . . . . . . . . . . . . . . . | 20 | 15 |
| Driveshaft retaining nut*: | | |
|    Stage 1 . . . . . . . . . . . . . . . . . . . . . . . . . . . . . . . . . . . . . . . . . . . . | 150 | 111 |
|    Stage 2 . . . . . . . . . . . . . . . . . . . . . . . . . . . . . . . . . . . . . . . . . . . . | Slacken the nut by 45° | |
|    Stage 3 . . . . . . . . . . . . . . . . . . . . . . . . . . . . . . . . . . . . . . . . . . . . | 250 | 185 |
| Front engine mounting/torque link to subframe. . . . . . . . . . . . . . . . | 55 | 41 |
| Hub bearing assembly to swivel hub*: | | |
|    Stage 1 . . . . . . . . . . . . . . . . . . . . . . . . . . . . . . . . . . . . . . . . . . . . | 90 | 66 |
|    Stage 2 . . . . . . . . . . . . . . . . . . . . . . . . . . . . . . . . . . . . . . . . . . . . | Angle-tighten a further 30° | |
|    Stage 3 . . . . . . . . . . . . . . . . . . . . . . . . . . . . . . . . . . . . . . . . . . . . | Angle-tighten a further 15° | |
| Lower arm to subframe*: | | |
|    Stage 1 . . . . . . . . . . . . . . . . . . . . . . . . . . . . . . . . . . . . . . . . . . . . | 90 | 66 |
|    Stage 2 . . . . . . . . . . . . . . . . . . . . . . . . . . . . . . . . . . . . . . . . . . . . | Angle-tighten a further 75° | |
|    Stage 3 . . . . . . . . . . . . . . . . . . . . . . . . . . . . . . . . . . . . . . . . . . . . | Angle-tighten a further 15° | |
| Lower arm balljoint clamp bolt nut*: . . . . . . . . . . . . . . . . . . . . . . . . . | 50 | 37 |
| Lower balljoint to lower arm. . . . . . . . . . . . . . . . . . . . . . . . . . . . . . . . | 35 | 26 |
| Rear engine mounting/torque link bracket to subframe. . . . . . . . . . . | 55 | 41 |
| Rear engine mounting/torque link bracket to transmission . . . . . . . . | 80 | 59 |
| Subframe mounting bolts: | | |
|    Stage 1 . . . . . . . . . . . . . . . . . . . . . . . . . . . . . . . . . . . . . . . . . . . . | 90 | 66 |
|    Stage 2 . . . . . . . . . . . . . . . . . . . . . . . . . . . . . . . . . . . . . . . . . . . . | Angle-tighten a further 45° | |
|    Stage 3 . . . . . . . . . . . . . . . . . . . . . . . . . . . . . . . . . . . . . . . . . . . . | Angle-tighten a further 15° | |
| Suspension strut piston rod nut* . . . . . . . . . . . . . . . . . . . . . . . . . . . . | 80 | 59 |
| Swivel hub to strut*: | | |
|    Stage 1 . . . . . . . . . . . . . . . . . . . . . . . . . . . . . . . . . . . . . . . . . . . . | 85 | 63 |
|    Stage 2 . . . . . . . . . . . . . . . . . . . . . . . . . . . . . . . . . . . . . . . . . . . . | Angle-tighten a further 75° | |
|    Stage 3 . . . . . . . . . . . . . . . . . . . . . . . . . . . . . . . . . . . . . . . . . . . . | Angle-tighten a further 15° | |
| **Rear suspension** | | |
| Brake hydraulic line union nuts . . . . . . . . . . . . . . . . . . . . . . . . . . . . . | 16 | 12 |
| Hub bearing assembly to trailing arm*: | | |
|    Stage 1 . . . . . . . . . . . . . . . . . . . . . . . . . . . . . . . . . . . . . . . . . . . . | 50 | 37 |
|    Stage 2 . . . . . . . . . . . . . . . . . . . . . . . . . . . . . . . . . . . . . . . . . . . . | Angle-tighten a further 30° | |
|    Stage 3 . . . . . . . . . . . . . . . . . . . . . . . . . . . . . . . . . . . . . . . . . . . . | Angle-tighten a further 15° | |
| Shock absorber: | | |
|    To body. . . . . . . . . . . . . . . . . . . . . . . . . . . . . . . . . . . . . . . . . . . . | 90 | 66 |
|    To trailing arm. . . . . . . . . . . . . . . . . . . . . . . . . . . . . . . . . . . . . . . | 130 | 96 |
| Torsion beam front mounting bracket*: | | |
|   Centre bolt: | | |
|      Stage 1 . . . . . . . . . . . . . . . . . . . . . . . . . . . . . . . . . . . . . . . . | 90 | 66 |
|      Stage 2 . . . . . . . . . . . . . . . . . . . . . . . . . . . . . . . . . . . . . . . . | Angle-tighten a further 60° | |
|      Stage 3 . . . . . . . . . . . . . . . . . . . . . . . . . . . . . . . . . . . . . . . . | Angle-tighten a further 15° | |
|   Bracket-to-underbody bolts: | | |
|      Stage 1 . . . . . . . . . . . . . . . . . . . . . . . . . . . . . . . . . . . . . . . . | 90 | 66 |
|      Stage 2 . . . . . . . . . . . . . . . . . . . . . . . . . . . . . . . . . . . . . . . . | Angle-tighten a further 30° | |
|      Stage 3 . . . . . . . . . . . . . . . . . . . . . . . . . . . . . . . . . . . . . . . . | Angle-tighten a further 15° | |
| **Steering** | | |
| Electro-hydraulic pump to steering gear and subframe. . . . . . . . . . . | 22 | 16 |
| Hydraulic pressure and return line union nuts: | | |
|   TRW steering gear . . . . . . . . . . . . . . . . . . . . . . . . . . . . . . . . . . . | 30 | 22 |
|   ZF steering gear . . . . . . . . . . . . . . . . . . . . . . . . . . . . . . . . . . . . . | 16 | 12 |
| Intermediate shaft to steering gear pinion and steering column* . . . . . | 24 | 18 |
| Steering column mounting bolts*. . . . . . . . . . . . . . . . . . . . . . . . . . . . | 22 | 16 |
| Steering gear to subframe*: | | |
|    Stage 1 . . . . . . . . . . . . . . . . . . . . . . . . . . . . . . . . . . . . . . . . . . . . | 45 | 33 |
|    Stage 2 . . . . . . . . . . . . . . . . . . . . . . . . . . . . . . . . . . . . . . . . . . . . | Angle-tighten a further 45° | |
|    Stage 3 . . . . . . . . . . . . . . . . . . . . . . . . . . . . . . . . . . . . . . . . . . . . | Angle-tighten a further 15° | |
| Steering wheel retaining bolt*. . . . . . . . . . . . . . . . . . . . . . . . . . . . . . . | 30 | 22 |
| Track rod end locking nut. . . . . . . . . . . . . . . . . . . . . . . . . . . . . . . . . . | 60 | 44 |
| Track rod end to swivel hub*: | | |
|    Stage 1 . . . . . . . . . . . . . . . . . . . . . . . . . . . . . . . . . . . . . . . . . . . . | 30 | 22 |
|    Stage 2 . . . . . . . . . . . . . . . . . . . . . . . . . . . . . . . . . . . . . . . . . . . . | Angle-tighten a further 90° | |
|    Stage 3 . . . . . . . . . . . . . . . . . . . . . . . . . . . . . . . . . . . . . . . . . . . . | Angle-tighten a further 15° | |
| Track rod to steering rack. . . . . . . . . . . . . . . . . . . . . . . . . . . . . . . . . . | 90 | 66 |
| **Roadwheels** | | |
| All models. . . . . . . . . . . . . . . . . . . . . . . . . . . . . . . . . . . . . . . . . . . . . . | 110 | 81 |

*Use new fasteners*

# 1 General information

The independent front suspension is of the MacPherson strut type, incorporating coil springs and integral telescopic shock absorbers. The MacPherson struts are located by transverse lower suspension arms, which utilise rubber inner mounting bushes, and incorporate a balljoint at the outer ends. The front swivel hubs, which carry the hub bearings, brake calipers and disc assemblies, are bolted to the MacPherson struts, and connected to the lower arms via the balljoints. A front anti-roll bar is fitted, which has link rods with balljoints at each end to connect it to the strut.

The rear suspension is of semi-independent type, consisting of a torsion beam and trailing arms, with double-conical coil springs and telescopic shock absorbers. The front ends of the trailing arms are attached to the vehicle underbody by horizontal bushes, and the rear ends are located by the shock absorbers, which are bolted to the underbody at their upper ends. The coil springs are mounted independently of the shock absorbers, and act directly between the trailing arms and the underbody. Each rear wheel bearing, hub and stub axle assembly is manufactured as a sealed unit, and cannot be dismantled.

The steering system is of the electro-hydraulic power steering (EHPS) type. This system utilises a conventional rack-and-pinion type steering gear mounted on the front subframe, with variable power assistance generated by a hydraulic pump, driven by an electric motor. The degree of power assistance available is governed by the speed of the electric motor which is controlled by the steering system electronic control unit. The ECU receives input signals on steering wheel position (from a steering angle sensor) and roadspeed (from the ABS wheel speed sensors) and calculates the amount of power assistance required. The hydraulic pump, electric motor and hydraulic fluid reservoir are mounted above the rack-and-pinion steering gear on the front subframe.

The steering column is linked to the steering gear by an intermediate shaft. The intermediate shaft has a universal joint fitted to its upper end, and is secured to the column by a clamp bolt. The lower end of the intermediate shaft is attached to the steering gear pinion by means of a clamp bolt.

# 2 Front swivel hub –
## removal and refitting

**Caution: The front wheel camber setting is controlled by the bolts securing the swivel hub to the front suspension strut. Before removing the bolts, mark the swivel**

**2.3a Depress the retaining tab and release the wheel speed sensor wiring connector from the strut bracket – models without a brake pad wear indicator**

*hub in relation to the strut accurately. On completion, the camber setting must be checked and adjusted by a suitably-equipped garage.*

**Note:** *A new driveshaft retaining nut, lower arm balljoint clamp bolt and nut, suspension strut-to-swivel hub nuts and bolts and a new track rod end retaining nut will be needed for refitting. The driveshaft outer joint splines may be a tight fit in the hub and it is possible that a puller/extractor will be required to draw the hub assembly off the driveshaft during removal.*

## Removal

**1** Firmly apply the handbrake, then jack up the front of the car and support it securely on axle stands (see *Jacking and vehicle support*). Remove the relevant front roadwheel.

**2.4a Depress the locking tab and release the wiring connector from the suspension strut**

**2.4c . . . then hold the upper part of the connector and twist the lower part in the direction of the arrow**

**2.3b Push the locking tab downward and disconnect the wheel speed sensor wiring from the connector – models without a brake pad wear indicator**

**2** Remove the front brake disc as described in Chapter 9.

**3** On models without a front brake pad wear indicator, depress the retaining tab and release the ABS wheel speed sensor wiring connector from the suspension strut bracket. Push the locking tab downward and disconnect the wheel speed sensor wiring from the connector **(see illustrations)**.

**4** On models with a front brake pad wear indicator depress the locking tab and release the wiring connector from the suspension strut. Slide the locking bar on the connector downward, then hold the upper part of the connector and twist the lower part to open the connector. Disconnect the ABS wheel speed sensor wire from the connector and also disconnect the brake pad wear warning indicator wire **(see illustrations)**.

**2.4b Slide the locking bar on the wiring connector downward . . .**

**2.4d Disconnect the wires from the connector – models with a brake pad wear indicator**

**TOOL TiP**

*A tool to hold the wheel hub stationary whilst the driveshaft retaining nut is slackened can be fabricated from two lengths of steel strip (one long, one short) and a nut an bolt; the nut and bolt forming the pivot of a forked tool.*

**5** To prevent rotation of the wheel hub as the driveshaft retaining nut is slackened, make up a holding tool and bolt the tool to the wheel hub using two wheel bolts **(see Tool Tip)**.

**6** With the holding tool in place, slacken and remove the driveshaft retaining nut using a socket and long bar. Where necessary, support the socket on an axle stand to prevent it slipping off the nut. This nut is very tight; make sure that there is no risk of pulling the car off the axle stands as the nut is slackened.

**7** Unscrew the nut securing the track rod end to the steering arm on the swivel hub, then use a balljoint separator tool to remove the track rod end **(see illustration)**.

**8** Unscrew the nut and remove the clamp

**2.9 Use a chisel or screwdriver as a wedge to expand the lower portion of the swivel hub**

**2.11b ... then free the driveshaft from the swivel hub**

**2.7 Use a balljoint separator tool to remove the track rod end**

bolt securing the front suspension lower arm balljoint to the swivel hub **(see illustration)**. Note that a new clamp bolt and nut will be required for refitting.

**9** Use a chisel or screwdriver as a wedge to expand the lower portion of the swivel hub **(see illustration)**.

**10** Using a lever, push down on the suspension lower arm to free the balljoint from the swivel hub, then move the swivel hub to one side and release the arm, taking care not to damage the balljoint rubber boot. It is advisable to place a protective cover over the rubber boot such as the plastic cap from an aerosol can, suitably cut to fit.

**11** The hub must now be freed from the end of the driveshaft. It may be possible to pull the hub off the driveshaft, but if the end of the driveshaft is tight in the hub, temporarily refit the driveshaft retaining nut to protect the

**2.11a Tap the end of the driveshaft with a soft-faced hammer ...**

**2.13 Slacken and remove the two nuts and bolts securing the suspension strut to the swivel hub**

**2.8 Unscrew the nut and remove the clamp bolt securing the lower arm balljoint to the swivel hub**

driveshaft threads, then tap the end of the driveshaft with a soft-faced hammer while pulling outwards on the swivel hub **(see illustrations)**. Alternatively, use a suitable puller to press the driveshaft through the hub.

**12** Mark the position of the suspension strut on the swivel hub by drawing a circle around the heads of the two retaining bolts. **Note:** *This is important to maintain the camber setting.*

**13** Slacken and remove the two nuts and bolts securing the suspension strut to the swivel hub, noting that new nuts and bolts will be required for refitting **(see illustration)**. Disengage the swivel hub from the strut and remove it from the car.

### Refitting

**14** Ensure that the driveshaft outer constant velocity joint and hub splines are clean, then slide the hub onto the driveshaft splines. Fit the new driveshaft retaining nut, tightening it by hand only at this stage.

**15** Engage the swivel hub with the suspension strut, and insert the new bolts from the front of the strut so that their threads are facing to the rear. Fit the new nuts, tightening them by hand only at this stage.

**16** Locate the lower arm balljoint in the swivel hub. Insert the new clamp bolt from the front of the swivel hub, so that its threads are facing to the rear. Fit the new nut to the clamp bolt, and tighten it to the specified torque.

**17** With the hub correctly located, align the strut-to-swivel hub bolt heads with the marks made on the strut during removal. Tighten the bolts to the specified torque and through the specified angles given in the Specifications, using a torque wrench and angle-tightening gauge.

**18** Engage the track rod balljoint in the swivel hub, then fit the new retaining nut and tighten it to the specified torque setting.

**19** Refit the brake disc together with the brake caliper and pads as described in Chapter 9.

**20** Reconnect the ABS wheel speed sensor wiring connector and, where applicable, the break pad wear warning indicator wire. Secure the wiring in the relevant support brackets and clips.

**21** Refit the brake hydraulic hose to the suspension strut and secure with the retaining clip.

**22** Using the method employed on removal to prevent rotation, tighten the driveshaft retaining nut through the stages given in the Specifications.

**23** Refit the roadwheel, then lower the vehicle to the ground and tighten the roadwheel bolts to the specified torque.

## 3 Front hub bearings – checking and renewal

**Note:** *The front hub bearing and integral ABS wheel speed sensor is a sealed unit and no repairs are possible. If the bearing is worn or the speed sensor is faulty, a new bearing assembly must be obtained.*

### Checking

**1** Firmly apply the handbrake, then jack up the front of the car and support it securely on axle stands (see *Jacking and vehicle support*). Remove the roadwheel.

**2** A dial test indicator (DTI) will be required to measure the amount of play in the bearing. Locate the DTI on the suspension strut and zero the probe on the brake disc.

**3** Lever the hub in and out and measure the amount of play in the bearing.

**4** To measure the bearing lateral and radial run-out, undo the two bolts securing the brake caliper mounting bracket to the swivel hub. Slide the mounting bracket, complete with brake caliper and pads off the brake disc, and tie it to the coil spring using wire or a cable tie.

**5** Undo the securing screw and remove the brake disc from the wheel hub.

**6** To check the lateral run-out, locate the DTI on the suspension strut and zero the probe on the front face of the hub flange. Rotate the hub and measure the run-out.

**7** To check the radial run-out, zero the DTI probe on the upper face of the extended portion at the centre of the hub. Rotate the hub and measure the run-out.

**8** If the play or run-out exceeds the specified amount, renew the hub bearing as described below.

**9** If the bearing is satisfactory, refit the brake disc and tighten its retaining screw securely.

**10** Slide the brake pads, caliper and mounting bracket over the disc and into position on the swivel hub. Fit the two caliper mounting bracket retaining bolts and tighten them to the specified torque (see Chapter 9).

**11** Refit the roadwheel, then lower the vehicle to the ground and tighten the roadwheel bolts to the specified torque.

### Renewal

**Note:** *New hub bearing retaining bolts will be required for refitting.*

**12** Carry out the operations described in Section 2, paragraphs 1 to 11.

**13** Undo the three bolts securing the bearing assembly to the swivel hub **(see illustration)**.

**3.13 Undo the three bolts (arrowed) securing the bearing assembly to the swivel hub . . .**

**14** Remove the bearing and the brake shield from the swivel hub **(see illustration)**.

**15** Thoroughly clean the swivel hub and brake shield, then place the shield in position on the swivel hub.

**16** Locate the wheel bearing over the brake shield and into the swivel hub. Position the bearing so that the wheel speed sensor wiring connector is toward the brake caliper side of the swivel hub (ie, towards the front of the vehicle). Align the retaining bolt holes and fit the three new bolts.

**17** Tighten the retaining bolts progressively to the specified Stage 1 torque setting using a torque wrench, and then through the specified Stage 2 and Stage 3 angles, using an angle tightening gauge **(see illustrations)**.

**18** Ensure that the driveshaft outer constant velocity joint and hub splines are clean, then slide the hub onto the driveshaft splines. Fit the new driveshaft retaining nut, tightening it by hand only at this stage.

**19** Locate the lower arm balljoint in the swivel hub. Insert the clamp bolt from the front of the swivel hub, so that its threads are facing to the rear. Fit the new nut to the clamp bolt, and tighten it to the specified torque.

**20** Engage the track rod balljoint in the swivel hub, then fit the new retaining nut and tighten it to the specified torque setting.

**21** Refit the brake disc together with the brake caliper and pads as described in Chapter 9.

**22** Reconnect the ABS wheel speed sensor wiring connector and, where applicable, the brake pad wear warning indicator wire. Secure

**3.14 . . . then remove the bearing assembly and brake shield from the hub**

the wiring in the relevant support brackets and clips.

**23** Refit the brake hydraulic hose to the suspension strut and secure with the retaining clip.

**24** Using the method employed on removal to prevent rotation, tighten the driveshaft retaining nut through the stages given in the Specifications.

**25** Refit the roadwheel, then lower the vehicle to the ground and tighten the roadwheel bolts to the specified torque.

## 4 Front suspension strut – removal, overhaul and refitting

**Note:** *New strut-to-swivel hub bolts and nuts, strut retaining clamp and strut-to-anti-roll bar link rod nut, will be required for refitting. Ideally, both front suspension struts should be renewed at the same time in order to maintain good steering and suspension characteristics.*

### Removal

**1** Apply the handbrake, then jack up the front of the vehicle and support it on axle stands (see *Jacking and vehicle support*). Remove the front roadwheel.

**2** Unclip the ABS wheel speed sensor wiring guide from the brake hydraulic hose, then extract the retaining clip and release the hydraulic hose from the suspension strut **(see illustrations)**.

**3.17a Tighten the retaining bolts to the Stage 1 torque setting using a torque wrench . . .**

**3.17b . . . and then through the Stage 2 and 3 angles, using an angle tightening gauge**

**4.2a Unclip the ABS wheel speed sensor wiring guide from the hydraulic hose . . .**

**4.2b . . . then extract the retaining clip . . .**

**4.2c . . . and release the hydraulic hose from the suspension strut**

**3** On models without a front brake pad wear indicator, depress the retaining tab and release the ABS wheel speed sensor wiring connector from the suspension strut bracket. Push the locking tab downward and disconnect the wheel speed sensor wiring from the connector **(see illustrations 2.3a and 2.3b)**.

**4** On models with a front brake pad wear indicator depress the locking tab and release the wiring connector from the suspension strut. Slide the locking bar on the connector downward, then hold the upper part of the connector and twist the lower part to open the connector. Disconnect the ABS wheel speed sensor wire from the connector and also disconnect the brake pad wear warning indicator wire **(see illustrations 2.4a to 2.4d)**.

**5** Unscrew the nut and disconnect the anti-roll bar link rod from the strut. Use a spanner on the special flats to hold the link while the nut is being loosened **(see illustration)**.

**6** Mark the position of the suspension strut on the swivel hub by drawing a circle around the heads of the two retaining bolts. **Note:** *This is important to maintain the camber setting.*

**7** Slacken and remove the two nuts and bolts securing the suspension strut to the swivel hub, noting that new nuts and bolts will be required for refitting. Disengage the top of the swivel hub from the strut **(see illustrations)**.

**8** Engage the help of an assistant to support the strut beneath the front wing. From within the engine compartment, prise apart the two halves of the strut retaining clamp by spreading open the serrations **(see illustration)**. Push up on the strut to relieve the tension on the clamp, and remove the two clamp halves from the strut tower. Note that the retaining clamp will be destroyed during removal and a new clamp must be obtained for refitting.

**9** Lower the strut and withdraw it from under the front wing.

### Overhaul

**Note 1:** *A spring compressor tool will be required for this operation. Before overhaul, mark the position of each component in relationship with each other for reassembly.*
**Note 2:** *A new piston rod nut will be required for reassembly.*

**10** With the suspension strut resting on a bench, or clamped in a vice, fit a spring compressor tool, and compress the coil spring to relieve the pressure on the spring seats **(see illustration)**. Ensure that the compressor tool is securely located on the spring, in accordance with the tool manufacturer's instructions.

**11** Using a screwdriver, prise out the plastic cap from the upper mounting **(see illustration)**.

**12** Mark the position of the spring on the top and bottom mountings, then counterhold the strut piston rod with an Allen key or suitable

**4.5 Unscrew the nut and disconnect the anti-roll bar link rod from the strut**

**4.7a Undo the two nuts and bolts securing the suspension strut to the swivel hub . . .**

**4.7b . . . then disengage the top of the swivel hub from the strut**

**4.8 Prise apart the two halves of the strut retaining clamp by spreading open the serations**

**4.10 Fit a spring compressor tool, and compress the coil spring**

**4.11 Prise out the plastic cap from the upper mounting**

4.12 Counterhold the strut piston rod with an Allen key or suitable bit, and unscrew the piston rod nut

4.13a Remove the strut upper mounting . . .

4.13b . . . upper spring seat with rubber gaiter . . .

4.13c . . . spring . . .

4.13d . . . and buffer, from the strut

bit, and unscrew the piston rod nut (see illustration).

**13** Remove the strut upper mounting, upper spring seat with rubber gaiter, spring and buffer from the strut (see illustrations).

**14** With the strut assembly now completely dismantled, examine all the components for wear, damage or deformation. Renew any of the components as necessary.

**15** Examine the strut for signs of fluid leakage. Check the strut piston for signs of pitting along its entire length, and check the strut body for signs of damage. While holding it in an upright position, test the operation of the strut by moving the piston through a full stroke, and then through short strokes of 50 to 100 mm. In both cases, the resistance felt should be smooth and continuous. If the resistance is jerky or uneven or if there is any visible sign of wear or damage to the strut, renewal is necessary.

**16** If any doubt exists as to the condition of the coil spring, carefully remove the spring compressors and check the spring for distortion and signs of cracking. Renew the spring if it is damaged or distorted, or if there is any doubt as to its condition.

**17** Inspect all other components for damage or deterioration, and renew any that are suspect.

**18** With the spring compressed with the compressor tool, locate the spring on the strut making sure that it is correctly seated with its lower end against the raised stop (see illustration).

**19** Refit the buffer, rubber gaiter, upper spring seat and the upper mounting.

**20** Refit the new piston rod nut and tighten it to the specified torque while counterholding the piston rod. Refit the plastic cap to the upper mounting.

**21** Slowly slacken the spring compressor tool to relieve the tension in the spring. Check that the ends of the spring locate correctly against the stops on the spring seats. If necessary,

turn the spring and the upper seat so that the components locate correctly before the compressor tool is removed. Remove the compressor tool when the spring is fully seated.

### Refitting

**22** Locate the strut in position under the front wing and engage the help of an assistant to retain it in place. Engage the two halves of the new strut retaining clamp with the strut upper mounting and push the two halves together so that the serrations engage. Using a pair of wide-opening grips or similar, squeeze the two clamp halves fully together (see illustration).

4.18 Locate the spring on the strut making sure that its lower end (A) is against the raised stop (B)

4.22 Engage the two halves of the strut retaining clamp with the strut upper mounting and squeze the two clamp halves fully together

**5.5 Front suspension lower arm inner mounting located on the subframe**

**23** Engage the swivel hub with the suspension strut, and insert the new bolts from the front of the strut so that their threads are facing to the rear. Fit the new nuts, tightening them by hand only at this stage.

**24** Align the strut-to-swivel hub bolt heads with the marks made on the strut during removal. Tighten the bolts to the specified torque and through the specified angles given in the Specifications, using a torque wrench and angle-tightening gauge.

**25** Locate the hydraulic hose in the strut bracket and secure with the retaining clip. Refit the ABS wheel speed sensor wiring guide to the brake hydraulic hose.

**26** Reconnect the ABS wheel speed sensor wiring connector and, where applicable, the brake pad wear warning indicator wire. Secure the wiring in the relevant support brackets and clips.

**27** Connect the anti-roll bar link rod to the strut and use a spanner on the flats to hold the link while tightening the nut to the specified torque.

**28** Refit the roadwheel, then lower the vehicle to the ground and tighten the roadwheel bolts to the specified torque.

## 5 Front suspension lower arm – removal, overhaul and refitting

**Note:** *New lower arm inner pivot bolts and lower arm balljoint clamp bolt and nut will be needed for refitting.*

### Removal

**1** Firmly apply the handbrake, then jack up

**6.2 Front suspension lower balljoint showing rivets securing it to the lower arm**

the front of the car and support it securely on axle stands (see *Jacking and vehicle support*). Remove the front roadwheel.

**2** Unscrew the nut and remove the clamp bolt securing the front suspension lower arm balljoint to the swivel hub **(see illustration 2.8)**. Note that a new clamp bolt and nut will be required for refitting.

**3** Use a chisel or screwdriver as a wedge to expand the lower portion of the swivel hub **(see illustration 2.9)**.

**4** Using a lever, push down on the suspension lower arm to free the balljoint from the swivel hub, then move the swivel hub to one side and release the arm, taking care not to damage the balljoint rubber boot. It is advisable to place a protective cover over the rubber boot such as the plastic cap from an aerosol can, suitably cut to fit.

**5** Note that the lower arm inner retaining bolt heads are facing the front of the vehicle. Unscrew and remove the bolts and withdraw the lower arm from the subframe **(see illustration)**. It will be necessary to slightly press the arms to release the rubber mountings.

### Overhaul

**6** The lower balljoint may be renewed as described in Section 6. The rubber bushes are a tight fit in the arm and must be pressed out. If a press is not available, the bushes can be drawn out using a long bolt, nut, washers and a socket or length of metal tubing.

**7** Prior to fitting the new bushes, coat them with silicone grease or soapy water. Press both bushes fully into the lower arm.

### Refitting

**8** Locate the lower arm on the subframe and fit the retaining bolts from the front of the vehicle. Hand-tighten the bolts at this stage.

**9** Locate the lower arm balljoint in the swivel hub. Insert the new clamp bolt from the front of the swivel hub, so that its threads are facing to the rear. Fit the new nut to the clamp bolt, and tighten it to the specified torque.

**10** Refit the front wheel and lower the vehicle to the ground.

**11** With the weight of the vehicle on the suspension, tighten the lower arm inner pivot bolts to the specified torque and in the stages given.

**12** Have the front wheel alignment settings checked on completion.

## 6 Front suspension lower balljoint – renewal

**Note:** *The original balljoint is riveted to the lower arm; service replacements are bolted in position.*

**1** Remove the front suspension lower arm as described in Section 5. **Note:** *If the fitted balljoint is a service replacement, it is not necessary to completely remove the arm but only to disconnect the balljoint from the*

bottom of the swivel hub then unbolt the old balljoint.

**2** Mount the lower arm in a vice, then drill the heads from the three rivets that secure the balljoint to the lower arm, using a 12.0 mm diameter drill **(see illustration)**.

**3** If necessary, tap the rivets from the lower arm, then remove the balljoint.

**4** Clean any rust from the rivet holes, and apply rust inhibitor.

**5** The new balljoint must be fitted using three special bolts, spring washers and nuts, available from a Vauxhall/Opel parts stockists.

**6** Ensure that the balljoint is fitted the correct way up, noting that the securing nuts are positioned on the underside of the lower arm. Tighten the nuts to the specified torque.

**7** Refit the front suspension lower arm as described in Section 5.

## 7 Front subframe – removal and refitting

**Note:** *Vauxhall/Opel technicians use special jigs to ensure that the subframe is correctly aligned. Without the use of these tools it is important to note the position of the subframe accurately before removal.*

### Removal

**1** Jack up the front and rear of the car and support it securely on axle stands (see *Jacking and vehicle support*). Preferably, position the car over an inspection pit, or on a lift. The help of an assistant will be needed for this procedure.

**2** Set the front wheels in the straight-ahead position, then remove the ignition key and lock the column by turning the steering wheel as required. Remove both front roadwheels and remove the lower liner from the right-hand wheel arch.

**3** Remove the front bumper as described in Chapter 11.

**4** Remove the plastic cover over the top of the engine.

**5** Remove the complete exhaust system as described in Chapter 4A.

**6** In the driver's footwell, unscrew the bolt securing the bottom of the steering column intermediate shaft to the steering gear pinion. Use paint or a suitable marker pen to make

**7.6 Unscrew the clamp bolt, then disconnect the intermediate shaft from the steering gear pinion**

alignment marks between the intermediate shaft and the steering gear pinion, then pull the shaft from the pinion and position to one side (see illustration).

7 Release the locking clip, then lift up the cooling system expansion tank and remove it from the mounting bracket. Place the tank to one side.

8 Retain the radiator in position by inserting a drill bit, or similar, through the holes provided on each of the radiator upper mounting brackets (see illustration). This is necessary as the radiator bottom mounting rubbers are located in the subframe.

9 Lift off the cover from the wiring junction box at the left-hand rear corner of the engine compartment. Undo the nut and disconnect the electro-hydraulic power steering system positive cable from the junction box terminal (see illustration).

10 Disconnect the wiring connector for the electro-hydraulic power steering system at the block connector adjacent to the ABS hydraulic modulator (see illustration).

11 Undo the bolt and disconnect the electro-hydraulic power steering system earth cable from the battery negative terminal clamp.

12 Working under the car, release the cable ties and retaining clips and release the power steering wiring harness from its body attachments. The wiring harness must be free to be removed with the subframe.

13 Connect a hoist to the engine/transmission assembly and support its weight. If available, the type of support bar which locates in the engine compartment side channels is to be preferred,

7.8 Insert a drill bit (arrowed) or similar, through the holes provided on the radiator mounting brackets (shown with radiator removed)

as this will ensure correct repositioning during refitting. Connect the hoist chains to the lifting brackets on the cylinder head.

14 Unscrew the nut and disconnect the anti-roll bar link rod from the strut. Use a spanner on the special flats to hold the link while the nut is being loosened (see illustration 4.5).

15 Unscrew the nut securing the track rod end to the steering arm on the swivel hub, then use a balljoint separator tool to remove the track rod end (see illustration 2.7).

16 Unscrew the nut and remove the clamp bolt securing the front suspension lower arm balljoint to the swivel hub (see illustration 2.8). Note that a new clamp bolt and nut will be required for refitting.

17 Use a chisel or screwdriver as a wedge to expand the lower portion of the swivel hub (see illustration 2.9).

7.9 Disconnect the power steering positive cable (arrowed) from the junction box terminal

18 Using a lever, push down on the suspension lower arm to free the balljoint from the swivel hub, then move the swivel hub to one side and release the arm, taking care not to damage the balljoint rubber boot. It is advisable to place a protective cover over the rubber boot such as the plastic cap from an aerosol can, suitably cut to fit.

19 On manual transmission models with a rod-type gearchange mechanism, note the position of the gearchange linkage located above the engine rear mounting, then disconnect it from the support bracket on the subframe (refer to Chapter 7A if necessary).

20 Undo the three bolts and detach the rear engine mounting/torque link bracket from the transmission.

21 Slacken and remove the nut securing the front engine mounting/torque link to the subframe bracket. Withdraw the through-bolt (see illustration).

22 Support the subframe with a length of wood on a trolley jack. Ideally, a purpose-made cradle should be used. Enlist the help of an assistant.

23 Accurately mark the position of the subframe and mounting bolts to ensure correct refitting. Note that Vauxhall/Opel technicians use a special jig with guide pins located through the alignment holes in the subframe and underbody.

24 Unscrew and remove the subframe mounting bolts, noting the position of each bolt, as they are of different lengths (see illustrations). There are two bolts at the front,

7.10 Disconnect the power steering wiring at the block connector (arrowed)

7.21 Undo the nut (arrowed) and remove the bolt securing the front engine mounting/ torque link to the subframe bracket

7.24a Unscrew the subframe front mounting bolts . . .

7.24b . . . side mounting bolts . . .

7.24c . . . and rear support bracket bolts

**7.25 Guide the steering gear pinion through the rubber grommet when lowering the subframe**

two bolts located above the lower suspension arms, and six bolts located on the triangular rear support brackets.

**25** With the help of an assistant, carefully lower the subframe taking care not to damage the wiring harness for the power steering. As it is being lowered, guide the steering gear pinion through the rubber grommet in the floor **(see illustrations)**.

**26** Remove the steering gear, front suspension lower arms and anti-roll bar with reference to Sections 18, 5 and 8. If necessary, the subframe mounting rubbers may be renewed, however, they must be renewed in pairs only (ie, left and right together). Use a metal tube, a long threaded bar, and two nuts and washers to force out the rubbers. If necessary, unbolt and remove the gearchange bracket (where fitted).

### Refitting

**27** Refitting is a reversal of removal, bearing in mind the following points:

 a) *Ensure that the radiator lower mounting pegs engage correctly in the subframe brackets as the subframe is refitted.*
 b) *Tighten all nuts and bolts to the specified torque and, where necessary, in the stages given. Note that new nuts/ bolts should be used on all disturbed fittings.*
 c) *Make sure that the subframe is correctly aligned with the underbody before fully tightening the mounting bolts.*

## 8  Front anti-roll bar – removal and refitting

**Note:** *It is recommended that all mounting nuts and bolts are renewed when refitting.*

### Removal

**1** Remove the front subframe assembly as described in Section 7.
**2** Prior to removal of the anti-roll bar, mark the position of each anti-roll bar mounting clamp rubber.
**3** Unscrew the retaining nut and disconnect the link rod from the ends of the anti-roll bar, discard the retaining nut; a new one should be used on refitting. Use a spanner on the flats to hold the link while the nut is being loosened.
**4** Unscrew the two bolts from each mounting clamp, and remove the clamp **(see illustration)**. As the last clamp is removed, support the anti-roll bar and remove it from the subframe.
**5** Inspect the mounting clamp rubbers for signs of damage and deterioration, and renew if necessary **(see illustrations)**. **Note:** *On later models, the mounting clamp rubbers are a modified two-piece design and cannot be renewed separately. If the rubbers are worn, a complete new anti-roll bar complete with integral mounting clamps will be required. Consult a Vauxhall/Opel dealer for further information.*

### Refitting

**6** Align the mounting rubbers with the marks made on the anti-roll bar prior to removal.
**7** Refit the anti-roll bar to the subframe, and fit the mounting clamps. Ensure that the clamp half is correctly engaged with the anti-roll bar rubbers, then tighten each clamp retaining bolt, by hand only at this stage.
**8** With the two clamps loosely installed, check the position of the anti-roll bar to the marks made on removal, then tighten the clamp bolts to the specified torque setting.
**9** Refit the link rods to the ends of the anti-roll bar using new retaining nuts, tighten to the specified torque setting.
**10** Refit the front subframe assembly as described in Section 7.

**11** Refit the roadwheels if not already done, then lower the vehicle to the ground and tighten the roadwheel bolts to the specified torque setting.

## 9  Rear hub bearings – checking and renewal

**Note:** *The rear hub bearing and integral ABS wheel speed sensor is a sealed unit and no repairs are possible. If the bearing is worn or the speed sensor is faulty, a new bearing assembly must be obtained.*

### Checking

**1** Chock the front wheels then jack up the rear of the car and securely support it on axle stands (see *Jacking and vehicle support*). Remove the roadwheel.
**2** Remove the brake disc as described in Chapter 9.
**3** A dial test indicator (DTI) will be required to measure the amount of radial and lateral run-out in the bearing. Zero the indicator on the outer edge of the hub flange.
**4** Lever the hub in and out and measure the amount of play in the bearing.
**5** To measure lateral run-out, locate the probe on the surface of the hub which contacts the disc. To measure radial run-out, locate the probe on the outer perimeter of the hub so that it is pointing towards the centre of the hub.
**6** Slowly turn the hub and note the maximum amount of run-out. If the run-out exceeds the amount given in the Specifications, renew the hub bearing unit as described below.
**7** Remove the indicator and refit the brake disc with reference to Chapter 9.
**8** Refit the roadwheel, then lower the vehicle to the ground and tighten the roadwheel bolts to the specified torque.

### Renewal

**Note:** *New hub bearing retaining nuts will be required for refitting.*

**9** Chock the front wheels then jack up the rear of the car and securely support it on axle stands (see *Jacking and vehicle support*). Remove the roadwheel.

**8.4 Anti-roll bar clamp mounting bolts (arrowed)**

**8.5a Remove the clamps from the rubber bushes . . .**

**8.5b . . . then remove the bushes and inspect for wear**

**10** Remove the rear brake disc as described in Chapter 9.

**11** Disconnect the wiring for the ABS wheel speed sensor located on the inside of the bearing assembly **(see illustration)**.

**12** Attach the brake caliper carrier plate to the rear coil spring with a plastic cable tie to prevent straining the hydraulic brake line.

**13** Support the bearing assembly and unscrew the four mounting nuts on the inside of the trailing arm. Withdraw the bearing and brake shield from the rear trailing arm. Note that the locating studs are spaced so that the bearing will only fit in one position.

**14** Thoroughly clean the trailing arm, bearing unit and brake shield mating faces, then place the shield in position on the bearing unit.

**15** Refit the bearing unit and brake shield to the trailing arm, and screw on four new retaining nuts.

**16** Tighten the retaining nuts progressively to the specified Stage 1 torque setting using a torque wrench, and then through the specified Stage 2 and Stage 3 angles, using an angle tightening gauge.

**17** Reconnect the ABS wheel speed sensor wiring connector.

**18** Refit the rear brake disc as described in Chapter 9.

### 10 Rear shock absorber –
removal, inspection and refitting

**Note:** *Always renew shock absorbers in pairs to maintain good road handling.*

### Removal

**1** Chock the front wheels then jack up the rear of the car and securely support it on axle stands (see *Jacking and vehicle support*). Remove the rear roadwheels.

**2** Using a trolley jack, slightly raise the trailing arm on the relevant side.

**3** Unscrew and remove the shock absorber lower mounting bolt from the trailing arm **(see illustration)**.

**4** Support the shock absorber, then unscrew and remove the upper mounting bolt and withdraw the shock absorber from the underbody bracket **(see illustration)**.

### Inspection

**5** The shock absorber can be tested by clamping the lower mounting eye in a vice, then fully extending and compressing the shock absorber several times. Any evidence of jerky movement or lack of resistance indicates the need for renewal.

**6** Examine the mounting rubbers in the shock absorber for excessive wear.

**7** If the shock absorber or its mounting rubbers are worn excessively, renew the complete shock absorber.

### Refitting

**8** Refitting is a reversal of removal, but tighten the mounting bolts to the specified torque.

### 11 Rear suspension coil spring
– removal and refitting

**Note:** *Due to the design of the rear suspension, it is important to note that only one coil spring should be removed at a time. Note that the rear springs should be renewed in pairs.*

### Removal

**1** Chock the front wheels then jack up the rear of the car and securely support it on axle stands (see *Jacking and vehicle support*). Remove the rear roadwheels.

**2** Using a trolley jack, slightly raise the trailing arm on the relevant side.

**3** Unscrew and remove the shock absorber lower mounting bolt from the trailing arm **(see illustration 10.3)**.

**9.11 Disconnecting the ABS wiring from the inside of the rear hub**

**4** Carefully lower the trailing arm as far as possible without straining the brake flexible hoses leading to the rear brakes.

**5** Remove the coil spring and spring seats from the underbody and trailing arm, and withdraw from under the vehicle. Note that the upper spring seat incorporates a damper buffer **(see illustrations)**.

### Refitting

**6** Refitting is a reversal of removal, but note the following points.

a) Ensure that the spring locates correctly on the upper and lower seats, as well as on the trailing arm and underbody.

b) Tighten the shock absorber lower mounting bolt to the specified torque.

c) If both springs are being renewed, repeat the procedure on the remaining side of the vehicle.

**10.3 Unscrew and remove the shock absorber lower mounting bolt from the trailing arm . . .**

**10.4 . . . and the upper mounting bolt from the underbody bracket**

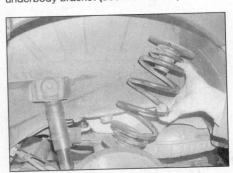

**11.5a Remove the rear coil spring, together with the spring seats . . .**

**11.5b . . . then remove the upper spring seat . . .**

**11.5c . . . and lower spring seat**

**12.2 Unclip and remove the centre console access panel**

**12.3 Unclip the cover from around the handbrake lever**

**12.4 Handbrake cable adjuster nut (arrowed)**

## 12 Rear suspension torsion beam and trailing arms – removal and refitting

**Note:** *New front mounting bracket retaining bolts will be required for refitting.*

### Removal

**1** Chock the front wheels then jack up the rear of the car and securely support it on axle stands (see *Jacking and vehicle support*). Remove the rear roadwheels.

**2** From inside the vehicle, unclip and remove the access panel in the centre console, beneath the handbrake lever **(see illustration)**.

**3** Unclip the cover from around the handbrake lever **(see illustration)**.

**4** Move the handbrake lever to the fully released position, then turn the cable adjuster nut anti-clockwise to remove all tension from the cables **(see illustration)**.

**5** Working on each side in turn, use a screwdriver to push the handbrake operating lever on the brake caliper downwards, and detach the cable end fitting from the lever **(see illustration)**.

**6** Prise out the handbrake outer cable retaining clip and withdraw the handbrake cable from the caliper bracket **(see illustrations)**.

**7** Remove the clips and disconnect the handbrake outer cables from the support brackets on the trailing arms. Also release the handbrake cables from the supports on the torsion beam.

**8** Disconnect the ABS rear wheel speed sensor wiring from the rear hubs, and unclip the wiring from the torsion beam.

**9** Remove the filler cap from the brake hydraulic fluid reservoir in the engine compartment, then tighten the cap down onto a piece of polythene sheeting. This will help prevent the fluid from draining from the system when the rear brake flexible hoses are disconnected.

**10** Unscrew the union nuts and disconnect the rear brake hydraulic pipes from the flexible hoses at the support brackets on the trailing arms on each side. Recover the retaining plates. Be prepared for some loss of brake fluid, and plug or tape over the ends of the lines and hoses to prevent entry of dust and dirt.

**11** Support the weight of the torsion beam and trailing arms using two trolley jacks. Alternatively, one trolley jack and a length of wood may be used, but the help of an assistant will be required.

**12** Unscrew the lower mounting bolts and detach both shock absorbers from the torsion beam.

**13** Carefully lower the torsion beam until it is possible to remove the coil springs and spring seats. Note that the upper spring seats incorporate buffers.

**14** Make sure that the torsion beam is supported, then unscrew and remove the front mounting bracket bolts from the underbody **(see illustration)**. Note that new bolts will be required for refitting.

**15** Lower the torsion beam to the ground and remove it from under the vehicle.

**16** The brake components can be removed from the trailing arms, referring to the relevant Sections of Chapter 9. The hub bearing units can be removed with reference to Section 9.

**17** If necessary, the front mounting brackets can be removed after unscrewing the retaining nut and withdrawing the centre through bolt. Note that a new nut and bolt will be required for refitting. Renewal of the front mounting bushes is a complex operation requiring numerous special tools and a hydraulic press. Bush renewal should therefore be entrusted to a Vauxhall/Opel dealer.

### Refitting

**18** Refit any components that were removed from the torsion beam, referring to the relevant Sections of this Chapter and Chapter 9, as applicable. If the front mounting brackets were removed from the trailing arms, refit the brackets using new nuts and bolts, but only tighten the nuts lightly at this stage.

**12.5 Push the handbrake operating lever on the brake caliper downwards, and detach the cable end fitting from the lever**

**12.6a Prise out the handbrake outer cable retaining clip . . .**

**12.6b . . . and withdraw the handbrake cable from the caliper bracket**

**12.14 Rear suspension torsion beam front mounting bracket**

**19** Check the condition of the threads in the front mounting bracket captive nuts on the underbody. If necessary, use a tap to clean out the threads.

**20** Support the torsion beam on the trolley jacks, and position the assembly under the rear of the vehicle.

**21** Raise the jacks, and fit the new mounting bracket bolts. Do not fully tighten the bolts at this stage.

**22** If the front mounting brackets have been removed from the trailing arms, position the torsion beam so that the distance between the coil spring contact surfaces on the trailing arms and underbody is 173.0 ± 10.0 mm. With the torsion beam in this position, tighten the front mounting bracket centre bolts on each side to the specified torque and angle settings in the stages given.

**23** Fully tighten the front mounting bracket-to-underbody bolts to the specified torque and angle settings in the stages given.

**24** Locate the upper and lower seats on the coil springs, then refit the springs on the torsion beam.

**25** Raise the torsion beam until the shock absorber lower mounting bolts can be inserted. Tighten the bolts to the specified torque.

**26** Refit the brake hydraulic pipes and flexible hoses together with the retaining plates and tighten the union nuts to the specified torque.

**27** Clip the wiring to the torsion beam and reconnect it to the ABS wheel speed sensors.

**28** Reconnect the handbrake cables to the caliper levers and fit the cables in the supports.

**29** Bleed the complete brake hydraulic system, as described in Chapter 9.

**30** Adjust the handbrake cable as described in Chapter 1, then refit the handbrake lever cover and centre console access panel.

**31** Refit the roadwheels and lower the vehicle to the ground.

## 13 Steering wheel –
removal and refitting

 **Warning: Make sure that the airbag safety recommendations given in Chapter 12 are followed to prevent personal injury.**

**Note:** *A new steering wheel retaining bolt will be required for refitting.*

### Removal

**1** Remove the airbag as described in Chapter 12.

**2** Set the front wheels in the straight-ahead position, then lock the column in position after removing the ignition key.

**3** Disconnect the wiring harness connector for the steering wheel switches **(see illustration)**.

**4** Unscrew the Torx retaining bolt securing the steering wheel to the column **(see illustration)**.

**13.3 Disconnect the wiring harness connector for the steering wheel switches**

**13.5 Alignment marks (arrowed) between the steering column shaft and steering wheel**

**5** Check that there are alignment marks between the steering column shaft and steering wheel **(see illustration)**. If no marks are visible, centre punch the wheel and column shaft to ensure correct alignment when refitting.

**6** Grip the steering wheel with both hands and carefully rock it from side-to-side to release it from the splines on the steering column. As the steering wheel is being removed, guide the wiring for the airbag through the aperture in the wheel, taking care not to damage the wiring connectors **(see illustration)**.

### Refitting

**7** Refit the steering wheel, aligning the marks made prior to removal. Route the airbag wiring connectors through the steering wheel aperture. **Note:** *Make sure the guide pin on the steering wheel centre hub locates correctly with the contact unit on the steering column,*

**14.4 Insert a thin rod into the lock housing hole, press the rod to release the detent spring, and pull out the lock cylinder**

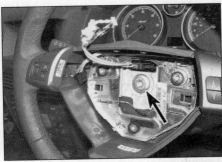

**13.4 Unscrew the steering wheel retaining bolt (arrowed)**

**13.6 Guide the wiring for the airbag through the aperture in the wheel**

*and that the two arrows on the contact unit are aligned.*

**8** Clean the threads in the steering column, coat the new retaining bolt threads with locking compound, then fit the bolt and tighten to the specified torque.

**9** Reconnect the wiring connector for the steering wheel switches.

**10** Release the steering lock, and refit the airbag as described in Chapter 12.

## 14 Ignition switch/
steering column lock –
removal and refitting

### Removal

**1** Disconnect the battery negative terminal (refer to *Disconnecting the battery* in the Reference Chapter).

**2** Remove the steering column shrouds as described in Chapter 11.

**3** Insert the ignition key into the ignition switch/lock, and turn it to position I.

**4** Insert a thin rod into the hole in the lock housing, press the rod to release the detent spring, and pull out the lock cylinder using the key **(see illustration)**.

### Refitting

**5** Insert the ignition switch/lock into the lock housing, while the key is in position I. Remove the rod from the lock housing.

**6** Refit steering column shrouds as described in Chapter 11, then reconnect the battery.

**15.9a Unscrew the steering column lower fastening clamp bolt . . .**

**15.9b . . . and the two upper mounting bolts (arrowed) . . .**

**15.9c . . . then slide the column upward to disengage the locating tongue (arrowed)**

## 15 Steering column – removal and refitting

**Note:** *It is recommended that all mounting nuts and bolts are renewed when refitting.*

### Removal

**1** Remove the steering wheel as described in Section 13.
**2** Remove the steering column shrouds as described in Chapter 11.
**3** Remove the lower trim panel beneath the facia on the driver's side as described in Chapter 11.
**4** Release the two retaining clips and remove the facia lower panel above the pedals.
**5** Remove the steering column electronics module as described in Chapter 12.

**6** If applicable, make sure the steering column adjustment handle is in the locked position.
**7** In the driver's footwell, unscrew the bolt securing the bottom of the steering column intermediate shaft to the steering gear pinion. Use paint or a suitable marker pen to make alignment marks between the intermediate shaft and the steering gear pinion, then pull the shaft from the pinion and position to one side **(see illustration 7.6)**.
**8** Undo the retaining bolt and disconnect the earth cable from the column. Unscrew the plastic retainer and release the wiring harness from the side of the column.
**9** Unscrew the steering column lower fastening clamp bolt, and the two upper mounting bolts. Slide the column upward to disengage the locating tongue, then withdraw the steering column from the facia crossmember, and remove the column from inside the vehicle **(see illustrations)**.

### Refitting

**10** Refitting is a reversal of removal, bearing in mind the following points:
a) *Tighten all nuts and bolts to the specified torque. Note that new nuts/bolts should be used on all disturbed fittings.*
b) *Ensure that the marks made on the steering column and intermediate shaft are correctly aligned.*
c) *Refit the steering column electronics module as described in Chapter 12.*
d) *Refit the steering column shrouds and facia footwell trim panel as described in Chapter 11.*
e) *Refit the steering wheel as described in Section 13.*

## 16 Steering column intermediate shaft – removal and refitting

**Note:** *New intermediate shaft upper and lower clamp bolts will be required for refitting.*

### Removal

**1** Set the front wheels in the straight-ahead position. Remove the ignition key and allow the steering lock to engage.
**2** Remove the steering column shrouds as described in Chapter 11.
**3** Remove the lower trim panel beneath the facia on the driver's side as described in Chapter 11.
**4** Release the two retaining clips and remove the facia lower panel above the pedals.
**5** Mark the steering column intermediate shaft upper and lower joints in relation to the steering column and steering gear pinion as an aid to refitting, then unscrew both clamp bolts **(see illustrations)**.
**6** Compress the telescopic intermediate shaft and slide the joints from the column and pinion **(see illustration)**. Withdraw the intermediate shaft from inside the vehicle.
**7** Inspect the intermediate shaft universal joints for excessive wear or damage. If either joint is worn or damaged, the complete shaft assembly must be renewed.

### Refitting

**8** Check that the front wheels and steering

**16.5a Unscrew the intermediate shaft upper clamp bolt (arrowed) . . .**

**16.5b . . . and lower clamp bolt (arrowed) . . .**

**16.6a Separate the intermediate shaft from the steering column . . .**

**16.6b . . . and steering gear pinion**

wheel are still in the straight-ahead position, and that the steering wheel is still locked.

**9** Slide the intermediate shaft lower joint onto the steering gear pinion, aligning the previously-made marks. Note that it will not be possible to insert the clamp bolt if the splines are not correctly aligned. Insert the new clamp bolt and tighten to the specified torque.

**10** Slide the upper end of the intermediate shaft onto the column splines, aligning the previously-made marks. Insert the new clamp bolt and tighten to the specified torque.

**11** Refit the steering column shrouds and facia footwell trim panel as described in Chapter 11.

## 17 Steering gear rubber gaiters – renewal

**1** Remove the relevant track rod end as described in Section 21.

**2** Remove the inner and outer securing clips **(see illustration)**, then slide the gaiter off the end of the track rod.

**3** Thoroughly clean the track rod, then slide the new gaiter into position. Note that a groove is provided in the track rod for the outer end of the gaiter to locate in.

**4** Fit the gaiter securing clips, using new clips if necessary, making sure that the gaiter is not twisted.

**5** Refit the track rod end as described in Section 21.

**6** Have the front wheel toe setting checked and adjusted at the earliest opportunity.

## 18 Steering gear – removal and refitting

**Note:** New steering gear mounting bolts will be required for refitting.

### Removal

**1** Set the front wheels in the straight-ahead position. Remove the ignition key and allow the steering lock to engage.

**2** Remove the front subframe as described in Section 7.

**3** On left-hand drive models, unbolt the rear engine mounting/torque link bracket from the subframe.

**4** Where fitted, unbolt the support bracket for the pressure and return lines from the subframe.

**5** Position a suitable container beneath the steering gear fluid unions to catch spilt hydraulic fluid.

**6** Unscrew the union nuts and disconnect the fluid pressure and return lines from the steering gear **(see illustration)**.

**7** Note the routing of the wiring loom then either disconnect it from the electro-hydraulic pump (where possible) or release it from the subframe. **Note:** On pumps supplied by TRW,

the wiring loom is supplied together with the pump and cannot be separated.

**8** Unscrew the mounting nuts and withdraw the electro-hydraulic pump together with the fluid reservoir and pressure/return lines from the subframe and steering gear.

**9** Unscrew the mounting bolts and remove the steering gear from the subframe **(see illustration)**. If necessary, remove the anti-roll bar first with reference to Section 8. The manufacturers recommend that the mounting bolts are renewed whenever removed.

**10** If necessary, remove the track rod ends and track rods with reference to Sections 21 and 22. **Note:** New steering gear assemblies are available from Vauxhall/Opel either with or without the track rods fitted. Also remove the rubber grommets from the pinion.

### Refitting

**11** Refit the track rods and track rod ends with reference to Sections 22 and 21. Also refit the rubber grommets to the pinion.

**12** Clean any dirt from the steering gear and subframe, then locate the steering gear in position. Insert the new mounting bolts and tighten to the specified torque, then through the specified angles.

**13** Where removed, refit the anti-roll bar with reference to Section 8.

**14** Refit the electro-hydraulic pump, together with the fluid reservoir and pressure/return lines to the subframe and steering gear, and tighten the mounting nuts to the specified torque.

**15** Reconnect the wiring loom to the electro-hydraulic pump and attach it to the subframe.

**16** Fit new rubber sealing rings to the pressure and return lines, then refit the lines to the steering gear and tighten the union nuts to the specified torque.

**17** Where fitted, refit the support bracket for the pressure and return lines to the subframe and tighten the mounting bolts securely.

**18** On left-hand drive models, refit the rear engine mounting/torque link bracket to the subframe and tighten to the specified torque.

**19** Refit the front subframe as described in Section 7.

**20** Bleed the power steering hydraulic system as described in Section 20.

**21** Have the front wheel toe setting checked and adjusted at the earliest opportunity.

**17.2 Steering gear rubber gaiter outer securing clip**

## 19 Electro-hydraulic power steering pump – removal and refitting

### Removal

**1** Remove the front subframe as described in Section 7.

**2** Position a suitable container beneath the power steering pump fluid unions to catch spilt hydraulic fluid.

**3** Disconnect the pressure and return lines from the power steering pump. Use a spanner to unscrew the pressure line union nut. If necessary, cut free the return line clip and update it with a screw-type clip.

**4** Note the routing of the wiring loom then either disconnect it from the electro-hydraulic pump (where possible) or release it from the subframe. **Note:** On pumps supplied by TRW, the wiring loom is supplied together with the pump and cannot be separated.

**5** Unscrew the mounting nuts and withdraw the electro-hydraulic pump, together with the bracket, wiring and fluid reservoir from the subframe and steering gear.

**6** Unscrew the mounting nuts and remove the electro-hydraulic pump and mounting bushes from the bracket. Check the rubber mounting bushes for wear and damage and renew them if necessary.

### Refitting

**7** Refit the pump and bushes to the bracket and tighten the mounting nuts.

**8** Refit the electro-hydraulic pump and

**18.6 Hydraulic fluid line connections on the steering gear**

**18.9 Steering gear mounting bolt retaining nut (arrowed)**

**21.2 Hold the track rod stationary while loosening the track rod end securing locknut**

**21.3 Unscrew the balljoint nut securing the track rod end to the steering arm on the swivel hub**

**21.4 Disconnect the track rod end from the steering arm on the swivel hub using a balljoint separator tool**

bracket on the subframe and steering gear and tighten the mounting nuts to the specified torque.

**9** Reconnect the wiring loom (where applicable) and secure it to the subframe. Make sure that the loom is routed as noted during removal.

**10** Fit a new rubber sealing ring to the pressure line, then reconnect the pressure and return lines to the power steering pump. Tighten the pressure line union nut securely, and fit a new clip to the return line.

**11** Refit the front subframe as described in Section 7

**12** Bleed the power steering hydraulic system as described in Section 20.

## 20 Power steering hydraulic system – bleeding

**Note:** *The system must be bled at room temperature – do not bleed the system immediately after using the vehicle on the road.*

**1** Check and top-up the power steering fluid level in the reservoir to the MAX mark on the dipstick as described in Chapter 1. If the system regularly requires more fluid, check the hoses for leaks.

**2** Start the engine, then switch it off again after approximately five seconds. Repeat this procedure two more times, pausing briefly between each stop/start and maintaining the fluid level in the reservoir.

**3** Now start the engine again and allow it to idle. Turn the steering to full left lock, then full right lock five times. Switch the engine off.

**4** Recheck the fluid level in the reservoir and top-up if necessary. Remove the funnel and tube and refit the reservoir filler cap.

**5** It is possible that some air may still remain in the system after bleeding but this will be expelled when the car is driven on the road.

## 21 Track rod end – removal and refitting

**Note:** *A new track rod end retaining nut will be needed for refitting.*

### Removal

**1** Apply the handbrake, then jack up the front of the vehicle, and support securely on axle stands (see *Jacking and vehicle support*). Remove the relevant roadwheel.

**2** Loosen the track rod end securing locknut on the track rod a quarter turn, while holding the track rod stationary with a second spanner on the flats provided **(see illustration)**. If necessary, use a wire brush to remove rust from the nut and threads and lubricate the threads with penetrating oil before unscrewing the nut. As an additional check, measure the visible amount of threads on the track rod using vernier calipers. This will ensure the track rod end is refitted in the same position.

**3** Unscrew and remove the balljoint nut securing the track rod end to the steering arm on the swivel hub **(see illustration)**.

**4** Disconnect the track rod end balljoint from the steering arm on the swivel hub using a balljoint separator tool, taking care not to damage the balljoint boot **(see illustration)**.

**5** Unscrew the track rod end from the track rod, counting the number of turns necessary to remove it and taking care not to disturb the locknut. **Note:** *The track rod ends are handed side-for-side. The right-hand track rod end is marked with an R and has a right-hand thread, whereas the left-hand one is marked with an L and has a **left-hand thread**.*

### Refitting

**6** Screw the track rod end onto the track rod the number of turns noted during removal. Check that the visible amount of threads on the track rod is as previously noted.

**7** Insert the track rod end balljoint in the steering arm on the swivel hub, then fit the nut and tighten to the specified torque, then through the angles given. If the balljoint stud turns as the nut is being tightened, press down on the track rod end to force the stud into the arm.

**8** Tighten the track rod end securing locknut on the track rod while holding the track rod stationary with a second spanner on the flats provided. If possible, tighten the nut to the specified torque using a special crow-foot adapter for the torque wrench.

**9** Refit the roadwheel, then lower the vehicle to the ground, and tighten the wheelbolts.

**10** Have the front wheel alignment checked and adjusted at the earliest opportunity.

## 22 Track rod – removal and refitting

### Removal

**1** Remove the track rod end from the relevant track rod as described in Section 21. Note, however, that on right-hand drive models it is necessary to remove both track rod ends and bellows when removing the left-hand track rod. Conversely, on left-hand drive models it is necessary to remove both track rod ends and bellows when removing the right-hand track rod.

**2** Where necessary, remove the wheel arch liner or trim from under the wheel arch by removing the fasteners (see Chapter 11).

**3** Release the clips and slide the rubber bellows from the steering gear and track rod. Remove the bellows from both sides where necessary (see paragraph 1). Where metal clips are fitted, either prise them free with a screwdriver, or carefully cut them off with a hacksaw.

**4** Turn the steering on full lock so that the rack protrudes from the steering gear on the relevant side. Mark the inner joint housing and rack in relation to each other to indicate how tight it is (see paragraph 6).

**5** Hold the rack stationary with a spanner on the flats provided, then unscrew and remove the track rod inner joint housing. Use either a large adjustable spanner or grips.

### Refitting

**6** Clean the threads and apply a little locking fluid to them, then screw the track rod inner joint housing into the rack and tighten to the specified torque. Because of its size and design, using a torque wrench may be difficult, in which case the joint housing should be tightened until the previously-made marks are aligned with each other.

**7** Refit the bellows making sure that the inner end is pushed fully onto the steering gear and the outer end is seated in the groove on the track rod. Use new clips if necessary.

8 Where necessary, refit the wheel arch liner or trim.

9 Refit the track rod end(s) as described in Section 21.

10 Have the front wheel alignment checked and adjusted at the earliest opportunity.

## 23 Wheel alignment and steering angles – general information

### Definitions

1 A car's steering and suspension geometry is defined in four basic settings – all angles are expressed in degrees (toe settings are also expressed as a measurement); the steering axis is defined as an imaginary line drawn through the axis of the suspension strut, extended where necessary to contact the ground.

2 **Camber** is the angle between each roadwheel and a vertical line drawn through its centre and tyre contact patch, when viewed from the front or rear of the car. Positive camber is when the roadwheels are tilted outwards from the vertical at the top; negative camber is when they are tilted inwards. Slight adjustment of the front camber angle is possible, by altering the position of the swivel hub at its attachment to the front suspension strut. The rear camber angle is not adjustable.

3 **Castor** is the angle between the steering axis and a vertical line drawn through each roadwheel's centre and tyre contact patch, when viewed from the side of the car. Positive castor is when the steering axis is tilted so that it contacts the ground ahead of the vertical; negative castor is when it contacts the ground behind the vertical. The castor angle is not adjustable.

4 **Toe** is the difference, viewed from above, between lines drawn through the roadwheel centres and the car's centre-line. 'Toe-in' is when the roadwheels point inwards, towards each other at the front, while 'toe-out' is when they splay outwards from each other at the front.

5 The front wheel toe setting is adjusted by screwing the track rod in or out of its balljoints, to alter the effective length of the track rod assembly. The rear wheel toe setting is not adjustable.

### Checking and adjustment

6 Due to the special measuring equipment necessary to check the wheel alignment and steering angles, and the skill required to use it properly, the checking and adjustment of these settings is best left to a Vauxhall/Opel dealer or similar expert. Note that most tyre-fitting shops now possess sophisticated checking equipment.

# Chapter 11
# Bodywork and fittings

## Contents

## Degrees of difficulty

| **Easy,** suitable for novice with little experience  | **Fairly easy,** suitable for beginner with some experience  | **Fairly difficult,** suitable for competent DIY mechanic  | **Difficult,** suitable for experienced DIY mechanic  | **Very difficult,** suitable for expert DIY or professional  |
|---|---|---|---|---|

## Specifications

| Torque wrench settings | Nm | lbf ft |
|---|---|---|
| Front seat belt anchorage bolts . . . . . . . . . . . . . . . . . . . . . . . . . . . . . . . . . . . . . . . | 25 | 18 |
| Front seat belt inertia reel nut . . . . . . . . . . . . . . . . . . . . . . . . . . . . . . . . . . . . . . . . | 20 | 15 |
| Front seat belt stalk and tensioner bolt . . . . . . . . . . . . . . . . . . . . . . . . . . . . . . . | 35 | 26 |
| Front seat mounting bolts . . . . . . . . . . . . . . . . . . . . . . . . . . . . . . . . . . . . . . . . . | 35 | 26 |
| Rear seat belt anchorage bolts . . . . . . . . . . . . . . . . . . . . . . . . . . . . . . . . . . . . . | 35 | 26 |
| Rear seat belt inertia reel bolt . . . . . . . . . . . . . . . . . . . . . . . . . . . . . . . . . . . . . . | 35 | 26 |
| Rear seat belt stalk retaining bolts . . . . . . . . . . . . . . . . . . . . . . . . . . . . . . . . . . . | 35 | 26 |
| Seat belt-to-height adjuster mounting bolts . . . . . . . . . . . . . . . . . . . . . . . . . . . . | 30 | 22 |

## 1 General information

The bodyshell is made of pressed-steel sections, and is available in three- and five-door Hatchback, and Estate versions. Most components are welded together, but some use is made of structural adhesives; the front wings are bolted on.

The bonnet is made of aluminium, whereas the doors, and some other vulnerable panels, are made of zinc-coated metal. These are further protected by being coated with an anti-chip primer, prior to being sprayed.

Extensive use is made of plastic materials, mainly on the interior, but also in exterior components. The front and rear bumpers are injection-moulded from a synthetic material which is very strong and yet light. Plastic components such as wheel arch liners are fitted to the underside of the vehicle, to improve the body's resistance to corrosion.

## 2 Maintenance – bodywork and underframe

The general condition of a vehicle's body-work is the one thing that significantly affects its value. Maintenance is easy, but needs to be regular. Neglect, particularly after minor damage, can lead quickly to further deterioration and costly repair bills. It is important also to keep watch on those parts of the vehicle not immediately visible, for instance the underside, inside all the wheel arches, and the lower part of the engine compartment.

The basic maintenance routine for the bodywork is washing – preferably with a lot of water, from a hose. This will remove all the loose solids which may have stuck to the vehicle. It is important to flush these off in such a way as to prevent grit from scratching the finish. The wheel arches and underframe need washing in the same way, to remove any accumulated mud, which will retain moisture and tend to encourage rust. Paradoxically enough, the best time to clean the underframe and wheel arches is in wet weather, when the mud is thoroughly wet and soft. In very wet weather, the underframe is usually cleaned of large accumulations automatically, and this is a good time for inspection.

Periodically, except on vehicles with a wax-based underbody protective coating, it is a good idea to have the whole of the underframe of the vehicle steam-cleaned, engine compartment included, so that a thorough inspection can be carried out to see what minor repairs and renovations are necessary. Steam-cleaning is available at many garages, and is necessary for the removal of the accumulation of oily grime, which sometimes is allowed to become thick in certain areas. If steam-cleaning facilities are not available, there are some excellent grease solvents available which can be brush-applied; the dirt can then be simply hosed off. Note that these methods should not be used on vehicles with wax-based underbody protective coating, or the coating will be removed. Such vehicles should be inspected annually, preferably just prior to Winter, when the underbody should be washed down, and any damage to the wax coating repaired. Ideally, a completely fresh coat should be applied. It would also be worth considering the use of such wax-based protection for injection into door panels, sills, box sections, etc, as an additional safeguard against rust damage, where such protection is not provided by the vehicle manufacturer.

After washing paintwork, wipe off with a chamois leather to give an unspotted clear finish. A coat of clear protective wax polish will give added protection against chemical pollutants in the air. If the paintwork sheen has dulled or oxidised, use a cleaner/polisher combination to restore the brilliance of the shine. This requires a little effort, but such dulling is usually caused because regular washing has been neglected. Care needs to be taken with metallic paintwork, as special non-abrasive cleaner/polisher is required to avoid damage to the finish. Always check that the door and ventilator opening drain holes and pipes are completely clear, so that water can be drained out. Brightwork should be treated in the same way as paintwork. Windscreens and windows can be kept clear of the smeary film which often appears, by the use of proprietary glass cleaner. Never use any form of wax or other body or chromium polish on glass.

## 3 Maintenance of upholstery and carpets – general

Mats and carpets should be brushed or vacuum-cleaned regularly, to keep them free of grit. If they are badly stained, remove them from the vehicle for scrubbing or sponging, and make quite sure they are dry before refitting. Seats and interior trim panels can be kept clean by wiping with a damp cloth. If they do become stained (which can be more apparent on light-coloured upholstery), use a little liquid detergent and a soft nail brush to scour the grime out of the grain of the material. Do not forget to keep the headlining clean in the same way as the upholstery. When using liquid cleaners inside the vehicle, do not over-wet the surfaces being cleaned. Excessive damp could get into the seams and padded interior, causing stains, offensive odours or even rot.

If the inside of the vehicle gets wet accidentally, it is worthwhile taking some trouble to dry it out properly, particularly where carpets are involved. Do not leave oil or electric heaters inside the vehicle for this purpose.

## 4 Minor body damage – repair

### Minor scratches

If the scratch is very superficial, and does not penetrate to the metal of the bodywork, repair is very simple. Lightly rub the area of the scratch with a paintwork renovator, or a very fine cutting paste, to remove loose paint from the scratch, and to clear the surrounding bodywork of wax polish. Rinse the area with clean water.

Apply touch-up paint to the scratch using a fine paint brush; continue to apply fine layers of paint until the surface of the paint in the scratch is level with the surrounding paintwork. Allow the new paint at least two weeks to harden, then blend it into the surrounding paintwork by rubbing the scratch area with a paintwork renovator or a very fine cutting paste. Finally, apply wax polish.

Where the scratch has penetrated right through to the metal of the bodywork, causing the metal to rust, a different repair technique is required. Remove any loose rust from the bottom of the scratch with a penknife, then apply rust-inhibiting paint to prevent the formation of rust in the future. Using a rubber or nylon applicator, fill the scratch with bodystopper paste. If required, this paste can be mixed with cellulose thinners to provide a very thin paste which is ideal for filling narrow scratches. Before the stopper-paste in the scratch hardens, wrap a piece of smooth cotton rag around the top of a finger. Dip the finger in cellulose thinners, and quickly sweep it across the surface of the stopper-paste in the scratch; this will ensure that the surface of the stopper-paste is slightly hollowed. The scratch can now be painted over as described earlier in this Section.

### Dents

When deep denting of the vehicle's bodywork has taken place, the first task is to pull the dent out, until the affected bodywork almost attains its original shape. There is little point in trying to restore the original shape completely, as the metal in the damaged area will have stretched on impact, and cannot be reshaped fully to its original contour. It is better to bring the level of the dent up to a point which is about 3 mm below the level of the surrounding bodywork. In cases where the dent is very shallow anyway, it is not worth trying to pull it out at all. If the underside of the dent is accessible, it can be hammered out gently from behind, using a mallet with a wooden or plastic head. Whilst doing this, hold a suitable block of wood firmly against the outside of the panel, to absorb the impact from the hammer blows and thus prevent a large area of the bodywork from being 'belled-out'.

Should the dent be in a section of the

bodywork which has a double skin, or some other factor making it inaccessible from behind, a different technique is called for. Drill several small holes through the metal inside the area – particularly in the deeper section. Then screw long self-tapping screws into the holes, just sufficiently for them to gain a good purchase in the metal. Now the dent can be pulled out by pulling on the protruding heads of the screws with a pair of pliers.

The next stage of the repair is the removal of the paint from the damaged area, and from an inch or so of the surrounding 'sound' bodywork. This is accomplished most easily by using a wire brush or abrasive pad on a power drill, although it can be done just as effectively by hand, using sheets of abrasive paper. To complete the preparation for filling, score the surface of the bare metal with a screwdriver or the tang of a file, or alternatively, drill small holes in the affected area. This will provide a really good 'key' for the filler paste.

To complete the repair, see the Section on filling and respraying.

### Rust holes or gashes

Remove all paint from the affected area, and from an inch or so of the surrounding 'sound' bodywork, using an abrasive pad or a wire brush on a power drill. If these are not available, a few sheets of abrasive paper will do the job most effectively. With the paint removed, you will be able to judge the severity of the corrosion, and therefore decide whether to renew the whole panel (if this is possible) or to repair the affected area. New body panels are not as expensive as most people think, and it is often quicker and more satisfactory to fit a new panel than to attempt to repair large areas of corrosion.

Remove all fittings from the affected area, except those which will act as a guide to the original shape of the damaged bodywork (eg headlight shells etc). Then, using tin snips or a hacksaw blade, remove all loose metal and any other metal badly affected by corrosion. Hammer the edges of the hole inwards, in order to create a slight depression for the filler paste.

Wire-brush the affected area to remove the powdery rust from the surface of the remaining metal. Paint the affected area with rust-inhibiting paint, if the back of the rusted area is accessible, treat this also.

Before filling can take place, it will be necessary to block the hole in some way. This can be achieved by the use of aluminium or plastic mesh, or aluminium tape.

Aluminium or plastic mesh, or glass-fibre matting, is probably the best material to use for a large hole. Cut a piece to the approximate size and shape of the hole to be filled, then position it in the hole so that its edges are below the level of the surrounding bodywork. It can be retained in position by several blobs of filler paste around its periphery.

Aluminium tape should be used for small or very narrow holes. Pull a piece off the roll, trim it to the approximate size and shape required, then pull off the backing paper (if used) and stick the tape over the hole; it can be overlapped if the thickness of one piece is insufficient. Burnish down the edges of the tape with the handle of a screwdriver or similar, to ensure that the tape is securely attached to the metal underneath.

### Filling and respraying

Before using this Section, see the Sections on dent, deep scratch, rust holes and gash repairs.

Many types of bodyfiller are available, but generally speaking, those proprietary kits which contain a tin of filler paste and a tube of resin hardener are best for this type of repair. A wide, flexible plastic or nylon applicator will be found invaluable for imparting a smooth and well-contoured finish to the surface of the filler.

Mix up a little filler on a clean piece of card or board – measure the hardener carefully (follow the maker's instructions on the pack), otherwise the filler will set too rapidly or too slowly. Using the applicator, apply the filler paste to the prepared area; draw the applicator across the surface of the filler to achieve the correct contour and to level the surface. As soon as a contour that approximates to the correct one is achieved, stop working the paste – if you carry on too long, the paste will become sticky and begin to 'pick-up' on the applicator. Continue to add thin layers of filler paste at 20-minute intervals, until the level of the filler is just proud of the surrounding bodywork.

Once the filler has hardened, the excess can be removed using a metal plane or file. From then on, progressively-finer grades of abrasive paper should be used, starting with a 40-grade production paper, and finishing with a 400-grade wet-and-dry paper. Always wrap the abrasive paper around a flat rubber, cork, or wooden block – otherwise the surface of the filler will not be completely flat. During the smoothing of the filler surface, the wet-and-dry paper should be periodically rinsed in water. This will ensure that a very smooth finish is imparted to the filler at the final stage.

At this stage, the 'dent' should be surrounded by a ring of bare metal, which in turn should be encircled by the finely 'feathered' edge of the good paintwork. Rinse the repair area with clean water, until all of the dust produced by the rubbing-down operation has gone.

Spray the whole area with a light coat of primer – this will show up any imperfections in the surface of the filler. Repair these imperfections with fresh filler paste or bodystopper, and once more smooth the surface with abrasive paper. Repeat this spray-and-repair procedure until you are satisfied that the surface of the filler, and the feathered edge of the paintwork, are perfect. Clean the repair area with clean water, and allow to dry fully.

The repair area is now ready for final spraying. Paint spraying must be carried out in a warm, dry, windless and dust-free atmosphere. This condition can be created artificially if you have access to a large indoor working area, but if you are forced to work in the open, you will have to pick your day very carefully. If you are working indoors, dousing the floor in the work area with water will help to settle the dust which would otherwise be in the atmosphere. If the repair area is confined to one body panel, mask off the surrounding panels; this will help to minimise the effects of a slight mis-match in paint colours. Bodywork fittings (eg chrome strips, door handles etc) will also need to be masked off. Use genuine masking tape, and several thicknesses of newspaper, for the masking operations.

Before commencing to spray, agitate the aerosol can thoroughly, then spray a test area (an old tin, or similar) until the technique is mastered. Cover the repair area with a thick coat of primer; the thickness should be built up using several thin layers of paint, rather than one thick one. Using 400-grade wet-and-dry paper, rub down the surface of the primer until it is really smooth. While doing this, the work area should be thoroughly doused with water, and the wet-and-dry paper periodically rinsed in water. Allow to dry before spraying on more paint.

Spray on the top coat, again building up the thickness by using several thin layers of paint. Start spraying at one edge of the repair area, and then, using a side-to-side motion, work until the whole repair area and about 2 inches of the surrounding original paintwork is covered. Remove all masking material 10 to 15 minutes after spraying on the final coat of paint.

Allow the new paint at least two weeks to harden, then, using a paintwork renovator, or a very fine cutting paste, blend the edges of the paint into the existing paintwork. Finally, apply wax polish.

### Plastic components

With the use of more and more plastic body components by the vehicle manufacturers (eg bumpers. spoilers, and in some cases major body panels), rectification of more serious damage to such items has become a matter of either entrusting repair work to a specialist in this field, or renewing complete components. Repair of such damage by the DIY owner is not really feasible, owing to the cost of the equipment and materials required for effecting such repairs. The basic technique involves making a groove along the line of the crack in the plastic, using a rotary burr in a power drill. The damaged part is then welded back together, using a hot-air gun to heat up and fuse a plastic filler rod into the groove. Any excess plastic is then removed, and the area rubbed down to a smooth finish. It is important that a filler rod of the correct plastic is used, as body components can be made of a variety of different types (eg polycarbonate, ABS, polypropylene).

**6.2a Undo the upper screw . . .**

**6.2b . . . and lower screw each side securing the bumper to the wheel arch**

**6.3 Release the three plastic rivets (arrowed) securing the lower centre of the bumper to the subframe**

**6.4 Pull out the centre pin and extract the expanding rivet each side**

Damage of a less serious nature (abrasions, minor cracks etc) can be repaired by the DIY owner using a two-part epoxy filler repair material. Once mixed in equal proportions, this is used in similar fashion to the bodywork filler used on metal panels. The filler is usually cured in twenty to thirty minutes, ready for sanding and painting.

If the owner is renewing a complete component himself, or if he has repaired it with epoxy filler, he will be left with the problem of finding a suitable paint for finishing which is compatible with the type of plastic used. At one time, the use of a universal paint was not possible, owing to the complex range of plastics encountered in body component applications. Standard paints, generally speaking, will not bond to plastic or rubber satisfactorily. However, it is now possible to obtain a plastic body parts finishing kit which

consists of a pre-primer treatment, a primer and coloured top coat. Full instructions are normally supplied with a kit, but basically, the method of use is to first apply the pre-primer to the component concerned, and allow it to dry for up to 30 minutes. Then the primer is applied, and left to dry for about an hour before finally applying the special-coloured top coat. The result is a correctly-coloured component, where the paint will flex with the plastic or rubber, a property that standard paint does not normally possess.

## 5 Major body damage repair – general

Where serious damage has occurred, or large areas need renewal due to neglect, it means that

complete new panels will need welding-in, and this is best left to professionals. If the damage is due to impact, it will also be necessary to check completely the alignment of the bodyshell, and this can only be carried out accurately by a Vauxhall/Opel dealer, or accident repair specialist, using special jigs. If the body is left misaligned, it is primarily dangerous as the car will not handle properly, and secondly, uneven stresses will be imposed on the steering, suspension and possibly transmission, causing abnormal wear, or complete failure, particularly to such items as the tyres.

## 6 Front bumper – removal and refitting

### Removal

**1** Remove the radiator grille as described in Section 20.
**2** Working under the wheel arch, undo the four retaining screws (two on each side) securing the wheel arch liner to the bumper **(see illustrations)**.
**3** Release the three plastic rivets securing the lower centre of the bumper to the front subframe **(see illustration)**.
**4** Pull out the centre pin and extract the expanding rivet each side, adjacent to the headlight **(see illustration)**.
**5** Where applicable, disconnect the foglight wiring connectors and headlight washer hoses from the rear of the bumper. Unclip the outside temperature sensor from the centre ventilation grille.
**6** With the aid of an assistant, pull the bumper upward and outward at the sides to disengage the guide rails **(see illustration)**.
**7** Unclip the bumper from the four front guide rails and carefully lift it off the car **(see illustration)**.

### Refitting

**8** Refitting is a reversal of the removal procedure, ensuring that all bumper fasteners are securely tightened.

## 7 Rear bumper – removal and refitting

### Removal

#### Saloon and Hatchback models

**1** Remove the rear light cluster each side as described in Chapter 12.
**2** Remove the rear number plate.
**3** Push out the centre pin and extract the expanding rivet each side securing the lower inner corner of the mudflap to the base of the bumper on each side **(see illustration)**.
**4** From under the wheel arch undo the three screws on each side and remove both mudflaps **(see illustrations)**.

**6.6 Pull the bumper upward and outward at the sides to disengage the guide rails**

**6.7 Unclip the bumper from the four front guide rails and lift it off the car**

**7.3 Push out the centre pin and extract the expanding rivet securing the mudflaps to the base of the bumper**

**7.4a Undo the three screws (arrowed) on each side . . .**

**7.4b . . . and remove both mudflaps**

**5** Undo the screw on each side above the mudflap location, securing the wheel arch liner to the bumper **(see illustration)**.

**6** Undo the two bumper rear retaining screws in the number plate aperture **(see illustration)**.

**7** Release the tailgate weatherstrip from the upper edge of the bumper **(see illustration)**.

**8** On models with parking distance sensors, disconnect the distance sensor main wiring connector from the underside of the bumper.

**9** With the aid of an assistant, pull the bumper upward and outward at the sides to disengage the side guide rails **(see illustration)**.

**10** Pull the bumper rearwards to disengage the rear guide rails and centre guide rails **(see illustration)**.

**11** When sufficient clearance exists, release the number plate light bulbholders from the light units. The bulbholders are a bayonet fitting in the light units **(see illustration)**.

**7.5 Undo the screw each side (arrowed) securing the wheel arch liner to the bumper**

**12** Carefully lift the bumper off the car **(see illustration)**.

### Estate models

**13** Remove the rear light cluster each side as described in Chapter 12.

**7.6 Undo the two screws in the number plate aperture**

**14** Undo the retaining screw each side in the rear light cluster aperture **(see illustration)**.

**15** Working under the wheel arch, undo the four retaining screws (two on each side)

**7.7 Release the tailgate weatherstrip from the upper edge of the bumper**

**7.9 Pull the bumper upward and outward at the sides to disengage the side guide rails**

**7.10 Pull the bumper rearwards to disengage the rear guide rails and centre guide rails**

**7.11 Release the number plate light bulbholders from the light units**

**7.12 Carefully lift the bumper off the car**

**7.14 Undo the retaining screw (arrowed) each side in the rear light cluster aperture**

7.15a  Undo the lower screw . . .

7.15b  . . . and the upper screw each side, securing the wheel arch liner to the bumper

7.16  Pull out the centre pin and extract the expanding rivet each side securing the bumper to the underbody brackets

7.18  Pull the bumper upward and outward at the sides to disengage the side guide rails

7.19  Pull the bumper rearwards to disengage the rear guide rails and carefully lift it off the car

securing the wheel arch liner to the bumper (see illustrations).

16  Pull out the centre pin and extract the expanding rivet each side securing the lower centre of the bumper to the underbody brackets (see illustration).

17  Release the tailgate weatherstrip from the upper edge of the bumper.

18  With the aid of an assistant, pull the bumper upward and outward at the sides to disengage the side guide rails (see illustration).

19  Pull the bumper rearwards to disengage the rear guide rails and carefully lift it off the car (see illustration).

### Refitting

20  Refitting is a reversal of the removal procedure, ensuring that all bumper fasteners are securely tightened.

9.4a  Insert a small screwdriver through the gap between the release handle and mounting bracket . . .

## 8  Bonnet and support strut – removal, refitting and adjustment

### Bonnet

#### Removal

1  Open the bonnet, and have an assistant support it.

2  Using a marker pen or paint, mark around the hinge positions on the bonnet.

3  Using a screwdriver prise out the retaining spring clip and disconnect the support strut from the bonnet.

4  With the aid of the assistant, unscrew the bolts securing the bonnet to the hinges on both sides.

5  Lift off the bonnet taking care not to damage the vehicle paintwork.

#### Refitting

6  Align the marks made on the bonnet before removal with the hinges, then refit and tighten the bonnet securing bolts.

7  Check the bonnet adjustment as follows.

#### Adjustment

8  Close the bonnet, and check that there is an equal gap (approximately 4.0 mm) at each side, between the bonnet and the wing panels. Check also that the bonnet sits flush in relation to the surrounding body panels.

9  The bonnet should close smoothly and positively without excessive pressure. If this is not the case, adjustment will be required.

10  To adjust the bonnet alignment, loosen the bonnet-to-hinge mounting bolts, and move the bonnet on the bolts as required (the bolt holes in the hinges are enlarged). If necessary, the scissor-type hinge mounting bolts may be loosened as well. Access to the hinge retaining bolts can be gained after removing the water deflector (see Section 20). To adjust the bonnet front height in relation to the front wings, adjustable rubber bump stops are fitted to the front corners of the bonnet. These may be screwed in or out as necessary. After making an adjustment, the bonnet striker must be adjusted so that the lock spring holds the bonnet firmly against the rubber bump stops. Loosen the locknut and screw the striker in or out as necessary.

### Support strut

#### Removal

11  Open the bonnet, and have an assistant support it.

12  Using a screwdriver prise out the retaining spring clips and disconnect the strut from bonnet and body. Note which way round the strut is fitted.

#### Refitting

13  Refitting is a reversal of removal.

## 9  Bonnet release cable – removal and refitting

### Removal

1  Remove the driver's side lower trim panel as described in Section 26.

2  Remove the water deflector as described in Section 20.

3  Remove the bonnet lock spring as described in Section 10.

4  Insert a small screwdriver through the gap between the release handle and mounting bracket, to depress the detent lug (see illustrations). With the lug depressed, lift the release handle off the mounting bracket.

5  Detach the outer cable from the release handle frame, then slip the inner cable end fitting out of the lever (see illustrations).

6  Release the cable from the support clips

9.4b . . . to depress the detent lug (arrowed)

9.5a Detach the outer cable from the release handle frame . . .

9.5b . . . then slip the inner cable end fitting out of the lever

and brackets in the engine compartment, then withdraw the cable through the rubber grommet and into the passenger compartment. As an aid to refitting, tie a length of string to the cable before removing it and leave the string in position ready for refitting.

### Refitting

**7** Refitting is a reversal of removal, but tie the string to the end of the cable, and use the string to pull the cable into position. Ensure that the cable is routed as noted before removal, and make sure that the grommet is correctly seated. On completion, refit the water deflector and the interior trim panels as described in Section 20 and 26.

### 10 Bonnet lock spring – removal and refitting

### Removal

**1** The bonnet is held in its locked position with a strong spring which engages with the striker on the front edge of the bonnet. The release cable is connected to the end of the spring.

**2** The striker may be removed from the bonnet by unscrewing the locknut, however measure its fitted length first as a guide to refitting it.

**3** To remove the lock spring, disengage the spring leg from the front crossmember, slide the other end of the spring off the release cable and remove the spring from the crossmember (see illustrations).

### Refitting

**4** Refitting is a reversal of removal.

### 11 Door – removal, refitting and adjustment

### Front door

#### Removal

**1** To remove a door, open it fully and support it under its lower edge on blocks or axle stands covered with pads of rag.

10.3a Disengage the bonnet lock spring leg from the front crossmember . . .

10.3b . . . slide the other end off the release cable and remove the spring from the crossmember

**2** Disconnect the wiring connector from the front edge of the door. To release the connector, pull out the locking clip, then twist the collar and pull the connector from the socket in the door (see illustrations).

11.2a Pull out the locking clip . . .

**3** Unscrew the Torx bolt securing the door check arm pivot to the A-pillar (see illustration).

**4** Where applicable, remove the plastic covers from the hinge pins (see illustration),

11.2b . . . then twist the collar and pull the connector from the socket

11.3 The front door check arm pivot is attached to the A-pillar with a Torx bolt

11.4 Removing the plastic covers from the front door hinge pins

**11.8 Front door lock striker on the B-pillar**

**11.9 Disconnecting the wiring from the front edge of the rear door**

**11.10 Rear door check arm**

**11.11 Removing the plastic covers from the rear door hinge pins**

**11.15 Rear door lock striker on the C-pillar**

then drive out the pins using a punch. Have an assistant support the door as the pins are driven out, then withdraw the door from the vehicle. If renewing a door, transfer all the serviceable fixings to the new door.

### Refitting

5 Refitting is a reversal of removal.

### Adjustment

6 The door hinges are welded onto the door frame and the body pillar, so that there is no provision for adjustment or alignment.

7 If the door can be moved up and down on its hinges due to wear in the hinge pins or their holes, it may be possible to drill out the holes and fit slightly oversize pins. Consult a Vauxhall/Opel dealer for further advice.

8 Door closure may be adjusted by altering the position of the lock striker on the body pillar, using an Allen key or a hexagon bit **(see illustration)**.

## *Rear door*

### Removal

9 Disconnect the wiring connector from the front edge of the door **(see illustration)**. To release the connector, twist the locking collar, then pull the connector from the socket in the door.

10 Unscrew the Torx bolt securing the door check arm pivot to the B-pillar **(see illustration)**.

11 Where applicable, remove the plastic covers from the hinge pins **(see illustration)**, then drive out the pins using a punch. Have an assistant support the door as the pins are driven out, then withdraw the door from the vehicle. If renewing a door, transfer all the serviceable fixings to the new door.

### Refitting

12 Refitting is a reversal of removal.

### Adjustment

13 The door hinges are welded onto the door frame and the body pillar, so that there is no provision for adjustment or alignment.

14 If the door can be moved up and down on its hinges due to wear in the hinge pins or their holes, it may be possible to drill out the holes and fit slightly oversize pins. Consult a Vauxhall/Opel dealer for further advice.

15 Door closure may be adjusted by altering the position of the lock striker on the body pillar, using an Allen key or a hexagon bit **(see illustration)**.

## 12 Door inner trim panel – removal and refitting

## *Front door*

### Removal

1 Carefully prise off the door mirror interior trim panel to release the three retaining clips **(see illustration)**.

2 Remove the foam insulation from the mirror interior trim panel and disconnect the speaker wiring connector **(see illustrations)**.

3 Using a plastic wedge or similar tool, carefully prise off the door grab handle plastic cover and undo the two screws now exposed **(see illustrations)**.

4 Pull open the door interior handle and prise off the trim plate using a small screwdriver. Undo the screw in the trim panel aperture **(see illustrations)**.

**12.1 Carefully prise off the door mirror interior trim panel**

**12.2a Remove the foam insulation from the mirror interior trim panel . . .**

**12.2b . . . and disconnect the speaker wiring connector**

12.3a  Prise off the door grab handle plastic cover . . .

12.3b  . . . and undo the two screws (arrowed) now exposed

12.4a  Pull open the door interior handle and prise off the trim plate . . .

12.4b  . . . then undo the screw (arrowed) in the trim panel aperture

12.5a  Undo the lower screws (arrowed) . . .

12.5b  . . . and rear screws (arrowed) securing the edge of the trim panel to the door

5  Undo the two lower screws (3 lower screws on 3-door Hatchback models) and two rear screws securing the edge of the trim panel to the door (see illustrations).

6  Using a wide-bladed screwdriver or removal tool, carefully prise the bottom and sides of the panel away from door to release the internal clips (see illustration). Lift the panel upward to release it from the window aperture.

7  Once the panel is free, reach behind and release the door lock operating cable from the interior handle. Disengage the inner cable end from the handle lever (see illustration).

8  Disconnect the wiring connectors from the window control switch and door interior handle, then remove the trim panel from the car (see illustrations).

### Refitting

9  Refitting is a reversal of removal.

### Rear door

#### Removal

10  Where a manual window regulator is fitted, locate a cloth rag between the handle and the trim panel and pull it to one side to release the spring clip. Remove the handle from the splined shaft and refit the spring clip to the handle.

11  Using a plastic wedge or similar tool, carefully prise off the door grab handle plastic cover and undo the two screws now exposed (see illustrations 12.3a and 12.3b).

12  Pull open the door interior handle and prise off the trim plate using a small screwdriver.

Undo the screw in the trim panel aperture (see illustrations 12.4a and 12.4b).

13  Undo the screw securing the lower edge

12.6  Carefully prise the bottom and sides of the panel away from door to release the internal clips

12.8a  Disconnect the wiring connectors from the window control switch . . .

of the trim panel to the door (see illustration).

14  Using a wide-bladed screwdriver or removal

12.7  Reach behind the panel and release the door lock operating cable from the interior handle

12.8b  . . . and door interior handle

**12.13 Undo the screw (arrowed) securing the lower edge of the rear trim panel to the door**

**12.14 Carefully prise the bottom and sides of the panel away from door to release the internal clips**

**13.3a Remove the screw (arrowed) from the rear edge of the door . . .**

**13.3b . . . to gain access to the handle locking screw (arrowed)**

tool, carefully prise the bottom and sides of the panel away from door to release the internal clips. Lift the panel upward to release it from the window aperture **(see illustration)**.
**15** Once the panel is free, reach behind and release the door lock operating cable from the

interior handle. Disengage the inner cable end from the handle lever **(see illustration 12.7)**.
**16** On models with electric windows, disconnect the wiring connector from the window control switch, then remove the trim panel from the car.

**13.4 With the exterior door handle held open, turn the handle locking screw anti-clockwise until it reaches its stop**

**13.5 Withdraw the fixed part of the handle, containing the lock cylinder, from the door**

**13.6 Disengage the exterior handle front pivot from the frame and remove the handle from the door**

**13.12a Prise out the blanking cap from the rear edge of the door . . .**

## Refitting

**17** Refitting is a reversal of removal.

## 13 Door handles and lock components – removal and refitting

### *Door interior handle*

#### Removal

**1** The door interior handle is an integral part of the door inner trim panel and cannot be individually removed. If there are any problems with the interior handle, a new inner trim panel will be required.

### *Front door exterior handle*

#### Removal

**2** On vehicles with the 'Open and Start' system, remove the door inner trim panel as described in Section 12, and disconnect the 'Open and Start' wiring harness connector.
**3** Open the door and remove the screw from the rear edge of the door to gain access to the handle locking screw **(see illustrations)**.
**4** Pull the exterior door handle outwards and hold it in that position. With the exterior door handle held in the open position, turn the handle locking screw anti-clockwise until it reaches its stop **(see illustration)**. The exterior door handle should now be fixed in the open position.
**5** Withdraw the fixed part of the handle, containing the lock cylinder, from the door **(see illustration)**.
**6** Slide the exterior door handle to the rear, disengage the front pivot from the handle frame and remove the handle from the door **(see illustration)**.

#### Refitting

**7** Engage the handle front pivot with the frame and move the handle back into position.
**8** Refit the fixed part of the handle with the lock cylinder to the door.
**9** Hold the exterior door handle and turn the handle locking screw clockwise to retain the handle.
**10** Check the operation of the handle then refit the blanking cap to the edge of the door.
**11** On vehicles with the 'Open and Start' system, reconnect the wiring connector then refit the door inner trim panel as described in Section 12.

### *Rear door exterior handle*

#### Removal

**12** Open the door and carefully prise out the blanking cap from the rear edge of the door to gain access to the handle locking screw **(see illustrations)**.
**13** Pull the exterior door handle outwards and hold it in that position. With the exterior door handle held in the open position, turn the handle locking screw anti-clockwise until it reaches its stop **(see illustration)**. The exterior door handle should now be fixed in the open position.

**13.12b** . . . to gain access to the handle locking screw (arrowed)

**14** Withdraw the fixed part of the handle from the door **(see illustration)**.

**15** Slide the exterior door handle to the rear, disengage the front pivot from the handle frame and remove the handle from the door **(see illustration 13.6)**.

### Refitting

**16** Engage the handle front pivot with the frame and move the handle back into position.
**17** Refit the fixed part of the handle to the door.
**18** Hold the exterior handle and turn the handle locking screw clockwise to retain the handle.
**19** Check the operation of the handle then refit the blanking cap to the edge of the door.

## *Front door lock cylinder*

### Removal

**20** Remove the exterior handle as described previously in this Section.

**13.13** With the exterior door handle held open, turn the handle locking screw anti-clockwise until it reaches its stop

**21** Unclip the trim cap and remove the cap from the lock cylinder housing.
**22** The lock cylinder body is an integral part of the housing and no further dismantling is possible.

### Refitting

**23** Refitting is a reversal of removal.

## *Front door exterior handle frame*

**Note:** *A pop-rivet gun and suitable rivets will be required when refitting. The rivet heads should be approximately 4.8 mm in diameter and 11 mm in length.*

### Removal

**24** Disconnect the battery negative terminal (refer to *Disconnecting the battery* in the Reference Chapter).
**25** Remove the exterior handle as described previously in this Section.
**26** Pull out the centre pin and remove the

**13.14** Withdraw the fixed part of the handle from the door

inner trim panel plastic guides from the door panel **(see illustration)**.
**27** Release the clips securing the wiring harness to the door **(see illustration)**.
**28** Carefully peel back the protective plastic sheet and remove the sheet from the door **(see illustration 13.58)**.
**29** Using an 8.5 mm drill bit, drill out the two rivets securing the window rear guide rail to the door, taking great care not to damage the door panel **(see illustration)**.
**30** Remove the guide rail through the door aperture **(see illustration)**.
**31** Undo the two screws securing the security cover to the exterior handle frame and door lock, and remove the cover through the door aperture **(see illustrations)**.
**32** Release the retaining clip and disconnect the lock operating rod from the lever on the exterior handle frame **(see illustration)**.
**33** Slacken the exterior handle frame front

**13.26** Pull out the centre pin and remove the inner trim panel plastic guides from the door panel

**13.27** Release the clips (arrowed) securing the wiring harness to the door

**13.29** Drill out the two rivets (arrowed) securing the window rear guide rail to the door

**13.30** Remove the guide rail through the door aperture

**13.31a** Undo the two screws (arrowed) securing the security cover to the exterior handle frame and door lock . . .

**13.31b** . . . and remove the cover through the door aperture

**13.32 Release the retaining clip (arrowed) and disconnect the lock operating rod from the lever on the exterior handle frame**

**13.33a Slacken the exterior handle frame front retaining screw approximately five turns . . .**

**13.33b . . . extract the rear guide clip, then slide the handle frame forward . . .**

retaining screw approximately five turns. Extract the rear guide clip, then slide the handle frame forward to release the rear locating lugs. Disengage the lock cylinder operating rod and remove the frame through the door aperture **(see illustrations)**.

**13.33c . . . disengage the lock cylinder operating rod and remove the frame through the door aperture**

34 Clean out the remains of the old rivets from inside the door.

### Refitting

35 Connect the lock cylinder operating rod, then place the exterior handle frame in

position in the door. Refit the rear guide clip, then tighten the front retaining screw securely.
36 Engage the lock operating rod with the lever on the exterior handle frame and push the retaining clip back into position on the rod.
37 Refit the security cover and secure with the two screws.
38 Position the window guide rail in the door and secure the guide rail with new pop rivets.
39 Refit the protective plastic sheet to the door ensuring it is firmly stuck with no air bubbles. If the sheet was damaged during removal it should be renewed. This entails cutting a new sheet to the correct size and shape using the old sheet as a template. The new sheet can then be attached to the door with fresh adhesive.
40 Refit the wiring harness clips and inner trim panel plastic guides to the door, ensuring they are firmly attached.
41 Refit the door inner trim panel as described in Section 12.
42 Refit the exterior handle as described previously in this Section, then reconnect the battery negative terminal.

### Rear door exterior handle frame

#### Removal

43 Disconnect the battery negative terminal (refer to *Disconnecting the battery* in the Reference Chapter).
44 Remove the exterior handle as described previously in this Section.
45 Remove the door inner trim panel as described in Section 12.
46 Remove the rear door lock as described later in this Section.
47 Slacken the exterior handle frame front retaining screw approximately five turns. Extract the rear guide clip, then slide the handle frame forward to release the rear locating lugs. Disengage the lock cylinder operating rod and remove the frame through the door aperture **(see illustrations 13.33a to 13.33c)**.

#### Refitting

48 Place the exterior handle frame in position in the door. Refit the rear guide clip, then tighten the front retaining screw securely.
49 Refit the rear door lock as described later in this Section.
50 Refit the door inner trim panel as described in Section 12.
51 Refit the exterior handle as described previously in this Section, then reconnect the battery negative terminal.

### Front door lock

#### Removal

52 Remove the front door exterior handle frame as described earlier in this Section.
53 Undo the three screws securing the lock to the door **(see illustration)**.
54 Withdraw the lock from its location, then lift the locking bar and disconnect the wiring connector. Remove the lock assembly through the upper door aperture **(see illustration)**.

**13.53 Undo the three screws (arrowed) securing the lock to the door**

**13.54 Disconnect the wiring connector, then remove the lock assembly through the upper door aperture**

**13.55a Release the locking clip and disconnect the outer cable . . .**

**13.55b . . . and inner cable from the lock**

**13.58 Carefully peel back the protective plastic sheet and remove the sheet from the door**

**13.59 Release the retaining clip (arrowed) and disconnect the lock operating rod from the lever on the exterior handle frame**

**13.61 Withdraw the lock from its location, then lift the locking bar and disconnect the wiring connector**

**55** If required, disconnect the operating cables from the lock linkage and bracket **(see illustrations)**.

### Refitting

**56** Refitting is a reversal of removal.

## *Rear door lock*

### Removal

**57** Remove the door inner trim panel as described in Section 12.

**58** Carefully peel back the protective plastic sheet and remove the sheet from the door **(see illustration)**.

**59** Release the retaining clip and disconnect the lock operating rod from the lever on the exterior handle frame **(see illustration)**.

**60** Undo the three screws securing the lock to the door **(see illustration 13.53)**.

**61** Withdraw the lock from its location, then lift the locking bar and disconnect the wiring connector **(see illustration)**.

**62** Remove the lock assembly through the door aperture.

**63** If required, disconnect the operating cables from the lock linkage and bracket **(see illustrations 13.55a and 13.55b)**.

### Refitting

**64** If removed, reconnect the operating cables to the lock linkage and bracket.

**65** Insert the lock assembly into the door and reconnect the wiring connector.

**66** Position the lock assembly in its location, refit the three retaining screws and tighten securely.

**67** Engage the lock operating rod with the lever on the exterior handle frame, and push the retaining clip back into position on the rod.

**68** Refit the protective plastic sheet to the door ensuring it is firmly stuck with no air bubbles. If the sheet was damaged during removal it should be renewed. This entails cutting a new sheet to the correct size and shape using the old sheet as a template. The new sheet can then be attached to the door with fresh adhesive.

**69** Refit the door inner trim panel as described in Section 12.

---

## 14 Door window glass and regulator – removal and refitting

### *Front door window glass*

**Note:** *A pop-rivet gun and suitable rivets will be required when refitting. The rivet heads should be approximately 4.8 mm in diameter and 11 mm in length.*

### Removal

**1** Open the door window fully.

**2** Remove the door inner trim panel as described in Section 12.

**3** Pull out the centre pin and remove the inner trim panel plastic guides from the door panel **(see illustration 13.26)**.

**4** Release the clips securing the wiring harness to the door **(see illustration 13.27)**.

**5** Carefully peel back the protective plastic sheet and remove the sheet from the door **(see illustration 13.58)**.

**6** Using a plastic wedge or similar tool, starting from the rear, tap up the door window inner waist seal from the door aperture. Lift the seal up and remove it from the door **(see illustration)**.

**7** Similarly, tap up the door window outer waist seal from the door aperture. Lift the seal up and remove it from the door **(see illustration)**.

**8** Using an 8.5 mm drill bit, drill out the two rivets securing the window rear guide rail to the door, taking great care not to damage the door panel. Remove the guide rail through the door aperture **(see illustrations)**.

**14.6 Tap up the door window inner waist seal from the door aperture, then lift the seal up and remove it from the door**

**14.7 Similarly, tap up the outer waist seal and remove it from the door**

**14.8a Drill out the two rivets (arrowed) securing the window rear guide rail to the door . . .**

**14.8b . . . then remove the guide rail through the door aperture**

**14.9 Undo the two bolts (arrowed) securing the window glass lower frame to the regulator front lifting arm**

9 Undo the two bolts securing the window glass lower frame to the regulator front lifting arm (see illustration).

10 Disengage the window glass lower frame from the regulator rear lifting arm and lift the glass up and out of the door (see illustrations).

11 Clean out the remains of the old rivets from inside the door.

### Refitting

12 Carefully lower the window glass into the door and engage the lower frame with the regulator rear lifting arm.

13 Locate the regulator front lifting arm over the window glass lower frame, refit the two retaining bolts and tighten securely.

14 Refit the window rear guide rail to the door and secure the guide rail with new pop rivets.

15 Refit the window inner and outer waist seals to the door aperture, ensuring that the retaining clips securely engage.

**14.10a Disengage the window glass lower frame from the regulator rear lifting arm (arrowed) . . .**

16 Refit the protective plastic sheet to the door ensuring it is firmly stuck with no air bubbles. If the sheet was damaged during removal it should be renewed. This entails cutting a new sheet to the correct size and shape using the old sheet as a template. The new sheet can then be attached to the door with fresh adhesive.

17 Refit the inner trim panel plastic guides and the wiring harness retaining clips.

18 Refit the door inner trim panel as described in Section 12.

### Rear door window glass

#### Removal

19 Open the door window fully.

20 Remove the door inner trim panel as described in Section 12.

21 On models with manual window regulators, remove the rubber seal from the regulator shaft.

**14.10b . . . and lift the glass up and out of the door**

22 On models with electric window regulators, release the clips securing the wiring harness to the door (see illustration).

23 Carefully peel back the protective plastic sheet and remove the sheet from the door (see illustration 13.58).

24 Using a plastic wedge or similar tool, starting from the rear, tap up the door window inner waist seal from the door aperture. Lift the seal up and remove it from the door.

25 Similarly, tap up the door window outer waist seal from the door aperture. Lift the seal up and remove it from the door (see illustration).

26 Carefully pull away the window guide channel from the rear guide rail (see illustration).

27 Undo the screws securing the upper and lower ends of the window rear guide rail to the door, then remove the guide rail (see illustrations).

**14.22 On models with electric window regulators, release the clips (arrowed) securing the wiring harness to the door**

**14.25 Tap up the door window outer waist seal, then lift the seal up and remove it from the door**

**14.26 Carefully pull away the window guide channel from the rear guide rail**

**14.27a Undo the screws securing the upper . . .**

**14.27b . . . and lower ends of the window rear guide rail to the door . . .**

**14.27c . . . then remove the guide rail**

**14.28a Disengage the window glass lower frame from the regulator lifting arms (arrowed) . . .**

**14.28b . . . and lift the glass up and out of the door**

**14.36 Remove the fixed window glass from the door**

**28** Disengage the window glass lower frame from the regulator lifting arms and lift the glass up and out of the door (see illustrations).

### Refitting

**29** Carefully lower the window glass into the door and engage the lower frame with the regulator lifting arms.
**30** Refit the window rear guide rail to the door and secure the guide rail with the two screws.
**31** Refit the window inner and outer waist seals to the door aperture, ensuring that the retaining clips securely engage.
**32** Refit the protective plastic sheet to the door ensuring it is firmly stuck with no air bubbles. If the sheet was damaged during removal it should be renewed. This entails cutting a new sheet to the correct size and shape using the old sheet as a template. The new sheet can then be attached to the door with fresh adhesive.
**33** Refit the wiring harness retaining clips or regulator shaft rubber seal, as applicable.
**34** Refit the door inner trim panel as described in Section 12.

### Rear door fixed window glass

#### Removal

**35** Carry out the operations described previously in paragraphs 19 to 27.

**36** Remove the fixed window glass from the door (see illustration).

### Refitting

**37** Locate the fixed window glass in the guide channel.
**38** Carry out the operations described in paragraphs 30 to 34.

### Front and rear door window regulator

**Note:** *A pop-rivet gun and suitable rivets will be required when refitting. The rivet heads should be approximately 4.8 mm in diameter and 11 mm in length.*

#### Removal

**39** Remove the front or rear door window glass as described previously in this Section.
**40** Where applicable, disconnect the wiring connector from the window regulator motor (see illustration).
**41** Using an 8.5 mm drill bit, drill out the six rivets securing the window regulator to the door, taking great care not to damage the door panel (see illustration).
**42** Remove the regulator through the door aperture.
**43** Clean out the remains of the old rivets from inside the door.

### Refitting

**44** Refit the regulator to the door and secure the regulator with new pop rivets.
**45** Reconnect the regulator wiring connector, where applicable.
**46** Refit the front or rear door window glass as described previously in this Section.

### 15 Tailgate and support struts
– removal, refitting and adjustment

### *Tailgate*

#### Removal

**1** On Hatchback models, unhook the lifting cords and remove the parcel shelf from the luggage compartment. Unscrew the parcel shelf lifting pins on each side.
**2** Remove the tailgate upper side trim panel, by prising it free at the sides, then at the centre to release the internal retaining clips. On some models, the panel is in two parts with a join at the centre. In this case, remove the left-hand panel first, followed by the right-hand panel. (see illustrations).
**3** Disconnect the tailgate main wiring harness connector, then release the grommet and pull

**14.40 Disconnect the wiring connector from the window regulator motor**

**14.41 Drill out the six rivets (arrowed) securing the window regulator to the door**

15.2a Remove the tailgate upper side trim panel, by prising it free at the sides . . .

15.2b . . . then at the centre to release the internal retaining clips

15.3a Disconnect the tailgate main wiring harness connector . . .

15.3b . . . then release the grommet and pull the wiring connector out of the tailgate

15.6 Extract the clips (arrowed) and carefully drive out the hinge pins, from outside to inside

15.9 Prise the spring clip from the top of the support strut and disconnect it from the ball on the tailgate

the wiring connector out of the tailgate (see illustrations).

4 Disconnect the tailgate washer hose from the jet and pull the hose out of the tailgate.

5 Have an assistant support the tailgate, then disconnect the tops of the support struts by prising out the spring clips with a small screwdriver. Lower the struts to the body.

6 Extract the clips and carefully drive out the hinge pins, from outside to inside, using a small drift, while the assistant supports the tailgate (see illustration). Withdraw the tailgate from the body.

### Refitting

7 Refitting is a reversal of removal, but apply a little grease to the pivots, and check that when closed the tailgate is positioned centrally within the body aperture and flush with the surrounding bodywork. If necessary, adjust the position of the rubber supports so that the tailgate is flush with the surrounding bodywork. After making adjustments, check that the striker enters the lock centrally and if necessary loosen the striker bolts to reposition it. Tighten the bolts on completion.

### *Support struts*

### Removal

8 Open the tailgate and note which way round the struts are fitted. Have an assistant support the tailgate in its open position.

9 Using a small screwdriver, prise the spring clip from the top of the strut and disconnect it from the ball on the tailgate (see illustration).

10 Similarly prise the spring clip from the bottom of the strut and disconnect it from the ball on the body. Withdraw the strut.

### Refitting

11 Refitting is a reversal of removal.

## 16 Tailgate lock components – removal and refitting

### *Removal*

1 On Hatchback models, unhook the lifting cords and remove the parcel shelf from the luggage compartment. Unscrew the parcel shelf lifting pins on each side.

2 Remove the tailgate upper side trim panel, by prising it free at the sides, then at the centre to release the internal retaining clips. On some models, the panel is in two parts with a join at the centre. In this case, remove the left-hand panel first, followed by the right-hand panel. (see illustrations 15.2a and 15.2b).

3 Pull out the expanding rivet and undo the retaining screw (where fitted), securing the lock cover panel to the base of the tailgate (see illustration). Remove the panel.

16.3 Pull out the expanding rivet (A) and undo the retaining screw (B) (where fitted)

16.4a On Estate models, pull out the expanding rivet each side . . .

16.4b . . . and unscrew the two screws at the top of the panel

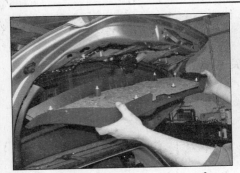

**16.5 Pull the lower trim panel away from the tailgate to release the remaining internal clips**

**16.6 Undo the three lock assembly retaining screws (arrowed)**

**16.7 Withdraw the lock through the tailgate aperture and disconnect the wiring connector**

**4** On Estate models, pull out the expanding rivet each side, securing the tailgate lower trim panel to the tailgate, and unscrew the two screws at the top of the panel **(see illustrations)**.

**5** On all models, pull the lower trim panel away from the tailgate to release the remaining internal clips and remove the panel from the tailgate **(see illustration)**.

**6** Undo the three lock assembly retaining screws **(see illustration)**.

**7** Withdraw the lock through the tailgate aperture and disconnect the wiring connector **(see illustration)**.

### *Refitting*

**8** Refitting is a reversal of removal.

### 17 Exterior mirrors and associated components – removal and refitting

### *Exterior mirror*

#### Removal

**1** Carefully prise off the door mirror interior trim panel to release the three retaining clips **(see illustration)**.

**2** Remove the foam insulation from the mirror interior trim panel and disconnect the speaker wiring connector **(see illustrations)**.

**3** On electrically operated mirrors, disconnect the wiring connector from the mirror **(see illustration)**.

**4** Undo the three retaining bolts and remove the mirror assembly from the door **(see illustration)**.

#### Refitting

**5** Refitting is a reversal of removal.

### *Mirror glass*

#### Removal

**6** Push in the upper inner (nearest the door) corner of the glass so that the lower outer corner of the glass is forced out from the centre.

**7** Using a plastic wedge, prise the outer edge of the glass outwards to release the internal retaining clips **(see illustration)**.

**8** Withdraw the mirror glass and, where applicable, disconnect the wiring connectors **(see illustration)**.

**17.1 Carefully prise off the door mirror interior trim panel to release the three retaining clips**

**17.2a Remove the foam insulation from the mirror interior trim panel . . .**

**17.2b . . . and disconnect the speaker wiring connector**

**17.3 On electrically operated mirrors, disconnect the wiring connector from the mirror**

**17.4 Undo the three retaining bolts (arrowed) and remove the mirror assembly from the door**

**17.7 Using a plastic wedge, prise the outer edge of the glass outwards to release the internal retaining clips**

17.8 Withdraw the mirror glass and, where applicable, disconnect the wiring connectors (arrowed)

17.10 Prise the upper edge of the outer cover away from the mirror body to release the four upper clips (arrowed)

### Refitting

9 Refitting is a reversal of removal. Carefully press the mirror glass into the housing until the centre retainer clips are engaged.

## Outer cover

### Removal

10 Carefully prise the upper edge of the outer cover away from the mirror body to release the four upper clips (see illustration).
11 Unhook the four lower clips and remove the outer cover from the mirror body (see illustration).

### Refitting

12 Refitting is a reversal of removal.

## 18 Windscreen and fixed window glass – general information

The windscreen, tailgate and rear quarter window glasses are cemented in position with a special adhesive and require the use of specialist equipment for their removal and refitting. Renewal of such fixed glass is considered beyond the scope of the home mechanic. Owners are strongly advised to have the work carried out by one of the many specialist windscreen fitting specialists.

## 19 Sunroof – general information

An electric sunroof was offered as an optional extra on most models, and is fitted as standard equipment on some models.
Due to the complexity of the sunroof mechanism, considerable expertise is needed to repair, renew or adjust the sunroof components successfully. Removal of the roof first requires the headlining to be removed, which is a complex and tedious operation in itself, and not a task to be undertaken lightly. Therefore, any problems with the sunroof should be referred to a Vauxhall/Opel dealer.

## 20 Body exterior fittings – removal and refitting

### Radiator grille

1 Push in the centre pins and extract the four expanding rivets securing the upper edge of the radiator grille to the body panel (see illustration). Note that the expanding rivet centre pins are likely to be lost when doing this

and new expanding rivets may be required for refitting.
2 Disengage the six lower lugs and remove the radiator grille from the car (see illustration).

## Wheel arch liners and body under-panels

3 The various plastic covers fitted to the underside of the vehicle are secured in position by a mixture of screws, nuts and retaining clips, and removal will be fairly obvious on inspection. Work methodically around the liner/panel, removing its retaining screws and releasing its retaining clips until it is free to be removed from the underside of the vehicle. Most clips used on the vehicle, with the exception of the fasteners which are used to secure the wheel arch liners, are simply prised out of position. The wheel arch liner clips are released by tapping their centre pins through the clip, and then removing the outer section of the clip; new clips will be required on refitting if the centre pins are not recovered.
4 When refitting, renew any retaining clips that may have been broken on removal, and ensure that the panel is securely retained by all the relevant clips, nuts and screws. Vauxhall/Opel also recommend that plastic nuts (where used) are renewed, regardless of their apparent condition, whenever they are disturbed.

17.11 Unhook the four lower clips (arrowed) and remove the outer cover from the mirror body

20.1 Push in the centre pins and extract the expanding rivets securing the upper edge of the radiator grille to the body panel

20.2 Disengage the six lower lugs and remove the radiator grille from the car

## Water deflector

**Note:** *The water deflector retaining clips, and the water deflector itself, are manufactured from extremely brittle plastic and are likely to break during the following operations. Be prepared to obtain new clips, and possibly a new water deflector!*

**5** Remove the windscreen wiper arms as described in Chapter 12.

**6** Open the bonnet, and pull up the rubber weatherseal from the flange at the rear of the engine compartment **(see illustration)**.

**7** Carefully prise free the water deflector from the base of the windscreen to release the five retaining clips **(see illustration)**.

**8** Disconnect the windscreen washer hose and remove the water deflector from the car.

**9** Refit the water deflector using a reversal of the removal procedure. Refit the wiper arms as described in Chapter 12.

## Body trim strips and badges

**10** The various body trim strips and badges are held in position with a special adhesive tape. Removal requires the trim/badge to be heated, to soften the adhesive, and then cut away from the surface. Due to the high risk of damage to the vehicle's paintwork during this operation, it is recommended that this task should be entrusted to a Vauxhall/Opel dealer.

---

### 21  Seats –
removal and refitting

![spanner icons]

⚠ *Warning: The front seats are equipped with seat belt tensioners, and side airbags may be built into the outer sides of the seats. The seat belt tensioners and side airbags may cause injury if triggered accidentally. If the tensioner has been triggered due to a sudden impact or accident, the unit must be renewed, as it cannot be reset. If a seat is to be disposed of, the tensioner must be triggered before the seat is removed from the vehicle. Due to safety considerations, tensioner renewal or seat disposal must be entrusted to a Vauxhall/ Opel dealer. Where side airbags are fitted, refer to Chapter 12 for the precautions*

**20.6  Pull up the rubber weatherseal from the flange at the rear of the engine compartment**

*which should be observed when dealing with an airbag system.*

**1** Disconnect the battery negative terminal (refer to *Disconnecting the battery* in the Reference Chapter). Wait 2 minutes for the capacitors to discharge, before working on the seat electrics.

### Front seat removal

**2** Slide the seat adjustment fully forward.

**3** Unclip the cover over the seat belt mounting, by releasing it at the rear, then disengaging the front locating tabs **(see illustration)**.

**4** Undo the seat belt retaining bolt **(see illustration)**.

**5** Slacken and remove the seat retaining bolts from the rear of the guide rails **(see illustration)**.

**6** Pull the seat backwards to disengage the guide rail front mounting lugs from the floor.

**21.3  Unclip the cover over the seat belt mounting**

**20.7  Carefully prise free the water deflector from the base of the windscreen to release the five retaining clips**

**7** Pull out the locking bar and disconnect the wiring connector from the underside of the seat, then remove the seat from the car.

### Rear seat removal

#### Cushion – Hatchback models

**8** Pull out the two release straps, while at the same time lifting the cushion up at the front **(see illustration)**.

**9** Push the cushion rearwards and upwards to disengage it at the rear and remove the cushion from the car.

#### Cushion – Estate models

**10** Pull out the two release straps, while at the same time lifting the cushion up at the front.

**11** Tip the cushion fully forward, then disengage the pivot arms from the brackets on the floor **(see illustration)**. Remove the cushion from the car.

**21.4  Undo the seat belt retaining bolt (arrowed)**

**21.5  Slacken and remove the seat retaining bolts (arrowed) from the rear of the guide rails**

**21.8  Pull out the two release straps, while at the same time lifting the rear seat cushion up at the front**

**21.11  Tip the cushion fully forward, then disengage the pivot arms from the brackets on the floor**

21.13a Undo the bolts (arrowed) securing the centre . . .

21.13b . . . and side seat belt buckles and seat hinge to the floor

21.14 Seat hinge rear securing bolts (arrowed)

21.15a Press the outer hinge pin locking collar in, to free the hinge pin . . .

21.15b . . . while at the same time pulling upward to release the backrest

### Backrest

**12** Remove the rear seat cushion as described previously in this Section.

**13** Undo the three bolts securing the seat belt buckles and seat hinge to the floor **(see illustrations)**.

**14** Fold the backrest forward and undo the three rear bolts securing the seat hinge to the floor **(see illustration)**.

**15** Using a screwdriver, press the outer hinge pin locking collar in, to free the hinge pin, while at the same time pulling upward to release the backrest **(see illustrations)**. Remove the backrest from the car.

### *Front seat refitting*

**16** Refitting is a reverse of the removal procedure, noting the following points:

a) *Remove all traces of old thread-locking compound from the threads of the seat retaining bolts, and clean the threaded holes*

in the vehicle floor, ideally by running a tap of the correct size and pitch down them.

b) *Apply a suitable thread-locking compound to the threads of the seat bolts. Refit the bolts, and tighten them to the specified torque setting.*

c) *Reconnect the seat wiring connector making sure it has locked securely, then reconnect the battery negative terminal.*

### *Rear seat refitting*

**17** Refitting is a reverse of the removal procedure.

### 22 Seat belt tensioning mechanism – general information

All models covered in this manual are fitted with a front seat belt pyrotechnic tensioner system. The system is designed to

instantaneously take up any slack in the seat belt in the case of a sudden frontal impact, therefore reducing the possibility of injury to the front seat occupants. Each front seat is fitted with its own system, the components of which are mounted on the seat frame.

The seat belt tensioner is triggered by a frontal impact causing a deceleration of six times the force of gravity or greater. Lesser impacts, including impacts from behind, will not trigger the system.

When the system is triggered, a pretensioned spring draws back the seat belt via a cable which acts on the seat belt stalk. The cable can move by up to 80.0 mm, which therefore reduces the slack in the seat belt around the shoulders and waist of the occupant by a similar amount.

There is a risk of injury if the system is triggered inadvertently when working on the vehicle, and it is therefore strongly recommended that any work involving the seat belt tensioner system is entrusted to a Vauxhall/Opel dealer. Refer to the warning given at the beginning of Section 23 before contemplating any work on the front seats.

### 23 Seat belt components – removal and refitting

⚠️ **Warning: The front seats are fitted with pyrotechnic seat belt tensioners which are triggered by the airbag control system. Before removing a seat belt, disconnect the battery and wait at least 2 minutes to allow the system capacitors to discharge.**

### *Front belt and reel*

#### Removal

**1** Unclip the cover over the seat belt mounting on the front seat, by releasing it at the rear, then disengaging the front locating tabs **(see illustration 21.3)**.

**2** Undo the seat belt retaining bolt **(see illustration 21.4)**.

**3** Remove the B-pillar inner trim panel and sill trim panel as described in Section 24.

**4** Undo the seat belt upper mounting bolt.

**5** Prise the cover from the lower outside of

23.5a Prise the cover from the lower outside of the B-pillar . . .

23.5b . . . for access to the front seat belt reel mounting nut

**23.10 Undo the retaining bolt (arrowed) and withdraw the tensioner from the seat**

**23.11 Release the cable retaining clip (arrowed) and remove the tensioner**

**23.15 Undo the seat belt lower mounting bolt (arrowed)**

the B-pillar for access to the front seat belt reel mounting nut **(see illustrations)**. Using a 13 mm socket, 65 mm deep on the inside, unscrew the nut taking care not to drop it inside the B-pillar. Note that an extension pin is provided to enable the nut to be removed safely.

**6** With the nut removed, remove the reel from the inside of the pillar.

### Refitting

**7** Refitting is a reversal of removal, but tighten the mounting bolts to the specified torque.

## Front belt stalk and tensioner

### Removal

**8** Remove the front seat as described in Section 21.

**9** From underneath the seat, slide out the wiring connector locking bar and disconnect the wiring connector. Unclip the wiring harness from the seat.

**10** Undo the retaining bolt and withdraw the tensioner from the seat **(see illustration)**.

**11** Release the cable retaining clip and remove the tensioner **(see illustration)**.

### Refitting

**12** Refitting is a reverse of the removal procedure, noting the following points:

 a) *Remove all traces of old thread-locking compound from the thread of the tensioner retaining bolt, and clean the threaded hole in the seat, ideally by running a tap of the correct size and pitch down it.*

 b) *Apply a suitable thread-locking compound to the thread of the tensioner retaining bolt. Refit the bolt, and tighten it to the specified torque setting.*

## Rear outer belt and reel

### Removal

**13** Remove the rear seat cushion as described in Section 21.

**14** Remove the relevant luggage compartment side trim panels as described in Section 24.

**15** Undo the seat belt lower mounting bolt **(see illustration)**.

**16** Undo the seat belt reel mounting bolt and remove the reel and belt from the car **(see illustration)**.

**23.16 Undo the seat belt reel mounting bolt (arrowed) and remove the reel and belt from the car**

**23.20 Rear seat belt stalk retaining bolts**

### Refitting

**17** Refitting is a reversal of removal, but tighten the mounting bolts to the specified torque.

## Rear centre belt and reel

**18** The inertia reel for the centre rear seat belt is located internally within the rear seat backrest. To gain access, the backrest must be removed and completely dismantled. This is a complex operation and considerable expertise is needed to remove and refit the seat upholstery and internal components without damage. Therefore, any problems with the centre seat belt and reel should be referred to a Vauxhall/Opel dealer.

## Rear belt stalk

### Removal

**19** Remove the rear seat cushion as described in Section 21.

**20** Undo the retaining bolt and remove the relevant stalk from the floor **(see illustration)**.

### Refitting

**21** Refitting is a reversal of removal, but tighten the mounting bolts to the specified torque.

---

**24 Interior trim –** removal and refitting

**1** The interior trim panels are secured by a combination of clips and screws. Removal

and refitting is generally self-explanatory, noting that it may be necessary to remove or loosen surrounding panels to allow a particular panel to be removed. The following paragraphs describe the general removal and refitting details of the major panels on 5-door Hatchback and Estate models. The procedures are generally similar on 3-door Hatchback models, although some differences will be encountered in the luggage compartment area.

## A-pillar trim panel

**2** Pull off the front door weather strip in the vicinity of the A-pillar trim panel.

**3** On models equipped with curtain airbags, pull out the airbag positioning clip from the trim panel **(see illustration)**.

**4** Pull the trim panel away from the A-pillar and remove it from the car **(see illustration)**.

**24.3 Pull out the airbag positioning clip from the trim panel**

24.4 Pull the trim panel away from the A-pillar and remove it from the car

24.9 Prise out the plastic cover at the top of the panel

24.10 Prise the upper and lower parts of the trim panel away from the B-pillar

24.11a Feed the seat belt through the opening . . .

24.11b . . . and remove the panel from the car

24.12 Lift the tongue at the base of the upper panel, then release the retaining pegs (arrowed) while pulling the panels apart

5 Refitting is a reversal of removal.

### B-pillar trim panel

6 Unclip the cover over the seat belt mounting on the front seat, by releasing it at the rear, then disengaging the front locating tabs (see illustration 21.3).
7 Undo the seat belt retaining bolt (see illustration 21.4).
8 Remove the side sill inner trim panel as described later in this Section.
9 Prise out the plastic cover at the top of the panel (see illustration).
10 Starting at the top, prise the upper and lower parts of the trim panel away from the B-pillar (see illustration).
11 Feed the seat belt through the opening and remove the panel from the car (see illustrations).
12 To separate the upper and lower parts of

the panel, lift the tongue at the base of the upper panel, then release the retaining peg at each side, while pulling the panels apart (see illustration).
13 Refitting is a reversal of removal, but tighten the seat belt retaining bolt to the specified torque.

### Side sill inner trim panel

14 Open the front and rear doors and pull the weatherstrip away from the B-pillar and the lower part of the door apertures.
15 Using a small screwdriver, carefully disengage the sill trim panel from the B-pillar lower trim (see illustration).
16 Lift the panel upwards to unclip it from the sill and remove the panel from the car (see illustration).
17 Refitting is a reversal of removal.

### Tailgate aperture upper centre trim panel

18 Open the tailgate.
19 Pull the panel away to release the internal clips, and remove the panel from the car (see illustration).
20 Refitting is a reversal of removal.

### Tailgate aperture lower centre trim panel

21 Open the tailgate.
22 Remove the luggage compartment floor covering.
23 Undo the four panel retaining screws (see illustration).
24 Pull the panel away to release the internal clips, and remove the panel from the car.
25 Refitting is a reversal of removal.

24.15 Disengage the side sill trim panel from the B-pillar lower trim

24.16 Lift the panel upwards to unclip it from the sill

24.19 Pull the tailgate aperture panel away to release the internal clips, and remove the panel from the car

**24.23  Undo the four lower panel retaining screws**

**24.27a  Pull the upper part of the panel away from the C-pillar and roof . . .**

**24.27b  . . . then disengage the panel from the lower side trim**

**24.31  Pull out the centre pin and extract the expanding rivet**

**24.32  Pull the panel away from the pillar to release the internal clips**

**24.33  Slide the seat belt out through the slot in the panel, then remove the panel from the car**

## D-pillar trim panel – Estate models

26  Remove the tailgate aperture upper centre trim panel as described previously.

27  Pull the upper part of the panel away from the C-pillar and roof to release the internal clips. Disengage the panel from the lower side trim panel and remove it from the car (see illustration).

28  Refitting is a reversal of removal.

## C-pillar lower trim panel

29  Remove the rear seat cushion and rear seat backrest as described in Section 21.

30  Remove the side sill inner trim panel as described previously.

31  Pull out the centre pin and extract the expanding rivet securing the base of the panel to the C-pillar (see illustration).

32  Pull the panel away from the pillar to release the internal clips (see illustration).

33  Slide the seat belt out through the slot in the panel, then remove the panel from the car (see illustration).

34  Refitting is a reversal of removal.

## Luggage compartment side trim panel – Hatchback models

35  Remove the luggage compartment floor covering.

36  Remove the C-pillar lower trim panel as described previously.

37  Undo the rear seat belt lower mounting bolt.

38  Prise out the plastic cover at the top of the panel upper part (see illustration).

39  Pull the panel out to disengage the retaining clips and release the panel from the pillar (see illustration).

40  Feed the seat belt through the panel opening and remove the panel from the car (see illustration).

41  Undo the three screws securing the panel lower part to the pillar (see illustration).

**24.38  Prise out the plastic cover at the top of the panel upper part**

**24.39  Pull the panel out to disengage the retaining clips**

**24.40  Feed the seat belt through the panel opening and remove the panel from the car**

**24.41  Undo the three screws (arrowed) securing the panel lower part to the pillar**

24.42 Pull the panel out to disengage the retaining clips and release the panel from the pillar

24.46 Remove the rear light cluster access panel from the lower part of the side trim panel

24.47 Carefully prise out the luggage compartment light, disconnect the wiring and remove the light

**42** Pull the panel out to disengage the retaining clips and release the panel from the pillar **(see illustration)**.
**43** Refitting is a reversal of removal, but tighten the seat belt mounting bolt to the specified torque.

### Luggage compartment side trim panel – Estate models

**44** Remove the luggage compartment floor covering.
**45** Remove the D-pillar trim panel and the C-pillar lower trim panel as described previously.
**46** Remove the rear light cluster access panel from the lower part of the side trim panel **(see illustration)**.
**47** Carefully prise out the luggage compart-

ment light, disconnect the wiring connector and remove the light **(see illustration)**.
**48** Using a forked tool, prise out the retaining plates at the front and rear of the upper part of the panel **(see illustration)**.
**49** Undo the retaining screw located at the front and rear corners of the panel upper part **(see illustrations)**.
**50** Lift the front end of the panel upper part, pull the panel out to disengage the retaining clips and remove the upper part from the car **(see illustration)**.
**51** Using a forked tool, prise out the retaining plates at the base of the lower part of the panel **(see illustration)**.
**52** Pull the panel out to disengage the retaining clips and remove the lower part from the car **(see illustration)**.

**53** Refitting is a reversal of removal.

### C-pillar upper trim panel – Estate models

**54** Remove the luggage compartment side trim panel as described previously.
**55** Undo the rear seat belt lower mounting bolt.
**56** Prise out the plastic cover at the top of the panel **(see illustration)**.
**57** Pull the panel out to disengage the retaining clips and release the panel from the C-pillar **(see illustration)**.
**58** Feed the seat belt through the panel opening and remove the panel from the car **(see illustration)**.
**59** Refitting is a reversal of removal, but tighten the seat belt mounting bolt to the specified torque.

24.48 Prise out the retaining plates at the front and rear of the upper part of the panel

24.49a Undo the retaining screw located at the front corner . . .

24.49b . . . and rear corner (arrowed) of the panel upper part

24.50 Lift the front end of the panel upper part, then pull the panel out to disengage the retaining clips

24.51 Prise out the retaining plates at the base of the lower part of the panel

24.52 Pull the panel out to disengage the retaining clips and remove the lower part from the car

24.56 Prise out the plastic cover at the top of the panel

24.57 Pull the panel out to disengage the retaining clips and release the panel from the C-pillar

24.58 Feed the seat belt through the panel opening and remove the panel from the car

## Interior mirror

60 On models fitted with a rain sensor, unclip and remove the sensor trim panel, then release the retaining clip(s) and disconnect the wiring connectors from the mirror assembly.

61 Press the retaining clip at the top of the interior mirror mounting bracket, then carefully release the interior mirror in the downwards direction to remove it from the windscreen.

62 Refitting is the reverse of removal.

## 25 Centre console – removal and refitting

### Removal

1 Disconnect the battery negative terminal (refer to *Disconnecting the battery* in the Reference Chapter).

2 Unclip and remove the access panel in the centre console, beneath the handbrake lever (see illustration).

3 Unclip the cover from around the handbrake lever (see illustration).

4 At the rear of the console, remove the stowage box by pulling it upward to release the retaining clips (see illustration).

5 Unscrew the nut, now exposed, securing the rear of the console to the floor (see illustration).

6 Move both front seats fully forward and undo the console rear retaining screws on both sides.

7 Undo the screw below the handbrake lever

securing the console to the support bracket (see illustration).

8 At the front of the console, prise out the trim caps and undo the screw each side securing

the console to the base of the facia (see illustrations).

9 Using a small screwdriver, carefully prise up the right-hand side of the ashtray, withdraw the

25.2 Unclip and remove the access panel beneath the handbrake lever

25.3 Unclip the cover from around the handbrake lever

25.4 Remove the stowage box by pulling it upward to release the retaining clips

25.5 Console rear retaining nut (A) and left-hand side retaining screw (B)

25.7 Undo the screw (arrowed) below the handbrake lever

25.8a Prise out the trim caps . . .

25.8b . . . and undo the screw (arrowed) each side

25.9a Carefully prise up the right-hand side of the ashtray . . .

25.9b . . . then withdraw the ashtray and disconnect the wiring connector

25.10a Undo the two screws securing the rear of the gear lever gaiter trim panel to the console . . .

25.10b . . . lift the panel up at the rear and disengage it from the console at the front

25.11 Undo the two screws (arrowed) securing the front of the console to the facia

ashtray from the centre console and disconnect the wiring connector (see illustrations).

10 Undo the two screws securing the rear of the gear lever gaiter trim panel to the centre console. Lift the panel up at the rear and disengage it from the centre console at the front (see illustrations).

11 Undo the two screws securing the front of the console to the centre of the facia (see illustration).

12 Lift the console up and slide it to the rear to disengage the front guides from the lugs on the facia (see illustrations).

13 Feed the gear lever gaiter trim panel through the console aperture and remove the console from the car.

### Refitting

14 Refitting is a reversal of removal.

## 26 Facia panel components – removal and refitting

### Glovebox

#### Removal

1 Open the glovebox lid and undo the four screws securing the glovebox to the facia (see illustration).

25.12a Lift the console up and slide it to the rear . . .

25.12b . . . to disengage the front guides (arrowed) from the lugs on the facia

26.1 Undo the four screws (arrowed) securing the glovebox to the facia

26.2 Withdraw the glovebox from the facia and disconnect the glovebox light wiring connector

**26.8a Undo the two centre panel lower retaining screws (arrowed) . . .**

**26.8b . . . then pull the panel away from the facia to release the upper retaining lugs (arrowed)**

**26.9 Lift up the locking bar and disconnect the wiring connector**

**2** Withdraw the glovebox from the facia, disconnect the glovebox light wiring connector and remove the glovebox from the car **(see illustration)**.

### Refitting

**3** Refitting is a reversal of removal.

## *Facia centre panel*

### Removal

**4** Disconnect the battery negative terminal (refer to *Disconnecting the battery* in the Reference Chapter).
**5** Remove the centre console as described in Section 25.
**6** Remove the radio/cassette/CD player as described in Chapter 12.
**7** Remove the heater control assembly as described in Chapter 3.
**8** Undo the two centre panel lower retaining screws, then pull the panel away from the facia to release the upper retaining lugs **(see illustrations)**.
**9** Lift up the locking bar and disconnect the wiring connector, then remove the panel from the car **(see illustration)**.

### Refitting

**10** Refitting is a reversal of removal.

## *Driver's side lower trim panel*

### Removal

**11** Remove the headlight switch as described in Chapter 12.
**12** Remove the steering column shrouds as described later in this Section.
**13** Working in the headlight switch aperture, undo the two screws securing the upper part of the panel to the facia **(see illustration)**.
**14** Undo the two panel lower securing screws beneath the steering column.
**15** Swivel the panel down and detach the lower lugs from the facia tube **(see illustration)**. Remove the panel from the car.

### Refitting

**16** Refitting is a reversal of removal.

## *Steering column shrouds*

### Removal

**17** Turn the steering wheel as necessary to access the left and right front retaining screws.

**26.13 Undo the two screws (arrowed) in the switch aperture securing the lower trim panel to the facia**

**18** Carefully prise off the screw trim cap and undo the front retaining screw now exposed **(see illustrations)**. Repeat this procedure on the other side of the shroud.

**26.15 Swivel the panel down and detach the lower lugs from the facia tube**

**19** Undo the lower shroud lower retaining screw **(see illustration)**.
**20** Carefully prise free the circular trim panel around the ignition switch **(see illustration)**.

**26.18a Carefully prise off the screw trim cap . . .**

**26.18b . . . and undo the front retaining screw now exposed**

**26.19 Undo the lower shroud lower retaining screw**

**26.20 Carefully prise free the circular trim panel around the ignition switch**

**26.21a  Lift up the upper column shroud and undo the right-hand retaining screw (arrowed) . . .**

**26.21b  . . . and left-hand retaining screw (arrowed) securing the lower shroud to the steering column**

**26.22  Remove the lower shroud from the steering column**

**26.23  Unclip the upper shroud from the instrument panel and remove it from the car**

**26.33  Carefully release the facia decorative strip using a plastic spatula or similar tool**

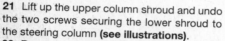

**26.35  Carefully prise out the sun sensor panel from the top of the facia**

**21**  Lift up the upper column shroud and undo the two screws securing the lower shroud to the steering column **(see illustrations)**.

**22**  Remove the lower shroud from the steering column **(see illustration)**.

**23**  Unclip the upper shroud from the instrument panel and remove it from the car **(see illustration)**.

### Refitting

**24**  Refitting is a reversal of removal.

## Complete facia assembly

**Note:** *This is an involved operation entailing the removal of numerous components and assemblies, and the disconnection of a multitude of wiring connectors. Make notes on the location of all disconnected wiring, or attach labels to the connectors, to avoid confusion when refitting.*

### Removal

**25**  Disconnect the battery negative terminal (refer to *Disconnecting the battery* in the Reference Chapter).

**26**  Remove the A-pillar trim panels on both sides as described in Section 24.

**27**  Remove the side sill inner trim panel on both sides as described in Section 24.

**28**  Remove the centre console as described in Section 25.

**29**  Remove the steering wheel as described in Chapter 10.

**30**  Remove the following facia panels as described previously in this Section:

a) Glovebox.
b) Facia centre panel.
c) Driver's side lower trim panel.
d) Steering column shrouds.

**31**  Remove the following components as described in Chapter 12:

a) Steering column electronics module.
b) Instrument panel.
c) Information display.

**32**  Remove the steering column as described in Chapter 10.

**33**  Carefully release the facia decorative strip on the passenger's side using a plastic spatula or similar tool **(see illustration)**.

**34**  Extract the plastic rivets and remove the footwell air duct on the driver's and passenger's side.

**35**  Carefully prise out the sun sensor panel from the top of the facia and disconnect the wiring connector (where fitted) **(see illustration)**.

**36**  Remove the trim caps at the left-hand and right-hand ends of the facia **(see illustration)**.

**37**  Undo the following fasteners securing the facia to the mounting brackets **(see illustrations)**:

a) 1 bolt in the sun sensor aperture.
b) 1 bolt at the left-hand and right-hand end.

**26.36  Remove the trim caps at the left-hand and right-hand ends of the facia**

**26.37a  Undo the bolt in the sun sensor aperture**

**26.37b  Undo the bolt (arrowed) at each end of the facia**

**26.37c Undo the bolt (arrowed) at the left-hand floor bracket . . .**

**26.37d . . . and the three bolts (arrowed) at the right-hand floor bracket**

**26.37e Undo the bolt (arrowed) at the lower corner of the facia each side**

*c) 4 bolts at the centre floor brackets.*
*d) 1 bolt each side at the lower left-hand and right-hand corners of the facia.*

**38** With the help of an assistant, carefully lift the facia from its location. Check that all wiring has been disconnected, then remove the facia from the car.

## Refitting

**39** Refitting is a reversal of removal ensuring that all wiring is correctly reconnected and all mountings securely tightened.

## *Facia crossmember*

**Note:** *This is an involved operation entailing the disconnection of a multitude of wiring connectors. Make notes on the location of all disconnected wiring, or attach labels to the connectors, to avoid confusion when refitting.*

## Removal

**40** Remove the facia as described previously in this Section.

**41** Remove the steering column as described in Chapter 10.
**42** Remove the passenger's airbag as described in Chapter 12.
**43** Remove the front doors as described in Section 11.
**44** Remove the brake pedal as described in Chapter 9.
**45** Remove the clutch pedal as described in Chapter 6.
**46** Undo the bolts securing the crossmember centre supports to the floor brackets.
**47** Disconnect all remaining earth cables and wiring connections, making careful notes as to their locations.
**48** From outside the car, undo the two bolts securing the crossmember to the A-pillar on each side **(see illustration)**.
**49** With the help of an assistant, check that all wiring has been disconnected, then remove the crossmember from the car.

**26.48 Undo the two bolts (arrowed) securing the crossmember to the A-pillar on each side**

## Refitting

**50** Refitting is a reversal of removal ensuring that all wiring is correctly reconnected and all mountings securely tightened.

# Chapter 12
# Body electrical systems

## Contents

## Degrees of difficulty

| | | | | |
|---|---|---|---|---|
| **Easy,** suitable for novice with little experience | **Fairly easy,** suitable for beginner with some experience | **Fairly difficult,** suitable for competent DIY mechanic | **Difficult,** suitable for experienced DIY mechanic | **Very difficult,** suitable for expert DIY or professional |

## Specifications

**System type** ................................................. 12 volt negative earth

**Bulbs** — **Wattage**

| Bulbs | Wattage |
|---|---|
| Direction indicator side repeater | 5 |
| Direction indicator | 21 |
| Front foglight | 55 |
| Headlight | 55 |
| Interior lights | 10 |
| Number plate light | 10 |
| Rear foglight | 21 |
| Reversing light | 21 |
| Sidelight | 5 |
| Stop/tail-light | 21/5 |

## 1 General information and precautions

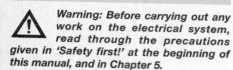

**Warning: Before carrying out any work on the electrical system, read through the precautions given in 'Safety first!' at the beginning of this manual, and in Chapter 5.**

1 The electrical system is of the 12 volt negative earth type. Power for the lights and all electrical accessories is supplied by a lead-acid type battery, which is charged by the engine-driven alternator.

2 This Chapter covers repair and service procedures for the various electrical components not associated with the engine. Information on the battery, alternator and starter motor can be found in Chapter 5.

3 It should be noted that, prior to working on any component in the electrical system, the battery negative terminal should first be disconnected, to prevent the possibility of electrical short-circuits and/or fires.

*Caution: Before proceeding, refer to 'Disconnecting the battery' in the Reference Chapter for further information.*

## 2 Electrical fault finding – general information

*Note: Refer to the precautions given in 'Safety first!' and in Section 1 before starting work. The following tests relate to testing of the main electrical circuits, and should not be used to test delicate electronic circuits (such as the anti-lock braking system or fuel injection system), particularly where an electronic control unit is used.*

### General

1 A typical electrical circuit consists of an electrical component, any switches, relays, motors, fuses, fusible links or circuit breakers related to that component, and the wiring and connectors which link the component to both the battery and the vehicle body. To help to pinpoint a problem in an electrical circuit, wiring diagrams are shown at the end of this Chapter.

2 Before attempting to diagnose an electrical fault, first study the appropriate wiring diagram to obtain a complete understanding of the components included in the particular circuit concerned. The possible sources of a fault can be narrowed down by noting if other components related to the circuit are operating properly. If several components or circuits fail at one time, the problem is likely to be related to a shared fuse or earth connection.

3 Electrical problems usually stem from simple causes, such as loose or corroded connections, a faulty earth connection, a blown fuse, a melted fusible link, or a faulty relay (refer to Section 3 for details of testing relays). Inspect the condition of all fuses, wires and connections in a problem circuit before testing the components. Use the wiring diagrams to determine which terminal connections will need to be checked in order to pinpoint the trouble-spot.

4 The basic tools required for electrical fault finding include a circuit tester or voltmeter (a 12 volt bulb with a set of test leads can also be used for certain tests); a self-powered test light (sometimes known as a continuity tester); an ohmmeter (to measure resistance); a battery and set of test leads; and a jumper wire, preferably with a circuit breaker or fuse incorporated, which can be used to bypass suspect wires or electrical components. Before attempting to locate a problem with test instruments, use the wiring diagram to determine where to make the connections.

5 To find the source of an intermittent wiring fault (usually due to a poor or dirty connection, or damaged wiring insulation), a 'wiggle' test can be performed on the wiring. This involves wiggling the wiring by hand to see if the fault occurs as the wiring is moved. It should be possible to narrow down the source of the fault to a particular section of wiring. This method of testing can be used in conjunction with any of the tests described in the following sub-Sections.

6 Apart from problems due to poor connections, two basic types of fault can occur in an electrical circuit – open-circuit, or short-circuit.

7 Open-circuit faults are caused by a break somewhere in the circuit, which prevents current from flowing. An open-circuit fault will prevent a component from working, but will not cause the relevant circuit fuse to blow.

8 Short-circuit faults are caused by a 'short' somewhere in the circuit, which allows the current flowing in the circuit to 'escape' along an alternative route, usually to earth. Short-circuit faults are normally caused by a breakdown in wiring insulation, which allows a feed wire to touch either another wire, or an earthed component such as the bodyshell. A short-circuit fault will normally cause the relevant circuit fuse to blow.

### Finding an open-circuit

9 To check for an open-circuit, connect one lead of a circuit tester or voltmeter to either the negative battery terminal or a known good earth.

10 Connect the other lead to a connector in the circuit being tested, preferably nearest to the battery or fuse.

11 Switch on the circuit, bearing in mind that some circuits are live only when the ignition switch is turned to a particular position.

12 If voltage is present (indicated either by the tester bulb lighting or a voltmeter reading, as applicable), this means that the section of the circuit between the relevant connector and the battery is problem-free.

13 Continue to check the remainder of the circuit in the same fashion.

14 When a point is reached at which no voltage is present, the problem must lie between that point and the previous test point with voltage. Most problems can be traced to a broken, corroded or loose connection.

### Finding a short-circuit

15 To check for a short-circuit, first disconnect the load(s) from the circuit (loads are the components which draw current from a circuit, such as bulbs, motors, heating elements, etc).

16 Remove the relevant fuse from the circuit, and connect a circuit tester or voltmeter to the fuse connections.

17 Switch on the circuit, bearing in mind that some circuits are live only when the ignition switch is turned to a particular position.

18 If voltage is present (indicated either by the tester bulb lighting or a voltmeter reading, as applicable), this means that there is a short-circuit.

19 If no voltage is present, but the fuse still blows with the load(s) connected, this indicates an internal fault in the load(s).

### Finding an earth fault

20 The battery negative terminal is connected to 'earth' – the metal of the engine/transmission unit and the car body – and most systems are wired so that they only receive a positive feed, the current returning via the metal of the car body. This means that the component mounting and the body form part of that circuit. Loose or corroded mountings can therefore cause a range of electrical faults, ranging from total failure of a circuit, to a puzzling partial fault. In particular, lights may shine dimly (especially when another circuit sharing the same earth point is in operation), motors (eg, wiper motors or the radiator cooling fan motor) may run slowly, and the operation of one circuit may have an apparently-unrelated effect on another. Note that on many vehicles, earth straps are used between certain components, such as the engine/transmission and the body, usually where there is no metal-to-metal contact between components, due to flexible rubber mountings, etc.

21 To check whether a component is properly earthed, disconnect the battery, and connect one lead of an ohmmeter to a known good earth point. Connect the other lead to the wire or earth connection being tested. The resistance reading should be zero; if not, check the connection as follows.

22 If an earth connection is thought to be faulty, dismantle the connection, and clean back to bare metal both the bodyshell and the wire terminal or the component earth connection mating surface. Be careful to remove all traces of dirt and corrosion, then use a knife to trim away any paint, so that a clean metal-to-metal joint is made. On reassembly, tighten the joint fasteners securely; if a wire terminal is being refitted, use serrated washers between the terminal

**3.2 Access to the fuses in the luggage compartment can be gained by opening the stowage compartment cover**

**3.3 Release the catches and lift off the fuse/relay box cover for access to the engine compartment fuses**

**3.4 Pull the fuse out of its terminals using the plastic removal tool provided**

and the bodyshell, to ensure a clean and secure connection. When the connection is remade, prevent the onset of corrosion in the future by applying a coat of petroleum jelly or silicone-based grease. Alternatively, at regular intervals, spray on a proprietary ignition sealer or a water-dispersant lubricant.

### 3 Fuses and relays – general information

#### Fuses

1 The main fuses are located behind the trim panel on the left-hand side of the luggage compartment, with additional fuses and relays located in the fuse/relay box on the left-hand side of the engine compartment.
2 To gain access to the luggage compartment fuses, turn the catches and open the cover **(see illustration)**.
3 To gain access to the engine compartment fuses, release the catches using a small screwdriver and lift off the fuse/relay box cover **(see illustration)**.
4 To remove a fuse, first switch off the circuit concerned (or the ignition), then pull the fuse out of its terminals using the plastic removal tool provided **(see illustration)**. The wire within the fuse is clearly visible; if the fuse is blown, it will be broken or melted.
5 Always renew a fuse with one of an identical rating; never use a fuse with a different rating from the original, nor substitute anything else. Never renew a fuse more than once without tracing the source of the trouble. The fuse rating is stamped on top of the fuse; note that the fuses are also colour-coded for easy recognition.
6 If a new fuse blows immediately, find the cause before renewing it again; a short to earth as a result of faulty insulation is most likely. Where a fuse protects more than one circuit, try to isolate the defect by switching on each circuit in turn (if possible) until the fuse blows again. Always carry a supply of spare fuses of each relevant rating on the vehicle, a spare of each rating should be clipped into the base of the fuse/relay box.

#### Relays

7 Most of the relays are located in the fuse/relay boxes in the luggage compartment and engine compartment **(see illustrations 3.2 and 3.3)**.
8 If a circuit or system controlled by a relay develops a fault and the relay is suspect, operate the system; if the relay is functioning, it should be possible to hear it click as it is energised. If this is the case, the fault lies with the components or wiring of the system. If the relay is not being energised, then either the relay is not receiving a main supply or a switching voltage, or the relay itself is faulty. Testing is by the substitution of a known good unit, but be careful; while some relays are identical in appearance and in operation, others look similar but perform different functions.
9 To renew a relay, first ensure that the ignition switch is off. The relay can then simply be pulled out from the socket and the new relay pressed in.

### 4 Switches – removal and refitting

**Note:** *Disconnect the battery negative terminal (refer to 'Disconnecting the battery' in the Reference Chapter) before removing any switch, and reconnect the terminal after refitting.*

#### Ignition switch/ steering column lock

1 Refer to Chapter 10.

#### Steering column switches

2 The direction indicator and windscreen wiper switches are an integral part of the steering column electronics module, and cannot be individually renewed.
3 To remove the steering column electronics module, which also contains the airbag rotary connector, proceed as described in Section 17.

#### Lighting switch assembly

4 With the light switch knob in the off position, press the knob in and turn it to the AUTO position (vehicles with automatic dipped beam activation), or to the vertical position (sidelights 'on'). The switch assembly internal catch is now unlocked and the switch assembly can be withdrawn from the facia **(see illustrations)**. Once the switch is released, turn the switch off.
5 Release the locking catch and disconnect the switch wiring connector.
6 Note that the switch assembly cannot be dismantled; if any of its functions are faulty, the complete assembly must be renewed.
7 Reconnect the wiring connector and push the switch back into the facia.

#### Facia centre switches

8 The facia centre switches are contained in the switch strip assembly located in the facia

**4.4a Press the switch knob in and turn it to the appropriate position . . .**

**4.4b . . . then withdraw the switch assembly from the facia**

**4.9a Turn the switch strip retaining catches a quarter of a turn . . .**

**4.9b . . . and withdraw the switch strip from the centre panel**

**4.16 Release the retaining clip and push the rear of the switch out of the trim panel**

**4.17 Disengage the control switch front locating tab (arrowed) and remove the switch**

**4.19a Carefully prise out the rear control switch assembly . . .**

**4.19b . . . and disconnect the wiring connector**

centre panel. If an individual switch is faulty the complete switch strip must be renewed. To gain access to the switch, remove the facia centre panel as described in Chapter 11, Section 26.

**9** With the facia centre panel removed, turn the switch strip retaining catches a quarter of a turn and withdraw the switch strip from the centre panel **(see illustration)**.

**10** Refit the switch strip and turn the retaining catches back a quarter of a turn to lock the assembly in position.

**11** Refit the facia centre panel as described in Chapter 11, Section 26.

## Heated rear window/ blower motor switch

**12** The heated rear window and blower motor switches are an integral part of the heater control assembly. Removal and refitting procedures are contained in Chapter 3.

### Handbrake warning light switch

**13** Refer to Chapter 9.

### Stop-light switch

**14** Refer to Chapter 9.

### Electric window/mirror switches

#### Front door

**15** Remove the front door inner trim panel as described in Chapter 11, Section 12.

**16** Carefully release the retaining clip and push the rear of the switch out of the trim panel **(see illustration)**.

**17** Disengage the switch front locating tab and remove the switch from the panel **(see illustration)**.

**18** Refitting is the reverse of removal.

#### Rear door

**19** Carefully prise out the switch assembly

and disconnect the wiring connector **(see illustrations)**.

**20** Refitting is the reverse of removal.

### Air conditioning system switch

**21** The air conditioning system control switch is an integral part of the heating/ventilation control unit, and cannot be removed. Should the switch become faulty, the complete control unit assembly must be renewed (see Chapter 3).

### Steering wheel switches

**22** Turn the steering wheel so that the switch retaining screw opening is accessible, then undo the retaining screw from the rear of the steering wheel **(see illustration)**.

**23** Unclip the switch surround from the steering wheel, then disconnect the wiring connector from the switch **(see illustration)**.

**24** Refitting is the reverse of removal.

**4.22 Undo the retaining screw from the rear of the steering wheel to release the switches**

**4.23 Unclip the switch surround from the steering wheel, then disconnect the switch wiring connector**

## 5 Bulbs (exterior lights) – renewal

### General

**1** Whenever a bulb is renewed, note the following points:

a) Make sure the switch is in the OFF position, for the respective bulb you are working on.

b) Remember that if the light has just been in use, the bulb may be extremely hot.

c) Always check the bulb contacts and

**5.1 Open the flap in the wheel arch liner for access to the outer bulbs in the headlight unit**

**5.2 Remove the outer plastic cover from the rear of the headlight**

**5.3 Rotate the dipped beam bulbholder anti-clockwise to release the bayonet fitting**

holder, ensuring that there is clean metal-to-metal contact between the bulb and its live(s) and earth. Clean off any corrosion or dirt before fitting a new bulb.

d) Wherever bayonet-type bulbs are fitted, ensure that the live contact(s) bear firmly against the bulb contact.

e) Always ensure that the new bulb is of the correct rating, and that it is completely clean before fitting it; this applies particularly to headlight/foglight bulbs.

### Halogen type headlight unit

**Note 1:** If working on the outer bulb in the headlight unit, turn the steering on to full lock for access under the wheel arch. Open the flap in the wheel arch liner for access to the rear of the headlight unit **(see illustration)**.

**Note 2:** If working on the inner bulb in the headlight unit, remove the air intake duct at the front of the air cleaner housing (right-hand side) or unclip the wiring harness connector from the front of the fuse/relay box (left-hand side).

**Note 3:** The outer bulb in the headlight unit is the dipped beam bulb and the inner bulb is the main beam bulb.

### Dipped beam

**2** Remove the plastic cover from the rear of the headlight unit **(see illustration)**.

**3** Rotate the bulbholder anti-clockwise to release the bayonet fitting, then withdraw the bulbholder from the light unit **(see illustration)**.

**4** Hold the bulb by its base and withdraw it

from the bulbholder **(see illustration)**. When handling the new bulb, use a tissue or clean cloth to avoid touching the glass with the fingers; moisture and grease from the skin can cause blackening and rapid failure of this type of bulb. If the glass is accidentally touched, wipe it clean using methylated spirit.

**5** Fit the new bulb to the bulbholder, then refit the bulbholder to the headlight unit. Turn the bulbholder clockwise to lock it in position.

**6** Refit the plastic cover to the rear of the headlight unit, then refit any components removed for access.

### Main beam

**7** Remove the plastic cover from the rear of the headlight unit **(see illustration)**.

**8** Disconnect the wiring connector from the rear of the bulb **(see illustration)**.

**9** Compress the legs of the retaining spring

**5.4 Hold the bulb by its base and withdraw it from the bulbholder**

clip and pivot the clip off the bulb. Lift the bulb out of the light unit **(see illustrations)**. When handling the new bulb, use a tissue or clean cloth to avoid touching the glass with the fingers; moisture and grease from the skin can cause blackening and rapid failure of this type of bulb. If the glass is accidentally touched, wipe it clean using methylated spirit.

**10** Fit the new bulb to the headlight unit and secure with the spring clip. Reconnect the wiring connector.

**11** Refit the plastic cover to the rear of the headlight unit, then refit any components removed for access.

### Front sidelight

**12** Remove the main beam plastic cover from the rear of the headlight unit **(see illustration 5.7)**.

**13** Withdraw the sidelight bulbholder from the

**5.7 Remove the inner plastic cover from the rear of the headlight**

**5.8 Disconnect the wiring connector (arrowed) from the rear of the bulb**

**5.9a Compress the legs of the retaining spring clip (arrowed) and pivot the clip off the bulb . . .**

**5.9b . . . then lift the bulb out of the light unit**

5.13a Withdraw the sidelight bulbholder from the rear of the headlight unit

5.13b The bulb is a push-fit in the bulbholder

5.15 Twist the indicator bulbholder anti-clockwise, and remove it from the rear of the headlight unit

5.16 The bulb is a bayonet fit in the bulbholder

rear of the headlight unit. The bulb is of the capless (push-fit) type, and can be removed by simply pulling it out of the bulbholder **(see illustrations)**.

14 Refitting is the reverse of the removal procedure, ensuring that the bulbholder is fully engaged. On completion, refit any components removed for access.

### Front indicator

15 Twist the indicator bulbholder anti-clockwise, and remove it from the rear of the headlight unit **(see illustration)**.

16 The bulb is a bayonet fit in the holder, and can be removed by pressing it and twisting in an anti-clockwise direction **(see illustration)**.

17 Refitting is a reverse of the removal procedure. On completion, refit any components removed for access.

## Xenon type headlight unit

⚠️ **Warning: Xenon dipped beam headlights operate at very high voltage. Do not touch the associated wiring when the headlights are switched on.**

**Note:** The outer bulb in the headlight unit is the main beam bulb and the inner bulb is the dipped beam bulb.

### Dipped beam

18 Remove the headlight unit as described in Section 7.

19 Undo the three screws and lift off the plastic cover at the rear of the headlight unit.

20 Disconnect the xenon starter unit from the bulb by turning it anti-clockwise.

21 Compress the legs of the retaining spring clip and pivot the clip off the bulb. Withdraw the bulb from the rear of the headlight unit.

22 When handling the new bulb, use a tissue or clean cloth to avoid touching the glass with the fingers; moisture and grease from the skin can cause blackening and rapid failure of this type of bulb. If the glass is accidentally touched, wipe it clean using methylated spirit.

23 Install the new bulb, ensuring that its locating tabs are correctly located in the headlight unit cut-outs. Secure the bulb with the retaining spring clip and reconnect the starter unit. Turn the starter unit clockwise to lock it in position

24 Refit the plastic cover to the rear of the unit, then refit the headlight unit as described in Section 7.

### Main beam

25 Renewal of the main beam bulb is as described previously in this Section for the halogen type headlight unit.

### Front sidelight

26 Renewal of the front sidelight bulb is as described previously in this Section for the halogen type headlight unit.

### Front indicator

27 Renewal of the front indicator bulb is as described previously in this Section for the halogen type headlight unit.

## Indicator side repeater

28 Push the light unit toward the front door, and release the front edge of the unit from the wing. If necessary, assist removal using a suitable plastic wedge, taking great care not damage the painted finish of the wing.

29 Withdraw the light unit from the wing, and pull the bulbholder out of the light unit. The bulb is of the capless (push-fit) type, and can be removed by simply pulling it out of the bulbholder.

30 Refitting is a reverse of the removal procedure.

## Front foglight

31 Reach up under the front bumper, twist the cover and free it from the foglight unit **(see illustration)**.

32 Release the spring clip and withdraw the foglight bulb from the light unit **(see illustration)**.

33 Disconnect the wiring connector and remove the bulb **(see illustration)**.

5.31 Twist the cover and free it from the foglight unit

5.32 Release the spring clip and withdraw the foglight bulb from the light unit

5.33 Disconnect the wiring connector and remove the bulb

**5.39 Disconnect the wiring connector from the bulbholder**

**5.40 Release the sealing grommet from the top of the light cluster**

**5.42 Unscrew the plastic nuts and withdraw the light cluster from the rear wing**

**5.43 On 5-door models, undo the three screws (arrowed) securing the bulbholder to the light cluster**

**5.44a On 5-door models, depress the two locking tabs on the side of the bulbholder . . .**

**5.44b . . . and withdraw the bulbholder from the light cluster**

**34** When handling the new bulb, use a tissue or clean cloth to avoid touching the glass with the fingers; moisture and grease from the skin can cause blackening and rapid failure of this type of bulb. If the glass is accidentally touched, wipe it clean using methylated spirit.

**35** Connect the wiring connector to the new bulb.

**36** Insert the new bulb, making sure it is correctly located, and secure it in position with the spring clip.

**37** Refit the cover to the rear of the unit.

### *Rear light cluster*

#### Hatchback models

**38** Turn the catch(es), where applicable, and remove the access cover from the luggage compartment trim panel.

**39** Reach in through the trim panel opening and disconnect the wiring connector from the bulbholder (see illustration).

**40** Using a small screwdriver, release the sealing grommet from the top of the light cluster (see illustration).

**41** Use the wheelbrace from the tool kit to slacken the two light cluster plastic retaining nuts.

**42** Hold the light cluster from the outside and unscrew the plastic nuts by hand the rest of the way. Withdraw the light cluster from the rear wing (see illustration).

**43** On 5-door models, undo the three screws securing the bulbholder to the rear of the light cluster (see illustration).

**44** On 5-door models, depress the two locking tabs on the side of the bulbholder and withdraw the bulbholder from the light cluster. (see illustrations). On 3-door models, release the four retaining clips and withdraw the bulbholder from the light cluster.

**45** The relevant bulb can then be renewed; all bulbs have a bayonet fitting (see illustration).

Note that the stop/tail-light bulb has offset locating pins, to prevent it being installed incorrectly.

**46** Refitting is the reverse of the removal sequence, bearing in mind the following points:

a) *Ensure that the bulbholder locates securely in position on the light cluster.*

b) *Ensure that the rubber seals are in place on the bulbholder, locating pegs and retaining studs before refitting the light cluster.*

c) *Re-engage the sealing grommet with the top of the light cluster after refitting.*

#### Estate models

**47** Press the catches and remove the access cover from the luggage compartment trim panel (see illustration).

**48** Reach in through the trim panel opening and use the wheelbrace from the tool kit to slacken the three light cluster plastic retaining nuts (see illustration).

**5.45 The relevant bulb can then be renewed**

**5.47 Remove the access cover from the luggage compartment trim panel**

**5.48 Slacken the three light cluster plastic nuts (arrowed)**

5.50 Withdraw the light cluster and disconnect the wiring connector

5.51a Lift off the rubber seal from the rear of the bulbholder . . .

5.51b . . . undo the three retaining screws (arrowed) . . .

5.51c . . . and separate the bulbholder from the light cluster

5.52 The relevant bulb can then be renewed

5.54 Carefully prise the number plate light unit out from its location

**49** Hold the light cluster from the outside and unscrew the plastic nuts by hand the rest of the way.
**50** Withdraw the light cluster from the rear wing and disconnect the wiring connector **(see illustration)**.

**51** Lift off the rubber seal from the rear of the bulbholder, then undo the three retaining screws and separate the bulbholder from the light cluster **(see illustrations)**.
**52** The relevant bulb can then be renewed; all bulbs have a bayonet fitting **(see illustration)**.

Note that the stop/tail-light bulb has offset locating pins, to prevent it being installed incorrectly.
**53** Refitting is the reverse of the removal sequence.

### Number plate light

**54** Using a small flat-bladed screwdriver, carefully prise the light unit out from its location **(see illustration)**.
**55** Twist the bulbholder to remove it from the light unit, and remove the bulb **(see illustrations)**.
**56** Refitting is a reverse of the removal procedure.

### High-level stop-light

**57** The high-level stop-light bulbs are of the LED (light emitting diode) type and cannot be individually renewed. Remove the complete light unit as described in Section 7.

5.55a Twist the bulbholder to remove it from the light unit . . .

5.55b . . . and remove the push-fit bulb

## 6 Bulbs (interior lights) – renewal

### General

**1** Refer to Section 5, paragraph 1.

### Front courtesy light

**2** Using a small screwdriver, carefully prise the light unit lens from the overhead console **(see illustration)**.
**3** Pull the relevant bulb from its socket **(see illustration)**.

6.2 Carefully prise the light unit lens from the overhead console

6.3 Pull the relevant bulb from its socket

**6.8 Carefully prise the luggage compartment light unit out of position and release the bulb from the contacts**

**6.10a Carefully prise up the right-hand side of the ashtray . . .**

**6.10b . . . withdraw the ashtray from the centre console and disconnect the wiring connector**

**6.13a Carefully prise the glovebox light unit out of position . . .**

**6.13b . . . then release the bulb from its contacts**

**6.16 Twist and remove the relevant bulb-holder from the rear of the information display**

**4** Install the new bulb, ensuring that it is securely held in position by the contacts, and clip the light unit lens back into position.

### Rear courtesy light

**5** Using a suitable screwdriver, carefully prise the right-hand side of the light unit out of position, and withdraw the light unit.
**6** Release the locking plate and disconnect the wiring connector. Remove the relevant bulb from the light unit.
**7** Install the new bulb, ensuring that it is securely held in position by the contacts. Refit the wiring connector and locking plate, then clip the light unit back into position.

### Luggage compartment light

**8** Using a suitable screwdriver, carefully prise the light unit out of position, and release the bulb from the light unit contacts **(see illustration)**.
**9** Install the new bulb, ensuring that it is securely held in position by the contacts, and clip the light unit back into position.

### Cigarette lighter/ ashtray illumination

**10** Using a small screwdriver, carefully prise up the right-hand side of the ashtray, withdraw the ashtray from the centre console and disconnect the wiring connector at the rear of the cigarette lighter socket **(see illustrations)**.
**11** Using a small screwdriver, depress the retaining lug and withdraw the bulbholder from the lighter socket. Remove the bulb from the bulbholder.
**12** Refitting is a reverse of the removal procedure.

### Glovebox light

**13** Open the glovebox. Using a small flat-bladed screwdriver, carefully prise the light unit out of position, then release the bulb from its contacts **(see illustrations)**. Install the new bulb, ensuring it is securely held in position by the contacts, and clip the light unit back into position.

### Switch illumination

**14** All the switches are fitted with illumination bulbs; some are also fitted with a bulb to show when the circuit concerned is operating. These bulbs are an integral part of the switch assembly, and cannot be obtained separately.

### Information display illumination

**15** Remove the information display unit as described in Section 10.
**16** Twist and remove the relevant bulbholder

**7.2a Undo the lower retaining bolt (arrowed) . . .**

from the rear of the unit **(see illustration)**. The bulbs are integral with the bulbholders.
**17** Fit the new bulbholder and bulb, then refit the information display unit as described in Section 10.

---

### 7 Exterior light units – removal and refitting

**Note:** *Disconnect the battery negative terminal (refer to 'Disconnecting the battery' in the Reference Chapter) before removing any light unit, and reconnect the terminal after refitting.*

### Headlight

⚠️ **Warning: Xenon dipped beam headlights operate at very high voltage. Do not touch the associated wiring when the headlights are switched on.**

**1** Remove the front bumper as described in Chapter 11, Section 6.
**2** Undo the three retaining bolts and withdraw the headlight unit from the vehicle. Disconnect the wiring connectors from rear of the headlight unit as it is withdrawn **(see illustrations)**.
**3** On models fitted with halogen type headlight units, the headlight beam adjustment motor can be removed and refitted as follows. Note that a new adjustment motor cover will be required to carry out this procedure.
**4** Using a suitable knife cut around the circumference of the adjustment motor cover at the joint between the cover and the rear of the headlight unit. Remove and discard the

**7.2b ... the upper outer retaining bolt (arrowed) ...**

**7.2c ... and the upper inner retaining bolt (arrowed)**

**7.2d ... then withdraw the headlight unit ...**

**7.2e ... and disconnect the wiring connector**

cover. Rotate the adjustment motor clockwise to free the motor from the rear of the headlight unit. Unclip the balljoint from the rear of the light reflector and disconnect the wiring connector.

**5** On refitting, align the motor balljoint with the light unit socket, and clip it into position. Engage the motor assembly with the light, and twist it anti-clockwise to secure it in position. Obtain a new adjustment motor cover and secure it to the headlight unit using three self-tapping screws in the holes provided.

**6** Refitting is a reverse of the removal procedure. On completion, check the headlight beam alignment using the information given in Section 8.

### Front indicator light

**7** The front direction indicator lights are integral with the headlight units. Removal and refitting is as described above.

### Indicator side repeater light

**8** Push the light unit toward the front door, and release the front edge of the unit from the wing. If necessary, assist removal using a suitable plastic wedge, taking great care not damage the painted finish of the wing.

**9** Withdraw the light unit from the wing, and disconnect its wiring connector. Tie a piece of string to the wiring, to prevent it falling back into the wing.

**10** On refitting, connect the wiring connector, and clip the light unit back into position.

### Front foglight

**11** Working under the front bumper, undo the three foglight retaining bolts, disconnect the wiring connector and remove the light unit from the bumper.

**12** Refit the light unit to the bumper, and securely tighten its retaining bolts.

**13** Reconnect the wiring connector.

### Rear light cluster

#### Hatchback models

**14** Turn the catch (es), where applicable, and remove the access cover from the luggage compartment trim panel.

**15** Reach in through the trim panel opening and disconnect the wiring connector from the bulbholder **(see illustration 5.39)**.

**16** Using a small screwdriver, release the sealing grommet from the top of the light cluster **(see illustration 5.40)**.

**17** Use the wheelbrace from the tool kit to slacken the two light cluster plastic retaining nuts.

**18** Hold the light cluster from the outside and unscrew the plastic nuts by hand the rest of the way. Withdraw the light cluster from the rear wing **(see illustration 5.42)**.

**19** Refitting is the reverse of the removal sequence, bearing in mind the following points:

a) *Ensure that the rubber seals are in place on the bulbholder, locating pegs and retaining studs before refitting the light cluster.*

b) *Re-engage the sealing grommet with the top of the light cluster after refitting.*

#### Estate models

**20** Press the catches and remove the access cover from the luggage compartment trim panel **(see illustration 5.47)**.

**21** Reach in through the trim panel opening and use the wheelbrace from the tool kit to slacken the three light cluster plastic retaining nuts **(see illustration 5.48)**.

**22** Hold the light cluster from the outside and unscrew the plastic nuts by hand the rest of the way.

**23** Withdraw the light cluster from the rear wing and disconnect the wiring connector **(see illustration 5.50)**.

**24** Refitting is the reverse of the removal sequence.

### Number plate light

**25** Using a small flat-bladed screwdriver, carefully prise the light unit out from its location **(see illustration 5.54)**.

**26** Twist the bulbholder to remove it from the light unit.

**27** Refitting is the reverse of the removal sequence.

### High-level stop-light

**28** Using a suitably protected spatula or similar thin tool, insert the tool between the light unit and tailgate at the lower right-hand corner. Push up on the tool, while at the same time pulling up on the light unit, to release the first of the six retaining clips. Work around the light unit to release the remaining clips and withdraw the unit from the tailgate **(see illustrations)**.

**29** Disconnect the wiring connector, and on Hatchback models, also disconnect the tailgate washer hose from the jet **(see**

**7.28a Using a thin tool, depress the retaining clips while at the same time pulling up on the light unit ...**

**7.28b ... then withdraw the unit from the tailgate**

**7.29a Disconnect the wiring connector . . .**

**7.29b . . . and on Hatchback models, also disconnect the tailgate washer hose from the jet**

illustrations). Remove the stop-light unit from the tailgate.

30 Reconnect the wiring connector and, where applicable, the washer hose, then push the light unit into the tailgate until it locks in position.

## 8  Headlight beam alignment – general information

1 Accurate adjustment of the headlight beam is only possible using optical beam-setting equipment, and this work should therefore be carried out by a Vauxhall/Opel dealer or suitably-equipped workshop.
2 For reference, the headlights can be adjusted using the adjuster assemblies fitted to the top of each light unit. The inner adjuster, alters the vertical position of the beam. The outer adjuster alters the horizontal aim of the beam.
3 Most models have an electrically-operated headlight beam adjustment system, controlled via a switch in the facia. The recommended settings are as follows.

0  Front seat(s) occupied
1  All seats occupied
2  All seats occupied, and load in luggage compartment
3  Driver's seat occupied and load in the luggage compartment

**Note:** *When adjusting the headlight aim, ensure that the switch is set to position 0.*

## 9  Instrument panel – removal and refitting

**Note:** *The instrument panel is a complete* sealed assembly, and no dismantling of the instrument panel is possible.

### Removal

1 Disconnect the battery negative terminal (refer to *Disconnecting the battery* in the Reference Chapter).
2 Remove the steering column shrouds as described in Chapter 11, Section 26.
3 Undo the two lower retaining screws, then pull the panel away from the facia at the bottom (**see illustrations**).
4 Disengage the top of the panel from the facia, disconnect the wiring connector and remove the panel from the car (**see illustration**).

### Refitting

5 Refitting is a reversal of removal.

## 10  Information display unit – removal and refitting

### Removal

1 Disconnect the battery negative terminal (refer to *Disconnecting the battery* in the Reference Chapter).
2 Remove the facia centre panel as described in Chapter 11, Section 26.
3 Undo the two lower retaining screws and withdraw the information display unit from the facia (**see illustrations**).
4 Disconnect the wiring connector and remove the unit from the car (**see illustration**).

**9.3a Undo the instrument panel left-hand lower retaining screw (arrowed) . . .**

**9.3b . . . and right-hand lower retaining screw (arrowed)**

**9.4 Disengage the top of the panel from the facia and disconnect the wiring connector**

**10.3a Undo the two screws (arrowed) . . .**

**10.3b . . . and withdraw the information display unit from the facia**

**10.4 Disconnect the wiring connector and remove the unit from the car**

**12.2 The horns are located under the front bumper on the right-hand side**

### Refitting

5 Refitting is a reversal of removal.

## 11 Cigarette lighter – removal and refitting

The cigarette lighter is an integral part of the ashtray. Proceed as described in Section 6, paragraphs 10 to 12.

## 12 Horn – removal and refitting

### Removal

1 Firmly apply the handbrake, then jack up the front of the car and support it securely on axle stands (see *Jacking and vehicle support*). Remove the wheel arch lower panel on the right-hand side.

2 Working under the bumper on the right-hand side, undo the retaining nut/bolt and remove the horn(s), disconnecting the wiring connector as it becomes accessible **(see illustration)**.

### Refitting

3 Refitting is the reverse of removal.

## 13 Wiper arm – removal and refitting

### Removal

1 Operate the wiper motor, then switch it off so that the wiper arm returns to the at-rest (parked) position.

 **HAYNES HINT** *Stick a piece of masking tape along the edge of the wiper blade, to use as an alignment aid on refitting.*

2 Unclip the wiper arm spindle nut cover (windscreen wiper arm), or pivot the cover up (tailgate wiper arm), then slacken and remove the spindle nut and washer **(see illustrations)**.

3 Using a suitable puller, free the wiper arm from the spindle and remove the arm **(see illustration)**. **Note:** *If both windscreen wiper arms are to be removed at the same time, mark them for identification. The arms are not interchangeable; the passenger-side wiper arm is longer than the driver's-side arm, and its shaft is also cranked slightly.*

### Refitting

4 Ensure that the wiper arm and spindle splines are clean and dry, then refit the arm to the spindle, aligning the wiper blade with the tape fitted on removal. Refit the spindle nut, tightening it securely, and clip the nut cover back in position.

## 14 Windscreen wiper motor and linkage – removal and refitting

### Removal

1 Disconnect the battery negative terminal (refer to *Disconnecting the battery* in the Reference Chapter).

2 Remove the wiper arms as described in the Section 13.

3 Remove the water deflector as described in Chapter 11, Section 20.

4 Undo the three retaining bolts, and withdraw the wiper motor and linkage assembly from the scuttle **(see illustrations)**.

5 Disconnect the wiring connector from the wiper motor and remove the assembly from the car **(see illustration)**.

6 If necessary, mark the relative positions of the motor shaft and linkage arm, then unscrew the retaining nut from the motor spindle. Free

**13.2a Unclip the windscreen wiper arm spindle nut cover . . .**

**13.2b . . . then slacken and remove the spindle nut . . .**

**13.2c . . . and collect the washer**

**13.3 Using a suitable puller, free the wiper arm from the spindle**

**14.4a Undo the four retaining bolts (arrowed) . . .**

**14.4b . . . and withdraw the wiper motor and linkage assembly**

the wiper linkage from the spindle, then remove the three motor retaining bolts, and separate the motor and linkage (see illustration).

### Refitting

**7** Where necessary, assemble the motor and linkage, and securely tighten the motor retaining bolts. Locate the linkage arm on the motor spindle, aligning the marks made prior to removal, and securely tighten its retaining nut.

**8** Reconnect the wiper motor wiring connector, then manoeuvre the motor assembly back into position in the vehicle. Refit the retaining bolts, and tighten them securely.

**9** Refit the water deflector as described in Chapter 11, Section 20.

**10** Install both the wiper arms as described in Section 13, and reconnect the battery negative terminal.

## 15 Tailgate wiper motor – removal and refitting

### Removal

**1** On Hatchback models, unhook the lifting cords and remove the parcel shelf from the luggage compartment. Unscrew the parcel shelf lifting pins on each side.

**2** Remove the tailgate upper side trim panel, by prising it free at the sides, then at the centre to release the internal retaining clips. On some models, the panel is in two parts with a join at the centre. In this case, remove the left-hand panel first, followed by the right-hand panel. (see illustrations).

**3** Pull out the expanding rivet and undo the retaining screw (where fitted), securing the lock cover panel to the base of the tailgate (see illustration). Remove the panel.

**4** On Estate models, pull out the expanding rivet each side, securing the tailgate lower trim panel to the tailgate, and unscrew the two screws at the top of the panel (see illustrations).

**5** On all models, pull the lower trim panel away from the tailgate to release the remaining internal clips and remove the panel from the tailgate (see illustration).

**6** Remove the wiper arm as described in Section 13.

**14.5 Disconnect the wiper motor wiring connector and remove the assembly from the car**

**15.2a Remove the tailgate upper side trim panel, by prising it free at the sides . . .**

**7** Disconnect the wiring connector, then slacken and remove the three wiper motor mounting bolts and remove the wiper motor (see illustration).

**15.3 Pull out the expanding rivet (A) and undo the retaining screw (B) (where fitted)**

**14.6 Wiper motor retaining bolts (arrowed)**

**15.2b . . . then at the centre to release the internal retaining clips**

### Refitting

**8** Refitting is the reverse of removal, ensuring the wiper motor retaining bolts are securely tightened.

**15.4a On Estate models, pull out the expanding rivet each side . . .**

**15.4b . . . and unscrew the two screws at the top of the panel**

**15.5 Pull the lower trim panel away from the tailgate to release the remaining internal clips**

**15.7 Tailgate wiper motor mounting bolts (arrowed)**

**16.2 Unscrew the bolt (arrowed) securing the filler neck to the bonnet crossmember**

**16.3 Disconnect the wiring connector (A) and washer hoses at the washer pump (B)**

**16.4 Washer reservoir retaining bolt (arrowed)**

**16.7 Ease the pump out from the reservoir and recover its sealing grommet**

**16.10 Depress the retaining clip, then prise the washer nozzle from the water deflector panel**

**16.16 Carefully extract the washer jet from the tailgate**

## 16 Windscreen/tailgate washer system components – removal and refitting

### Washer system reservoir

**1** Remove the front bumper as described in Chapter 11, Section 6.

**2** Unscrew the bolt securing the filler neck to the bonnet crossmember **(see illustration)**.

**3** Disconnect the wiring connector(s) and washer hoses at the washer pump(s), then release the wiring and hoses from the side of the reservoir **(see illustration)**.

**4** Undo the retaining bolt (two bolts on some models, according to equipment) and lower the reservoir out from under the car **(see illustration)**.

**5** Refitting is the reverse of removal, ensuring that the washer hose(s) are securely connected.

### Washer pump

**6** Remove the front bumper as described in Chapter 11, Section 6.

**7** Disconnect the pump washer hoses, then carefully ease the pump out from the reservoir and recover its sealing grommet **(see illustration)**.

**8** Refitting is the reverse of removal, using a new sealing grommet if the original one shows signs of damage or deterioration.

### Windscreen washer jets

**9** Remove the water deflector as described in Chapter 11, Section 20

**10** Depress the retaining clip, then carefully prise the nozzle from the water deflector panel **(see illustration)**.

**11** Disconnect the nozzle from its fluid hose(s), and remove it from the vehicle.

**12** On refitting, securely connect the nozzle to the hose, and clip it into position in the water deflector panel. Refit the water deflector panel, then check the operation of the jet. If necessary, adjust the nozzle using a pin, aiming the spray to a point slightly above the centre of the swept area.

### Tailgate washer jet

#### Hatchback models

**13** Remove the high-level stop-light as described in Section 7.

**14** Release the two retaining lugs and remove the washer jet from the stop-light unit.

**15** When refitting, ensure that the jet is clipped securely in position. Check the operation of

**17.6 Undo the three bolts (arrowed) securing the electronics module to the steering column**

the jet. If necessary, adjust the nozzle using a pin, aiming the spray to a point slightly above the centre of the swept area.

#### Estate models

**16** Carefully extract the washer jet from the tailgate **(see illustration)**.

**17** Disconnect the fluid hose and remove the jet from the car.

**18** When refitting, ensure that the jet is clipped securely in position. Check the operation of the jet. If necessary, adjust the nozzle using a pin, aiming the spray to a point slightly above the centre of the swept area.

## 17 Steering column electronics module – removal and refitting

### Removal

**1** Disconnect the battery negative terminal (refer to *Disconnecting the battery* in the Reference Chapter) and wait for 2 minutes.

**2** Remove the driver's airbag as described in Section 24.

**3** Set the roadwheels in the straight-ahead position and ensure they remain in that position during the removal and refitting procedures.

**4** Remove the steering wheel as described in Chapter 10.

**5** Remove the steering column shrouds as described in Chapter 11, Section 26.

**6** Undo the three bolts securing the module to the steering column **(see illustration)**.

**7** Withdraw the module from the steering

**17.7 Withdraw the module from the steering column and disconnect the wiring connector**

**17.8a Insert a thin rod down the slot on the side of the stalk to depress the internal retaining lug . . .**

**17.8b . . . then withdraw the stalk from the electronics module**

column, disconnect the wiring connector and remove the module **(see illustration)**.

**8** If required the direction indicator and wiper switch stalks can be removed from the module as follows. Insert a 1.5 mm diameter rod down the slot on the side of the stalk. Push the rod in fully, to depress the internal retaining lug and withdraw the stalk from the module **(see illustrations)**. Note that this procedure merely allows the stalks to be removed, the actual direction indicator and wiper switches themselves are an integral part of the electronics module and cannot be removed.

### Refitting

**9** If removed, push the switch stalks back into position in the module until they lock into place.
**10** Refit the electronics module to the steering wheel using a reverse of the removal procedure.

### 18 Radio/cassette/CD player – removal and refitting

**Note:** *The following removal and refitting procedure is for the range of radio/cassette/ CD units which Vauxhall/Opel fit as standard equipment. Removal and refitting procedures of non-standard units may differ slightly.*

### Removal

**1** All the radio/cassette/CD players fitted by Vauxhall have DIN standard fixings. Two

special tools, obtainable from most car accessory shops, are required for removal. Alternatively, suitable tools can be fabricated from 3 mm diameter wire, such as welding rod.
**2** Disconnect the battery negative terminal (refer to *Disconnecting the battery* in the Reference Chapter).
**3** Insert the tools into the holes on the front of the unit, and push them until they snap into place. The radio/cassette/CD player can then be slid out of the facia **(see illustration)**.
**4** Disconnect the wiring and aerial connections at the rear of the unit, and remove the unit from the car.

### Refitting

**5** To refit the radio/cassette player/CD, reconnect the wiring and simply push the unit into the facia until the retaining lugs snap into

**18.3 Removing the radio/cassette/CD player using welding rod to compress the internal clips**

place. On completion, reconnect the battery and enter the radio security code, where applicable.

### 19 Speakers – removal and refitting

### Front door small (tweeter) speaker

**1** Carefully prise off the door mirror interior trim panel to release the three retaining clips **(see illustration)**.
**2** Remove the foam insulation from the mirror interior trim panel and disconnect the speaker wiring connector **(see illustrations)**.
**3** Withdraw the speaker from the panel **(see illustration)**.
**4** Refitting is the reverse of removal.

**19.1 Carefully prise off the door mirror interior trim panel to release the three retaining clips**

**19.2a Remove the foam insulation from the mirror interior trim panel . . .**

**19.2b . . . and disconnect the speaker wiring connector**

**19.3 Withdraw the speaker from the mirror trim panel**

**19.6 Door loudspeaker retaining screws (arrowed)**

### Door main speaker

**Note:** *On 3-door Hatchback models, a rear speaker is fitted behind the rear interior trim panel. Remove the trim panel and proceed as described in paragraphs 6 and 7.*

**5** Remove the door inner trim panel as described in Chapter 11.

**6** Undo the retaining screws, then free the speaker from its location **(see illustration)**. Disconnect the wiring connectors and remove the speaker.

**7** Refitting is the reverse of removal.

### 20 Radio aerial – general information

**1** Where required, the aerial mast can be unscrewed from the base unit.

**2** Removal of the base unit entails removal of the headlining, which is a complicated operation, considered to be outside the scope of this manual. Therefore, any problems relating to the aerial base unit or wiring should be entrusted to a Vauxhall/Opel dealer.

### 21 Anti-theft alarm system – general information

**Note:** *This information is applicable only to the anti-theft alarm system fitted by Vauxhall/Opel as standard equipment.*

**1** Most models in the range are fitted with an anti-theft alarm system as standard equipment. The alarm is automatically armed and disarmed when the deadlocks are operated using the driver's door lock or remote control key. The alarm has switches on all the doors (including the tailgate), the bonnet, the radio/cassette/CD player and the ignition and starter circuits. If the tailgate, bonnet or any of the doors are opened whilst the alarm is set, the alarm horn will sound and the hazard warning lights will flash. The alarm also has an immobiliser function which makes the ignition and starter circuits inoperable whilst the alarm is triggered.

**2** The alarm system performs a self-test every time it is switched on; this test takes approximately 10 seconds. During the

self-test, the LED (light emitting diode) in the hazard warning light switch will come on. If the LED flashes, then either the tailgate, bonnet or one of the doors is open, or there is a fault in the circuit. After the initial 10-second period, the LED will flash to indicate that the alarm is switched on. On unlocking the driver's door lock, the LED will illuminate for approximately 1 second, then go out, indicating that the alarm has been switched off.

**3** With the alarm set, if the tailgate is unlocked, the tailgate switch sensing will automatically be switched off, but the door and bonnet switches will still be active. Once the tailgate is shut and locked again, the tailgate switch sensing will be switched back on after approximately 10 seconds.

**4** Should the alarm system develop a fault, the vehicle should be taken to a Vauxhall/Opel dealer for examination.

### 22 Heated seat components – general information

On models with heated seats, a heater mat is fitted to both the seat back and seat cushion. Renewal of either heater mat involves peeling away the upholstery, removing the old mat, sticking the new mat in position and then refitting the upholstery. Note that upholstery removal and refitting requires considerable skill and experience if it is to be carried out successfully, and is therefore best entrusted to your Vauxhall/Opel dealer. In practice, it will be very difficult for the home mechanic to carry out the job without ruining the upholstery.

### 23 Airbag system – general information and precautions

#### General information

A driver's airbag is fitted as standard equipment on all models. The airbag is fitted in the steering wheel centre pad. Additionally, a passenger's airbag located in the facia, side airbags located in the front seats, and curtain airbags located in the headlining are optionally available.

The system is armed only when the ignition is switched on, however, a reserve power source maintains a power supply to the system in the event of a break in the main electrical supply. The steering wheel and facia airbags are activated by a 'g' sensor (deceleration sensor), and controlled by an electronic control unit located under the centre console. The side airbags and curtain airbags are activated by severe side impact and operate independently of the main system. A separate electrical supply, control unit and sensor is provided for the side/curtain airbags on each side of the car.

The airbags are inflated by a gas generator,

which forces the bag out from its location in the steering wheel, facia, seat back frame, or headlining.

#### Precautions

 **Warning: The following precautions must be observed when working on vehicles equipped with an airbag system, to prevent the possibility of personal injury.**

#### General precautions

The following precautions **must** be observed when carrying out work on a vehicle equipped with an airbag:

a) *Do not disconnect the battery with the engine running.*

b) *Before carrying out any work in the vicinity of the airbag, removal of any of the airbag components, or any welding work on the vehicle, de-activate the system as described in the following sub-Section.*

c) *Do not attempt to test any of the airbag system circuits using test meters or any other test equipment.*

d) *If the airbag warning light comes on, or any fault in the system is suspected, consult a Vauxhall/Opel dealer without delay. Do not attempt to carry out fault diagnosis, or any dismantling of the components.*

#### Precautions when handling an airbag

a) *Transport the airbag by itself, bag upward.*

b) *Do not put your arms around the airbag.*

c) *Carry the airbag close to the body, bag outward.*

d) *Do not drop the airbag or expose it to impacts.*

e) *Do not attempt to dismantle the airbag unit.*

f) *Do not connect any form of electrical equipment to any part of the airbag circuit.*

#### Precautions when storing an airbag

a) *Store the unit in a cupboard with the airbag upward.*

b) *Do not expose the airbag to temperatures above 80°C.*

c) *Do not expose the airbag to flames.*

d) *Do not attempt to dispose of the airbag – consult a Vauxhall/Opel dealer.*

e) *Never refit an airbag which is known to be faulty or damaged.*

### De-activation of airbag system

The system must be de-activated before carrying out any work on the airbag components or surrounding area:

a) *Switch on the ignition and check the operation of the airbag warning light on the instrument panel. The light should illuminate when the ignition is switched on, then extinguish.*

b) *Switch off the ignition.*

c) *Remove the ignition key.*

d) *Switch off all electrical equipment.*

e) *Disconnect the battery negative terminal (refer to 'Disconnecting the battery' in the Reference Chapter).*

**24.2a Insert a screwdriver into the holes at the rear of the steering wheel (shown with steering wheel removed) . . .**

**24.2b . . . to depress the airbag internal spring retainers (arrowed – shown with airbag removed)**

**24.3 Release the locking clips, then disconnect the wiring connectors**

f) *Insulate the battery negative terminal and the end of the battery negative lead to prevent any possibility of contact.*

g) *Wait for at least two minutes before carrying out any further work. Wait at least ten minutes if the airbag warning light did not operate correctly.*

## Activation of airbag system

To activate the system on completion of any work, proceed as follows:

a) *Ensure that there are no occupants in the vehicle, and that there are no loose objects around the vicinity of the steering wheel. Close the vehicle doors and windows.*

b) *Ensure that the ignition is switched off then reconnect the battery negative terminal.*

c) *Open the driver's door and switch on the ignition, without reaching in front of the steering wheel. Check that the airbag warning light illuminates briefly then extinguishes.*

d) *Switch off the ignition.*

e) *If the airbag warning light does not operate as described in paragraph c), consult a Vauxhall/Opel dealer before driving the vehicle.*

**24 Airbag system components –** removal and refitting

⚠ **Warning: Refer to the precautions given in Section 23 before attempting to carry out work on any of the airbag components.**

**1** De-activate the airbag system as described in the previous Section, then proceed as described under the relevant heading.

### Driver's airbag

**2** Turn the steering wheel through 90° so that the two holes at the rear of the steering wheel spokes are accessible. Insert a screwdriver into the holes, one at a time, to depress the internal spring retainers, and at the same time pull the airbag unit away from the steering wheel to release it **(see illustrations)**.

**3** Release the locking clips, then disconnect the wiring connectors at the rear of the airbag unit **(see illustration)**. Remove the airbag unit. Note that the airbag must not be knocked or dropped, and should be stored the correct way up, with its padded surface uppermost.

**4** Refitting is a reversal of the removal procedure.

### Passenger's airbag

**5** Remove the complete facia assembly as described in Chapter 11, Section 26.

**6** Undo the bolt securing the airbag to the facia crossmember **(see illustration)**. Withdraw the airbag and disconnect the wiring connector(s). Note that the airbag must not be knocked or dropped, and should be stored the correct way up (as mounted in the vehicle).

**7** Refitting is a reversal of the removal procedure, tightening the retaining bolt securely.

### Side airbags

**8** The side airbags are located internally within the front seat back and no attempt should be made to remove them. Any suspected

**24.6 Passenger's airbag retaining bolt (arrowed)**

problems with the side airbag system should be referred to a Vauxhall/Opel dealer.

### Curtain airbags

**9** The curtain airbags are located behind the headlining above the doors on each side and no attempt should be made to remove them. Any suspected problems with the curtain airbag system should be referred to a Vauxhall/Opel dealer.

### Airbag control unit

**10** The airbag control unit is located beneath the centre console and no attempt should be made to remove it. Any suspected problems with the control unit should be referred to a Vauxhall/Opel dealer.

### Airbag rotary connector

**11** The airbag rotary connector is an integral part of the steering column electronics module. Removal and refitting procedures for the module are contained in Section 17.

## VAUXHALL ASTRA wiring diagrams

**Diagram 1**

### Key to symbols

Dashed outline denotes part of a larger item, containing in this case an electronic or solid state device.

**XE2/11** - Connector No. **XE2**, pin No. **11**

Solenoid actuator

Heating element

Earth point & location

Wire colour (red with yellow tracer) — Rd/Ye —

Bulb

Switch

Fuse/fusible link **F26**

Resistor

Variable resistor

Variable resistor

Wire splice, soldered joint, or unspecified connector

Connecting wires

Diode

Light-emitting diode

Item number **12**

Motor/pump **M**

### Engine fusebox ④
(without rear electronic control unit)

| Fuse | Rating | Circuit protected |
|---|---|---|
| F1 | 20A | ABS |
| F2 | 30A | ABS |
| F3 | 30A | Heater blower, climate control system |
| F4 | 30A | Heater blower, heating, air conditioning |
| F5 | 30A | Engine cooling fan |
| | 40A | Engine cooling fan |
| F6 | 20A | Engine cooling fan |
| | 30A | Engine cooling fan |
| | 40A | Engine cooling fan |
| F7 | 20A | Central locking |
| F8 | 10A | Front washer, tailgate |
| F9 | 30A | Heated rear window, heated mirrors |
| F10 | 7.5A | Diagnostic connector |
| F11 | 7.5A | Instruments |
| F12 | 7.5A | Mobile telephone, audio system, display |
| F13 | 5A | Interior light |
| F14 | 30A | Front wiper |
| F15 | 30A | Front wiper |
| F16 | 5A | Horn, ABS, stop light switch, air conditioning |
| F17 | 25A | Diesel filter or air conditioning |
| F18 | 25A | Starter |
| F19 | 30A | Transmission electronics |
| F20 | 15A | Horn |
| F21 | 20A | Engine electronics |
| F22 | 7.5A | Engine electronics |
| F23 | 5A | Headlight levelling |
| F24 | 15A | Fuel pump |
| F25 | 5A | Reversing lights |
| F26 | 10A | Engine electronics |
| F27 | 7.5A | Heating, air conditioning, air quality sensor |
| F28 | - | Spare |
| F29 | 5A | Power steering |
| F30 | 10A | Engine electronics |
| F31 | 15A | Rear wiper |
| F32 | 5A | Stop light switch |
| F33 | 5A | Headlight levelling, light switch, clutch switch, instrument cluster, driver's door control unit |
| F34 | 7.5A | Steering column control unit |
| F35 | 20A | Infotainment system |
| F36 | 15A | Cigar lighter, front accessory socket |

### Engine fusebox ④
(with rear electronic control unit)

| Fuse | Rating | Circuit protected |
|---|---|---|
| F1 | 20A | ABS |
| F2 | 30A | ABS |
| F3 | 30A | Heater blower, climate control system |
| F4 | 30A | Heater blower, heating, air conditioning |
| F5 | 30A | Engine cooling fan |
| | 40A | Engine cooling fan |
| F6 | 20A | Engine cooling fan |
| | 30A | Engine cooling fan |
| | 40A | Engine cooling fan |
| F7 | 10A | Front washer |
| F8 | 15A | Horn |
| F9 | 25A | Headlight washer |
| F10 | - | Spare |
| F11 | - | Spare |
| F12 | - | Spare |
| F13 | 15A | Front foglights |
| F14 | 30A | Front wiper |
| F15 | 30A | Front wiper |
| F16 | 5A | Electronic control units, open & start system, ABS, stop light switch, TwinTop |
| F17 | 25A | Diesel filter heater |
| F18 | 25A | Starter |
| F19 | 30A | Transmission electronics |
| F20 | 10A | Air conditioning |
| F21 | 20A | Engine electronics |
| F22 | 7.5A | Engine electronics |
| F23 | 10A | Adaptive forward lighting, headlight levelling |
| F24 | 15A | Fuel pump |
| F25 | 15A | Transmission electronics |
| F26 | 10A | Engine electronics |
| F27 | 5A | Power steering |
| F28 | 5A | Transmission electronics |
| F29 | 7.5A | Transmission electronics |
| F30 | 10A | Engine electronics |
| F31 | 10A | Adaptive forward lighting |
| F32 | 5A | Stop light switch, air conditioning, clutch switch |
| F33 | 5A | Adaptive forward lighting, headlight levelling, light switch |
| F34 | 7.5A | Steering column control unit |
| F35 | 20A | Infotainment system |
| F36 | 7.5A | Mobile telephone, audio system, display |

H33731

## VAUXHALL ASTRA wiring diagrams

Diagram 2

### Rear fusebox 14
(without rear electronic control unit)

| Fuse | Rating | Circuit protected |
|------|--------|-------------------|
| F1 | 15A | Luggage compartment accessory socket |
| F2 | 15A | Rear accessory socket |
| F3 | 30A | Front electic windows |
| F4 | 30A | Rear electric windows |
| F5 | 7.5A | Heated mirrors |
| F6 | 10A | Air conditioning |

### Rear fusebox 14
(with rear electronic control unit)

| Fuse | Rating | Circuit protected |
|------|--------|-------------------|
| F1 | 25A | Front electric windows |
| F2 | - | Spare |
| F3 | 7.5A | Instrument cluster |
| F4 | 5A | Heating, air conditioning, climate control |
| F5 | 7.5A | Airbags |
| F6 | - | Spare |
| F7 | - | Spare |
| F8 | - | Spare |
| F9 | - | Spare |
| F10 | - | Spare |
| F11 | 25A | Heated rear window |
| F12 | 15A | Rear wiper |
| F13 | 5A | Parking distance sensors |
| F14 | 7.5A | Heating, air conditioning |
| F15 | - | Spare |
| F16 | 5A | Seat occupancy recognition, open & start system |
| F17 | 5A | Rain sensor, air quality sensor, tyre pressure monitor, interior mirror |
| F18 | 5A | Instruments, switches |
| F19 | - | Spare |
| F20 | 10A | CDC |
| F21 | 7.5A | Heated mirrors |
| F22 | 20A | Sunroof |
| F23 | 25A | Rear electric windows |
| F24 | 7.5A | Diagnostic connector |
| F25 | - | Spare |
| F26 | 7.5A | Retractable mirrors |
| F27 | 5A | Ultrasonic alarm sensor |
| F28 | - | Spare |
| F29 | 15A | Cigar lighter, front accessory socket |
| F30 | 15A | Rear accessory socket |
| F31 | - | Spare |
| F32 | - | Spare |
| F33 | 15A | Open & start |
| F34 | 25A | Sunroof, TwinTop |
| F35 | 15A | Rear accessory socket |
| F36 | 20A | Towing equipment |
| F37 | 5A | Interior light |
| F38 | 25A | Central locking |
| F39 | 15A | LH seat heater |
| F40 | 15A | RH seat heater |
| F41 | - | Spare |
| F42 | - | Spare |
| F43 | - | Spare |
| F44 | - | Spare |

### Earth locations

| | |
|---|---|
| E1 | Battery -ve terminal |
| E2 | On rear of engine |
| E3 | LH front wheel arch |
| E4 | LH front chassis leg |
| E5 | RH front chassis leg |
| E6 | LH front inner wing |
| E7 | LH front inner wing |
| E8 | Base of LH 'A' pillar |
| E9 | LH dashboard crossmember |
| E10 | Bracket on steering column |
| E11 | RH dashboard crossmember |
| E12 | Centre dashboard crossmember |
| E13 | Base of RH 'A' pillar |
| E14 | Transmission tunnel |
| E15 | Transmission tunnel |
| E16 | LH 'C' pillar |
| E17 | Near LH rear light |
| E18 | Below battery |
| E19 | Not used |
| E20 | Below battery |
| E21 | Near battery |
| E22 | Lh rear of engine |
| E23 | LH rear of engine |
| E24 | LH rear of engine |
| E25 | RH rear compartment (Twin Top only) |

### Key to circuits

| | |
|---|---|
| Diagram 1 | Information for wiring diagrams |
| Diagram 2 | Information for wiring diagrams |
| Diagram 3 | Typical starting, charging & engine cooling fans |
| Diagram 4 | Typical horn, stop & reversing lights, sidelights, tail lights, number plate lights, headlights |
| Diagram 5 | Typical foglights, direction indicators & hazard warning lights, trailer socket, headlight levelling (without xenon headlights) |
| Diagram 6 | Typical headlight levelling (with xenon headlights), interior lighting, cigar lighter & accessory socket, heated rear window |
| Diagram 7 | Typical heater & wash/wipe |
| Diagram 8 | Typical audio system, sunroof & electric mirrors |
| Diagram 9 | Typical electric windows, central locking |

H33732

## Wire colours

| | | | |
|---|---|---|---|
| Bk | Black | Pk | Pink |
| Ye | Yellow | Vt | Violet |
| Bu | Blue | Og | Orange |
| Bn | Brown | Wh | White |
| Gn | Green | Lgn | Light Green |
| Gy | Grey | Lbu | Light Blue |
| Pu | Purple | Dgn | Dark Green |
| Bg | Beige | DBu | Dark Blue |
| Rd | Red | | |

## Key to items

1 Battery
2 Alternator
3 Starter motor
4 Engine fusebox
a = under bonnet control unit
k1 = starter relay
k3 = terminal 15 relay
k11 = engine cooling fan relay
k12 = engine cooling fan relay
k13 = engine cooling fan relay

5 Steering column control unit
6 Engine cooling fan
7 Engine cooling fan relay

## Diagram 3

H33733

### Typical starting & charging

### Typical engine cooling fan - dual fan

### Typical engine cooling fan - single fan

## Wire colours

| | | | |
|---|---|---|---|
| **Bk** | Black | **Pk** | Pink |
| **Ye** | Yellow | **Vt** | Violet |
| **Bu** | Blue | **Og** | Orange |
| **Bn** | Brown | **Wh** | White |
| **Gn** | Green | **Lgn** | Light Green |
| **Gy** | Grey | **Lbu** | Light Blue |
| **Pu** | Purple | **Dgn** | Dark Green |
| **Bg** | Beige | **DBu** | Dark Blue |
| **Rd** | Red | | |

\* 5 door hatch
\*\* 3 door hatch
\*\*\* Estate

## Key to items

1 Battery
4 Engine fusebox
  a = under bonnet control unit
  k2 = engine control relay
5 Steering column control unit
10 Horn
11 Horn switch
12 Stop light switch
13 Reversing light switch
14 Rear fusebox
  a = rear control unit

15 LH rear light unit
  a = stop/tail light
  b = reversing light
  c = tail light
16 RH rear light unit
  (as above)
17 High level stop light
18 Number plate light
19 Instrument cluster
20 Light switch
  a = auto/side/headlights

21 LH headlight
  a = sidelight
  b = main beam
  c = main beam aperture actuator
  d = xenon control unit
  e = xenon ignition unit
  f = dip beam
22 RH headlight
  (as above)

**Diagram 4**

H33734

### Typical horn

### Typical stop & reversing lights

### Typical side, tail & number plate lights

### Typical headlights

## Wire colours

| | | | |
|---|---|---|---|
| **Bk** | Black | **Pk** | Pink |
| **Ye** | Yellow | **Vt** | Violet |
| **Bu** | Blue | **Og** | Orange |
| **Bn** | Brown | **Wh** | White |
| **Gn** | Green | **Lgn** | Light Green |
| **Gy** | Grey | **Lbu** | Light Blue |
| **Pu** | Purple | **Dgn** | Dark Green |
| **Bg** | Beige | **DBu** | Dark Blue |
| **Rd** | Red | | |

*     5 door hatch
**   3 door hatch
*** Estate

## Key to items

1 Battery
4 Engine fusebox
  a   = under bonnet control unit
  k3  = terminal 15 relay
  k16 = front foglight relay
5 Steering column control unit
14 Rear fusebox
  a   = rear control unit
  b   = trailer control unit
15 LH rear light unit
  d   = direction indicator
16 RH rear light unit
  d   = direction indicator
  e   = foglight

19 Instrument cluster
20 Light switch
  b   = front foglight
  c   = rear foglight
  d   = headlight levelling adjuster
21 LH headlight
  g   = hazard warning
  h   = headlight levelling adjuster
22 RH headlight
  (as above)
25 LH front foglight
26 RH front foglight

27 Centre console switch
  a   = hazard warning switch
28 LH indicator side repeater
29 RH indicator side repeater
30 Engine maxifusebox
31 Trailer socket

## Diagram 5

H33735

### *Typical foglights*

### *Typical trailer socket*

### *Typical direction indicators & hazard warning lights*

### *Typical headlight levelling - without xenon headlights*

## Wire colours

| | | | |
|---|---|---|---|
| **Bk** | Black | **Pk** | Pink |
| **Ye** | Yellow | **Vt** | Violet |
| **Bu** | Blue | **Og** | Orange |
| **Bn** | Brown | **Wh** | White |
| **Gn** | Green | **Lgn** | Light Green |
| **Gy** | Grey | **Lbu** | Light Blue |
| **Pu** | Purple | **Dgn** | Dark Green |
| **Bg** | Beige | **DBu** | Dark Blue |
| **Rd** | Red | | |

## Key to items

1 Battery
4 Engine fusebox
  a  = under bonnet control unit
  k3  = terminal 15 relay
5 Steering column control unit
14 Rear fusebox
  a  = rear control unit
  k1  = terminal 15 relay
  K3  = heated rear window relay
19 Instrument cluster
20 Light switch
  e  = interior lighting dimmer
21 LH headlight
  h  = headlight levelling adjuster
22 RH headlight
  h  = headlight levelling adjuster
30 Engine maxifusebox
35 Headlight levelling control unit
36 Vehicle level sensor
37 Driver's door courtesy light
41 Glovebox light
42 Luggage compartment light
43 LH vanity mirror light
44 RH vanity mirror light
45 Front accessory socket/cigar lighter
46 Rear accessory socket
47 Heated rear window
38 Passenger's door courtesy light
39 Front interior light
40 Rear interior light

## Diagram 6

H33736

### Typical headlight levelling - with xenon headlights

High speed CAN

### Typical interior lighting

Low speed CAN

Low speed CAN

### Typical cigar lighter & accessory sockets

### Typical heated rear window

Low speed CAN

See diagram 8
Heated mirrors

## Wire colours

| | | | |
|---|---|---|---|
| **Bk** | Black | **Pk** | Pink |
| **Ye** | Yellow | **Vt** | Violet |
| **Bu** | Blue | **Og** | Orange |
| **Bn** | Brown | **Wh** | White |
| **Gn** | Green | **Lgn** | Light Green |
| **Gy** | Grey | **Lbu** | Light Blue |
| **Pu** | Purple | **Dgn** | Dark Green |
| **Bg** | Beige | **DBu** | Dark Blue |
| **Rd** | Red | | |

## Key to items

1 Battery
4 Engine fusebox
  a = under bonnet control unit
  k5 = front wiper relay (low/hi speed)
  k6 = front wiper relay (on/off)
  k7 = headlight washer relay
  k15 = heater blower relay
5 Steering column control unit
14 Rear fusebox
  a = rear control unit
  k1 = terminal 15 relay

19 Instrument cluster
30 Engine maxifusebox
50 Heater unit
  a = control unit
  b = heater blower resistors
  c = heater blower motor
  d = recirculation flap motor
  e = air distribution flap motor
  f = mixed air flap motor
51 Front and rear washer pump
52 Headlight washer pump

53 Rain sensor
54 Front wiper motor
55 Rear wiper motor
56 Wash/wipe switch

**Diagram 7**

H33737

*Typical heater*

*Typical wash/wipe*

**Diagram 8**

## Wire colours

| | | | |
|---|---|---|---|
| **Bk** | Black | **Pk** | Pink |
| **Ye** | Yellow | **Vt** | Violet |
| **Bu** | Blue | **Og** | Orange |
| **Bn** | Brown | **Wh** | White |
| **Gn** | Green | **Lgn** | Light Green |
| **Gy** | Grey | **Lbu** | Light Blue |
| **Pu** | Purple | **Dgn** | Dark Green |
| **Bg** | Beige | **DBu** | Dark Blue |
| **Rd** | Red | | |

## Key to items

1 Battery
4 Engine fusebox
14 Rear fusebox
  a = under bonnet control unit
19 Instrument cluster
30 Engine maxifusebox
60 Audio unit
61 Antenna module
62 Instrument panel centre speaker
63 LH front door speaker
64 LH front tweeter
65 RH front door speaker
66 RH front tweeter
67 LH rear speaker
68 RH rear speaker
69 Sunroof switch
70 Sunroof motor
71 Sunscreen switch
72 Sunscreen motor
73 LH door mirror assembly
  a = heating element
  b = mirror retraction
  c = mirror adjustment
74 RH door mirror assembly
  (as above)
75 Driver's door switch
  a = control unit
  b = mirror retraction control
  c = switch illumination
  d = mirror control

H33738

**Typical audio system**

**Typical sunroof**

**Typical electric mirrors**

See Diagram 6
Heated rear window

## Wire colours

| | | | |
|---|---|---|---|
| **Bk** | Black | **Pk** | Pink |
| **Ye** | Yellow | **Vt** | Violet |
| **Bu** | Blue | **Og** | Orange |
| **Bn** | Brown | **Wh** | White |
| **Gn** | Green | **Lgn** | Light Green |
| **Gy** | Grey | **Lbu** | Light Blue |
| **Pu** | Purple | **Dgn** | Dark Green |
| **Bg** | Beige | **DBu** | Dark Blue |
| **Rd** | Red | | |

## Key to items

1 Battery
14 Rear fusebox
  a  = under bonnet control unit
19 Instrument cluster
27 Centre console switch
30 Engine maxifusebox
75 Driver's door switch
  e  = rear window isolation
  f  = LH front window
  g  = LH rear window
  h  = RH rear window
  i  = RH front window

80 Front passenger door switch
81 LH rear door switch
82 RH rear door switch
83 Driver's window motor
84 Passenger's window motor
85 LH rear window motor
86 RH rear window motor
87 Driver's door lock motor
88 Passenger's door lock motor
89 LH rear door lock motor
90 RH rear door lock motor
91 Tailgate lock motor

92 Tailgate lock switch
93 Fuel filler flap lock

**Diagram 9**

H33739

### Typical electric windows

### Typical central locking

# Dimensions and weights

**Note:** *All figures are approximate and may vary according to model. Refer to manufacturer's data for exact figures.*

## Dimensions

Overall length:
| | |
|---|---|
| 3-door Hatchback | 4290 mm |
| 5-door Hatchback | 4249 mm |
| Estate | 4515 mm |
| Overall width (including door mirrors) | 2032 mm |

Overall height (unladen):
| | |
|---|---|
| 3-door Hatchback | 1435 mm |
| 5-door Hatchback | 1460 mm |
| Estate | 1500 mm |

Wheelbase:
| | |
|---|---|
| Hatchback | 2614 mm |
| Estate | 2703 mm |
| Turning circle diameter (wall to wall) | 11.20 metres |
| Front track | 1488 mm |
| Rear track | 1488 mm |

## Weights

Kerb weight:

1.4 litre models:
| | |
|---|---|
| Hatchback | 1220 to 1260 kg |
| Estate | 1278 to 1298 kg |

1.6 litre models:
| | |
|---|---|
| Hatchback | 1265 to 1290 kg |
| Estate | 1315 to 1335 kg |

1.8 litre models:
| | |
|---|---|
| Hatchback | 1278 to 1298 kg |
| Estate | 1325 to 1370 kg |
| Gross vehicle weight | Refer to information contained on the vehicle identification plate |

Maximum roof load (including weight of rack):
| | |
|---|---|
| Hatchback | 75 kg |
| Estate | 100 kg |

# Conversion factors

## Length (distance)

| | | | | |
|---|---|---|---|---|
| Inches (in) | x 25.4 | = Millimetres (mm) | x 0.0394 | = Inches (in) |
| Feet (ft) | x 0.305 | = Metres (m) | x 3.281 | = Feet (ft) |
| Miles | x 1.609 | = Kilometres (km) | x 0.621 | = Miles |

## Volume (capacity)

| | | | | |
|---|---|---|---|---|
| Cubic inches (cu in; in³) | x 16.387 | = Cubic centimetres (cc; cm³) | x 0.061 | = Cubic inches (cu in; in³) |
| Imperial pints (Imp pt) | x 0.568 | = Litres (l) | x 1.76 | = Imperial pints (Imp pt) |
| Imperial quarts (Imp qt) | x 1.137 | = Litres (l) | x 0.88 | = Imperial quarts (Imp qt) |
| Imperial quarts (Imp qt) | x 1.201 | = US quarts (US qt) | x 0.833 | = Imperial quarts (Imp qt) |
| US quarts (US qt) | x 0.946 | = Litres (l) | x 1.057 | = US quarts (US qt) |
| Imperial gallons (Imp gal) | x 4.546 | = Litres (l) | x 0.22 | = Imperial gallons (Imp gal) |
| Imperial gallons (Imp gal) | x 1.201 | = US gallons (US gal) | x 0.833 | = Imperial gallons (Imp gal) |
| US gallons (US gal) | x 3.785 | = Litres (l) | x 0.264 | = US gallons (US gal) |

## Mass (weight)

| | | | | |
|---|---|---|---|---|
| Ounces (oz) | x 28.35 | = Grams (g) | x 0.035 | = Ounces (oz) |
| Pounds (lb) | x 0.454 | = Kilograms (kg) | x 2.205 | = Pounds (lb) |

## Force

| | | | | |
|---|---|---|---|---|
| Ounces-force (ozf; oz) | x 0.278 | = Newtons (N) | x 3.6 | = Ounces-force (ozf; oz) |
| Pounds-force (lbf; lb) | x 4.448 | = Newtons (N) | x 0.225 | = Pounds-force (lbf; lb) |
| Newtons (N) | x 0.1 | = Kilograms-force (kgf; kg) | x 9.81 | = Newtons (N) |

## Pressure

| | | | | |
|---|---|---|---|---|
| Pounds-force per square inch (psi; lbf/in²; lb/in²) | x 0.070 | = Kilograms-force per square centimetre (kgf/cm²; kg/cm²) | x 14.223 | = Pounds-force per square inch (psi; lbf/in²; lb/in²) |
| Pounds-force per square inch (psi; lbf/in²; lb/in²) | x 0.068 | = Atmospheres (atm) | x 14.696 | = Pounds-force per square inch (psi; lbf/in²; lb/in²) |
| Pounds-force per square inch (psi; lbf/in²; lb/in²) | x 0.069 | = Bars | x 14.5 | = Pounds-force per square inch (psi; lbf/in²; lb/in²) |
| Pounds-force per square inch (psi; lbf/in²; lb/in²) | x 6.895 | = Kilopascals (kPa) | x 0.145 | = Pounds-force per square inch (psi; lbf/in²; lb/in²) |
| Kilopascals (kPa) | x 0.01 | = Kilograms-force per square centimetre (kgf/cm²; kg/cm²) | x 98.1 | = Kilopascals (kPa) |
| Millibar (mbar) | x 100 | = Pascals (Pa) | x 0.01 | = Millibar (mbar) |
| Millibar (mbar) | x 0.0145 | = Pounds-force per square inch (psi; lbf/in²; lb/in²) | x 68.947 | = Millibar (mbar) |
| Millibar (mbar) | x 0.75 | = Millimetres of mercury (mmHg) | x 1.333 | = Millibar (mbar) |
| Millibar (mbar) | x 0.401 | = Inches of water (inH₂O) | x 2.491 | = Millibar (mbar) |
| Millimetres of mercury (mmHg) | x 0.535 | = Inches of water (inH₂O) | x 1.868 | = Millimetres of mercury (mmHg) |
| Inches of water (inH₂O) | x 0.036 | = Pounds-force per square inch (psi; lbf/in²; lb/in²) | x 27.68 | = Inches of water (inH₂O) |

## Torque (moment of force)

| | | | | |
|---|---|---|---|---|
| Pounds-force inches (lbf in; lb in) | x 1.152 | = Kilograms-force centimetre (kgf cm; kg cm) | x 0.868 | = Pounds-force inches (lbf in; lb in) |
| Pounds-force inches (lbf in; lb in) | x 0.113 | = Newton metres (Nm) | x 8.85 | = Pounds-force inches (lbf in; lb in) |
| Pounds-force inches (lbf in; lb in) | x 0.083 | = Pounds-force feet (lbf ft; lb ft) | x 12 | = Pounds-force inches (lbf in; lb in) |
| Pounds-force feet (lbf ft; lb ft) | x 0.138 | = Kilograms-force metres (kgf m; kg m) | x 7.233 | = Pounds-force feet (lbf ft; lb ft) |
| Pounds-force feet (lbf ft; lb ft) | x 1.356 | = Newton metres (Nm) | x 0.738 | = Pounds-force feet (lbf ft; lb ft) |
| Newton metres (Nm) | x 0.102 | = Kilograms-force metres (kgf m; kg m) | x 9.804 | = Newton metres (Nm) |

## Power

| | | | | |
|---|---|---|---|---|
| Horsepower (hp) | x 745.7 | = Watts (W) | x 0.0013 | = Horsepower (hp) |

## Velocity (speed)

| | | | | |
|---|---|---|---|---|
| Miles per hour (miles/hr; mph) | x 1.609 | = Kilometres per hour (km/hr; kph) | x 0.621 | = Miles per hour (miles/hr; mph) |

## Fuel consumption*

| | | | | |
|---|---|---|---|---|
| Miles per gallon, Imperial (mpg) | x 0.354 | = Kilometres per litre (km/l) | x 2.825 | = Miles per gallon, Imperial (mpg) |
| Miles per gallon, US (mpg) | x 0.425 | = Kilometres per litre (km/l) | x 2.352 | = Miles per gallon, US (mpg) |

## Temperature

Degrees Fahrenheit = (°C x 1.8) + 32          Degrees Celsius (Degrees Centigrade; °C) = (°F - 32) x 0.56

*It is common practice to convert from miles per gallon (mpg) to litres/100 kilometres (l/100km), where mpg x l/100 km = 282*

Spare parts are available from many sources, including maker's appointed garages, accessory shops, and motor factors. To be sure of obtaining the correct parts, it will sometimes be necessary to quote the vehicle identification number. If possible, it can also be useful to take the old parts along for positive identification. Items such as starter motors and alternators may be available under a service exchange scheme – any parts returned should be clean. Our advice regarding spare parts is as follows.

## Officially appointed garages

This is the best source of parts which are peculiar to your car, and which are not otherwise generally available (eg, badges, interior trim, certain body panels, etc). It is also the only place at which you should buy parts if the vehicle is still under warranty.

## Accessory shops

These are very good places to buy materials and components needed for the maintenance of your car (oil, air and fuel filters, light bulbs, drivebelts, greases, brake pads, touch-up paint, etc). Components of this nature sold by a reputable shop are of the same standard as those used by the car manufacturer.

Besides components, these shops also sell tools and general accessories, usually have convenient opening hours, charge lower prices, and can often be found close to home. Some accessory shops have parts counters where components needed for almost any repair job can be purchased or ordered.

## Motor factors

Good factors will stock all the more important components which wear out comparatively quickly, and can sometimes supply individual components needed for the overhaul of a larger assembly (eg, brake seals and hydraulic parts, bearing shells, pistons, valves). They may also handle work such as cylinder block reboring, crankshaft regrinding, etc.

## Tyre and exhaust specialists

These outlets may be independent, or members of a local or national chain. They frequently offer competitive prices when compared with a main dealer or local garage, but it will pay to obtain several quotes before making a decision. When researching prices, also ask what 'extras' may be added – for instance fitting a new valve and balancing the wheel are both commonly charged on top of the price of a new tyre.

## Other sources

Beware of parts or materials obtained from market stalls, car boot sales or similar outlets. Such items are not invariably sub-standard, but there is little chance of compensation if they do prove unsatisfactory. In the case of safety-critical components such as brake pads, there is the risk not only of financial loss, but also of an accident causing injury or death.

Second-hand components or assemblies obtained from a car breaker can be a good buy in some circumstances, but his sort of purchase is best made by the experienced DIY mechanic.

# Vehicle identification

Modifications are a continuing and unpublished process in vehicle manufacture, quite apart from major model changes. Spare parts manuals and lists are compiled upon a numerical basis, the individual vehicle numbers being essential to correct identification of the component required.

When ordering spare parts, always give as much information as possible. Quote the car model, year of manufacture and vehicle identification and/or engine numbers as appropriate.

The *vehicle identification plate* is attached to the front right-hand side door pillar **(see illustration)** and includes the Vehicle Identification Number (VIN), vehicle weight information and paint and trim colour codes.

The *Vehicle Identification Number (VIN)* is given on the vehicle identification plate and is also stamped into the body floor panel between the right-hand front seat and the door sill panel **(see illustration)**; lift the flap in the carpet to see it.

Vauxhall/Opel use a 'Car pass' scheme for vehicle identification. This is a card which is issued to the customer when the car is first purchased. It contains important information, eg, VIN number, key number and radio code. It also includes a special code for diagnostic equipment, therefore it must be kept in a secure place and not in the vehicle.

*The engine number* is stamped on a horizontal flat located on the front of the cylinder block, at the transmission end. The first part of the engine number gives the engine code – eg, Z14XEP.

## Engine codes

| | |
|---|---|
| 1.4 litre (1364 cc) DOHC 16-valve engine (66kW) | Z14XEP |
| 1.4 litre (1364 cc) DOHC 16-valve engine (55kW) | Z14XEL |
| 1.6 litre (1598 cc) DOHC 16-valve engine (77kW) | Z16XEP |
| 1.8 litre (1796 cc) DOHC 16-valve engine (92kW) | Z18XE |
| 1.8 litre (1796 cc) DOHC 16-valve VVT engine (103kW) | Z18XER |

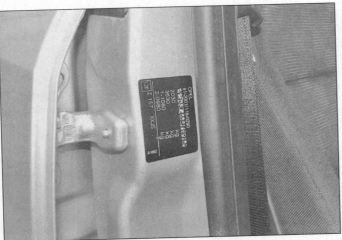

**Vehicle Identification Number (VIN) plate attached to the front right-hand side door pillar**

**The VIN number is stamped into the body floor next to the right-hand front seat**

Whenever servicing, repair or overhaul work is carried out on the car or its components, observe the following procedures and instructions. This will assist in carrying out the operation efficiently and to a professional standard of workmanship.

## Joint mating faces and gaskets

When separating components at their mating faces, never insert screwdrivers or similar implements into the joint between the faces in order to prise them apart. This can cause severe damage which results in oil leaks, coolant leaks, etc upon reassembly. Separation is usually achieved by tapping along the joint with a soft-faced hammer in order to break the seal. However, note that this method may not be suitable where dowels are used for component location.

Where a gasket is used between the mating faces of two components, a new one must be fitted on reassembly; fit it dry unless otherwise stated in the repair procedure. Make sure that the mating faces are clean and dry, with all traces of old gasket removed. When cleaning a joint face, use a tool which is unlikely to score or damage the face, and remove any burrs or nicks with an oilstone or fine file.

Make sure that tapped holes are cleaned with a pipe cleaner, and keep them free of jointing compound, if this is being used, unless specifically instructed otherwise.

Ensure that all orifices, channels or pipes are clear, and blow through them, preferably using compressed air.

## Oil seals

Oil seals can be removed by levering them out with a wide flat-bladed screwdriver or similar implement. Alternatively, a number of self-tapping screws may be screwed into the seal, and these used as a purchase for pliers or some similar device in order to pull the seal free.

Whenever an oil seal is removed from its working location, either individually or as part of an assembly, it should be renewed.

The very fine sealing lip of the seal is easily damaged, and will not seal if the surface it contacts is not completely clean and free from scratches, nicks or grooves. If the original sealing surface of the component cannot be restored, and the manufacturer has not made provision for slight relocation of the seal relative to the sealing surface, the component should be renewed.

Protect the lips of the seal from any surface which may damage them in the course of fitting. Use tape or a conical sleeve where possible. Where indicated, lubricate the seal lips with oil before fitting and, on dual-lipped seals, fill the space between the lips with grease.

Unless otherwise stated, oil seals must be fitted with their sealing lips toward the lubricant to be sealed.

Use a tubular drift or block of wood of the appropriate size to install the seal and, if the seal housing is shouldered, drive the seal down to the shoulder. If the seal housing is unshouldered, the seal should be fitted with its face flush with the housing top face (unless otherwise instructed).

## Screw threads and fastenings

Seized nuts, bolts and screws are quite a common occurrence where corrosion has set in, and the use of penetrating oil or releasing fluid will often overcome this problem if the offending item is soaked for a while before attempting to release it. The use of an impact driver may also provide a means of releasing such stubborn fastening devices, when used in conjunction with the appropriate screwdriver bit or socket. If none of these methods works, it may be necessary to resort to the careful application of heat, or the use of a hacksaw or nut splitter device. Before resorting to extreme methods, check that you are not dealing with a left-hand thread!

Studs are usually removed by locking two nuts together on the threaded part, and then using a spanner on the lower nut to unscrew the stud. Studs or bolts which have broken off below the surface of the component in which they are mounted can sometimes be removed using a stud extractor.

Always ensure that a blind tapped hole is completely free from oil, grease, water or other fluid before installing the bolt or stud. Failure to do this could cause the housing to crack due to the hydraulic action of the bolt or stud as it is screwed in.

For some screw fastenings, notably cylinder head bolts or nuts, torque wrench settings are no longer specified for the latter stages of tightening, "angle-tightening" being called up instead. Typically, a fairly low torque wrench setting will be applied to the bolts/nuts in the correct sequence, followed by one or more stages of tightening through specified angles.

When checking or retightening a nut or bolt to a specified torque setting, slacken the nut or bolt by a quarter of a turn, and then retighten to the specified setting. However, this should not be attempted where angular tightening has been used.

## Locknuts, locktabs and washers

Any fastening which will rotate against a component or housing during tightening should always have a washer between it and the relevant component or housing.

Spring or split washers should always be renewed when they are used to lock a critical component such as a big-end bearing retaining bolt or nut. Locktabs which are folded over to retain a nut or bolt should always be renewed.

Self-locking nuts can be re-used in non-critical areas, providing resistance can be felt when the locking portion passes over the bolt or stud thread. However, it should be noted that self-locking stiffnuts tend to lose their effectiveness after long periods of use, and should then be renewed as a matter of course.

Split pins must always be replaced with new ones of the correct size for the hole.

When thread-locking compound is found on the threads of a fastener which is to be re-used, it should be cleaned off with a wire brush and solvent, and fresh compound applied on reassembly.

## Special tools

Some repair procedures in this manual entail the use of special tools such as a press, two or three-legged pullers, spring compressors, etc. Wherever possible, suitable readily-available alternatives to the manufacturer's special tools are described, and are shown in use. In some instances, where no alternative is possible, it has been necessary to resort to the use of a manufacturer's tool, and this has been done for reasons of safety as well as the efficient completion of the repair operation. Unless you are highly-skilled and have a thorough understanding of the procedures described, never attempt to bypass the use of any special tool when the procedure described specifies its use. Not only is there a very great risk of personal injury, but expensive damage could be caused to the components involved.

## Environmental considerations

When disposing of used engine oil, brake fluid, antifreeze, etc, give due consideration to any detrimental environmental effects. Do not, for instance, pour any of the above liquids down drains into the general sewage system, or onto the ground to soak away. Many local council refuse tips provide a facility for waste oil disposal, as do some garages. You can find your nearest disposal point by calling the Environment Agency on 08708 506 506 or by visiting www.oilbankline.org.uk.

OIL CARE

FOLLOW THE CODE

**Note: It is illegal and anti-social to dump oil down the drain. To find the location of your local oil recycling bank, call 08708 506 506 or visit www.oilbankline.org.uk.**

The jack supplied with the vehicle tool kit should only be used for changing roadwheels – see *Wheel changing* at the front of this manual. Ensure the jack head is correctly engaged before attempting to raise the vehicle. When carrying out any other kind of work, raise the vehicle using a hydraulic jack, and always supplement the jack with axle stands positioned under the vehicle jacking points.

When jacking up the vehicle with a trolley jack, position the jack head under one of the relevant jacking points. Use a block of wood between the jack or axle stand and the sill – the block of wood should have a groove cut into it , in which the welded flange of the sill will locate. **Do not** jack the vehicle under the sump or any of the steering or suspension components. Supplement the jack using axle stands **(see illustrations)**.

 **Warning: Never work under, around, or near a raised vehicle, unless it is adequately supported in at least two places.**

**Front jacking point for hydraulic jack or axle stands**

**Rear jacking point for hydraulic jack or axle stands**

**Axle stands should be placed under, or adjacent to the jacking point (arrowed)**

# Disconnecting the battery

Numerous systems fitted to the vehicle require battery power to be available at all times, either to ensure their continued operation (such as the clock) or to maintain control unit memories which would be erased if the battery were to be disconnected. Whenever the battery is to be disconnected therefore, first note the following, to ensure that there are no unforeseen consequences of this action:

a) *First, on any vehicle with central locking, it is a wise precaution to remove the key from the ignition, and to keep it with you, so that it does not get locked in, if the central locking should engage accidentally when the battery is reconnected.*

b) *Depending on model and specification, the Vauxhall/Opel anti-theft alarm system may be of the type which is automatically activated when the vehicle battery is disconnected and/or reconnected. To prevent the alarm sounding on models so equipped, switch the ignition on, then off, and disconnect the battery within15 seconds. If the alarm is activated when the battery is reconnected, switch the ignition on then off to deactivate the alarm.*

c) *If a security-coded audio unit is fitted, and the unit and/or the battery is disconnected, the unit will not function again on reconnection until the correct*

security code is entered. Details of this procedure, which varies according to the unit fitted, are given in the vehicle audio system operating instructions. Ensure you have the correct code before you disconnect the battery. If you do not have the code or details of the correct procedure, but can supply proof of ownership and a legitimate reason for wanting this information, a Vauxhall/Opel dealer may be able to help.

d) *The engine management electronic control unit is of the 'self-learning' type, meaning that as it operates, it also monitors and stores the settings which give optimum engine performance under all operating conditions. When the battery is disconnected, these settings are lost and the ECU reverts to the base settings programmed into its memory at the factory. On restarting, this may lead to the engine running/idling roughly for a short while, until the ECU has re-learned the optimum settings. This process is best accomplished by taking the vehicle on a road test (for approximately 15 minutes), covering all engine speeds and loads, concentrating mainly in the 2500 to 3500 rpm region.*

e) *On models equipped with automatic transmission, the transmission selector lever assembly incorporates an*

electrically-operated selector lever lock mechanism that prevents the lever being moved out of the P position unless the ignition is switched on and the brake pedal is depressed. If the selector lever is in the P position and the battery is disconnected, it will not be possible to move the selector lever out of position P by the normal means. Although it is possible to manually override the system (see Chapter 7B), it is sensible to move the selector lever to the N position before disconnecting the battery.

f) *On models with electric windows, it will be necessary to reprogramme the motors to restore the one-touch function of the buttons, after reconnection of the battery. To do this, fully close both front windows. With the windows closed, depress the up button of the driver's side window for approximately 5 seconds, then release it and depress the passenger side window up button for approximately 5 seconds.*

g) *On models with an electric sliding sunroof, it will be necessary to fully open and fully close the sunroof after battery reconnection, to recalibrate the sensors.*

h) *On all models, when reconnecting the battery after disconnection, switch on the ignition and wait 10 seconds to allow the electronic vehicle systems to stabilise and re-initialise.*

### Introduction

A selection of good tools is a fundamental requirement for anyone contemplating the maintenance and repair of a motor vehicle. For the owner who does not possess any, their purchase will prove a considerable expense, offsetting some of the savings made by doing-it-yourself. However, provided that the tools purchased meet the relevant national safety standards and are of good quality, they will last for many years and prove an extremely worthwhile investment.

To help the average owner to decide which tools are needed to carry out the various tasks detailed in this manual, we have compiled three lists of tools under the following headings: *Maintenance and minor repair*, *Repair and overhaul*, and *Special*. Newcomers to practical mechanics should start off with the *Maintenance and minor repair* tool kit, and confine themselves to the simpler jobs around the vehicle. Then, as confidence and experience grow, more difficult tasks can be undertaken, with extra tools being purchased as, and when, they are needed. In this way, a *Maintenance and minor repair* tool kit can be built up into a *Repair and overhaul* tool kit over a considerable period of time, without any major cash outlays. The experienced do-it-yourselfer will have a tool kit good enough for most repair and overhaul procedures, and will add tools from the *Special* category when it is felt that the expense is justified by the amount of use to which these tools will be put.

### Maintenance and minor repair tool kit

The tools given in this list should be considered as a minimum requirement if routine maintenance, servicing and minor repair operations are to be undertaken. We recommend the purchase of combination spanners (ring one end, open-ended the other); although more expensive than open-ended ones, they do give the advantages of both types of spanner.

☐ *Combination spanners:*
  *Metric - 8 to 19 mm inclusive*
☐ *Adjustable spanner - 35 mm jaw (approx.)*
☐ *Spark plug spanner (with rubber insert) - petrol models*
☐ *Spark plug gap adjustment tool - petrol models*
☐ *Set of feeler gauges*
☐ *Brake bleed nipple spanner*
☐ *Screwdrivers:*
  *Flat blade - 100 mm long x 6 mm dia*
  *Cross blade - 100 mm long x 6 mm dia*
  *Torx - various sizes (not all vehicles)*
☐ *Combination pliers*
☐ *Hacksaw (junior)*
☐ *Tyre pump*
☐ *Tyre pressure gauge*
☐ *Oil can*
☐ *Oil filter removal tool*
☐ *Fine emery cloth*
☐ *Wire brush (small)*
☐ *Funnel (medium size)*
☐ *Sump drain plug key (not all vehicles)*

### Repair and overhaul tool kit

These tools are virtually essential for anyone undertaking any major repairs to a motor vehicle, and are additional to those given in the *Maintenance and minor repair* list. Included in this list is a comprehensive set of sockets. Although these are expensive, they will be found invaluable as they are so versatile - particularly if various drives are included in the set. We recommend the half-inch square-drive type, as this can be used with most proprietary torque wrenches.

The tools in this list will sometimes need to be supplemented by tools from the *Special* list:

☐ *Sockets (or box spanners) to cover range in previous list (including Torx sockets)*
☐ *Reversible ratchet drive (for use with sockets)*
☐ *Extension piece, 250 mm (for use with sockets)*
☐ *Universal joint (for use with sockets)*
☐ *Flexible handle or sliding T "breaker bar" (for use with sockets)*
☐ *Torque wrench (for use with sockets)*
☐ *Self-locking grips*
☐ *Ball pein hammer*
☐ *Soft-faced mallet (plastic or rubber)*
☐ *Screwdrivers:*
  *Flat blade - long & sturdy, short (chubby), and narrow (electrician's) types*
  *Cross blade – long & sturdy, and short (chubby) types*
☐ *Pliers:*
  *Long-nosed*
  *Side cutters (electrician's)*
  *Circlip (internal and external)*
☐ *Cold chisel - 25 mm*
☐ *Scriber*
☐ *Scraper*
☐ *Centre-punch*
☐ *Pin punch*
☐ *Hacksaw*
☐ *Brake hose clamp*
☐ *Brake/clutch bleeding kit*
☐ *Selection of twist drills*
☐ *Steel rule/straight-edge*
☐ *Allen keys (inc. splined/Torx type)*
☐ *Selection of files*
☐ *Wire brush*
☐ *Axle stands*
☐ *Jack (strong trolley or hydraulic type)*
☐ *Light with extension lead*
☐ *Universal electrical multi-meter*

**Sockets and reversible ratchet drive**

**Brake bleeding kit**

**Torx key, socket and bit**

**Hose clamp**

**Angular-tightening gauge**

## Special tools

The tools in this list are those which are not used regularly, are expensive to buy, or which need to be used in accordance with their manufacturers' instructions. Unless relatively difficult mechanical jobs are undertaken frequently, it will not be economic to buy many of these tools. Where this is the case, you could consider clubbing together with friends (or joining a motorists' club) to make a joint purchase, or borrowing the tools against a deposit from a local garage or tool hire specialist. It is worth noting that many of the larger DIY superstores now carry a large range of special tools for hire at modest rates.

The following list contains only those tools and instruments freely available to the public, and not those special tools produced by the vehicle manufacturer specifically for its dealer network. You will find occasional references to these manufacturers' special tools in the text of this manual. Generally, an alternative method of doing the job without the vehicle manufacturers' special tool is given. However, sometimes there is no alternative to using them. Where this is the case and the relevant tool cannot be bought or borrowed, you will have to entrust the work to a dealer.

- ☐ Angular-tightening gauge
- ☐ Valve spring compressor
- ☐ Valve grinding tool
- ☐ Piston ring compressor
- ☐ Piston ring removal/installation tool
- ☐ Cylinder bore hone
- ☐ Balljoint separator
- ☐ Coil spring compressors (where applicable)
- ☐ Two/three-legged hub and bearing puller
- ☐ Impact screwdriver
- ☐ Micrometer and/or vernier calipers
- ☐ Dial gauge
- ☐ Stroboscopic timing light
- ☐ Dwell angle meter/tachometer
- ☐ Fault code reader
- ☐ Cylinder compression gauge
- ☐ Hand-operated vacuum pump and gauge
- ☐ Clutch plate alignment set
- ☐ Brake shoe steady spring cup removal tool
- ☐ Bush and bearing removal/installation set
- ☐ Stud extractors
- ☐ Tap and die set
- ☐ Lifting tackle
- ☐ Trolley jack

## Buying tools

Reputable motor accessory shops and superstores often offer excellent quality tools at discount prices, so it pays to shop around.

Remember, you don't have to buy the most expensive items on the shelf, but it is always advisable to steer clear of the very cheap tools. Beware of 'bargains' offered on market stalls or at car boot sales. There are plenty of good tools around at reasonable prices, but always aim to purchase items which meet the relevant national safety standards. If in doubt, ask the proprietor or manager of the shop for advice before making a purchase.

## Care and maintenance of tools

Having purchased a reasonable tool kit, it is necessary to keep the tools in a clean and serviceable condition. After use, always wipe off any dirt, grease and metal particles using a clean, dry cloth, before putting the tools away. Never leave them lying around after they have been used. A simple tool rack on the garage or workshop wall for items such as screwdrivers and pliers is a good idea. Store all normal spanners and sockets in a metal box. Any measuring instruments, gauges, meters, etc, must be carefully stored where they cannot be damaged or become rusty.

Take a little care when tools are used. Hammer heads inevitably become marked, and screwdrivers lose the keen edge on their blades from time to time. A little timely attention with emery cloth or a file will soon restore items like this to a good finish.

## Working facilities

Not to be forgotten when discussing tools is the workshop itself. If anything more than routine maintenance is to be carried out, a suitable working area becomes essential.

It is appreciated that many an owner-mechanic is forced by circumstances to remove an engine or similar item without the benefit of a garage or workshop. Having done this, any repairs should always be done under the cover of a roof.

Wherever possible, any dismantling should be done on a clean, flat workbench or table at a suitable working height.

Any workbench needs a vice; one with a jaw opening of 100 mm is suitable for most jobs. As mentioned previously, some clean dry storage space is also required for tools, as well as for any lubricants, cleaning fluids, touch-up paints etc, which become necessary.

Another item which may be required, and which has a much more general usage, is an electric drill with a chuck capacity of at least 8 mm. This, together with a good range of twist drills, is virtually essential for fitting accessories.

Last, but not least, always keep a supply of old newspapers and clean, lint-free rags available, and try to keep any working area as clean as possible.

**Micrometers**

**Dial test indicator ("dial gauge")**

**Strap wrench**

**Compression tester**

**Fault code reader**

This is a guide to getting your vehicle through the MOT test. Obviously it will not be possible to examine the vehicle to the same standard as the professional MOT tester. However, working through the following checks will enable you to identify any problem areas before submitting the vehicle for the test.

It has only been possible to summarise the test requirements here, based on the regulations in force at the time of printing. Test standards are becoming increasingly stringent, although there are some exemptions for older vehicles.

An assistant will be needed to help carry out some of these checks.

*The checks have been sub-divided into four categories, as follows:*

**1** Checks carried out **FROM THE DRIVER'S SEAT**

**2** Checks carried out **WITH THE VEHICLE ON THE GROUND**

**3** Checks carried out **WITH THE VEHICLE RAISED AND THE WHEELS FREE TO TURN**

**4** Checks carried out on **YOUR VEHICLE'S EXHAUST EMISSION SYSTEM**

---

**1** Checks carried out **FROM THE DRIVER'S SEAT**

### Handbrake

☐ Test the operation of the handbrake. Excessive travel (too many clicks) indicates incorrect brake or cable adjustment.
☐ Check that the handbrake cannot be released by tapping the lever sideways. Check the security of the lever mountings.

### Footbrake

☐ Depress the brake pedal and check that it does not creep down to the floor, indicating a master cylinder fault. Release the pedal, wait a few seconds, then depress it again. If the pedal travels nearly to the floor before firm resistance is felt, brake adjustment or repair is necessary. If the pedal feels spongy, there is air in the hydraulic system which must be removed by bleeding.

☐ Check that the brake pedal is secure and in good condition. Check also for signs of fluid leaks on the pedal, floor or carpets, which would indicate failed seals in the brake master cylinder.
☐ Check the servo unit (when applicable) by operating the brake pedal several times, then keeping the pedal depressed and starting the engine. As the engine starts, the pedal will move down slightly. If not, the vacuum hose or the servo itself may be faulty.

### Steering wheel and column

☐ Examine the steering wheel for fractures or looseness of the hub, spokes or rim.
☐ Move the steering wheel from side to side and then up and down. Check that the steering wheel is not loose on the column, indicating wear or a loose retaining nut. Continue moving the steering wheel as before, but also turn it slightly from left to right.
☐ Check that the steering wheel is not loose on the column, and that there is no abnormal

movement of the steering wheel, indicating wear in the column support bearings or couplings.

### Windscreen, mirrors and sunvisor

☐ The windscreen must be free of cracks or other significant damage within the driver's field of view. (Small stone chips are acceptable.) Rear view mirrors must be secure, intact, and capable of being adjusted.

290mm

☐ The driver's sunvisor must be capable of being stored in the "up" position.

### Seat belts and seats

**Note:** *The following checks are applicable to all seat belts, front and rear.*

☐ Examine the webbing of all the belts (including rear belts if fitted) for cuts, serious fraying or deterioration. Fasten and unfasten each belt to check the buckles. If applicable, check the retracting mechanism. Check the security of all seat belt mountings accessible from inside the vehicle.

☐ Seat belts with pre-tensioners, once activated, have a "flag" or similar showing on the seat belt stalk. This, in itself, is not a reason for test failure.

☐ The front seats themselves must be securely attached and the backrests must lock in the upright position.

### Doors

☐ Both front doors must be able to be opened and closed from outside and inside, and must latch securely when closed.

## 2 Checks carried out WITH THE VEHICLE ON THE GROUND

### Vehicle identification

☐ Number plates must be in good condition, secure and legible, with letters and numbers correctly spaced – spacing at (A) should be at least twice that at (B).

☐ The VIN plate and/or homologation plate must be legible.

### Electrical equipment

☐ Switch on the ignition and check the operation of the horn.

☐ Check the windscreen washers and wipers, examining the wiper blades; renew damaged or perished blades. Also check the operation of the stop-lights.

☐ Check the operation of the sidelights and number plate lights. The lenses and reflectors must be secure, clean and undamaged.

☐ Check the operation and alignment of the headlights. The headlight reflectors must not be tarnished and the lenses must be undamaged.

☐ Switch on the ignition and check the operation of the direction indicators (including the instrument panel tell-tale) and the hazard warning lights. Operation of the sidelights and stop-lights must not affect the indicators - if it does, the cause is usually a bad earth at the rear light cluster.

☐ Check the operation of the rear foglight(s), including the warning light on the instrument panel or in the switch.

☐ The ABS warning light must illuminate in accordance with the manufacturers' design. For most vehicles, the ABS warning light should illuminate when the ignition is switched on, and (if the system is operating properly) extinguish after a few seconds. Refer to the owner's handbook.

### Footbrake

☐ Examine the master cylinder, brake pipes and servo unit for leaks, loose mountings, corrosion or other damage.

☐ The fluid reservoir must be secure and the fluid level must be between the upper (A) and lower (B) markings.

☐ Inspect both front brake flexible hoses for cracks or deterioration of the rubber. Turn the steering from lock to lock, and ensure that the hoses do not contact the wheel, tyre, or any part of the steering or suspension mechanism. With the brake pedal firmly depressed, check the hoses for bulges or leaks under pressure.

### Steering and suspension

☐ Have your assistant turn the steering wheel from side to side slightly, up to the point where the steering gear just begins to transmit this movement to the roadwheels. Check for excessive free play between the steering wheel and the steering gear, indicating wear or insecurity of the steering column joints, the column-to-steering gear coupling, or the steering gear itself.

☐ Have your assistant turn the steering wheel more vigorously in each direction, so that the roadwheels just begin to turn. As this is done, examine all the steering joints, linkages, fittings and attachments. Renew any component that shows signs of wear or damage. On vehicles with power steering, check the security and condition of the steering pump, drivebelt and hoses.

☐ Check that the vehicle is standing level, and at approximately the correct ride height.

### Shock absorbers

☐ Depress each corner of the vehicle in turn, then release it. The vehicle should rise and then settle in its normal position. If the vehicle continues to rise and fall, the shock absorber is defective. A shock absorber which has seized will also cause the vehicle to fail.

## Exhaust system

☐ Start the engine. With your assistant holding a rag over the tailpipe, check the entire system for leaks. Repair or renew leaking sections.

**3** Checks carried out **WITH THE VEHICLE RAISED AND THE WHEELS FREE TO TURN**

*Jack up the front and rear of the vehicle, and securely support it on axle stands. Position the stands clear of the suspension assemblies. Ensure that the wheels are clear of the ground and that the steering can be turned from lock to lock.*

## Steering mechanism

☐ Have your assistant turn the steering from lock to lock. Check that the steering turns smoothly, and that no part of the steering mechanism, including a wheel or tyre, fouls any brake hose or pipe or any part of the body structure.
☐ Examine the steering rack rubber gaiters for damage or insecurity of the retaining clips. If power steering is fitted, check for signs of damage or leakage of the fluid hoses, pipes or connections. Also check for excessive stiffness or binding of the steering, a missing split pin or locking device, or severe corrosion of the body structure within 30 cm of any steering component attachment point.

## Front and rear suspension and wheel bearings

☐ Starting at the front right-hand side, grasp the roadwheel at the 3 o'clock and 9 o'clock positions and rock gently but firmly. Check for free play or insecurity at the wheel bearings, suspension balljoints, or suspension mountings, pivots and attachments.
☐ Now grasp the wheel at the 12 o'clock and 6 o'clock positions and repeat the previous inspection. Spin the wheel, and check for roughness or tightness of the front wheel bearing.

☐ If excess free play is suspected at a component pivot point, this can be confirmed by using a large screwdriver or similar tool and levering between the mounting and the component attachment. This will confirm whether the wear is in the pivot bush, its retaining bolt, or in the mounting itself (the bolt holes can often become elongated).

☐ Carry out all the above checks at the other front wheel, and then at both rear wheels.

## Springs and shock absorbers

☐ Examine the suspension struts (when applicable) for serious fluid leakage, corrosion, or damage to the casing. Also check the security of the mounting points.
☐ If coil springs are fitted, check that the spring ends locate in their seats, and that the spring is not corroded, cracked or broken.
☐ If leaf springs are fitted, check that all leaves are intact, that the axle is securely attached to each spring, and that there is no deterioration of the spring eye mountings, bushes, and shackles.

☐ The same general checks apply to vehicles fitted with other suspension types, such as torsion bars, hydraulic displacer units, etc. Ensure that all mountings and attachments are secure, that there are no signs of excessive wear, corrosion or damage, and (on hydraulic types) that there are no fluid leaks or damaged pipes.
☐ Inspect the shock absorbers for signs of serious fluid leakage. Check for wear of the mounting bushes or attachments, or damage to the body of the unit.

## Driveshafts (fwd vehicles only)

☐ Rotate each front wheel in turn and inspect the constant velocity joint gaiters for splits or damage. Also check that each driveshaft is straight and undamaged.

## Braking system

☐ If possible without dismantling, check brake pad wear and disc condition. Ensure that the friction lining material has not worn excessively, (A) and that the discs are not fractured, pitted, scored or badly worn (B).

☐ Examine all the rigid brake pipes underneath the vehicle, and the flexible hose(s) at the rear. Look for corrosion, chafing or insecurity of the pipes, and for signs of bulging under pressure, chafing, splits or deterioration of the flexible hoses.
☐ Look for signs of fluid leaks at the brake calipers or on the brake backplates. Repair or renew leaking components.
☐ Slowly spin each wheel, while your assistant depresses and releases the footbrake. Ensure that each brake is operating and does not bind when the pedal is released.

☐ Examine the handbrake mechanism, checking for frayed or broken cables, excessive corrosion, or wear or insecurity of the linkage. Check that the mechanism works on each relevant wheel, and releases fully, without binding.

☐ It is not possible to test brake efficiency without special equipment, but a road test can be carried out later to check that the vehicle pulls up in a straight line.

## Fuel and exhaust systems

☐ Inspect the fuel tank (including the filler cap), fuel pipes, hoses and unions. All components must be secure and free from leaks.

☐ Examine the exhaust system over its entire length, checking for any damaged, broken or missing mountings, security of the retaining clamps and rust or corrosion.

## Wheels and tyres

☐ Examine the sidewalls and tread area of each tyre in turn. Check for cuts, tears, lumps, bulges, separation of the tread, and exposure of the ply or cord due to wear or damage. Check that the tyre bead is correctly seated on the wheel rim, that the valve is sound and properly seated, and that the wheel is not distorted or damaged.

☐ Check that the tyres are of the correct size for the vehicle, that they are of the same size

and type on each axle, and that the pressures are correct.

☐ Check the tyre tread depth. The legal minimum at the time of writing is 1.6 mm over at least three-quarters of the tread width. Abnormal tread wear may indicate incorrect front wheel alignment.

## Body corrosion

☐ Check the condition of the entire vehicle structure for signs of corrosion in load-bearing areas. (These include chassis box sections, side sills, cross-members, pillars, and all suspension, steering, braking system and seat belt mountings and anchorages.) Any corrosion which has seriously reduced the thickness of a load-bearing area is likely to cause the vehicle to fail. In this case professional repairs are likely to be needed.

☐ Damage or corrosion which causes sharp or otherwise dangerous edges to be exposed will also cause the vehicle to fail.

## 4 Checks carried out on YOUR VEHICLE'S EXHAUST EMISSION SYSTEM

### Petrol models

☐ The engine should be warmed up, and running well (ignition system in good order, air filter element clean, etc).

☐ Before testing, run the engine at around 2500 rpm for 20 seconds. Let the engine drop to idle, and watch for smoke from the exhaust. If the idle speed is too high, or if dense blue or black smoke emerges for more than 5 seconds, the vehicle will fail. Typically, blue smoke signifies oil burning (engine wear); black smoke means unburnt fuel (dirty air cleaner element, or other fuel system fault).

☐ An exhaust gas analyser for measuring carbon monoxide (CO) and hydrocarbons (HC) is now needed. If one cannot be hired or borrowed, have a local garage perform the check.

### CO emissions (mixture)

☐ The MOT tester has access to the CO limits for all vehicles. The CO level is measured at idle speed, and at 'fast idle' (2500 to 3000 rpm). The following limits are given as a general guide:
   *At idle speed* – Less than 0.5% CO
   *At 'fast idle'* – Less than 0.3% CO
   *Lambda reading* – 0.97 to 1.03

☐ If the CO level is too high, this may point to poor maintenance, a fuel injection system problem, faulty lambda (oxygen) sensor or catalytic converter. Try an injector cleaning treatment, and check the vehicle's ECU for fault codes.

### HC emissions

☐ The MOT tester has access to HC limits for all vehicles. The HC level is measured at 'fast idle' (2500 to 3000 rpm). The following limits are given as a general guide:
   *At 'fast idle'* – Less then 200 ppm

☐ Excessive HC emissions are typically caused by oil being burnt (worn engine), or by a blocked crankcase ventilation system ('breather'). If the engine oil is old and thin, an oil change may help. If the engine is running badly, check the vehicle's ECU for fault codes.

### Diesel models

☐ The only emission test for diesel engines is measuring exhaust smoke density, using a calibrated smoke meter. The test involves accelerating the engine at least 3 times to its maximum unloaded speed.

**Note:** *On engines with a timing belt, it is VITAL that the belt is in good condition before the test is carried out.*

☐ With the engine warmed up, it is first purged by running at around 2500 rpm for 20 seconds. A governor check is then carried out, by slowly accelerating the engine to its maximum speed. After this, the smoke meter is connected, and the engine is accelerated quickly to maximum speed three times. If the smoke density is less than the limits given below, the vehicle will pass:
   *Non-turbo vehicles*: 2.5m-1
   *Turbocharged vehicles*: 3.0m-1

☐ If excess smoke is produced, try fitting a new air cleaner element, or using an injector cleaning treatment. If the engine is running badly, where applicable, check the vehicle's ECU for fault codes. Also check the vehicle's EGR system, where applicable. At high mileages, the injectors may require professional attention.

## Engine

- [ ] Engine fails to rotate when attempting to start
- [ ] Engine rotates, but will not start
- [ ] Engine difficult to start when cold
- [ ] Engine difficult to start when hot
- [ ] Starter motor noisy or excessively-rough in engagement
- [ ] Engine starts, but stops immediately
- [ ] Engine idles erratically
- [ ] Engine misfires at idle speed
- [ ] Engine misfires throughout the driving speed range
- [ ] Engine hesitates on acceleration
- [ ] Engine stalls
- [ ] Engine lacks power
- [ ] Engine backfires
- [ ] Oil pressure warning light illuminated with engine running
- [ ] Engine runs-on after switching off
- [ ] Engine noises

## Cooling system

- [ ] Overheating
- [ ] Overcooling
- [ ] External coolant leakage
- [ ] Internal coolant leakage
- [ ] Corrosion

## Fuel and exhaust systems

- [ ] Excessive fuel consumption
- [ ] Fuel leakage and/or fuel odour
- [ ] Excessive noise or fumes from exhaust system

## Clutch

- [ ] Pedal travels to floor – no pressure or very little resistance
- [ ] Clutch fails to disengage (unable to select gears)
- [ ] Clutch slips (engine speed increases, with no increase in vehicle speed)
- [ ] Judder as clutch is engaged
- [ ] Noise when depressing or releasing clutch pedal

## Manual transmission

- [ ] Noisy in neutral with engine running
- [ ] Noisy in one particular gear
- [ ] Difficulty engaging gears
- [ ] Jumps out of gear
- [ ] Vibration
- [ ] Lubricant leaks

## Automatic transmission

- [ ] Fluid leakage
- [ ] Transmission fluid brown, or has burned smell
- [ ] General gear selection problems
- [ ] Transmission will not downshift (kickdown) with accelerator pedal fully depressed
- [ ] Engine will not start in any gear, or starts in gears other than Park or Neutral
- [ ] Transmission slips, shifts roughly, is noisy, or has no drive in forward or reverse gears

## Driveshafts

- [ ] Vibration when accelerating or decelerating
- [ ] Clicking or knocking noise on turns (at slow speed on full-lock)

## Braking system

- [ ] Vehicle pulls to one side under braking
- [ ] Noise (grinding or high-pitched squeal) when brakes applied
- [ ] Excessive brake pedal travel
- [ ] Brake pedal feels spongy when depressed
- [ ] Excessive brake pedal effort required to stop vehicle
- [ ] Judder felt through brake pedal or steering wheel when braking
- [ ] Brakes binding
- [ ] Rear wheels locking under normal braking

## Suspension and steering

- [ ] Vehicle pulls to one side
- [ ] Wheel wobble and vibration
- [ ] Excessive pitching and/or rolling around corners, or during braking
- [ ] Wandering or general instability
- [ ] Excessively-stiff steering
- [ ] Excessive play in steering
- [ ] Lack of power assistance
- [ ] Tyre wear excessive

## Electrical system

- [ ] Battery will not hold a charge for more than a few days
- [ ] Ignition/no-charge warning light remains illuminated with engine running
- [ ] Ignition/no-charge warning light fails to come on
- [ ] Lights inoperative
- [ ] Instrument readings inaccurate or erratic
- [ ] Horn inoperative, or unsatisfactory in operation
- [ ] Windscreen wipers inoperative, or unsatisfactory in operation
- [ ] Windscreen washers inoperative, or unsatisfactory in operation
- [ ] Electric windows inoperative, or unsatisfactory in operation
- [ ] Central locking system inoperative, or unsatisfactory in operation

# Introduction

The vehicle owner who does his or her own maintenance according to the recommended service schedules should not have to use this section of the manual very often. Modern component reliability is such that, provided those items subject to wear or deterioration are inspected or renewed at the specified intervals, sudden failure is comparatively rare. Faults do not usually just happen as a result of sudden failure, but develop over a period of time. Major mechanical failures in particular are usually preceded by characteristic symptoms over hundreds or even thousands of miles. Those components which do occasionally fail without warning are often small and easily carried in the vehicle.

With any fault-finding, the first step is to decide where to begin investigations. Sometimes this is obvious, but on other occasions, a little detective work will be necessary. The owner who makes half a dozen haphazard adjustments or replacements may be successful in curing a fault (or its symptoms), but will be none the wiser if the fault recurs, and ultimately may have spent more time and money than was necessary. A calm and logical approach will be found to be more satisfactory in the long run. Always take into account any warning signs or abnormalities that may have been noticed in the period preceding the fault – power loss, high or low gauge readings, unusual smells, etc – and remember that failure of components such as fuses or spark plugs may only be pointers to some underlying fault.

The pages which follow provide an easy-reference guide to the more common problems which may occur during the operation of the vehicle. These problems and their possible causes are grouped under headings denoting various components or systems, such as Engine, Cooling system, etc. The general

Chapter which deals with the problem is also shown in brackets; refer to the relevant part of that Chapter for system-specific information. Whatever the fault, certain basic principles apply. These are as follows:

*Verify the fault.* This is simply a matter of being sure that you know what the symptoms are before starting work. This is particularly important if you are investigating a fault for someone else, who may not have described it very accurately.

*Don't overlook the obvious.* For example, if the vehicle won't start, is there fuel in the tank? (Don't take anyone else's word on this particular point, and don't trust the fuel gauge either!) If an electrical fault is indicated, look for loose or broken wires before digging out the test gear.

*Cure the disease, not the symptom.* Substituting a flat battery with a fully-charged one will get you off the hard shoulder, but if the underlying cause is not attended to, the new battery will go the same way. Similarly, changing oil-fouled spark plugs for a new set will get you moving again, but remember that the reason for the fouling (if it wasn't simply an incorrect grade of plug) will have to be established and corrected.

*Don't take anything for granted.* Particularly, don't forget that a 'new' component may itself be defective (especially if it's been rattling around in the boot for months), and don't leave components out of a fault diagnosis sequence just because they are new or recently-fitted. When you do finally diagnose a difficult fault, you'll probably realise that all the evidence was there from the start.

*Consider what work, if any, has recently been carried out.* Many faults arise through careless or hurried work. For instance, if any work has been performed under the bonnet, could some of the wiring have been dislodged or incorrectly routed, or a hose trapped? Have all the fasteners been properly tightened? Were new, genuine parts and new gaskets used? There is often a certain amount of detective work to be done in this case, as an apparently-unrelated task can have far-reaching consequences.

# Engine

## Engine fails to rotate when attempting to start

☐ Battery terminal connections loose or corroded (see *Weekly checks*)
☐ Battery discharged or faulty (Chapter 5A)
☐ Broken, loose or disconnected wiring in the starting circuit (Chapter 5A)
☐ Defective starter solenoid or ignition switch (Chapter 5A or 12)
☐ Defective starter motor (Chapter 5A)
☐ Starter pinion or flywheel ring gear teeth loose or broken (Chapter 2A, 2B, 2C or 5A)
☐ Engine earth strap broken or disconnected (Chapter 5A)
☐ Engine suffering 'hydraulic lock' (eg from water drawn into the engine after traversing flooded roads, or from a serious internal coolant leak) – consult a main dealer for advice
☐ Automatic transmission not in position P or N (Chapter 7B)

## Engine rotates, but will not start

☐ Fuel tank empty
☐ Battery discharged (engine rotates slowly) (Chapter 5A)
☐ Battery terminal connections loose or corroded (see *Weekly checks*)
☐ Ignition components damp or damaged (Chapter 1 or 5B)
☐ Immobiliser fault, or 'uncoded' ignition key being used (Chapter 12 or Roadside repairs)
☐ Broken, loose or disconnected wiring in the ignition circuit (Chapter 1 or 5B)
☐ Worn, faulty or incorrectly-gapped spark plugs (Chapter 1)
☐ Fuel injection/engine management system fault (Chapter 4A or 4B)
☐ Major mechanical failure (eg timing belt/chain snapped) (Chapter 2A, 2B or 2C)

## Engine difficult to start when cold

☐ Battery discharged (Chapter 5A)
☐ Battery terminal connections loose or corroded (see *Weekly checks*)
☐ Worn, faulty or incorrectly-gapped spark plugs (Chapter 1)
☐ Other ignition system fault (Chapter 1 or 5B)
☐ Fuel injection/engine management system fault (Chapter 4A or 4B)
☐ Wrong grade of engine oil used (*Weekly checks*, Chapter 1)
☐ Low cylinder compression (Chapter 2A, 2B or 2C)

## Engine difficult to start when hot

☐ Air filter element dirty or clogged (Chapter 1)
☐ Fuel injection/engine management system fault (Chapter 4A or 4B)
☐ Low cylinder compression (Chapter 2A, 2B or 2C)

## Starter motor noisy or excessively-rough in engagement

☐ Starter pinion or flywheel ring gear teeth loose or broken (Chapter 2, 2B, 2C or 5A)
☐ Starter motor mounting bolts loose or missing (Chapter 5A)
☐ Starter motor internal components worn or damaged (Chapter 5A)

## Engine starts, but stops immediately

☐ Loose or faulty electrical connections in the ignition circuit (Chapter 1 or 5B)
☐ Vacuum leak at the throttle housing or inlet manifold (Chapter 4A)
☐ Blocked injectors/fuel injection system fault (Chapter 4A)

## Engine idles erratically

☐ Air filter element clogged (Chapter 1)
☐ Vacuum leak at the throttle housing, inlet manifold or associated hoses (Chapter 4A or 4B)
☐ Worn, faulty or incorrectly-gapped spark plugs (Chapter 1)
☐ Uneven or low cylinder compression (Chapter 2A, 2B or 2C)
☐ Camshaft lobes worn (Chapter 2A, 2B or 2C)
☐ Blocked injectors/fuel injection system fault (Chapter 4A)

## Engine misfires at idle speed

☐ Worn, faulty or incorrectly-gapped spark plugs (Chapter 1)
☐ Vacuum leak at the throttle housing, inlet manifold or associated hoses (Chapter 4A or 4B)
☐ Blocked injectors/fuel injection system fault (Chapter 4A)
☐ Uneven or low cylinder compression (Chapter 2A, 2B or 2C)
☐ Disconnected, leaking, or perished crankcase ventilation hoses (Chapter 4B)

## Engine misfires throughout the driving speed range

☐ Fuel pump faulty, or delivery pressure low (Chapter 4A)
☐ Fuel tank vent blocked, or fuel pipes restricted (Chapter 4A or 4B)
☐ Vacuum leak at the throttle housing, inlet manifold or associated hoses (Chapter 4A or 4B)
☐ Worn, faulty or incorrectly-gapped spark plugs (Chapter 1)
☐ Faulty ignition module (Chapter 5B)
☐ Uneven or low cylinder compression (Chapter 2A, 2B or 2C)
☐ Blocked injector/fuel injection system fault (Chapter 4A)
☐ Blocked catalytic converter (Chapter 4A or 4B)
☐ Engine overheating (Chapter 3)

## Engine hesitates on acceleration

☐ Worn, faulty or incorrectly-gapped spark plugs (Chapter 1)
☐ Vacuum leak at the throttle housing, inlet manifold or associated hoses (Chapter 4A or 4B)
☐ Blocked injectors/fuel injection system fault (Chapter 4A)

# Engine (continued)

### Engine stalls

- [ ] Vacuum leak at the throttle housing, inlet manifold or associated hoses (Chapter 4A or 4B)
- [ ] Fuel pump faulty, or delivery pressure low (Chapter 4A)
- [ ] Fuel tank vent blocked, or fuel pipes restricted (Chapter 4A or 4B)
- [ ] Blocked injectors/fuel injection system fault (Chapter 4A or 4B)

### Engine lacks power

- [ ] Air filter element blocked (Chapter 1)
- [ ] Fuel pipes blocked or restricted (Chapter 4A)
- [ ] Worn, faulty or incorrectly-gapped spark plugs (Chapter 1)
- [ ] Engine overheating (Chapter 3)
- [ ] Accelerator pedal position sensor faulty (Chapter 4A)
- [ ] Vacuum leak at the throttle housing, inlet manifold or associated hoses (Chapter 4A or 4B)
- [ ] Blocked injectors/fuel injection system fault (Chapter 4A or 4B)
- [ ] Fuel pump faulty, or delivery pressure low (Chapter 4A)
- [ ] Uneven or low cylinder compression (Chapter 2A, 2B or 2C)
- [ ] Blocked catalytic converter (Chapter 4A or 4B)
- [ ] Brakes binding (Chapter 1 or 9)
- [ ] Clutch slipping (Chapter 6)

### Engine backfires

- [ ] Vacuum leak at the throttle housing, inlet manifold or associated hoses (Chapter 4A or 4B)
- [ ] Blocked injectors/fuel injection system fault (Chapter 4A)
- [ ] Blocked catalytic converter (Chapter 4A or 4B)
- [ ] Faulty ignition module (Chapter 5B)

### Oil pressure warning light illuminated with engine running

- [ ] Low oil level, or incorrect oil grade (see *Weekly checks*)
- [ ] Faulty oil pressure switch, or wiring damaged (Chapter 5A)
- [ ] Worn engine bearings and/or oil pump (Chapter 2A, 2B, 2C or 2D)
- [ ] High engine operating temperature (Chapter 3)
- [ ] Oil pump pressure relief valve defective (Chapter 2A, 2B or 2C)
- [ ] Oil pump pick-up strainer clogged (Chapter 2A, 2B or 2C)

### Engine runs-on after switching off

- [ ] Excessive carbon build-up in engine (Chapter 2A, 2B or 2C)
- [ ] High engine operating temperature (Chapter 3)
- [ ] Fuel injection/engine management system fault (Chapter 4A)

### Engine noises

#### Pre-ignition (pinking) or knocking during acceleration or under load

- [ ] Ignition timing incorrect/ignition system fault (Chapter 1 or 5B)
- [ ] Incorrect grade of spark plug (Chapter 1)
- [ ] Incorrect grade of fuel (Chapter 4A)
- [ ] Knock sensor faulty (Chapter 4A)
- [ ] Vacuum leak at the throttle housing, inlet manifold or associated hoses (Chapter 4A or 4B)
- [ ] Excessive carbon build-up in engine (Chapter 2A, 2B or 2C)
- [ ] Fuel injection/engine management system fault (Chapter 4A)

#### Whistling or wheezing noises

- [ ] Leaking inlet manifold or throttle housing gasket (Chapter 4A)
- [ ] Leaking exhaust manifold gasket or pipe-to-manifold joint (Chapter 4A)
- [ ] Leaking vacuum hose (Chapter 4A, 4B or 9)
- [ ] Blowing cylinder head gasket (Chapter 2A, 2B or 2C)
- [ ] Partially blocked or leaking crankcase ventilation system (Chapter 4B)

#### Tapping or rattling noises

- [ ] Worn valve gear or camshaft (Chapter 2A, 2B or 2C)
- [ ] Ancillary component fault (coolant pump, alternator, etc) (Chapter 3, 5A, etc)

#### Knocking or thumping noises

- [ ] Worn big-end bearings (regular heavy knocking, perhaps less under load) (Chapter 2D)
- [ ] Worn main bearings (rumbling and knocking, perhaps worsening under load) (Chapter 2D)
- [ ] Piston slap – most noticeable when cold, caused by piston/bore wear (Chapter 2D)
- [ ] Ancillary component fault (coolant pump, alternator, etc) (Chapter 3, 5A, etc)
- [ ] Engine mountings worn or defective (Chapter 2A, 2B or 2C)
- [ ] Front suspension or steering components worn (Chapter 10)

# Cooling system

### Overheating

- [ ] Insufficient coolant in system (see *Weekly checks*)
- [ ] Thermostat faulty (Chapter 3)
- [ ] Radiator core blocked, or grille restricted (Chapter 3)
- [ ] Cooling fan faulty (Chapter 3)
- [ ] Inaccurate coolant temperature sensor (Chapter 3)
- [ ] Airlock in cooling system (Chapter 1 or 3)
- [ ] Expansion tank pressure cap faulty (Chapter 3)
- [ ] Engine management system fault (Chapter 4A or 4B)

### Overcooling

- [ ] Thermostat faulty (Chapter 3)
- [ ] Inaccurate coolant temperature sensor (Chapter 3)
- [ ] Cooling fan faulty (Chapter 3)
- [ ] Engine management system fault (Chapter 4A or 4B)

### External coolant leakage

- [ ] Deteriorated or damaged hoses or hose clips (Chapter 1)
- [ ] Radiator core or heater matrix leaking (Chapter 3)
- [ ] Expansion tank pressure cap faulty (Chapter 3)
- [ ] Coolant pump internal seal leaking (Chapter 3)
- [ ] Coolant pump gasket leaking (Chapter 3)
- [ ] Boiling due to overheating (Chapter 3)
- [ ] Cylinder block core plug leaking (Chapter 2D)

### Internal coolant leakage

- [ ] Leaking cylinder head gasket (Chapter 2A, 2B or 2C)
- [ ] Cracked cylinder head or cylinder block (Chapter 2A, 2B, 2C or 2D)

### Corrosion

- [ ] Infrequent draining and flushing (Chapter 1)
- [ ] Incorrect coolant mixture or inappropriate coolant type (see *Weekly checks*)

# Fuel and exhaust systems

### Excessive fuel consumption

☐ Air filter element dirty or clogged (Chapter 1)
☐ Fuel injection system fault (Chapter 4A or 4B)
☐ Engine management system fault (Chapter 4A or 4B)
☐ Crankcase ventilation system blocked (Chapter 4B)
☐ Tyres under-inflated (see *Weekly checks*)
☐ Brakes binding (Chapter 1 or 9)
☐ Fuel leak, causing apparent high consumption (Chapter 1, 4A or 4B)

### Fuel leakage and/or fuel odour

☐ Damaged or corroded fuel tank, pipes or connections (Chapter 4A or 4B)
☐ Evaporative emissions system fault (Chapter 4B)

### Excessive noise or fumes from exhaust system

☐ Leaking exhaust system or manifold joints (Chapter 1 or 4A)
☐ Leaking, corroded or damaged silencers or pipe (Chapter 1 or 4A)
☐ Broken mountings causing body or suspension contact (Chapter 1 or 4A)

# Clutch

**Note:** *Fault finding for the Easytronic semi-automatic clutch should be entrusted to a Vauxhall/Opel dealer.*

### Pedal travels to floor – no pressure or very little resistance

☐ Air in hydraulic system/faulty master or release cylinder (Chapter 6)
☐ Faulty hydraulic release system (Chapter 6)
☐ Clutch pedal return spring detached or broken (Chapter 6)
☐ Broken clutch release bearing (Chapter 6)
☐ Broken diaphragm spring in clutch pressure plate (Chapter 6)

### Clutch fails to disengage (unable to select gears)

☐ Air in hydraulic system/faulty master or release cylinder (Chapter 6)
☐ Faulty hydraulic release system (Chapter 6)
☐ Clutch disc sticking on transmission input shaft splines (Chapter 6)
☐ Clutch disc sticking to flywheel or pressure plate (Chapter 6)
☐ Faulty pressure plate assembly (Chapter 6)
☐ Clutch release mechanism worn or incorrectly assembled (Chapter 6)

### Clutch slips (engine speed increases, with no increase in vehicle speed)

☐ Faulty hydraulic release system (Chapter 6)
☐ Clutch disc linings excessively worn (Chapter 6)
☐ Clutch disc linings contaminated with oil or grease (Chapter 6)
☐ Faulty pressure plate or weak diaphragm spring (Chapter 6)

### Judder as clutch is engaged

☐ Clutch disc linings contaminated with oil or grease (Chapter 6)
☐ Clutch disc linings excessively worn (Chapter 6)
☐ Faulty or distorted pressure plate or diaphragm spring (Chapter 6).
☐ Worn or loose engine or transmission mountings (Chapter 2A, 2B or 2C)
☐ Clutch disc hub or transmission input shaft splines worn (Chapter 6)

### Noise when depressing or releasing clutch pedal

☐ Worn clutch release bearing (Chapter 6)
☐ Worn or dry clutch pedal bushes (Chapter 6)
☐ Worn or dry clutch master cylinder piston (Chapter 6)
☐ Faulty pressure plate assembly (Chapter 6)
☐ Pressure plate diaphragm spring broken (Chapter 6)
☐ Broken clutch disc cushioning springs (Chapter 6)

# Manual transmission

**Note:** *Fault finding for the Easytronic transmission should be entrusted to a Vauxhall dealer/Opel.*

### Noisy in neutral with engine running

☐ Lack of oil (Chapter 7A or 7C)
☐ Input shaft bearings worn (noise apparent with clutch pedal released, but not when depressed) (Chapter 7A)*
☐ Clutch release bearing worn (noise apparent with clutch pedal depressed, possibly less when released) (Chapter 6)

### Noisy in one particular gear

☐ Worn, damaged or chipped gear teeth (Chapter 7A)*

### Difficulty engaging gears

☐ Clutch fault (Chapter 6)
☐ Worn, damaged, or poorly-adjusted gearchange (Chapter 7A)
☐ Lack of oil (Chapter 7A or 7C)
☐ Worn synchroniser units (Chapter 7A)*

### Jumps out of gear

☐ Worn, damaged, or poorly-adjusted gearchange (Chapter 7A)
☐ Worn synchroniser units (Chapter 7A)*
☐ Worn selector forks (Chapter 7A)*

### Vibration

☐ Lack of oil (Chapter 7A or 7C)
☐ Worn bearings (Chapter 7A)*

### Lubricant leaks

☐ Leaking driveshaft or selector shaft oil seal (Chapter 7A)
☐ Leaking housing joint (Chapter 7A)*
☐ Leaking input shaft oil seal (Chapter 7A)*

*Although the corrective action necessary to remedy the symptoms described is beyond the scope of the home mechanic, the above information should be helpful in isolating the cause of the condition, so that the owner can communicate clearly with a professional mechanic.*

# Automatic transmission

**Note:** *Due to the complexity of the automatic transmission, it is difficult for the home mechanic to properly diagnose and service this unit. For problems other than the following, the vehicle should be taken to a dealer service department or automatic transmission specialist. Do not be too hasty in removing the transmission if a fault is suspected, as most of the testing is carried out with the unit still fitted. Remember that, besides the sensors specific to the transmission, many of the engine management system sensors described in Chapter 4 are essential to the correct operation of the transmission.*

### Fluid leakage

☐ Automatic transmission fluid is usually dark red in colour. Fluid leaks should not be confused with engine oil, which can easily be blown onto the transmission by airflow.
☐ To determine the source of a leak, first remove all built-up dirt and grime from the transmission housing and surrounding areas using a degreasing agent, or by steam-cleaning. Drive the vehicle at low speed, so airflow will not blow the leak far from its source. Raise and support the vehicle, and determine where the leak is coming from. The following are common areas of leakage:
a) Fluid pan
b) Dipstick tube (Chapter 7B)
c) Transmission-to-fluid cooler unions (Chapter 7B)

### Transmission fluid brown, or has burned smell

☐ Transmission fluid level low (Chapter 7B)

### General gear selection problems

☐ Chapter 7B deals with checking the selector cable on automatic transmissions. The following are common problems which may be caused by a faulty cable or sensor:

a) Engine starting in gears other than Park or Neutral.
b) Indicator panel indicating a gear other than the one actually being used.
c) Vehicle moves when in Park or Neutral.
d) Poor gear shift quality or erratic gear changes.

### Transmission will not downshift (kickdown) with accelerator pedal fully depressed

☐ Low transmission fluid level (Chapter 7B)
☐ Engine management system fault (Chapter 4A)
☐ Faulty transmission sensor or wiring (Chapter 7B)
☐ Incorrect selector cable adjustment (Chapter 7B)

### Engine will not start in any gear, or starts in gears other than Park or Neutral

☐ Faulty transmission sensor or wiring (Chapter 7B)
☐ Engine management system fault (Chapter 4A)
☐ Incorrect selector cable adjustment (Chapter 7B)

### Transmission slips, shifts roughly, is noisy, or has no drive in forward or reverse gears

☐ Transmission fluid level low (Chapter 7B)
☐ Faulty transmission sensor or wiring (Chapter 7B)
☐ Engine management system fault (Chapter 4A)

**Note:** *There are many probable causes for the above problems, but diagnosing and correcting them is considered beyond the scope of this manual. Having checked the fluid level and all the wiring as far as possible, a dealer or transmission specialist should be consulted if the problem persists.*

# Driveshafts

## Vibration when accelerating or decelerating

- ☐ Worn inner constant velocity joint (Chapter 8)
- ☐ Bent or distorted driveshaft (Chapter 8)

## Clicking or knocking noise on turns (at slow speed on full-lock)

- ☐ Worn outer constant velocity joint (Chapter 8)
- ☐ Lack of constant velocity joint lubricant, possibly due to damaged gaiter (Chapter 8)

# Braking system

*Note: Before assuming that a brake problem exists, make sure that the tyres are in good condition and correctly inflated, that the front wheel alignment is correct, and that the vehicle is not loaded with weight in an unequal manner. Apart from checking the condition of all pipe and hose connections, any faults occurring on the anti-lock braking system should be referred to a Vauxhall/Opel dealer for diagnosis.*

## Vehicle pulls to one side under braking

- ☐ Worn, defective, damaged or contaminated brake pads/shoes on one side (Chapter 1 or 9)
- ☐ Seized or partially-seized brake caliper piston/wheel cylinder (Chapter 1 or 9)
- ☐ A mixture of brake pad/shoe lining materials fitted between sides (Chapter 1 or 9)
- ☐ Brake caliper/backplate mounting bolts loose (Chapter 9)
- ☐ Worn or damaged steering or suspension components (Chapter 1 or 10)

## Noise (grinding or high-pitched squeal) when brakes applied

- ☐ Brake pad/shoe friction lining material worn down to metal backing (Chapter 1 or 9)
- ☐ Excessive corrosion of brake disc/drum (may be apparent after the vehicle has been standing for some time (Chapter 1 or 9)
- ☐ Foreign object (stone chipping, etc) trapped between brake disc and shield (Chapter 1 or 9)

## Excessive brake pedal travel

- ☐ Faulty master cylinder (Chapter 9)
- ☐ Air in hydraulic system (Chapter 1, 6 or 9)
- ☐ Faulty vacuum servo unit (Chapter 9)

## Brake pedal feels spongy when depressed

- ☐ Air in hydraulic system (Chapter 1, 6 or 9)
- ☐ Deteriorated flexible rubber brake hoses (Chapter 1 or 9)
- ☐ Master cylinder mounting nuts loose (Chapter 9)
- ☐ Faulty master cylinder (Chapter 9)

## Excessive brake pedal effort required to stop vehicle

- ☐ Faulty vacuum servo unit (Chapter 9)
- ☐ Disconnected, damaged or insecure brake servo vacuum hose (Chapter 9)
- ☐ Primary or secondary hydraulic circuit failure (Chapter 9)
- ☐ Seized brake caliper/wheel cylinder piston (Chapter 9)
- ☐ Brake pads/shoes incorrectly fitted (Chapter 9)
- ☐ Incorrect grade of brake pads/shoes fitted (Chapter 9)
- ☐ Brake pad/shoe linings contaminated (Chapter 1 or 9)

## Judder felt through brake pedal or steering wheel when braking

*Note: Under heavy braking on models equipped with ABS, vibration may be felt through the brake pedal. This is a normal feature of ABS operation, and does not constitute a fault*

- ☐ Excessive run-out or distortion of discs/drums (Chapter 1 or 9)
- ☐ Brake pad/shoe linings worn (Chapter 1 or 9)
- ☐ Brake caliper/backplate mounting bolts loose (Chapter 9)
- ☐ Wear in suspension or steering components or mountings (Chapter 1 or 10)
- ☐ Front wheels out of balance (see *Weekly checks*)

## Brakes binding

- ☐ Seized brake caliper/wheel cylinder piston (Chapter 9)
- ☐ Incorrectly-adjusted handbrake mechanism (Chapter 9)
- ☐ Faulty master cylinder (Chapter 9)

## Rear wheels locking under normal braking

- ☐ Rear brake pad/shoe linings contaminated or damaged (Chapter 1 or 9)
- ☐ Rear brake discs/drums warped (Chapter 1 or 9)

# Suspension and steering

**Note:** *Before diagnosing suspension or steering faults, be sure that the trouble is not due to incorrect tyre pressures, mixtures of tyre types, or binding brakes.*

## Vehicle pulls to one side

- [ ] Defective tyre (see *Weekly checks*)
- [ ] Excessive wear in suspension or steering components (Chapter 1 or 10)
- [ ] Incorrect front wheel alignment (Chapter 10)
- [ ] Accident damage to steering or suspension components (Chapter 1)

## Wheel wobble and vibration

- [ ] Front wheels out of balance (vibration felt mainly through the steering wheel) (see *Weekly checks*)
- [ ] Rear wheels out of balance (vibration felt throughout the vehicle) (see *Weekly checks*)
- [ ] Roadwheels damaged or distorted (see *Weekly checks*)
- [ ] Faulty or damaged tyre (see *Weekly checks*)
- [ ] Worn steering or suspension joints, bushes or components (Chapter 1 or 10)
- [ ] Wheel bolts loose (Chapter 1)

## Excessive pitching and/or rolling around corners, or during braking

- [ ] Defective shock absorbers (Chapter 1 or 10)
- [ ] Broken or weak spring and/or suspension component (Chapter 1 or 10)
- [ ] Worn or damaged anti-roll bar or mountings (Chapter 1 or 10)

## Wandering or general instability

- [ ] Incorrect front wheel alignment (Chapter 10)
- [ ] Worn steering or suspension joints, bushes or components (Chapter 1 or 10)
- [ ] Roadwheels out of balance (see *Weekly checks*)
- [ ] Faulty or damaged tyre (see *Weekly checks*)
- [ ] Wheel bolts loose (Chapter 1)
- [ ] Defective shock absorbers (Chapter 1 or 10)
- [ ] Power steering system fault (Chapter 10)

## Excessively-stiff steering

- [ ] Seized steering linkage balljoint or suspension balljoint (Chapter 1 or 10)
- [ ] Incorrect front wheel alignment (Chapter 10)
- [ ] Steering rack damaged (Chapter 10)
- [ ] Power steering system fault (Chapter 10)

## Excessive play in steering

- [ ] Worn steering column/intermediate shaft joints (Chapter 10)
- [ ] Worn track rod balljoints (Chapter 1 or 10)
- [ ] Worn steering rack (Chapter 10)
- [ ] Worn steering or suspension joints, bushes or components (Chapter 1 or 10)

## Lack of power assistance

- [ ] Power steering system fault (Chapter 10)
- [ ] Faulty steering rack (Chapter 10)

## Tyre wear excessive

### Tyres worn on inside or outside edges

- [ ] Tyres under-inflated (wear on both edges) (see *Weekly checks*)
- [ ] Incorrect camber or castor angles (wear on one edge only) (Chapter 10)
- [ ] Worn steering or suspension joints, bushes or components (Chapter 1 or 10)
- [ ] Excessively-hard cornering or braking
- [ ] Accident damage

### Tyre treads exhibit feathered edges

- [ ] Incorrect toe-setting (Chapter 10)

### Tyres worn in centre of tread

- [ ] Tyres over-inflated (see *Weekly checks*)

### Tyres worn on inside and outside edges

- [ ] Tyres under-inflated (see *Weekly checks*)

### Tyres worn unevenly

- [ ] Tyres/wheels out of balance (see *Weekly checks*)
- [ ] Excessive wheel or tyre run-out
- [ ] Worn shock absorbers (Chapter 1 or 10)
- [ ] Faulty tyre (see *Weekly checks*)

# Electrical system

**Note:** *For problems associated with the starting system, refer to the faults listed under 'Engine' earlier in this Section.*

## Battery will not hold a charge for more than a few days

- [ ] Battery defective internally (Chapter 5A)
- [ ] Battery terminal connections loose or corroded (see *Weekly checks*)
- [ ] Auxiliary drivebelt worn or incorrectly adjusted (Chapter 1)
- [ ] Alternator not charging at correct output (Chapter 5A)
- [ ] Alternator or voltage regulator faulty (Chapter 5A)
- [ ] Short-circuit causing continual battery drain (Chapter 5A or 12)

## Ignition/no-charge warning light remains illuminated with engine running

- [ ] Auxiliary drivebelt broken, worn, or incorrectly adjusted (Chapter 1)
- [ ] Internal fault in alternator or voltage regulator (Chapter 5A)
- [ ] Broken, disconnected, or loose wiring in charging circuit (Chapter 5A or 12)

## Ignition/no-charge warning light fails to come on

- [ ] Warning light bulb blown (Chapter 12)
- [ ] Broken, disconnected, or loose wiring in warning light circuit (Chapter 5A or 12)
- [ ] Alternator faulty (Chapter 5A)

# Electrical system

## Lights inoperative

- [ ] Bulb blown (Chapter 12)
- [ ] Corrosion of bulb or bulbholder contacts (Chapter 12)
- [ ] Blown fuse (Chapter 12)
- [ ] Faulty relay (Chapter 12)
- [ ] Broken, loose, or disconnected wiring (Chapter 12)
- [ ] Faulty switch (Chapter 12)

## Instrument readings inaccurate or erratic

### Fuel or temperature gauges give no reading

- [ ] Faulty gauge sender unit (Chapter 3 or 4)
- [ ] Wiring open-circuit (Chapter 12)
- [ ] Faulty gauge (Chapter 12)

### Fuel or temperature gauges give continuous maximum reading

- [ ] Faulty gauge sender unit (Chapter 3 or 4)
- [ ] Wiring short-circuit (Chapter 12)
- [ ] Faulty gauge (Chapter 12)

## Horn inoperative, or unsatisfactory in operation

### Horn operates all the time

- [ ] Horn push either earthed or stuck down (Chapter 12)
- [ ] Horn cable-to-horn push earthed (Chapter 12)

### Horn fails to operate

- [ ] Blown fuse (Chapter 12)
- [ ] Cable or connections loose, broken or disconnected (Chapter 12)
- [ ] Faulty horn (Chapter 12)

### Horn emits intermittent or unsatisfactory sound

- [ ] Cable connections loose (Chapter 12)
- [ ] Horn mountings loose (Chapter 12)
- [ ] Faulty horn (Chapter 12)

## Windscreen wipers inoperative, or unsatisfactory in operation

### Wipers fail to operate, or operate very slowly

- [ ] Wiper blades stuck to screen, or linkage seized or binding (Chapter 12)
- [ ] Blown fuse (Chapter 12)
- [ ] Battery discharged (Chapter 5A)
- [ ] Cable or connections loose, broken or disconnected (Chapter 12)
- [ ] Faulty relay (Chapter 12)
- [ ] Faulty wiper motor (Chapter 12)

### Wiper blades sweep over too large or too small an area of the glass

- [ ] Wiper blades incorrectly fitted, or wrong size used (see *Weekly checks*)
- [ ] Wiper arms incorrectly positioned on spindles (Chapter 12)
- [ ] Excessive wear of wiper linkage (Chapter 12)
- [ ] Wiper motor or linkage mountings loose or insecure (Chapter 12)

### Wiper blades fail to clean the glass effectively

- [ ] Wiper blade rubbers dirty, worn or perished (see *Weekly checks*)
- [ ] Wiper blades incorrectly fitted, or wrong size used (see *Weekly checks*)
- [ ] Wiper arm tension springs broken, or arm pivots seized (Chapter 12)
- [ ] Insufficient windscreen washer additive to adequately remove road film (see *Weekly checks*)

## Windscreen washers inoperative, or unsatisfactory in operation

### One or more washer jets inoperative

- [ ] Blocked washer jet
- [ ] Disconnected, kinked or restricted fluid hose (Chapter 12)
- [ ] Insufficient fluid in washer reservoir (see *Weekly checks*)

### Washer pump fails to operate

- [ ] Broken or disconnected wiring or connections (Chapter 12)
- [ ] Blown fuse (Chapter 12)
- [ ] Faulty washer switch (Chapter 12)
- [ ] Faulty washer pump (Chapter 12)

### Washer pump runs for some time before fluid is emitted from jets

- [ ] Faulty one-way valve in fluid supply hose (Chapter 12)

## Electric windows inoperative, or unsatisfactory in operation

### Window glass will only move in one direction

- [ ] Faulty switch (Chapter 12)

### Window glass slow to move

- [ ] Battery discharged (Chapter 5A)
- [ ] Regulator seized or damaged, or in need of lubrication (Chapter 11)
- [ ] Door internal components or trim fouling regulator (Chapter 11)
- [ ] Faulty motor (Chapter 11)

### Window glass fails to move

- [ ] Blown fuse (Chapter 12)
- [ ] Faulty relay (Chapter 12)
- [ ] Broken or disconnected wiring or connections (Chapter 12)
- [ ] Faulty motor (Chapter 11)

## Central locking system inoperative, or unsatisfactory in operation

### Complete system failure

- [ ] Remote handset battery discharged, where applicable (Chapter 1)
- [ ] Blown fuse (Chapter 12)
- [ ] Faulty relay (Chapter 12)
- [ ] Broken or disconnected wiring or connections (Chapter 12)
- [ ] Faulty motor (Chapter 11)

### Latch locks but will not unlock, or unlocks but will not lock

- [ ] Remote handset battery discharged, where applicable (Chapter 1)
- [ ] Faulty master switch (Chapter 12)
- [ ] Broken or disconnected latch operating rods or levers (Chapter 11)
- [ ] Faulty relay (Chapter 12)
- [ ] Faulty motor (Chapter 11)

### One solenoid/motor fails to operate

- [ ] Broken or disconnected wiring or connections (Chapter 12)
- [ ] Faulty operating assembly (Chapter 11)
- [ ] Broken, binding or disconnected latch operating rods or levers (Chapter 11)
- [ ] Fault in door latch (Chapter 11)

# A

**ABS (Anti-lock brake system)** A system, usually electronically controlled, that senses incipient wheel lockup during braking and relieves hydraulic pressure at wheels that are about to skid.

**Air bag** An inflatable bag hidden in the steering wheel (driver's side) or the dash or glovebox (passenger side). In a head-on collision, the bags inflate, preventing the driver and front passenger from being thrown forward into the steering wheel or windscreen.

**Air cleaner** A metal or plastic housing, containing a filter element, which removes dust and dirt from the air being drawn into the engine.

**Air filter element** The actual filter in an air cleaner system, usually manufactured from pleated paper and requiring renewal at regular intervals.

*Air filter*

**Allen key** A hexagonal wrench which fits into a recessed hexagonal hole.

**Alligator clip** A long-nosed spring-loaded metal clip with meshing teeth. Used to make temporary electrical connections.

**Alternator** A component in the electrical system which converts mechanical energy from a drivebelt into electrical energy to charge the battery and to operate the starting system, ignition system and electrical accessories.

**Ampere (amp)** A unit of measurement for the flow of electric current. One amp is the amount of current produced by one volt acting through a resistance of one ohm.

**Anaerobic sealer** A substance used to prevent bolts and screws from loosening. Anaerobic means that it does not require oxygen for activation. The Loctite brand is widely used.

**Antifreeze** A substance (usually ethylene glycol) mixed with water, and added to a vehicle's cooling system, to prevent freezing of the coolant in winter. Antifreeze also contains chemicals to inhibit corrosion and the formation of rust and other deposits that would tend to clog the radiator and coolant passages and reduce cooling efficiency.

**Anti-seize compound** A coating that reduces the risk of seizing on fasteners that are subjected to high temperatures, such as exhaust manifold bolts and nuts.

**Asbestos** A natural fibrous mineral with great heat resistance, commonly used in the composition of brake friction materials.

Asbestos is a health hazard and the dust created by brake systems should never be inhaled or ingested.

**Axle** A shaft on which a wheel revolves, or which revolves with a wheel. Also, a solid beam that connects the two wheels at one end of the vehicle. An axle which also transmits power to the wheels is known as a live axle.

**Axleshaft** A single rotating shaft, on either side of the differential, which delivers power from the final drive assembly to the drive wheels. Also called a driveshaft or a halfshaft.

# B

**Ball bearing** An anti-friction bearing consisting of a hardened inner and outer race with hardened steel balls between two races.

**Bearing** The curved surface on a shaft or in a bore, or the part assembled into either, that permits relative motion between them with minimum wear and friction.

*Bearing*

**Big-end bearing** The bearing in the end of the connecting rod that's attached to the crankshaft.

**Bleed nipple** A valve on a brake wheel cylinder, caliper or other hydraulic component that is opened to purge the hydraulic system of air. Also called a bleed screw.

**Brake bleeding** Procedure for removing air from lines of a hydraulic brake system.

*Brake bleeding*

**Brake disc** The component of a disc brake that rotates with the wheels.

**Brake drum** The component of a drum brake that rotates with the wheels.

**Brake linings** The friction material which contacts the brake disc or drum to retard the vehicle's speed. The linings are bonded or riveted to the brake pads or shoes.

**Brake pads** The replaceable friction pads that pinch the brake disc when the brakes are applied. Brake pads consist of a friction material bonded or riveted to a rigid backing plate.

**Brake shoe** The crescent-shaped carrier to which the brake linings are mounted and which forces the lining against the rotating drum during braking.

**Braking systems** For more information on braking systems, consult the *Haynes Automotive Brake Manual*.

**Breaker bar** A long socket wrench handle providing greater leverage.

**Bulkhead** The insulated partition between the engine and the passenger compartment.

# C

**Caliper** The non-rotating part of a disc-brake assembly that straddles the disc and carries the brake pads. The caliper also contains the hydraulic components that cause the pads to pinch the disc when the brakes are applied. A caliper is also a measuring tool that can be set to measure inside or outside dimensions of an object.

**Camshaft** A rotating shaft on which a series of cam lobes operate the valve mechanisms. The camshaft may be driven by gears, by sprockets and chain or by sprockets and a belt.

**Canister** A container in an evaporative emission control system; contains activated charcoal granules to trap vapours from the fuel system.

*Canister*

**Carburettor** A device which mixes fuel with air in the proper proportions to provide a desired power output from a spark ignition internal combustion engine.

**Castellated** Resembling the parapets along the top of a castle wall. For example, a castellated balljoint stud nut.

**Castor** In wheel alignment, the backward or forward tilt of the steering axis. Castor is positive when the steering axis is inclined rearward at the top.

**Catalytic converter** A silencer-like device in the exhaust system which converts certain pollutants in the exhaust gases into less harmful substances.

*Catalytic converter*

**Circlip** A ring-shaped clip used to prevent endwise movement of cylindrical parts and shafts. An internal circlip is installed in a groove in a housing; an external circlip fits into a groove on the outside of a cylindrical piece such as a shaft.

**Clearance** The amount of space between two parts. For example, between a piston and a cylinder, between a bearing and a journal, etc.

**Coil spring** A spiral of elastic steel found in various sizes throughout a vehicle, for example as a springing medium in the suspension and in the valve train.

**Compression** Reduction in volume, and increase in pressure and temperature, of a gas, caused by squeezing it into a smaller space.

**Compression ratio** The relationship between cylinder volume when the piston is at top dead centre and cylinder volume when the piston is at bottom dead centre.

**Constant velocity (CV) joint** A type of universal joint that cancels out vibrations caused by driving power being transmitted through an angle.

**Core plug** A disc or cup-shaped metal device inserted in a hole in a casting through which core was removed when the casting was formed. Also known as a freeze plug or expansion plug.

**Crankcase** The lower part of the engine block in which the crankshaft rotates.

**Crankshaft** The main rotating member, or shaft, running the length of the crankcase, with offset "throws" to which the connecting rods are attached.

*Crankshaft assembly*

**Crocodile clip** See Alligator clip

## D

**Diagnostic code** Code numbers obtained by accessing the diagnostic mode of an engine management computer. This code can be used to determine the area in the system where a malfunction may be located.

**Disc brake** A brake design incorporating a rotating disc onto which brake pads are squeezed. The resulting friction converts the energy of a moving vehicle into heat.

**Double-overhead cam (DOHC)** An engine that uses two overhead camshafts, usually one for the intake valves and one for the exhaust valves.

**Drivebelt(s)** The belt(s) used to drive accessories such as the alternator, water pump, power steering pump, air conditioning compressor, etc. off the crankshaft pulley.

*Accessory drivebelts*

**Driveshaft** Any shaft used to transmit motion. Commonly used when referring to the axleshafts on a front wheel drive vehicle.

**Drum brake** A type of brake using a drum-shaped metal cylinder attached to the inner surface of the wheel. When the brake pedal is pressed, curved brake shoes with friction linings press against the inside of the drum to slow or stop the vehicle.

## E

**EGR valve** A valve used to introduce exhaust gases into the intake air stream.

**Electronic control unit (ECU)** A computer which controls (for instance) ignition and fuel injection systems, or an anti-lock braking system. For more information refer to the *Haynes Automotive Electrical and Electronic Systems Manual*.

**Electronic Fuel Injection (EFI)** A computer controlled fuel system that distributes fuel through an injector located in each intake port of the engine.

**Emergency brake** A braking system, independent of the main hydraulic system, that can be used to slow or stop the vehicle if the primary brakes fail, or to hold the vehicle stationary even though the brake pedal isn't depressed. It usually consists of a hand lever that actuates either front or rear brakes mechanically through a series of cables and linkages. Also known as a handbrake or parking brake.

**Endfloat** The amount of lengthwise movement between two parts. As applied to a crankshaft, the distance that the crankshaft can move forward and back in the cylinder block.

**Engine management system (EMS)** A computer controlled system which manages the fuel injection and the ignition systems in an integrated fashion.

**Exhaust manifold** A part with several passages through which exhaust gases leave the engine combustion chambers and enter the exhaust pipe.

## F

**Fan clutch** A viscous (fluid) drive coupling device which permits variable engine fan speeds in relation to engine speeds.

**Feeler blade** A thin strip or blade of hardened steel, ground to an exact thickness, used to check or measure clearances between parts.

*Feeler blade*

**Firing order** The order in which the engine cylinders fire, or deliver their power strokes, beginning with the number one cylinder.

**Flywheel** A heavy spinning wheel in which energy is absorbed and stored by means of momentum. On cars, the flywheel is attached to the crankshaft to smooth out firing impulses.

**Free play** The amount of travel before any action takes place. The "looseness" in a linkage, or an assembly of parts, between the initial application of force and actual movement. For example, the distance the brake pedal moves before the pistons in the master cylinder are actuated.

**Fuse** An electrical device which protects a circuit against accidental overload. The typical fuse contains a soft piece of metal which is calibrated to melt at a predetermined current flow (expressed as amps) and break the circuit.

**Fusible link** A circuit protection device consisting of a conductor surrounded by heat-resistant insulation. The conductor is smaller than the wire it protects, so it acts as the weakest link in the circuit. Unlike a blown fuse, a failed fusible link must frequently be cut from the wire for replacement.

## G

**Gap** The distance the spark must travel in jumping from the centre electrode to the side electrode in a spark plug. Also refers to the spacing between the points in a contact breaker assembly in a conventional points-type ignition, or to the distance between the reluctor or rotor and the pickup coil in an electronic ignition.

*Adjusting spark plug gap*

**Gasket** Any thin, soft material - usually cork, cardboard, asbestos or soft metal - installed between two metal surfaces to ensure a good seal. For instance, the cylinder head gasket seals the joint between the block and the cylinder head.

*Gasket*

**Gauge** An instrument panel display used to monitor engine conditions. A gauge with a movable pointer on a dial or a fixed scale is an analogue gauge. A gauge with a numerical readout is called a digital gauge.

## H

**Halfshaft** A rotating shaft that transmits power from the final drive unit to a drive wheel, usually when referring to a live rear axle.

**Harmonic balancer** A device designed to reduce torsion or twisting vibration in the crankshaft. May be incorporated in the crankshaft pulley. Also known as a vibration damper.

**Hone** An abrasive tool for correcting small irregularities or differences in diameter in an engine cylinder, brake cylinder, etc.

**Hydraulic tappet** A tappet that utilises hydraulic pressure from the engine's lubrication system to maintain zero clearance (constant contact with both camshaft and valve stem). Automatically adjusts to variation in valve stem length. Hydraulic tappets also reduce valve noise.

## I

**Ignition timing** The moment at which the spark plug fires, usually expressed in the number of crankshaft degrees before the piston reaches the top of its stroke.

**Inlet manifold** A tube or housing with passages through which flows the air-fuel mixture (carburettor vehicles and vehicles with throttle body injection) or air only (port fuel-injected vehicles) to the port openings in the cylinder head.

## J

**Jump start** Starting the engine of a vehicle with a discharged or weak battery by attaching jump leads from the weak battery to a charged or helper battery.

## L

**Load Sensing Proportioning Valve (LSPV)** A brake hydraulic system control valve that works like a proportioning valve, but also takes into consideration the amount of weight carried by the rear axle.

**Locknut** A nut used to lock an adjustment nut, or other threaded component, in place. For example, a locknut is employed to keep the adjusting nut on the rocker arm in position.

**Lockwasher** A form of washer designed to prevent an attaching nut from working loose.

## M

**MacPherson strut** A type of front suspension system devised by Earle MacPherson at Ford of England. In its original form, a simple lateral link with the anti-roll bar creates the lower control arm. A long strut - an integral coil spring and shock absorber - is mounted between the body and the steering knuckle. Many modern so-called MacPherson strut systems use a conventional lower A-arm and don't rely on the anti-roll bar for location.

**Multimeter** An electrical test instrument with the capability to measure voltage, current and resistance.

## N

**NOx** Oxides of Nitrogen. A common toxic pollutant emitted by petrol and diesel engines at higher temperatures.

## O

**Ohm** The unit of electrical resistance. One volt applied to a resistance of one ohm will produce a current of one amp.

**Ohmmeter** An instrument for measuring electrical resistance.

**O-ring** A type of sealing ring made of a special rubber-like material; in use, the O-ring is compressed into a groove to provide the sealing action.

**Overhead cam (ohc) engine** An engine with the camshaft(s) located on top of the cylinder head(s).

**Overhead valve (ohv) engine** An engine with the valves located in the cylinder head, but with the camshaft located in the engine block.

**Oxygen sensor** A device installed in the engine exhaust manifold, which senses the oxygen content in the exhaust and converts this information into an electric current. Also called a Lambda sensor.

## P

**Phillips screw** A type of screw head having a cross instead of a slot for a corresponding type of screwdriver.

**Plastigage** A thin strip of plastic thread, available in different sizes, used for measuring clearances. For example, a strip of Plastigage is laid across a bearing journal. The parts are assembled and dismantled; the width of the crushed strip indicates the clearance between journal and bearing.

*Plastigage*

**Propeller shaft** The long hollow tube with universal joints at both ends that carries power from the transmission to the differential on front-engined rear wheel drive vehicles.

**Proportioning valve** A hydraulic control valve which limits the amount of pressure to the rear brakes during panic stops to prevent wheel lock-up.

## R

**Rack-and-pinion steering** A steering system with a pinion gear on the end of the steering shaft that mates with a rack (think of a geared wheel opened up and laid flat). When the steering wheel is turned, the pinion turns, moving the rack to the left or right. This movement is transmitted through the track rods to the steering arms at the wheels.

**Radiator** A liquid-to-air heat transfer device designed to reduce the temperature of the coolant in an internal combustion engine cooling system.

**Refrigerant** Any substance used as a heat transfer agent in an air-conditioning system. R-12 has been the principle refrigerant for many years; recently, however, manufacturers have begun using R-134a, a non-CFC substance that is considered less harmful to the ozone in the upper atmosphere.

**Rocker arm** A lever arm that rocks on a shaft or pivots on a stud. In an overhead valve engine, the rocker arm converts the upward movement of the pushrod into a downward movement to open a valve.

**Rotor** In a distributor, the rotating device inside the cap that connects the centre electrode and the outer terminals as it turns, distributing the high voltage from the coil secondary winding to the proper spark plug. Also, that part of an alternator which rotates inside the stator. Also, the rotating assembly of a turbocharger, including the compressor wheel, shaft and turbine wheel.

**Runout** The amount of wobble (in-and-out movement) of a gear or wheel as it's rotated. The amount a shaft rotates "out-of-true." The out-of-round condition of a rotating part.

## S

**Sealant** A liquid or paste used to prevent leakage at a joint. Sometimes used in conjunction with a gasket.

**Sealed beam lamp** An older headlight design which integrates the reflector, lens and filaments into a hermetically-sealed one-piece unit. When a filament burns out or the lens cracks, the entire unit is simply replaced.

**Serpentine drivebelt** A single, long, wide accessory drivebelt that's used on some newer vehicles to drive all the accessories, instead of a series of smaller, shorter belts. Serpentine drivebelts are usually tensioned by an automatic tensioner.

*Serpentine drivebelt*

**Shim** Thin spacer, commonly used to adjust the clearance or relative positions between two parts. For example, shims inserted into or under bucket tappets control valve clearances. Clearance is adjusted by changing the thickness of the shim.

**Slide hammer** A special puller that screws into or hooks onto a component such as a shaft or bearing; a heavy sliding handle on the shaft bottoms against the end of the shaft to knock the component free.

**Sprocket** A tooth or projection on the periphery of a wheel, shaped to engage with a chain or drivebelt. Commonly used to refer to the sprocket wheel itself.

**Starter inhibitor switch** On vehicles with an automatic transmission, a switch that prevents starting if the vehicle is not in Neutral or Park.

**Strut** See MacPherson strut.

## T

**Tappet** A cylindrical component which transmits motion from the cam to the valve stem, either directly or via a pushrod and rocker arm. Also called a cam follower.

**Thermostat** A heat-controlled valve that regulates the flow of coolant between the cylinder block and the radiator, so maintaining optimum engine operating temperature. A thermostat is also used in some air cleaners in which the temperature is regulated.

**Thrust bearing** The bearing in the clutch assembly that is moved in to the release levers by clutch pedal action to disengage the clutch. Also referred to as a release bearing.

**Timing belt** A toothed belt which drives the camshaft. Serious engine damage may result if it breaks in service.

**Timing chain** A chain which drives the camshaft.

**Toe-in** The amount the front wheels are closer together at the front than at the rear. On rear wheel drive vehicles, a slight amount of toe-in is usually specified to keep the front wheels running parallel on the road by offsetting other forces that tend to spread the wheels apart.

**Toe-out** The amount the front wheels are closer together at the rear than at the front. On front wheel drive vehicles, a slight amount of toe-out is usually specified.

**Tools** For full information on choosing and using tools, refer to the *Haynes Automotive Tools Manual*.

**Tracer** A stripe of a second colour applied to a wire insulator to distinguish that wire from another one with the same colour insulator.

**Tune-up** A process of accurate and careful adjustments and parts replacement to obtain the best possible engine performance.

**Turbocharger** A centrifugal device, driven by exhaust gases, that pressurises the intake air. Normally used to increase the power output from a given engine displacement, but can also be used primarily to reduce exhaust emissions (as on VW's "Umwelt" Diesel engine).

## U

**Universal joint or U-joint** A double-pivoted connection for transmitting power from a driving to a driven shaft through an angle. A U-joint consists of two Y-shaped yokes and a cross-shaped member called the spider.

## V

**Valve** A device through which the flow of liquid, gas, vacuum, or loose material in bulk may be started, stopped, or regulated by a movable part that opens, shuts, or partially obstructs one or more ports or passageways. A valve is also the movable part of such a device.

**Valve clearance** The clearance between the valve tip (the end of the valve stem) and the rocker arm or tappet. The valve clearance is measured when the valve is closed.

**Vernier caliper** A precision measuring instrument that measures inside and outside dimensions. Not quite as accurate as a micrometer, but more convenient.

**Viscosity** The thickness of a liquid or its resistance to flow.

**Volt** A unit for expressing electrical "pressure" in a circuit. One volt that will produce a current of one ampere through a resistance of one ohm.

## W

**Welding** Various processes used to join metal items by heating the areas to be joined to a molten state and fusing them together. For more information refer to the *Haynes Automotive Welding Manual*.

**Wiring diagram** A drawing portraying the components and wires in a vehicle's electrical system, using standardised symbols. For more information refer to the *Haynes Automotive Electrical and Electronic Systems Manual*.

**Note:** *References throughout this index are in the form* **"Chapter number"** • **"Page number"**. *So, for example, 2C•15 refers to page 15 of Chapter 2C.*

**Note:** *References throughout this index are in the form* "**Chapter number**" • "**Page number**". *So, for example, 2C•15 refers to page 15 of Chapter 2C.*

**Note:** *References throughout this index are in the form* **"Chapter number"** • **"Page number"**. *So, for example, 2C•15 refers to page 15 of Chapter 2C.*

# Haynes Manuals – The Complete UK Car List

| Title | Book No. |
|---|---|
| **ALFA ROMEO** Alfasud/Sprint (74 - 88) up to F * | 0292 |
| Alfa Romeo Alfetta (73 - 87) up to E * | 0531 |
| **AUDI** 80, 90 & Coupe Petrol (79 - Nov 88) up to F | 0605 |
| Audi 80, 90 & Coupe Petrol (Oct 86 - 90) D to H | 1491 |
| Audi 100 & 200 Petrol (Oct 82 - 90) up to H | 0907 |
| Audi 100 & A6 Petrol & Diesel (May 91 - May 97) H to P | 3504 |
| Audi A3 Petrol & Diesel (96 - May 03) P to 03 | 4253 |
| Audi A4 Petrol & Diesel (95 - 00) M to X | 3575 |
| Audi A4 Petrol & Diesel (01 - 04) X to 54 | 4609 |
| **AUSTIN** A35 & A40 (56 - 67) up to F * | 0118 |
| Austin/MG/Rover Maestro 1.3 & 1.6 Petrol (83 - 95) up to M | 0922 |
| Austin/MG Metro (80 - May 90) up to G | 0718 |
| Austin/Rover Montego 1.3 & 1.6 Petrol (84 - 94) A to L | 1066 |
| Austin/MG/Rover Montego 2.0 Petrol (84 - 95) A to M | 1067 |
| Mini (59 - 69) up to H * | 0527 |
| Mini (69 - 01) up to X | 0646 |
| Austin/Rover 2.0 litre Diesel Engine (86 - 93) C to L | 1857 |
| Austin Healey 100/6 & 3000 (56 - 68) up to G * | 0049 |
| **BEDFORD** CF Petrol (69 - 87) up to E | 0163 |
| Bedford/Vauxhall Rascal & Suzuki Supercarry (86 - Oct 94) C to M | 3015 |
| **BMW** 316, 320 & 320i (4-cyl) (75 - Feb 83) up to Y * | 0276 |
| BMW 320, 320i, 323i & 325i (6-cyl) (Oct 77 - Sept 87) up to E | 0815 |
| BMW 3- & 5-Series Petrol (81 - 91) up to J | 1948 |
| BMW 3-Series Petrol (Apr 91 - 99) H to V | 3210 |
| BMW 3-Series Petrol (Sept 98 - 03) S to 53 | 4067 |
| BMW 520i & 525e (Oct 81 - June 88) up to E | 1560 |
| BMW 525, 528 & 528i (73 - Sept 81) up to X * | 0632 |
| BMW 5-Series 6-cyl Petrol (April 96 - Aug 03) N to 03 | 4151 |
| BMW 1500, 1502, 1600, 1602, 2000 & 2002 (59 - 77) up to S * | 0240 |
| **CHRYSLER** PT Cruiser Petrol (00 - 03) W to 53 | 4058 |
| **CITROËN** 2CV, Ami & Dyane (67 - 90) up to H | 0196 |
| Citroën AX Petrol & Diesel (87 - 97) D to P | 3014 |
| Citroën Berlingo & Peugeot Partner Petrol & Diesel (96 - 05) P to 55 | 4281 |
| Citroën BX Petrol (83 - 94) A to L | 0908 |
| Citroën C15 Van Petrol & Diesel (89 - Oct 98) F to S | 3509 |
| Citroën C3 Petrol & Diesel (02 - 05) 51 to 05 | 4197 |
| Citroen C5 Petrol & Diesel (01-08) Y to 08 | 4745 |
| Citroën CX Petrol (75 - 88) up to F | 0528 |
| Citroën Saxo Petrol & Diesel (96 - 04) N to 54 | 3506 |
| Citroën Visa Petrol (79 - 88) up to F | 0620 |
| Citroën Xantia Petrol & Diesel (93 - 01) K to Y | 3082 |
| Citroën XM Petrol & Diesel (89 - 00) G to X | 3451 |
| Citroën Xsara Petrol & Diesel (97 - Sept 00) R to W | 3751 |
| Citroën Xsara Picasso Petrol & Diesel (00 - 02) W to 52 | 3944 |
| Citroen Xsara Picasso (03-08) | 4784 |
| Citroën ZX Diesel (91 - 98) J to S | 1922 |
| Citroën ZX Petrol (91 - 98) H to S | 1881 |
| Citroën 1.7 & 1.9 litre Diesel Engine (84 - 96) A to N | 1379 |
| **FIAT** 126 (73 - 87) up to E * | 0305 |
| Fiat 500 (57 - 73) up to M * | 0090 |
| Fiat Bravo & Brava Petrol (95 - 00) N to W | 3572 |
| Fiat Cinquecento (93 - 98) K to R | 3501 |
| Fiat Panda (81 - 95) up to M | 0793 |
| Fiat Punto Petrol & Diesel (94 - Oct 99) L to V | 3251 |
| Fiat Punto Petrol (Oct 99 - July 03) V to 03 | 4066 |
| Fiat Punto Petrol (03-07) 03 to 07 | 4746 |
| Fiat Regata Petrol (84 - 88) A to F | 1167 |
| Fiat Tipo Petrol (88 - 91) E to J | 1625 |
| Fiat Uno Petrol (83 - 95) up to M | 0923 |
| Fiat X1/9 (74 - 89) up to G * | 0273 |
| **FORD** Anglia (59 - 68) up to G * | 0001 |

| Title | Book No. |
|---|---|
| Ford Capri II (& III) 1.6 & 2.0 (74 - 87) up to E * | 0283 |
| Ford Capri II (& III) 2.8 & 3.0 V6 (74 - 87) up to E | 1309 |
| Ford Cortina Mk I & Corsair 1500 ('62 - '66) up to D* | 0214 |
| Ford Cortina Mk III 1300 & 1600 (70 - 76) up to P * | 0070 |
| Ford Escort Mk I 1100 & 1300 (68 - 74) up to N * | 0171 |
| Ford Escort Mk I Mexico, RS 1600 & RS 2000 (70 - 74) up to N * | 0139 |
| Ford Escort Mk II Mexico, RS 1800 & RS 2000 (75 - 80) up to W * | 0735 |
| Ford Escort (75 - Aug 80) up to V * | 0280 |
| Ford Escort Petrol (Sept 80 - Sept 90) up to H | 0686 |
| Ford Escort & Orion Petrol (Sept 90 - 00) H to X | 1737 |
| Ford Escort & Orion Diesel (Sept 90 - 00) H to X | 4081 |
| Ford Fiesta (76 - Aug 83) up to Y | 0334 |
| Ford Fiesta Petrol (Aug 83 - Feb 89) A to F | 1030 |
| Ford Fiesta Petrol (Feb 89 - Oct 95) F to N | 1595 |
| Ford Fiesta Petrol & Diesel (Oct 95 - Mar 02) N to 02 | 3397 |
| Ford Fiesta Petrol & Diesel (Apr 02 - 07) 02 to 57 | 4170 |
| Ford Focus Petrol & Diesel (98 - 01) S to Y | 3759 |
| Ford Focus Petrol & Diesel (Oct 01 - 05) 51 to 05 | 4167 |
| Ford Galaxy Petrol & Diesel (95 - Aug 00) M to W | 3984 |
| Ford Granada Petrol (Sept 77 - Feb 85) up to B * | 0481 |
| Ford Granada & Scorpio Petrol (Mar 85 - 94) B to M | 1245 |
| Ford Ka (96 - 02) P to 52 | 3570 |
| Ford Mondeo Petrol (93 - Sept 00) K to X | 1923 |
| Ford Mondeo Petrol & Diesel (Oct 00 - Jul 03) X to 03 | 3990 |
| Ford Mondeo Petrol & Diesel (July 03 - 07) 03 to 56 | 4619 |
| Ford Mondeo Diesel (93 - 96) L to N | 3465 |
| Ford Orion Petrol (83 - Sept 90) up to H | 1009 |
| Ford Sierra 4-cyl Petrol (82 - 93) up to K | 0903 |
| Ford Sierra V6 Petrol (82 - 91) up to J | 0904 |
| Ford Transit Petrol (Mk 2) (78 - Jan 86) up to C | 0719 |
| Ford Transit Petrol (Mk 3) (Feb 86 - 89) C to G | 1468 |
| Ford Transit Diesel (Feb 86 - 99) C to T | 3019 |
| Ford Transit Diesel (00-06) | 4775 |
| Ford 1.6 & 1.8 litre Diesel Engine (84 - 96) A to N | 1172 |
| Ford 2.1, 2.3 & 2.5 litre Diesel Engine (77 - 90) up to H | 1606 |
| **FREIGHT ROVER** Sherpa Petrol (74 - 87) up to E | 0463 |
| **HILLMAN** Avenger (70 - 82) up to Y | 0037 |
| Hillman Imp (63 - 76) up to R * | 0022 |
| **HONDA** Civic (Feb 84 - Oct 87) A to E | 1226 |
| Honda Civic (Nov 91 - 96) J to N | 3199 |
| Honda Civic Petrol (Mar 95 - 00) M to X | 4050 |
| Honda Civic Petrol & Diesel (01 - 05) X to 55 | 4611 |
| Honda CR-V Petrol & Diesel (01-06) | 4747 |
| Honda Jazz (01 - Feb 08) 51 - 57 | 4735 |
| **HYUNDAI** Pony (85 - 94) C to M | 3398 |
| **JAGUAR** E Type (61 - 72) up to L * | 0140 |
| Jaguar MkI & II, 240 & 340 (55 - 69) up to H * | 0098 |
| Jaguar XJ6, XJ & Sovereign; Daimler Sovereign (68 - Oct 86) up to D | 0242 |
| Jaguar XJ6 & Sovereign (Oct 86 - Sept 94) D to M | 3261 |
| Jaguar XJ12, XJS & Sovereign; Daimler Double Six (72 - 88) up to F | 0478 |
| **JEEP** Cherokee Petrol (93 - 96) K to N | 1943 |
| **LADA** 1200, 1300, 1500 & 1600 (74 - 91) up to J | 0413 |
| Lada Samara (87 - 91) D to J | 1610 |
| **LAND ROVER** 90, 110 & Defender Diesel (83 - 07) up to 56 | 3017 |
| Land Rover Discovery Petrol & Diesel (89 - 98) G to S | 3016 |
| Land Rover Discovery Diesel (Nov 98 - Jul 04) S to 04 | 4606 |
| Land Rover Freelander Petrol & Diesel (97 - Sept 03) R to 53 | 3929 |
| Land Rover Freelander Petrol & Diesel (Oct 03 - Oct 06) 53 to 56 | 4623 |

| Title | Book No. |
|---|---|
| Land Rover Series IIA & III Diesel (58 - 85) up to C | 0529 |
| Land Rover Series II, IIA & III 4-cyl Petrol (58 - 85) up to C | 0314 |
| **MAZDA** 323 (Mar 81 - Oct 89) up to G | 1608 |
| Mazda 323 (Oct 89 - 98) G to R | 3455 |
| Mazda 626 (May 83 - Sept 87) up to E | 0929 |
| Mazda B1600, B1800 & B2000 Pick-up Petrol (72 - 88) up to F | 0267 |
| Mazda RX-7 (79 - 85) up to C * | 0460 |
| **MERCEDES-BENZ** 190, 190E & 190D Petrol & Diesel (83 - 93) A to L | 3450 |
| Mercedes-Benz 200D, 240D, 240TD, 300D & 300TD 123 Series Diesel (Oct 76 - 85) | 1114 |
| Mercedes-Benz 250 & 280 (68 - 72) up to L * | 0346 |
| Mercedes-Benz 250 & 280 123 Series Petrol (Oct 76 - 84) up to B * | 0677 |
| Mercedes-Benz 124 Series Petrol & Diesel (85 - Aug 93) C to K | 3253 |
| Mercedes-Benz A-Class Petrol & Diesel (98-04) S to 54 | 4748 |
| Mercedes-Benz C-Class Petrol & Diesel (93 - Aug 00) L to W | 3511 |
| Mercedes-Benz C-Class (00-06) | 4780 |
| **MG**A (55 - 62) * | 0475 |
| MGB (62 - 80) up to W | 0111 |
| MG Midget & Austin-Healey Sprite (58 - 80) up to W * | 0265 |
| **MINI** Petrol (July 01 - 05) Y to 05 | 4273 |
| **MITSUBISHI** Shogun & L200 Pick-Ups Petrol (83 - 94) up to M | 1944 |
| **MORRIS** Ital 1.3 (80 - 84) up to B | 0705 |
| Morris Minor 1000 (56 - 71) up to K | 0024 |
| **NISSAN** Almera Petrol (95 - Feb 00) N to V | 4053 |
| Nissan Almera & Tino Petrol (Feb 00 - 07) V to 56 | 4612 |
| Nissan Bluebird (May 84 - Mar 86) A to C | 1223 |
| Nissan Bluebird Petrol (Mar 86 - 90) C to H | 1473 |
| Nissan Cherry (Sept 82 - 86) up to D | 1031 |
| Nissan Micra (83 - Jan 93) up to K | 0931 |
| Nissan Micra (93 - 02) K to 52 | 3254 |
| Nissan Micra Petrol (03-07) 52 to 57 | 4734 |
| Nissan Primera Petrol (90 - Aug 99) H to T | 1851 |
| Nissan Stanza (82 - 86) up to D | 0824 |
| Nissan Sunny Petrol (May 82 - Oct 86) up to D | 0895 |
| Nissan Sunny Petrol (Oct 86 - Mar 91) D to H | 1378 |
| Nissan Sunny Petrol (Apr 91 - 95) H to N | 3219 |
| **OPEL** Ascona & Manta (B Series) (Sept 75 - 88) up to F * | 0316 |
| Opel Ascona Petrol (81 - 88) | 3215 |
| Opel Astra Petrol (Oct 91 - Feb 98) | 3156 |
| Opel Corsa Petrol (83 - Mar 93) | 3160 |
| Opel Corsa Petrol (Mar 93 - 97) | 3159 |
| Opel Kadett Petrol (Nov 79 - Oct 84) up to B | 0634 |
| Opel Kadett Petrol (Oct 84 - Oct 91) | 3196 |
| Opel Omega & Senator Petrol (Nov 86 - 94) | 3157 |
| Opel Rekord Petrol (Feb 78 - Oct 86) up to D | 0543 |
| Opel Vectra Petrol (Oct 88 - Oct 95) | 3158 |
| **PEUGEOT** 106 Petrol & Diesel (91 - 04) J to 53 | 1882 |
| Peugeot 205 Petrol (83 - 97) A to P | 0932 |
| Peugeot 206 Petrol & Diesel (98 - 01) S to X | 3757 |
| Peugeot 206 Petrol & Diesel (02 - 06) 51 to 06 | 4613 |
| Peugeot 306 Petrol & Diesel (93 - 02) K to 02 | 3073 |
| Peugeot 307 Petrol & Diesel (01 - 04) Y to 54 | 4147 |
| Peugeot 309 Petrol (86 - 93) C to K | 1266 |
| Peugeot 405 Petrol (88 - 97) E to P | 1559 |
| Peugeot 405 Diesel (88 - 97) E to P | 3198 |
| Peugeot 406 Petrol & Diesel (96 - Mar 99) N to T | 3394 |
| Peugeot 406 Petrol & Diesel (Mar 99 - 02) T to 52 | 3982 |

\* Classic reprint

| Title | Book No. |
|---|---|
| Peugeot 505 Petrol (79 - 89) up to G | 0762 |
| Peugeot 1.7/1.8 & 1.9 litre Diesel Engine (82 - 96) up to N | 0950 |
| Peugeot 2.0, 2.1, 2.3 & 2.5 litre Diesel Engines (74 - 90) up to H | 1607 |
| **PORSCHE** 911 (65 - 85) up to C | 0264 |
| Porsche 924 & 924 Turbo (76 - 85) up to C | 0397 |
| **PROTON** (89 - 97) F to P | 3255 |
| **RANGE ROVER** V8 Petrol (70 - Oct 92) up to K | 0606 |
| **RELIANT** Robin & Kitten (73 - 83) up to A * | 0436 |
| **RENAULT** 4 (61 - 86) up to D * | 0072 |
| Renault 5 Petrol (Feb 85 - 96) B to N | 1219 |
| Renault 9 & 11 Petrol (82 - 89) up to F | 0822 |
| Renault 18 Petrol (79 - 86) up to D | 0598 |
| Renault 19 Petrol (89 - 96) F to N | 1646 |
| Renault 19 Diesel (89 - 96) F to N | 1946 |
| Renault 21 Petrol (86 - 94) C to M | 1397 |
| Renault 25 Petrol & Diesel (84 - 92) B to K | 1228 |
| Renault Clio Petrol (91 - May 98) H to R | 1853 |
| Renault Clio Diesel (91 - June 96) H to N | 3031 |
| Renault Clio Petrol & Diesel (May 98 - May 01) R to Y | 3906 |
| Renault Clio Petrol & Diesel (June '01 - '05) Y to 55 | 4168 |
| Renault Espace Petrol & Diesel (85 - 96) C to N | 3197 |
| Renault Laguna Petrol & Diesel (94 - 00) L to W | 3252 |
| Renault Laguna Petrol & Diesel (Feb 01 - Feb 05) X to 54 | 4283 |
| Renault Mégane & Scénic Petrol & Diesel (96 - 99) N to T | 3395 |
| Renault Mégane & Scénic Petrol & Diesel (Apr 99 - 02) T to 52 | 3916 |
| Renault Megane Petrol & Diesel (Oct 02 - 05) 52 to 55 | 4284 |
| Renault Scenic Petrol & Diesel (Sept 03 - 06) 53 to 06 | 4297 |
| **ROVER** 213 & 216 (84 - 89) A to G | 1116 |
| Rover 214 & 414 Petrol (89 - 96) G to N | 1689 |
| Rover 216 & 416 Petrol (89 - 96) G to N | 1830 |
| Rover 211, 214, 216, 218 & 220 Petrol & Diesel (Dec 95 - 99) N to V | 3399 |
| Rover 25 & MG ZR Petrol & Diesel (Oct 99 - 04) V to 54 | 4145 |
| Rover 414, 416 & 420 Petrol & Diesel (May 95 - 98) M to R | 3453 |
| Rover 45 / MG ZS Petrol & Diesel (99 - 05) V to 55 | 4384 |
| Rover 618, 620 & 623 Petrol (93 - 97) K to P | 3257 |
| Rover 75 / MG ZT Petrol & Diesel (99 - 06) S to 06 | 4292 |
| Rover 820, 825 & 827 Petrol (86 - 95) D to N | 1380 |
| Rover 3500 (76 - 87) up to E * | 0365 |
| Rover Metro, 111 & 114 Petrol (May 90 - 98) G to S | 1711 |
| **SAAB** 95 & 96 (66 - 76) up to R * | 0198 |
| Saab 90, 99 & 900 (79 - Oct 93) up to L | 0765 |
| Saab 900 (Oct 93 - 98) L to R | 3512 |
| Saab 9000 (4-cyl) (85 - 98) C to S | 1686 |
| Saab 9-3 Petrol & Diesel (98 - Aug 02) R to 02 | 4614 |
| Saab 9-3 Petrol & Diesel (02-07) 52 to 57 | 4749 |
| Saab 9-5 4-cyl Petrol (97 - 04) R to 54 | 4156 |
| **SEAT** Ibiza & Cordoba Petrol & Diesel (Oct 93 - Oct 99) L to V | 3571 |
| Seat Ibiza & Malaga Petrol (85 - 92) B to K | 1609 |
| **SKODA** Estelle (77 - 89) up to G | 0604 |
| Skoda Fabia Petrol & Diesel (00 - 06) W to 06 | 4376 |
| Skoda Favorit (89 - 96) F to N | 1801 |
| Skoda Felicia Petrol & Diesel (95 - 01) M to X | 3505 |
| Skoda Octavia Petrol & Diesel (98 - Apr 04) R to 04 | 4285 |
| **SUBARU** 1600 & 1800 (Nov 79 - 90) up to H * | 0995 |

| Title | Book No. |
|---|---|
| **SUNBEAM** Alpine, Rapier & H120 (67 - 74) up to N * | 0051 |
| **SUZUKI** SJ Series, Samurai & Vitara (4-cyl) Petrol (82 - 97) up to P | 1942 |
| Suzuki Supercarry & Bedford/Vauxhall Rascal (86 - Oct 94) C to M | 3015 |
| **TALBOT** Alpine, Solara, Minx & Rapier (75 - 86) up to D | 0337 |
| Talbot Horizon Petrol (78 - 86) up to D | 0473 |
| Talbot Samba (82 - 86) up to D | 0823 |
| **TOYOTA** Avensis Petrol (98 - Jan 03) R to 52 | 4264 |
| Toyota Carina E Petrol (May 92 - 97) J to P | 3256 |
| Toyota Corolla (80 - 85) up to C | 0683 |
| Toyota Corolla (Sept 83 - Sept 87) A to E | 1024 |
| Toyota Corolla (Sept 87 - Aug 92) E to K | 1683 |
| Toyota Corolla Petrol (Aug 92 - 97) K to P | 3259 |
| Toyota Corolla Petrol (July 97 - Feb 02) P to 51 | 4286 |
| Toyota Hi-Ace & Hi-Lux Petrol (69 - Oct 83) up to A | 0304 |
| Toyota RAV4 Petrol & Diesel (94-06) L to 55 | 4750 |
| Toyota Yaris Petrol (99 - 05) T to 05 | 4265 |
| **TRIUMPH** GT6 & Vitesse (62 - 74 ) up to N * | 0112 |
| Triumph Herald (59 - 71) up to K * | 0010 |
| Triumph Spitfire (62 - 81) up to X | 0113 |
| Triumph Stag (70 - 78) up to T * | 0441 |
| Triumph TR2, TR3, TR3A, TR4 & TR4A (52 - 67) up to F * | 0028 |
| Triumph TR5 & 6 (67 - 75) up to P * | 0031 |
| Triumph TR7 (75 - 82) up to Y * | 0322 |
| **VAUXHALL** Astra Petrol (80 - Oct 84) up to B | 0635 |
| Vauxhall Astra & Belmont Petrol (Oct 84 - Oct 91) B to J | 1136 |
| Vauxhall Astra Petrol (Oct 91 - Feb 98) J to R | 1832 |
| Vauxhall/Opel Astra & Zafira Petrol (Feb 98 - Apr 04) R to 04 | 3758 |
| Vauxhall/Opel Astra & Zafira Diesel (Feb 98 - Apr 04) R to 04 | 3797 |
| Vauxhall/Opel Astra Petrol (04 - 08) | 4732 |
| Vauxhall/Opel Astra Diesel (04 - 08) | 4733 |
| Vauxhall/Opel Calibra (90 - 98) G to S | 3502 |
| Vauxhall Carlton Petrol (Oct 78 - Oct 86) up to D | 0480 |
| Vauxhall Carlton & Senator Petrol (Nov 86 - 94) D to L | 1469 |
| Vauxhall Cavalier Petrol (81 - Oct 88) up to F | 0812 |
| Vauxhall Cavalier Petrol (Oct 88 - 95) F to N | 1570 |
| Vauxhall Chevette (75 - 84) up to B | 0285 |
| Vauxhall/Opel Corsa Diesel (Mar 93 - Oct 00) K to X | 4087 |
| Vauxhall Corsa Petrol (Mar 93 - 97) K to R | 1985 |
| Vauxhall/Opel Corsa Petrol (Apr 97 - Oct 00) P to X | 3921 |
| Vauxhall/Opel Corsa Petrol & Diesel (Oct 00 - Sept 03) X to 53 | 4079 |
| Vauxhall/Opel Corsa Petrol & Diesel (Oct 03 - Aug 06) 53 to 06 | 4617 |
| Vauxhall/Opel Frontera Petrol & Diesel (91 - Sept 98) J to S | 3454 |
| Vauxhall Nova Petrol (83 - 93) up to K | 0909 |
| Vauxhall/Opel Omega Petrol (94 - 99) L to T | 3510 |
| Vauxhall/Opel Vectra Petrol & Diesel (95 - Feb 99) N to S | 3396 |
| Vauxhall/Opel Vectra Petrol & Diesel (Mar 99 - May 02) T to 02 | 3930 |
| Vauxhall/Opel Vectra Petrol & Diesel (June 02 - Sept 05) 02 to 55 | 4618 |
| Vauxhall/Opel 1.5, 1.6 & 1.7 litre Diesel Engine (82 - 96) up to N | 1222 |
| **VW** 411 & 412 (68 - 75) up to P * | 0091 |
| VW Beetle 1200 (54 - 77) up to S | 0036 |
| VW Beetle 1300 & 1500 (65 - 75) up to P | 0039 |

| Title | Book No. |
|---|---|
| VW 1302 & 1302S (70 - 72) up to L * | 0110 |
| VW Beetle 1303, 1303S & GT (72 - 75) up to P | 0159 |
| VW Beetle Petrol & Diesel (Apr 99 - 07) T to 57 | 3798 |
| VW Golf & Jetta Mk 1 Petrol 1.1 & 1.3 (74 - 84) up to A | 0716 |
| VW Golf, Jetta & Scirocco Mk 1 Petrol 1.5, 1.6 & 1.8 (74 - 84) up to A | 0726 |
| VW Golf & Jetta Mk 1 Diesel (78 - 84) up to A | 0451 |
| VW Golf & Jetta Mk 2 Petrol (Mar 84 - Feb 92) A to J | 1081 |
| VW Golf & Vento Petrol & Diesel (Feb 92 - Mar 98) J to R | 3097 |
| VW Golf & Bora Petrol & Diesel (April 98 - 00) R to X | 3727 |
| VW Golf & Bora 4-cyl Petrol & Diesel (01 - 03) X to 53 | 4169 |
| VW Golf & Jetta Petrol & Diesel (04 - 07) 53 to 07 | 4610 |
| VW LT Petrol Vans & Light Trucks (76 - 87) up to E | 0637 |
| VW Passat & Santana Petrol (Sept 81 - May 88) up to E | 0814 |
| VW Passat 4-cyl Petrol & Diesel (May 88 - 96) E to P | 3498 |
| VW Passat 4-cyl Petrol & Diesel (Dec 96 - Nov 00) P to X | 3917 |
| VW Passat Petrol & Diesel (Dec 00 - May 05) X to 05 | 4279 |
| VW Polo & Derby (76 - Jan 82) up to X | 0335 |
| VW Polo (82 - Oct 90) up to H | 0813 |
| VW Polo Petrol (Nov 90 - Aug 94) H to L | 3245 |
| VW Polo Hatchback Petrol & Diesel (94 - 99) M to S | 3500 |
| VW Polo Hatchback Petrol (00 - Jan 02) V to 51 | 4150 |
| VW Polo Petrol & Diesel (02 - May 05) 51 to 05 | 4608 |
| VW Scirocco (82 - 90) up to H * | 1224 |
| VW Transporter 1600 (68 - 79) up to V | 0082 |
| VW Transporter 1700, 1800 & 2000 (72 - 79) up to V * | 0226 |
| VW Transporter (air-cooled) Petrol (79 - 82) up to Y * | 0638 |
| VW Transporter (water-cooled) Petrol (82 - 90) up to H | 3452 |
| VW Type 3 (63 - 73) up to M * | 0084 |
| **VOLVO** 120 & 130 Series (& P1800) (61 - 73) up to M * | 0203 |
| Volvo 142, 144 & 145 (66 - 74) up to N * | 0129 |
| Volvo 240 Series Petrol (74 - 93) up to K | 0270 |
| Volvo 262, 264 & 260/265 (75 - 85) up to C * | 0400 |
| Volvo 340, 343, 345 & 360 (76 - 91) up to J | 0715 |
| Volvo 440, 460 & 480 Petrol (87 - 97) D to P | 1691 |
| Volvo 740 & 760 Petrol (82 - 91) up to J | 1258 |
| Volvo 850 Petrol (92 - 96) J to P | 3260 |
| Volvo 940 petrol (90 - 98) H to R | 3249 |
| Volvo S40 & V40 Petrol (96 - Mar 04) N to 04 | 3569 |
| Volvo S40 & V50 Petrol & Diesel (Mar 04 - Jun 07) 04 to 07 | 4731 |
| Volvo S60 Petrol & Diesel (01-08) | 4793 |
| Volvo S70, V70 & C70 Petrol (96 - 99) P to V | 3573 |
| Volvo V70 / S80 Petrol & Diesel (98 - 05) S to 55 | 4263 |

### DIY MANUAL SERIES

| Title | Book No. |
|---|---|
| The Haynes Air Conditioning Manual | 4192 |
| The Haynes Car Electrical Systems Manual | 4251 |
| The Haynes Manual on Bodywork | 4198 |
| The Haynes Manual on Brakes | 4178 |
| The Haynes Manual on Carburettors | 4177 |
| The Haynes Manual on Diesel Engines | 4174 |
| The Haynes Manual on Engine Management | 4199 |
| The Haynes Manual on Fault Codes | 4175 |
| The Haynes Manual on Practical Electrical Systems | 4267 |
| The Haynes Manual on Small Engines | 4250 |
| The Haynes Manual on Welding | 4176 |

* Classic reprint

# Preserving Our Motoring Heritage

< The Model J Duesenberg Derham Tourster. Only eight of these magnificent cars were ever built – this is the only example to be found outside the United States of America

Almost every car you've ever loved, loathed or desired is gathered under one roof at the Haynes Motor Museum. Over 300 immaculately presented cars and motorbikes represent every aspect of our motoring heritage, from elegant reminders of bygone days, such as the superb Model J Duesenberg to curiosities like the bug-eyed BMW Isetta. There are also many old friends and flames. Perhaps you remember the 1959 Ford Popular that you did your courting in? The magnificent 'Red Collection' is a spectacle of classic sports cars including AC, Alfa Romeo, Austin Healey, Ferrari, Lamborghini, Maserati, MG, Riley, Porsche and Triumph.

## A Perfect Day Out

Each and every vehicle at the Haynes Motor Museum has played its part in the history and culture of Motoring. Today, they make a wonderful spectacle and a great day out for all the family. Bring the kids, bring Mum and Dad, but above all bring your camera to capture those golden memories for ever. You will also find an impressive array of motoring memorabilia, a comfortable 70 seat video cinema and one of the most extensive transport book shops in Britain. The Pit Stop Cafe serves everything from a cup of tea to wholesome, home-made meals or, if you prefer, you can enjoy the large picnic area nestled in the beautiful rural surroundings of Somerset.

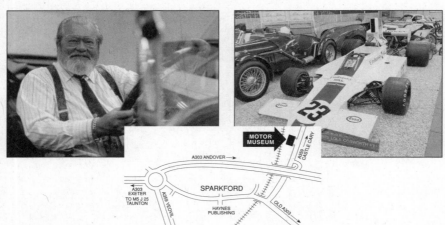

> John Haynes O.B.E., Founder and Chairman of the museum at the wheel of a Haynes Light 12.

< Graham Hill's Lola Cosworth Formula 1 car next to a 1934 Riley Sports.

The Museum is situated on the A359 Yeovil to Frome road at Sparkford, just off the A303 in Somerset. It is about 40 miles south of Bristol, and 25 minutes drive from the M5 intersection at Taunton.

Open 9.30am - 5.30pm (10.00am - 4.00pm Winter) 7 days a week, *except Christmas Day, Boxing Day and New Years Day*

Special rates available for schools, coach parties and outings  Charitable Trust No. 292048